STRUCTURED PL/I (PL/C) PROGRAMMING

STRUCTURED PL/I (PL/C) PROGRAMMING

Jean-Paul Tremblay
Richard B. Bunt
Judith A. Richardson

Department of Computational Science
University of Saskatchewan, Saskatoon
Canada

McGraw-Hill Book Company

New York   St. Louis   San Francisco   Auckland   Bogotá   Düsseldorf
Johannesburg   London   Madrid   Mexico   Montreal
New Delhi   Panama   Paris   São Paulo   Singapore   Sydney   Tokyo   Toronto

STRUCTURED PL/I (PL/C) PROGRAMMING

1 2 3 4 5 6 7 8 9 0   EBEB   7 8 3 2 1 0 9

This book was set in Souvenir by the authors.
The editors were Charles E. Stewart and Annette Hall;
the designer was Robin Hessel
the production supervisor was Dominick Petrellese
Edwards Brothers Incorporated was printer and binder.

Library of Congress Cataloging in Publication Data

Tremblay, Jean-Paul, date
    Structured PL/I (PL/C) programming.

    Bibliography: p.
    Includes index.
    1.   PL/I (Computer program language) 2. PL/C
(Computer program language) I. Bunt, Richard B.,
date joint author. II. Richardson, Judith A.,
joint author. III. Title.
QA76.73.P25T73   001.6'424   79-17904
ISBN 0-07-065173-6

CONTENTS

APPENDIX REFERENCE SUMMARY FOR PL/I AND PL/C   400

INDEX   429

PREFACE

The first course in a computer science curriculum is certainly one of the most important. For most students this constitutes their initial exposure to fundamental notions such as the algorithm, and to the description of solutions in a manner sufficiently precise for computer interpretation. It is important that these notions be properly taught for, as the ancient Roman poet Horace observed, "A new cask will long preserve the tincture of the liquor with which it was first impregnated."

To this end we have prepared a package of instructional materials which reflects our own view of how the first course should be organized and taught. The cornerstone of this package is a book entitled "An Introduction to Computer Science: An Algorithmic Approach" (Tremblay/Bunt, 1979). This book presents computer science concepts in an algorithmic framework, with a strong emphasis on problem solving and solution development. We feel this to be particularly important for the first course.

Clearly the use of a programming language is an important part of the first course too. For that reason we have prepared a series of supplementary integrated programming guides (of which this is one) to provide the needed support. The supplementary guides are not intended to re-teach the ideas of the main book, but rather to *supplement* them with the programming concepts required to implement them in a particular programming language (here, PL/I), and thereby provide the student with the practical programming framework that we feel to be important.

Any book on the PL/I language must set careful terms of reference. The "language" for any programmer is, in fact, defined by the compiler that he or she is using. One of the original PL/I compilers was IBM's F-level PL/I compiler, now superseded by the newer Checkout and Optimizing compilers. Several other computer manufacturers offer PL/I-like languages in their software support: Honeywell, for example, has a language called EPL for its MULTICS operating system, and Digital Equipment Corporation offers a language called CPL with its DECSYSTEM 10 and 20 operating systems. A number of student-oriented compilers have emerged from universities: prominent among these are the University of Toronto's SP/k, Brooklyn Polytechnic Institute's PLAGO, the University of Maryland's PLUM, and Cornell University's PL/C. Our discussion in this book centers primarily on the PL/I programming language as it is implemented in the PL/C compiler. On occasion, however, we venture into full PL/I as supported by IBM, when language features that we require are not supported by PL/C.

It has been our experience that students learn by "viewing." This is particularly true in the case of programming where it seems that there are immense barriers of bewilderment for many students at the outset. To try to flatten these barriers we present worked-out sample programs, in many cases complete with actual run output. These have been programmed using the compilers available to us at the University of Saskatchewan; namely, release 7.6 of the PL/C compiler and version 5.4 of the IBM F-level PL/I compiler. In addition to examples presented for the sake of illustration, most chapters end with a number of more detailed applications that attempt to draw together the material presented in the chapter. These are the same applications that are discussed in the main book; their choice reflects our emphasis on the nonnumeric aspects of computing. As in the main body, this same bias is carried over into the exercises as well. Exercises are found at the end of most sections and at the end of most chapters.

Much has been said and written in the past few years about the merits of an approach to programming loosely termed "structured programming." Studies of the programming task itself have shown that adherence to certain basic principles can result in the production of better quality programs. Our approach is based on many of these principles, and our presentation and examples are designed accordingly. Chapter 7, on programming style, examines the process of programming itself in more depth.

Finally, since we view this guide both as an instructional vehicle and a reference document, we have included as an appendix a lengthy reference summary of the PL/I language (and, in particular, the PL/C language).

SUMMARY BY CHAPTERS

The book begins with a brief introduction to programming from a PL/I perspective.

Chapter 2 provides an introduction to basic concepts of computing and programming as well as the first examples of complete PL/I programs. Some simple applications are described.

The notion of "flow of control" is introduced in Chapter 3, along with two fundamental PL/I control structures: the IF and the DO. Solutions to several fairly elaborate applications are developed.

The concept of the array is the topic of Chapter 4. Processing of single-dimensional arrays, or vectors, is discussed first. The chapter then moves to a consideration of arrays of higher dimension. Some typical applications of vectors and arrays are discussed. Among these are the important applications of searching and sorting.

String processing is the topic of Chapter 5. The representation of strings in a computer and basic PL/I operations on strings are described. A number of simple applications involving string processing are developed. More advanced topics are deferred to Chapter 9. Chapter 5 also deals for the first time with the concepts of formatted I/0 — in particular the GET EDIT and PUT EDIT statements of PL/I.

Chapter 6 deals with functions and procedures. Topics discussed include the correspondence of arguments and parameters, the way in which functions and procedures are invoked and values are returned in PL/I, and the general question of scope in programs. Three applications involving the use of functions and procedures are considered.

Programming style is the topic of Chapter 7. This we feel to be an important chapter of the main book. In this book we try to consider the effects of style on the production of PL/I programs. Examples of actual programs are included to illustrate the points made.

Chapter 8 deals with the subject of numerical computation. PL/I programs are given for the solution of problems discussed in the main book. These include root finding, numerical integration, the solution of simultaneous linear equations, and curve fitting. For some of the material in this chapter, familiarity with elementary calculus would be an asset.

Chapter 9 returns to the topic of string processing, with the presentation dealing with more advanced applications such as KWIC indexing and text editing.

Chapter 10 offers an introduction to the support of linear data structures in PL/I. Simple structures such a linear lists, stacks, and queues are discussed, as are PL/I capabilities to manage these structures. Important PL/I features such as pointer variables, controlled and based storage, structures, and recursion are presented for the first time. A number of important applications are described. These include the compilation of expressions, the symbolic manipulation of polynomials, and simulation. Also discussed in this chapter are hash-table techniques.

Chapter 11 considers the PL/I support for the most important non-linear data structure — the tree. Topics include the representation of trees in PL/I and the application of trees to problems such as the symbolic manipulation of expressions, searching, and sorting.

As already mentioned, the book concludes with an appendix containing a detailed reference summary of the PL/I language.

HOW TO USE THIS BOOK

This book is intended for use in conjunction with the book by Tremblay and Bunt entitled "An Introduction to Computer Science: An Algorithmic Approach" (Tremblay/Bunt, 1979). The material covered by these two books encompasses courses CS1 and CS2 in the revised curriculum proposals of the Association for Computing Machinery (Austing et al., 1979).

As was done in the main book, we make assumptions as to the nature of available computing facilities. For convenience of presentation we assume a card reader/line printer environment throughout. Since we recognize that this may not be the case for many students, the dependency on such matters is minor. Should an alternative environment exist, a simple comment from the instructor should suffice to overcome any possible problems of comprehension.

ACKNOWLEDGMENTS

A project of this scale cannot be completed without the able assistance of many people. We are, of course, indebted to all those who assisted us both directly and indirectly. Marilyn Archibald was an active participant in the early stages of the project, and contributed significantly to the first four chapters. Grant Cheston devoted a great deal of time to the reading of our notes and contributed many valuable suggestions. Our proof readers, including Lyle Opseth, Murray Mazer, Cheryl Ernewein, and Dave Hrenewich, showed patience and diligence. Lyle Opseth also programmed many of the examples in the book. Murray Mazer and Guy Friswell assisted in the programming of some examples. We are grateful for the support and comments of our colleagues and students in the Department of

Computational Science at the University of Saskatchewan, who have class-tested preliminary versions of our books over the past three years. We appreciate the efforts of the Department of Printing Services at the University of Saskatchewan, and in particular Mr. Bill Snell who provided us with an automatic typesetting capability that made it possible to meet a difficult schedule. Finally, one of the authors (Bunt) owes a large debt of thanks to the Research Division of the IBM Corporation at Yorktown Heights, New York, for a very enjoyable and productive sabbatical leave during which this project was completed.

Jean-Paul Tremblay

Richard B. Bunt

Judith A. Richardson

REFERENCES

AUSTING, R. H., BARNES, B. H., BONNETTE, D. T., ENGEL, G. L., and STOKES D. G.: "CURRICULUM '78: Recommendation for the Undergraduate Program in Computer Science," *Communications of the ACM*, Vol. 22, No. 3, March 1979, pp. 147-166.

TREMBLAY, J. P. and BUNT, R. B.: *An Introduction to Computer Science: An Algorithmic Approach*, McGraw-Hill Book Co., New York, 1979.

STRUCTURED PL/I (PL/C) PROGRAMMING

CHAPTER

1

INTRODUCTION
TO PL/I
PROGRAMMING

Interactions involving humans are most effectively carried out through the medium of language. Language permits the expression of thoughts and ideas, and without it, communication, as we know it, would be very difficult indeed.

In computer programming, a programming language serves as the means of communication between the person with a problem and the computer used to help solve it. Languages are said to affect the thought and culture of those who use them. Eskimos, for example, have a large vocabulary simply on the subject of snow. An effective programming language enhances both the development and the expression of computer programs. It must bridge the gap between the too often unstructured nature of human thought and the precision required for computer execution. The programming language shapes the thought processes of the programmer, and the quality of the language has a large effect on the quality of the programs produced with it.

1-1 INTRODUCTION

This book is intended to supplement the text *An Introduction to Computer Science: An Algorithmic Approach*. Its purpose is to provide an introduction to the programming language PL/I, sufficient to enable you to implement the algorithms of the main text.

As much as possible, we attempt to parallel the presentation of the main text. In our presentation, we assume that the pertinent sections of the main text have been read. The algorithmic language of the main text has been designed for easy translation into several popular programming languages, including PL/I. For easy references, Appendix A contains a brief summary of the procedure for translating from the algorithmic language into PL/I.

The purpose of this chapter is to define a perspective for the material in this book by providing a brief overview of the development and use of the PL/I language.

1-2 A SHORT HISTORY OF THE PL/I LANGUAGE

In the early days of computing, programming was a very formidable task. Many of the early computers were "hard wired" to perform a specific task: to change the "program" required rewiring components. John von Neumann was the first to propose the concept of the stored program, that is, the idea that the instructions of the program be stored in the memory of the computer along with the data. Before long, people began to look for more convenient ways of specifying these instructions, moving from low level (i.e., machine-oriented) symbolic assembly languages through to higher level problem-oriented programming languages.

One of the first general purpose problem-oriented programming languages was FORTRAN (FORmula TRANslator), introduced in 1954 and designed for the solution of scientific numerical problems. FORTRAN was instrumental in demonstrating the value and cost effectiveness of problem-oriented programming languages, and soon other such languages began to appear, with COBOL (COmmon Business Oriented Language) for business applications, ALGOL (ALGOrithmic Language) for problems in numerical mathematics, LISP for list processing applications primarily in artificial intelligence, and SNOBOL for applications involving string manipulation, proving to be the most enduring.

Late in 1963, a committee consisting of IBM personnel and customers began to consider the design of a new programming language, intended originally as a major FORTRAN enhancement. During the design process, features were borrowed from the other languages mentioned previously and incorporated, perhaps in slightly different form, into the new language, which was eventually named PL/I. The first official PL/I manual was published in 1965, and the first compiler was available in 1966.

PL/I is a very large and a very general language, with features appropriate to the solution of a very wide range of problems. Its use as a teaching language has been enhanced by the development of student-oriented compilers, perhaps the most popular of which is PL/C, developed at Cornell University. Such compilers support only those features of PL/I appropriate to student programmers and offer powerful error diagnostic capabilities to aid in learning the language. Also, the cost of running programs under PL/C is low, thus permitting its use in large classes.

1-3 THE USE OF A PROGRAMMING LANGUAGE

As described earlier, a programming language serves to aid in the transformation of a problem solution into an executable computer program. In fact, a language that is well-designed enhances not only the *expression* of the solution, but also its *development* as well.

Once a problem solution has been formulated in terms of a computer program in some programming language, it must then be translated into the machine language of the computer on which the program is to be run. Machine language is not programmer-oriented; machine language programs are nothing more than long strings of numbers, but written in such a way as to be meaningful to the computer. The translation of a program written in a high level programming language (sometimes called the *source program*) to its machine language equivalent (sometimes called the *object program*) is handled through a special program known as a *compiler*.

For a given programming language, there may be many compilers. For example, there will be a different compiler for every different type of machine that supports the language. Even on the same machine, there may be several compilers for the same language. For example, in addition to the regular compiler (say, the regular PL/I compiler) there may be one or more student compilers (such as PL/C) that support perhaps fewer features of the language but offer special instructional capabilities.

Often the action of a compiler appears transparent to the programmer, but never completely so. For example, the compiler can often detect errors made in the writing of the program that would prevent it from running correctly. Other errors may escape its detection, and not be discovered until the translated machine language program (or the object program) is actually in execution. The distinction between *compile-time* and *run-time* is described more completely in Chap. 2.

1-4 THE APPROACH OF THE BOOK

Although we are dealing with the *language* PL/I, where possible, we will be running our example programs under the PL/C *compiler*. There are some subtle differences that ought not to affect the beginning programmer, but may be of more concern as more progamming experience is acquired. A list of the major differences can be found in the Appendices.

When first learning the PL/I language, it is very easy to be overpowered by detail. Since PL/I is by design intended for a wide range of applications, almost every feature of the language comes with many variants and options, most of which are unimportant to the beginning programmer. We have tried to ease this problem through a layered presentation that matches the presentation of the main text. When a feature of the language is first introduced, it is described in such a way as to be useful immediately to the beginning programmer. Variations and additional options are deferred until motivated by actual problem requirements.

Much has been said and written in recent years on an approach to programming known as "structured programming." Structured programming is really little more than that application of a particular discipline to the practice of programming. The evidence seems clear that students produce better programs in a shorter time span with this philosophy. The presentation in this book is consistent with the teachings of structured programming.

With this short introduction, you are now ready to begin your study of the PL/I language.

BIBLIOGRAPHY

BACKUS, J.W., et al.: "The FORTRAN Automatic Coding System" (ed., S. Rosen), in *Programming Systems and Languages,* McGraw-Hill Book Company, New York, 1967.

CONWAY, R.W., and WILCOX, T.R.: *"Design and Implementation of a Diagnostic Compiler for PL/I",* Communications of the ACM, Vol. 16, No. 3, March 1973, 169-179.

IBM System 360 Operation System: PL/I Language Specifications, IBM Corp., C28-6571-0, Data Processing Division, White Plains, N.Y., 1965.

SAMMET, J.E.: *Programming Languages: History and Fundamentals,* Prentice-Hall Inc., Englewood Cliffs, N.J., 1969.

TREMBLAY, J.P., and BUNT, R.B.: *An Introduction to Computer Science: An Algorithmic Approach,* McGraw-Hill Book Company, New York, 1979.

CHAPTER

FUNDAMENTAL PL/I CONCEPTS

This chapter introduces several of the fundamental concepts of programming in the PL/I language. The presentation closely follows that of Chap. 2 in the main text. The chapter begins with a simple overview of solving problems in PL/I, including data, its representation and manipulation, and the use of variables. Simple input and output operations are discussed. This discussion should be sufficient to allow the novice programmer to write very simple PL/I programs. The process of preparing a program to run under the PL/C compiler is explained and some instruction on program execution, debugging, and tracing is given. The chapter concludes with complete PL/I programs for the applications developed in Chap. 2 of the main text.

2-1 DATA, DATA TYPES, AND PRIMITIVE OPERATIONS

The computer is used to perform tasks involving pieces of information or *data*. By submitting a series of instructions to the computer by means of a program, the programmer specifies exactly how these data are to be processed. The PL/I language allows the programmer to provide several different types of data. In this section we discuss various data types, their representations in a PL/C program, and the kinds of operations that can be used to manipulate data.

2-1.1 Data Types

In PL/I, four broad classes of data can be used: the familiar numeric, character, and logical types along with the special type, pointer. These are described in more detail in the main text. Each of these various data modes has a distinct internal representation and different machine instructions are used for each. In order for the computer to interpret the data correctly, rules for expressing data of each type in programs must be followed by the programmer.

Numeric data in PL/I can be represented in several different ways: as fixed-point numbers, floating-point numbers, complex numbers, or imaginary numbers. Usually all of these types are represented in base 10 (using decimal digits), although base 2 (using binary digits 0 and 1) may be used if desired.

Fixed-point numbers are written as a string of one or more digits, and may or may not contain a decimal point. If a decimal point is not included, it is assumed to fall after the rightmost digit in the number, thereby making the number an integer. Fixed-point numbers with a decimal point correspond to real numbers in decimal representation. Numbers may be signed as either positive or negative. In the case that the sign is not written, the number is assumed to be positive. The range of fixed-point values permitted is a function of the particular computing system used. In the IBM 360/370 fixed-point values may range from –99999 to 99999. The following examples of fixed-point decimal constants:

$$1$$
$$+1.0$$
$$0$$
$$-427.695$$
$$99999$$

Floating-point numbers are specified by any signed or unsigned string of digits, optionally containing a decimal point, followed by the letter E (for exponent), and a signed or unsigned integer exponent. The integer exponent must be expressed with decimal digits. Floating-point form is interpreted to mean that the number preceding the letter E is to be multiplied by 10 raised to the power given by the integer after the E. This form is sometimes referred to as "scientific notation" and is useful when writing very large or very small numbers. As with fixed-point values, the allowable magnitude of floating-point values depends on the computing system used. In the IBM 360/370, all values must fall between 1E–79 to 1E75. Also, the exponent decimal integer may not contain more than two digits and the string to the left of the E is limited to sixteen significant digits or less. Examples of floating-point decimal constants are:

```
4.13414133E7
+2.22E+01
   75E0
 -3E-18
```

Fixed- and floating-point constants may, as mentioned previously, also be written in binary form, that is, using the binary digits 0 and 1, instead of decimal digits. In this case, the programmer must also include the letter B immediately following the constant, in order that the computer may distinguish intended binary constants from decimal constants. When writing floating-point binary constants, the integer exponent must still appear in decimal form. This feature is really intended for special applications. Thus, we will dwell on it no further at this time.

The remaining numeric data types (complex and imaginary) are based on the fixed- and floating-point forms discussed, but are beyond the scope of this book.

The *character string* is the second major data type in the PL/I language. A character string is a sequence of character symbols, where each character must be either an alphabetic letter, one of the digits (0123456789), or one of the set of special characters <blank,(; |&$*)+-_!/,⌐ >?:@#'=%. For presentation purposes, character strings are often enclosed in single quotes. The quotes themselves are not considered part of the string, only as markers for the start and end of the string (or *delimiters*). A string which has no characters between the quotes (not even the blank character) is called the *empty*, or *null*, string and is written simply as '' (i.e., two single quotes written consecutively).

The character string format just described may present a problem if the desired string contains, within itself, a quotation mark. The problem is solved by using two consecutive single quotes to represent one quote which is embedded in the string. For example, the correct string representation for the contraction of 'COULD NOT' is not 'COULDN'T', but 'COULDN''T'. The following are examples of valid string constants:

```
'COMPUTER SCIENCE'
       '67'
   '$.50 PIECES'
     '3+3-4=-1'
     '5?AB6+*'
```

There is a variation of this format for character strings which can be used in PL/I, but not in PL/C. This altered format uses a *repetition factor* and will be discussed in Chap. 5.

The length of a character string is defined as the number of characters in the string (including the blank characters). An embedded pair of quotes is counted as just one character, since it actually represents only one single quote. Thus, the length of the string 'DON''T' is 5 and not 6. The null string is defined to have length 0. The maximum length that any string constant may have varies from compiler to compiler, but is typically quite large. In PL/C, however, this maximum length is 256 characters.

A third data type in PL/I is the logical type, where each data constant is called a *bit string*. Bit strings are commonly used to represent the two truth values, "true" and "false". The bit string that represents the truth value "true" is written '1'B, while the bit string for the value "false" is written '0'B. Applications involving logical data are considered in Chap. 9.

The pointer data type is less commonly used than those already described and is presented in Chap. 10.

For the computer to interpret the data correctly, it must be specified in a certain format. The programmer, therefore, must determine the particular type of data he or she plans to use, and then follow the rules for expressing values of that type. The type of data chosen also determines the possible operations that may be used to manipulate its values. This subject is the topic of the next section.

2-1.2 Data Manipulation

The numeric operation is a fundamental component of PL/I. The symbols and use of the numeric operators are described in this seciton. With one exception, the symbols used here are the same as those of the algorithmic language in the main text. Numeric functions are also available and are discussed in Sec. 2-2.

NUMERIC OPERATORS

The operators used in PL/I are of two types, *binary* and *unary*. Binary operators are used in operations which contain two operands. The binary operators include:

1. For subtraction –, e.g., 3 – 4,
2. For addition +, e.g., 4 + 3,
3. For multiplication *, e.g., 3 * 4,
4. For division /, e.g., 4 / 4,
5. For exponentiation **, e.g., 4 ** 3 represents 4 raised to the third power.

In the algorithmic notation, the symbol ↑ was used for exponentiation (e.g., 4 ↑ 3). In traditional mathematics, the notation 4^3 is used.

Unary operators are used which have only a single operand, such as the unary plus (+) and minus (–). These operators are used to indicate a positive or negative number in an operation. Later, additional examples of unary operators are presented.

TYPES OF NUMERIC OPERATION

The operators may be used with fixed-point operands, with floating-point operands, or with any combination of these. When two operands of differing types are involved in a binary operation, a copy of one of the values is converted to the other's type. If one operand is of floating-point type and the other is of fixed-point type, a copy of the fixed-point operand is converted into a floating-point operand and the operation is carried out with the two floating-point operands. The one exception to this rule is that exponents that are integers are not converted during exponentiation. Some examples of the different types of operations are:

Operation	Type of Result
5.6E02 + 7.8E33	floating-point
4 + 3	fixed-point
4.32 – 8.9	fixed-point
2.33E45 / 8	floating-point
5 ** 7.45E–34	floating-point
5.99E23 * 3.87E34	floating-point

Division involving fixed-point numbers is the one combination of operands that can cause problems. PL/I handles constants in such a way that fixed-point division does not always result in the correct answer. To make sure that divisions are performed correctly, the programmer should always ensure that at least one of the operands used in a division operation is of type floating-point. For example the division

$$\frac{6}{2}$$

should be written as 6E0 / 2, 6 / 2E0, 6 / 2.0E+0,6.0E+0 / 2, or 6.0E+0 / 2.0E+0, but not as 6 / 2.

Any numeric operation raises the possibility of certain problems. Two such problems are overflow and underflow.

Overflow is an error condition that occurs when the result of a computation is too large to be represented in the storage space for fixed-point or floating-point values.

Overflow can occur when:

1. Adding two large positive or negative numbers,
2. Subtracting a large positive number from a large negative number, or subtracting a large negative number from a large positive number,
3. Multiplying two large numbers, negative or positive,
4. Dividing a very large number by a very small one,
5. Raising a number to a very large power.

Underflow is an error which occurs when the result of computation is too small to be represented in the storage space for fixed-point or floating-point values.

Underflow can occur when:

1. Multiplying two very small numbers,
2. Dividing a very small number by a very large number,
3. Raising a number to a very small power.

It is the responsibily of the programmer to ensure that the results of the computations fall within the limits of the fixed-point and floating-point number values that can be stored. Since the value of the overflowed or underflowed number retained by the computer would be incomplete, and, therefore, usually worthless in any computation in which it may be subsequently required, the usual response of the computer to overflow or underflow conditions is to print an overflow or underflow error message and teminate execution of the program. In some computations, however, a warning message may not be given, and the computer may continue to execute using the incomplete value. The programmer must be very careful, therefore, in situations in which the data values are such that overflow or underflow may occur.

In this section, operators, types of operations, and problems that can occur when using operators have been discussed. The variable, involving its use and representation, is the topic of the next section.

Exercises for Sec. 2-1

1. Give the type of each of the following constants:

    (i)   723   (v)   −2456
    (ii)   723E0   (vi)   −63E−11
    (iii) '723'   (vii) 45E+26
    (iv)   +723E+1   (viii) 786

2. Give the result and its type for each of the following operations:

    (i)   6 + 3   (v)   76 / 10 + 2
    (ii)   .536E3 − 536   (vi)   35E−1 / 3.5 − 2
    (iii) 5 * 30   (vii) 2 ** 3
    (iv)   .77E2 / .11E+2   (vii) 4 * 2 − 3E0

2-2 VARIABLES AND EXPRESSIONS

We have seen in the previous section that PL/I allows various types of data values. This section introduces the concept of a variable and gives rules for the use of variables in PL/I programs. Also, the *assignment* statement of PL/I is explored. Finally, we look at combining simple operations into complex expressions.

2-2.1 Variables and Their Declaration

A *variable* in a programming language stands for a location in memory that is capable of holding a value and is referenced by a *variable name* (or *identifier*). In PL/I, some rules are imposed on the naming of variables. These are very similar to the naming rules given in the main text for variables in the algorithmic language. First, a variable name must begin with a letter (or one of the special characters, #, @, and $) and can contain no blanks or special characters other than the dollar sign ($), pound sign (#), the "at" character (@) or the underscore (_). In other words, only the letters A through Z, the digits 0 through 9, and the special characters, $, #, @, and _ may be used. The maximum size for a variable name is 31 characters. Some subsets of PL/I may impose further restrictions on the naming of variables by not allowing the use of certain *keywords* of the language. Words like END, DECLARE, and DO, for example, have special meaning in the PL/I language. Even though their use as identifiers may not be forbidden (except in some compilers, such as PL/C), it may cause confusion in reading the program, and should be avoided in any case. Examples of correct and incorrect identifiers follow.

LOG	valid
$MONEY	valid
X3	valid
BANK_ACC	valid
#8778	valid
J@B	valid
WHEN?	invalid (? is not allowed in an identifier.)
X+Z	invalid (+ is a special symbol.)
VARIABLE NAME	invalid (Blanks are not allowed within variable names.)

1AB   invalid (Variable name must start with a letter.)
THIS_SEQUENCE_IS_TOO_LONG_FOR_A_VARIABLE_NAME   invalid
                     (Variable name cannot be more than 31 characters long.)

Although a variable can change its value many times during the execution of a program, it can hold only one type of data value throughout. Thus, all the values it is given during a program must be of the same type. The type of data values a variable can hold is defined by its *type attributes*.

All variables used in a program must be introduced by means of declaration statements. These declarations simultaneously associate memory locations with the variables and serve to tell the compiler the particular data type that the variable will hold (and therefore, the storage representation to use for its values). This is not unlike making a reservation for a table in a restaurant. PL/I type decalaration statements may appear anywhere in a program, but usually are placed at the beginning.

To declare a variable which is to hold only integer or fixed-point values, the programmer writes the following:

DECLARE *variable-name* FIXED;

where FIXED is the type attributed for the variable. Notice the semicolon (;) marking the end of statement. In PL/I, all statements must be terminated by a semicolon. An example of a declaration statement, the following statement

DECLARE SUM FIXED;

tells the compiler that the memory location for the variable SUM will be expected to hold integer values. If the programmer desires a variable to hold floating-point values, then he or she writes a declaration of the following form:

DECLARE *variable-name* FLOAT;

For example, the following causes the location for the variable TOTAL to accept only floating-point values:

DECLARE TOTAL FLOAT;

An additional type attribute can be used to specify the number base to be used to represent the number internally. Numbers can be stored either in decimal or in binary form. For example, the declarations

DECLARE SUM FIXED BINARY;
DECLARE TOTAL FLOAT DECIMAL;

indicate that the variable SUM and TOTAL may hold only values which are, respectively, fixed-point in binary form, and floating-point in decimal form. For most applications, however, the beginning programmer will need to specify only FIXED or FLOAT and let the compiler determine the rest.

Variables which will accept character strings as values to be stored in their storage locations are declared using the following:

DECLARE *variable-name* CHARACTER(*length*);

where *length* is a constant or an expression (see Sec. 2-2.2) which indicates the length of the character strings which the *variable-name* will hold. For example, the following:

DECLARE TEXT CHARACTER(5);

defines the variable TEXT to represent values which are character strings of length 5. It is important to note that if, during the execution of the program, a variable, which is declared to accept character strings of a certain length, is given a string value of length less than that length, then the computer automatically adds enough blank characters on the immediate right of the string value to fill it out to the required length, before storing it in the variable's location. For example, if the variable TEXT (declared to have a length of five in the previous example) were assigned the string 'THE', 'THE' would be stored as 'THEbb' where the two b's represent added blanks.

Unfortunately, the padding of the string value with blanks may cause problems and/or inefficiencies in certain string applications. In order to avoid this problem, the VARYING attribute may be added to the declaration of the string variable. The VARYING attribute indicates that the variable may hold character strings that are less than or equal to the maximum declared length. For example, the following declaration

DECLARE TEXT CHARACTER(5) VARYING;

defines the variable TEXT to represent character string values of up to five characters in length. If no TEXT is assigned a value which is less than five characters in length, the string value would be stored without the addition of extra blanks. If a string variable is assigned a value which is greater in length than the string variable's maximum declared length, the value will be truncated on its right to reduce it to the necessary length. For example, if the string 'THIS BOOK' is assigned to the variable TEXT, only 'THISb' will be held in the memory location for TEXT.

When several variables are to be declared in a program, the programmer may, instead of writing a separate DECLARE statement for each one, write only one DECLARE statement which includes all or any number of variables. For example, instead of declaring the variables SUM and TOTAL using two separate declarations, as follows:

DECLARE TOTAL FLOAT;

DECLARE SUM FIXED;

the following, single declaration could be written, given the same result:

DECLARE TOTAL FLOAT, SUM FIXED;

The comma is necessary to indicate to the compiler where the attributes of one variable's name end and the next variable name begins. Again, a semicolon is used to terminate the statement.

Another useful simplification is known as *factoring*. When several variables are declared to be the same type, they may be grouped into one declaration, as in the following example:

DECLARE (COUNT, SUM, VALUE) FIXED;

Notice the use of parentheses to identify the list of variables.

At this point, you should be able to write declaration statements necessary to solve the type of problem given in Chap. 2 of the main text. The DECLARE statement has many more features than we have given here. These features, however, are not needed until the problem requirements become more elaborate and their early disussion will only confuse the issue. Consequently, we will deal with these details in the Appendices.

We have described the declaration of numeric and string variables in this section. The declaration of logical and pointer variables will be discussed in later chapters, as the need for variables of these types arises.

In the next section, we turn to the use of arithmetic expressions in PL/I.

2-2.2 Evaluation of Expressions

The arithmetic expression is a basic element of the PL/I language. An *expression* can be:

1. A constant,
2. A variable,
3. Two or more constants or variables (or combinations of constants and variables) separated by operators.

The following are all examples of expressions.

```
5
6.387
APPLE
LENGTH
- 7
+3.9
A + B
3 / 9
78 * 8.9
3 ** 45
INT + 5 / 6
(98 - 78 / (34 * 78)
7 * A + 3 / 2 - 6
6 + 89 - 34 * (65 - 43) ** 34 / 67 * (11 - 7)
```

The order in which the terms of an expression are evaluated is based on the rules of precedence described in the main text. For example, in the statement

$$7.0 + 6.0 * 3.0 - 2.0$$

the multiplication is done first, followed by the addition and subtraction, yielding the following sequence of intermediate results:

6.0 * 3.0 = *18.0* Intermediate result: *7.0 + 18.0 - 2.0*
7.0 + 18.0 = *25.0* intermediate result: *25.0 - 2.0*
25.0 - 2.0 = *23.0*

The rules of precedence for PL/I are summarized in Table 2-1.

NUMERIC BUILT-IN FUNCTIONS

PL/I provides many built-in functions that can be used in expressions. Built-in functions allow the programmer to perform frequently used operations which cannot be easily handled by the arithmetic operators. The general form of a built-in function is

function name(expression)

The expression which appears in the parentheses following the function name is called the *argument*. The argument (or arguments in the case of functions with more than one argument) of the built-in function is evaluated and then the indicated function is performed with that value. For example, the expression

SQRT(5 + 4)

is evaluated in the following manner. First, the expression 5 + 4 is evaluated, leaving an intermediate result of SQRT(9). Then, this function is evaluated and a final value of 3 results.

A built-in function may be the argument of another built-in function. For example, the statement

LOG (ABS(25 - 80))

results in the natural log of the absolute value of 25 - 80.

The type of result from the evaluation of a built-in function is determined by the type of function and the argument (or arguments) it possesses. In most cases, the argument of a function may be any numeric data type. A list of the commonly used built-in functions appears in Table 2-2. Restrictions on their use with certain numeric data types are described.

Table 2-1 Order of precedence for PL/I operators

	Operation	Symbol	Order of Evaluation
1.	Parentheses	( )	inner to outer, (i.e., inner-most first)
2.	Exponentiation	**	right to left
	Unary plus, minus	+, −	
3.	Multiplication	*	left to right
	Division	/	
4.	Addition	+	left to right
	Subtraction	−	

Table 2-2 Some useful built-in functions

Function Name	Argument and Type	Meaning and Type of Result
ABS(n)	n: a real, integer, or complex expression	absolute value: result is $|n|$, same type as n
SQRT(n)	n: a floating-point expression (If n is not floating-point, it is converted.)	square root: result is n, type floating-point
TRUNC(n)	n: may not be complex	truncate: result is the largest integer smaller than or equal to n
ROUND(n,q)	n: a signed or unsigned integer constant	round: if q = 0, result is n rounded to the nearest integer if q > 0, result is n rounded to the qth digit to the right of the decimal point if q < 0, result is n rounded to the q+1th digit to the left of the decimal point
LOG(n)	n: a floating-point expression (If n is not floating-point, it will be converted. n must be greater than 0.)	logarithm base e: result is the natural (Naperian) logarithm of n, type floating-point
LOG10(n)	n: a floating-point expression (If n is not floating-point, it will be converted. n may not be complex and n must be greater than 0.)	logarithm base 10: result is the base 10 logarithm of n, type floating-point

Table 2-2 Some useful built-in functions (cont'd.)

Function Name	Argument and Type	Meaning and Type of Result
EXP(n)	n: a floating-point expression (if n is not floating-point, it will be converted. n is the number of radians.)	exponent: result e^n, type floating-point
CEIL(n)	n: may not be complex	ceiling: result is the smallest integer greater than or equal to n
FLOOR(n)	n: may not be complex	floor: result is the largest integer not greater than n
SIN(n)	n: a floating-point expression (If n is not floating-point, it will be converted. n is the number of radians.)	sine: result is the sine of n radians, type floating-point
SIND(n)	n: a floating-point expression (If n is not floating-point, it will be converted. n is the number of degrees.)	sine: result is sine of n degrees type floating-point
COS(n)	n: a floating-point expression (If n is not floating-point, it will be converted. n is the number of radians.)	cosine: result is cosine of n radians, type floating-point
COSD(n)	n: a floating-point expression (If n is not floating-point, it will be converted. n is the number of degrees.)	cosine: result is cosine of n degrees, type floating-point
TAN(n)	n: a floating-point expression (If n is not floating-point, it will be converted. n is the number of radians.)	tangent: result is tangent n radians, type floating-point
TAND(n)	n: a floating-point expression (If n is not floating-point, it will be converted. n is the number of degrees.)	tangent: result is tangent of n degrees, type floating-point

2-2.3   The Assignment Statement

SIMPLE ASSIGNMENT

The assignment operation allows the programmer to give a variable a value during the execution of a program. In PL/I, the assignment operator is the equal sign (=), rather than the left-pointing arrow(←) used in the main text. Unfortunately, this can lead to confusion with the equality relation. An assignment operation in PL/I is indicated by a statement of the form
   variable = expression;
where the expression can be any valid PL/I expression.

The rules governing assignment statements in PL/I closely parallel those of the algorithmic language of the main text. The following are examples of correct and incorrect assignment statements.

X = 3.0;	correct
Y = 8.0E0;	correct
A = 2.0 + 3.0;	correct
NAME = 'JUDY';	correct
X + Y = A * B;	incorrect (The item on the left hand side of the assignment operator, X + Y, is an expression, not a variable.)
NUM = 4.777	incorrect (Semi colon, needed at the end of the statement, is missing.)
3.0 = R;	incorrect (The item on the left hand side of the assignment operator, 3.0, is a constant, not a variable.)

TYPE CONVERSIONS

As was the case in the algorithmic language, the concept of type is important in the processing of assignment statements in PL/I. It is expected that the value on the righthand side of the assignment operator be of the same type as the variable to which it is being assigned. Where this is not the case, PL/I will attempt to convert the value to conform. Conversion is possible, for example, where both are numeric (fixed or float) types. However, if one is numeric and one nonnumeric, a conversion error results, as might be expected. Consider the following program segment:

```
DECLARE NAME CHARACTER (10) VARYING,
     NUM1 FIXED,
     NUM2 FLOAT;
     NAME = 'RICHARDSON';
     NUM1 = 16;
     NUM2 = 24E5;
     NUM2 = -4;
     NUM1 = 2.567
     NUM1 = NAME;
```

Three variables are declared in the first statement: a string variable NAME, a fixed-point variable NUM1, and a floating-point variable NUM2. In the first three assignment statements, the type of the value being assigned matches that of the variable to which it is being assigned. In the fourth case (NUM2 = -4;), it does not.

However, since both are numeric, conversion is possible. The fixed-point integer constant (–4) is automatically converted to floating-point (–4E0), and then the assignment is carried out. In the next assignment statement, a real value (2.567) is assigned to a fixed-point variable. In this case, the real value is *truncated* (i.e., the fractional part is removed) to yield an integer. This integer result (2) is then assigned to NUM1. In the fifth case (NUM1 = NAME;), once again the types do not match. This time, no conversion can be performed, however, and a conversion error results.

The complete set of rules governing type conversion in PL/I are quite complicated, and once again, are beyond the scope of this book. At the level described here, the rules are the same as those given in the main text (for example, reals are truncated if necessary before being assigned to integer variables). This simple-minded approach is sufficient for a large number of applications and thus we will not go into further detail.

EXTENDED ASSIGNMENT

A useful variation of the assignment statement is the extended assignment statement. The extended assignment statement allows in one statement the assignment of one value to a number of different variables. The extended assignment statement represented by

$variable_1 \leftarrow variable_2 \leftarrow \ldots variable_n \leftarrow$ expression

in the algorithmic notation has the following format in PL/I.

$variable_1, variable_2, \ldots, variable_n$ = expression;

The value of the expression is assigned to each of the variables from left to right. The preceding extended assignment statement, therefore, is equivalent to the following sequence of simple assignment statements.

$variable_1$ = expression;
$variable_2$ = expression;

.

.

.

$variable_n$ = expression;

The following are examples of extended assignment statements.

I, J, K, L, = 7.777;	correct
A, B, C = 5 /3	correct
A, X + T, B = 5;	incorrect (X + T is an expression, not a variable.)
K, 5, J = 6;	incorrect (5 is a constant, not a variable.)

This concludes our discussion on variables and expressions. In the first part of this discussion, the concept of a variable was introduced. The rules for naming and declaring variables were given. The evaluation of expressions was the topic of Sec. 2-2.2. Included under this heading the precedence of operators was explained and an example was used to illustrate the evaluation of expressions. Finally, in Sec. 2-2.4 the function and rules for use of the assignment and extended assignment statements were explained.

We now move on to two important aspects of programming, input and output.

Exercises for Sec. 2-2

1. Which of the following variable names are valid?

   (i)   WATER
   (ii) $STAR
   (iii) 76354
   (iv) NUM@
   (v)   #A37_621
   (vi) TAX
   (vii) THE_END_OF_THIS_QUESTION?

2. Evaluate the following expressions, giving the intermediate and final results:

   (i) $-7 + 8 * 3$
   (ii) $32 / 4E0 - 9 * 2$
   (iii) $7 ** 2 ** 3$
   (iv) $11 - 9 + 2 - 3$
   (v) $60 / 3E0 + (5 * 2) * 2 ** 2$
   (vi) $24 * (2 + 3) - 45$
   (vii) $6 ** 2 - 8 * (3 * 1)$
   (viii) $45 / 5E1 + 2$

3. Assume that A, B and C have been declared as FLOAT variables and that I, J and K have been declared as integer variables. Given A = 5E0, B = 5E0 and I = 4, what is the final value requested in each of the following:

   (i)   C = A * B – I;   C = ———
   (ii)   K = I / 4 * 6 – B;   K = ———
   (iii) C = B / A + 1.53 – 2;   C = ———
   (iv)   K = TRUNC(B / A + 4.7);   K = ———
   (v)   J = ROUND(A / (5 / I), 0);   J = ———
   (vi)   K = ABS(A – B) * 2 + I;   K = ———
   (vii) K, J, C = B / A – I + 2;   K = ———
                                                  J = ———
                                                  C = ———
   (viii) C, K = B / A + 1 – .5;   C = ———
                                                  K = ———

2-3 SIMPLE INPUT AND OUTPUT

In any computing environment, input and output provide the final interface between the programmer and the computer executing the program. Input statements in the program allow the computer to read data during the execution of the program. This allows the programmer to write general programs that can be used repeatedly on different sets of data, the exact values of which the programmer need not know at the time the program is written. Without output statements, most programs would be useless, as the users would have no way of knowing what results were obtained.

The PL/I language provides a number of different methods of input and output. Methods that are easy to use have certain restrictions associated with them. For more advanced applications, where the format of the input data or the printed results, for example, is of particular importance, more sophisticated methods must be used. The discussion of these methods will be deferred until Chap. 5.

LIST-DIRECTED INPUT

The simplest type of input and output is free-style or format-free. This corresponds almost exactly to the form of input/output employed in the main text. One type of free-style input statement available in PL/I is the list-directed input statement,

GET LIST (*input list*);

The *input list* consists of one or more variables separated by commas. Each variable in the input list corresponds to an item in the data (which we will assume to be on punched cards). For example, the following program segment:

    DECLARE (A, B, C) FIXED
    GET LIST (A, B, C);

    Data card:
    7, 8, 9

causes the data card to be scanned. The first value on the card, 7, is assigned to A. The second value, 8, is assigned to B, and the third value, 9, is assigned to C. The data type of the variable and corresponding data item should be the same. If the data types are not the same, conversions are performed according to the same rules as for the assignment statement; an error message is printed when the conversion cannot be done.

The items on the data card must be separated by a comma and/or one or more blanks. Blanks or commas may, therefore, not appear within a single numeric data item. Twelve thousand and forty-three is, for example, represented on a data card as 12043, not as 12,043. Data may appear in any column of the data card and may even be split across card boundaries. Since the data may be split across card boundaries, the programmer must be careful when punching data cards. The following two sets of data cards are not equivalent, though they may appear the same.

Set 1:

    6.0   7   8   52
    ↑
    col. 1

    34   6
    ↑
    col. 1

Set 2:

```
6.0      7      8           52
↑                           ↑
col. 1                      col. 80

34      6
↑
col. 1
```

Set 1 contains the six values 6.0, 7, 8, 52, 34, and 6. Set 2 contains the five values 6.0, 7, 8, 5234, and 6, as there are no blanks or commas between 52 and 34.

Character strings must be enclosed in single quotes. Again, the quotes serve only to delimit the string and are not part of the string itself. The data card
'DAY OF THE MONTH' 'YEAR'
contains the two character strings 'DAY OF THE MONTH' and 'YEAR'.

If there are more values on the data card than there are variables in the GET LIST statement, the remaining values are ignored. If another input statement occurs in the program, reading resumes from where the previous input statement stopped. Each value is read only once. Consider the following program segment and data card.

```
DECLARE (LENGTH, WIDTH, HEIGHT) FIXED;
DECLARE NAME CHARACTER(20) VARYING;
GET LIST (NAME);
GET LIST (LENGTH, WIDTH);
GET LIST (HEIGHT);
```

Data card:
'BOX' 7 5 8

This causes the assignment of 'BOX' to NAME, and the assignment of 7, 5, and 8 to LENGTH, WIDTH, and HEIGHT, respectively. If there are not enough data items on a card to *satisfy* the GET statement (i.e., to give each of the variables in the input list a value), more data cards will be read until all the variables have values. In the example,

```
DECLARE (NUMBER, COUNT) FIXED;
DECLARE (AVERAGE, MEAN) FLOAT;
GET LIST (NUMBER, AVERAGE, COUNT, MEAN);
```

Data cards:
```
7
    8.978E–03
9
        10.345E23
```

the first card is scanned and 7 is assigned to NUMBER. Since there are no more values on that card, the next card is scanned and 8.978E–03 is assigned to AVERAGE. Finally, the last two cards are scanned and COUNT and MEAN are assigned the values 9, and 10.345E23, respectively.

DATA-DIRECTED INPUT

Another type of free-style PL/I input statement, known as data-directed input, has the form,

GET DATA (*input list*);

This statement is very similar to the GET LIST statement, except for the form in which the data must be represented on the data card. In order to use the GET DATA statement, the names of the variables in the input list must appear on the data card along with their values, as in the following:

variable$_1$ = constant$_1$, variable$_2$ = constant$_2$,. . ., variable$_n$ = constant$_n$;

Banks and/or commas are used to separate each variable and datum pair. A semicolon must follow the list of data items for a particular GET DATA statement. Here is an example of the use of the GET DATA statement.

```
DECLARE (ID, VINTAGE, VOLUME, NUMBER) FIXED;
GET DATA (ID, VOLUME, VINTAGE, NUMBER);

Data cards:
  VINTAGE = 1961,
  NUMBER = 78,
  VOLUME = 24,
  ID = 3345;
```

Notice that in data-directed input, the order of the variables in the input list does not necessarily have to correspond to the order of the items on the data card. The input list may contain more variables than are given in the data stream. In this case, the variables which are not contained in the data stream retain their old values and are not affected by the input statement. For example, in this program segment

```
DECLARE(NUMBER, AGE, HEIGHT, WEIGHT) FIXED;
NUMBER = 34;
HEIGHT = 76;
GET DATA (NUMBER, HEIGHT, WEIGHT, AGE);

Data card;
HEIGHT = 56   WEIGHT = 100   AGE = 13;
```

WEIGHT and AGE are given the values 100 and 13, respectively. HEIGHT, which was assigned the value 76, receives the new value 56. The value of NUMBER, which was 34 before the GET DATA statement, remains the same after, since there was no item in the data stream corresponding to NUMBER.

One option that can be added to the GET LIST and GET DATA statements is SKIP(*expression*), which causes data cards to be skipped during input. This option may be placed between the GET and LIST or the GET and DATA, or at the end of the statement before the semicolon. The expression within parentheses is evaluated to yield an integer value which indicates the number of cards to be skipped (including the card currently being processed). If the value of the expression is less than one, SKIP(1) is assumed, otherwise, the value of the integer is used. If no expression appears with the SKIP option, a value of one is assumed. The following example illustrates the use of the SKIP option.

```
DECLARE (A, B, C) FIXED;
GET SKIP(2) LIST (A, B,C);
```

Data cards:
```
 1
         2
 3    4    5
```

assigns 3, 4, and 5 to A, B, and C, respectively. The first two data cards are skipped. If the data cards are arranged in the following order:

```
1
2
3
4
5
```

the same assignment results. Here is another example of the use of the SKIP option.

```
DECLARE (A, B, C, D) FIXED;
GET DATA (A, B);
GET DATA (C, D) SKIP;
```

Data cards:
```
A = 7, B = 9;   5,   6,   7,
C = 8,   D = 11;
```

In this program segment, the first GET statement causes 7 to be assigned to A, and 9 to be assigned to B. The next GET statement causes the computer to skip to the next card before reading; thus, the remaining values on the first card are ignored. The value 8 from the second card is assigned to C, and the value is assigned to D. SKIP is always processed first; that is, it is processed before any input takes place.

Finally, GET LIST and GET DATA statements may be intermixed within the same program. For example, this program segment

```
DECLARE (X, Y, Z) FIXED;
DECLARE NAME CHARACTER(20) VARYING;
GET DATA (X, Y);
GET LIST (Z, NAME);
```

Data card:
```
X = 6, Y = 7; 10 'CHARLIE'
```

assigns the value 6 to X, 7 to 10 to Z and the string, 'CHARLIE', to NAME.

LIST-DIRECTED OUTPUT

PL/I offers output methods similar to those described for input. *List-directed* output, for example, is free-style oriented and has the following form:

PUT LIST (*list of variables, constants, expressions or literals, separated by commas*);

The list of variables, constants, expressions, and literals enclosed in parentheses comprises the *output list* for the PUT statement. As in the main text, we will assume (unless stated otherwise) that the output device is a line printer. Each print line is divided into *print fields,* 24 spaces or *print positions* wide. Each item in the output is printed in the first available print field. The items are left adjusted (i.e., placed as far left as possible) in the print field.

Numeric values may not in fact appear to be left adjusted in the print field, since they are printed according to their type attributes with leading zeros suppressed. Here are some examples of the different output generated for the value 5.

DECLARED TYPE	APPEARANCE IN OUTPUT
FLOAT	b5.00000E+00bbbbbbbbbbbb
FIXED	bbbbbbb5bbbbbbbbbbbbbbbb

The b's represent spaces that appear in the print field. Spaces appearing before the "5" indicate suppressed zeros.

Character strings are printed, without enclosing quotes, in the first available print field. If the character string is wider than 24 characters, the string is continued on the next print field. If the character string is exactly 24 characters or a multiple of 24, it is printed in one or more print fields (depending on its length), and the next print field is skipped.

When variables appear in the output list, the value of the variable is printed, not the variable name. For example, the following PUT statement prints the values of the variables NAME and AGE.

```
DECLARE NAME CHARACTER(20) VARYING;
DECLARE AGE FIXED;
NAME = 'MARILYN';
AGE = 22;
PUT LIST (NAME, AGE);
```

Output:
MARILYNbbbbbbbbbbbbbbbbbbbbbbbbbb22

The b's that appear between the output items have been placed in this text (and will be used in the remainder of this section) to represent blanks for the purpose of showing the position of the printed items; they do not appear in the actual print out.

Constants in the output list are copied directly into the next available field. Here is an example of constants in an output list.

```
PUT LIST (1, 2, 3);
Output:
bbb1bbbbbbbbbbbbbbbbbbbbbbbb2bbbbbbbbbbbbbbbbbbbbbbbb3
```

Expressions in the output list are evaluated, and then the value of the expression is printed. The following example illustrates this:

```
PUT LIST (5 + 6, 7 * 3);
```

Output:
bbb11bbbbbbbbbbbbbbbbbbbbbbb21

The term *literal* is used to denote a string constant appearing in an output list. It is simply a string of characters enclosed by single quotes. When a literal appears in the output list, whatever is contained within the quotes is copied directly onto the print line in the first available print field. Here is an example of two literals.

```
PUT LIST ('COMPUTER SCIENCE', 'MATH');
```

Output:
COMPUTER SCIENCEbbbbbbbbbMATH

If the literal is 24 characters long, it is printed in one print field and the following print field is skipped. For example, the PUT statement,

```
PUT LIST ('THIS STRING IS 24 CHARS.', 'THIRD FIELD');
```

Output:
THIS STRING IS 24 CHARS.bbbbbbbbbbbbbbbbbbbbbbbbTHIRD FIELD

causes the first string to be printed in the first print field. The second print field is skipped, and the second literal is printed in the third field.

If the literal is longer than 24 characters, it is continued into the next field(s). The next item in the output is printed in the next available field after the literal, unless the literal is a multiple of 24. In the case where the literal is a multiple of 24, the field that follows the end of the literal is left blank, and printing resumes in the next field. For example,

```
PUT LIST ('THIS STRING IS LONGER THAN 24 CHARACTERS', 'NEXT ITEM');
```

Output:
THIS STRING IS LONGER THAN 24 CHARACTERSbbbbbbbbbNEXT ITEM

contains two literals. The first literal stretches over one field and part of another. The next literal is printed in the next available field, which happens to be the third print field.

If a quote is to be contained within a literal, two quote marks must be used, as in the following PUT statement:

```
PUT LIST ('RYAN''S FANCY');
```

Output:
RYAN'S FANCY

Literals are very useful in output statements because they give the programmer a way of identifying parts of the output. in this way, literals can make the output easier to read. For example, the following program segment prints the value of MARK.

```
DECLARE MARK FIXED;
MARK = 67;
PUT LIST ('MARK=', MARK);
```

Output:
MARK=bbbbbbbbbbbbbbbbbbbbbbbbbbb67

PL/I allows literals to be split across card boundaries in print statements. Some subsets of PL/I may, however, restrict the literal to one card, and not allow the literal to be broken across a card boundary.

If there are not enough print fields in one line to contain all the items in the output list, printing continues on the next line. The following program segment produces two lines of output.

```
DECLARE (AGE, HEIGHT, WEIGHT) FIXED;
DECLARE NAME CHARACTER(26) VARYING;
AGE = 45;
HEIGHT = 72;
WEIGHT = 200;
NAME = 'JACK';
PUT LIST ('NAME=', NAME, 'AGE=', AGE 'HEIGHT=', HEIGHT,
          'WEIGHT=', WEIGHT);
```

Output:
NAME=(19 spaces)JACK(20 spaces)AGE=(26 spaces)45(16 spaces)
HEIGHT=(6 spaces)72(16 spaces)WEIGHT=(22 spaces)200

This particular example assumes a print line length of 120 characters. The line length may differ on different printers. The blank spaces between output items are indicated in parentheses. The parentheses and their contents do not appear in the actual print out. They have been inserted here so that the entire print line could be shown on one text line.

If there is more than one output statement, the second output statement causes printing to resume in the next available print field, if possible. For example, the following pair of PUT statements results in one line of output.

```
DECLARE COLOUR CHARACTER(23) VARYING;
DECLARE ID FIXED;
COLOUR = 'BLUE';
ID = 3345;
PUT LIST (ID);
PUT LIST (COLOUR);
```

Output:
bbbb3345bbbbbbbbbbbbbbbbbbbBLUE

If a variable in a PUT statement has not received a value at the time the statement is executed, then one or more question marks (depending on the variable type) may be printed. here is an example of an output statement which contains variables which are assumed not to have values.

```
DECLARE (MARK, SCORE) FIXED;
DECLARE (AVG1, AVG2) FLOAT;
DECLARE NAME CHARACTER (14);
PUT LIST (MARK, SCORE, AVG1, AVG2, NAME);
```

Output:
(8 spaces)?(23 spaces)?(17 spaces)?.?????E+??(13 spaces)?.?????E+??(12 spaces)blank field

The spaces between each output item have been reduced so that the entire output line could be printed on one text line. Notice that the charactr string (declared, but not given a value) is left as an empty field.

Blank fields may be placed in the output in order to align certain items in columns or to improve the readability of the output. Blank fields may be indicated as blank literals in the output list. For example, the following output statement places a blank field between two literals.

PUT LIST ('FIRST FIELD', ' ', 'THIRD FIELD');

Output:
FIRST FIELDbbbbbbbbbbbbbbbbbbbbbbbbbbbbbbbbbbbbbbbbbbbbTHIRD FIELD

DATA-DIRECTED OUTPUT

Another form of free-style output statement is known as *data-directed* output. This statement has the following form:

PUT DATA (*list of variables*);

The PUT DATA statement causes all the variables that are listed in the output list to be printed with their names as well as their values.

$variable_1 = constant_1 \ldots variable_n = constant_n;$

Each variable-constant pair is placed in one print field, and the list is ended with a semicolon. Character strings are enclosed in quotes. Expressions, constants or literals are *not* allowed in the output list for the PUT DATA statement. The items are printed in the same order as they appear in the output list. For example, the PUT DATA statement in the following program:

```
DECLARE (A, B, C) FIXED;
A = 34;
B = 45;
C = 234;
PUT DATA (A, B, C);
```

Output:
A=bbbbbb34bbbbbbbbbbbbbbbB=bbbbbb45bbbbbbbbbbbbbbbC=bbbbb234;

outputs the values of A, B, and C, respectively.

If the value of a variable is not known when the PUT DATA statement is reached, a question mark(s) is printed after the equal sign, according to the type of the variable. Here is an example of a PUT DATA statement where the values of some the variables are not known.

```
DECLARE PAY FIXED;
DECLARE EMPLOYEE CHARACTER(24) VARYING;
EMPLOYEE = 'JUDY';
PUT DATA (EMPLOYEE, PAY);
```

Output:
EMPLOYEE='JUDY'bbbbbbbbbbPAY=bbbbbbb?;

The space between output items has been omitted to allow the output to be printed on one text line.

Data-directed output is very useful as an easy way of generating informative printouts during the debugging and testing phases of the program, when the need for tracing often arises.

There are several options that can be used with the PUT LIST and PUT DATA statements to allow finer control of the appearance of the output. These options may appear between 'PUT' and 'LIST' or 'DATA', or after the output list. One such option in SKIP(*expression*). The SKIP(*expression*) option causes lines to be skipped before the printing of items in the output list. The expression is evaluated and, if necessary, the resulting value is converted to an integer. If the integer value of the expression is greater than zero, the number of lines skipped is equal to that value. It is important to note that the number of lines skipped includes the current line. The current line is the last line that output occurred on, or if this is the first output statement, or if the last output line is full, the current line is the first blank line. Here is an example which may help to eliminate some of the confusion concerning the use of SKIP.

```
DECLARE (MARK, TEST) FIXED;
DECLARE STUDENT CHARACTER(25) VARYING;
STUDENT = 'M. BRILLIANT';
TEST = 5;
MARK = 100;
PUT SKIP(2) LIST (STUDENT);
PUT SKIP(2) DATA (TEST, MARK);
```

Output:
(blank line)
(blank line)
M. BRILLIANT
(blank line)
TEST=bbbbbbb5bbbbbbbbbbbbMARK=bbbbb100;

The first output statement causes the current line (i.e., the first blank line since this is the first output statement) and the next line to be skipped. The second output line causes the remainder of the current line, which contains 'M. BRILLIANT', and the next line to be skipped, and output resumes on the fifth line.

If no expression appears with the SKIP option, a value of one is assumed. SKIP(1) starts the output on the next line. Here is an example of SKIP used without an expression.

```
DECLARE (VOLUME, AREA) FIXED;
VOLUME = 45;
AREA = 67;
PUT SKIP DATA (AREA, VOLUME);
```

Output:
(blank line)
AREA=bbbbbb67bbbbbbbbbbbbVOLUME=bbbbbb45;

If the value of the expression is less than or equal to zero, the output will start at the beginning of the current line. Consider the following example.

```
DECLARE (AGE, WEIGHT) FIXED;
AGE = 34;
WEIGHT = 145;
PUT SKIP LIST (' ', WEIGHT);
PUT SKIP (0) LIST (AGE);
```

Output:
bbbbbb34bbbbbbbbbbbbbbbbbbbbbb145

In this example, the first output statement causes a line to be skipped; then, the first field is skipped (notice the blank literal at the beginning of the output list), and the value of WEIGHT is printed in the second print field. The next output statement, which gives SKIP a value of zero, causes the value of AGE to be printed on the same line in the first field. This field, because of the blank literal, is empty. Other print options are discussed in Sec. 5-3.

Finally, PUT LIST and PUT DATA statements may both appear in the same program. An example of the mixing of PUT LIST and PUT DATA statements is shown in the following program segment.

```
DECLARE (MARK1, MARK2, MARK3) FIXED;
DECLARE AVERAGE FLOAT;
DECLARE STUDENT CHARACTER(20) VARYING;
STUDENT = 'J. JONES';
MARK1 = 78;
MARK2 = 89;
MARK3 = 88;
AVERAGE = (MARK1 + MARK2 + MARK3) / 3.0E0;
PUT LIST ('STUDENT''S MARKS AND AVERAGE');
PUT SKIP(3) LIST ('STUDENT''S NAME IS', STUDENT);
PUT DATA (MARK1, MARK2, MARK3) LINE (12);
PUT SKIP LIST ('FINAL AVERAGE IS', AVERAGE);
PUT SKIP(2) LIST ('FAREWELL TO FORMAT-FREE I/0');
```

Output:
STUDENT'S MARKS AND AVERAGE
   (blank line)
   (blank line)
STUDENT'S NAME ISbbbbbbbbJ. JONES
   (blank line)
   (blank line)
   (blank line)
   (blank line)
   (blank line)
   (blank line)
   (blank line)
MARK1=bbbbbb78bbbbbbbbbbbMARK2=bbbbbb89bbbbbbbbbbbMARK3=bbbbbb88;
FINAL AVERAGE ISbbbbbbbbbb8.50000E+01
(blank line)
FAREWELL TO FORMAT-FREE I/0

In this example, the printer prints the first literal on the first line. The next statement causes the printer to skip three lines (i.e., leave two blank lines) and print the literal with the student's name. The marks are then printed. The fourth output statement causes the printer to skip to the next line and print the average. Finally, the printer skips a line and prints,

FAREWELL TO FORMAT-FREE I/0.

This brings us to the end of the section on free-style input and output. In this section, the principles and rules governing free-style input and output have been discussed. We now have assembled a body of information sufficient to write simple PL/I programs. In the next sections, the steps involved in preparing a program for execution on a computer and in interpreting the information that is returned are described. A number of complete sample programs are given and discussed.

Exercises for Sec. 2-3

1. Describe the results of the following three print statements:

    PUT LIST ('STATEMENT ONE');
    PUT SKIP LIST ('STATEMENT TWO');
    PUT LIST ('STATEMENT THREE');

2. Give the values of the variables MARK, SUM and ACCOUNT following the input statement
    GET LIST (MARK, AVERAGE, NAME, SUM, SOC_INS, ACCOUNT);
    assuming the following input data values:
    65, 62, 'JOE GREEN', 42, 655302111, 57321

3. Write a program to read a person's name in the form given name followed by surname and print the name in the form surname followed by given name.

    Example: Input 'URIAH', 'HEEP'
              Output HEEP, URIAH

2-4   PREPARING A PL/C PROGRAM

The process of preparing and running any program is often needlessly perplexing for the novice programmer. However, after the first several times, the procedure will become more familiar. Again following the lead of the main text, we will assume that programs are submitted to the computer through punched cards and output is handled by a line printer.

The first step is the coding of the program statements. This process is aided by the use of a special coding form, such as that shown in Fig. 2-1. This form contains printed rows of squares, the 80 squares in a row corresponding to the 80 columns on a punch card. Usually, one statement is printed in each row on the coding sheet. Later, each row will be keypunched on a separate card. Only one character may be printed in a square.

After the program statements have been printed on the coding forms, the next step is usually to have the program keypunched on program punch cards. A keypunch machine (see Fig. 2-2) has a keyboard similar to that of a typewriter, but

PL/I CODING FORM
UNIVERSITY OF SASKATCHEWAN
COMPUTATION CENTER

Name of Program _____

Coded by _____   Date _____

Checked by _____   Page _____ of _____

NOTE: Although PL/I coding is by definition independant of format, the computation centre requests that, for kepunching efficiency, each line start in column 2, 6, 11, 16, 21, 26, 31, 36, or 41 if possible, and that unnecessary blanks be omitted.

```
/* PROGRAM TO FIND THE AVERAGE OF THREE MARKS */

AVERAGE: PROCEDURE OPTIONS (MAIN);

    DECLARE (MARK1, MARK2, MARK3) FIXED;
    DECLARE (AVG, SUM) FLOAT;

    GET LIST (MARK1, MARK2, MARK3);
    SUM = MARK1 + MARK2 + MARK3;
    AVG = SUM / 3;

    PUT SKIP DATA (MARK1, MARK2, MARK3);
    PUT SKIP(2) LIST ('AVERAGE =', AVG);

END AVERAGE;
```

Fig. 2-1   A coding form

has automatic facilities for punching holes in cards. For every character the keypunch operator types, the machine prints the character at the top of the card and punches a certain combination of holes below. Every character is assigned its own unique pattern of holes. The computer is able to interpret the pattern of holes and thereby understand what character the combination represents.

Various compilers have various rules concerning the positioning of program statements on the card. For the PL/C compiler, all program statements must be punched somewhere in columns 2 to 72 of the punch cards. Blanks (signified on the card by no holes punched in the column) may appear anywhere within a statement (except, of course, in the middle of an identifier, constant, or keyword). In order to improve the readability of the program, the convention of punching only one statement per card is usually adopted. Several statements, however, may appear on one card. If a PL/C statement is too long to be punched on one card, it may be continued onto the next card (starting between columns 2 and 72). If this happens, the programmer must ensure that the point in the statement where the next card is begun does not fall in the middle of a constant, keyword, or identifier. Column 1 and columns 73 through 80 are not normally considered in the processing of the PL/C program. The latter columns (73 through 80) may be used to number the cards in order or else can be left empty.

All PL/C program statements must be followed by a semicolon. Two special statements are used to mark the beginning and end of every PL/C program. The first statement in a program must always be a PROCEDURE statement of the following form:

program-name: PROCEDURE OPTIONS(MAIN);

where the *program-name* must be valid PL/C identifier containing seven characters or less. This name uniquely identifies the program. The final statement in a program must always be an END statement, in either of two forms:

END;

or

END *program-name*;

If the second END format is used, then the *program-name* is the name on the PROCEDURE OPTIONS(MAIN); statement. This approach can be useful for reasons that will be seen in Chap. 3. This particular END statement indicates the physical

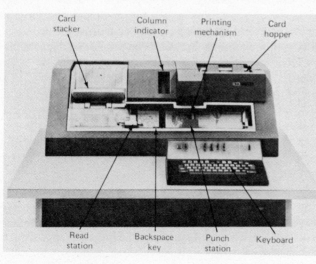

Fig. 2-2   A keypunch machine

end of the program statements and, if executed, terminates the program. PL/C allows any program statement to be assigned a unique *label*, where each label must be a valid identifier, which precedes the statement it names. A labelled statement has the following form:

> *label: program statement;*

Later, we will see situations in which this feature can be used.

It is good programming practice to include, directly in a program, various narrative explanations or comments. These can be used, for example, to describe the purpose of a particular statement or group of statements or to state conditions in effect at certain points of the program. In this way, other people who may look at the program can read these comments along with the actual statements and thereby understand the program more readily. Comments interspersed with the program statements aid the reader in clarifying the purpose and meaning of the instructions, but play no part in the actual processing of the PL/C statements. In order to distinguish between PL/C program statements and comments, a comment is always preceded by the pair of symbols /* and followed by the pair */ (sometimes referred to as comment brackets or delimiters). When punching both the beginning and terminating pairs, no blanks may appear between the * and / symbols. An example of an acceptable comment is the following:

> /* THIS PROGRAM READS 3 NUMBERS AND AVERAGES THEM */

A restriction often imposed in PL/C programs is that a comment may not continue across a card boundary onto the next card. If the programmer desires to include a comment which cannot entirely fit on one card, then he or she must end the comment with the closing symbols */ on the first card and continue it on the next by beginning a second comment there with the /* symbols. As with program statements, no part of a comment should appear in column 1 or columns 73 through 80 of any card. As an example, consider the following comments:

> /* IF THE INPUT NUMBERS SUM TO A NUMBER GREATER THAN THIRTY, */
> /* THEN PRINT OUT AN ERROR MESSAGE */

Finally, PL/C programs are entirely free-form, meaning that any number of blanks may appear within or between program statements. This means that the programmer has complete freedom in where statements can appear on cards. They can be grouped or spread out at will. For example, the programmer may insert blank unpunched cards at various locations among his program statement cards. When the computer prints out the program, it produces a blank line for every blank card encountered and thus improves the spacing of the program statements. This approach can reduce the clutter of the program listing, and thereby increase its readability. Also, program statements may be made more readable by indenting and including blanks within and around the program statement.

Input data are also usually keypunched on cards, although the rules for keypunching data cards are different from those for program statements. The format for data cards was discussed in Sec. 2-3.

After a program and necessary data have been keypunched on cards, the set of all these cards (the *card deck*) is almost ready to be input to the computer for processing. Prior to this step, however, the programmer must arrange the cards in the following order. At the front of the input card deck must appear certain *control cards* — special cards containing information needed by the computer concerning the program, such as the identification of the programmer and computer account

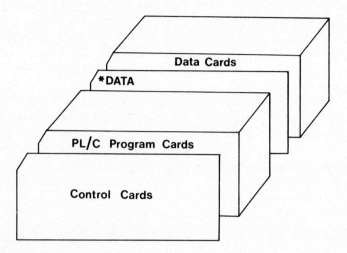

Fig. 2-3   Layout of a program deck

and the programming language used. Control cards, usually one or two in number, will normally be supplied by the class instructor or by the computer installation itself. Following these come the program statement cards in the exact order in which the statements appeared on the coding sheet. Then starting in column 1 may appear a card with

*DATA

punched on it. A *DATA card tells the compiler that the remaining cards in the deck, if any, are data cards. Finally, the data cards should appear at the end of the deck. If no data cards are required by the program, then the *DATA card may be omitted from the deck. Figure 2-3 illustrates the complete layout of a program deck.

The deck is now ready to be input to the card reader, which reads the cards and passes the information to the computer for processing. The program output is normally printed on paper by a line printer. This printout consists of a complete listing of the submitted PL/C program, followed by any output generated by its execution. Any error messages generated by the processing of the program are printed as well.

The guide for preparing a PL/C program just given should aid the begining programmer in successfully running his or her first jobs. After some practice, the novice should become familiar with the use of a keypunch, card reader, and line printer. Also with practice, the coding and card layout rules in PL/C will become less difficult to remember, along with the required card deck sequence rules. The final step mentioned in running a job was receiving the printed output. The programmer must then try to discover why errors occurred by re-creating exactly the steps that the computer performed. This important aspect of programming is the subject of the next section.

Exercises for Sec. 2-4

1.   What are control cards?

2.   What is the purpose of a *DATA card?

2-5 PROCESSING SIMPLE PL/I PROGRAMS

Once a program has been prepared according to the steps outlined in Sec. 2-4, it is ready to be submitted to the computer. The first stage of its processing involves execution of another program called the *compiler*, whose function it is to translate your program into an equivalent program in machine language ready for execution. During the compilation of a program, the compiler reports, and may attempt to correct, any errors that have been made in the use of the programming language. After the program has been compiled successfully, it is executed. Figure 2-4 contains the printout from the processing of a simple program. Let's examine it.

The printout begins with a line identifying the compiler used:

*PLC

After this line, lines entitled 'OPTIONS IN EFFECT" appear. These lines tell the programmer the settings of the various options available in the processing of PL/C programs. For example, for this run, the maximum number of pages is 30, and the maximum number of lines is 2000.

The next line printed is a page header which contains, among other things, the contents of the card that immediately follows the control cards. Since this line appears at the top of all pages to come, it is helpful to place a descriptive comment card here. The other information given includes the date and time that this particular run was made.

The next printed line contains six headings,

STMT LEVEL NEST BLOCK MLVL SOURCE TEXT

The statement numbers appear under the STMT heading. Each statement in the program is numbered by the compiler. These numbers are provided in order to help in referencing statements (for example, in error messages). Notice that comments are not statements and therefore, are not numbered. The next four headings, LEVEL, NEST, BLOCK, and MLVL, provide further information concerning the program, the meaning and use of which is not important at the present time. Under the SOURCE TEXT heading appear the source program statements exactly as they appear on the punched cards submitted to the computer.

Following this listing of the source program, a summary of all errors and possible errors (i.e., warnings) that can be detected only after the entire program has been compiled are printed. Such errors, for example, would include the failure to declare a key variable. Since declarations can occur anywhere within a program, the lack of a declaration only be detected after the entire program has been processed. In this program, one warning appears in this section, namely,

WARNING: NO FILE SPECIFIED. SYSIN/SYSPRINT ASSUMED.

This warning indicates that no input or output files have been specified; and, therefore, the standard input file (SYSIN) and the standard output file (SYSPRINT) have been used. SYSIN and SYSPRINT refer to the card reader and line printer, respectively. This warning is, in fact, to be expected under the assumptions that we have made concerning input and output at the present time, and should not be of concern for the time being.

After the compiler has finished translating the program, the program is executed. First, three data values are read in (the values used in this run were 65, 72, and 83). The variables, MARK1, MARK2, and MARK3, are asigned the values 65, 72, and 83, respectively, from the data cards (not shown). In the next statement, the sum of MARK1, MARK2, and MARK3 is calculated and assigned to the variable SUM. Next, the sum of the marks is divided by three to produce the

```
*PLC

*OPTIONS IN EFFECT*    TIME=(0,15.00),PAGES=30,LINES=2000,NOATR,NOXREF,FLAGW,NOCMNTS,SORMGIN=(2,72,1),ERRORS=(50,50),TABSIZE=29200,
*OPTIONS IN EFFECT*    SOURCE,OPLIST,NOCMPRS,HDRPG,AUXIO=10000,LINECT=60,NOALIST,MONITOR=(UDEF,BNDRY,SUBRG,AUTO),MCALL,NOMTEXT,
*OPTIONS IN EFFECT*    DUMP=(S,F,L,E,U,R),DUMPE=(S,F,L,E,U,R),DUMPT=(S,F,L,E,U,R)
```

```
/* PROGRAM TO FIND THE AVERAGE OF THREE MARKS */                      PL/C-R7.6-004 07/31/78  9:46 PAGE    1

  STMT LEVEL NEST BLOCK MLVL   SOURCE TEXT

                                     /* PROGRAM TO FIND THE AVERAGE OF THREE MARKS */

    1                                AVERAGE: PROCEDURE OPTIONS (MAIN);

    2    1          1                    DECLARE (MARK1, MARK2, MARK3) FIXED;
    3    1          1                    DECLARE (AVG, SUM) FLOAT;

    4    1          1                    GET LIST (MARK1, MARK2, MARK3);
    5    1          1                    SUM = MARK1 + MARK2 + MARK3;
    6    1          1                    AVG = SUM / 3;

    7    1          1                    PUT SKIP DATA (MARK1, MARK2, MARK3);
    8    1          1                    PUT SKIP(2) LIST ('AVERAGE =', AVG);
    9    1          1                END AVERAGE;

ERRORS/WARNINGS DETECTED DURING CODE GENERATION:

      WARNING: NO FILE SPECIFIED. SYSIN/SYSPRINT ASSUMED. (CGOC)


MARK1=      65        MARK2=      72        MARK3=      83;

AVERAGE =                  .7.33333E+01


IN STMT    9  PROGRAM RETURNS FROM MAIN PROCEDURE.
```

Fig. 2-4   Program to find the average of three marks

average, which is assigned to the variable AVG. The output, which is generated by the PUT statements in the program, is printed on a new page, and a copy of it follows.

```
MARK1=      65        MARK2=      72        MARK3=      83;
AVERAGE =                  7.33333E+01

IN STMT    9  PROGRAM RETURNS FROM MAIN PROCEDURE.
```

In this program, the output consists of the three marks and the average, which have been titled using literals. After the output, the message
      IN STMT n PROGRAM RETURNS FROM MAIN PROCEDURE.
signals the end of execution. "n" is the number of the last statement executed, which in this program is the "END AVERAGE;" statement (statement number 9).
      Finally, on the next output printer page the *post-mortem dump* appears. A copy of this program's post-mortem dump appears in Fig. 2-5. The contents of this part of the printout are discussed later in this section.
      The program of Fig. 2-6 is somewhat more difficult. This program reads in the radius of a circle in metres and finds the circumference and area of that circle. This computation is also repeated for a second circle whose radius is two metres larger than the first.

```
/* PROGRAM TO FIND THE AVERAGE OF THREE MARKS */                    PL/C-R7   POST-MORTEM DUMP   PAGE   1


IN STMT   9  SCALARS AND BLOCK-TRACE:

***** MAIN PROCEDURE AVERAGE

SUM= 2.20000E+02      AVG= 7.33333E+01      MARK3=    83       MARK2=    72       MARK1=    65



NON-0 PROCEDURE EXECUTION COUNTS:
NAME        STMT COUNT  NAME      STMT COUNT  NAME      STMT COUNT  NAME      STMT COUNT  NAME      STMT COUNT
AVERAGE     0001 00001
```

```
        COMPILATION STATISTICS  (0009 STATEMENTS)    |            EXECUTION STATISTICS
SECONDS  ERRORS  WARNINGS  PAGES  LINES  CARDS  INCL'S | SECONDS  ERRORS  WARNINGS  PAGES  LINES  CARDS  INCL'S  AUX I/O
  .24       0        1       1     31     16      0   |   .01       0        0        1      8      1      0       0
--------------------------------------------------------+----------------------------------------------------------------
BYTES    SYMBOL TABLE  INTERMEDIATE CODE   OBJECT CODE  |  STATIC CORE   AUTOMATIC CORE    DYNAMIC CORE   TOTAL STORAGE
USED        697( 1K)      294(  1K)        246(  1K)   |   344(  1K)      482(  1K)        0(  0K)       1698(  2K)
UNUSED    16103(113K)  166870(162K)     283530(276K)   | 282738(276K)  282738(276K)   166870(162K)    282738(276K)
```

THIS PROGRAM MAY BE RERUN WITHOUT CHANGE IN A REGION 276K BYTES SMALLER USING TABLESIZE=   175

Fig. 2-5   Post-mortem dump of averaging program

```
                        /* AREA AND CIRCUMFERENCE */

                        STMT LEVEL NEST BLOCK MLVL  SOURCE TEXT


                                           /* AREA AND CIRCUMFERENCE */

                          1                CIRCLE: PROCEDURE OPTIONS (MAIN);

                          2   1        1   DECLARE (AREA, CIR, PI) FLOAT;
                          3   1        1   DECLARE RADIUS FIXED;

                          4   1        1   GET LIST (RADIUS);
                          5   1        1   PI = 3.14159;
                          6   1        1   AREA = PI * RADIUS * RADIUS;
                          7   1        1   CIR = PI * RADIUS * 2;

                          8   1        1   PUT SKIP DATA (RADIUS, AREA, CIR);

                                           /* CALCULATE AND PRINT SECOND RADIUS, AREA */
                                           /* AND CIRCUMFERENCE */

                          9   1        1   PUT SKIP(2) LIST ('SECOND RADIUS');

                         10   1        1   RADIUS = RADIUS + 2;
                         11   1        1   AREA = PI * RADIUS * RADIUS;
                         12   1        1   CIR = PI * RADIUS * 2;

                         13   1        1   PUT SKIP DATA (RADIUS, AREA, CIR);
                         14   1        1   END CIRCLE;

                        ERRORS/WARNINGS DETECTED DURING CODE GENERATION:

                            WARNING: NO FILE SPECIFIED. SYSIN/SYSPRINT ASSUMED. (CGOC)


                        RADIUS=      7        AREA= 1.53937E+02     CIR= 4.39822E+01;

                        SECOND RADIUS
                        RADIUS=      9        AREA= 2.54468E+02     CIR= 5.65486E+01;


                        IN STMT   14  PROGRAM RETURNS FROM MAIN PROCEDURE.
```

Fig. 2-6   Program to find the area and circumference of two circles

The variables used in this program are declared in statements 2 and 3. The next statement reads in the radius of the circle. The variable PL is initialized to 3.14159 and in statements 6, 7, and 8, the values of AREA and CIR are calculated and printed. Following this, a comment section describes the purpose of the rest of the program. The radius is increased by two metres, and new values for AREA and CIR are calculated and printed. The output from this program appears at the end of the program.

DEBUGGING

Both of the examples discussed to this point were correct programs. Often, however, despite the *best* intentions of the programmer, errors are made during the writing of programs. These errors often result from misuse of some feature of the programming language or a misunderstanding of exactly what certain statements do in a program. The computer often aids in finding these errors by printing error messages, if for example, statements are not properly specified or an illegal operation is attempted. It is the programmer's task to remove all these errors from the program; this important process is usually referred to as *debugging*.

There are three types of errors that are common in programs. The first type of error is the *syntax error* (or *compile-time error*). A syntax error is a violation of one of the grammatical rules of the programming language itself, for example, illegally forming one of the statements. As was previously mentioned, syntax errors are detected during the compilation of the program. If a syntax error is discovered by the PL/C compiler, an error message is printed and an attempt is made to correct the error. Sometimes the programmer is lucky, and the proper correction is made, as in the program given in Fig. 2-7.

The error in this program occurs in statement 6, as indicated by the message from the compiler. 'LIST' is missing from the PUT statement. As stated in the error message, the offending statement has been replaced by a corrected version.

```
/* VOLUME OF A SPHERE */

STMT LEVEL NEST BLOCK MLVL   SOURCE TEXT


                        /* VOLUME OF A SPHERE */

  1                     VOLUME: PROCEDURE OPTIONS(MAIN);

  2    1         1        DECLARE (RADIUS, PI, VOLUME) FLOAT;

  3    1         1        RADIUS = 7.8;
  4    1         1        PI = 3.14159;
  5    1         1        VOLUME = 4 / 3E0 * PI * RADIUS ** 3;
  6    1         1        PUT ('VOLUME =', VOLUME);
   ERROR IN STMT    6  IMPROPER I/O PHRASE (SY22)
        FOR STMT    6 PL/C USES  PUT LIST ('VOLUME =',VOLUME);

  7    1         1        END VOLUME;
ERRORS/WARNINGS DETECTED DURING CODE GENERATION:

     WARNING: NO FILE SPECIFIED. SYSIN/SYSPRINT ASSUMED. (CGOC)


VOLUME =              1.98779E+03


IN STMT    7  PROGRAM RETURNS FROM MAIN PROCEDURE.
```

Fig. 2-7   Correctly diagnosed syntax error

Unfortuntately, the computer cannot read minds; syntax errors are not always corrected in the way the programmer wishes. This can lead to disastrous results, and thus one should not blindly follow the correction. This problem is illustrated in Fig. 2-8. In this program, the positions of 'LIST' and 'SKIP' have been accidentally interchanged in the PUT statement. A correction is made by the PL/C compiler, but clearly it is not the one desired. This correction causes more errors that are detected at the end of compilation. These errors are listed under ERRORS/WARNINGS IN USE OR DEFINITION OF SYMBOLS:

If the statement in error cannot be understood or corrected by the PL/C compiler, a null statement (denoted simply by ";") is used to replace it, as in the example program of Fig. 2-9. In this example, the error occurs in statement 2. A minus sign has been used instead of an equal sign. The statement should read

RADIUS = 7.8;

The second type of error occurs during the execution of a program and is appropriately called an *execution error* (or *run-time error*). An execution error occurs when the program directs the computer to perform an operation that, for some reason, it cannot perform. When an execution error occurs, the computer prints an error message and attempts to correct the error. Consider the example program which appears in Fig. 2-10.

```
/* VOLUME OF A SPHERE */

STMT LEVEL NEST BLOCK MLVL   SOURCE TEXT


                                    /* VOLUME OF A SPHERE */

    1                          VOLUME: PROCEDURE OPTIONS(MAIN);

    2    1         1               DECLARE (RADIUS, PI, VOLUME) FLOAT;

    3    1         1               RADIUS = 7.8;
    4    1         1               PI = 3.14159;
    5    1         1               VOLUME = 4 / 3E0 * PI * RADIUS ** 3;
    6    1         1               PUT LIST SKIP ('VOLUME =', VOLUME);
     ERROR IN STMT     6 MISSING ( IN COLUMN 15 (SY02)
     ERROR IN STMT     6 MISSING ) IN COLUMN 40 (SY04)
           FOR STMT    6 PL/C USES  PUT LIST (SKIP ('VOLUME =',VOLUME));

    7    1         1               END VOLUME;

ERRORS/WARNINGS IN USE OR DEFINITION OF SYMBOLS:

     ERROR IN STMT     6 NAME NEVER DECLARED, OR AMBIGUOUSLY QUALIFIED (SM50)
     ERROR IN STMT     6 $UFIXVAR HAS TOO MANY SUBSCRIPTS.  SUBSCRIPT LIST DELETED (SM4E)
           FOR STMT    6 PL/C USES  PUT LIST ($UFIXVAR);
           DECLARED IN BLOCK                 0


ERRORS/WARNINGS DETECTED DURING CODE GENERATION:

     WARNING: NO FILE SPECIFIED. SYSIN/SYSPRINT ASSUMED. (CGOC)



         0



IN STMT   7 PROGRAM RETURNS FROM MAIN PROCEDURE.
```

Fig. 2-8   Incorrectly diagnosed syntax error

```
/* VOLUME OF A SPHERE */

STMT LEVEL NEST BLOCK MLVL   SOURCE TEXT


                            /* VOLUME OF A SPHERE */

    1                       VOLUME: PROCEDURE OPTIONS(MAIN);

    2    1        1            DECLARE (RADIUS, PI, VOLUME) FLOAT;

    3    1        1            RADIUS - 7.8;
        ERROR IN STMT    3  IMPROPER SYNTAX, TRANSLATION SUSPENDED IN COLUMN 13 (SY17)
            FOR STMT    3 PL/C USES  ;
    4    1        1            PI = 3.14159;
    5    1        1            VOLUME = 4 / 3E0 * PI * RADIUS ** 3;
    6    1        1            PUT SKIP LIST ('VOLUME =', VOLUME);
    7    1        1         END VOLUME;

ERRORS/WARNINGS DETECTED DURING CODE GENERATION:

    WARNING: NO FILE SPECIFIED. SYSIN/SYSPRINT ASSUMED. (CGOC)



***** ERROR IN STMT    3  DELETED STATEMENT ENCOUNTERED (EX32)
***** ERROR IN STMT    5  RADIUS  HAS NOT BEEN INITIALIZED.  IT IS SET TO ZERO. (EX5D)
VOLUME =                  0.00000E+00


IN STMT    7  PROGRAM RETURNS FROM MAIN PROCEDURE.
```

Fig. 2-9   Syntax error replaced by a null statement

```
/* VOLUME OF A SPHERE */

STMT LEVEL NEST BLOCK MLVL   SOURCE TEXT


                            /* VOLUME OF A SPHERE */

    1                       VOLUME: PROCEDURE OPTIONS(MAIN);

    2    1        1            DECLARE (RADIUS, PI, VOLUME) FLOAT;

    3    1        1            RADIUS = 7.8;
    4    1        1            PI = 3.14159;
    5    1        1            VOLUME = 4 / 3E0 * PIE * RADIUS **3;
    6    1        1            PUT SKIP LIST ('VOLUME =', VOLUME);
    7    1        1         END VOLUME;

ERRORS/WARNINGS DETECTED DURING CODE GENERATION:

    WARNING: NO FILE SPECIFIED. SYSIN/SYSPRINT ASSUMED. (CGOC)



***** ERROR IN STMT    5  PIE  HAS NOT BEEN INITIALIZED.  IT IS SET TO ZERO. (EX5D)
VOLUME =                  0.00000E+00


IN STMT    7  PROGRAM RETURNS FROM MAIN PROCEDURE.
```

Fig. 2-10   Execution error

In this example, the computer is unable to calculate a value for VOLUME in statement 5, since the variable PIE was never initialized. The error is, in fact, a keypunching error. PIE should have been PI. The statement should read:

VOLUME = 4 / 3E0 * *PI* * RADIUS ** 3;

PL/C attempts to correct this error by assigning a value of 0 to PIE and uses this value to calculate the volume.

Sometimes, the computer is unable to make any corection that will allow the program to continue executing. In such an instance execution stops because the error is *fatal*. An example of such a program is given in Fig. 2-11. This program attempts to read in the value of RADIUS, but no data cards were provided. Thus, it is unable to do this, and execution stops.

The third type of error is more insidious than the other two, as it is perhaps the most difficult type of error to detect. This detection difficulty arises because it usually does not generate any error message. In the case of this type of error, messages appear only if an execution error is generated later in the program. For example, at one point in a program, a variable may, through an error, be given a value of zero. If this variable is used as a divisor in another part of the program, the computer at that point prints an error message, since dividing by zero is an illegal operation (although the error actually occurred when the variable was given the value 0). If, however, this error does not cause a problem during execution, the error may remain undetected invalidating the results of the program. Some of the causes of error of this third type are keypunching mistakes in constants, hidden truncation of values, and misuse of operators and their precedence. The program which appears in Fig. 2-12 contains two errors of this type.

In this example, a mistake has been made in assigning the value of PI in statement 4. PI has been assigned the value 3.14259 instead of 3.14159. The second error occurs in statement 5. The value of RADIUS should be raised to the third power rather than multiplied by three, as this statement indicates.

A correct program to find the volume of a sphere with radius 7.8 is given in Fig. 2-13.

```
/* VOLUME OF A SPHERE */

STMT LEVEL NEST BLOCK MLVL  SOURCE TEXT


                                    /* VOLUME OF A SPHERE */

      1                             VOLUME: PROCEDURE OPTIONS(MAIN);

      2    1            1             DECLARE (RADIUS, PI, VOLUME) FLOAT;

      3    1            1             GET LIST (RADIUS);
      4    1            1             PI = 3.14159;
      5    1            1             VOLUME = 4 / 3E0 * PI * RADIUS ** 3;
      6    1            1             PUT SKIP LIST ('VOLUME =', VOLUME);
      7    1            1           END VOLUME;

ERRORS/WARNINGS DETECTED DURING CODE GENERATION:

   WARNING: NO FILE SPECIFIED. SYSIN/SYSPRINT ASSUMED. (CGOC)


***** ERROR IN STMT   3 END OF FILE REACHED. (EX02)
ABOVE ERROR IS FATAL.  PROGRAM IS STOPPED.
```

Fig. 2-11   Fatal execution error

```
/* VOLUME OF A SPHERE */

STMT LEVEL NEST BLOCK MLVL  SOURCE TEXT

                            /* VOLUME OF A SPHERE */

    1                       VOLUME: PROCEDURE OPTIONS(MAIN);

    2   1         1             DECLARE (RADIUS, PI, VOLUME) FLOAT;

    3   1         1             RADIUS = 7.8;
    4   1         1             PI = 3.14259;
    5   1         1             VOLUME = 4 / 3E0 * PI * RADIUS * 3;
    6   1         1             PUT SKIP LIST ('VOLUME =', VOLUME);
    7   1         1         END VOLUME;

ERRORS/WARNINGS DETECTED DURING CODE GENERATION:

    WARNING: NO FILE SPECIFIED. SYSIN/SYSPRINT ASSUMED. (CGOC)


VOLUME =            9.80488E+01


IN STMT   7  PROGRAM RETURNS FROM MAIN PROCEDURE.
```

Fig. 2-12   Logical errors

One of the ways to find errors that are not detected by the computer (i.e., errors that are caused by faulty logic or by not providing for every case that could occur in the data) is through *program testing*. The main text offers useful comments on methods of program testing. Program testing involves executing the program with carefully selected data, and is a skill that one acquires through continual practice. To start you on the right track, we offer some general guidelines. Test data should always be chosen with regard to the program specifications, rather than to fit the program itself. When the correct results are known, the results of the program can be easily verified. The data should be

```
/* VOLUME OF A SPHERE */

STMT LEVEL NEST BLOCK MLVL  SOURCE TEXT

                            /* VOLUME OF A SPHERE */

    1                       VOLUME: PROCEDURE OPTIONS(MAIN);

    2   1         1             DECLARE (RADIUS, PI, VOLUME) FLOAT;

    3   1         1             RADIUS = 7.8;
    4   1         1             PI = 3.14159;
    5   1         1             VOLUME = 4 / 3E0 * PI * RADIUS ** 3;
    6   1         1             PUT SKIP LIST ('VOLUME =', VOLUME);
    7   1         1         END VOLUME;

ERRORS/WARNINGS DETECTED DURING CODE GENERATION:

    WARNING: NO FILE SPECIFIED. SYSIN/SYSPRINT ASSUMED. (CGOC)


VOLUME =            1.98779E+03


IN STMT   7  PROGRAM RETURNS FROM MAIN PROCEDURE.
```

Fig. 2-13   Correct volume of a sphere program

representative of the program specifications, rather than of the program itself. This is to ensure that the test is of what the program was supposed to do, rather than what it was written to do; this approach to testing will often detect omissions in the implementation of a problem. Care must be taken to ensure that the data are representative of all possible cases. This does not mean that all possible data must be tested; but, it does mean that all possible situations should be tested. For example, consider the problem of writing a program that reads in an employee's name and hours worked, and calculates the amount of pay received per hour, given a fixed weekly salary. The program is then to print the employee's name, hours worked, weekly and hourly salary. The program which appears in Fig. 2-14 is one possible solution. This program has been tested using the test data,

    'JOHN DOE'   40

This program appears to satisfy the specifications of the problem, but not all situations have been tested. Suppose, for some reason (a paid vacation, for example), an employee did not work at all that week and, therefore, the "hours" entry on his card was 0. Running this program with this employee's information would result in an error, as an attempt to divide by zero would be made in statement 7. A test of this program should have included this possiblity.

Often, extra output statements can be inserted to help locate errors. These extra statements are used to print intermediate values or messages, which allow the programmer to follow the execution of the program. The program of Fig. 2-15 illustrates this method of locating errors.

```
/* PROGRAM TO CALCULATE HOURLY PAY */

STMT LEVEL NEST BLOCK MLVL  SOURCE TEXT


                                /* PROGRAM TO CALCULATE HOURLY PAY */

    1                           PAY: PROCEDURE OPTIONS (MAIN);

    2     1         1               DECLARE (HOURS, HOURLY_PAY) FLOAT;
    3     1         1               DECLARE WEEKLY_PAY FIXED;
    4     1         1               DECLARE EMPLOYEE CHARACTER (25) VARYING;

    5     1         1               GET LIST (EMPLOYEE, HOURS);
    6     1         1               WEEKLY_PAY = 150.00;
    7     1         1               HOURLY_PAY = WEEKLY_PAY / HOURS;

    8     1         1               PUT SKIP LIST ('EMPLOYEE''S PAY');
    9     1         1               PUT SKIP (2) LIST ('EMPLOYEE: ', EMPLOYEE);
   10     1         1               PUT SKIP (3) LIST ('WEEKLY PAY =', WEEKLY PAY);
   11     1         1               PUT SKIP LIST ('HOURLY PAY =', HOURLY_PAY);
   12     1         1           END PAY;

ERRORS/WARNINGS DETECTED DURING CODE GENERATION:

    WARNING: NO FILE SPECIFIED. SYSIN/SYSPRINT ASSUMED. (CGOC)


EMPLOYEE'S PAY

EMPLOYEE:          JOHN DOE


WEEKLY PAY =              150
HOURLY PAY =       3.75000E+00


IN STMT   12  PROGRAM RETURNS FROM MAIN PROCEDURE.
```

Fig. 2-14   Program to calculate hourly pay

```
/* PROGRAM TO FIND THE AVERAGE OF THREE NUMBERS */

STMT LEVEL NEST BLOCK MLVL   SOURCE TEXT


                             /* PROGRAM TO FIND THE AVERAGE OF THREE NUMBERS */

   1                         AVERAGE: PROCEDURE OPTIONS(MAIN);

   2    1         1          DECLARE (A, B, C) FIXED;
   3    1         1          DECLARE (SUM, AVG) FLOAT;

   4    1         1          A = 68;
   5    1         1          B = 72;
   6    1         1          C = 31;
   7    1         1          SUM = A + B - C;
   8    1         1          PUT DATA (A, B, C, SUM);
   9    1         1          AVG = SUM / 3;
  10    1         1          PUT SKIP LIST ('THE AVERAGE IS', AVG);
  11    1         1          END AVERAGE;

ERRORS/WARNINGS DETECTED DURING CODE GENERATION:

     WARNING: NO FILE SPECIFIED. SYSIN/SYSPRINT ASSUMED. (CGOC)



A=     68           B=     72          C=     31          SUM= 1.09000E+02;
THE AVERAGE IS          3.63333E+01



IN STMT   11  PROGRAM RETURNS FROM MAIN PROCEDURE.
```

Fig. 2-15 Example of output statements used to find errors

Statement 8 in this program prints the values of A, B, C, and SUM. It is clear from this printout that, for the given values of A, B, and C, the value of SUM is too small. A recheck of the program indicates an obvious mistake. Statement 7 should be SUM = A + B + C, not SUM = A + B - C. Though the use of this extra print statement was not necessary to find the error in this particular program, it might be important in a situation in which a similar error was embedded in a program containing hundreds of statements.

PL/C provides a facility that may offer additional help in finding errors. This is the post-mortem dump that was previously mentioned. This dump gives a listing of all the variables in the program and their final values. From this listing, variables that never received values or were improperly defined are easily detected. Note, however, that this listing gives the *final* values only — it does not give any of the intermediate values. For intermediate values, the programmer must rely on output statements.

This dump also counts the number of times each label in the program is encountered during execution. This feature may be useful in counting the number of times that key statements are executed. This can be done simply by labelling them, and then checking the dump. The rest of the post-mortem dump includes statistics concerning the program. These are divided into two tables: one of compilation statistics and the other of execution statistics. The novice programmer need not worry about these statistics. The post-mortem dump for the program to compute the volume of a sphere is shown in Fig. 2-16.

This ends the discussion on the preparation and execution of simple PL/C programs. In this section, examples of executed programs were shown. The concepts of program testing and debugging were discussed, and the types of errors found in programs were illustrated.

In the next section, more elaborate sample programs are given.

```
/* VOLUME OF A SPHERE */


IN STMT    7  SCALARS AND BLOCK-TRACE:

***** MAIN PROCEDURE VOLUME

VOLUME= 1.98779E+03     PI= 3.14158E+00        RADIUS= 7.79999E+00


NON-0 PROCEDURE EXECUTION COUNTS:
NAME        STMT COUNT  NAME       STMT COUNT  NAME       STMT COUNT  NAME       STMT COUNT  NAME       STMT COUNT
VOLUME      0001 00001


     COMPILATION STATISTICS  (0007 STATEMENTS)         ¦            EXECUTION STATISTICS
SECONDS  ERRORS  WARNINGS  PAGES  LINES  CARDS  INCL'S  ¦ SECONDS  ERRORS  WARNINGS  PAGES  LINES  CARDS  INCL'S  AUX I/O
   .22      0       1        1     28     12      0     ¦   .00       0       0        1      6      0      0        0
------------------------------------------------------------------------------------------------------------------------
BYTES    SYMBOL TABLE    INTERMEDIATE CODE    OBJECT CODE  ¦ STATIC CORE   AUTOMATIC CORE   DYNAMIC CORE    TOTAL STORAGE
USED        871(  1K)       182(  1K)          208(  1K)   ¦   346(  1K)      390(  1K)         0(  0K)        1637(  2K)
UNUSED    15929(113K)    166870(162K)       283526(276K)   ¦282814(276K)   282814(276K)    166870(162K)     282799(276K)

THIS PROGRAM MAY BE RERUN WITHOUT CHANGE IN A REGION 276K BYTES SMALLER USING TABLESIZE=  218
```

Fig. 2-16   Post-mortem dump of volume of a sphere program

Exercises for Sec. 2-5

1. Name three types of programming errors.

2. What is program testing?

3. How may the post-mortem dump be used to assist in locating errors?

2-6   APPLICATIONS

In this section, complete PL/C programs are given for the applications discussed in Sec. 2-6 of the main text. In each case, the reader is expected to have followed through the relevant material in the main text carefully, from problem specification, through the process of algorithm design, to the production of the final algorithm itself. The programs given in this section have resulted from a straightforward implementation of the algorithms given in the main text. The same solution approach has been used and, where possible, the same names have been used for the variables. Sample input and output are given for each program.

The subsection numbering employed parallels that of the main text.

2-6.1   Reporting Student Grades

This section presents the programmed solution to the problem of reporting student grades given in Sec. 2-6.1 of the main text. The problem as given in the main text is to calculate the final grade of a student given his/her mark in three aspects of a year's work. The three marks to be considered are the result of the midterm examination which is to count 30% towards the final mark, the mark given for the laboratory work which is to count 20%, and finally, the result of the final examination which is to account for the remaining 50%. The input data is to consist of the student's name and mark in each of the three designated areas. The variables used in the PL/C solution given in Fig. 2-17 are:

Variable name	Type	Usage
LAB_WORK	FIXED	Mark received for lab work
MIDTERM_EXAM	FIXED	Mark received on midterm exam
FINAL_EXAM	FIXED	Mark received on final exam
GRADE	FLOAT	Final grade
NAME	CHARACTER(20) VARYING	Student's name

The data card used with this program contained the following values:

'ARTHUR FONZARELLI' 72, 68, 65

```
/*CALCULATE FINAL GRADE FROM THREE ASPECTS OF A STUDENT'S WORK */

STMT LEVEL NEST BLOCK MLVL  SOURCE TEXT


                            /*CALCULATE FINAL GRADE FROM THREE ASPECTS OF A STUDENT'S WORK */

  1                         REPORT: PROCEDURE OPTIONS(MAIN);

  2    1         1          DECLARE (LAB_WORK, MIDTERM_EXAM, FINAL_EXAM) FIXED,
                                GRADE FLOAT,
                                NAME CHARACTER(20) VARYING;

                            /* INPUT */
  3    1         1          GET LIST (NAME, LAB_WORK, MIDTERM_EXAM, FINAL_EXAM);

                            /* COMPUTE FINAL GRADE */
  4    1         1          GRADE = 0.20 * LAB_WORK + 0.30 * MIDTERM_EXAM + 0.50 * FINAL_EXAM;

                            /* DISPLAY RESULTS */
  5    1         1          PUT SKIP LIST ('STUDENT NAME:', NAME);
  6    1         1          PUT SKIP LIST ('LABORATORY WORK:', LAB_WORK);
  7    1         1          PUT SKIP LIST ('MIDTERM EXAMINATION:', MIDTERM_EXAM);
  8    1         1          PUT SKIP LIST ('FINAL EXAMINATION:', FINAL_EXAM);
  9    1         1          PUT SKIP LIST ('FINAL GRADE:', GRADE);

 10    1         1          END REPORT;

ERRORS/WARNINGS DETECTED DURING CODE GENERATION:

    WARNING: NO FILE SPECIFIED. SYSIN/SYSPRINT ASSUMED. (CGOC)


STUDENT NAME:          ARTHUR FONZARELLI
LABORATORY WORK:          72
MIDTERM EXAMINATION:      68
FINAL EXAMINATION:        65
FINAL GRADE:          6.72999E+01


IN STMT   10  PROGRAM RETURNS FROM MAIN PROCEDURE.
```

Fig. 2-17 Program for the reporting student grades problem

In statement 4, the student's name and three aspects of his year's work are read into the respective variables. The student's final grade is calculated in statement 4. Statements 5 to 9 print the input information and the student's grade. Note that the three items comprising the final grades are declared to be of type integer, while the final grade itself is of type float. This results in different output format. In statement 10, execution is terminated.

2-6.2 Gauging Inflation

The program presented in this section is the solution to the gauging inflation problem given in Sec. 2-6.2 of the main text. The problem is to calculate the algebraic and percentage differences in the prices of the same product bought a month apart. The input values are the name of the product followed by its price this month and the price paid last month. The variables used in the PL/C program which appears in Fig. 2-18 are:

Variable name	Type	Usage
ITEM	CHARACTER(20) VARYING	Description of item
CURRENT_PRICE	FLOAT	Price paid this month
OLD_PRICE	FLOAT	Price paid last month
ALG_DIFF	FLOAT	Algebraic difference
PC_DIFF	FLOAT	Percentage difference

The following data card was used with this program.

'COOKING OIL', 4.79, 4.38

In statement 3, the three input values are read into ITEM, CURRENT_PRICE, and OLD_PRICE, respectively. The fourth statement uses the current price and old price to calculate the algebraic difference (ALG_DIFF). The percentage difference (PC_DIFF) is calculated in statement 5. Statements 6 through 10 print the input values and the calculated algebraic and percentage differences for that item. In statement 11, execution of the program is terminated.

2-6.3 Pari-Mutuel Payoffs

The program given in Fig. 2-19 is a solution to the pari-mutuel payoff problem given in Sec. 2-6.3 of the main text. This problem concerns pari-mutuel betting at a horse racetrack. Under this system, persons who bet on the winning horse share the total amount which was bet for the race minus a percentage of the total for the racetrack expenses (including purses for the races) and for taxes. The rate of taxation is 10.6% of all money bet. In addition, the race track owners take another 12% to cover expenses. The remaining money is divided among those who bet on the winning horse in proportion to their bets.

The problem, then, is to write a PL/C program which takes as input data, the total amount bet on a race, the name of the winning horse for the race, and the amount bet on that horse, in that order and calculates the payoff on a 2 dollar bet. The variables used in the following PL/C solution are:

Variable name	Type	Usage
WIN_POOL	FLOAT	Total amount bet in the race
WINNER	CHARACTER(20) VARYING	Name of winning horse
BET	FLOAT	Amount bet on winning horse
RATIO	FLOAT	Payoff ratio for each dollar bet
TRACK_SHARE	FLOAT	Track owners' share
GOVT_SHARE	FLOAT	Governments' share (taxes)
PAYOFF	FLOAT	Amount paid on a $2 bet

The sample data card run with the above program contained the following input values:

10000   'COMPUTER DELIGHT'

In statement 3, the three input data values are read into the respective variables. Statements 4 and 5 compute the track's and taxes' shares of the amount bet (10000), and statement 6 reduces the WIN_POOL amount accordingly. The payoff ratio for each dollar bet on the winning horse COMPUTER DELIGHT is computed in statement 7, by dividing the value of

```
/* CALCULATE THE ALGEBRAIC AND PERCENTAGE DIFFERENCE IN PRICE */

STMT LEVEL NEST BLOCK MLVL   SOURCE TEXT


                        /* CALCULATE THE ALGEBRAIC AND PERCENTAGE DIFFERENCE IN PRICE */
                        /* OF IDENTICAL ITEMS BOUGHT IN DIFFERENT MONTHS */

  1                     GUAGE: PROCEDURE OPTIONS(MAIN);

  2    1        1       DECLARE ITEM CHARACTER(20) VARYING,
                            (CURRENT_PRICE, OLD_PRICE, ALG_DIFF, PC_DIFF) FLOAT;

                        /* INPUT */
  3    1        1       GET LIST (ITEM, CURRENT_PRICE, OLD_PRICE);

                        /* COMPUTE ALGEBRAIC DIFFERENCE IN PRICE */
  4    1        1       ALG_DIFF = CURRENT_PRICE - OLD_PRICE;

                        /* COMPUTE PERCENTAGE INCREASE */
  5    1        1       PC_DIFF = ALG_DIFF / OLD_PRICE * 100;

                        /* OUTPUT */
  6    1        1       PUT SKIP LIST ('ITEM PURCHASED:', ITEM);
  7    1        1       PUT SKIP LIST ('PRICE THIS MONTH:', '$', CURRENT_PRICE);
  8    1        1       PUT SKIP LIST ('PRICE LAST MONTH:', '$', OLD_PRICE);
  9    1        1       PUT SKIP LIST ('ALGEBRAIC DIFFERENCE:', '$', ALG_DIFF);
 10    1        1       PUT SKIP LIST ('PERCENTAGE DIFFERENCE:', PC_DIFF, '%');

 11    1        1       END GUAGE;

ERRORS/WARNINGS DETECTED DURING CODE GENERATION:

    WARNING: NO FILE SPECIFIED. SYSIN/SYSPRINT ASSUMED. (CGOC)



ITEM PURCHASED:        COOKING OIL
PRICE THIS MONTH:      $                  4.78999E+00
PRICE LAST MONTH:      $                  4.37999E+00
ALGEBRAIC DIFFERENCE:  $                  4.09999E-01
PERCENTAGE DIFFERENCE: 9.36073E+00            %


IN STMT   11  PROGRAM RETURNS FROM MAIN PROCEDURE.
```

Fig. 2-18   Program for the gauging inflation problem

```
/* COMPUTE THE PAYOFF FOR A STANDARD $2 BET */

STMT LEVEL NEST BLOCK MLVL   SOURCE TEXT


                                  /* COMPUTE THE PAYOFF FOR A STANDARD $2 BET */

  1                               PAYOFF:  PROCEDURE OPTIONS(MAIN);

  2     1          1              DECLARE WINNER CHARACTER(20) VARYING,
                                         (BET, WIN_POOL, GOVT_SHARE, TRACK_SHARE, RATIO,
                                         PAYOFF) FLOAT;

                                  /*  INPUT */
  3     1          1              GET LIST (WIN_POOL, WINNER, BET);

                                  /* DETERMINE GOVERNMENT'S AND TRACK'S SHARE OF POOL */
  4     1          1              GOVT_SHARE = 0.106 * WIN_POOL;
  5     1          1              TRACK_SHARE = 0.12 * WIN_POOL;

                                  /* REDUCE POOL ACCORDINGLY */
  6     1          1              WIN_POOL = WIN_POOL - (GOVT_SHARE + TRACK_SHARE);

                                  /* COMPUTE PAYOFF RATIO FOR EACH DOLLAR WAGERED */
  7     1          1              RATIO = WIN_POOL / BET;

                                  /* COMPUTE POSTED PAYOFF */
  8     1          1              PAYOFF = RATIO * 2.0;

                                  /* OUTPUT */
  9     1          1              PUT SKIP LIST (WINNER, 'WINS AND PAYS $', PAYOFF);

                                  /* FINISHED */
 10     1          1          END PAYOFF;

ERRORS/WARNINGS DETECTED DURING CODE GENERATION:

    WARNING: NO FILE SPECIFIED. SYSIN/SYSPRINT ASSUMED. (CGOC)


COMPUTER DELIGHT       WINS AND PAYS $       2.81454E+01


IN STMT   10  PROGRAM RETURNS FROM MAIN PROCEDURE.
```

Fig. 2-19 Program for the pari-mutual payoffs problem

on COMPUTER DELIGHT, which is the value of BET (550). This value is then doubled to give the payoff on a $2 bet. Statement 9 serves to print the results of the computations. In statement 11, execution is terminated.

The reader, at this point, should be familiar with the basic concepts of PL/I programming. In this chapter, data and data types were introduced, along with principles of data manipulation. The use of variables in PL/I programming was discussed. Expressions and their evaluation were the topics of the next section, and the PL/I assignment statement was also presented. The set of fundamental programming tools discussed thus far was completed with the section on input and output. The remainder of the chapter concerned the approach to preparing, and executing PL/C programs, and the reader was provided with sample problems and solutions.

In the next chapter, more complex programming concepts are given to expand the reader's programming capabilities.

EXERCISES FOR CHAPTER 2

1. The Canadian weather office has recently undergone a conversion to the metric system.
    (i) Write a program to find the Fahrenheit equivalent of a Celsius temperature (integer value) input to the program (conversion formula: $F = 9/5 \, C° + 32$). Test your program by finding the Fahrenheit equivalent of 26 degrees Celsius.
    (ii) Write a program that read a rainfall amount given in inches (real value) and prints its equivalent in millimetres (conversion formula: 25.4 millimetres = 1 inch). Test your program by finding the millimetre equivalent of 1.75 inches.

2. The roots of a quadratic equation of the form
    $$ax^2 + bx + c = 0$$
    are real if and only if the discriminant given by
    $$b^2 - 4ac$$
    is nonnegative. Write a program to read the values of the coefficients a, b, and c and print the coefficients and the value of the discriminant.
    Example   Input: 2 3 1
                 Output: COEFFICIENTS ARE: 2 3 1
                             DISCRIMINANT IS: 1
    Test your program on the values a = 5, b = 6, and c = 8.

3. The cost to the consumer of a new car is the sum of the wholesale cost of the car, the dealer's percentage markup and the provincial or state sales tax (applied to the "marked up" price). Assuming a dealer's markup of 12% on all units and a sales tax of 6%, write a program to read the wholesale cost of the car and print the consumer's cost. Using your program, find the consumer's cost of a car that has a wholesale cost of $7500.

4. Honest John's Used Car Company pays its sales staff a salary of $250 per month plus a commission of $15 for each car they sell plus 5% of the value of the sale. Each month, Honest John's bookkeeper prepares a single punched card for each salesperson, containing his/her name, the number of cars sold and the value of the cars sold.
    Write a program to compute and display a salesperson's salary for a given month. include in the output the salesperson's name and salary. Test your program on the data values
        'DON SWIFT', 4, 32000

5. Three masses m_1, m_2, and m_3 are separated by distances r_{12}, r_{13}, and r_{23}, as shown in Fig. 2-20. If G is the universal gravitational constant, the binding energy holding the mass particles together is given by the following formula:
    $$E = G \left(\frac{m_1 m_2}{r_{12}} + \frac{m_1 m_3}{r_{13}} + \frac{m_2 m_3}{r_{23}} \right)$$
    Write a program to read values of m_1, m_2, m_3, r_{12}, r_{13}, and r_{23}; then compute and print the binding energy along with the initial data values. For mass in kilograms and distance in metres, $G = 6.67 \times 10^{-11}$ newton- metre^2 / kg^2. The values of m_1, m_2, and m_3 are punched on the first data card, and values

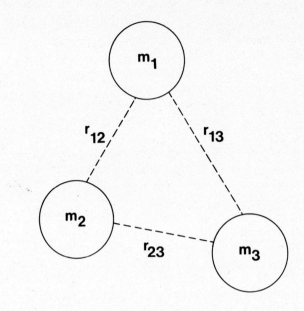

Fig. 2-20   Distances between three masses

of r_{12}, r_{13}, and r_{23} are punched on the second. Assume that all data are punched as real values. Using your program, find the binding energy given the following data:

637E24	3651E36	4531E29
96E65	531E50	75E45

6. The cost of hail insurance in a typical farming community is 3.5% of the desired amount of coverage per acre, multiplied by the number of acres seeded.

    Assuming that the crop possibilities are limited to wheat, oats and barley, write a program that reads the desired coverage and the number of acres planted for each of the three crops and computes the total cost of hail insurance for this customer.

    Test your program on the following data:

Desired Coverage Per Acre	*Number of Acres*
30.00	140
25.00	240
30.0	300

7. Although the speed of light remains constant regardless of the relative speeds of the light source and the observer, the measured frequency and wavelength do change — an effect first predicted by Johann Doppler and thereby dubbed the "Doppler effect." The wavelength λ emitted by a source moving towards an observer with velocity v appears to be compressed by an amount $\triangle\lambda$, which is given by the formula

$$\triangle\lambda = \frac{v\lambda}{c}$$

where c is the speed of light.

Suppose an airplane is travelling towards a radio station at a constant velocity of 360 km/hour (or 10^4 cm. per sec.). If the radio station is broadcasting at a wavelength of 30 metres, the change in wavelength due to the Doppler effect is

$$\triangle\lambda \;=\; \frac{\mathrm{v}\lambda}{\mathrm{c}}$$

$$=\; \frac{(10^4 \text{ cm per sec}) \times (3 \times 10^3 \text{ cm})}{(3 \times 10^{10} \text{ cm per sec})} \;=\; 10^{-3} \text{ cm.}$$

Thus the pilot of this airplane must adjust his receiving set to a wavelength of 3000 cm. *minus* 10^{-3} cm., or 2999.999 cm., until he reaches the station and then to a wavelength of 3000.001 cm. as he moves away from the station.

Write a program to read the broadcast length (in metres) of a radio station and the speed of an approaching plane (in km/hour) and then print out the actual setting (in cm.) at which the pilot will receive the signal. Note that your program will have to make the necessary conversions before calculating the change in wavelength (conversions are: 1000 m. = 1 km., 100 cm. = 1 m.). Use your program to find the proper wavelength setting if a pilot travelling at 440 km/hour wishes to receive a radio station with a broadcast wavelength of 25 metres.

CHAPTER

DECISION
STRUCTURES

The preceding chapter presented some basic tools in PL/I programming which allow the programmer to design and run simple programs involving input of values, computations, and output of results. More complex problems, however, require the use of additional capabilities in a programming language. This chapter introduces the PL/I capabilities of choosing one course of action from several alternatives and of causing the repeated execution of a group of statements. Central to both of these constructs is the concept of a decision: in the former, to determine which alternative to take; in the latter, whether to perform the set of statements one more time. The basis for these decisions is written in a program as expressions called "conditions" which are also developed at this point. Programs using the concepts introduced in this chapter are then presented.

3-1 INTRODUCTION

Chapter 3 of the main text presents key programming constructs to affect the flow of control through an algorithm or program. These constructs, known as *control structures*, represent a major factor in determining the power and usability of a programming language.

The PL/I language offers a wide range of powerful control structures that match those introduced in the algorithmic language. The implementation of two control structures in PL/I is presented in this chapter, along with some discussion of their applications.

3-2 THE SELECTION FROM ALTERNATIVE ACTIONS

3-2.1 The IF...THEN...ELSE Statement

The If...then...else statement represented by

```
If condition
then statement
else statement
```

in the algorithmic language has a direct counterpart in PL/I. The general form of the IF statement in PL/I is

```
IF condition
THEN single statement to do if condition is true;
ELSE  single statement to do if condition is false;
```

As an aid to improved readability, we have adopted the convention that the "IF", "THEN", and "ELSE" all begin in the same column.

As in the algorithmic language, the PL/I IF statement is a double alternative statement; that is, there are two alternative actions. If the expressed condition is true, the "true alternative" (or "THEN clause") is executed; otherwise, the "false alternative" (or "ELSE clause") is executed.

The condition is expressed as a PL/I logical expression, that is, an expression which can have only two values, "true" or "false". These values are usually represented in PL/I as bit strings '1'B (true) and '0'B (false). As is done in the algorithmic language, the condition is normally expressed using *relational operators*, to compare two operands. Table 3-1 shows the relational operators used in the algorithmic language and their representation in PL/I.

In PL/I, as in the algorithmic language, logical expressions may also contain the logical connectives, *and, not,* and *or*. The use of these operators in conditional statements is discussed in Sec. 3-4. Here are some examples of logical expressions in PL/I.

Table 3-1   Relational operators and their symbols

Operator	Algorithmic Language Symbol	PL/I Symbol
Greater than	$>$	$>$
Less than	$<$	$<$
Equal	$=$	$=$
Greater than or equal to	$\geq$	$>=$
Less than or equal to	$\leq$	$<=$
Not equal	$\neq$	$\neg=$

A = B	(In this context, this is an expression which is "true" if the value of A equals that of B. Notice that this is easily confused with the assignment of B to A.)
3 < 7	
'1'B	(logical constant)
'0'B	(logical constant)
SWITCH	(A variable that has been declared LOGICAL.)
'CAT' = 'DOG'	

The last example is a comparison between two strings. Character strings can be compared using any of the relational operators. In this chapter, we compare strings only for equality (i.e., whether the strings are equal or not) for which the interpretation is clear. Complete rules governing the comparison of character strings are left to Chap. 5.

Here is a simple example of a PL/I IF...THEN...ELSE statement.

```
IF A < B
THEN PUT LIST ('A IS SMALLER THAN B');
ELSE  PUT LIST ('B IS SMALLER THAN OR EQUAL TO A');
```

In many cases, more than one statement is required in the true or false alternative. For this to be done in PL/I, the alternative must be contained in a *DO group.* The DO group has the form

```
DO;
statement₁
statement₂
     .

     .

     .
statementₙ
END;
```

The "DO" and "END" which enclose the statements of the DO group signal that these statements are to be considered as one statement. The following is an example of an IF structure which contains more than one statement in both the true and false alternatives.

```
IF COUNT >= COUNT1
THEN DO;
     COUNT = COUNT + 1;
     PUT LIST ('TRUE ALTERNATIVE SELECTED.');
     PLACE = 7 * 34;
     END;
ELSE DO;
     COUNT1 = COUNT1 + 2;
     PUT LIST ('FALSE ALTERNATIVE SELECTED.');
     PLACE = 8 * 34;
     END;
```

DO groups may be used in both the true and false alternatives, or they may be used in only one alternative. An example in which the true alternative is one statement and the false alternative is a DO group is the following:

```
IF NUM < SUM
THEN PUT LIST ('TRUE ALTERNATIVE SELECTED.');
ELSE DO;
     COUNT = COUNT + 1;
     PUT LIST ('FALSE ALTERNATIVE SELECTED.');
     END;
```

As in the algorithmic language, the PL/I IF statement can also be used if there is just one alternative. In the following program segment, for example, if the variable NUM is less than zero, then one is added to COUNT; otherwise, nothing is done.

```
DECLARE (NUM, COUNT) FIXED;
COUNT = 0;
NUM = - 6;
IF NUM < 0
THEN COUNT = COUNT + 1;
```

In this example there is no ELSE clause. The action of the single alternative IF statement is to perform the statement included within the IF statement, if the condition is true. If the condition is false, execution continues with the next executable statement after the true alternative. The following is another example of a single alternative IF structure.

```
DECLARE (MARK, SUM) FIXED;
IF MARK < 50
THEN DO;
     PUT LIST ('STUDENT HAS FAILED');
     SUM = SUM + MARK;
     END;
```

In this example if MARK is less than 50, the literal 'STUDENT HAS FAILED' is printed and MARK is added to SUM.

The IF...THEN...ELSE structure also allows the testing of a number of conditions that may occur in sequence. The next section illustrates a way of testing conditions, through the use of nested IF statements.

3-2.2 Nested IF Statements

In PL/I, as in the algorithmic language, it is often desirable to include an IF statement in one of the alternatives of another IF...THEN...ELSE statement. This second IF statement is said to be *nested* within the first IF statement.

For example, consider the following program segment which reads in a student's name and mark, and prints a message if the student has passed (i.e., mark is greater than or equal to 50). If the student has received a passing grade, a further check is made to see if he or she is an "A" student (i.e., the mark is greater than or equal to 80).

```
DECLARE MARK FIXED;
DECLARE NAME CHARACTER(20) VARYING;
GET LIST (NAME, MARK);
IF MARK >= 50
THEN DO;
      PUT LIST (NAME, 'HAS PASSED.');
      IF MARK >= 80
      THEN PUT SKIP LIST (NAME, 'IS AN "A" STUDENT.');
      ELSE PUT SKIP LIST (NAME, 'IS NOT AN "A" STUDENT.');
      END;
```

In this program, the student's name and mark are read in. If the mark is greater than or equal to 50, the student's name and the literal, HAS PASSED. are printed. In addition, if the mark is greater than or equal to 80, the student's name and the literal IS AN 'A' STUDENT are printed. If, however, the mark is between 50 and 79 inclusively, the name of the student and the message IS NOT AN 'A' STUDENT. is printed.

As was pointed out in the main text, the programmer must be very careful when using nested IF statements. For example, consider the following program segment.

```
DECLARE MARK FIXED;
DECLARE NAME CHARACTER(20) VARYING;
GET LIST (NAME, MARK);
IF MARK >= 50
THEN IF MARK >= 80
      THEN PUT SKIP LIST (NAME, 'IS AN "A" STUDENT.');
ELSE PUT SKIP LIST (NAME, 'HAS FAILED.');
```

The intent of the program is to have the ELSE belong to the first IF statement (i.e., IF MARK >= 50), and the indenting appears to suggest that this is the case, but is it? The answer is no. The ELSE is always associated with the innermost preceding IF that does not have an ELSE; in this case, that is, IF MARK >= 80.

There are two ways that the desired interpretation can be achieved. One way is to put the nested IF statement in a DO group, as is done in the following example.

```
DECLARE MARK FIXED;
DECLARE NAME CHARACTER(20) VARYING;
GET LIST (NAME, MARK);
IF MARK >= 50
THEN DO;
      IF MARK >= 80
      THEN PUT LIST (NAME, 'IS AN "A" STUDENT.');
      END;
ELSE PUT SKIP LIST (NAME, 'HAS FAILED.');
```

Another method is to insert a *dummy* ELSE. A dummy ELSE is simply an ELSE followed by a semicolon. The following example uses this technique.

```
DECLARE MARK FIXED;
DECLARE NAME CHARACTER (20) VARYING;
GET LIST (NAME, MARK);
IF MARK >= 50
THEN IF MARK >= 80
      THEN PUT SKIP LIST (NAME, 'IS AN "A" STUDENT.');
      ELSE;
ELSE PUT SKIP LIST (NAME, 'HAS FAILED.');
```

In this version, the dummy "ELSE" inserted after the THEN clause of the nested IF causes the ELSE clause following the second IF to be interpreted as belonging to the outermost IF statement. The erroneous version of this particular program segment serves to illustrate another important point; namely, that indenting only acts as a guide to the human reader; it has no effect whatsoever on the actions of the computer.

Many IF statements can, of course, be nested within one another. An example of a multilevel nesting of such statements is contained in the following program.

```
DECLARE (A, B, C, D, E) FLOAT;
GET LIST (A, B, C, D, E);
IF A < B
THEN DO;
      PUT LIST ('A IS LESS THAN B');
      IF A < C
      THEN DO;
            PUT SKIP LIST ('A IS LESS THAN C');
            IF A < D
            THEN DO;
                  PUT SKIP LIST ('A IS LESS THAN D');
                  IF A < E
                  THEN DO;
                        PUT SKIP LIST ('A IS LESS THAN E');
                        END;
                  END;
            END;
      END;
```

In this program, A is compared to B. If A is less than B, a message is printed and then A is compared to C. If A is less than C, another message is printed and then A is compared to D. If A is less than D, a third message is printed and then A is compared to E. If A is less than E, a final message is printed. Notice that if A is not less than B, nothing is printed.

In this section, the PL/I IF statement was introduced. This control structure allows decisions to be made during the execution of the program, based on certain conditions that are usually unknown before run time. Nested IF statements were also introduced. The programmer is again cautioned that undisciplined use of this type of structure might impair the clarity of programs and so proper care must be exercised when using nested IF statements.

The next section deals with another control structure which allows the programmer to alter the flow of control during execution. The looping structure allows the programmer to have sections of a program repeated during execution.

Exercises for Sec. 3-2

1. Write a program to read in the base and height of a triangle and print out the area of the triangle (area = ½ * base * height). During the preparation of data for this algorithm, it is entirely possible that a mistake be made that may inadvertently result in one of the values base or height being negative. Clearly, this is undesirable since it will result in a negative area being printed. Design into your program the capability to check for negative values on input. If one is encountered, you should print it out along with a message identifying it as the base or height (this may make it easier for someone to correct the error). Test your program on the values base = 34 and height = –64.

2. Write a program to read the lengths of the three sides of a triangle (S1, S2, S3) and determine what type of triangle it is based on the following cases:
   Let A denote the largest of S1, S2 and S3, and B and C the other two.
   Then,

if $A = B + C$	, no triangle is formed;
if $A^2 = B^2 = C^2$	, an equilateral triangle is formed;
if $A^2 = B^2 + C^2$	, a right-angled triangle is formed;
if $A^2 > B^2 + C^2$	, an obtuse triangle is formed;
if $A^2 < B^2 + C^2$	, an acute triangle is formed.

   Your program should print the lengths of the three sides, followed by the triangle's type
   (i.e., SIDES ARE: 3 4 5
      TYPE OF TRIANGLE: RIGHT_ANGLED)
   Use your program to decide what type of triangle has sides of lengths 6, 7, and 8.

3. (i) Write a program to read an integer value and determine whether the value is even or odd.
   (ii) Generalize the program written in question (i) to decide, given m and n, whether, n divides m. (i.e., there is no remainder for m/n)

3-3 LOOPING

As described in the main text, the programmer may indicate the repetition of a group of statements using a construct called a *loop*. The general format for any loop is usually as follows:

> *loop control statement*
> > *group of statements which are to be repeated*

The group of statements to be repeated is called the *range* of the loop; the number of times that the range is repeated is determined by the loop control statement which must directly precede the range. The loop end statement serves to indicate the end of the statements that make up the range, but is not always required in some kinds of loops.

In the algorithmic language, we introduced two forms of loop: the conditional loop and the counted loop. The conditional loop in the algorithmic notation was given as

> Repeat while condition
> > *statement*$_1$
> > *statement*$_2$
> > .
> > .
> > .
> > *statement*$_n$

where *statement*$_1$ thru *statement*$_n$ were statements to be performed while the condition was true. Another form of the conditional loop was

> Repeat thru step *N* while condition

where step *N* referred to the last step of the range. In the algorithmic language the counted loop was given as

> Repeat for *name* = *start-value, start-value + 1, . . ., end-value*
> > *statement*$_1$
> > *statement*$_2$
> > .
> > .
> > .
> > *statement*$_n$

where *statement*$_1$ thru *statement*$_n$ represent the range of the loop or

> Repeat thru step *N* for *name* = *start-value, start-value + increment, . . .,*
> > *end-value*

where *N* represents the last step in the range. Both of these forms have direct parallels in PL/I. In this section we look first at the types of loop provided in PL/I, discussing the rules for their use. We then discuss the concept of writing loops inside loops or loop nesting.

3-3.1 Conditional Loops

The general form of the conditional loop in PL/I is

```
DO WHILE (condition);
    range statement₁
    range statement₂
        .
        .
        .
    range statementₙ
END;
```

where the first statement is the loop control statement. The *condition* is a valid PL/I logical expression which is evaluated to a truth value of either "true" or "false". (Note that unlike the IF statement, the condition must be enclosed in parentheses and the statement must be followed by a semicolon.) The *range statements* are a group of any valid PL/I statements. The keyword END must be placed immediately following the last statement in the group of range statements to indicate the exact position in the program where the loop's range physically ends. The interpretation given is identical to that of the "Repeat ... while" construct of the algorithmic language. Upon encountering the loop control statement for the first time, the condition is evaluated using the present values of all variables found in the condition. If the truth value resulting from this evaluation is "false," then the loop will not be performed at all and the next statement executed will be the one which follows the loop's corresponding END statement. If, however, the truth value is "true," then the statements in the range are executed. After this execution, control returns to the loop control statement and the condition is once again evaluated. Note that the values of the variables involved in the condition may have been changed in the loop. If the truth value obtained from this evaluation is "false," then the range is not performed any more and control is relinquished to the statement after the corresponding END. If the truth value is "true," the process of loop execution and subsequent condition testing occurs again. This process continues until a condition evaluation produces a "false" value. For example, consider the following segment (notice the indentation convention that we adopt for the statements in the range of a loop);

```
DECLARE (COUNT, NUM, SUM) FIXED;
COUNT = 0;   SUM = 0;
NUM = 6;
DO WHILE (SUM < NUM);
    COUNT = COUNT + 1;
    SUM = SUM + 2;
END;
PUT LIST (SUM, COUNT);
```

Execution of this segment produces the following output:

6   3

Notice that if this program segment were altered somewhat, by changing the assignment statement

NUM = 6;

to

NUM = 0;

then execution of the segment would produce the output:

          0   0

since the condition would yield a value of "false" upon the initial evaluation, and thus, the loop range is not entered even once.

The conditional loop uses the truth value of the condition for each loop repetition to determine if the range statements will be repeated once more. Thus, the number of times the repetition actually occurs is not fixed, but dependent upon the logical value of the condition. As shown in the main text, there are certain applications where the loop range must be performed a fixed number of times, controlled by a counter, and independent of any condition. This type of loop is known as the counted loop and is the subject of the next section.

3-3.2   Counted Loops

The PL/I *counted loop* differs in form from that given in the algorithmic language, although the general principle is very similar.

Both forms of the counted loop involve a loop control statement based on a special *loop variable* that takes on a sequence of values. The essential difference lies in the specification of this sequence. In the algorithmic language, the sequence is expressed in the form

$val_1, val_2, \ldots, val_n$

In PL/I, it is expressed in the form

start-value TO end-value BY step-value

where *start-value, end-value*, and *step-value* are each arithmetic expressions. BY and TO are special keywords. The complete construct has the following general form:

DO *loop variable* = *start-value TO end-value BY step-value;*
    range statement$_1$
    range statement$_2$
       .
       .
       .
    last range statement
END;

The loop control statement is followed by the list of statements comprising the range, and then the loop end statement END;. The END; serves to indicate the physical point in the program statements where the range statements end.

The execution of a counted loop in PL/I proceeds as follows. First, the expressions for the start-value, end-value, and step-value entries are all evaluated and stored, and the value of the start-value expression is assigned to the loop variable. A test comparison is then made between the value of the loop variable and the end-value. If the loop variable value is greater than the end-value, and the step-value is positive, then the loop's range statements are not executed even once. Instead, control immediately passes to the statement following the loop's END; statement. If, however, the loop variable value is less than or equal to the end-value, with the step-value being positive, then loop execution continues as follows. The loop range statements are performed once, followed by an increment of the loop variable. This increment is done automatically by adding the step-value to the loop variable value. Next, another test comparison between the incremented loop variable and the end-value is made. Again, if the value of the former is less than or equal to the latter (assuming the step-value is a positive value), then the range is executed once again, followed by another increment of the loop variable and a subsequent comparison. This process continues until the loop variable has a value greater than the end-value, at which point the loop is finally terminated.

Note that the preceding description of the execution applies to a counted loop with a positive step-value. If, however, a negative value is obtained from the step-value expression, then the loop execution proceeds in basically the same fashion as just described. The only change is that, for each test comparison made, the loop is terminated if the loop variable value is, not greater than, but less than the end-value. Thus, if the value of the loop variable is greater than or equal to the end-value, then the loop execution continues.

For example, consider the following program segment:

```
DECLARE (COUNT, SUM) FIXED;
SUM = 0;
DO COUNT = 1 TO 3 BY 1;
    SUM = SUM + COUNT;
END;
PUT LIST ('SUM = ', SUM);
```

In this loop, the loop variable is COUNT. The start-value, end-value, and step-value entries are 1, 3, and 1, respectively. The range of the loop consists of only a single statement, an assignment statement. Execution of the loop begins with the storing of the values of the start-value, end-value, and step-value, and the assignment of the start-value 1 to COUNT. The initial comparison is then made between the COUNT value 1 and the end-value 3. Since the step-value 1 is positive and the COUNT value 1 is less than the end-value 3, the one statement that makes up the range is performed. After this, SUM has the value 1. The increment of the COUNT value to 2 is then done automatically, using the step-value 1, and the subsequent comparison between the COUNT value 2 and the end-value 3 causes execution of the range statement to take place once again, since 2 is not greater than 3. The assignment statement leaves the value 3 in SUM (since COUNT now has the value 2); the subsequent incrementing of COUNT then results in it getting the value 3. Once again, the comparison is made and COUNT is found to be equal to the end-value 3. Thus, the range statement is repeated once more, leaving the value 6 in SUM. COUNT is next incremented to 4 and the comparison finds that this time the value of COUNT is greater than 3. Therefore, the loop is terminated and the PUT statement is the next statement executed.

In many cases, the value of the loop variable never actually becomes equal to the end-value, but misses it during the succession of values. For example, if the loop control statement for a loop is

    DO I = 5 TO 2 BY –2;

the successive values of I will be 5, 3, and then 1. When the last of these values, 1, is given to I, the I value is less than the end-value 2 and, consequently, the loop execution terminates. Thus, the loop variable I is never given the value 2, the end-value, during the execution. This poses no problems, since the comparisons made test, not if the loop variable value is equal to the end-value, but if it is less than (or, in the case of a positive step-value, greater than) the end-value.

Note that it is possible for a counted loop to have its range executed zero times. This happens when the start-value given is greater than the end-value (or, if the step-value is negative, when the start-value is less than the end-value). For example, the program segment:

```
DECLARE J FIXED, LIMIT FIXED;
LIMIT = 4;
DO J = 5 TO LIMIT BY 2;
    PUT LIST (J);
END;
next statement
```

causes the assignment of the value 5 to the loop variable J and then performs the initial comparison. Since the step-value 2 is positive and the J value 5 is greater than the end-value 4, the loop is terminated immediately, with control passing to the next statement after the END;. Thus, the PUT statement comprising the range is never executed.

There are several extensions and variations of this basic counted loop format that serve to extend the power of the loop control statement. These are dealt with in the Appendices.

There are several important points that should be noted concerning the use of counted loops. Frequently, the step-value entry is omitted. In that case, the compiler automatically assumes a step-value of 1.

Although a statement in the range of a loop is permitted to change the value of the loop variable, you would be wise to avoid this practice, since the number of times the loop will be executed is changed once the loop variable value is tampered with. For example, consider the following program segment:

```
DECLARE VARB FIXED, NAME CHARACTER (20) VARYING;
DO VARB = 6 TO 8 BY 1;
    GET LIST (NAME)
    PUT LIST ('NAME IS', NAME);
    VARB = VARB + 2;
END;
```

In the loop control statement, the programmer has indicated he or she intends the loop range to be repeated three times, for values of VARB of 6, 7, and 8. This will not occur. Instead, after the first pass through the range, the value of VARB has the value of 6+2, or 8. The subsequent loop variable increment then leaves VARB holding the value 9, and therefore, the ensuing test comparison finds that 9 is greater than the end-value 8 and the loop is then terminated. Thus the loop range is executed only once. In this case the actual loop execution contradicts the intent as implied in the loop control statement. This can make this program unnecessarily difficult to understand.

If the statements in the range change the values of any of the variables that are used in the expressions for the start-value, end-value, or step-value, this will have no effect on the number of repetitions. This is because the three expressions are evaluated only once, at the very start of the loop execution. The resulting values are then stored and used for all increments and test comparisons made during the execution. For example, the following program segment

```
DECLARE CTR FIXED, NUM FIXED, NAME CHARACTER (20) VARYING;
NUM = 1;
DO CTR = -2 TO 10 BY NUM;
    GET LIST (NAME);
    PUT LIST (NAME);
    NUM = NUM + 1;
END;
```

causes the loop range to be performed for values of CTR of -2, -1, 0, . . . 7, 8, 9, 10. The step-value is always 1, even though the value of the variable NUM is changed with each repetition, and upon loop termination, it has the value 14.

Another notable characteristic of counted loops is that, upon completion of the loop execution and normal exit to the statement after the corresponding END;, the loop variable contains the value used in the final comparison (which must have failed). This is important should that value be used in a computation in the program following the loop. For example, after execution of the following segment

```
DECLARE (CTR, FIRST) FIXED,
    EXPON FLOAT;
FIRST = 0;
DO CTR = FIRST - 1 TO FIRST + 8.2;
    GET LIST (EXPON);
    PUT LIST (CTR ** EXPON);
END;
```

the value of the loop variable CTR is 9.

In all the examples given thus far, the loop variable and the variables in the expressions in the loop control have all been of type FIXED. Variables of type FLOAT may be used in those contexts as well. The programmer must be aware, however, when using FLOAT variables in the loop control entries, that the actual sequence of values taken on by the loop variable may not be exactly as intended because of the way FLOAT values are stored internally. For example, the following segment:

```
DECLARE I FLOAT, NUM FLOAT;
NUM = 2.2;
DO I = NUM TO 4.2;
    PUT LIST (I);
END;
```

causes the correct number of repetitions, but the sequence of values that are given to the variable I are 2.19999E0, 3.19999E0, 4.19999E0, and not the expected sequence 2.2, 3.2, 4.2. These values result because of the way floating-point numbers are stored internally. With this method of internal storage some floating point values cannot be represented exactly and so are approximated as shown by these results.

The counted loop is a very useful structure in situations where a group of statements must be repeated a definite number of times, under control of a counter. The programmer should be able to determine, for a given application requiring a loop, whether a counted or conditional loop is more appropriate. It is true that, in PL/I, the counted loop actually need never be used, since an equivalent conditional loop can always be written instead. The general form of a conditional loop which simulates a counted loop having the specification of form *start-value TO end-value BY step-value*, and with a positive step-value, is as follows:

```
LOOPVAL = start-value;
ENDVAL = end-value;
STEPVAL = step-value;
DO WHILE(LOOPVAL <= ENDVAL);
    range statement₁
    range statement₂
      .

      .

      .
    range statementₙ
    LOOPVAL = LOOPVAL + STEPVAL;
END;
```

For counted loops with negative step-values, the conditional loop form just given must be changed by replacing the DO WHILE statement by:

```
DO WHILE (LOOPVAL >= ENDVAL);
```

From this format we see that, although it is possible, the simulation of counted loops by conditional loops is somewhat awkward. If counted repetition is required, it is much less cumbersome for the programmer to use a counted loop instead of a conditional loop. For counted loops, the compiler looks after many of the execution details, such as assigning the start-value, incrementing the loop variable, and performing the comparisons. In many other looping situations, though, the conditional loop will be found to be more useful, since its repetition is based on conditions, and not on a fixed sequence of values assigned to a loop variable.

3-3.3 Loop-controlled Input

Section 3-3 of the main text dealt with the problem of loop-controlled input and presented three ways in which this might be handled. Counter-controlled input and sentinel-controlled input are logical schemes that can be implemented in any programming language.

For example, suppose a program is required for a consumer study which is comparing the prices of goods in two stores. Suppose further we are told that the data deck is composed of an arbitrary number of cards, each containing three data values: the name of a product sold in both stores, the price of that product in the first store, and the price of the product in the second store. The two prices are always different. The very first data card in the deck contains only one value, an integer, which is the number of data cards following. The program must, for each set of values, print the product name, the name of the store ('STORE1' or 'STORE2') whose price for the product is higher than the other store's, and the products price. A PL/I solution for this problem is given here, utilizing a counted loop to perform counter-controlled input. The variables PRICE1 and PRICE2 represent the respective prices of STORE1 and STORE2; PROD holds the product name.

```
PRICES: PROCEDURE OPTIONS(MAIN);
      DECLARE (NUM, COUNT, PRICE1, PRICE2) FIXED,
          PROD CHARACTER(20) VARYING;
      GET LIST (NUM);
      DO COUNT = 1 TO NUM;
          GET LIST (PROD, PRICE1, PRICE2);
          IF PRICE1 > PRICE2
          THEN PUT LIST (PROD, 'STORE1 IS MORE EXPENSIVE', PRICE1);
          ELSE  IF PRICE2 > PRICE1
                  THEN PUT LIST (PROD, 'STORE2 IS MORE EXPENSIVE',
                                        PRICE2);
      END;
   END PRICES;
```

In this approach, the programmer has controlled the input loop by ensuring that the number of cards is, first of all, read as a value into a variable (NUM). This variable is subsequently used as the end-value in a counted loop which starts the loop variable COUNT at 1 and successively increments it by 1. Thus, the loop is performed the correct number of times for the number of accompanying sets of data values.

To demonstrate the use of sentinel-controlled input using a conditional loop, suppose the consumer prices problem were altered such that the extra integer at the front of the data is no longer provided. Instead, we are told that an extra set of values:

'END' 0.0 0.0

will be added at the end of the regular data cards. The altered solution is now as follows:

```
PRICES: PROCEDURE OPTIONS(MAIN);
      DECLARE (PRICE1, PRICE2) FIXED,
          PROD CHARACTER(20) VARYING;
      GET LIST (PROD, PRICE1, PRICE2);
```

```
  DO WHILE (PROD ¬ = 'END');
      IF PRICE1 > PRICE2
      THEN PUT LIST (PROD, 'STORE1 IS MORE EXPENSIVE', PRICE1);
      ELSE  IF PRICE2 > PRICE1
              THEN PUT LIST (PROD, 'STORE2 IS MORE EXPENSIVE',
                                    PRICE2);
              ELSE PUT LIST (PROD, 'PRICE IS THE SAME');
      GET LIST (PROD, PRICE1, PRICE2);
  END;
END PRICES;
```

The third approach described in the main text for controlling input loops is the "end of file" method which is indicated in the algorithmic language by the phase, "If there is no more data", or by the condition, "while there is input data". This phrase is very language dependent. PL/I provides such a feature through the use of a special feature known as an "on condition". No extra data cards are required. Instead, the programmer specifies an action to be taken in the event that an end of file is detected in the following way. An ON ENDFILE construct is specified in the program and has the form

ON ENDFILE (SYSIN) *action*

where *action* may be a single statement such as a GO TO statement or a group of statements know as a BEGIN block. The word SYSIN refers to the file into which the program statements and data are read. If another input file is used, then its name should be specified in the ON ENDFILE statement.

A GO TO statement consists of the words
GO TO *label*

This statement specifies that execution of the program is to continue with the statement with the label, *label*. PL/C allows any program statement to be assigned a unique *label*, where each label must be a valid identifier, which precedes the statement it names. A labelled statement has the following form:

label: program statement;

Since the GO TO allows branching to other parts of the program, the use of many GO TO's may obscure the flow structure of the program. For this reason the use of the GO TO statement is discouraged and this troublesome statement will only be used when necessary in the remainder of this book.

A BEGIN block is composed of a group of valid statements preceded by the statement BEGIN; and directly followed by the statement END;. Once an ON ENDFILE(SYSIN) statement is executed, the "action" statement(s) becomes associated with all GET statements encountered in the program, until another ON ENDFILE(SYSIN) construct is executed. This means that if any GET statement executed finds there is insufficient data left for it to perform the input, then the "action" statements will automatically be executed at that time. When used with an input loop, this construct usually physically precedes the loop in the program. The interpretation given to this input method is as follows. The computer continues the looping and reading in of values until it finds that there is no more data left to input. When this happens, the loop's GET statement fails in its attempt to read yet another set of data values and control is then automatically passed to the statement(s) in the "action" portion of the ON ENDFILE(SYSIN) construct. These statements are performed at that point; under no other circumstances are they ever executed in the program. The programmer indicates, in these statements, exactly what should occur after the last data value has been read and processed. In most cases, this action will be some action that will trigger loop termination. After those statements have been performed, control is passed to the statement following the GET statement which had attempted the unsuccessful input.

The most convenient type of input loop using this approach is a conditional loop. The condition in the loop control statement in this context tests whether or not the end of the input data has been reached. As long as there are more data to be read, the condition yields a value of "true." After the last values have been read, however, the next execution of the loop's GET statement causes the "action" statements of the ON ENDFILE(SYSIN) construct to be performed. These actions must, in some manner, cause the condition in the loop control to give a "false" value in its next evaluation. This is turn brings about loop termination.

For example, suppose the consumer prices problem is again changed, so that no special data card is provided with the regular data cards. In this situation, we must use the end-of-file detection approach with a conditional input loop and an ON ENDFILE(SYSIN) statement. The solution is now as follows:

```
PRICES: PROCEDURE OPTIONS(MAIN);
    DECLARE ENDFLAG CHARACTER(3) VARYING,
        (PRICE1, PRICE2) FIXED, PROD CHARACTER(20) VARYING;
    ENDFLAG = 'OFF';
    ON ENDFILE(SYSIN) ENDFLAG = 'ON';
    GET LIST (PROD, PRICE1, PRICE2);
    DO WHILE (ENDFLAG = 'OFF');
        IF PRICE1 > PRICE2
        THEN PUT LIST (PROD, 'STORE1 IS MORE EXPENSIVE', PRICE1);
        ELSE  IF PRICE2 > PRICE1
                THEN PUT LIST (PROD, 'STORE2 IS MORE EXPENSIVE',
                                PRICE2);
                ELSE PUT LIST (PROD, 'PRICE IS THE SAME');
        GET LIST (PROD, PRICE1, PRICE2);
    END;
END PRICES;
```

In this approach, the string variable ENDFLAG serves as an indicator for controlling the input loop. After declaration, it is initialized to the value 'OFF', and it continues to hold that value until after the input data has been read and processed, when its value is changed to 'ON'. Therefore, the conditional loop terminates when the value of ENDFLAG is no longer 'OFF', but 'ON'. Assuming there is at least one set of data provided, the first GET statement reads in the first of the input sets of data. The loop is then entered, since the first evaluation of the condition gives a "true" value. The prices are compared and the associated results printed. The GET statement at the bottom of the loop then attempts to read in the next set of values. If there are no more data values, then that GET statement fails. Consequently, the "action" portion of the ON ENDFILE(SYSIN) is executed, causing the value of ENDFLAG to be changed to 'ON'. Control is then passed to the statement after the GET satement, which is the loop end. The subsequent evaluation of the condition in the loop control, in that case, gives a "false" value and the loop terminates. If, however, the GET statement succeeds in finding another set of values to input, then the value of ENDFLAG remains 'OFF'. In this case, the evaluation of the condition in the loop control yields a "true" value and the loop is performed once again. This process continues until the loop's GET statement fails in an attempt to input another set of values, causing the "action" statements to be performed and the setting of the value of ENDFLAG to 'ON'.

Observe that correct action is taken by the program for the special case of no data cards being present. In such an instance the first GET statement outside the loop fails in its attempt to input a set of data values and, therefore, the "action" statements in the ON ENDFILE(SYSIN) construct are then performed. This causes the changing of the value of ENDFLAG to 'ON'. Thus, when the condition in the loop control statement is evaluated the first time, a "false" value results. The loop is then bypassed entirely and an end to program execution occurs.

3-3.4 Nested Loops

As described in the main text, a nested loop is one which is embedded within the range of another loop. This means that the nested loop has *all* its repetitions executed entirely for *each* of the repetitions of the "outer' loop. Both types of loops in PL/I may be nested, although certain rules for doing so must be followed. An example of a valid nesting of two loops is as follows:

```
DECLARE VALUE FLOAT, VAR FIXED;
GET LIST (VALUE)
DO WHILE (VALUE < 9999);
    DO VAR = 1 TO 9;
        PUT LIST (VALUE ** (VAR +1));
    END;
    GET LIST (VALUE);
END;
```

Execution of this segment causes the outer loop to repeat until a value greater than or equal to 9999 is read into VALUE, and for each of its repetitions, the inner loop repeats for values of the loop variable VAR of 1, 2, 3, ..., 8, and 9.

Nested loops of any type must be entirely contained within the range of the loop which envelops them. Therefore, no part of the range of the nested loop may be physically outside the range of the "outer" loop. The compiler matches every loop END statement with the nearest preceding unmatched loop control statement, starting with the innermost loop, Thus, if part of the intended range of the nested loop is outside the bounds of the outer loop's intended range, then the result of the matching of the END statements with the loop control statements, as performed by the compiler, produces a different interpretation of the nesting than was desired by the programmer. For example, the following shows invalid nesting of two loops. The first loop is

```
DO COUNT1 = 2 TO 5 BY 2;
    PUT LIST (COUNT1);
    COUNT2 = COUNT2 ** 2;
END;
```

and the second loop, a conditional loop, is

```
DO WHILE (COUNT2 < (COUNT1 + 2) ** 2);
    PUT LIST (COUNT2);
    COUNT2 = COUNT2 + 1;
END;
```

An incorrect nesting of these two loops follows.

```
DECLARE (COUNT1, COUNT2) FIXED;
DO COUNT1 = 2 TO 5 BY 2;
    PUT LIST (COUNT1);
    COUNT2 = COUNT1 ** 2;
    DO WHILE (COUNT2 < (COUNT1 + 2) ** 2);
END;
    PUT LIST (COUNT2);
    COUNT2 = COUNT2 + 1;
END;
```

In this example, the compiler matches the first END statement with the conditional loop control statement and the last END with the counted loop control, thereby producing entirely different loop ranges than were originally intended. Notice again that the indentation scheme has no effect on the actions of the compiler.

By now you probably have noticed that the END statement is a ubiquitous statement in the PL/I language. Unfortunately, this makes the programs more difficult to read than they need to be. A consistent indentation convention can alleviate this problem somewhat. So can the use of labels. For example, any DO statement can be labelled and this label can be specified on its terminating END statement. This practice was also advocated in the previous chapter for the END statement marking the physical end of the program.

The next section deals in more depth with the concept of conditions in PL/I. Many applications the use of conditions which are much more complex than the simple relations used in examples thus far. Additional operators to allow the formation of such conditional expression will be presented.

Exercises for Sec. 3-3

1. In each of the following segments, give the value printed for the variable VAR. Assume FIXED variables throughout.
    (a)
```
VAR = 0;
DO INDEX = 1 TO 15;
    VAR = VAR +1;
END;
PUT LIST (VAR);
```

(b)
```
VAR = 0;
DO INDEX = 4 TO 36 BY 4;
    VAR = VAR + 1;
END;
PUT LIST (VAR);
```
(c)
```
VAR = 0;
DO WHILE (VAR – 0);
    VAR = VAR – 1;
END;
PUT LIST (VAR);
```
(d)
```
VAR = 0;
DO INDEX1 = 1 TO 15;
    DO INDEX2 = 5 TO 9;
        VAR = VAR + 1;
    END;
END;
PUT LIST (VAR);
```
(e)
```
VAR = 0;
DO WHILE (VAR >= 0);
    VAR = VAR + 1;
    DO WHILE (VAR >= –2);
        VAR = VAR – 1;
    END;
END;
PUT LIST (VAR);
```

2. Penny Programmer is worried about her performance in her computer science class. On her first program, she made one mistake; on her second, she made two; on the third, four, and so on. It appears that she makes twice the number of mistakes on each program as she made on the program before. The class runs for thirteen weeks, with two programming problems per week. Write a program to compute the number of errors Penny can expect on her final program, at her current rate of performance.

3. Saskatchewan fishing regulations impose a limit on the total poundage of a day's catch. Suppose that you take your portable computer terminal with you on your next fishing trip, and you require a program to tell you when you have exceeded your limit.

   Write a program that first reads the daily limit (in total pounds) and then reads input values one by one (the weights of the fish recorded as they are caught) and prints a message at the point when the limit is exceeded. A weight of 0 indicates the end of input. After each fish is recorded, your program should print the total poundage caught up to that time.

   Test your program on the following input values:

50
6
7
3
8
6
10
3
7
6
8
5
0

4. Manny Motorist has just returned from a recent motoring holiday. At each stop for gas, he recorded his odometer reading and the amount of gas purchased. In addition, he purchased gas and took odometer readings prior to leaving for the trip and immediately upon return. Write a program to read first the total number of stops made (including the first and the last) and then the data recorded for gas purchases and compute

(i) the gas mileage achieved between every pair of stops on the trip, and
(ii) the gas mileage achieved through the entire trip.

The following is a record of Manny's trip.

Gas purchased	Odometer reading
15 gal.	4500
10 gal.	4700
18 gal.	5060
15 gal.	5360
10 gal.	5560
14 gal.	5840
10 gal.	6040
20 gal.	6440
15 gal.	6740
10 gal.	6940

5. The Who-Do-You Trust Company plans to use a computer to prepare customer statements for their deposit accounts. For each customer, a set of data cards is prepared, containing information on his deposits and withdrawals for that month. The data for each customer begins with a special card containing his name, address and balance forwarded from the previous month. This is then followed by transaction cards, which contain the customer's name, a description of the transaction and the amount of the transaction. Account withdrawals will have a negative amount of transaction. Typical input would be as follows:

. The last card is a "dummy" card
. with customer name of 'LASTCARD'

.

'N. WOLFE', '914 WEST 35TH ST.', 18075.00

'A. BUNKER', 'CASH WITHDRAWAL', -75.00

'A. BUNKER', 'MACY S', -50.00

'A. BUNKER', 'PAY CHEQUE', 500.00

'A. BUNKER', '704 HOWSER ST.', 1000.00

A typical customer set

Write a program to produce a statement of account for each customer. These statements appear as follows:

WHO-DO-YOU TRUST COMPANY
416 FIFTH AVE.
NEW YORK

TO: A. BUNKER
704 HOWSER ST.

ITEM	DEPOSITS	WITHDRAWALS	TOTAL
OPENING BALANCE	1000.00		1000.00
PAY CHEQUE	500.00		1500.00
MACYS		50.00	1450.00
CASH WITHDRAWAL		75.00	1375.00
SERVICECHARGE		.50	1374.50
INTEREST PAID	3.75		1378.25

The service charge must be calculated for each customer at a rate of 25¢ for each withdrawal. Interest is to be calculated by your program at 1% on any final balance over $1000.00. A new customer's leading card is detected by a change in name.

Test your program on the following data:

'J. GREEN'	'432 JACKSON AVE.'	1200.00
'J. GREEN'	'PAYLESS DRUGS'	-45.00
'J. GREEN'	'PAY CHEQUE'	850.00
'J. GREEN'	'DOMINION'	-50.00
'G. BROWN'	'648 WALKER DR.'	46.00
'G. BROWN'	'CASH WITHDRAWAL'	-30.00
'G. BROWN'	'PAY CHEQUE'	700.00
'M. BLACK'	'73 ALLEN ST.'	5000.00
'M. BLACK'	'SAAN STORE'	-45.00
'M. BLACK'	'SAM'S JEWELRY'	-75.00
'M. BLACK'	'WONDERLAND FOODS'	-60.00

3-4 USE OF COMPOUND CONDITIONS

In Sec. 3-4 of the main text, a set of logical connectives "and," "or," and "not" was introduced to allow the formation of compound conditions. Similar connectives are provided in PL/I, denoted by the symbols & (and), | (or), and (not). The truth tables for the connectives, &, |, and ¬ , are shown in Table 3-2, where C1 and C2 denoted simple conditions.

Here are three examples of compound conditions. The simple conditions, 30 <= 40 (which is true) and 50 <= 30 (which is false), are used.

(30 <= 40) & (50 <= 30)
(30 <= 40) | (50 <= 30)
¬ (30 <= 40)

In the first example, the first simple condition is true and the second is false. In this case, the "and" operator evaluates to compound condition as false. Again in the second example, the first simple condition is true and the second is false. Table 3-2 indicates that when one condition is true and the other false, the "or" compound condition is true. Finally, the third compound condition is false. The "not" operator has the effect of reversing the value of the simple condition (which is true); therefore, the compound condition is false.

The PL/I declaration of a logical variable which is to contain a logical value (i.e., '0'B or '1'B) is accomplished through the use of the BIT(1) attribute. For example, the statment

DECLARE FLAG BIT(1);

declares the logical variable FLAG.

Table 3-2 Truth tables of PL/I logical connectives

1. "and" (conjunction) denoted by &

C1	C2	C1 & C2
TRUE	TRUE	TRUE
TRUE	FALSE	FALSE
FALSE	TRUE	FALSE
FALSE	FALSE	FALSE

2. "or" (disjunction) denoted by |

C1	C2	C1 | C2
TRUE	TRUE	TRUE
TRUE	FALSE	TRUE
FALSE	TRUE	TRUE
FALSE	FALSE	FALSE

3. "not" (negation) denoted by ¬

C1	¬ C1
TRUE	FALSE
FALSE	TRUE

PRECEDENCE OF LOGICAL AND RELATIONAL OPERATORS

To provide a natural interpretation of conditions, while at the same time avoiding excessive use of parentheses, the logical connectives are given lower precedence than the relational operators, which in turn, have a lower precedence than the numeric operators and the built-in functions. Care must be taken, however, with the "not" operator, since it has a precedence which is equal to the exponentiation or unary plus or minus operations. It is for this reason that parentheses should always enclose conditions to which the not operator applies. A complete table of the precedence rules appears in Table 3-3.

To illustrate, here is an example of a more complex condition.

$$5 + 6 <= * 9 \& \neg (7 - 11 <= 4)$$

In this example, the expression within parentheses is evaluated first. Within this expression, the arithmetic operation is evaluated first, leaving an intermediate result of

$$5 + 6 <= 7 * 9 \& \neg (-4 <= 4)$$

and then the relational operation is performed leaving the result

$$5 + 6 <= 7 * 9 \& \neg ('1'B)$$

Then the "not" operation is evaluated, leaving an intermediate result of

$$5 + 6 <= 7 * 9 \& '0'B$$

Next, the rest of the arithmetic operations are evaluated from left to right, leaving intermmediate results of first

$$5 + 6 <= 63 \& '0'B$$

and then

$$11 <= 63 \& '0'B$$

Next, the remaining relational operation is evaluated, leaving an intermediate result of

Table 3-3   Precedence of operators and logical connectives

Operation	Operator	Order of Evaluation
1. Built-in functions		left to right
2. Exponentiation	**	right to left
Unary plus and	+	
Minus	–	
Logical "not"	¬	
3. Multiplication and	*	left to right
Division	/	
4. Addition and	+	
Subtraction	–	
5. Relational Operators	=	left to right
	>=	
	<=	
	¬=	
	<	
	>	
6. And	&	left to right
7. Or	|	left to right

'1'B & '0'B

Finally, the last logical operation, &, is evaluated giving a final result of '0'B (false).

COMPOUND CONDITIONS IN DECISION STRUCTURES

As was previously mentioned, compound conditions can be used in IF statements and in DO WHILE statements. Compound conditions are often used to clarify programs in which complex nesting might otherwise be required. Unfortunately, complex compound conditions can also cause confusion and, therefore, nesting and compound conditions should be used together judiciously to produce the clearest possible programs.

The choice of either using nesting or using compound conditions depends on the circumstances of the program and must be left to the programmer's judgement. The following two programs have been written using nesting (Program 1) and compound conditions (Program 2). Both programs read in three distinct numbers and determine the largest of the three values.

```
/*PROGRAM 1: THE LARGEST OF THREE VALUES (NESTED VERSION) */
MAXIMUM: PROCEDURE OPTIONS(MAIN):
    /* DECLARE VARIABLES */
    DECLARE (A, B, C, MAX) FLOAT;
    /*READ THREE VALUES */
    GET LIST (A, B, C);
    /*FIND LARGEST VALUE*/
    IF A > B
    THEN IF A > C
         THEN MAX = A;
         ELSE  MAX = C;
    ELSE IF B > C
         THEN MAX = B;
         ELSE  MAX = C;
    PUT LIST('THE LARGEST VALUE IS', MAX);
END MAXIMUM;
```

```
/* PROGRAM 2: THE LARGEST OF THREE VALUES (COMPOUND CONDITIONS) */
MAXIMUM: PROCEDURE OPTIONS (MAIN)
    /*DECLARE VARIABLES */
    DECLARE (A, B, C, MAX) FLOAT:
    /* READ VALUES */
    GET LIST (A, B, C);
    /* FIND LARGEST VALUE */
    IF A > B & A > C
    THEN MAX = A;
    IF B > A & B > C
    THEN MAX = B;
    IF C > A & C > B
    THEN MAX = C;
    PUT LIST ('THE LARGEST VALUE IS', MAX);
END MAXIMUM;
```

This concludes the section on compound conditions. The next section illustrates problems that have solved using some of the concepts that are described in this chapter.

Exercises for Sec. 3-4

1. Suppose I and J are FIXED variables with values 4 and 8, respectively. Which of the following conditions are true?
    (i) $2 * I < = J$
    (ii) $2 * I - 1 < J$
    (iii) $I > 0 \& I < = 10$
    (iv) $I > 25 | (I < 50 \& J < 50)$
    (v) $I < 4 | J > 5$
    (vi) $\neg(I > 6)$

2. Students are recommended for graduate fellowships according to their overall undergraduate average. The nature of the recommendations is based on the following table:

Average	Recommendation
$\geq 90\%$	highest recommendation
$\geq 80\%$ but $< 90\%$	strong recommendation
$\geq 70\%$ but $< 80\%$	recommended
$< 70\%$	not recommended

    A card is prepared for each student applicant according to the following format:
    student's name, overall average
    Design a program to read the deck of cards for the applicants and prepare a list giving the name of each student, his or her average and the recommendation. At the end of the list (denoted by a sentinel) card with student name 'END-OF LIST'), give the overall average of the applicants and a count of the number recommendations of each type.
    Use your program to evaluate the following list of applicants:

Student	Overall Average
M. ALLEN	85
K. BELL	65
R. CORMAN	90
L. DICKSON	70
J. ELLIOT	95
S. FORMAN	75
D. GRAY	55
H. HUGHES	81

3. Students were given five examinations (A, B, C, D, E). Statistics are required to determine the number that
    (i)   passed all exams
    (ii) passed A, B, and D, but not C or E
    (iii) passed A and B, C or D, but not E
    Write a program to compute these statistics for the following set of marks (each out of 100). Each line represents the marks received by one student.

Student's Marks

45	60	55	70	40
65	70	89	90	77
35	45	75	60	55
50	65	55	40	75
65	72	35	66	42
75	85	90	85	75
100	90	95	92	89
45	70	65	55	42
23	32	46	35	41
65	54	49	55	60

3-5 APPLICATIONS

This section gives PL/C program solutions to the application problems found in Sec. 3-5 of the main text.

3-5.1 Book Store Orders

The program which appears in Fig. 3-1 is a solution to the book store order problem given in Sec. 3-5.1. The problem is to estimate the number of books that the book store should order and the profit the book store will make in the coming academic term. For each book that is to be used, a card has been prepared containing the following information:

1. the book order number (a 6 digit code)
2. the quantity in stock ·
3. classification of the book
   (1 for a prescribed text and 2 for a text recommended for supplementary reading)
4. estimated student enrolment in course requiring this book
5. indication whether this book is being used for the first time (1 indicates that the book is being used for the first time and 0 indicates that the book has been used before)
6. wholesale cost of the book.

It has been found that for required tests that have been previously used, sales are 60% of estimated enrolment and for new books that are required sales are 85% of estimated enrolment. Sales for books required for supplementary reading have been estimated at 25% for books that have been previously used and 40% for new books. The number of books required is based on these figures. The number to order is determined by subtracting the number currently in stock form the number required. If the result is negative, more books are held in stock than are required and the extra books are to be returned. In this case a message indicating the overstocked condition and the number of books to be returned is required. The profit margin is based on a 25% mark up on books with a wholesale value of ten dollars or less and a 20% mark up on all other books. Given this information, the following report is to be generated.

ORDER NO.	ON HAND	TO ORDER	PROFIT MARGIN
386054	13	67	200
389854	IS OVERSTOCKED 7 COPIES TO RETURN		

.	.	.	.
.	.	.	.
		.	.

| TOTAL PROFIT | 25653.72 |

The variables used in this program are

Variable name	Type	Usage
IDENT	CHARACTER(6)	Book identification number
STOCK	FIXED	Quantity currently in stock
TYPE	FIXED	Classification of the book as pre-scribed text or supplementary reading
ENROLMENT	FIXED	Estimated course enrolment
NEW	FIXED	Indicates text as new or pre-viously used
COST	FLOAT	Wholesale cost of the book
NUMBER_REQUIRED	FIXED	Number of copies required
ORDER	FIXED	Number of copies to be ordered
PROFIT	FLOAT	Profit margin on this book
TOTAL_PROFIT	FLOAT	Total profit margin
END_FLAG	CHARACTER(3) VARYING	Indicates end of data

The following input values were used in this program

'394072'	20	1	80	1	20.40
'794362'	10	2	10	0	10.20
'767231'	25	1	100	1	11.95
'472315'	12	2	50	0	14.36
'399789'	20	1	135	1	25.30
'699233'	30	2	14	0	23.00
'629111'	15	1	123	1	14.70
'567124'	21	2	179	0	12.30
'791121'	24	1	60	1	26.40
'654315'	6	1	43	1	12.50
'731717'	7	2	110	0	13.75

Statements 3 and 4 initialize the TOTAL_PROFIT to 0 and the END_FLAG to 'OFF'. Statement 5 indicates that the variable END_FLAG is to be assigned the value 'ON' when the end of the data has been reached. In statement 8, the loop that is to handle the processing of the book orders is begun. Information concerning a book is read in statement 9. For each book, the number required is calculated using information concerning the books type and whether or not the book has

```
/* PROGRAM TO DETERMINE THE PROFIT MARGIN ON BOOK ORDERS */

STMT LEVEL NEST BLOCK MLVL   SOURCE TEXT

                                    /* PROGRAM TO DETERMINE THE PROFIT MARGIN ON BOOK ORDERS */

     1                              BSTORE: PROCEDURE OPTIONS (MAIN);

     2     1           1            DECLARE IDENT CHARACTER(6),    /* BOOK IDENTIFICATION NUMBER */
                                            STOCK FIXED,           /* QUANTITY IN STOCK */
                                            TYPE FIXED,            /* CLASSIFICATION OF THE BOOK */
                                            ENROLMENT FIXED,       /* ESTIMATED COURSE ENROLMENT */
                                            NEW FIXED,             /* NEW TEXT OR USED PREVIOUSLY */
                                            COST FLOAT,            /* WHOLESALE COST */
                                            NUMBER_REQUIRED FIXED,    /* NUMBER NEEDED */
                                            ORDER FIXED,           /* NUMBER TO BE ORDERED */
                                            PROFIT FLOAT,          /* PROFIT MARGIN ON BOOK */
                                            TOTAL_PROFIT FLOAT,    /* TOTAL PROFIT MARGIN */
                                            END_FLAG CHARACTER(3) VARYING; /* END OF DATA FLAG */

                                    /* INITIALIZE */
     3     1           1            TOTAL_PROFIT = 0.00;
     4     1           1            END_FLAG = 'OFF';

     5     1           1            ON ENDFILE (SYSIN) END_FLAG = 'ON';

                                    /* PRINT REPORT HEADINGS */
     7     2           2            PUT SKIP LIST ('IDENTIFICATION', 'ON HAND', 'TO ORDER',
                                       'PROFIT MARGIN');

                                    /* PROCESS BOOKS */
     8     1           1            DO WHILE (END_FLAG = 'OFF');
                                       /* READ INFORMATION FOR NEXT BOOK */
     9     1     1     1               GET LIST (IDENT, STOCK, TYPE, ENROLMENT, NEW, COST);
    10     1     1     1               IF END_FLAG = 'ON'
    11     1     1     1               THEN DO;
    12     1     2     1                  PUT SKIP LIST ('TOTAL PROFIT', TOTAL_PROFIT);
    13     1     2     1                  EXIT;
    14     1     2     1                  END;

                                       /* DETERMINE NUMBER OF COPIES REQUIRED */
    15     1     1     1               IF TYPE = 1
    16     1     1     1               THEN IF NEW = 1          /* PRESCRIBED TEXT */
    17     1     1     1                  THEN NUMBER_REQUIRED = ROUND(0.85 * ENROLMENT, 0);
    18     1     1     1                  ELSE NUMBER_REQUIRED = ROUND(0.60 * ENROLMENT, 0);
    19     1     1     1               ELSE IF NEW = 1          /* SUPPLEMENTARY READING */
    20     1     1     1                  THEN NUMBER_REQUIRED = ROUND(0.40 * ENROLMENT, 0);

    21     1     1     1                  ELSE NUMBER_REQUIRED = ROUND(0.25 * ENROLMENT, 0);

                                       /* DETERMINE SIZE OF ORDER AND, IF NECESSSARY, ISSUE */
                                       /* OVERSTOCKED NOTICE */

    22     1     1     1               ORDER = NUMBER_REQUIRED - STOCK;
    23     1     1     1               IF ORDER < 0
    24     1     1     1               THEN PUT SKIP LIST (IDENT, 'IS OVERSTOCKED:', ABS(ORDER),
                                          'COPIES TO RETURN');

                                       /* DETERMINE PROFIT ON THIS BOOK */
    25     1     1     1               IF COST <= 10.00
    26     1     1     1               THEN PROFIT = NUMBER_REQUIRED * 0.25 * COST;
    27     1     1     1               ELSE PROFIT = NUMBER_REQUIRED * 0.20 * COST;

                                       /* UPDATE TOTAL PROFIT STATISTIC */
    28     1     1     1               TOTAL_PROFIT = TOTAL_PROFIT + PROFIT;

                                       /* PRINT LINE FOR THIS BOOK */
    29     1     1     1               PUT SKIP LIST (IDENT, STOCK, ORDER, PROFIT);
    30     1     1     1               END;

    31     1           1            END BSTORE;

ERRORS/WARNINGS DETECTED DURING CODE GENERATION:

     WARNING: NO FILE SPECIFIED. SYSIN/SYSPRINT ASSUMED. (CGOC)
```

Fig. 3-1 Program for book store orders problem

```
IDENTIFICATION        ON HAND              TO ORDER          PROFIT MARGIN
394072                  20                     48            2.77439E+02
794362            IS OVERSTOCKED:               7            COPIES TO RETURN
794362                  10                     -7            6.11999E+00
767231                  25                     60            2.03149E+02
472315                  12                      1            3.73359E+01
399789                  20                     95            5.81899E+02
699233            IS OVERSTOCKED:              26            COPIES TO RETURN
699233                  30                    -26            1.83999E+01
629111                  15                     90            3.08699E+02
567124                  21                     24            1.10699E+02
791121                  24                     27            2.69279E+02
654315                   6                     31            9.24999E+01
731717                   7                     21            7.69999E+01
TOTAL PROFIT       1.98252E+03

IN STMT   13  PROGRAM IS STOPPED.
```

Fig. 3-1   Program for book store orders problem (cont'd.)

been used before. The size of the order, ORDER, is calculated by subtracting the number in stock, STOCK, from the number required, NUMBER_REQUIRED. If there are more books in stock than are required (i.e., ORDER is negative), a message indicating the number of books to be returned is printed. The profit for this book is calculated and then added to the total profit. Finally, the identification number, the number in stock, the number to order, and the profit to be made on this book are printed. The total profit is printed and execution is terminated when all input values have been processed.

3-5.2 Mortgage Payments

The program in Fig. 3-2 is a solution to the mortgage payment problem given in Sec. 3-5.2 of the main text. The calculation of monthly payments on a mortgage depends on three components — the principal involved, the mortgage rate, and the length of the term for the mortgage. The basic formula used in the calculation is

$$\text{Monthly Payment} = \frac{P * IR * (IR + 1) ** N}{(IR + 1) ** N - 1}$$

Where P is the principal, IR is the interest rate per month, and N is the number of months in the term. (Normally, the customer is given the interest rate and term of his mortgage in yearly figures, and therefore, these must be converted to montly figures for use in the formula.)

Each monthly payment is the sum of the montly interest required, as dictated by the monthly interest rate applied to the outstanding principal, and a portion of the principal. That is, for any month, given by P * IR, and an amount deducted from the outstanding principal in an attempt to reduce it to zero over the mortgage term.

The problem is then to write a PL/C program that takes as input the amount of the principal of a mortgage, the yearly interest rate, and the term in years of that mortgage. The output produced must contain the calculated monthly payment and

```
/* COMPUTE MONTHLY MORTGAGE PAYMENT */

STMT LEVEL NEST BLOCK MLVL   SOURCE TEXT


                                      /* COMPUTE MONTHLY MORTGAGE PAYMENT */
                                      /* FOR EACH TERM YEAR, PRINT AND TOTAL UP THE MONTHLY */
                                      /* INTEREST PAYMENTS AND MONTHLY PAYMENTS ON THE PRINCIPAL */

  1                                   MORTPAY:  PROCEDURE OPTIONS(MAIN);

  2    1          1                   DECLARE PRINC FLOAT,     /* PRINCIPAL AMOUNT */
                                              IRATE FLOAT,     /* YEARLY INTEREST RATE */
                                              TERM FIXED,      /* TERM, IN YEARS */
                                              IR FLOAT,        /* MONTHLY INTEREST RATE */
                                              N FIXED,         /* TERM, IN MONTHS */
                                              PAYMNT FLOAT,    /* CALCULATED MONTHLY PAYMENT*/
                                              INTTOT FLOAT,    /* YEARLY TOTAL OF INTEREST PAYMENTS */
                                              PRTOT FLOAT,     /* YEARLY TOTAL OF PRINCIPAL PAYMENTS */
                                              MONINT FLOAT,    /* MONTHLY INTEREST PAYMENT */
                                              MONPR FLOAT,     /* MONTHLY PRINCIPAL PAYMENT */
                                              (YEAR, MONTH) FIXED;     /* LOOP VARIABLES */

                                      /* INPUT DATA VALUES AND CHECK THEIR VALIDITY */
  3    1          1                   GET LIST (PRINC, IRATE, TERM);

  4    1          1                   IF (PRINC <= 0) | (IRATE <= 0) | (TERM <= 0)
                                      THEN
  5    1          1                       PUT SKIP (2) LIST ('INVALID INPUT VALUE.');
  6    1          1                   ELSE DO;

                                      /* CONVERT YEARLY FIGURES TO MONTHLY, AND */
                                      /* COMPUTE MONTHLY PAYMENT */
  7    1    1     1                   IR = IRATE / 12;
  8    1    1     1                   N = TERM * 12;
  9    1    1     1                   PAYMNT = (PRINC * IR * (IR+1) ** N) / ((IR+1) ** N - 1);
 10    1    1     1                   PUT SKIP(2) LIST ('MONTHLY PAYMENT IS $', PAYMNT);
 11    1    1     1                   PUT SKIP(2) LIST ('     YEAR', '  MONTH',
                                          'AMT PAID TO PRINCIPAL', 'AMT PAID TO INTEREST');

                                      /* FOR EACH YEAR, PRINT THE MONTHLY AND YEARLY STATISTICS */
 12    1    1     1                   DO YEAR = 1 TO TERM;

                                          /* INITIALIZE YEARLY TOTALS */
 13    1    2     1                   INTTOT = 0;
 14    1    2     1                   PRTOT = 0;

                                          /* FOR EACH MONTH, COMPUTE AMOUNTS, PRINT AND */
                                          /* UPDATE TOTALS */
 15    1    2     1                   DO MONTH = 1 TO 12;
 16    1    3     1                       MONINT = IR * PRINC;
 17    1    3     1                       MONPR = PAYMNT - MONINT;
 18    1    3     1                       INTTOT = INTTOT + MONINT;
 19    1    3     1                       PRTOT = PRTOT + MONPR;

                                          /* PRINT AMOUNTS FOR THE MONTH */
 20    1    3     1                       PUT SKIP LIST (YEAR, MONTH, MONPR, MONINT);

 21    1    3     1                       PRINC = PRINC - MONPR;
 22    1    3     1                   END;

                                          /* PRINT TOTALS FOR THE YEAR */
 23    1    2     1                   PUT SKIP LIST ('YEAR END SUMMARY:');
 24    1    2     1                   PUT SKIP LIST ('PRINCIPAL PAID:', PRTOT);
 25    1    2     1                   PUT SKIP LIST ('INTEREST PAID:', INTTOT);
 26    1    2     1                   PUT SKIP LIST ('OUTSTANDING PRINCIPAL:', PRINC);
 27    1    2     1                   END;

 28    1    1     1                   END;
 29    1          1                   END MORTPAY;

ERRORS/WARNINGS DETECTED DURING CODE GENERATION:

    WARNING: NO FILE SPECIFIED. SYSIN/SYSPRINT ASSUMED. (CGOC)
```

Fig. 3-2 Program for mortgage payments problem

```
MONTHLY PAYMENT IS $      1.61335E+02
```

YEAR	MONTH	AMT PAID TO PRINCIPAL	AMT PAID TO INTEREST
1	1	1.19669E+02	4.16666E+01
1	2	1.20666E+02	4.06694E+01
1	3	1.21672E+02	3.96638E+01
1	4	1.22686E+02	3.86499E+01
1	5	1.23708E+02	3.76275E+01
1	6	1.24739E+02	3.65966E+01
1	7	1.25778E+02	3.55571E+01
1	8	1.26826E+02	3.45089E+01
1	9	1.27883E+02	3.34521E+01
1	10	1.28949E+02	3.23864E+01
1	11	1.30024E+02	3.13118E+01
1	12	1.31107E+02	3.02282E+01

```
YEAR END SUMMARY:
PRINCIPAL PAID:       1.50371E+03
INTEREST PAID:        4.32318E+02
OUTSTANDING PRINCIPAL: 3.49628E+03
```

YEAR	MONTH	AMT PAID TO PRINCIPAL	AMT PAID TO INTEREST
2	1	1.32200E+02	2.91357E+01
2	2	1.33301E+02	2.80340E+01
2	3	1.34412E+02	2.69232E+01
2	4	1.35532E+02	2.58031E+01
2	5	1.36662E+02	2.46736E+01
2	6	1.37801E+02	2.35348E+01
2	7	1.38949E+02	2.23864E+01
2	8	1.40107E+02	2.12285E+01
2	9	1.41274E+02	2.00609E+01
2	10	1.42452E+02	1.88837E+01
2	11	1.43639E+02	1.76966E+01
2	12	1.44836E+02	1.64996E+01

```
YEAR END SUMMARY:
PRINCIPAL PAID:       1.66117E+03
INTEREST PAID:        2.74860E+02
OUTSTANDING PRINCIPAL: 1.83511E+03
```

YEAR	MONTH	AMT PAID TO PRINCIPAL	AMT PAID TO INTEREST
3	1	1.46043E+02	1.52926E+01
3	2	1.47260E+02	1.40756E+01
3	3	1.48487E+02	1.28484E+01
3	4	1.49724E+02	1.16110E+01
3	5	1.50972E+02	1.03633E+01
3	6	1.52230E+02	9.10523E+00
3	7	1.53499E+02	7.83664E+00
3	8	1.54778E+02	6.55748E+00
3	9	1.56068E+02	5.26766E+00
3	10	1.57368E+02	3.96709E+00
3	11	1.58680E+02	2.65569E+00
3	12	1.60002E+02	1.33335E+00

```
YEAR END SUMMARY:
PRINCIPAL PAID:       1.83511E+03
INTEREST PAID:        1.00914E+02
OUTSTANDING PRINCIPAL: -1.14496E-10
```

```
IN STMT   29  PROGRAM RETURNS FROM MAIN PROCEDURE.
```

Fig. 3-2 Program for mortgage payments problem (cont'd.)

for each of the term years the payments to interest and the principal for each month of the year, and year-ends total of these monthly amounts. The variables used in the following PL/C program are

Variable name	Type	Usage
PRINC	FLOAT	Principal amount
IRATE	FLOAT	Yearly interest rate
TERM	FIXED	Term, in years
IR	FLOAT	Montly interest rate
N	FIXED	Term, in months
PAYMNT	FLOAT	Calculated monthly payment

INTTOT	FLOAT	Yearly total of interest payments
PRTOT	FLOAT	Yearly total of principal payments
MONINT	FLOAT	Monthly interest payment
MONPR	FLOAT	Monthly principal payment
YEAR	FIXED	Loop variable
MONTH	FIXED	Loop variable

The data card used in the run consisted of the following values:

5000. .10 3

Statement 2 contains the declarations for the variables used. The next statement serves to read the input values. The IF statement beginning in statement 4 checks the data values that have been input for the three variables to ensure that they are reasonable and have viable values. It is assumed that if any of the principal amount, the interest rate, or the term length values is less than or equal to 0, then such a data value was most likely mispunched on the data card, and therefore, execution is not continued. Otherwise, the values are accepted as valid, and the processing proceeds within the ELSE clause of the IF...THEN...ELSE statement. In statement 12, a counted loop is used to cause the repetitions of the yearly computations, once for each year in the term. Statement 15 is the loop control for the inner counted loop, which controls the twelve repetitions of the monthly calculations, one for each month of the year, YEAR.

3-5.3   Cheque Reconciliation

The program presented in Fig. 3-3 is the solution to the cheque reconciliation problem given in Sec. 3-5.3 of the main text.

The management of the Red Nose Winery company requires a program to reconcile cheques issued to their employees. For each cheque issued, a card is prepared containing the cheque number and the amount for which the cheque was written. At the end of each month similar cards are prepared for the cashed cheques. The cards containing information on the issued and cashed cheques are merged manually and are used as input for the program. The program is to list the cheques that have been issued but have not yet been cashed and the cheque number and the two amounts of any cheque that has been issued and cashed for differing amounts. After all the cheques have been processed, the total amount of the cheques cashed and the total amount of the cheques outstanding (i.e., cheques that have not been cashed) are to be printed. The variables used in this program are

Variable name	Type	Usage
CASHED	FLOAT	Total amount of cheques cashed
OUTSTANDING	FLOAT	Total amount of cheques outstanding
CARD_REQUIRED	FIXED	Type of card required

CHEQUE1_NO	FIXED	Identification number of issued cheque
CHEQUE1_AMT	FLOAT	Amount of issued cheque
CHEQUE2_NO	FIXED	Identification number of cashed cheque
CHEQUE2_AMT	FLOAT	Amount of cashed cheque
END_FLAG	CHARACTER(3) VARYING	End of data flag

The following data cards were used with this program.

23871	48.50
23871	48.50
23872	150.00
23873	36.00
23873	236.00
23874	200.00
23875	230.00
23875	130.00
23876	150.00
23876	150.00
23877	75.00
23877	175.00
23878	75.00
23879	45.00
23880	50.00
23880	50.00

Statements 3 through 6 initialize variables to be used in the program. In statement 9, a loop which controls the processing of the cheques is begun. If the variable CARD_REQUIRED equals 1, the information concerning the next cheque is read. If there are no more cheques, the amount of total cashed and total outstanding is printed, and execution of the program is terminated. If there is indeed more data, the input values are read into CHEQUE1_NO and CHEQUE1_AMT, respectively. The following data card is read. If the end of the data is reached at this point, the last cheque was uncashed; therefore, the amount outstanding is updated accordingly, and the totals of cashed and outstanding cheques are printed. If, however, the end of the data is not reached, the next input values are read into CHEQUE2_NO and CHEQUE2_AMT, respectively. If the indentification numbers of the two cheques (i.e., CHEQUE1_NO and CHEQUE2_NO) are the same, then the amounts of the cheque issued and cashed are compared. If the two amounts are identical, the value of the cheque is added to the total of cashed cheques; otherwise, a message is printed indicating that the cheques have been issued and cashed for different amounts. In statement 32, the flag CARD_REQUIRED is set to 1 to indicate that a complete pair of cards has been read and the next card read contains information concerning an issued cheque.

If it is found in the comparison made in statement 27 that the cheque numbers are not identical, then the issued cheque has not been cashed. In statement 35, the outstanding total is updated by adding the amount of the

```
/* PROGRAM TO RECONCILE DATA ON CHEQUES ISSUED AND CHEQUES CASHED */

STMT LEVEL NEST BLOCK MLVL   SOURCE TEXT


                             /* PROGRAM TO RECONCILE DATA ON CHEQUES ISSUED AND CHEQUES CASHED */

  1                          RECON: PROCEDURE OPTIONS(MAIN);

  2    1          1          DECLARE CASHED FLOAT,        /* TOTAL AMOUNT OF CHEQUES CASHED */
                                     OUTSTANDING FLOAT,   /* TOTAL AMOUNT OUTSTANDING */
                                     CARD_REQUIRED FIXED, /* TYPE OF CARD REQUIRED */
                                     CHEQUE1_NO FIXED,    /* NO. OF CHEQUE ISSUED */
                                     CHEQUE1_AMT FLOAT,   /* AMOUNT OF CHEQUE ISSUED */
                                     CHEQUE2_NO FIXED,    /* NO. OF CHEQUE CASHED */
                                     CHEQUE2_AMT FLOAT,   /* AMOUNT OF CHEQUE CASHED */
                                     END_FLAG CHARACTER(3) VARYING; /* END OF DATA FLAG */

                             /* INITIALIZE */
  3    1          1          CASHED = 0.0;
  4    1          1          OUTSTANDING = 0.0;
  5    1          1          CARD_REQUIRED = 1;
  6    1          1          END_FLAG = 'OFF';
  7    1          1          ON ENDFILE(SYSIN) END_FLAG = 'ON';

                             /* PROCESS CHEQUES */
  9    2          2          DO WHILE (END_FLAG = 'OFF');

                                 /* READ FIRST CARD OF A PAIR IF NOT PREVIOUSLY READ */
 10    1    1     1              IF CARD_REQUIRED = 1
 11    1    1     1              THEN GET LIST(CHEQUE1_NO, CHEQUE1_AMT);
 12    1    1     1              IF END_FLAG = 'ON'
 13    1    1     1              THEN DO;
 14    1    2     1                  PUT SKIP LIST ('TOTAL CASHED = $', CASHED);
 15    1    2     1                  PUT SKIP LIST ('TOTAL OUTSTANDING = $', OUTSTANDING);
 16    1    2     1                  EXIT;
 17    1    2     1                  END;

                                 /* READ SECOND CARD OF PAIR */
 18    1    1     1              GET LIST (CHEQUE2_NO, CHEQUE2_AMT);
 19    1    1     1              IF END_FLAG = 'ON'
 20    1    1     1              THEN DO;   /* LAST CHEQUE WAS NOT CASHED */
 21    1    2     1                  PUT SKIP LIST (CHEQUE1_NO, CHEQUE1_AMT);
 22    1    2     1                  PUT SKIP LIST ('TOTAL CASHED = $', CASHED);
 23    1    2     1                  OUTSTANDING = OUTSTANDING + CHEQUE1_AMT;
 24    1    2     1                  PUT SKIP LIST ('TOTAL OUTSTANDING = $', OUTSTANDING);
 25    1    2     1                  EXIT;
 26    1    2     1                  END;

                                 /* PROCESS THE PAIR OF CARDS */
 27    1    1     1              IF CHEQUE1_NO = CHEQUE2_NO
 28    1    1     1              THEN DO;

 29    1    2     1                  IF CHEQUE1_AMT = CHEQUE2_AMT

                                     /* ISSUED AND CASHED FOR THE SAME AMOUNT */
 30    1    2     1                  THEN CASHED = CASHED + CHEQUE1_AMT;

                                     /* ISSUED AND CASHED FOR DIFFERENT AMOUNTS */
 31    1    2     1                  ELSE PUT SKIP LIST (CHEQUE1_NO, CHEQUE1_AMT,
                                                         CHEQUE2_AMT);
 32    1    2     1                  CARD_REQUIRED = 1;  /* COMPLETE PAIR HAS BEEN READ */
 33    1    2     1                  END;
 34    1    1     1              ELSE DO;
                                     /* CHEQUE NOT CASHED YET */
 35    1    2     1                  PUT SKIP LIST (CHEQUE1_NO, CHEQUE1_AMT);
 36    1    2     1                  OUTSTANDING = OUTSTANDING + CHEQUE1_AMT;

                                     /* SECOND CARD BECOMES FIRST CARD OF NEXT PAIR */
 37    1    2     1                  CHEQUE1_NO = CHEQUE2_NO;
 38    1    2     1                  CHEQUE1_AMT = CHEQUE2_AMT;
 39    1    2     1                  CARD_REQUIRED = 2;
 40    1    2     1                  END;
 41    1    1     1                  END;

 42    1          1          END RECON;

ERRORS/WARNINGS DETECTED DURING CODE GENERATION:
```

Fig. 3-3   Program for cheque reconciliation problem

```
WARNING: NO FILE SPECIFIED. SYSIN/SYSPRINT ASSUMED. (CG0C)


    23872                    1.50000E+02
    23873                    3.60000E+01              2.36000E+02
    23874                    2.00000E+02
    23875                    2.30000E+02              1.30000E+02
    23877                    7.50000E+01              1.75000E+02
    23878                    7.50000E+01
    23879                    4.50000E+01
TOTAL CASHED = $             2.48500E+02
TOTAL OUTSTANDING = $        4.70000E+02



    IN STMT   16  PROGRAM IS STOPPED.
```

Fig. 3-3   Program for cheque reconciliation problem (cont'd.)

uncashed cheque, and statements 37 and 38 transfer the information concerning the second card to the variables representing the issued cheque. The flag, CARD_REQUIRED, is assigned the value 2, indicating that the issued cheque has already been read and information concerning the cashed cheque is required.

This concludes the chapter on decision structures. In Sec. 3-2, the IF statement, which allows selection from alternative actions, was introduced. The next section dealt with the repetition of instructions, using the different forms of the loop structure. Next under discussion was the use of complex conditions in both the DO WHILE and IF statements. Finally, in the last section, the important concepts of this chapter were illustrated, through the use of three programmed examples.

In the next chapter, the programmer is introduced to further programming techniques which involve an important data structure, the array.

EXERCISES FOR CHAPTER 3

1. Write a program to compute the sum of the squares of the first 100 integers.

2. Commercial fishermen are required to report monthly information on their catch to the Department of Fisheries. This data is analyzed regularly to determine the growth or reduction of the various species of fish and to indicate any possible trouble. From the catch reports and previous data, a card is prepared containing the following information:
    region fished (integer code from 1 to 20), species name (character),
        number caught this year (integer), number caught last year (integer)
    e.g., 16, 'HALIBUT', 20485, 18760
        This sample card indicates that in region 16, a total of 20,485 halibut were caught, as compared to 18,760 in the same month last year.
        Write a program to read the following data:

5,	'SALMON',	25632,	19276
4,	'COD',	35789,	40256
12,	'HERRING',	56792,	20543
19,	'TUNA',	30625,	21872
1,	'HALIBUT',	20892,	23671
7,	'WHITEFISH',	30925,	30900
6,	'SALMON',	39625,	29521
13,	'HERRING',	45631,	40872
-1,	'FISH',	0,	0

Note that data is terminated by a card with a negative region number. After reading the data, your program should flag any unusual growth or reduction in catches. An unusual growth or reduction is defined as one in which the percentage change exceeds 30%, where percentage change is defined as

$$\frac{\text{(this year)} - \text{(last year)}}{\text{(last year)}} \times 100\%$$

3. The Saskatchewan Government Insurance Office has compiled data on all traffic accidents in the province over the past year. For each driver involved in an accident, a card has been prepared with the following pieces of information:

year driver was born (integer), sex ('M' or 'F'),
registration code (1 for Saskatchewan
registration, 0 for everything else)

Design a program to read the deck of data cards and print the following summary statistics on drivers involved in accidents:

(i)   percentage of drivers under 25 years of age
(ii) percentage of drivers who are female
(iii) percentage of drivers who are males between the ages of 18 and 25
(iv) percentage of drivers with out-of-province registration.

Use the end of file method to signal the end of input.
Using your program, calculate the four statistics for the following list of data:

1947	'M'	1
1962	'F'	0
1958	'M'	1
1936	'F'	1
1957	'M'	1
1945	'F'	0
1961	'M'	1
1948	'F'	0
1955	'F'	1
1950	'M'	1

4. The city police department has accumulated information on speeding violations over a period of time. The department has divided the city into four quadrants and wishes to have statistics on speeding violations by quadrant. For each violation, a card is prepared containing the following information:

vehicle registration number (eight digit code),
quadrant in which offense occured (1-4),
speed limit in kilometers per hour (integer),
actual speed travelled in kilometers per hour (integer).

This set of cards is terminated by a special card with a vehicle registration number of 0.

Write a program to produce two reports. First, give a listing of speeding fines collected, where the fine is calculated as the sum of court costs ($20) plus $1.25 for every mile per hour by which the speed limit was exceeded. Prepare a table with the following headings:

SPEEDING VIOLATIONS
VEHICLE REGISTRATION SPEED RECORDED (MPH) SPEED LIMIT (MPH) FINE

This report is to be followed by a second report in which an analysis of violations by quadrant is given. For each of the four quadrants, give the number of violations processed and the average fine.

Test your program on the list of traffic violations given in Table 3-4.

5. (a) Write a program to compute and tabulate the values of the function

$$f(x, y) = \frac{x^2 - y^2}{x^2 + y^2}$$

for x = 2, 4, 6, 8
and y = 6, 9, 12, 15, 18, 21.

(b) Write a program to compute the number of points with integer-valued coordinates that are contained within the ellipse

$$\frac{x^2}{16} + \frac{y^2}{25} = 1$$

(Notes:
1. Points on the ellipse are considered to be within it.
2. Range of coordinate values is limited by the major and minor axes of of the ellipse.
   i.e., $-4 \leqslant x \leqslant 4$
   and $-5 \leqslant y \leqslant 5$.)

Table 3-4 Traffic violations

Registration Number	Quadrant	Speed Limit	Actual Speed
45631288	2	25	30
76822131	1	40	55
65331245	3	65	73
55129871	4	70	78
61234891	3	25	35
77891348	1	10	15
67543111	2	25	32
98432918	3	25	29
79144855	4	65	78
23579812	1	30	45

6. (a) Design a program to compute the amount of savings you would have at the end of ten years, if you were to deposit $100 each month. Assume a constant annual interest rate of 6%, compounded every six months (that is, interest in the amount of 3% is awarded each six months).

    (b) We want to invest a sum of money that will grow to be X dollars in Y years time. If the interest rate is R percent, then the amount we have to invest (the present value of X) is given by the formula

$$\frac{X}{(1 + .01 * R)^Y}$$

Write a program that will print out a table of the present value of $5000 at 7.5% interest, for periods of one to twenty years, in steps of two years.

7. Assume that a particular store sells all of its merchandise for a price of $1.00 or less. Assume further that all customers pay for each purchase with a $1.00 bill.

    Design a program that reads in the purchase price of an article, and calculates the number of each type of coin to be given in change so that the smallest number of coins is returned. For example, if the purchase price is 65¢ the change will be 1 quarter, 1 dime, and 2 pennies.

    Using your program, find the change to be received from a purchase of 14¢ assuming the customer pays with a $1.00 bill.

CHAPTER

4

VECTORS AND ARRAYS

A subscripted variable in a programming language such as PL/I is a variable that represents an element in a finite ordered set. In this chapter, we examine the use of PL/I subscripted variables to implement the important data structures known as vectors and arrays, as discussed in Chap. 4 of the main text. We begin with a consideration of vectors and operations that can be performed on them. Sorting and searching are very important operations on vectors; these are discussed in Sec. 4-2. We then turn to arrays of higher dimensions. The chapter closes with complete PL/C programs for the applications discussed in the main text.

4-1   VECTORS AND OPERATIONS ON VECTORS

This section explains the rules for use of vectors in the PL/I language, introducing the common operations that may be performed on vectors. In the algorithmic language a vector is represented by a variable name and an element of the vector is represented by the variable name followed by the index of the element enclosed in square parentheses. In PL/I, a vector and its elements have representations similar to those of the algorithmic language. In PL/I each element in represented as

vector-name (subscript)

The *vector-name* is the name of the set and can be any valid PL/I variable name. The *subscript* entry must yield an integer value which identifies a particular element in the set. (Note that rather than square parentheses, round parentheses are used in PL/I to enclose the subscript.)

Before a vector or any of its elements may be used in a program, the vector must be declared in a DECLARE statement. For example, the statement

DECLARE PRICE(100) FLOAT;

identifies PRICE as the name of a vector. The 100, which appears in the parentheses following the vector-name, defines the *upper bound* (i.e., the value of the maximum possible subscript) of the vector. The *lower bound*, which is the smallest possible subscript, is assumed to be 1 for this vector. Elements of this vector, therefore, may be referenced by subscripts ranging from 1 to 100. The type attribute specified (i.e., FLOAT) applies to all the elements of the vector. All vector elements are stored in consecutive storage locations in the computer's memory.

Often a lower bound of other than 1 is desired for a vector. For example, suppose a vector CARS is to be used to contain the number of cars produced in the years 1957 through 1965. This vector could be referenced by subscripts ranging from 1 to 9, but a more meaningful designation is to use subscripts that range from 1957 to 1965. A subscript lower bound of other than 1 must appear in the declaration statement. The statement

DECLARE CARS(1957:1965) FLOAT;

declares CARS to be a vector of nine elements which are referenced by subscripts that range from 1957 to 1965. In this example, 1957 is the lower bound and 1965 is the upper bound. Observe that a colon is used to separate the two bounds. The *size* of any vector (i.e., the number of elements in the vector) can thus be determined by the following formula:

Vector size = upper bound – lower bound + 1

In most cases, the specified lower and upper bounds in a declaration statement must be positive or negative constants. An exception to this rule is presented in Chap. 6.

In order to refer to a specific element of a vector in a program, it is necessary to use a subscript to identify that element. In PL/I, a subscript may be any valid PL/I expression which results in a numeric value less than or equal to the declared upper bound and greater than or equal to the declared lower bound. If the resulting numeric value contains a fractional component, the fracitonal part is ignored. For example, the subscripted variable

NUM(12.867)

refers to the twelfth element of the vector NUM. If the vector NUM is declared in a program with the following statement

DECLARE NUM(15) FIXED;

a subscript reference to NUM(25) or NUM(-11) in the program is invalid. Subscripted variables may appear anywhere that simple variables of the same type are used. This means that subscripted variables may be used in expressions which are subscripts. For example, the statement

MARK(NUM(I) - 2) = 3;

is valid, if the expression NUM(I) - 2 yields a valid subscript for MARK.

To illustrate the use of vectors in a PL/I program, let us consider the following problem. Suppose we are given a list of stores and their retail prices for bread. We require a program that will print out a list of all the stores that have prices which exceed the average of the retail prices read in. Using data from 100 stores, the following program uses vectors to solve this problem.

```
/* RETAIL PRICE OF BREAD */
PRICE: PROCEDURE OPTIONS(MAIN);
     DECLARE I FIXED;
     DECLARE (PRICES(100), SUM, AVG) FLOAT;
     DECLARE STORE(100) CHARACTER(20) VARYING;
     SUM = 0.0;
     DO I = 1 TO 100;
          GET LIST (STORE(I), PRICES(I));
          SUM = SUM + PRICES(I);
     END;
     AVG = SUM / 100.0;
     DO I = 1 TO 100;
          IF PRICES(I) > AVG
          THEN PUT SKIP LIST (STORE(I), PRICES(I));
     END;
END PRICE;
```

Often, during the execution of a program it may be necessary to perform a certain operation on an entire vector. PL/I facilitates this by allowing the programmer to specify the entire vector in expressions and in operations. In order to specify the entire vector, the vector name is written without a subscript. For example, the assignment statement in this program segment

```
DECLARE SUM(10) FLOAT;
SUM = 0.0;
```

results in each of the ten elements of the vector SUM being assigned the value 0.0. When more than one vector is specified in an expression or an assignment statement, the bounds of all the vectors must be identical. Note that when single vector elements are used in an expression or assignment statement (rather than the entire vector), the bounds of the associated vectors need not be the same.

Vectors may also appear as arguments of built-in functions. When a vector is used as an argument of a built-in function which accepts a single value or variable as an argument, the function is applied to each element of the vector in turn. For example, the statements

        DECLARE (SUM(5), DEV(5)) FIXED;

            .
            .
            .

        DEV = SQRT(SUM);

place the square root of each element of SUM in the corresponding element of DEV.

Entire vectors may also be specified in input and output statements, much in the manner as is done in the main text. For example, the statements

        DECLARE MARK(10) FIXED;
        GET LIST (MARK);

result in the first ten data values being assigned to MARK(1) through MARK(10) in consecutive order (i.e., the first data value is assigned to MARK(1), the second to MARK(2), etc.). The output statement

        PUT LIST (MARK);

results in the ten elements of MARK being printed in consecutive order, beginning with MARK(1) and ending with MARK(10).

In order to illustrate some of the concepts presented in this section, the example given in Fig. 4-1 is presented. The problem is to find the range (i.e., the difference between the largest and smallest element) of a list of values. For example, the range of the following list

        2   4   6   7   9   3   12   4   2

is 10 (i.e., 12(largest value) − 2(smallest value) = 10).

The variables used in the following program, which calculates the range of a list of ten values, are

Variables	Type	Usage
VALUE(10)	FIXED	Vector of values for which the range is to be found
MAX	FIXED	Value of the largest element
MIN	FIXED	Value of the smallest element
RANGE	FIXED	Range of the vector VALUE
I	FIXED	Loop variable

The data used in this program are

7 9 11 5 6 9 20 30 52 5

After the appropriate variables have been declared, the list of values is read in and printed. MAX and MIN are both set initially to the value of the first element of the vector VALUE. A loop is then entered in which each element of the vector is compared with the present values of MAX and MIN. If an element is greater than the current value of MAX, MAX is assigned the value of that element. If the element is less than the current value of MIN, the value of that element is assigned to MIN. When all the elements have been processed, the range is computed by subtracting MIN from MAX. This value is then assigned to the variable RANGE. The value of the range is then printed.

This concludes our discussion of simple vector operations. The next section deals with the important applications of sorting and searching with vectors.

Exercises for Sec. 4-1

1. Write a program that will determine the largest and second largest elements of a list containing no more than 50 real numbers. The data is to consist of an integer specifying the number of elements in the list followed by the elements of the list.

```
/* RANGE OF A VECTOR */

STMT LEVEL NEST BLOCK MLVL  SOURCE TEXT


                            /* RANGE OF A VECTOR */

  1                         RAN: PROCEDURE OPTIONS(MAIN);

  2    1         1            DECLARE (VALUE(10), MAX, MIN, RANGE, I) FIXED;

  3    1         1            GET LIST (VALUE);
  4    1         1            PUT SKIP LIST ('VECTOR');
  5    1         1            PUT SKIP LIST (VALUE);
  6    1         1            MAX, MIN = VALUE(1);

  7    1         1            DO I = 1 TO 10;
  8    1    1    1                IF VALUE(I) > MAX
  9    1    1    1                THEN MAX = VALUE(I);
 10    1    1    1                IF VALUE(I) < MIN
 11    1    1    1                THEN MIN = VALUE(I);
 12    1    1    1            END;
 13    1         1            RANGE = MAX - MIN;
 14    1         1            PUT SKIP LIST ('RANGE IS', RANGE);
 15    1         1          END RAN;

ERRORS/WARNINGS DETECTED DURING CODE GENERATION:

    WARNING: NO FILE SPECIFIED. SYSIN/SYSPRINT ASSUMED. (CGOC)


VECTOR
        7                 9              11              5           6        9
       20                30              52              5
RANGE IS                 47


IN STMT   15  PROGRAM RETURNS FROM MAIN PROCEDURE.
```

Fig. 4-1 Program to find the range of a list of values

Using your program, find the largest and second largest elements in the following list.

75.63
71.77
68.31
82.94
66.11
79.81
67.79
92.34
88.11

2. Design a program which reads an unsorted vector A or n integers, and prints the vector in the same sequence after ignoring duplicate values found in the given vector. The number of remaining elements (m) is also required. For example, given the vector

A_1 A_2 A_3 A_4 A_5 A_6 A_7 A_8 A_9 A_{10}
15   31   23   15   75   23   41   15   31   85

of ten integers, the compressed vector returned would be

$\mathbf{A_1}$ A_2 A_3 A_4 A_5 A_6 A_7 A_8 A_9 A_{10}
15   31   23   75   41   85

with m = 6.
Test your program on the following input values.

16, 21, 23, 16, 25, 21, 41, 31, 23

3. Formulate a program to convert decimal (base 10) integers to their octal (base 8) representations by successive divisions. Let NUMBER denote the integer to be converted and BASE the base to which the integer is to be converted (8 in our case).

For example, to compute the octal representation of 150, it is repeatedly divided by eight and the resulting remainders are saved in order.

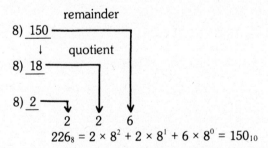

$$226_8 = 2 \times 8^2 + 2 \times 8^1 + 6 \times 8^0 = 150_{10}$$

Using your program find the octal representation of 1022.

4. As the shaft concrete lining was poured at a nearby potash mine, samples of the concrete were taken and tested for maximum strength. The record book of shaft depth versus concrete strength has been keypunched as follows:
-first card contains the starting shaft depth and the total number of test results for consecutive one foot increments down the shaft
-the following cards all contain ten test results per card, but the last card may contain less than ten results depending on the total number of results taken.

Example input:

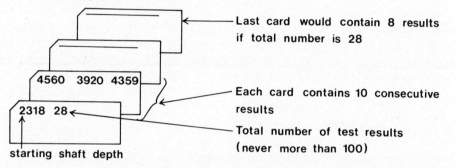

Last card would contain 8 results if total number is 28

Each card contains 10 consecutive results

Total number of test results (never more than 100)

starting shaft depth

A running average of eight results is used as an indication of the average concrete strength and would indicate any extremely weak section in the shaft. The running average is the average of the readings at that depth and the next seven feet below. The running average for each of the last seven feet is the average of the remaining readings.

Obtain a program to generate a running average table as follows:

DEPTH	TEST RESULT	RUNNING AVERAGE
2318	4560	4341
2319	3920	4265
.	.	.
.	.	.
.	.	.
2339	4820	4515
.	.	.
.	.	.
2345	4500	4500

The "length" of the running average, in this case eight feet, varies with each application. After you have a solution to the preceding problem, generalize your program so only one data card must be changed to change the length of the average.

With your program, print a running average table for the following values.

2500 (starting shaft depth)   11 (no. of test results)
Test Results

5500, 6511, 5615, 6000, 5791, 5821,
5651, 6345, 5796, 6312, 6200

5. An important problem in statistics concerns the predictability of the value of one variable from the value of another variable. Two variables that can be used in this way with good chance of success are said to be *strongly correlated*. The strength of correlation is determined by the *correlation coefficient*.

    We wish to conduct an experiment to determine the strength of correlation between a student's final high school average and his or her performance on first year university classes. Following final examinations, a card is prepared for each first year student containing two real values: high school average (H) and first year average (F). Assume there are N students involved in this study. (N is never greater than 100). Design an algorithm to read this data into two vector H[i] and F[i], i = 1, 2, ..., N. Then compute the correlation coefficient R according to the following formula

$$\frac{N \, \Sigma \, H[i]F[i] - \Sigma \, H[i] \, \Sigma \, F[i]}{(N \, \Sigma \, H[i]^2 - (\Sigma \, H[i])^2)(N \, \Sigma \, F[i]^2 - (\Sigma \, F[i])^2)}$$

If the correlation coefficient exceeds 0.85, a message is to be printed saying that these variables appear to be strongly correlated.

Test your program on the following input values.

12 (no. of students)	
78	65
85	80
65	50
80	75
90	88
67	62
79	75
80	80
69	54
75	70
70	70
82	80

6. Write a program which generates a yearly sales report. The report is to give a breakdown of sales for each month of the year, and, in addition, a yearly total. Each sales transaction is recorded on a card as follows:

    Sales amount, Month number

    where each month of the year is numbered from 1 to 12. The number of input cards is unknown and these cards are not in any sequence. Use an end of file to detect the end of the data.

    Use your program to generate a report for the following input values.

    6032 2
    6030 6

```
7841   1
7963   12
8967   11
3852   3
7789   4
8561   4
9921   12
6754   1
6251   1
```

4-2   SORTING AND SEARCHING WITH VECTORS

This section deals with two important applications that commonly involve vectors. These are sorting and searching. In Sec. 4-2.1 techniques of sorting, with particular emphasis on the selection sort, are discussed. In the next section, searching is introduced. Finally, in Sec. 4-2.3, merging and merge-sorting are presented. Programs are given for each technique.

4-2.1   Selection Sort

The technique of selection sorting is discussed in Sec. 4-3.1 of the main text. Suppose, for example, we wish to sort a vector into ascending (i.e., increasing) order. Using the selection method, the vector is scanned for the smallest element, and this element is assigned to the first element of a vector that is to contain the sorted elements. In order to distinguish the element that has already been selected, it is replaced in the original vector by some distinguishing value that is known not to exist as one of the elements of the vector. The original vector is then scanned (ignoring the distinguishing value) and the second smallest element is found. This element is then placed in the second position of the new vector. Its value in the original vector is replaced by the distinguishing value. The sort continues in this manner until each element of the original vector has been placed in the sorted vector.

The process of scanning the vector and selecting the next element in the ordering is called a *pass*. In a vector of n elements, this method of sorting requires n passes, with one element selected on each pass. A program to perform this selection sort appears in Fig. 4-2. The data values used in this program are:

```
14
5 10 1 7 9 23 46 32 12 4 2 8 7 11
```

The variables used are

Variable	Type	Usage
K(100)	FIXED	Vector containing list of values to be sorted
OUTPUT(100)	FIXED	Sorted vector
NUM	FIXED	Number of values to be sorted
PASS	FIXED	Number of current pass

| MIN | FIXED | Subscript which references current smallest element |
| I | FIXED | Loop variable |

In this program the unsorted vector K is read in and printed. The selection sort is then begun. A counted loop controls the passes made. During each pass, the smallest element is selected (ignoring elements that have been given the

```
/* SELECTION SORT (VERSION 1) */

STMT LEVEL NEST BLOCK MLVL  SOURCE TEXT

                          /* SELECTION SORT (VERSION 1) */
    1                     SELECT1: PROCEDURE OPTIONS(MAIN);

                              /* DECLARE VARIABLES */
    2    1          1         DECLARE (K(100), OUTPUT(100), PASS, MIN, NUM, I) FIXED;

                              /* READ IN VECTOR */
    3    1          1         GET LIST (NUM);
    4    1          1         DO I = 1 TO NUM;
    5    1    1     1             GET LIST (K(I));
    6    1    1     1         END;

                              /* PRINT UNSORTED VECTOR */
    7    1          1         PUT SKIP LIST ('UNSORTED VECTOR');
    8    1          1         PUT SKIP;
    9    1          1         DO I = 1 TO NUM;
   10    1    1     1             PUT LIST (K(I));
   11    1    1     1         END;

                              /* MAKE ONE PASS FOR EACH ELEMENT */
   12    1          1         DO PASS = 1 TO NUM;
   13    1    1     1             MIN = 1;

                                  /* FIND SMALLEST ELEMENT */
   14    1    1     1             DO I = 2 TO NUM;
   15    1    2     1                 IF K(I) < K(MIN) & K(I) ¬= 999
   16    1    2     1                 THEN MIN = I;
   17    1    2     1             END;
   18    1    1     1             OUTPUT(PASS) = K(MIN);
   19    1    1     1             K(MIN) = 999;
   20    1    1     1         END;

                              /* PRINT SORTED VECTOR */
   21    1          1         PUT SKIP LIST ('SORTED VECTOR');
   22    1          1         PUT SKIP;
   23    1          1         DO I = 1 TO NUM;
   24    1    1     1             PUT LIST (OUTPUT(I));
   25    1    1     1         END;
   26    1          1     END SELECT1;

ERRORS/WARNINGS DETECTED DURING CODE GENERATION:

    WARNING: NO FILE SPECIFIED. SYSIN/SYSPRINT ASSUMED. (CGOC)
```

```
UNSORTED VECTOR
        5              10              1              7              9             23
       46              32             12              4              2              8
        7              11
SORTED VECTOR
        1               2              4              5              7              7
        8               9             10             11             12             23
       32              46
```

```
IN STMT   26  PROGRAM RETURNS FROM MAIN PROCEDURE.
```

Fig. 4-2   Selection sort (version 1)

distinguishing value 999) and placed in the vector OUTPUT. It is then replaced in the original vector by the value 999. Finally, after all the passes have been made, the sorted vector OUTPUT is printed. This particular selection sort may present problems if the vector to be sorted is large or if one of the elements in the vector happens to be the special value 999. If the vector to be sorted is large, then a large amount of storage space may be required for the two vectors (original and sorted copy). Also, since the number of passes required is equal to the number of elements and each element must be checked on each pass, the time consumed in sorting a very large vector may be impractical. Notice that the vector K is declared to accommodate up to 100 elements. In any particular run (such as the one shown) there may be fewer elements. The actual number is given by N.

Another version of the selection sort, which saves both storage space and computing time, involves using the original vector to hold the selected elements, as described in the main text. The program given in Fig. 4-3 uses this method to sort the numbers

5 10 1 7 9 23 46 32 12 4 2 8 7 11

into ascending order. The following variables are used in this program.

Variable	Type	Usage
K(100)	FIXED	Vector containing list of values to be sorted
NUM	FIXED	Number of values to be sorted
PASS	FIXED	Number of current pass
MIN	FIXED	Subscript which references current smallest element
I	FIXED	Loop variable
NEXT	FIXED	Subscript used to reference the first element of the remaining unsorted elements
TEMP	FIXED	Temporarily holds the value of an element during an exchange

As in the first version of the selection sort, the vector to be sorted is read in. The first counted loop controls the number of passes. The second counted loop controls the search of the remaining elements in the vector. If the smallest element found is not already in the correct position, it is exchanged for the current element in that position. When $n - 1$ passes have been completed, the now sorted vector is printed.

Sorting may be performed on nonnumerical elements as well as numerical elements. For examples of sorting involving character string elements, see Chap. 5.

This concludes the section on selection sorts. In the next section, methods of searching for elements in vectors are introduced.

4-2.2   Basic Searching

Searching refers to the process of scanning a vector for a particular element. Two types of search were discussed in the main text; namely, the *linear* search and the *binary* search.

A linear search involves scanning the elements of a vector in sequential order (i.e., element by element) until the desired element is found. A program to perform this task is given in Fig. 4-4. The data values used in this run were

```
14
5 10 1 7 9 23 46 32 12 4 2 8 11 6
12
```

The following variables appears in this program.

Variable	Type	Usage
K(100)	FIXED	Vector to be searched
N	FIXED	Number of elements in vector
I	FIXED	Loop variable
X	FIXED	Value sought

```
/* SELECTION SORT (VERSION 2) */

STMT LEVEL NEST BLOCK MLVL   SOURCE TEXT

                                /* SELECTION SORT (VERSION 2) */

    1                           SELECT2: PROCEDURE OPTIONS(MAIN);

                                    /* DECLARE VARIABLES */
    2    1           1              DECLARE (K(100), PASS, MIN, NUM, I, NEXT, TEMP) FIXED;

                                    /* READ IN VECTOR */
    3    1           1              GET LIST (NUM);
    4    1           1              DO I = 1 TO NUM;
    5    1    1      1                  GET LIST (K(I));
    6    1    1      1              END;

                                    /* PRINT UNSORTED VECTOR */
    7    1           1              PUT SKIP LIST ('UNSORTED VECTOR');
    8    1           1              PUT SKIP;
    9    1           1              DO I = 1 TO NUM;
   10    1    1      1                  PUT LIST (K(I));
   11    1    1      1              END;

                                    /* REPEAT FOR  NUM - 1 PASSES */
   12    1           1              DO PASS = 1 TO NUM - 1;
   13    1    1      1                  MIN = PASS;
   14    1    1      1                  NEXT = PASS + 1;
   15    1    1      1                  DO I = NEXT TO NUM;
   16    1    2      1                      IF K(I) < K(MIN)
   17    1    2      1                      THEN MIN = I;
   18    1    2      1                  END;
   19    1    1      1                  IF MIN ¬= PASS
   20    1    1      1                  THEN DO;
   21    1    2      1                      TEMP = K(PASS);
   22    1    2      1                      K(PASS) = K(MIN);
   23    1    2      1                      K(MIN) = TEMP;
   24    1    2      1                      END;
   25    1    1      1              END;
                                    /* PRINT SORTED VECTOR */
   26    1           1              PUT SKIP LIST ('SORTED VECTOR');
   27    1           1              PUT SKIP;
   28    1           1              DO I = 1 TO NUM;
   29    1    1      1                  PUT LIST (K(I));
   30    1    1      1              END;
   31    1           1          END SELECT2;

ERRORS/WARNINGS DETECTED DURING CODE GENERATION:

    WARNING: NO FILE SPECIFIED. SYSIN/SYSPRINT ASSUMED. (CGOC)
```

Fig. 4-3   Selection sort (version 2)

```
UNSORTED VECTOR
     5               10              1               7               9               23
    46               32             12               4               2                8
     7               11
SORTED VECTOR
     1                2              4               5               7                7
     8                9             10              11              12               23
    32               46
```

IN STMT   31 PROGRAM RETURNS FROM MAIN PROCEDURE.

Fig. 4-3   Selection sort (version 2) (cont'd.)

After the appropriate variables are declared, the vector and particular element sought are read in and printed. The search then proceeds in a sequential manner until the desired element is found or the end of the vector is reached. If the element is found, the message SUCCESSFUL SEARCH and the position of the element in the vector is printed; otherwise, the end of the vector is reached and the message UNSUCCESSFUL SEARCH is printed.

A more efficient method of searching, which can be performed only on sorted vectors, is the *binary search*. Suppose the elements of a vector are stored in ascending order. A binary search performed on this vector proceeds in the following manner. The middle (or approximately the middle) element of the vector is chosen. If the value sought is greater than the middle element, the search continues with the second half of the vector. If, on the other hand, the value sought is less than the value of the middle element, the search continues with the first half of the vector. A new middle element, which is the middle of the new search interval, is found. The process is repeated with this new search interval and again the appropriate half (now one quarter of the whole vector) is chosen. This process is repeated until the element sought is found or until the search interval is empty, the latter indicating that the desired element is not present in the vector. A PL/I program to perform a binary search appears in Fig. 4-5. This program performs a binary search for the element 45 in the ordered vector:

   10 11 25 30 39 45 56 72 88

The variables that appear in this program are:

Variable	Type	Usage
K(100)	FIXED	Vector of values to be searched
LOW	FIXED	Subscript of smallest element in current search interval
HIGH	FIXED	Subscript of largest element in current search interval
MIDDLE	FIXED	Subscript of middle element in current search interval
N	FIXED	Number of values in K
X	FIXED	Value sought
I	FIXED	Loop variable

Notice in statement 14 that the built-in function TRUNC is used to obtain an integer value that is less than or equal to the calculated middle value. This is done to ensure that the subscript used to locate the middle element of the vector is always an integer. X is then compared with the middle element. If X is less than the middle element, then the variable HIGH is set to MIDDLE − 1, and the search interval becomes the bottom half of the present search interval. If X is greater than the value of the middle element, then LOW is assigned the value of MIDDLE + 1, and the search interval is reduced to the top half of the current search interval. The position of the middle element in this new search interval is then calculated. This process continues until X equals the value of the middle element (i.e., the search is successful), or until the search interval is empty (this is indicated by a value of LOW which is larger than the value of HIGH).

```
/* LINEAR SEARCH */

STMT LEVEL NEST BLOCK MLVL  SOURCE TEXT


                                /* LINEAR SEARCH */

     1                          LSEARCH: PROCEDURE OPTIONS(MAIN);

                                    /* DECLARE VARIABLES */
     2    1            1             DECLARE (K(100), N, I, X) FIXED;

                                    /* READ IN VECTOR  */
     3    1            1             GET LIST (N);
     4    1            1             DO I = 1 TO N;
     5    1    1       1                 GET LIST (K(I));
     6    1    1       1             END;
                                    /* READ IN ELEMENT SOUGHT */
     7    1            1             GET LIST (X);

                                    /* PRINT VECTOR TO BE SEARCHED AND VALUE SOUGHT */
     8    1            1             PUT SKIP LIST ('VECTOR');
     9    1            1             PUT SKIP;
    10    1            1             DO I = 1 TO N;
    11    1    1       1                 PUT LIST (K(I));
    12    1    1       1             END;
    13    1            1             PUT SKIP LIST ('VALUE SOUGHT EQUALS', X);

                                    /* CHECK EACH ELEMENT UNTIL X IS FOUND */
    14    1            1             DO I = 1 TO N;
    15    1    1       1                 IF K(I) = X
    16    1    1       1                 THEN DO;
    17    1    2       1                     PUT SKIP LIST ('SUCCESSFUL SEARCH. VALUE IN POSITION',
                                                 I);
    18    1    2       1                     EXIT;
    19    1    2       1                     END;
    20    1    1       1             END;
    21    1            1             PUT SKIP LIST ('UNSUCCESSFUL SEARCH');
    22    1            1         END LSEARCH;

ERRORS/WARNINGS DETECTED DURING CODE GENERATION:

    WARNING: NO FILE SPECIFIED. SYSIN/SYSPRINT ASSUMED. (CGOC)


VECTOR
          5                  10             1              7              9              23
         46                  32            12              4              2               8
         11                   6
VALUE SOUGHT EQUALS          12
SUCCESSFUL SEARCH. VALUE IN POSITION          9



IN STMT   18  PROGRAM IS STOPPED.
```

Fig. 4-4 Linear search

```
/* BINARY SEARCH */

STMT LEVEL NEST BLOCK MLVL   SOURCE TEXT

                                        /* BINARY SEARCH */

  1                                     BSEARCH: PROCEDURE OPTIONS(MAIN);

                                        /* DECLARE VARIABLES */
  2    1         1                      DECLARE (LOW, HIGH, K(100), N, I, MIDDLE, X) FIXED;

                                        /* READ IN VECTOR */
  3    1         1                      GET LIST (N);
  4    1         1                      DO I = 1 TO N;
  5    1    1    1                      GET LIST (K(I));
  6    1    1    1                      END;

                                        /* READ IN ELEMENT SEARCHED FOR */
  7    1         1                      GET LIST (X);

                                        /* PRINT VECTOR AND VALUE SOUGHT */
  8    1         1                      PUT SKIP LIST ('VECTOR');
  9    1         1                      PUT SKIP;
 10    1         1                      DO I = 1 TO N;
 11    1    1    1                      PUT LIST (K(I));
 12    1    1    1                      END;
 13    1         1                      PUT SKIP LIST ('VALUE SOUGHT EQUALS', X);

                                        /* INITIALIZE VARIABLES */
 14    1         1                      LOW = 1;
 15    1         1                      HIGH = N;
 16    1         1                      DO WHILE (LOW <= HIGH);
 17    1    1    1                      MIDDLE = TRUNC((LOW + HIGH) / 2.0);
 18    1    1    1                      IF X < K(MIDDLE)
 19    1    1    1                      THEN HIGH = MIDDLE - 1;
 20    1    1    1                      ELSE DO;
 21    1    2    2                      IF X > K(MIDDLE)
 22    1    2    2                      THEN LOW = MIDDLE + 1;
 23    1    2    2                      ELSE DO;
 24    1    3    3                      PUT SKIP LIST ('SUCCESSFUL SEARCH.',
                                                     'VALUE IN POSITION', MIDDLE);
 25    1    3    3                      EXIT;
 26    1    3    3                      END;
 27    1    2    2                      END;
 28    1    1    1                      END;

 29    1         1                      PUT SKIP LIST ('UNSUCCESSFUL SEARCH');
 30    1         1                      END BSEARCH;

ERRORS/WARNINGS DETECTED DURING CODE GENERATION:

  WARNING: NO FILE SPECIFIED. SYSIN/SYSPRINT ASSUMED. (CGOC)

VECTOR
       10      25      30      39      45
       56      88
       11
       72
       45
VALUE SOUGHT EQUALS              45
SUCCESSFUL SEARCH.    VALUE IN POSITION        6

IN STMT   25   PROGRAM IS STOPPED.
```

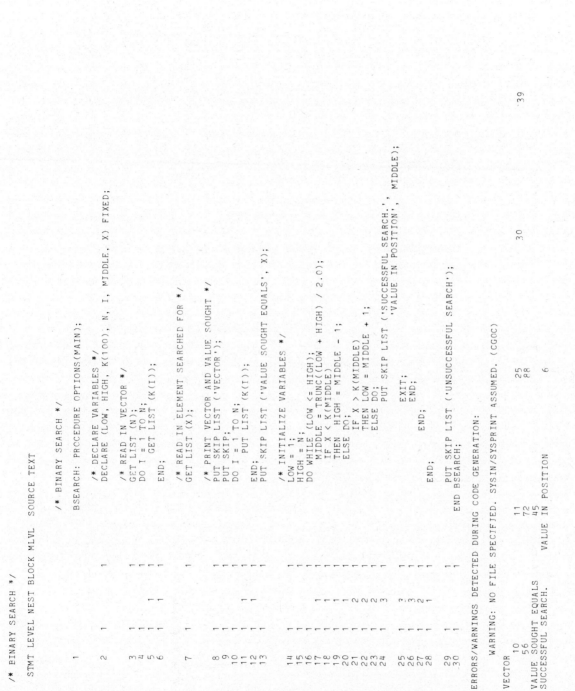

Fig. 4-5 Binary search

We close this section with a more elaborate problem. The city of Lowly Heights is experiencing a housing shortage. As a consequence, the price of rental accommodations has become unreasonable. In order to keep down the inflationary price of new apartments in the city, the city fathers have decided to implement a basic maximum allowable rent for apartments. This maximum is based on the amount of floor space contained in the apartment. The schedule of areas and corresponding rents is as follows.

Floor space	145	165	180	190	220	235	245	270	280	300	340	350
Rent	90	100	125	140	150	165	175	190	200	210	225	250

If the floor space is below 145 square feet, the apartment is exempt from rent control. If the floor space is above 350 square feet, the apartment is to be placed in a special category. The problem is to write a program that reads in the location of an apartment and the amount of floor space it contains and finds the maximum allowable rent that, according to the previous table, may be charged. If the floor space is below 145 square feet or above 350 square feet, the messages, "IS NOT COVERED UNDER RENT CONTROL", and "REFER TO SPECIAL CATEGORY", respectively are to be printed. In addition, a record must be kept of the number of apartments that fall into each of the 12 space and rent categories just given. The floor space read in is rounded to the nearest rent category. The program must generate the following reports:

APARTMENT REPORT

LOCATION	MAXIMUM ALLOWABLE RENT
APT. 5 SPRUCE CRES.	150
APT. 7 WRANGLER ROAD	90
APT. 9 CHARLY HTS.	125
APT. 4 WILLOW AVE.	190

and

REPORT ON RENTAL ACCOMMODATIONS

APPROXIMATE AREA	MAXIMUM ALLOWABLE RENT	NUMBER OF UNITS
145	90	1
165	100	0
.	.	.
.	.	.
.	.	.
350	250	0

A general outline of the steps involved in solving this problem follows.

1) Read in the data on the first apartment.
2) Repeat the following process until there is no more data:
   (i) Check whether the floor space is below or above the specified minimum and maximum, and if so, print the appropriate message;
      otherwise, use a binary search to find the position of the designated floor

space in the vector of areas and use that position to determine the rent for the apartment.

Print the location of the apartment and the maximum rent. Increment a counter which keeps track of the number of units of that area.

(ii) Read in data concerning the next apartment.

3) Print a report consisting of the various apartment floor spaces, the maximum rent that can be charged for each, and the number of apartments in that category.

The variables used in the program of Fig. 4-6 are

Variable	Type	Usage
AREA (12)	FIXED	Vector of floor spaces
RENT(12)	FIXED	Vector of rents
NUM(12)	FIXED	Number of available units in each category
LOW	FIXED	Subscript which points to the beginning of the search interval
HIGH	FIXED	Subscript which points to end of the search interval
MIDDLE	FIXED	Subscript which points to the middle of the search interval
I	FIXED	Loop variable
LOCATION	CHARACTER(24) VARYING	Address of the rental unit
SPACE	FIXED	Amount of floor space in the rental unit

The data for the program given in Fig. 4-6 include information given in the rent schedule and a list of appartments and their rents. The input list of apartments and areas used in this program follows.

'APT. 5 234 ELM ST.'	165
'APT. 12 452 SCYRA DRIVE'	270
'APT. 5 452 JASMIN ST.'	220
'APT. 4 125 YEOMAN AVE.'	235
'APT. 23 756 ROVER LANE'	270
'APT. 3 52 TARA COURT'	350
'APT. 6 25 SORRO PLACE'	145
'APT. 6 10 JOY ST.'	125
'APT. 2 335 GOPHER LANE'	165
'APT. 15 234 APPLE CRES.'	190
'APT. 1 24 RODE ST.'	165
'APT. 4 124 GRAY ST.'	280
'APT. 8 45 RYERS CRES.'	180
'APT. 25 435 TALLY DRIVE'	300
'APT. 42 534 RIVER ST.'	190
'END'	0

```
                                         /* APARTMENT RENTAL REPORT */

                         STMT LEVEL NEST BLOCK MLVL  SOURCE TEXT


                                                     /* APARTMENT RENTAL REPORT */
               1                                     REPORT: PROCEDURE OPTIONS(MAIN);

                                                         /* DECLARE AND INITIALIZE VARIABLES */
               2    1           1                     DECLARE (AREA(12), RENT(12), NUM(12)) FIXED;
               3    1           1                     DECLARE LOCATION CHARACTER(24) VARYING;
               4    1           1                     DECLARE (SPACE, LOW, HIGH, MIDDLE, I) FIXED;

               5    1           1                     DO I = 1 TO 12;
               6    1    1      1                         GET LIST (AREA(I), RENT(I));
               7    1    1      1                     END;
               8    1           1                     NUM = 0;

                                                         /* PRINT HEADER */
               9    1           1                     PUT LIST ('APARTMENT REPORT');
              10    1           1                     PUT SKIP LIST ('LOCATION', 'MAXIMUM ALLOWABLE RENT');

                                                         /* READ FIRST CARD */
              11    1           1                     GET LIST (LOCATION, SPACE);

                                                         /* PROCESS CARDS UNTIL TRAILER REACHED */
              12    1           1                     DO WHILE (LOCATION ¬= 'END');

                                                             /* CHECK IF AREA IS BELOW 145 */
              13    1    1      1                         IF SPACE < 145
              14    1    1      1                         THEN PUT SKIP LIST (LOCATION,
                                                               'IS NOT COVERED UNDER RENT CONTROL.');
              15    1    1      1                         ELSE IF SPACE > 350
              16    1    1      1                             THEN PUT SKIP LIST (LOCATION,
                                                                   'REFER TO SPECIAL CATEGORY.');
              17    1    1      1                         ELSE DO;
              18    1    2      1                             LOW = 1;
              19    1    2      1                             HIGH = 12;
              20    1    2      1                             DO WHILE (LOW <= HIGH);
              21    1    3      1                                 MIDDLE = TRUNC((LOW + HIGH) / 2.0);
              22    1    3      1                                 IF SPACE < AREA(MIDDLE)
              23    1    3      1                                 THEN HIGH = MIDDLE - 1;
              24    1    3      1                                 ELSE DO;
              25    1    4      1                                     IF SPACE > AREA(MIDDLE)
              26    1    4      1                                     THEN LOW = MIDDLE + 1;
              27    1    4      1                                     ELSE DO;
              28    1    5      1                                         PUT SKIP LIST (LOCATION,

                                                                               RENT(MIDDLE));
              29    1    5      1                                         NUM(MIDDLE) = NUM(MIDDLE) + 1;
              30    1    5      1                                         LOW = HIGH + 1;
              31    1    5      1                                         END;
              32    1    4      1                                     END;
              33    1    3      1                                 END;
              34    1    2      1                             END;
              35    1    1      1                         GET LIST (LOCATION, SPACE);
              36    1    1      1                     END;

                                                         /* PRINT SECOND REPORT */
              37    1           1                     PUT SKIP(3) LIST ('REPORT ON TOTAL RENTAL ACCOMMODATIONS');
              38    1           1                     PUT SKIP(2) LIST ('FLOOR SPACE', 'MAXIMUM RENT',
                                                           'NUMBER OF UNITS');
              39    1           1                     DO I = 1 TO 12;
              40    1    1      1                         PUT SKIP LIST (AREA(I), RENT(I), NUM(I));
              41    1    1      1                     END;
              42    1           1                 END REPORT;

         ERRORS/WARNINGS DETECTED DURING CODE GENERATION:

              WARNING: NO FILE SPECIFIED. SYSIN/SYSPRINT ASSUMED. (CG0C)


         APARTMENT REPORT
         LOCATION               MAXIMUM ALLOWABLE RENT
         APT. 5 234 ELM ST.          100
         APT. 12 452 SCYRA DRIVE     190
         APT. 5 452 JASMIN ST.       150
         APT. 4 125 YEOMAN AVE.      165
```

Fig. 4-6   Apartment report program

```
APT. 23 756 ROVER LANE      190
APT. 3 52 TARA COURT        250
APT. 6 25 SORRO PLACE        90
APT. 6 10 JOY ST.       IS NOT COVERED UNDER RENT CONTROL.
APT. 2 335 GOPHER LANE      100
APT. 15 234 APPLE CRES.     140
APT. 1 24 RODE ST.          100
APT. 4 124 GRAY ST.         200
APT. 8 45 RYERS CRES.       125
APT. 25 435 TALLY DRIVE     210
APT. 42 534 RIVER ST.       140


REPORT ON TOTAL RENTAL ACCOMMODATIONS

FLOOR SPACE          MAXIMUM RENT        NUMBER OF UNITS
    145                   90                   1
    165                  100                   3
    180                  125                   1
    190                  140                   2
    220                  150                   1
    235                  165                   1
    245                  175                   0
    270                  190                   2
    280                  200                   1
    300                  210                   1
    340                  225                   0
    350                  250                   1


IN STMT    42  PROGRAM RETURNS FROM MAIN PROCEDURE.
```

Fig. 4-6   Apartment report program (cont'd.)

At the start of the program, the schedule of rental rates and floor spaces is read. A loop processes each of the apartments, using a binary search to locate the appropriate rent. The location and allowable rent are printed for each apartment. In addition, a counter which contains the number of apartments in this category is incremented. When all apartments have been processed, a counted loop is used to print the number of apartments that fall into each category.

4-2.3   Merging and Merge Sorting

As described in the main text, merging vectors is the process of taking two sorted vectors and combining them into a single sorted vector. In this section, we present first a program that performs a merge, then a program that uses the technique of merging to effect a sort.

The program given in Fig. 4-7 merges two integer vectors that have been sorted in ascending order. The variables used in this program are

Variable	Type	Usage
A(100)	FIXED	Vector to be merged
B(100)	FIXED	Vector to be merged
C(200)	FIXED	Merged vector
N	FIXED	Number of elements in vector A
M	FIXED	Number of elements in vector B

```
/* PROGRAM TO MERGE TWO VECTORS */

STMT LEVEL NEST BLOCK MLVL   SOURCE TEXT


                                    /* PROGRAM TO MERGE TWO VECTORS */

   1                                MERGE: PROCEDURE OPTIONS(MAIN);

                                        /* DECLARE VARIABLES */
   2    1         1                 DECLARE (A(100), B(100), C(200)) FIXED;
   3    1         1                 DECLARE (N, M, I, J, K, R) FIXED;

                                        /* READ IN AND PRINT THE TWO VECTORS */
   4    1         1                 GET LIST (N, M);
   5    1         1                 PUT SKIP LIST ('VECTOR A');
   6    1         1                 PUT SKIP;
   7    1         1                 DO I = 1 TO N;
   8    1    1    1                     GET LIST (A(I));
   9    1    1    1                     PUT LIST (A(I));
  10    1    1    1                 END;
  11    1         1                 PUT SKIP LIST ('VECTOR B');
  12    1         1                 PUT SKIP;
  13    1         1                 DO I = 1 TO M;
  14    1    1    1                     GET LIST (B(I));
  15    1    1    1                     PUT LIST (B(I));
  16    1    1    1                 END;

                                        /* INITIALIZE VARIABLES */
  17    1         1                 I, J, K = 1;

                                        /* PROCESS VECTORS UNTIL THE END OF ONE IS REACHED */
  18    1         1                 DO WHILE ((I <= N) & (J <= M));
  19    1    1    1                     IF A(I) <= B(J)
  20    1    1    1                     THEN DO;
  21    1    2    1                         C(K) = A(I);
  22    1    2    1                         I = I + 1;
  23    1    2    1                         K = K + 1;
  24    1    2    1                         END;
  25    1    1    1                     ELSE DO;
  26    1    2    1                         C(K) = B(J);
  27    1    2    1                         J = J + 1;
  28    1    2    1                         K = K + 1;
  29    1    2    1                         END;
  30    1    1    1                 END;

                                        /* ADD REMAINING ELEMENTS TO SORTED VECTOR */
  31    1         1                 IF I > N

  32    1         1                 THEN DO;
  33    1    1    1                     DO R = J TO M;
  34    1    2    1                         C(K) = B(R);
  35    1    2    1                         K = K + 1;
  36    1    2    1                     END;
  37    1    1    1                     END;
  38    1         1                 ELSE DO;
  39    1    1    1                     DO R = I TO N;
  40    1    2    1                         C(K) = A(R);
  41    1    2    1                         K = K + 1;
  42    1    2    1                     END;
  43    1    1    1                     END;

                                        /* PRINT MERGED VECTOR */
  44    1         1                 PUT SKIP LIST('MERGED VECTOR');
  45    1         1                 PUT SKIP;
  46    1         1                 DO I = 1 TO N + M;
  47    1    1    1                     PUT LIST (C(I));
  48    1    1    1                 END;
  49    1         1                 END MERGE;

ERRORS/WARNINGS DETECTED DURING CODE GENERATION:

    WARNING: NO FILE SPECIFIED. SYSIN/SYSPRINT ASSUMED. (CGOC)
```

Fig. 4-7 Program to merge two vectors

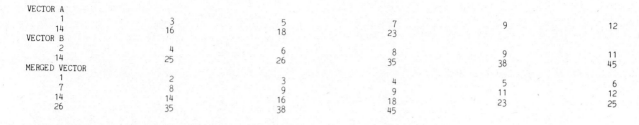

IN STMT 49 PROGRAM RETURNS FROM MAIN PROCEDURE.

Fig. 4-7 Program to merge two vectors (cont'd.)

I	FIXED	Subscript
J	FIXED	Subscript
K	FIXED	Subscript
R	FIXED	Loop variable

In this program, a card which contains two integers, N, the number of elements in the first vector, and M, the number of elements in the second, is read in. The first element of each vector is checked and the smallest is selected and placed in vector C. This process continues until all the elements of vector A or vector B have been used. The remaining unprocessed elements are then added to the vector containing the merged elements. Finally, the merged vector is printed.

Multiple merging or *K-way merging* is the merging of a number of sorted vectors into one sorted vector. The following program uses this method to sort a vector that contains 2^m elements where 2^m is less than 128. The program can be modified to handle vectors with a number of elements that are not an exact power of two, although this is not done here. The variables used in this program are:

Variable	Type	Usage
K(128)	FIXED	Vector to be sorted
C(128)	FIXED	Output sorted vector
N	FIXED	Number of elements in vector K
I	FIXED	Used as a subscript
J	FIXED	Used as a subscript
T	FIXED	Used as a subscript
R	FIXED	Loop variable
PASS	FIXED	Number of current pass
P	FIXED	Subscript of the first element of first subvector
Q	FIXED	Subscript of the first element of second subvector

S	FIXED	Subscript of last element in subvector
LAST	FIXED	Number of passes to be made
SIZE	FIXED	Size of the current subvector
SUBPASS	FIXED	Number of subpasses
S1	FIXED	Loop variable

The vector to be sorted is read in, and the number of passes needed to sort the vector is calculated. The number of passes needed for a vector of 2^m elements is m. In order to calculate m, it is necessary to find the log value of the number of elements to the base two. The built-in function LOG2 performs this task. The value 0.5 is then added to the log value obtained so as to round this result to the nearest integer. The variable SIZE refers to the number of elements contained in a subvector during a particular pass. The variables P and Q contain the first elements of the subvectors to be merged on a particular subpass. The variable SUBPASS contains the number of subpasses to be performed during that pass. Each subpass consists of merging two subvectors and placing the result in vector C if PASS is odd, or in vector K if the pass is even. Whether the pass is even or odd is tested by dividing PASS by 2.0 and comparing the resulting value with TRUNC(PASS/2.0). If the PASS is odd, the results are not equal because of the truncation performed by TRUNC(PASS/2.0). If the PASS is even, the results are the same. After each subpass is completed, the values of P and Q are updated, and the next subpass with the next two subvectors is performed until all subvectors within the vector have been processed. The next pass is then initiated, and this process continues until the entire vector has been sorted. If the number of passes required is odd, then the sorted vector C is recopied into vector K. Finally, the sorted vector K is printed.

This ends our discussion of vectors (one dimensional arrays in PL/I). In this section, some vector applications were introduced. In Sec. 4-2.1, two versions of the selection sort were presented. Searching was the topic of Sec. 4-2.2. Programs which illustrated linear and binary searches were given. Finally in Sec. 4-2.3, the process of merging and its use as a sorting technique were introduced.

In the next section, arrays with more than one dimension are presented. The multidimensional array and its use with certain operations are discussed.

Exercises for Sec. 4-2

1. Given a vector X on n integer elements where n is odd, write a program to calculate the median of this vector. The median is the value such that half the numbers are greater than that value and half are less. For example, given the vector X

X_1	X_2	X_3	X_4	X_5	X_6	X_7	X_8	X_9
17	-3	21	2	9	-4	6	8	11

   containing nine elements, the execution of your program should give a value of 8.

2. Program M_SORT given in this text only works if $n = 2^m$. Extend this program so it can handle any value of n.

3. A large firm has plants in five different cities. The firm employs a total of n employees. Each employee record contains (in part) the following fields:

1. Employee name
2. City
3. Employee number

These records are not kept in any order. Assume that the City field is coded with an integer value of 1 to 5. The information on the employees can be represented by three vectors: NAME, CITY, and NUMBER. Write a program which sorts all the employees records such that they are printed by increasing employee number within each city. That is, the format is as follows:

1st City

      name number
      name number
       .
       .
       .
      name number

2nd City

      name number
      name number
       .
       .
       .
      name number
       .
       .
       .

5th City

      name number
      name number
       .
       .
       .
      name number

4. Management information systems are becoming more common. They allow an administrator to type a request into a computer and obtain the answer to the request. In this problem, we will consider one such request; given the name of an employee, find the department in which the employee works. These requests come in the form of the keyword 'DEPARTMENT' followed by the name of the employee. The last of these requests has a keyword of 'FINISHED'.

    In order to respond to such requests, the following information is available. First there is a file of employee information. This file contains the employee's name and the name of his supervisor. This information is in

```
/* MERGE SORT */

STMT LEVEL NEST BLOCK MLVL  SOURCE TEXT

                                  /* MERGE SORT */

     1                            M_SORT: PROCEDURE OPTIONS(MAIN);

                                       /* DECLARE VARIABLES */
     2    1              1              DECLARE (K(128), C(128), PASS, P, Q, I) FIXED;
     3    1              1              DECLARE (J, R, S, T, N, LAST) FIXED;
     4    1              1              DECLARE (SIZE, SUBPASS, S1) FIXED;

                                       /* READ IN VECTOR */
     5    1              1              GET LIST (N);
     6    1              1              PUT SKIP LIST ('UNSORTED VECTOR');
     7    1              1              PUT SKIP;
     8    1              1              DO I = 1 TO N;
     9    1    1         1                 GET LIST (K(I));
    10    1    1         1                 PUT LIST (K(I));
    11    1    1         1              END;

                                       /* CALCULATE NUMBER OF PASSES */
    12    1              1              LAST = LOG2(N + 0.0) + 0.5;
    13    1              1              DO PASS = 1 TO LAST;
    14    1    1         1                 SIZE = 2 ** (PASS - 1);
    15    1    1         1                 P = 1;
    16    1    1         1                 Q = P + SIZE;
    17    1    1         1                 SUBPASS = N / (2 ** PASS);

                                       /* PERFORM THE SUBPASSES */
    18    1    1         1              DO S1 = 1 TO SUBPASS;
    19    1    2         1                 I = P;
    20    1    2         1                 J = Q;
    21    1    2         1                 T = P;
    22    1    2         1                 DO WHILE (1 + I - P <= SIZE & 1 + J - Q <= SIZE);
                                              /* IF THE PASS IS ODD */
    23    1    3         1                     IF PASS / 2.0 ¬= TRUNC(PASS / 2.0)
    24    1    3         1                     THEN DO;
    25    1    4         1                        IF K(I) <= K(J)
    26    1    4         1                        THEN DO;
    27    1    5         1                           C(T) = K(I);
    28    1    5         1                           I = I + 1;
    29    1    5         1                           T = T + 1;
    30    1    5         1                           END;
    31    1    4         1                        ELSE DO;
    32    1    5         1                           C(T) = K(J);

    33    1    5         1                           J = J + 1;
    34    1    5         1                           T = T + 1;
    35    1    5         1                           END;
    36    1    4         1                        END;

    37    1    3         1                  ELSE DO;
    38    1    4         1                     IF C(I) <= C(J)
    39    1    4         1                     THEN DO;
    40    1    5         1                        K(T) = C(I);
    41    1    5         1                        I = I + 1;
    42    1    5         1                        T = T +1;
    43    1    5         1                        END;
    44    1    4         1                     ELSE DO;
    45    1    5         1                        K(T) = C(J);
    46    1    5         1                        J = J +1;
    47    1    5         1                        T = T +1;
    48    1    5         1                        END;
    49    1    4         1                     END;
    50    1    3         1                  END;

                                       /* COPY REMAINING ELEMENTS INTO OUTPUT AREA */
    51    1    2         1              IF 1 + I - P > SIZE
    52    1    2         1              THEN DO;
    53    1    3         1                 S = Q + SIZE - 1;
                                          /* IF PASS IS ODD */
    54    1    3         1                 IF PASS / 2.0 ¬= TRUNC(PASS / 2.0)
    55    1    3         1                 THEN DO;
    56    1    4         1                    DO R = J TO S BY 1;
    57    1    5         1                       C(T) = K(R);
    58    1    5         1                       T = T + 1;
    59    1    5         1                       END;
    60    1    4         1                    END;
```

Fig. 4-8   Merge sort

```
61   1   3   1                        ELSE DO;
62   1   4   1                             DO R = J TO S BY 1;
63   1   5   1                                  K(T) = C(R);
64   1   5   1                                  T = T +1;
65   1   5   1                             END;
66   1   4   1                        END;
67   1   3   1                   END;
68   1   2   1              ELSE DO;
69   1   3   1                   S = P + SIZE - 1;
                                 /* IF PASS IS ODD */
70   1   3   1                   IF PASS / 2.0 ¬= TRUNC(PASS / 2.0)
71   1   3   1                   THEN DO;
72   1   4   1                        DO R = I TO S BY 1;
73   1   5   1                             C(T) = K(R);
74   1   5   1                             T = T +1;
75   1   5   1                        END;
76   1   4   1                   END;
77   1   3   1                   ELSE DO;
78   1   4   1                        DO R = I TO S BY 1;
79   1   5   1                             K(T) = C(R);
80   1   5   1                             T = T +1;
81   1   5   1                        END;
82   1   4   1                   END;
83   1   3   1              END;


84   1   2   1                   P = Q + SIZE;
85   1   2   1                   Q = P + SIZE;
86   1   2   1              END;
87   1   1   1         END;
                       /* RECOPY VECTOR IF NEEDED */
88   1       1         IF LAST / 2.0 ¬= TRUNC(LAST / 2.0)
                       THEN
89   1       1              DO I = 1 TO N BY 1;
90   1   1   1                   K(I) = C(I);
91   1   1   1              END;

                       /*PRINT SORTED VECTOR */
92   1       1         PUT SKIP LIST ('SORTED VECTOR');
93   1       1         PUT SKIP;
94   1       1         DO I = 1 TO N;
95   1   1   1              PUT LIST (K(I));
96   1   1   1         END;
97   1       1    END M_SORT;
```

ERRORS/WARNINGS DETECTED DURING CODE GENERATION:

    WARNING: NO FILE SPECIFIED. SYSIN/SYSPRINT ASSUMED. (CG0C)


```
UNSORTED VECTOR
     5              10              1               7               9               23
    46              32              12              4               2               8
     7              11              21              33
SORTED VECTOR
     1               2              4               5               7               7
     8               9              10              11              12              21
    23              32              33              46
```

IN STMT   97 PROGRAM RETURNS FROM MAIN PROCEDURE.

Fig. 4-8   Merge sort (cont'd.)

alphabetical order by employee name, and the last record in the file has a sentinel employee name of 'ZZZZZ'.

The company has a large number of employees, the current number (which changes from time to time) is 134. Since the number of employees is large and the file is in alphabetical order by employee name, when seeking the record for a specific employee, a binary search should be used.

It is known that every supervisor is also the manager of some department. Thus in order to determine the department in which an employee works, we must determine the name of the department that the employee's supervisor manages. This information can be determined from a second file, the department file. This file contains the name of each department and the name of the manager of the department. This file is ordered by department name. Note there is always less than 50 departments.

Write a program to respond to this type of request. For your data, assume the department file comes first, preceded by a number specifying the number of records (departments) in the department file. The employee file comes next. Last comes the requests for information.

4-3 ARRAYS

An array in PL/I, like a vector, is an ordered set consisting of a fixed number of data elements. Unlike a vector, however, more than one subscript must be used after the variable name to single out a particular element. To represent a two-dimensional table, for example, we require a subscripted variable having two subscripts, where, by convention, the first always specifies the row number and the second the column number. Thus, if the array that represents the table is TOTALS, the TOTALS(2, 1) indicates the value in the second row and first column of the array.

Note that the two subscripts are separated by a comma. If the table contained 5 rows and 3 columns, the array named TOTALS would require enough memory space to accommodate the 5 rows of values, with each row having 3 columns (that is, 15 memory locations must be reserved by the computer for that array).

Arrays such as the TOTALS array are examples of "two-dimensional" arrays —the rows constituting one dimension and the columns the second. For any two-dimensional array, two subscripts are always used with the array name and has the form:

array-name (subscript$_1$, subscript$_2$)

where *subscript$_1$* refers to the number of the row desired and *subscript$_2$* to the number of the column. The vector structure is actually just an array, with only a single dimension and thus requires only 1 subscript. Generally, if an array structure contains "n" dimensions, then "n" subscripts must be used following the array name in order to select a particular element in the array. Arrays having more than two dimensions are mentioned later in this section.

As in one-dimensional arrays, (and for all arrays, for that matter), elements in a two-dimensional array must all be of the same type and the range of *each* subscript must be from some lower bound to some upper bound for that subscript. In fact, the rules for specifying both subscripts are identical to those given in Sec. 4-1 for a vector subscript. When arrays of two dimensions are used, the bounds on both subscripts must be declared in a DECLARE statement, just as is required for vectors. For example, the TOTALS array described previously may be declared by the following:

DECLARE TOTALS(5, 3) FIXED;

or by

DECLARE TOTALS(1:5, 1:3) FIXED;

The declaration just given informs the compiler that the storage allocated for the array TOTALS must accommodate a table with 5 rows and 3 columns, with the successive rows numbered 1, 2, 3, 4, and 5 and the columns numbered 1, 2, and 3.

Array names may appear in GET and PUT statements in the same manner as vector names, either with or without appended subscripts. When used in a PUT statement without subscripts, all entries in the array are printed, regardless of whether or not each has been given a value. When used as such in a GET statement, values are read in for all array entries. For example, execution of the following:

    DECLARE TABLE(5, 2) FLOAT;
    GET LIST (TABLE);
    PUT LIST (TABLE);

causes ten data items to be input to the array TABLE and subsequently the printing of all ten elements. It is important to note, however, the particular order that the compiler uses when doing this. This is determined by the order in which the elements are stored in memory. PL/I always stores array values row by row, not column by column. That is, the entries of the first row are followed by the entries of the second row, then the third, and so on for all rows in the array. This convention determines the order in which they are read by a statement like

    GET LIST (TABLE);

The same order is used for printing out array values.

If the programmer wishes the values in an array to be printed out in an order other than the storage order, or if the programmer does not want all entries in the array to be printed out, then subscripts must be used with the array name with possibly some form of looping feature. The same is true for reading in values to the array. For example, in the program segment:

    DECLARE NAMES (3, 4) CHARACTER (20) VARYING,
        VARB FIXED;
        .
        .
        .
    DO VARB = 1 TO 4;
        PUT LIST (NAMES(1, VARB));
    END;

only the array elements NAMES(1, 1), NAMES(1, 2), NAMES(1, 3), and NAMES(1, 4), that is, the four elements of the first row of the array NAMES are printed in that order.

To print out the entire NAMES array by columns, that is, such that the entries of the first column are printed, then the second column entries, and so on for all the columns, nested looping must be used, as follows:

    DECLARE (ROW, COL) FIXED,
        NAMES (3, 4) CHARACTER (20) VARYING;
        .
        .
        .

```
DO COL = 1 TO 4;
    DO ROW = 1 TO 3;
        PUT LIST (NAMES(ROW, COL))
    END;
END;
```

Array entries may be assigned values in assignment statements, just as discussed for vector elements. The assignment of a value to a single array entry requires that both subscripts be used in the array reference to specify that element. To assign the same value to the entire array, the array name may be used on the left-hand side of the assignment operator without subscripts. For example, the segment

```
DECLARE NAMES (4, 0:2) CHARACTER(3) VARYING;
NAMES = 'XYZ';
```

assigns the character string 'XYZ' to all 12 entries of the array NAMES. Note that in this situation, if the right-hand side is composed of a single expression value, then that value is assigned to each entry of the array. If the right-hand side is, instead the name of another array, which is also without subscripts, then the value of each entry of the array on the right-hand side is assigned to the corresponding entry of the array on the left side. For example, the following program segment

```
DECLARE (TOTALS(5, 2), ACCOUNT(5, 2)) FLOAT;

         .
         .
         .

GET LIST (ACCOUNT);
TOTALS = ACCOUNT;
```

assigns the values read into ACCOUNT to the array TOTALS. In this form of assignment, it is important to note that the arrays on the left-hand and right-hand sides must have the same number of dimensions and identical bounds for each dimension. For example, if the declaration in the previous segment is changed to

```
DECLARE (TOTALS(6, 2), ACCOUNT(5, 2)) FLOAT;
```

then the subsequent assignment statement in the segment results in an error message. Note that the following declaration, when used in place of the preceding declaration in the segment, is also not acceptable:

```
DECLARE (TOTALS(0:4, 2), ACCOUNT(5, 2)) FLOAT;
```

Although both arrays contain two dimensions and both contain the same number of rows and columns, the bounds on the ranges of the row numbers differ, and therefore, the assignment statement cannot be performed.

Array references may also be used in PL/I expressions. In this context, unless the array reference specifies only a single entry in an array, it is once again necessary that all arrays that appear in the expression have identical dimensions and subscript bounds. For example, consider the following segment:

```
DECLARE (ARR1(2, 4), ARR2(2, 4)) FIXED,
        (VALUE(-2:0, 6), RESULT(2, 4)) FLOAT;
    .
    .
    .
VALUE = SQRT(2E0);
    .
    .
    .
RESULT = (ARR1 - VALUE(0, 6)) + 5 * ARR2;
```

The evaluation of the expression found in the second assignment statement produces a result which is an array with the same dimension and subscript bound as ARR1 and ARR2. This array is stored in the array RESULT on the left-hand side of the assignment. The segment is executed in the same manner as the following expanded version:

```
DECLARE (ARR1(2, 4), ARR2(2, 4), VAR1, VAR2) FIXED,
        (VALUE(-2:0, 6), RESULT(2, 4)) FLOAT;
    .
    .
    .
VALUE = SQRT(2E0);
    .
    .
    .
DO VAR1 = 1 TO 2;
    DO VAR2 = 1 TO 4;
        RESULT(VAR1, VAR2) = (ARR1(VAR1, VAR2) -
            VALUE(0, 6)) + 5 * ARR2(VAR1, VAR2);
    END;
END;
```

As with vectors, two-dimensional arrays may also be used as arguments to built-in functions which accept single value arguments. In this case, the operation is performed on each entry of the argument array and the result stored as the corresponding entry in the new array produced.

MULTI-DIMENSIONAL ARRAYS

Up until now, we have dealt mainly with one-dimensional arrays (usually called vectors) and two-dimensional arrays (often called matrices). PL/I allows arrays to be defined with many dimensions. Basically the same rules apply to arrays with three or more dimensions as those discussed thus far for arrays of lower dimension. The storage order given for two-dimensional arrays may be generalized to apply to arrays of any dimension. That is, array entries are stored in consecutive storage locations in an order such that every subscript is taken through its entire range of values for *each* of the values of the range of the subscript on its immediate left. Arrays of dimension greater than, say, three, are usually avoided by programmers, since they are more difficult to visualize, and thus to manipulate.

The program given in Fig. 4-9 illustrates one application of a three dimensional array. This program is based on the algorithm given in Sec. 4-4 of the main text. In this problem a program is required to find the average condition of all known antique cars from a particular year. Information concerning all reported cars is to be stored in a three-dimensional array named CARS where the first subscript represents the manufacturers code (an integer from 0 to 30), the second represents the year the car was built (from 1900 to 1950), and the third represents the cars condition (an integer from 1 to 4). Each element of the array contains the number of cars found that were built by the manufacturer in the year and in the condition given by the three subscripts. The variables used in this program are:

Variable	Type	Usage
CARS(0:30, 1900:1950, 4)	FIXED	Number of cars of each make year and condition found
YEAR	FIXED	Year car was made
COUNT	FIXED	Number of cars found in a certain year
AVG_COND	FLOAT	Average condition of cars
MAKE	FIXED	Make of car
COND	FIXED	Condition of car
NUM	FIXED	Number of cars of a certain year with a certain make and condition
I	FIXED	Loop variable

The input values used in this run were:

3	1946	3
5	1949	1
20	1936	4
25	1948	2
16	1949	2
11	1905	1
30	1922	3
24	1901	2
26	1907	4
15	1949	3
1949		

Information concerning ten cars is read in and the appropriate elements of the array CARS is incremented. Once this is done, the year for which information is requested is read. The counters COUNT and AVG_COUNT are initialized to zero. Two counted loops are then used to calculate the weighted average of the cars' conditions. Finally, the requested year, number of cars recorded for that year, and the average condition of the cars is printed.

This section has presented the concept of structure dimension focusing on the array data structure of dimension two. Operations with two-dimensional arrays were discussed by expanding on those given for vectors. The capability of defining several dimensions in arrays greatly increases the scope of problems that may be solved with the subscripted variable. Section 4-4 illustrates some particular applications which require the use of arrays in order to program efficient solutions to them.

Exercises for Sec. 4-3

1. A matrix A of the form

$$\begin{pmatrix} a_{11} & a_{12} & \dots & a_{1m} \\ a_{21} & a_{22} & \dots & a_{2m} \\ \cdot & \cdot & & \cdot \\ \cdot & \cdot & & \cdot \\ \cdot & \cdot & & \cdot \\ a_{n1} & a_{n2} & \dots & a_{nm} \end{pmatrix}$$

is symmetric if

$$a_{ij} = a_{ij} \text{ for } 1 \leqslant i \leqslant n \text{ and } 1 \leqslant j \leqslant m.$$

Write a program which reads a matrix (never greater than 10 x 10) and determines whether or not it is symmetric. Assume that the elements of the matrix are integers. Test your program on the symmetric matrix

$$\begin{pmatrix} 1 & 4 & 7 \\ 4 & 2 & 9 \\ 7 & 9 & 3 \end{pmatrix}$$

2. Given the two matrices A and B where

$$A = \begin{pmatrix} a_{11} & a_{12} & \dots & a_{1m} \\ a_{21} & a_{22} & \dots & a_{2m} \\ \cdot & \cdot & & \cdot \\ \cdot & \cdot & & \cdot \\ \cdot & \cdot & & \cdot \\ a_{n1} & a_{n2} & \dots & a_{nm} \end{pmatrix} \qquad B = \begin{pmatrix} b_{11} & b_{12} & \dots & b_{1r} \\ b_{21} & b_{22} & \dots & b_{2r} \\ \cdot & \cdot & & \cdot \\ \cdot & \cdot & & \cdot \\ \cdot & \cdot & & \cdot \\ b_{m1} & b_{m2} & \dots & b_{mr} \end{pmatrix}$$

the *product* of A and B is given by

$$C = \begin{pmatrix} c_{11} & c_{12} & \dots & c_{1r} \\ c_{21} & c_{22} & \dots & c_{2r} \\ \cdot & \cdot & & \cdot \\ \cdot & \cdot & & \cdot \\ \cdot & \cdot & & \cdot \\ c_{n1} & c_{n2} & \dots & c_{nr} \end{pmatrix}$$

where

$$c_{ij} = \sum_{k=1}^{m} a_{ik} * b_{kj}$$

For example, given

$$A = \begin{pmatrix} 1 & 2 & 3 \\ 4 & 5 & 6 \end{pmatrix} \quad \text{and} \quad B = \begin{pmatrix} 1 & 4 \\ 2 & 5 \\ 3 & 6 \end{pmatrix}$$

the product is

$$C = \begin{pmatrix} 14 & 32 \\ 32 & 77 \end{pmatrix}$$

Using your program find the product of A and B where

$$A = \begin{pmatrix} 1 & 4 & 6 \\ 3 & 2 & 9 \\ 1 & 6 & 7 \end{pmatrix} \quad \text{and} \quad B = \begin{pmatrix} 6 & 5 \\ 7 & 2 \\ 8 & 1 \end{pmatrix}$$

3. A study concerning the occurrence of traffic accidents is being conducted in Saskatoon. For convenience the city is divided into a grid as follows:

where the rows and column headings denote the streets or avenues in the city. Fox example, 7 traffic accidents have occured at the intersection of 2nd and 4th avenues. An unknown number of accident data are to be read in. Each accident gives the grid location of a traffic accident and takes the form of a pair of numbers. For example, the pair 2,4 describes the location of an accident at the intersection of 2nd and 4th avenues. Formulate a program which reads in this information and counts the number of accidents at each intersection. Furthermore, produce a list of the 10 most dangerous intersections. Use an end of file test to determine the end of the data.

4. Using the three-dimensional array CARS described in this section, write a program to compute the following statistics:

    (i) the number of cars made before 1910 with condition rated good or excellent

    (ii) the most popular make of car, as judged by the number recorded

    (iii) of all the manufacturers identify the one whose cars appear to be in the best average condition.

Test your program on the data used with the program CAR_REPORT.

```
/* REPORT ON ANTIQUE CARS */

 STMT LEVEL NEST BLOCK MLVL  SOURCE TEXT

                              /* REPORT ON ANTIQUE CARS */

   1                          CAR_RPT: PROCEDURE OPTIONS(MAIN);


   2    1         1           DECLARE CARS(0:30, 1900:1950, 4) FIXED, /* ARRAY OF ANTIQUE CARS*/
                                      YEAR FIXED,            /* YEAR CAR WAS MADE */
                                      COUNT FIXED,           /* NUMBER OF CARS FOUND IN A CERTAIN*/
                                                             /* YEAR */
                                      AVG_COND FLOAT,        /* AVERAGE CONDITION OF CARS  */
                                      MAKE FIXED,            /* MAKE OF CAR */
                                      COND FIXED,            /* CONDITION OF CAR */
                                      NUM FIXED,             /* NUMBER OF CARS OF A CERTAIN MAKE */
                                                             /* CONDITION  AND YEAR */
                                      I FIXED;               /* LOOP VARIABLE */

                              /* INITIALIZE ARRAY */
   3    1         1           CARS = 0;

                              /* READ DATA ON CARS */
   4    1         1           DO I = 1 TO 10;
   5    1    1    1               GET LIST (MAKE, YEAR, COND);
   6    1    1    1               CARS(MAKE, YEAR, COND) = CARS(MAKE, YEAR, COND) + 1;
   7    1    1    1           END;

                              /* READ REQUESTED YEAR */
   8    1         1           GET LIST (YEAR);

                              /* INITIALIZE COUNTERS */
   9    1         1           COUNT = 0;
  10    1         1           AVG_COND = 0;

                              /* PROCESS ALL MAKES OF CAR FOR THAT YEAR */
  11    1         1           DO MAKE = 0 TO 30;
  12    1    1    1               DO COND = 1 TO 4;
  13    1    2    1                   NUM = CARS(MAKE, YEAR, COND);
  14    1    2    1                   IF NUM ¬= 0
  15    1    2    1                   THEN DO;
  16    1    3    1                       AVG_COND = AVG_COND + COND * NUM;
  17    1    3    1                       COUNT = COUNT + NUM;
  18    1    3    1                       END;
  19    1    2    1                   END;
  20    1    1    1               END;

                              /* OUTPUT COMPUTED STATISTICS */
  21    1         1           PUT SKIP LIST ('YEAR:', YEAR, 'CARS RECORDED:', COUNT,
                                  'AVERAGE CONDITION:', AVG_COND / COUNT);

  22    1         1       END CAR_RPT;

ERRORS/WARNINGS DETECTED DURING CODE GENERATION:

    WARNING: NO FILE SPECIFIED. SYSIN/SYSPRINT ASSUMED. (CGOC)


YEAR:                    1949           CARS RECORDED:            3           AVERAGE CONDITION:
 2.00000E+00


IN STMT   22  PROGRAM RETURNS FROM MAIN PROCEDURE.
```

Fig. 4-9 Car report program

4-4 APPLICATIONS OF VECTORS AND ARRAYS

This section presents PL/C programs for the applications introduced in Sec. 4-5 of the main text.

4-4.1　Family Allowance Payments

The program which appears in Fig. 4-10 is a solution to the family allowance payments problem given in Sec. 4-5.1 of the main text. The problem is to calculate the monthly family allowance payment for the families in the kingdom of Fraziland. These monthly payments are based on the family's yearly income and on the number of children according to Table 4-1.

Variable	Type	Usage
SCHED(9, 0:6)	FIXED	Schedule of payments
INCOME	FIXED	Family's income
CHILDREN	FIXED	Number of children
END_FLAG	CHARACTER(3) VARYING	End of data flag
R	FIXED	Row subscript
C	FIXED	Column subscript
I	FIXED	Loop variable
J	FIXED	Loop variable

The input values for this run were

0	17	19	20	22	24	25
0	16	18	19	21	23	24
0	15	17	18	20	22	23
0	14	16	17	19	21	22
0	13	15	16	18	20	21
0	12	14	15	17	19	20
0	11	13	14	16	18	19
0	10	12	13	15	17	18
0	9	11	12	14	16	17

Table 4-1　Schedule of Family Allowance Payments

Yearly Income	Number of Children						
	0	1	2	3	4	5	6 and up
less than $3000	0	17	19	20	22	24	25
$3000 - 3999	0	16	18	19	21	23	24
$4000 - 4999	0	15	17	18	20	22	23
$5000 - 5999	0	14	16	17	19	21	22
$6000 - 6999	0	13	15	16	18	20	21
$7000 - 7999	0	12	14	15	17	19	20
$8000 - 8999	0	11	13	14	16	18	19
$9000 - 9999	0	10	12	13	15	17	18
$10,000 and over	0	9	11	12	14	16	17

For each family a card containing the yearly income of the family and the number of children in the family is prepared. Given this information, the program is to calculate and print the amount of payment. The following variables are used in this program.

7600	3
3950	4
2500	0
12700	8
5634	7
9820	5
4000	6
13872	1
42561	1
2500	2

Statements 6 to 10 read in the schedule of family allowance payments. Statement 11 begins a loop which handles the calculation and printing of payments for each of the families. In statement 12, information concerning the family's income and number of children is read. Using this information, the appropriate row and column subscripts are obtained. In statement 23, the payment for this particular family is printed. Finally, when all the data have been read, 'ON' is assigned to END_FLAG, and in statement 14, execution of the program is terminated.

4-4.2 Overweights Anonymous

The program given in Fig. 4-11 is based on the overweights anonymous problem given is Sec. 4-5.2 of the main text. In this problem fifteen members (rather than 50 as stated in the main text) of the Saskatoon branch of the Overweights Anonymous have been selected for a study of the effectiveness of the group's program. For each selected member a card has been prepared containing the subject's recorded weight (rounded to the nearest pound) for the last twelve months. Using this information the group wishes to determine the following:

1. The average weight change for all subjects over the entire 12 month period.
2. The number of subjects whose total weight exceeded the average.
3. The average monthly weight change per subject.
4. The number of instances during the year in which a subject lost more than the average monthly weight change during a single month.

The variables used in the following solution program are:

Variable	Type	Usage
POUNDS(15, 12)	FIXED	Array for input data
Y_COUNT	FIXED	Number exceeding yearly average loss
M_COUNT	FIXED	Number of times monthly average loss is exceeded
TEMP	FIXED	Temporary sum
SUBJECT	FIXED	Loop variable
MONTH	FIXED	Loop variable

| PY_AVG | FLOAT | Average weight loss for the year |
| PM_AVG | FLOAT | Average weight loss for a month for one subject |

```
/* PROGRAM TO COMPUTE THE MONTHLY FAMILY ALLOWANCE PAYMENTS */

STMT LEVEL NEST BLOCK MLVL   SOURCE TEXT

                                  /* PROGRAM TO COMPUTE THE MONTHLY FAMILY ALLOWANCE PAYMENTS */

  1                               BENEFIT: PROCEDURE OPTIONS(MAIN);

  2     1           1             DECLARE SCHED(9, 0:6) FIXED, /* SCHEDULE OF PAYMENTS */
                                          INCOME FIXED,         /* FAMILY'S INCOME */
                                          CHILDREN FIXED,       /* NO OF CHILDREN */
                                          END_FLAG CHARACTER(3) VARYING,  /* END OF DATA FLAG */
                                          R FIXED,              /* ROW SUBSCRIPT */
                                          C FIXED,              /* COLUMN SUBSCRIPT */
                                          (I, J) FIXED;         /* LOOP VARIABLES */

                                  /* INITIALIZE */
  3     1           1             END_FLAG = 'OFF';
  4     1           1             ON ENDFILE(SYSIN) END_FLAG = 'ON';

                                  /* READ IN SCHEDULE OF FAMILY ALLOWANCE PAYMENTS */
  6     2           2             DO I = 1 TO 9;
  7     1      1    1                 DO J = 0 TO 6;
  8     1      2    1                     GET LIST (SCHED(I, J));
  9     1      2    1                 END;
 10     1      1    1             END;

                                  /* PROCESS FAMILIES */
 11     1           1             DO WHILE (END_FLAG = 'OFF');

                                      /* READ DATA FOR NEXT FAMILY */
 12     1      1    1                 GET LIST (INCOME, CHILDREN);
 13     1      1    1                 IF END_FLAG = 'ON'
 14     1      1    1                 THEN EXIT;

                                      /* DETERMINE APPROPRIATE ROW SUBSCRIPT */
 15     1      1    1                 IF INCOME < 3000
 16     1      1    1                 THEN R = 1;
 17     1      1    1                 ELSE IF INCOME >= 10000
 18     1      1    1                     THEN R = 9;
 19     1      1    1                     ELSE R = TRUNC((INCOME - 1000) / 1000);

                                      /* DETERMINE APPROPRIATE COLUMN SUBSCRIPT */
 20     1      1    1                 IF CHILDREN >= 6
 21     1      1    1                 THEN C = 6;
 22     1      1    1                 ELSE C = CHILDREN;

                                      /* SELECT CORRECT PAYMENT */
 23     1      1    1                 PUT SKIP LIST ('PAYMENT IS', SCHED(R, C));
 24     1      1    1             END;

 25     1           1             END BENEFIT;

ERRORS/WARNINGS DETECTED DURING CODE GENERATION:

        WARNING: NO FILE SPECIFIED. SYSIN/SYSPRINT ASSUMED. (CGOC)


PAYMENT IS              15
PAYMENT IS              21
PAYMENT IS               0
PAYMENT IS              17
PAYMENT IS              22
PAYMENT IS              17
PAYMENT IS              23
PAYMENT IS               9
PAYMENT IS               9
PAYMENT IS              19


IN STMT   14  PROGRAM IS STOPPED.
```

Fig. 4-10 Program for family allowance payments problem

In the solution, statements 8 to 15 read the data values into the array POUNDS and simultaneously compute the running total of the subjects' weight losses for the year. Next, the average of the year's weight losses is computed. Another pass through the array elements is then performed in order to arrive at two figures; namely, the total number of subjects whose weight loss for the year exceeds the average (statement 20) and the sum of the subjects' averages of their monthly weight losses (statements 22 to 24). The subjects' average for the latter is computed in statement 25. The third pass through the array entries then occurs to count the number of times this average is surpassed.

4-4.3 The Global Hockey League

The program in Fig. 4-12 is a solution to the Global Hockey League problem given in Sec. 4-5.3 of the main text. In this problem a newly-formed hockey organization, the Global Hockey League, is developing a system for processing all league game results, using a computer. This involves recording wins and losses for all teams and the current point totals. Upon completion of each league game, the result is sent to the league headquarters, in the following format.

home-team's name home-team's score visiting-team's name visiting-team's score

For example, the following is a sample set of results:

'BURMA'   5   'CHILE'   4

The league is currently composed of 12 teams. A team is given 2 points for every win, 1 point for every tie, and no points for a game lost. These point totals, along with separate totals for each team's number of wins, losses, ties, and games played are kept as running totals and are updated regularly, after an appropriate number of new game results are received at the headquarters. After each update the latest league standings are produced as a report in the following form:

TEAM   GAMES PLAYED   WINS   LOSSES   TIES   POINTS
team$_1$
team$_2$
        .
        .
        .
team$_{12}$

The report lists the teams, with their respective statistics, in decreasing order of points.

The headquarters desires a program to be written which first inputs the current league standings (the team's totals), and stores them appropriately. Next, it must input as data a batch of the latest game results received (punched one set of results to a card, in the same format as received). For each result card, it must update the current team totals for the teams involved. After having processed all the results input, the program must then print out a new standings report in the form just given. The variables used in this program are

```
/* FOR 15 SUBJECTS, COMPUTE THE REQUESTED TOTALS AND AVERAGES */

STMT LEVEL NEST BLOCK MLVL   SOURCE TEXT


                                    /* FOR 15 SUBJECTS, COMPUTE THE REQUESTED TOTALS AND AVERAGES */
    1                               WEIGHT: PROCEDURE OPTIONS(MAIN);

    2    1          1               DECLARE (POUNDS(15, 12), /* ARRAY FOR SUBJECTS' WEIGHTS */
                                            Y_COUNT,         /* NUMBER EXCEEDING YEARLY AVERAGE LOSS */
                                            M_COUNT,         /* NUMBER OF TIMES MONTHLY AVERAGE */
                                                             /* LOSS EXCEEDED */
                                            SUBJECT, MONTH,  /* LOOP VARIABLES */
                                            TEMP) FIXED,     /* TEMPORARY SUM */
                                           (PY_AVG,          /* AVERAGE LOSS FOR THE YEAR */
                                            PM_AVG) FLOAT;   /* AVERAGE LOSS FOR A MONTH FOR */
                                                             /* 1 SUBJECT */

                                    /* INITIALIZE */
    3    1          1               Y_COUNT = 0;
    4    1          1               M_COUNT = 0;
    5    1          1               PY_AVG = 0;
    6    1          1               PM_AVG = 0;

                                    /* INPUT THE DATA TABLE AND SUM THE WEIGHT LOSSES FOR THE YEAR */
                                    /* FOR ALL SUBJECTS */
    7    1          1               PUT LIST ('SUBJECT WEIGHTS:');
    8    1          1               DO SUBJECT = 1 TO 15;
    9    1    1     1                   PUT SKIP(2);
   10    1    1     1                   DO MONTH = 1 TO 12;
   11    1    2     1                       GET LIST (POUNDS(SUBJECT, MONTH));
   12    1    2     1                       PUT LIST (POUNDS(SUBJECT, MONTH));
   13    1    2     1                   END;
   14    1    1     1                   PY_AVG = PY_AVG + (POUNDS(SUBJECT, 1) - POUNDS(SUBJECT, 12));
   15    1    1     1               END;

                                    /* COMPUTE PER SUBJECT YEARLY AVERAGE WEIGHT LOSS */
   16    1          1               PY_AVG = PY_AVG / 15;
   17    1          1               PUT SKIP LIST ('PER SUBJECT, PER YEAR WEIGHT CHANGE IS', PY_AVG);

                                    /* COUNT NUMBER EXCEEDING THIS AVERAGE AND SUM THE AVERAGE */
                                    /* MONTHLY WEIGHT LOSSES OF ALL SUBJECTS */
   18    1          1               DO SUBJECT = 1 TO 15;
   19    1    1     1                   IF POUNDS(SUBJECT, 1) - POUNDS(SUBJECT, 12) > PY_AVG
   20    1    1     1                       THEN Y_COUNT = Y_COUNT + 1;
   21    1    1     1                   TEMP = 0;
   22    1    1     1                   DO MONTH = 2 TO 12;

   23    1    2     1                       TEMP = TEMP + (POUNDS(SUBJECT, MONTH - 1) -
                                                    POUNDS(SUBJECT, MONTH));
   24    1    2     1                   END;
   25    1    1     1                   PM_AVG = PM_AVG + TEMP / 11E0;

   26    1    1     1               END;
   27    1          1               PUT SKIP LIST ('  NUMBER OF SUBJECTS EXCEEDING THIS FIGURE IS',
                                           Y_COUNT);

                                    /* COMPUTE THE AVERAGE OF THE MONTHLY AVERAGES OF THE SUBJECTS */
   28    1          1               PM_AVG = PM_AVG / 15;
   29    1          1               PUT SKIP LIST ('PER SUBJECT, PER MONTH WEIGHT CHANGE IS', PM_AVG);

                                    /* COUNT THE NUMBER EXCEEDING THIS AVERAGE */
   30    1          1               DO MONTH = 2 TO 12;
   31    1    1     1                   DO SUBJECT = 1 TO 15;
   32    1    2     1                       IF POUNDS(SUBJECT, MONTH - 1) - POUNDS(SUBJECT, MONTH)
                                                    > PM_AVG
   33    1    2     1                           THEN M_COUNT = M_COUNT + 1;
   34    1    2     1                   END;
   35    1    1     1               END;
   36    1          1               PUT SKIP LIST ('  NUMBER OF TIMES THIS FIGURE EXCEEDED IS',
                                           M_COUNT);

   37    1          1               END WEIGHT;

ERRORS/WARNINGS DETECTED DURING CODE GENERATION:

    WARNING: NO FILE SPECIFIED. SYSIN/SYSPRINT ASSUMED. (CGOC)
```

Fig. 4-11 Program for overweights anonymous problem

```
SUBJECT WEIGHTS:

    165        164        164        162        163        162
    162        161        160        160        155        155

    175        175        173        173        171        170
    169        170        168        168        164        165

    210        212        209        207        207        207
    204        203        201        201        201        200

    222        220        223        220        216        214
    214        212        210        210        208        205

    140        138        136        135        134        130
    128        127        126        125        126        125

    179        175        175        175        172        170
    168        169        165        164        163        162

    191        190        190        188        186        185
    184        184        182        181        180        172

    189        190        189        188        188        187
    187        187        186        186        183        182

    211        210        209        207        206        205
    205        203        201        200        199        194

    256        254        253        250        248        246
    245        243        242        239        236        230

    301        295        292        290        288        288
    289        291        286        285        284        280

    176        174        170        168        168        165
    166        164        163        162        160        158

    151        150        149        147        145        146
    142        140        138        135        133        132

    199        198        196        194        194        194
    192        189        185        182        182        180

    239        238        235        237        232        231
    228        227        226        223        221        221
PER SUBJECT, PER YEAR WEIGHT CHANGE IS      1.61999E+01
  NUMBER OF SUBJECTS EXCEEDING THIS FIGURE IS        10
PER SUBJECT, PER MONTH WEIGHT CHANGE IS     1.47272E+00
  NUMBER OF TIMES THIS FIGURE EXCEEDED IS          76


IN STMT   37  PROGRAM RETURNS FROM MAIN PROCEDURE.
```

Fig. 4-11 Program for overweights anonymous problem (cont'd.)

Variable	Type	Usage
STATS(12, 5)	FIXED	Array for teams' statistics
TEAMS(12)	CHARACTER(15)	Vector for teams' names
ROW	FIXED	Loop variable
COLUMN	FIXED	Loop variable
SCORE1	FIXED	Team's score
SCORE2	FIXED	Team's score
ROW1	FIXED	Save position in array
ROW2	FIXED	Save position in array
PASS	FIXED	Loop variable in sort
TOP	FIXED	Save subscript in sort
TEAM	FIXED	Loop counter

ENDFLAG	FIXED	Flag for end of input
TEMP	FIXED	Save value when switching elements
TEAM1	CHARACTER(15)	Team's name
TEAM2	CHARACTER(15)	Team's name

The data used in the previous run consisted of the following values:

'BURMA'	14	8	2	4	20
'CHILE'	14	8	3	3	19
'HAMMOND'	14	7	3	4	18
'KENTUCKY'	14	8	4	2	18
'LABRADOR'	14	6	3	5	17
'LOUISIANA'	14	6	5	3	15
'MOBILE'	14	5	7	2	12
'PEKING'	14	4	8	2	10
'SCOTLAND'	14	2	11	1	5
'TORONTO'	14	12	2	0	24
'TRAFALGAR'	14	5	7	2	12
'VICHY'	14	9	2	3	21
'BURMA'	5	'SCOTLAND'			3
'LOUISIANA'	2	'CHILE'			2
'VICHY'	1	'MOBILE'			6
'CHILE'	5	'PEKING'			5
'HAMMOND'	7	'TORONTO'			5
'TORONTO'	9	'LABRADOR'			0
'BURMA'	0	'PEKING'			1

Statements 4 to 9 serve to read in the current standings in the appropriate order. Next, a conditional loop is constructed to input the game result cards one at a time. For each game result, a search is made of the TEAMS vector to locate in it the respective input names (statements 14 through 19). The appropriate statistical totals are then updated by using nested IF...THEN... ELSE statements. When the input game results have all been processed, execution is passed to statement 40, where the computation of the new point totals begins. Satements 43 to 60 perform the selection sort of the arrays. Finally, the report on the latest totals is output.

4-4.4 Computer Dating Service

The program which appears in Fig. 4-13 is a solution to the dating service problem given in Sec. 4-5.4 of the main text. In this problem, Universal Dating Inc., a nationwide dating service, requires a program that will chose the most compatable candidates for an applicant based on the ratings of some factors. Each factor is rated with a number between 1 and 7 according to the following code:

1 - intense dislike
2 - moderate dislike
3 - mild dislike
4 - neutral
5 - mild like

6 - moderate like
7 - intense like

The input data begins with a card containing the date, the number of candidates, and the number of factors surveyed. Then for each candidate a card containing the candidate's name, sex (1 for male, 2 for female), and the ratings of the factors by increasing factor number (i.e., the first rating is for factor 1, the second for factor 2, etc.) follows. These cards are followed by cards containing the name, sex, and factor ratings for applicants. The most compatible dates are chosen from the candidates for each of the applicants using the least squares method. That is, each of the factor ratings are compared and the squares of the differences between the factor ratings of an applicant and candidate are summed. The candidate (or candidates) with the least sum of squares are considered the most compatable. The program, therefore, is to select and print the most suited candidates for each applicant based on the previously stated criteria. The variables used in this program are

Variable	Type	Usage
N	FIXED	Number of candidates
M	FIXED	Number of factors
RATINGS(10, 10)	FIXED	Candidate's rating of factors
SEX(10)	FIXED	Candidate's sex
FACTOR(10)	FIXED	Applicant's rating of factors
A_SEX	FIXED	Applicant's sex
STAT(10)	FIXED	Sum of squares statistics for the candidates
BEST(10)	FIXED	Candidates with smallest sum of squares statistics
ACCEPT	FIXED	Number of candidates with least sum of squares
MIN	FIXED	Least sum of squares
DATE	CHARACTER(20) VARYING	Current date
APPLICANT_ID	CHARACTER(20) VARYING	Applicant's name
NAME(10)	CHARACTER(20) VARYING	Candidates' names
I	FIXED	Index variables
J	FIXED	Index variables
ENDFLAG	CHARACTER(3) VARYING	End of data flag

The following input values were used in this run.

'MARCH 1, 1979'	5	3		
'MARY MATCH'	2	1	6	5
'TIM TALL'	1	2	4	5
'FRED FUN'	1	2	5	7
'GARY GALLANT'	1	1	6	7

```
/* UPDATE CURRENT TEAM STANDINGS USING NEW GAME RESULTS */

STMT LEVEL NEST BLOCK MLVL  SOURCE TEXT


                                /* UPDATE CURRENT TEAM STANDINGS USING NEW GAME RESULTS */
                                /* PRINT REPORT ON THE UPDATED LEAGUE STANDINGS */
   1                           HOCKEY:  PROCEDURE OPTIONS(MAIN);

   2    1        1             DECLARE (STATS(12, 5),    /* TEAMS' STATISTICS */
                                        ROW, COLUMN,     /* LOOP VARIABLES */
                                        SCORE1, SCORE2,  /* TEAMS' SCORES */
                                        ROW1, ROW2,      /* TO SAVE LOCATIONS IN ARRAY */
                                        PASS,            /* LOOP VARIABLE IN SORT */
                                        TOP,             /* TO SAVE SUBSCRIPT IN SORT */
                                        TEAM,            /* LOOP COUNTER */
                                        TEMP) FIXED,     /* SAVES VALUE WHEN SWITCHING ELEMENTS */
                                        ENDFLAG CHARACTER(3) VARYING, /* FLAG FOR END OF INPUT */
                                       (TEAMS(12),       /* TEAMS' NAMES VECTOR */
                                        TEAM1,           /* TEAM NAME */
                                        TEAM2) CHARACTER(15);  /* TEAM NAME */

                                /* INITIALIZE */
   3    1        1             ENDFLAG = 'OFF';

                                /* INPUT THE CURRENT TOTALS */
   4    1        1             DO ROW = 1 TO 12;
   5    1   1    1                  GET LIST (TEAMS(ROW));
   6    1   1    1                  DO COLUMN = 1 TO 5;
   7    1   2    1                      GET LIST (STATS(ROW, COLUMN));
   8    1   2    1                  END;
   9    1   1    1             END;

                                /* INPUT THE FIRST OF THE NEW GAME RESULT CARDS */
  10    1        1             ON ENDFILE(SYSIN) ENDFLAG = 'ON';
  12    2        2             GET LIST (TEAM1, SCORE1, TEAM2, SCORE2);

                                /* BEGIN LOOP TO INPUT AND PROCESS NEW GAME RESULTS */
  13    1        1             DO WHILE (ENDFLAG = 'OFF');

                                  /* FIND THE POSITIONS OF THE 2 TEAMS NAMES IN THE VECTOR */
  14    1   1    1                 DO ROW = 1 TO 12;
  15    1   2    1                     IF TEAMS(ROW) = TEAM1
  16    1   2    1                     THEN ROW1 = ROW;
  17    1   2    1                     ELSE IF TEAMS(ROW) = TEAM2
  18    1   2    1                         THEN ROW2 = ROW;
  19    1   2    1                 END;

                                  /* UPDATE THE GAMES PLAYED TOTALS FOR BOTH TEAMS */
  20    1   1    1                 STATS(ROW1, 1) = STATS(ROW1, 1) + 1;
  21    1   1    1                 STATS(ROW2, 1) = STATS(ROW2, 1) + 1;

                                  /* DETERMINE GAME OUTCOME AND UPDATE TOTALS ACCORDINGLY */
  22    1   1    1                 IF SCORE1 > SCORE2
  23    1   1    1                 THEN DO;
  24    1   2    1                     STATS(ROW1, 2) = STATS(ROW1, 2) + 1;
  25    1   2    1                     STATS(ROW2, 3) = STATS(ROW2, 3) + 1;
  26    1   2    1                     END;
  27    1   1    1                 ELSE DO;
  28    1   2    1                     IF SCORE2 > SCORE1
  29    1   2    1                     THEN DO;
  30    1   3    1                         STATS(ROW1, 3) = STATS(ROW1, 3) + 1;
  31    1   3    1                         STATS(ROW2, 2) = STATS(ROW2, 2) + 1;
  32    1   3    1                         END;
  33    1   2    1                     ELSE DO;
  34    1   3    1                         STATS(ROW1, 4) = STATS(ROW1, 4) + 1;
  35    1   3    1                         STATS(ROW2, 4) = STATS(ROW2, 4) + 1;
  36    1   3    1                         END;
  37    1   2    1                     END;

                                  /* READ IN NEXT GAME RESULT CARD */
  38    1   1    1                 GET LIST (TEAM1, SCORE1, TEAM2, SCORE2);
  39    1   1    1             END;

                                /* COMPUTE UPDATED POINT TOTALS */
  40    1   1    1             DO ROW = 1 TO 12;
  41    1   1    1                 STATS(ROW, 5) = 2 * STATS(ROW, 2) + STATS(ROW, 4);
  42    1   1    1             END;
```

Fig. 4-12 Program for the global hockey league problem

```
                                    /* SORT BY DECREASING ORDER OF POINTS */
43    1          1          DO PASS = 1 TO 11;
44    1    1     1              TOP = PASS;
                                    /* FIND THE LARGEST OF THE UNSORTED ELEMENTS */
45    1    1     1              DO ROW = TOP + 1 TO 12;
46    1    2     1                  IF STATS(ROW, 5) > STATS(TOP, 5)
47    1    2     1                  THEN TOP = ROW;
48    1    2     1              END;

                                    /* INTERCHANGE ROWS */
49    1    1     1              IF PASS ¬= TOP
50    1    1     1              THEN DO;
51    1    2     1                  DO COLUMN = 1 TO 5;
52    1    3     1                      TEMP = STATS(PASS, COLUMN);
53    1    3     1                      STATS(PASS, COLUMN) = STATS(TOP, COLUMN);
54    1    3     1                      STATS(TOP, COLUMN) = TEMP;
55    1    3     1                  END;
56    1    2     1                  TEAM1 = TEAMS(PASS);
57    1    2     1                  TEAMS(PASS) = TEAMS(TOP);
58    1    2     1                  TEAMS(TOP) = TEAM1;

59    1    2     1              END;
60    1    1     1          END;

                                    /* PRINT HEADINGS FOR THE REPORT */
61    1          1          PUT SKIP LIST (' TEAM', ' GAMES PLAYED', '      WINS',
                                ' LOSSES', '     TIES', '    POINTS');
                                    /* PRINT NEW TOTALS */
62    1          1          PUT SKIP;
63    1          1          DO TEAM = 1 TO 12;
64    1    1     1              PUT SKIP LIST (TEAMS(TEAM));
65    1    1     1              DO COLUMN = 1 TO 5;
66    1    2     1                  PUT LIST (STATS(TEAM, COLUMN));
67    1    2     1              END;
68    1    1     1          END;

69    1          1          END HOCKEY;
```

ERRORS/WARNINGS DETECTED DURING CODE GENERATION:

   WARNING: NO FILE SPECIFIED. SYSIN/SYSPRINT ASSUMED. (CGOC)

TEAM	GAMES PLAYED	WINS	LOSSES	TIES	POINTS
TORONTO	16	13	3	0	26
BURMA	16	9	3	4	22
CHILE	16	8	3	5	21
VICHY	15	9	3	3	21
HAMMOND	15	8	3	4	20
KENTUCKY	14	8	4	2	18
LABRADOR	15	6	4	5	17
LOUISIANA	15	6	5	4	16
MOBILE	15	6	7	2	14
PEKING	16	5	8	3	13
TRAFALGAR	14	5	7	2	12
SCOTLAND	15	2	12	1	5

IN STMT 69 PROGRAM RETURNS FROM MAIN PROCEDURE.

Fig. 4-12 Program for the global hockey league problem (cont'd.)

'LINDA LOVE'	2	2	4	6
'BARBARA BEAUTY'	2	2	5	6
'JIM BLACK'	1	2	5	6

   In statement 6, the date, number of candidates, and number of factors are read into DATE, N, and M, respectively. Statements 7 through 12 serve to read the candidate profiles. In statement 13, a loop to process each of the applicants is begun. The first step in the process is the reading of the applicant's identification number, sex, and factor ratings. Statements 23 to 28 designate a loop which calculates the least squares statistic for each candidate of opposite sex to the applicant. The candidates (or candidate) of opposite sex to the applicant with the smallest least square statistic are then selected. Finally the date, applicant's name, and the names of the candidate which are best suited to the applicant are printed.

```
/* GENERATE FROM THE CANDIDATES GIVEN, THE ONE THAT IS MOST SUITED */
STMT LEVEL NEST BLOCK MLVL   SOURCE TEXT


                            /* GENERATE FROM THE CANDIDATES GIVEN, THE ONE THAT IS MOST SUITED */
                            /* TO AN APPLICANT'S PROFILE */
   1                        DATING: PROCEDURE OPTIONS(MAIN);

   2    1         1         DECLARE (N, M) FIXED,        /* NUMBER OF CANDIDATES AND FACTORS */
                                    (I, J) FIXED,        /* INDEX VARIABLES */
                                    RATINGS(10, 10) FIXED, /* CANDIDATE'S RATINGS */
                                    SEX(10) FIXED,       /* CANDIDATE'S SEX */
                                    FACTOR(10) FIXED,    /* APPLICANT'S RATINGS */
                                    A_SEX FIXED,         /* APPLICANT'S SEX */
                                    STAT(10) FIXED,      /* SUM OF SQUARES STATISTICS FOR */
                                                         /* THE CANDIDATES */
                                    BEST(10) FIXED,      /* CANDIDATES WITH SMALLEST SUM OF */
                                                         /* SQUARES STATISTICS */
                                    ACCEPT FIXED,        /* NUMBER OF CANDIDATES WITH LEAST */
                                                         /* SUM OF SQUARES */
                                    MIN FIXED,           /* LEAST SUM OF SQUARES */
                                    DATE CHARACTER(20) VARYING,
                                    (APPLICANT_ID,       /* APPLICANT'S NAME */
                                    NAME(10)) CHARACTER(20) VARYING,  /* CANDIDATE'S NAMES */
                                    ENDFLAG CHARACTER(3) VARYING;

                            /* INITIALIZE */
   3    1         1         ENDFLAG = 'OFF';
   4    1         1         ON ENDFILE(SYSIN) ENDFLAG = 'ON';

                            /* INPUT DATE, NUMBER OF CANDIDATES, AND NUMBER OF FACTORS */
   6    2         2         GET LIST (DATE, N, M);

                            /* INPUT THE CANDIDATE PROFILES */
   7    1         1         DO I = 1 TO N;
   8    1    1    1             GET LIST (NAME(I), SEX(I));
   9    1    1    1             DO J = 1 TO M;
  10    1    2    1                 GET LIST (RATINGS(I, J));
  11    1    2    1             END;
  12    1    1    1         END;

                            /* PROCESS ALL APPLICANTS */
  13    1         1         DO WHILE (ENDFLAG = 'OFF');

                                /* READ IN APPLICANT'S PROFILE */
  14    1    1    1             GET LIST (APPLICANT_ID, A_SEX);

  15    1    1    1             IF ENDFLAG = 'ON'
  16    1    1    1             THEN EXIT;
  17    1    1    1             DO J = 1 TO M;
  18    1    2    1                 GET LIST (FACTOR(J));

  19    1    2    1             END;

                                /* COMPUTE THE CANDIDATE'S SUM OF SQUARES STATISTICS */
  20    1    1    1             DO I = 1 TO N;     /* INITIALIZE STATISTICS */
  21    1    2    1                 STAT(I) = 0;
  22    1    2    1             END;
  23    1    1    1             DO I = 1 TO N;
  24    1    2    1                 IF A_SEX ¬= SEX(I)
  25    1    2    1                 THEN DO J = 1 TO M;
  26    1    3    1                     STAT(I) = STAT(I) + (RATINGS(I, J) -
                                                         FACTOR(J)) ** 2;
  27    1    3    1                 END;
  28    1    2    1             END;
```

Fig. 4-13   Program for the computer dating service problem

```
29  1  1  1     /* DETERMINE THE MINIMUM SUM OF SQUARES STATISTIC */
30  1  1  1     I = 1;
31  1  2  1     DO WHILE (A_SEX = SEX(I));
32  1  2  1         I = I + 1;
33  1  1  1     END;
34  1  1  1     MIN = STAT(I);
35  1  2  1     DO J = I TO N;
36  1  2  1         IF A_SEX ¬= SEX(J)
37  1  2  1         THEN IF STAT(J) < MIN
38  1  2  1                 THEN MIN = STAT(J);
                END;

39  1  1  1     /* SELECT THOSE CANDIDATES WITH SMALLEST STATISTIC */
40  1  1  1     ACCEPT = 0;
41  1  2  1     DO I = 1 TO N;
42  1  2  1         IF A_SEX ¬= SEX(I)
43  1  2  1         THEN IF STAT(I) = MIN
44  1  3  1                 THEN DO;
45  1  3  1                     ACCEPT = ACCEPT + 1;
46  1  3  1                     BEST(ACCEPT) = I;
47  1  2  1                     END;
                END;

48  1  1  1     /* OUTPUT THE DESIRED REPORT FOR THIS APPLICANT */
49  1  1  1     PUT SKIP;
50  1  1  1     PUT SKIP LIST ('DATE IS ', DATE);
51  1  1  1     PUT SKIP LIST ('APPLICANT''S NAME IS:', APPLICANT_ID);
52  1  1  1     PUT SKIP LIST ('THE BEST MATCHED CANDIDATES ARE:');
53  1  2  1     DO I = 1 TO ACCEPT;
54  1  2  1         PUT SKIP LIST (NAME(BEST(I)));
55  1  1  1     END;
                END;

56  1     1  END DATING;
```

ERRORS/WARNINGS DETECTED DURING CODE GENERATION:

```
    WARNING: NO FILE SPECIFIED. SYSIN/SYSPRINT ASSUMED. (CGOC)

DATE IS              MARCH 1, 1979
APPLICANT'S NAME IS:    BARBARA BEAUTY
THE BEST MATCHED CANDIDATES ARE:
FRED FUN

DATE IS              MARCH 1, 1979
APPLICANT'S NAME IS:    JIM BLACK
THE BEST MATCHED CANDIDATES ARE:
LINDA LOVE

IN STMT   16  PROGRAM IS STOPPED.
```

Fig. 4-13 Program for the computer dating service problem (cont'd.)

This concludes the discussion of arrays. In Sec. 4-1 operations on vectors in PL/I were introduced. Section 4-2 presented methods of sorting and searching vectors. In Sec. 4-3 arrays of more than one dimension were disscussed. Finally, in Sec. 4-4 programmed solutions to the applications discussed in Sec. 4-5 of the main text were given. In the next chapter operations and applications involving strings are considered.

EXERCISES FOR CHAPTER 4

1. It has been discovered by the leaders of two international espionage organizations (called CONTROL and KAOS) that a number of employees are on the payrolls of both groups! A secret meeting is to be held

for loyal employees of CONTROL and KOAS (i.e., excluding those on both payrolls) to determine a suitable course of action to be taken against the "double agents".

Design a program which will accomplish the following task:

Read as input two alphabetically ordered list of names, one name per data card, the first list containing the names of agents on the CONTROL payroll and the second containing names of agents on the KAOS payroll. (Each of the two lists is followed by a card with the name 'ZZZZ'.) Then scan the two lists together and print in alphabetical order the names of those agents who should be invited to the proposed meeting (i.e., all those whose name appears on one list but not on both).

Example input:

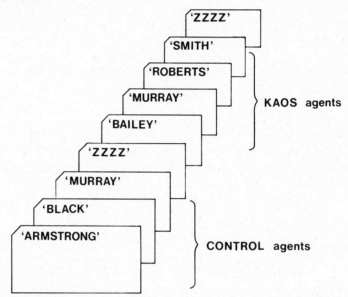

Corresponding Example Output:

    ARMSTRONG
    BAILEY
    BLACK
    ROBERTS
    SMITH

2. At any school or university the task of drafting an exam timetable is both difficult and time consuming. An aid to the development of an exam timetable is a program which would "check out" all students against a tentative exam timetable and determine if any exam conflicts exist (an exam conflict means the student writes more than one exam at any one time). Input to the program consists of the tentative exam timetable and student records indicating the classes taken by each student. This input is punched on cards as follows:

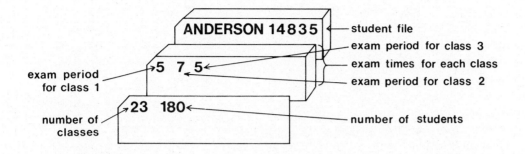

The first card contains two numbers - the number of classes and the number of students. The next set of cards indicate the exam period for each class with the first card indicating the exam periods for classes 1 to 10; the second card indicating the exam periods for classes 11 to 20, etc.

The final set of cards consists of the student's name and the number of classes the student takes. Each student always takes five classes. In the example illustrated, Anderson takes classes numbered 1, 4, 8, 3, and 5. Both classes 1 and 3 have been scheduled for exam period 5, therefore Anderson has an exam conflict. Your program must print the names of all students who have exam timetable conflicts.

3.   Assume that the Saskatchewan Real Estate Board has conducted a survey of each of its licensees. Each licensee fills in a questionnaire of the following form:

Item	Answer Code
License type	1 = broker
	2 = salesperson
Residence town	840 towns coded from 1 to 840
Age	Age in years
Sex	1 = male
	2 = female
Education	1 = less than high school diploma
	2 = high school diploma
	3 = technical institute or community college
	4 = college degree

Write a program which analyzes these questionnairs. In particular, calculate the following for the group of respondents:

(a) Total number of respondents.
(b) Percentage brokers and percentage salesmen.

Calculate the following separately for brokers and salespersons:

(a) Number of respondents from each town.
(b) Average age
(c) Percentage male and percentage female
(d) Number of respondents in each educational classification.

The input data for each questionnaire consists of five questionnaire answer codes representing license type, residence town, age, sex, and education. Use an end of file test to determine the end of the data.

4. A profile of student attitudes towards a certain course is being determine by a method that requires each student in the course to assess the degree of his or her feelings of like or dislike towards certain factors. Each student is requested to rate each factor by associating a number with every factor, according to the following scale of values:

1 - intense dislike	4 - neutral
2 - moderate dislike	5 - mild like
3 - mild dislike	6 - moderate like
	7 - intense like

It is required to formulate a program which will perform a simple analysis of this data and produce a report giving:

(a) the average rating of each factor
(b) information on the students whose ratings are "closest" to the average ratings.
More will be said about what is meant by "closest" shortly.

The input data is punched on cards and consists of one header card followed by a number of survey cards, one for each student surveyed. The header card contains 3 data items:

- name of the course
- the number of students surveyed
- the number of factors surveyed

Each survey card contains a student's identification number and this student's ratings of the factors by increasing factor number. That is, the first rating is for factor 1, the second rating is for factor 2, and so on.
The sample input data

Course Name	Number of students	Number of factors
'CMPT 180A'	5	3
	10175	1 6 5
	12791	2 4 5
	9981	2 5 7
	38005	1 6 7
	27091	2 4 6
	student number	ratings for factors 1, 2, and 3 respectively

describes the ratings obtained on three factors from five students in course CMPT 180A.
As mentioned earlier, the program must produce the average rating for each factor in the course and output the student or students whose ratings are

"closest" to the average ratings. The "closeness" is measured by the statistic S_j which is computed for the $_j$th student from his or her ratings for the various factors and the average for each of these factors. The lower the S_j value for a student, the "closer" the student's ratings are to the averages. S_i is defined as follows:

$$S_i = \sqrt{\sum_{j=1}^{n} (r_{ij} - \bar{r}_j)^2}$$

where S_i is the "closeness" statistic for person i

    n is the number of factors surveyed

    r_{ij} is the ith student's rating of the jth factor

    $\bar{r}_j$ is the average rating of the jth factor

The output report is to consist of

(a) name of the course

(b) the "smallest" (i.e., the smallest S_j) statistic for the course

(c) the average rating for each factor

(d) for each of these "closest" students, the difference between each of their ratings and the corresponding averages

(e) the identification numbers of those students "closest" to the averages

A sample report of the previous data follows:

ATTITUDE REPORT FOR COMPT 180A
SMALLEST S: 1.077

FACTOR		AVERAGE VALUE
1	1.60	
2	5.00	
3	6.00	

CLOSEST STUDENTS
STUDENT NUMBER: 9981

FACTOR		DIFF. FROM AVG.
1	0.40	
2	0.00	
3	1.00	

STUDENT NUMBER: 27091

FACTOR		DIFF. FROM AVG.
1	0.40	
2	−1.00	
3	0.00	

5. The College of Arts and Science wishes to determine the age distribution of the faculty members in its various departments. In particular, they want to know for each department, how many faculty members are in each of the following categories.

```
< 20
20 - 29
30 - 39
40 - 49
50 - 59
> 59
```

The following data have been prepared for the program. The first card gives the number of departments in the College. This is followed by the names of the departments in alphabetical order. These names are in quotes. After all the department names comes the information on the individual faculty members. This information consists of the faculty member's name (in quotes), the name of the department in which the faculty member is located, and the faculty member's age. This information is in alphabetical order by the name of the faculty member. The following is a set of sample data:

```
33
'ANATOMY'
'ANTHROPOLOGY'

    .

    .

    .

'SOCIOLOGY'
'ABBOT'            'HISTORY'            37
'ACKERMAN'         'PSYCHOLOGY'         53

    .              .                    .

    .              .

'ZOOK'             'ART'                42
'END'              'DATA'               0
```

Give a program that will use this data to output the age distribution for each department.

Output from the program should have the following format:

DEPARTMENT	AGE CATEGORIES					
	< 20	20 - 29	30 - 39	40 - 49	50 - 59	> 59
ANATOMY	0	2	5	4	2	2
ANTHROPOLOGY	0	1	2	4	2	1
.			.			
.			.			
SOCIOLOGY	0	4	5	6	4	1

CHAPTER

5

STRINGS
AND
THINGS

Although the concept of a string was introduced in Chap. 2, this chapter formally introduces the basic notions of string processing. The first section deals with the concatenation of strings and the rules that govern their comparison. Section 5-2 discusses several primitive string-handling functions. Section 5-3 introduces an alternative to free-style input and output — edited input and output. Finally, the chapter terminates with complete PL/I programs for the applications developed in Chap. 5 of the main text.

5-1 STRING CONCEPTS AND TERMINOLOGY

The definition of a string constant was given in Sec. 2-1.1. Recall from Sec. 22.1 that string variables could be declared as having a fixed or variable length. A variable-length string was specified by using the VARYING attribute. Unless otherwise specified, we will always use variable-length strings in this book. Also recall that the PL/I character set or alphabet is the following:

b.(<+|&!$*);¬–/,%_>?:#@'=ABCDEFGHIJKLMNOPQRSTUVWXYZ0123456789

In PL/I, the concatenation operator is denoted by "||". Note that there are no blanks between the two vertical strokes. Thus, "||" replaces the symbol "o" in the algorithmic notation of the main text. For example, the concatenation of the two strings 'SASKA' and 'TOON' is specified by the expression

'SASKA' || 'TOON'

The result of evaluating this expression is the string 'SASKATOON'. In general, a string expression can contain string variables as well as string constants. For example, the program segment

```
DECLARE (A, B, C) CHARACTER(20) VARYING;
A = 'COMPUTE';
B = 'SCIENCE';
C = A || 'Rb' || B;
```

declares A, B, and C to be string variables and generates a value for C of

'COMPUTER SCIENCE'.

The concatenation operator has higher precedence than the relational operators but lower than binary addition and subtraction.

In the earlier chapters the notion of testing strings for equality and inequality was introduced. The relational operations in PL/I were given in Table 3-1. Recall that for certain operators (such as < and >) PL/I requires two symbols in order to specify the relational operation. The comparison feature for "=" and "≠" can be expanded to include the other four relational operators. The basis of this comparison is the collating sequence of a character set. The collating sequence of the PL/I character set is defined to be

b.(<+|&!$*);¬–/,%_>?:#@'=ABCDEFGHIJKLMNOPQRSTUVWXYZ0123456789

Any character in this ordered set is said to "lexically precede" any character to its right in this set. When two strings having an unequal number of characters are compared, the shorter string is first padded on the right with blanks until the two strings contain the same number of characters. The comparison is only performed after this padding process. For example, in comparing the strings 'JOE' and 'JOHN', one blank is inserted in 'JOE' thus giving the string 'JOEb'. These two strings, 'JOEb' and 'JOHN', are then compared on a character-by-character basis in a left-to-right scan of the strings. In the current example the condition

'JOE' = 'JOHN'

is false. However, the condition,

'JOE' < 'JOHN'

is true since 'E' lexically precedes 'H'. Other examples of conditions involving strings are given in the following:

'BILL' < 'BILLY'	true
'BOB' <= 'ALAN'	false
'TREMBLAY' > 'BUNT'	true
'AND' = 'ANDb'	true

Note that the space in PL/I plays a different role than was the case in the algorithmic notation of the main text.

The comparison of character strings is very important in the sorting of string data. Such a sorting operation is required in many data processing and string manipulation applications. As an example, the following program performs a selection sort on a set of names.

```
/*PROGRAM TO SORT A SET OF NAMES*/
SELECT: PROCEDURE OPTIONS(MAIN);
      DECLARE (NAME(100), TEMP) CHARACTER(20) VARYING:
      DECLARE (PASS, MIN_INDEX, I, N) FIXED;
      /*READ IN NAMES*/
      GET LIST (N);
      DO I = 1 to N;
            GET LIST (NAME(I));
      END;
      /*PERFORM SELECTION SORT*/
      MIN_INDEX = PASS;
      DO PASS = 1 TO N - 1;
            DO I = PASS + 1 TO N;
                  IF NAME(I) < NAME(MIN_INDEX)
                  THEN MIN_INDEX = I;
            END;
            IF MIN_INDEX ¬ = PASS
            THEN DO:
                  TEMP = NAME(PASS);
                  NAME(PASS) = NAME(MIN_INDEX);
                  NAME(MIN_INDEX) = TEMP;
                  END;
      END;
      /*PRINT SORTED LIST*/
      DO I = 1 to N;
            PUT SKIP LIST (NAME(I));
      END;
END SELECT;
```

So far, the only string operation that we have introduced is concatenation. Clearly, if we are going to write string manipulation programs, a greater variety of operators is required. Some of these operators are introduced in the next section.

5-2 BASIC STRING OPERATIONS

The notions of string manipulation in the previous section involved the concatenation and the comparison of two strings. Other primitive operations which are required by a string-manipulation system include the following:

1) Obtain the length of a string.
2) Extract a portion (i.e., a substring) of a string.
3) Search and replace (if necessary) a given substring within a string.

The programming aspects of these primitive operations in PL/I are discussed in this section.

The length of a string in PL/I is given by the built-in function LENGTH. For example, the function reference

LENGTH('COMPUTER SCIENCE')

would yield an integer value of 16. Since the result of invoking the function is numeric, it can be used in an arithmetic computation. For example, the expression.

LENGTH('TREMBLAY') + LENGTH('BUNT')

would yield a value of 12. In general, the argument of the LENGTH function can be any string expression. The length of the empty string (i.e., '') is defined as zero.

The task of extracting a particular substring from a given string is accomplished in PL/I by using the SUBSTR function. This function is very similar to the function SUB of the main text. The form of the SUBSTR function is the following:

SUBSTR(*string-expression, initial-position, length*)

where

string-expression yeilds a string from which a substring is desired,
initial-position is the character position in the original string at which the substring begins, and
length denotes the length of the desired substring.

For example, the function reference

SUBSTR('MONTREAL, QUEBEC', 1, 8)

returns after its execution the string value 'MONTREAL'. The expression

SUBSTR('CLEVELAND, OHIO', 12, 4)

on the other hand, returns a value of 'OHIO'. It should be emphasized that the substring being referenced within a given string must actually exist. If any reference is made to characters outside the given string, then a compiler error will result. For example, the expression

    SUBSTR('OTTAWA', 7)

results in an error as the string 'OTTAWA' does not contain seven characters. The expression

    SUBSTR('TORONTO', 5, 5)

will also result in an error as the total length of the string 'TORONTO' is less than the sum of the initial-position (5) and the length of the substring (5).

    In particular instances it may be desirable to omit the third (length) argument in the function reference. In such a case the function is invoked as

    SUBSTR(*string-expression, initial-position*)

and the desired substring which is returned begins at the position indicated by the second argument, and runs through to the end of the given string. For example, the result of the expression

    SUBSTR('J P TREMBLAY', 5)

is the string 'TREMBLAY'. The same result is obtained from the expression

    SUBSTR('J P TREMBLAY', 5, 8).

    As another example, the following PL/I program transforms a name which has the input form

    first-name middle-name last-name

to the output form

    last-name, first initial middle-initial

```
/*GIVEN A NAME IN THE FORM FIRST-NAME MIDDLE-NAME LAST-NAME*/
/*THIS PROGRAM GENERATES AN EQUIVALENT NAME IN THE FORM*/
/*LAST-NAME, FIRST-INITIAL MIDDLE-INITIAL*/

NAME_ED: PROCEDURE OPTIONS(MAIN);

    DECLARE (NAME, LAST, DESIRED_NAME) CHARACTER(30) VARYING;
    DECLARE (FI, MI) CHARACTER(1) VARYING;
    DECLARE I FIXED;

    /*READ NAME*/
    GET LIST (NAME);

    /*OBTAIN FIRST INITIAL*/
    FI = SUBSTR(NAME, 1, 1);
```

```
/*SCAN THE NAME FOR THE FIRST BLANK*/
I = 1;
DO WHILE (SUBSTR(NAME, I, 1) ¬ = ' '));
      I = I + 1;
END;

/*OBTAIN THE SECOND INITIAL*/
MI = SUBSTR(NAME, I + 1, 1);

/*GET RID OF FIRST NAME AND BLANK*/
NAME = SUBSTR(NAME, I + 1);

/*SCAN THE NAME FOR THE SECOND BLANK*/
I = 1;
DO WHILE (SUBSTR(NAME, I, 1)¬ = ' ');
      I = I + 1;
END;

/*OBTAIN THE LAST NAME*/
LAST = SUBSTR(NAME, I + 1);

/*OUTPUT THE DESIRED NAME*/
DESIRED_NAME = LAST || ', ' || FI || ' ' || MI;
PUT SKIP LIST (DESIRED_NAME);
END NAME_ED;
```

The name to be transformed is read in. The SUBSTR function is then used to obtain the first intial. A DO WHILE loop is begun which scans NAME for the first blank. When the first blank is reached, the condition "SUBSTR(NAME, I, 1) = ' '" is false and the loop terminates. The second initial is then assigned to MI. The statement

```
NAME = SUBSTR(NAME, I + 1)
```

removes the first name and following blank from the string. Another DO WHILE loop is used to find the next blank, and the remaining string after this blank is assigned to LAST. Finally, the transformed name is created and the resulting string printed.

The function SUBSTR can also be used as a pseudo-variable on the left-hand side of an assignment statement. When it is used in this manner, however, the length of the replacing string on the right-hand side of the statement must be exactly the same as that of the substring being replaced. For example, the statement

```
SUBSTR(S, 4, 3) = 'ABC';
```

where S = '0123456789' changes S to a value of '012ABC6789'. In this example the substring '345' has been replaced by the string 'ABC'. In the statement

```
SUBSTR(S, 4, 3) = '';
```

however, the new value of S becomes '012bbb6789'. In this case the empty string of the right-hand side of the assignment statement has been padded with three blanks — the length of the substring being replaced. The statement

    SUBSTR(S, 4, 3) = 'ABCD';

yields the same result for S as the first example (i.e., '012ABC6789') just given. Note that in this case the fourth character (D) is dropped. Clearly, this restriction severely affects the usability of the SUBSTR function as a pseudo-variable. In the program given earlier for the editing of a given name, the positions of each blank in the name had to be determined. Although it was possible to determine these positions by using the SUBSTR function, this approach was somewhat tedious.

An alternate way of accomplishing the same editing task is simplified by the introduction of the built-in function INDEX. This function is identical in every respect to its counterpart in the main text. The function, in its general form, is

    INDEX(S, P)

where S denotes the subject string which is to be examined for the leftmost occurrence of the given pattern string P. If the search is successful, then the result of invoking this function is an integer which gives the leftmost position in the subject where the pattern string begins; otherwise, a value of zero is returned.

The following program is a reformulation of the program NAME_ED given earlier:

```
/*GIVEN A NAME IN THE FORM FIRST-NAME MIDDLE-NAME LAST-NAME*/
/*THIS PROGRAM USES THE INDEX AND SUBSTR FUNCTIONS TO PRINT*/
/*AN EQUIVALENT NAME IN THE FORM LAST-NAME, FIRST-INITIAL*/
/*MIDDLE-INITIAL*/

NAME_ED: PROCEDURE OPTIONS(MAIN);
      DECLARE (NAME, LAST, DESIRED_NAME) CHARACTER(30) VARYING;
      DECLARE (FI, MI) CHARACTER(1) VARYING;
      DECLARE I FIXED;

      /*READ NAME*/
      GET LIST (NAME);

      /*OBTAIN FIRST INITIAL*/
      FI = SUBSTR(NAME, 1, 1);

      /*SCAN THE NAME FOR THE FIRST BLANK*/
      I = INDEX(NAME, ' ');

      /*OBTAIN SECOND INITIAL*/
      MI = SUBSTR(NAME, I + 1, 1);

      /*GET RID OF FIRST NAME AND BLANK*/
      NAME = SUBSTR(NAME, I + 1);

      /*SCAN THE NAME FOR THE SECOND BLANK*/
      I = INDEX(NAME, ' ');
```

```
                /*OBTAIN THE LAST NAME*/
                LAST = SUBSTR(NAME, I + 1);

                /*OUTPUT THE DESIRED NAME*/
                DESIRED_NAME = LAST || ', ' || FI || ' ' || MI;
                PUT SKIP LIST(DESIRED_NAME);
            END NAME_ED;
```

The second version of this program is very similar to the first version, with the DO WHILE statements having been replaced by statements containing the INDEX function.

Another useful built-in function is the PL/I VERIFY function. The form of this function is

VERIFY(S, P)

where S and P denote the subject string and the pattern string, respectively. The result returned by VERIFY is an integer indicating the position of the first character in the subject string (i.e., S), which is not a character in the pattern string (i.e., P). If all characters in S are in P, then the result returned is 0. For example,

VERIFY('bbbABCD', 'b')

yields a value of 4 while

VERIFY('bbbABCD', 'bABCD')

yields a value of 0.

Other PL/I string-handling functions exist which are useful in very special situations. The reader is advised to consult the Appendices for descriptions of these functions.

The applications of the functions discussed in this section will be exhibited in Sec. 5-4. Before doing this, however, the basis of programmer-controlled input and output is examined in the next section.

Exercises for Sec. 5-2

1. Give the results of the following expressions:

    (i)   LENGTH('MACARONI' || 'AND' || 'CHEESE')
    (ii) SUBSTR('JOE' || 'LARRY' || 'MOE', 4, 5) ||
          SUBSTR('JOE' || 'LARRY' || 'MOE', 1, 3) ||
          SUBSTR('JOE' || 'LARRY' || 'MOE', 9, 3)
    (iii) SUBSTR('LANGUAGE', LENGTH('DOG') + 2)

2. (i) You are given two cards with names written on them. Each name is separated by a comma, e.g., JOHN, SUE, ..., JIM.
    Assume that a name appears only once on any one card. Write a program

that will read two cards and print out the union of the names on both cards. The union is the set of all the names that appear on one list or the other list or both lists (if on both, only print once).
Typical input and output are as follows:

JOHN, MARY, JIM, JERRY, SUE, BOB, BARB
BILL, BARB, JILL, BOB, SUE, JOHN
UNION IS JOHN, MARY, JIM, JERRY, SUE, BOB, BARB, BILL, JILL

(ii) Repeat part (i) and print the intersection of the names on both cards. The intersection is the set of all names that appear on both lists. For the input data just given, the output is

INTERSECTION IS JOHN, JIM, SUE, BARB

Note that the output suggested in this problem is one possible form of the result.

3. Write a program that inputs the name of a person which is punched on one card in the form

'EMILEbJEANbPAULbTREMBLAY'

and outputs

TREMBLAY, E.J.P.

(Note that the character 'b' represents a blank.) Your algorithm should handle an arbitrary number of names before the surname (up to a maximum of ten).

4. Write a program which inputs a string and replaces all occurrences of MRS.b' or 'MISSb' by 'MS.b' and all occurrences of 'CHAIRMAN' by 'CHAIRPERSON'. (Note that the character 'b' represents a blank.)

5. Devise a program that the deletes all occurrences of trailing blanks in a given string. For example, the string 'R.B.bBUNTbbbb' should be transformed to the string 'R.B.bBUNT'. (Note that the character 'b' represents a blank.)

6. Write a program which inputs a string S and a replication factor N, and replicates the given string N times. For example, the results for the input

'HO!', 3

would be

'HO!HO!HO!'

5-3   EDITED INPUT AND OUTPUT

In Sec. 2-3 the GET LIST and PUT LIST statements were introduced. Though useful, these statements have several disadvantages in that the programmer has little control over the format with which information may be read or printed. For example, suppose we wish to print a table of integers such as that the first integer appeared in column 1, the second in column 3, the third in column 5, and so on. With the PUT LIST statement, this desired output format is not possible. Edited input and output statements provide us with the ability to have much closer control over the format of input and output. The edited input and output statements in PL/I are

GET EDIT (*input list*) (*format list*);

and

PUT EDIT (*output list*) (*format list*);

The *input list* and *output list* were previously described in Sec. 2-3. The *format list* contains *format items* and *control items*. The format items control the style of the information to be read or printed. The control items determine the position of the next datum in input or the position of the next printed item. Each element of the input or output list is associated with an element in the format list in a left-to-right manner; that is, the first element in the input or output list is described by the first format item, the second element is described by the second format item, etc.

The following discussion concerns some of the more useful format and control items. A complete list of the format and control items is given in the Appendices.

A(w) Format

The A(w) format is used for the input and output of character strings. When used in input statements, the next w columns (assuming w is greater than zero) are read. If w is less than or equal to zero, the input is ignored and the null string is assigned to the associated variable instead. For example, in the following program segment

```
DECLARE STRING CHARACTER(8),
        BLANK CHARACTER(4);
GET EDIT (STRING, BLANK) (A(8), A(0));
```

STRING receives the value contained in the next eight columns of input and the empty string is assigned to BLANK. Note that when the A format is used in a GET EDIT statement, the character string on the data card is not enclosed in quotation marks as is required in the GET LIST statement. For example, suppose a data card contained the following values starting in column 1.

THE LAST RACE

If the statement

GET EDIT (STRING) (A(8));

were executed. The variable STRING would contain the string

'THE LAST'

If A(w) is used in a PUT EDIT statement, then the associated item in the output list is printed in the next w columns in the current line of output. If w is less than zero, nothing is printed, and the associated item in the output list is skipped. If the value to be printed is longer than the w columns specified, then only the leftmost w characters are printed.

Another feature of the A(w) format is that it may be used in output statements without the "(w)". When it is used in this form, the character string is printed in a field equal to the length of the string. The following statement:

PUT EDIT ('TOMO', 'RROW') (A, A(4));

uses the A(w) format to print

TOMORROW

The statement

PUT EDIT ('MARY HAD A LITTLE LAMB') (A(4));

prints the word

MARY

while

PUT EDIT ('MARY HAD A LITTLE LAMB') (A);

prints

MARY HAD A LITTLE LAMB

E Format

The E format item is used in the reading or writing of floating-point numbers. This format may also be used with fixed-point numbers. When used with fixed-point numbers, an exponent of 0 is assumed. The form of the E format is

E(w, d, s)

or

E(w, d)

w is the size of the print field (i.e., how many columns the floating-point number will occupy). Note that w must include space for the complete number including sign and exponent. If the number given is too long for the specified format, then it will be rounded to fit. d specifies the number of digits to the right of the decimal point and s (which must be less than 17) specifies the number of significant digits (i.e., how many digits should be presented). If s is not present, the number of significant digits is assumed to be d + 1.

When used in input operations, the data item associated with the E format may be any signed or unsigned floating-point or fixed-point constant located within the specified field. If the constant has no decimal point, then a decimal point is assumed to the right of the d rightmost digits; otherwise, the given decimal point is used. The value of s, if given, is ignored in input operations. The following are examples of the E format in GET EDIT statements. Assuming that the data card contains the value

56.76E 24

the statement

GET EDIT (NUMBER) (E(8, 2));

reads in the value

56.76E 24

If the input statement were

GET EDIT (NUMBER) (E(8, 1));

the same value, namely,

56.76E 24

would be read. Notice that the decimal point given in the number is used and the d specification (here, 1) is ignored.

On output, the floating-point number is printed in the next w columns in the following form

(optional –) (s – d digits).(d digits)E(+ or –)(exponent)

If d = 0, then no decimal point will be printed. The following are examples of the E format used in PUT EDIT statements. The b's represent blank spaces in the print field.

Statement	*Output*
PUT EDIT (132.66) (E (10, 1, 3);	bb13.3E+01
PUT EDIT (132.66) (E (12, 4));	bb1.3266E+02
PUT EDIT (132.66) (E (16, 8));	bbb.0013266E+06
PUT EDIT (132.66) (E (12, 4, 6));	b13.2660E+01

F Format

The F format is used to read or write fixed-point numbers. This format may also be used with floating-point numbers in which case the floating-point numbers are converted to fixed-point numbers which fit the specified format. The form of the F format is

      F(w)

or

      F(w, d)

or

      F(w, d, s)

When used in input statements, the next w columns are read in as a fixed-point number. If the number contained in the w columns contains a decimal point, then this decimal point is used; otherwise, a decimal point is assumed to be d digits (if d is given) to the right of the number. If d is omitted or equal to zero, then the decimal point is assumed to be to the right of the number. Blanks may precede or follow the number in the specified field, but blanks embedded in the number are not allowed. Preceding blanks are treated as zeros; trailing blanks are ignored. An entirely blank field is interpreted to be zero. if an s value is given, the number read is multiplied by 10 raised to the power of s before being assigned to the associated variable.

Assuming that a data card contains the following values

      131416713215

starting in column 1, the statement

      GET EDIT (AGE, MARK, ANSWER (F(2), F(2, 0), F(3, 2));

results in the values 13, 15, and 1.67 being read into AGE, MARK, and ANSWER, respectively. If the statement

      GET EDIT (AGE, MARK) (F(3), F(2, 0, 1));

is executed, AGE and MARK receive the values 132 and 150, respectively.

When the F format is used in PUT EDIT statement, the value to be printed is converted to fixed-decimal form (if necessary), rounded to fit the format (again, if necessary), and printed right-adjusted in a field w columns wide. If d is omitted or equal to zero, then the value is printed in integer form; otherwise, a decimal point is printed d digits to the right of the number. If an s value is present, then the number is multiplied by 10 raised to the power of s before being printed. The following examples illustrate the F format in output statements.

Statement	*Output*
PUT EDIT (56321) (F5));	56321
PUT EDIT (56321) (F(6, 2));	563.21
PUT EDIT (56321) (F(8, 3));	bb56.321
PUT EDIT (56321) (F(10, 0, 1));	bbb563210

COLUMN(w) Control Item

The COLUMN(w) control item written as

COLUMN(w)

or

COL(w)

is used to position the input of values at a certain card column or the output of values at a certain printer column. If the column w has already been passed, reading begins at column w on the next card or in the case of PUT EDIT statements printing begins at column w of the next line. For example, the statement

PUT EDIT ('HAPPY') (COL(45), A);

prints the word 'HAPPY' starting at column 45. The statement

GET EDIT (NUMBER) (COL(1), F(10));

reads the first 10 columns of the data card.

X(w) Control Item

The X(w) control item causes w columns to be skipped on input or output. If w is less than or equal to zero, then no columns are skipped. Since both COLUMN(w) and X(w) are control items, they are not associated with any element in the input or output list. Their only function is to indicate the position where reading or writing is to take place. The statement

PUT EDIT ('HAPPY', 'DAYS', 'ARE', 'HERE', 'AGAIN')
        (A, X(1), A, X(1), A, X(1), A, X(4), A);

causes the line

HAPPYbDAYSbAREbHEREbbbbAGAIN

to be printed.

Notice that the X control item and the COLUMN control item are different. The X control item is used to skip columns while the COLUMN control item is used to specify a specific column where reading or writing is to begin. The difference between the two control items can be clearly seen by the following statement which produces the same output as the previous example but has been rewritten using the COL control item.

PUT EDIT ('HAPPY', 'DAYS', 'ARE', 'HERE', 'AGAIN')
        (COL(1), A, COL(7), A, COL(12), A, COL(16), A, COL(24), A);

In this example, blanks have been inserted between the words by positioning the next word to be printed in a specific column rather than by skipping one column as was done in the previous example.

As was mentioned earlier, the elements of the input or output list are associated with the format items in a left-to-right manner. If there are more format items than there are elements in the input or output list, then the unused format items are ignored. If, however, there are fewer format items than elements, then the format items are reused starting from the first format item. For example, in the PUT statement

```
PUT EDIT('JOE', 4.5, 'GREEN', 5.5) (A, X(1), F(3,1));
```

'JOE' is printed using the A format, one column is skipped, and then 4.5 is printed using the F(3, 1) format. Since the end of the format list has been reached, the formats are reused for the remaining items. 'GREEN' is printed using the A format, the next column is skipped, and finally, 5.5 is printed using the F(3, 1) format.

Format items may also be used repeatedly through the use of *replication factors* in the format list. For example, in the statement

```
PUT EDIT (A, B, C) ( (2) E(13, 2), F(6, 1));
```

the "(2)" before the E format item indicates that E(13, 2) is to be used twice (i.e., once for the printing of A and a second time for the printing of B). This statement is equivalent to the statement

```
PUT EDIT (A, B, C) (E(13, 2), E (13, 2), F(6, 1));
```

The replication factor which appears in parentheses before the format item can be a constant, a variable, or an expression. If the value of the replication factor is less than or equal to zero, then the format item following it is skipped.

In Sec. 2-3, the SKIP option was introduced to allow vertical spacing when using the PUT LIST and PUT DATA statements. The SKIP option can also be used with the PUT EDIT statement. The rules for use of the SKIP option with the PUT EDIT statement are the same as those given for the PUT LIST and PUT DATA statements. Besides the SKIP option, PL/I offers other options that may be used with the PUT LIST, PUT EDIT, or PUT DATA statements. These options allow the programmer better control over the vertical position of his or her output. One of these options is LINE(*expression*). LINE(*expression*) causes output to be printed at certain lines on the page. The expression is evaluated as an integer. This result is used to indicate the line on the current page where the output is to appear. For example, the statement

```
PUT LINE(15) LIST ('THIS APPEARS ON LINE 15');
```

causes the literal to appear on the fifteenth line of the current page.

If the integer value of the expresison is less than or equal to zero, a value of 1 is assumed. If the printer has already passed the indicated line, or if the line number is greater than the number of lines on a page, the output is printed at the top of the next page. The statements

```
PUT LINE(25) LIST ('THIS APPEARS ON LINE 25.');
PUT LINE(14) LIST ('THIS APPEARS AT THE TOP OF A NEW PAGE');
PUT LINE(-77) LIST ('THIS APPEARS ON THE NEXT PAGE');
```

result in two pages of output. The first output statement places its literal on the twenty-fifth line of the first page. Since the printer has passed the fourteenth line, the second literal is placed on the first line of the next page. The negative expression in the third statement causes a value of 1 to be assumed, and the last literal is printed over top of the second literal, as the current line is still line 1.

A third print option is PAGE. The PAGE option causes all the remaining lines in the current page to be skipped and the output to be placed on the first line of the new page. For example,

    PUT LIST ('NEW PAGE') PAGE;

causes the literal 'NEW PAGE' to be placed at the top of the next page.

The PAGE option can be used with the LINE(*expression*) option to place the output on a certain line on a new page. The statement

    PUT LINE (11) LIST ('NEW PAGE') PAGE;

results in the literal ('NEW PAGE') being placed on the eleventh line of the next page. The order of the PAGE and LINE options is immaterial. The following two statements produce identical results.

    PUT PAGE LIST ('NEW PAGE') LINE (11);
    PUT LINE(11) PAGE LIST ('NEW PAGE');

Another feature of the PL/I language which facilitates the input and output of values is the *implied* counted loop. An implied counted loop may be used to specify the elements of the vector which are to be read in or printed out. For example, the GET statement in the following program segment uses a counted loop to input values for the vector WEIGHT.

    DECLARE (WEIGHT(25), I) FIXED DECIMAL;
    GET LIST ((WEIGHT(I) DO I = 1 TO 15));

(Notice that the vector-name and associated counted loop control is surrounded by parentehses.) The implied counted loop used in this example operates in the following manner. First, the loop variable I is assigned the start-value of 1, and the first data value is assigned to WEIGHT(I) (i.e., WEIGHT(1)). I is then incremented to 2, and the second data value is assigned to WEIGHT(2). This process continues until finally the fifteenth data value is assigned to WEIGHT(15). Additional vectors may be referenced by the same counted loop by placing them before the counted loop and separating them from each other by commas. For example, the PUT statement in the following program segment:

    DECLARE (HEIGHT(24), WEIGHT(0:25)) FIXED;
            .
            .
            .
    PUT LIST ((I, WEIGHT(I), HEIGHT(I) DO I = 1 TO 5 BY 2));

prints the values 1, WEIGHT(1), HEIGHT(1) 3, WEIGHT(3), HEIGHT(3), 5, WEIGHT(5), and HEIGHT(5). The vector(s) and counted loop control surrounded by parentheses is considered to be one item in the input and output lists, and is separated from the other items by a comma. The input and output statements may include a combination of single element variables, vectors, and vector elements specified by subscripts and/or implied loops. The following program segment illustrates a number of valid input and output statement.

```
DECLARE (MARK(0:100), I, AVG, NUMBER(45)) FIXED;
GET LIST ((MARK(I) DO I = 1 TO 7), AVG);
GET LIST ((NUMBER(I) DO I = 10 TO 1 BY -1));
GET LIST ((NUMBER(I) DO I = 10 TO 45), (MARK(I) DO I = 7 TO 100));
        .
        .
        .
PUT SKIP LIST (NUMBER, (MARK(I) DO I = 1 TO 5), AVG);
```

The second input statement illustrates a negative value used as an increment for the counted loop. This input statement results in the assignment of ten consecutive data values to the vector elements NUMBER(10) through NUMBER(1), in that order. Notice that the statement

```
GET LIST ((NUMBER(I) DO I = 1 TO 10));
```

does not result in the same assignment as the previously mentioned input statement. In the third input statement, the variable I is used as the loop variable for both vectors specified by counted loops. This is permissible, as the output signalled by the first counted loop is completed before the output designated by the second counted loop is begun.

Implied loops may also be used one within the other or *nested*. This ability is useful for the input or output of multidimensional arrays. For example, values may be read into a 3 x 4 array NAMES using the following statement.

```
GET LIST (((NAMES(ROW, COL) DO ROW = 1 TO 3) DO COL = 1 TO 4));
```

The inner implied loop control (in this case DO ROW = 1 TO 3) is contained within the inner parentheses and implies that for each repetition caused by the outer control (here, DO COL = 1 TO 4), all the repetitions of the inner control are performed. In the example, the order of the successive subscript pairs generated reads values first into, NAMES(1, 1), then NAMES(2, 1), then NAMES(3, 1), then NAMES(1, 2), then NAMES(2, 2), and so on.

This section has introduced several concepts concerning edited input and output. The PUT EDIT and GET EDIT statements can be used to format output and in the reading of formatted data. In addition other features of the PUT statement were introduced to give the programmer greater control in input or output operations. In the next section problems are solved using some of the concepts presented in this chapter.

Exercises for Sec. 5-3

1.   Give the results of the following PUT EDIT statements:

  (i) PUT EDIT ('ABBOTT AND COSTELLO') (A(9));
  (ii) PUT EDIT (56.78) (F(5, 1));
  (iii) PUT EDIT (65.33) (E(13, 4));
  (iv) PUT EDIT ('THE', 'LAST') (A, X(1), A);
  (v) PUT EDIT (7777) (E(12, 2));
  (vi) PUT EDIT (7777) (F(5, 1));
  (vii) PUT EDIT (7777 (F(6));
  (viii) PUT EDIT (14, 24, 36.6) (F(2), F(1, 1), F(5, 1, 1));

2. Write GET EDIT statements that will read the following information:

  (i) A five digit integer in columns 5 through 10
  (ii) A string of unknown length starting in column 10
  (iii) A real number in columns 20 through 30

3. Given a card containing the vollowing information

Card column	1	2	3	4	5	6	7	8
Values	1	1	7	8	5	6	7	9

what would the values of MARK, SUM, and AVERAGE be after each of the following input statements:

  (i) GET EDIT (MARK, SUM, AVERAGE) (F(2), F(2), F(2));
  (ii) GET EDIT (MARK, SUM, AVERAGE) (F(3, 1), F(2, 1), F(4));
  (iii) GET EDIT (MARK, SUM, AVERAGE) (F(4, 2), F(3, 1, 1), F(1));

4. Write a program which reads in a 4 x 4 array column by column and prints the array row by row.

For example,

Input	1	2	3	4
	5	6	7	8
	9	10	11	12
	13	14	15	16

Output	1	5	9	13
	2	6	10	14
	3	7	11	15
	4	8	12	16

5-4 BASIC STRING APPLICATIONS

This section presents PL/C programs for the applications introduced in Sec. 5-4 of the main text.

5-4.1 Analysis of Textual Material

The problem as stated in the main text concerns the analysis of natural language text. In this problem English text is to be analyzed in order to produce a frequency table which gives the words used in the text (listed in alphabetical order) and the frequency with which they appear. For example, the line

'THE LAST MILE WAS THE HARDEST'

results in the following frequency table.

WORD	FREQUENCY
HARDEST	1
LAST	1
MILE	1
THE	2
WAS	1

In solving this problem we assume that the words are separated by one blank and that all punctuation marks have been removed. Furthermore we assume that the words of the text are not hyphenated or broken across card boundaries. The number of cards containing the text is unknown, though it is known that the number of distinct words is less than 100 and no word contains more than 20 characters. For convenience we assume that the text contains no more than 256 characters (including separating blanks). A solution to this problem is given in Fig. 5-1. The following variables are used in this program.

Variable	Type	Usage
WORD(100)	CHARACTER(20) VARYING	Vector containing words used in text
FREQ(100)	FIXED	Vector containing count of number of times word used
TEXT	CHARACTER(256) VARYING	Text to be analyzed
NEXT	FIXED	Next free vector element
CARD	CHARACTER(80) VARYING	Input line of text
P	FIXED	Position of the leftmost blank
I	FIXED	Index variable
PASS	FIXED	Current pass in selection sort
MIN_INDEX	FIXED	Index of smallest element in pass
WORD_COUNT	FIXED	Number of distinct words
NEW_WORD	CHARACTER(20) VARYING	Current word
END_FLAG	CHARACTER(3) VARYING	End of data flag
TEMP_WORD	CHARACTER(20) VARYING	Temporary variable used in exchange
TEMP_FREQ	FIXED	Temporary variable used in exchange

The data analyzed by this program was the passage

```
/* ANALYSIS OF THE FREQUENCY OF WORDS IN ENGLISH TEXT */
STMT LEVEL NEST BLOCK MLVL   SOURCE TEXT


                              /* ANALYSIS OF THE FREQUENCY OF WORDS IN ENGLISH TEXT */
    1                         W_FREQ: PROCEDURE OPTIONS(MAIN);

    2    1         1          DECLARE WORD(100) CHARACTER(20) VARYING,     /* WORD TABLE */
                                  FREQUENCY(100) FIXED,             /* FREQUENCY TABLE */
                                  TEXT CHARACTER(256) VARYING, /* TEXT TO BE ANALYZED */
                                  NEXT FIXED,              /* NEXT FREE VECTOR ELEMENT */
                                  CARD CHARACTER(80) VARYING, /* INPUT LINE OF TEXT */
                                  P FIXED,               /* POSITION OF THE LEFTMOST BLANK */
                                  I FIXED,                      /* INDEX VARIABLE */
                                  PASS FIXED,           /* CURRENT PASS IN SELECTION SORT */
                                  MIN_INDEX FIXED,     /* INDEX OF SMALLEST ELEMENT IN PASS*/
                                  WORD_COUNT FIXED,     /* NUMBER OF DISTINCT WORDS */
                                  NEW_WORD CHARACTER(20) VARYING, /* CURRENT WORD */
                                  END_FLAG CHARACTER (3) VARYING, /* END OF DATA FLAG */
                                  TEMP_WORD CHARACTER (20) VARYING, /* TEMPORARY VARIABLE */
                                  TEMP_FREQ FIXED;         /* TEMPORARY VARIABLE */

                              /* INITIALIZE */
    3    1         1          NEXT = 1;
    4    1         1          FREQUENCY = 0;
    5    1         1          END_FLAG = 'OFF';
    6    1         1          ON ENDFILE(SYSIN) END_FLAG = 'ON';

                              /* READ IN PASSAGE OF NARRATIVE TEXT */
    8    2         2          TEXT = '';
    9    1         1          GET LIST (CARD);
   10    1         1          DO WHILE (END_FLAG = 'OFF');
   11    1    1    1              TEXT = TEXT || CARD;
   12    1    1    1              GET LIST (CARD);
   13    1    1    1          END;

                              /* PROCESS TEXT */
   14    1         1          P = INDEX(TEXT, ' ');
   15    1         1          DO WHILE (P ¬= 0);

                                  /* SCAN THE NEXT WORD OF TEXT */
   16    1    1    1              NEW_WORD = SUBSTR(TEXT, 1, P - 1);
   17    1    1    1              IF LENGTH(TEXT) = P
   18    1    1    1              THEN TEXT = '';
   19    1    1    1              ELSE TEXT = SUBSTR(TEXT, P + 1);

                                  /* SEARCH AND UPDATE WORD TABLE FOR THE WORD JUST SCANNED */
   20    1    1    1              I = 1;
   21    1    1    1              WORD(NEXT) = NEW_WORD;
   22    1    1    1              DO WHILE (WORD(I) ¬= NEW_WORD);
   23    1    2    1                  I = I + 1;
   24    1    2    1              END;
   25    1    1    1              IF I = NEXT
   26    1    1    1              THEN NEXT = NEXT + 1;

                                  /* UPDATE FREQUENCY COUNT OF THE WORD JUST SCANNED */
   27    1    1    1              FREQUENCY(I) = FREQUENCY(I) + 1;

                                  /* OBTAIN POSITION OF NEXT BLANK IN THE REMAINING NARRATIVE */
                                  /* TEXT */
   28    1    1    1              P = INDEX(TEXT, ' ');
   29    1    1    1          END;
```

Fig. 5-1   Program to analyze the frequency of words in English text

'YOU CAN FOOL SOME OF THE PEOPLE ALL OF THE TIME AND ALL
OF THE PEOPLE SOME OF THE TIME BUT NOT ALL OF THE PEOPLE
ALL OF THE TIME'

The program begins by reading the text to be analyzed. In statement 15 a
loop is begun to scan each word of the text. New words are added to the WORD

```
                                      /* USING A SELECTION SORT, SORT THE WORD TABLE AND */
                                      /* ASSOCIATED FREQUENCY COUNT */
     30    1          1               WORD_COUNT = NEXT - 1;
     31    1          1               DO PASS = 1 TO WORD_COUNT - 1;
     32    1    1     1                   MIN_INDEX = PASS;
     33    1    1     1                   DO I = PASS + 1 TO WORD_COUNT;
     34    1    2     1                       IF WORD(I) < WORD(MIN_INDEX)
     35    1    2     1                       THEN MIN_INDEX = I;
     36    1    2     1                   END;
     37    1    1     1                   IF MIN_INDEX ¬= PASS
     38    1    1     1                   THEN DO;
     39    1    2     1                       TEMP_WORD = WORD(PASS);
     40    1    2     1                       WORD(PASS) = WORD(MIN_INDEX);
     41    1    2     1                       WORD(MIN_INDEX) = TEMP_WORD;
     42    1    2     1                       TEMP_FREQ = FREQUENCY(PASS);
     43    1    2     1                       FREQUENCY(PASS) = FREQUENCY(MIN_INDEX);
     44    1    2     1                       FREQUENCY(MIN_INDEX) = TEMP_FREQ;
     45    1    2     1                       END;
     46    1    1     1                   END;

                                      /* PRINT DESIRED REPORT */
     47    1          1               PUT EDIT ('WORD', 'FREQUENCY')(X(1), A, X(15), A);
     48    1          1               DO I = 1 TO WORD_COUNT;
     49    1    1     1                   PUT SKIP EDIT (WORD(I), FREQUENCY(I))(A(20), X(2), F(3));
     50    1    1     1               END;
     51    1          1           END W_FREQ;

ERRORS/WARNINGS DETECTED DURING CODE GENERATION:

        WARNING: NO FILE SPECIFIED. SYSIN/SYSPRINT ASSUMED. (CGOC)


WORD                FREQUENCY
ALL                     4
AND                     1
BUT                     1
CAN                     1
FOOL                    1
NOT                     1
OF                      6
PEOPLE                  3
SOME                    2
THE                     6
TIME                    3
YOU                     1



IN STMT   51  PROGRAM RETURNS FROM MAIN PROCEDURE.
```

Fig. 5-1 Program to analyze the frequency of words in English text (cont'd.)

vector and the frequency count for the words is updated accordingly. Statements 30 thru 46 comprise a selection sort which sorts the WORD vector into alphabetic order. Finally, the frequency table is printed and execution of the program is terminated.

The second problem involving text analysis concerns the calculation of statistics for a passage of natural language (i.e., English) text. Three statistics which are of interest are

1) The number of sentences in the passage of text,
2) The average number of words in a sentence, and
3) The average number of symbols per word.

In solving this problem we assume words in the passage are separated by one blank. Secondly, we assume that commas, colons, semicolons, question marks, exclamation marks, hyphens, and periods are valid punctuation symbols which are not to be considered as textual characters in the calculation of the previously mentioned statistics. Sentences are denoted by a period, and for convenience we assume that periods are not allowed for any other purpose. The last sentence of the text is followed by a blank, the symbol "@", and another blank. Finally, the text to be analyzed contains at least one sentence and contains no more than 256 characters. The solution to this problem is given in Fig. 5-2. The following variables were used in this solution.

Variable	Type	Usage
SENTENCE_CTR	FLOAT	Number of sentences in narrative text
AVG_WORDS	FLOAT	Average number of words per sentence
AVG_SYMBOLS	FLOAT	Average number of symbols per word
CARD	CHARACTER(80) VARYING	Input line of text
WORD	CHARACTER(20) VARYING	Word in text
TEXT	CHARACTER(256) VARYING	Text to be analyzed
P	FIXED	Position of the leftmost blank in text
SYMBOL_CTR	FLOAT	Number of symbols in text
WORD_CTR	FLOAT	Number of words in text
END_FLAG	CHARACTER(3) VARYING	End of data flag

This program was used to analyze the following text taken from Chap. 1.

'INTERACTIONS INVOLVING HUMANS ARE MOST EFFECTIVELY CARRIED OUT THROUGH THE MEDIUM OF LANGUAGE. LANGUAGE PERMITS THE EXPRESSION OF THOUGHTS AND IDEAS, AND WITHOUT IT, COMMUNICATION, AS WE KNOW IT, WOULD BE VERY DIFFICULT INDEED. @ '

The text to be analyzed is read into the string variable TEXT. In statement 13 a WHILE loop is begun which scans through the text counting the number of sentences, words, and symbols that appear. If the special symbol "@" is found, the average number of words (AVG_WORDS) and average number of symbols (AVG_SYMBOLS) is computed and printed along with the number of sentences (SENTENCE_CTR) found in the text. If a period is encountered, the sentence counter is incremented. Finally the symbol counter is incremented by the length of the word found. If the word ends in a punctuation mark the symbol counter is decremented by one to reflect the true number of nonpunctuation symbols.

5-4.2   Justification of Text

The program given in Fig. 5-3 is a solution to the problem given in Sec. 5-4.2 of the main text. This problem concerns the justification of text. To reduce the complexity of this problem we assume that words are not to be split between lines and each line (except for the last line of text) is to be both left and right justified. Extra blanks used in the justification of text are to be distributed evenly between the words of a line. As in the previous application each word is separated from each other word by a blank and each punctuation symbol is followed by a blank. The text to be justified is read as data and is preceded by an integer representing the number (a maximum of 100) of characters per line of justified text. The following variables were used in the solution to this problem.

Variable	Type	Usage
TEXT	CHARACTER(256) VARYING	Text to be justified
CARD	CHARACTER(80) VARYING	Input text
RMARGIN	FIXED	number of characters in a justified line of text
BLANKS	FIXED	Number of blanks to be inserted to justify line
BFIELD	CHARACTER(20) VARYING	String of blanks
I	FIXED	Index variable used in scanning line of text
J	FIXED	Loop variable
LINE	CHARACTER(100) VARYING	Justified line of text
END_FLAG	CHARACTER(3) VARYING	End of data flag

The text justified during this run contained the following passage.

'INTERACTIONS INVOLVING HUMANS ARE MOST EFFECTIVELY CARRIED OUT THROUGH THE MEDIUM OF LANGUAGE. LANGUAGE PERMITS THE EXPRESSION OF THOUGHTS AND IDEAS, AND WITHOUT IT, COMMUNCIATIONS, AS WE KNOW IT WOULD BE VERY DIFFICULT INDEED.'

In statement 7 the number of characters per justified line of text (i.e., RMARGIN) is read. The next statements accomplish the reading in of the text to be justified. In statement 13 a loop is begun to justify the input text. A check is made to see if a word ends at the right margin. If this is the case, then no justification is required and LINE is assigned a substring of TEXT up to the end of that word; otherwise, blanks must be inserted to justify the text. The number of blanks needed is calculated, then in statement 27 a loop is begun to insert the blanks into the text. Finally, in statement 41 the justified text is printed, and in the next statement the line of justified text is removed from TEXT. When the length of TEXT is less than the length of justified text, the loop to justify text is terminated and the final line of text is printed unjustified.

5-4.3 Form Letter Generation

The program presented in this section is a solution to the form letter generation problem given in Sec. 5-4.3 of the main text. The problem as given in the main text is to write a program for generating personalized form letters. The input data are to consist of a number of cards, each card containing a line of the letter. The lines of the form letter contain certain keywords which are to be replaced by information concerning the recipient of the letter in order to make the letter more personal. The keywords to be used in this form letter are

```
/* CALCULATION OF STATISTICS FOR NARRATIVE TEXT */

STMT LEVEL NEST BLOCK MLVL   SOURCE TEXT


                                        /* CALCULATION OF STATISTICS FOR NARRATIVE TEXT */
      1                                 TEXT_AN: PROCEDURE OPTIONS(MAIN);

      2     1          1                DECLARE SENTENCE_CTR FLOAT,  /* NUMBER OF SENTENCES */
                                                AVG_WORDS FLOAT,      /* AVERAGE NUMBER OF WORDS PER */
                                                                        /* SENTENCE */
                                                AVG_SYMBOLS FLOAT,    /* AVERAGE NUMBER OF SYMBOLS PER */
                                                                        /* WORD */
                                                CARD CHARACTER(80) VARYING, /* INPUT LINE OF TEXT */
                                                WORD CHARACTER(20) VARYING, /* WORD IN TEXT */
                                                TEXT CHARACTER(256) VARYING, /* TEXT TO BE ANALYZED */
                                                P FIXED,                /* POSITION OF LEFTMOST BLANK */
                                                SYMBOL_CTR FLOAT,       /* NUMBER OF SYMBOLS IN TEXT */
                                                WORD_CTR FLOAT,         /* NUMBER OF WORDS IN TEXT */
                                                END_FLAG CHARACTER(3) VARYING; /* END OF DATA FLAG */

                                        /* INITIALIZE */
      3     1          1                WORD_CTR, SYMBOL_CTR, SENTENCE_CTR = 0;
      4     1          1                END_FLAG = 'OFF';
      5     1          1                ON ENDFILE(SYSIN) END_FLAG = 'ON';

                                        /* READ IN THE TEXTUAL MATERIAL */
      7     2          2                TEXT = '';
      8     1          1                GET LIST (CARD);
      9     1          1                DO WHILE (END_FLAG = 'OFF');
     10     1    1     1                    TEXT = TEXT || CARD;
     11     1    1     1                    GET LIST (CARD);
     12     1    1     1                END;

                                        /* PROCESS TEXTUAL MATERIAL */
     13     1          1                DO WHILE ('1'B);
     14     1    1     1                    P = INDEX(TEXT, ' ');
     15     1    1     1                    WORD = SUBSTR(TEXT, 1, P - 1);
     16     1    1     1                    IF LENGTH(TEXT) = P
     17     1    1     1                    THEN TEXT = '';
     18     1    1     1                    ELSE TEXT = SUBSTR(TEXT, P + 1);

                                        /* END OF TEXT */
     19     1    1     1                    IF WORD = '@'
     20     1    1     1                    THEN DO;
     21     1    2     1                        AVG_WORDS = WORD_CTR / SENTENCE_CTR;
     22     1    2     1                        AVG_SYMBOLS = SYMBOL_CTR / WORD_CTR;
     23     1    2     1                        PUT SKIP EDIT ('THE NUMBER OF SENTENCES IS',
                                                        SENTENCE_CTR) (A, F(3));
     24     1    2     1                        PUT SKIP EDIT
                                                  ('THE AVERAGE NUMBER OF WORDS IN A SENTENCE IS',
                                                        AVG_WORDS) (A, X(1), F(6,3));
     25     1    2     1                        PUT SKIP EDIT
                                                  ('THE AVERAGE NUMBER OF SYMBOLS IN A WORD IS',
                                                        AVG_SYMBOLS) (A, X(1), F(6,3));
     26     1    2     1                        EXIT;
     27     1    2     1                        END;
                                        /* END OF SENTENCE */
     28     1    1     1                    IF INDEX(WORD, '.') ¬= 0
     29     1    1     1                    THEN SENTENCE_CTR = SENTENCE_CTR + 1;

                                        /* UPDATE THE WORD COUNTER */
     30     1    1     1                    WORD_CTR = WORD_CTR + 1;

                                        /* UPDATE THE SYMBOL COUNTER */
     31     1    1     1                    SYMBOL_CTR = SYMBOL_CTR + P - 1;
     32     1    1     1                    IF INDEX(WORD, ',') ¬= 0 | INDEX(WORD, ':') ¬= 0
                                              | INDEX(WORD, ';') ¬= 0 | INDEX(WORD, '!') ¬= 0
                                              | INDEX(WORD, '?') ¬= 0 | INDEX(WORD, '-') ¬= 0
                                              | INDEX(WORD, '.') ¬= 0
     33     1    1     1                    THEN SYMBOL_CTR = SYMBOL_CTR - 1;
     34     1    1     1                END;
     35     1                          END TEXT_AN;

ERRORS/WARNINGS DETECTED DURING CODE GENERATION:

     WARNING: NO FILE SPECIFIED. SYSIN/SYSPRINT ASSUMED. (CGOC)
```

Fig. 5-2   Program to calculate statistics for narrative text

```
THE NUMBER OF SENTENCES IS  2
THE AVERAGE NUMBER OF WORDS IN A SENTENCE IS 17.000
THE AVERAGE NUMBER OF SYMBOLS IN A WORD IS  5.529


IN STMT  26 PROGRAM IS STOPPED.
```

Fig. 5-2   Program to calculate statistics for narrative text (cont'd.)

Keyword	Replacement information
DATE	Date given in the customer's information
ADDRESS	Customer's address
CITY	Customer's city
PROVINCE	Customer's province
N	Number of weeks until salesman's visit
X	Customer's full name (i.e., MR. R.B. BROWN)
Z	Customer's last name (i.e., MR. BROWN)

In addition to these keywords, an indentation code represented by "#number" is used to specify the indentation to be used for the following line. The number (containing no more than two digits) represents the number of characters the line is to be indented. The end of the form letter is denoted by a card containing the string '**'. Following this card, information concerning an unknown number of recipients is given. For each recipient (or customer) the following information is given.

'Dateb'
'MR. (or MRS., etc.)bInitialsbSurnameb'
'Street Addressb'
'City,bProvinceb'
'Number of weeks before salesman's visitb'

where b represents a blank within the strings. The program is to read in the form letter and for each customer produce a personalized form letter using the information given for that customer. A program which solves this problem is given in Fig. 5-4. The variables used in this program are

Variable	Type	Usage
LETTER(50)	CHARACTER(100) VARYING	Form letter
NUM_LINES	FIXED	Number of lines in the form letter
DATE	CHARACTER(30) VARYING	Date to be placed on the letter
NAME	CHARACTER(30) VARYING	Customer's name
ADDRESS	CHARACTER(40) VARYING	Customer's address
CITY_PROV	CHARACTER(40) VARYING	Customer's city and province
WEEKS	CHARACTER(10) VARYING	Weeks until salesman's visit
LAST_NAME	CHARACTER(20) VARYING	Customer's last name
PROVINCE	CHARACTER(20) VARYING	Customer's province
RESULT	CHARACTER(40) VARYING	String to replace keyword
VALUE	FIXED	Number of spaces line is to be indented

```
/* PROGRAM TO JUSTIFY NARRATIVE TEXT */

STMT LEVEL NEST BLOCK MLVL  SOURCE TEXT


                                     /* PROGRAM TO JUSTIFY NARRATIVE TEXT */
     1                               JUSTIFY: PROCEDURE OPTIONS(MAIN);

     2    1         1                DECLARE TEXT CHARACTER(256) VARYING, /* TEXT TO BE JUSTIFIED*/
                                       CARD CHARACTER(80) VARYING, /* INPUT TEXT */
                                       RMARGIN FIXED,        /* SPECIFIED RIGHT MARGIN */
                                       BLANKS FIXED,         /* NO. OF BLANKS TO BE INSERTED */
                                       BFIELD CHARACTER(20) VARYING,  /* BLANK STRING */
                                       I FIXED,              /* INDEX VARIABLE */
                                       J FIXED,              /* LOOP VARIABLE */
                                       LINE CHARACTER(100) VARYING, /* EDITED LINE OF TEXT */
                                       END_FLAG CHARACTER(3) VARYING; /* END OF DATA FLAG */

                                     /* INITIALIZE */
     3    1         1                TEXT = '';
     4    1         1                END_FLAG = 'OFF';
     5    1         1                ON ENDFILE(SYSIN) END_FLAG = 'ON';

                                     /* READ IN ENGLISH TEXT AND CHARACTERS PER LINE */
     7    2         2                GET LIST (RMARGIN);
     8    1         1                GET LIST (CARD);
     9    1         1                DO WHILE (END_FLAG = 'OFF');
    10    1    1    1                    TEXT = TEXT || CARD;
    11    1    1    1                    GET LIST (CARD);
    12    1    1    1                END;

                                     /* JUSTIFY TEXT */
    13    1         1                DO WHILE (LENGTH(TEXT) > RMARGIN);
    14    1    1    1                    IF SUBSTR(TEXT, RMARGIN, 1) ¬= ' ' &
                                          SUBSTR(TEXT, RMARGIN+1, 1) = ' '
    15    1    1    1                    THEN LINE = SUBSTR(TEXT, 1, RMARGIN);/* NO JUSTIFICATION */
                                                                             /* REQUIRED */
    16    1    1    1                    ELSE DO; /*BLANKS MUST BE INSERTED IN THE OUTPUT LINE */
                                             /* CHECK TO SEE IF POSITION RMARGIN CONTAINS A */
                                             /* NONBLANK CHARACTER */
    17    1    2    1                        I = RMARGIN - 1;
    18    1    2    1                        IF SUBSTR(TEXT, RMARGIN, 1) ¬= ' '
    19    1    2    1                        THEN DO;

    20    1    3    1                            DO WHILE (SUBSTR(TEXT, I, 1) ¬= ' ');
    21    1    4    1                                I = I - 1;
    22    1    4    1                            END;
    23    1    3    1                        END;

    24    1    2    1                        I = I - 1;

                                             /* ESTABLISH A LOOP FOR INSERTING BLANKS */
    25    1    2    1                        BLANKS = RMARGIN - I;
    26    1    2    1                        BFIELD = ' ';
    27    1    2    1                        DO J = 1 TO BLANKS;
                                             /* SUCCESSIVELY ADD BLANKS TO THE BLANK FIELDS */
                                             /* SEPARATING WORDS */
    28    1    3    1                            DO WHILE (INDEX(SUBSTR(TEXT, I, LENGTH(BFIELD)),
                                                   BFIELD) = 0);
    29    1    4    1                                I = I - 1;
    30    1    4    1                                IF I = 0
    31    1    4    1                                THEN DO;
    32    1    5    1                                    I = RMARGIN - BLANKS + J - 1;
    33    1    5    1                                    BFIELD = BFIELD || ' ';
    34    1    5    1                                    END;
    35    1    4    1                            END;

    36    1    3    1                            TEXT = SUBSTR(TEXT, 1, I) || ' '
                                                   || SUBSTR(TEXT, I + 1);
    37    1    3    1                            I = I - 1;
    38    1    3    1                        END;
    39    1    2    1                        LINE = SUBSTR(TEXT, 1, RMARGIN);
    40    1    2    1                    END;

                                     /* OUTPUT JUSTIFIED LINE */
    41    1    1    1                    PUT SKIP EDIT (LINE) (X(5), A);
    42    1    1    1                    TEXT = SUBSTR(TEXT, RMARGIN + 1);
    43    1    1    1                    IF SUBSTR(TEXT, 1, 1) = ' '
    44    1    1    1                    THEN TEXT = SUBSTR(TEXT, 2);
    45    1    1    1                END;
```

Fig. 5-3   Program to justify text

```
                                      /* OUTPUT LAST LINE */
    46    1         1            PUT SKIP EDIT (TEXT) (X(5), A);
    47    1         1        END JUSTIFY;
ERRORS/WARNINGS DETECTED DURING CODE GENERATION:

     WARNING: NO FILE SPECIFIED. SYSIN/SYSPRINT ASSUMED. (CGOC)

     INTERACTIONS INVOLVING HUMANS ARE MOST EFFECTIVELY
     CARRIED OUT THROUGH THE MEDIUM OF  LANGUAGE.
     LANGUAGE PERMITS THE EXPRESSION OF  THOUGHTS  AND
     IDEAS, AND WITHOUT IT, COMMUNICATION, AS  WE  KNOW
     IT, WOULD BE VERY DIFFICULT INDEED.


IN STMT   47 PROGRAM RETURNS FROM MAIN PROCEDURE.
```

Fig. 5-3   Program to justify text (cont'd.)

NUMBER	CHARACTER(2) VARYING	String containing line indent
BLANKS	CHARACTER(80) VARYING	String of 80 blanks
LINE	CHARACTER(80) VARYING	Input line of letter
KEY	CHARACTER(10) VARYING	Keyword in form letter
CHAR	CHARACTER(1)	Character in NUMBER string
END_FLAG	CHARACTER(3) VARYING	End of data flag

The following data were used in this run.

```
'#40 187 MAIN STREET'
'#40 WINNIPEG 1, MANITOBA'
'#40 *DATE*'
'*X*'
'*ADDRESS*'
'*CITY*, *PROVINCE*'

'DEAR *Z*'
    THE BUSINESS WORLD IS RAPIDLY CHANGING AND OUR CORPORATION'
'HAS BEEN KEEPING PACE WITH THE NEW REQUIREMENTS FORCED UPON OFFICE'
'MACHINERY, WE ARE GIVING, YOU *Z*, AS A KEY FIGURE IN THE *CITY*'
'BUSINESS COMMUNITY, AN OPPORTUNITY TO BECOME FAMILIAR WITH THE'
'LATEST ADVANCEMENTS IN OUR EQUIPMENT. A REPRESENTATIVE OF OUR'
'CORPORATION IN *PROVINCE* WILL BE SEEING YOU IN *N* WEEKS. HE WILL'
'TAKE SEVERAL MACHINES TO *CITY* WHICH ARE INDICATIVE OF A WHOLE NEW'
'LINE OF OFFICE MACHINES WE HAVE RECENTLY DEVELOPED.'
    OUR SALES REPRESENTATIVE IS LOOKING FORWARD TO HIS VISIT IN *CITY*'
'HE KNOWS THAT THE MACHINES HE SELLS COULD BECOME AN INTEGRAL PART'
'OF YOUR OFFICE ONLY A FEW DAYS AFTER IMPLEMENTATION.'

'*#40 SINCERELY,'
'#40 ROGER SMITH, MANAGER'
'#40 OFFICE DEVICES CORPORATION'
'**'
```

```
/*  PROGRAM TO GENERATE PERSONALIZED FORM LETTERS */

STMT LEVEL NEST BLOCK MLVL  SOURCE TEXT

                                    /*  PROGRAM TO GENERATE PERSONALIZED FORM LETTERS */
    1                               FORM: PROCEDURE OPTIONS(MAIN);
    2    1              1           DECLARE LETTER(50) CHARACTER(100) VARYING, /* FORM LETTER */
                                        NUM_LINES FIXED,      /* NO. OF LINES IN FORM LETTER */
                                        DATE CHARACTER(30) VARYING,
                                        NAME CHARACTER(30) VARYING, /* CUSTOMER'S NAME */
                                        ADDRESS CHARACTER(40) VARYING, /* CUSTOMER'S ADDRESS */
                                        CITY_PROV CHARACTER(40) VARYING,
                                        WEEKS CHARACTER(10) VARYING, /*WEEKS UNTIL VISIT */
                                        LAST_NAME CHARACTER (20) VARYING, /* CUSTOMER'S LAST */
                                                                  /* NAME */
                                        PROVINCE CHARACTER(20) VARYING, /* CUSTOMER'S PROVINCE */
                                        CITY CHARACTER(20) VARYING, /* CUSTOMER'S CITY */
                                        (I, J, K, CC) FIXED,
                                        RESULT CHARACTER(40) VARYING, /* KEYWORD REPLACEMENT */
                                        VALUE FIXED,          /* NO OF SPACES TO BE INDENTED */
                                        NUMBER CHARACTER(2) VARYING, /* STRING CONTAINING */
                                                                  /* INDENT */
                                        BLANKS CHARACTER(80), /* A STRING OF 80 BLANKS */
                                        LINE CHARACTER(80) VARYING, /* INPUT LINE  OF LETTER */
                                        KEY CHARACTER(10) VARYING, /* KEYWORD IN FORM LETTER */
                                        CHAR CHARACTER(1),    /*CHARACTER IN NUMBER */
                                        END_FLAG CHARACTER(3) VARYING; /* END OF DATA FLAG */

                                    /* INITIALIZE */
    3    1              1           END_FLAG = 'OFF';
    4    1              1           ON ENDFILE(SYSIN) END_FLAG = 'ON';

                                    /* INPUT  FORM LETTER */
    6    2              2           GET LIST (LINE);
    7    1              1           NUM_LINES = 0;
    8    1              1           DO WHILE(SUBSTR(LINE, 1, 2) ¬= '**');
    9    1    1         1               NUM_LINES = NUM_LINES + 1;
   10    1    1         1               LETTER(NUM_LINES) = LINE;
   11    1    1         1               GET LIST (LINE);
   12    1    1         1           END;
```

Fig. 5-4   Program to generate a personalized form letter

*JANUARY 1, 1978'
'MR. R.B. BROWN'
'1712 ELK DRIVE'
'JASPER ALBERTA'
'FOUR'
'JANUARY 10, 1978'
'MRS. C.T. ALLAN'
'336 RIVER ST.'
'REGINA, SASKATCHEWAN'
'SEVEN'

Statement 8 of the program begins a loop to read the lines of the form letter. In statement 14 a loop to produce the personalized form letters for each of the customers is begun. The information concerning the recipient is read in and then split into the components that are to used in the personalized letter. Each line of the form letter is then scanned and the keywords are replaced by the appropriate customer information. After this is done, the line is indented (if necessary). The line of the form letter is then printed.

This concludes our discussion of string applications. In this chapter, the concepts of string manipulation and operations on strings have been discussed. In Sec. 5-2 basic string functions were introduced. The next section presented several

```
                                /* ENGAGE THE LOOP TO WRITE PERSONALIZED LETTERS */
  13     1          1           BLANKS = '                                                    ' ||
                                '                                '; /* A STRING OF  80 BLANKS */
  14     1          1           DO WHILE (END_FLAG = 'OFF');
  15     1     1    1               GET LIST (DATE, NAME, ADDRESS, CITY_PROV, WEEKS);
  16     1     1    1               IF END_FLAG = 'ON'
  17     1     1    1               THEN EXIT;

                                    /* SPLIT UP THE PERSONALIZED DATA FOR ONE CUSTOMER */
  18     1     1    1               I = INDEX(NAME, ' ');
  19     1     1    1               J = INDEX(SUBSTR(NAME, I + 1), ' ');
  20     1     1    1               LAST_NAME = SUBSTR(NAME, 1, I-1) || ' ' ||
                                       SUBSTR(NAME, I + J + 1);
  21     1     1    1               I = INDEX(CITY_PROV, ',');
  22     1     1    1               PROVINCE = SUBSTR(CITY_PROV, I + 2);
  23     1     1    1               CITY = SUBSTR(CITY_PROV, 1, I-1);

                                    /* GENERATE A PERSONALIZED LETTER FOR CURRENT CUSTOMER */
  24     1     1    1               DO CC = 1 TO NUM_LINES;

                                        /* GET THE NEXT LINE OF THE FORM LETTER */
  25     1     2    1                   LINE = LETTER(CC);

                                        /* PERFORM ALL KEYWORDS SUBSTITUTIONS */
  26     1     2    1                   I = 0;
  27     1     2    1                   J = 0;
  28     1     2    1                   K = INDEX(LINE, '*');
  29     1     2    1                   DO WHILE (K ¬= 0);
  30     1     3    1                       I = K + J + I;
  31     1     3    1                       J = INDEX(SUBSTR(LINE, I+1), '*');
  32     1     3    1                       KEY = SUBSTR(LINE, I, J+1);
  33     1     3    1                       IF KEY = '*DATE*'
  34     1     3    1                       THEN RESULT = DATE;
  35     1     3    1                       ELSE IF KEY = '*ADDRESS*'
  36     1     3    1                           THEN RESULT = ADDRESS;
  37     1     3    1                           ELSE IF KEY = '*CITY*'
  38     1     3    1                               THEN RESULT = CITY;
  39     1     3    1                               ELSE IF KEY = '*PROVINCE*'
  40     1     3    1                                   THEN RESULT = PROVINCE;
  41     1     3    1                                   ELSE IF KEY = '*N*'
  42     1     3    1                                       THEN RESULT = WEEKS;
  43     1     3    1                                       ELSE IF KEY = '*X*'
  44     1     3    1                                           THEN RESULT = NAME;
  45     1     3    1                                           ELSE IF KEY = '*Z*'
  46     1     3    1                                               THEN RESULT = LAST_NAME;
  47     1     3    1                       LINE  = SUBSTR(LINE, 1, I-1) || RESULT ||
                                               SUBSTR(LINE, I + J + 1);
  48     1     3    1                       J = LENGTH(RESULT);
  49     1     3    1                       IF LENGTH(LINE) < I + J + 1
  50     1     3    1                       THEN K = 0;
  51     1     3    1                       ELSE K = INDEX(SUBSTR(LINE, I+ J + 1), '*');
  52     1     3    1                   END;
                                        /* PERFORM INDENTATION, IF REQUIRED */
  53     1     2    1                   IF SUBSTR(LINE, 1, 1) = '#'
  54     1     2    1                   THEN DO;
  55     1     3    1                       I = INDEX(LINE, ' ');
  56     1     3    1                       VALUE = 0;
  57     1     3    1                       NUMBER = SUBSTR(LINE, 2, I - 2);
  58     1     3    1                       IF LENGTH(NUMBER) = 2
  59     1     3    1                       THEN DO;
  60     1     4    1                           CHAR = SUBSTR(NUMBER, 1, 1);
  61     1     4    1                           VALUE = (INDEX('0123456789', CHAR) - 1) * 10;
  62     1     4    1                           NUMBER = SUBSTR(NUMBER, 2);
  63     1     4    1                           END;
  64     1     3    1                       VALUE = VALUE + INDEX('0123456789', NUMBER) -1;
  65     1     3    1                       LINE = SUBSTR( BLANKS, 1, VALUE) ||
                                               SUBSTR(LINE, I+1);
  66     1     3    1                       END;

                                        /* OUTPUT NEXT LINE OF PERSONALIZED LETTER */
  67     1     2    1                   PUT SKIP EDIT (LINE) (X(5), A);
  68     1     2    1                   END;
  69     1     1    1               PUT SKIP(3);
  70     1     1    1           END;
  71     1          1           END FORM;
ERRORS/WARNINGS DETECTED DURING CODE GENERATION:
        WARNING: NO FILE SPECIFIED. SYSIN/SYSPRINT ASSUMED. (CGOC)
```

Fig. 5-4   Program to generate a personalized form letter (cont'd.)

```
                                            187 MAIN STREET
                                            WINNIPEG 1, MANITOBA
                                            JANUARY 1, 1978

        MR. R.B. BROWN
        1712 ELK DRIVE
        JASPER, ALBERTA

        DEAR MR. BROWN
             THE BUSINESS WORLD IS RAPIDLY CHANGING AND OUR CORPORATION
        HAS BEEN KEEPING PACE WITH THE NEW REQUIREMENTS FORCED UPON OFFICE
        MACHINERY. WE ARE GIVING, YOU, MR. BROWN, AS A KEY FIGURE IN THE JASPER
        BUSINESS COMMUNITY, AN OPPORTUNITY TO BECOME FAMILIAR WITH THE
        LATEST ADVANCEMENTS IN OUR EQUIPMENT. A REPRESENTATIVE OF OUR
        CORPORATION IN ALBERTA WILL BE SEEING YOU IN FOUR WEEKS.  HE WILL
        TAKE SEVERAL MACHINES TO JASPER WHICH ARE INDICATIVE OF A WHOLE NEW
        LINE OF OFFICE MACHINES WE HAVE RECENTLY DEVELOPED.
             OUR SALES REPRESENTATIVE IS LOOKING FORWARD TO HIS VISIT IN JASPER.
        HE KNOWS THAT THE MACHINES HE SELLS COULD BECOME AN INTEGRAL PART
        OF YOUR OFFICE ONLY A FEW DAYS AFTER IMPLEMENTATION.

                                            SINCERELY,

                                            ROGER SMITH, MANAGER
                                            OFFICE DEVICES CORPORATION




                                            187 MAIN STREET
                                            WINNIPEG 1, MANITOBA
                                            JANUARY 10, 1978

        MRS. C.T. ALLAN
        336 RIVER ST.
        REGINA, SASKATCHEWAN

        DEAR MRS. ALLAN
             THE BUSINESS WORLD IS RAPIDLY CHANGING AND OUR CORPORATION
        HAS BEEN KEEPING PACE WITH THE NEW REQUIREMENTS FORCED UPON OFFICE
        MACHINERY. WE ARE GIVING, YOU, MRS. ALLAN, AS A KEY FIGURE IN THE REGINA
        BUSINESS COMMUNITY, AN OPPORTUNITY TO BECOME FAMILIAR WITH THE
        LATEST ADVANCEMENTS IN OUR EQUIPMENT. A REPRESENTATIVE OF OUR
        CORPORATION IN SASKATCHEWAN WILL BE SEEING YOU IN SEVEN WEEKS.  HE WILL
        TAKE SEVERAL MACHINES TO REGINA WHICH ARE INDICATIVE OF A WHOLE NEW
        LINE OF OFFICE MACHINES WE HAVE RECENTLY DEVELOPED.
             OUR SALES REPRESENTATIVE IS LOOKING FORWARD TO HIS VISIT IN REGINA.
        HE KNOWS THAT THE MACHINES HE SELLS COULD BECOME AN INTEGRAL PART
        OF YOUR OFFICE ONLY A FEW DAYS AFTER IMPLEMENTATION.

                                            SINCERELY,

                                            ROGER SMITH, MANAGER
                                            OFFICE DEVICES CORPORATION




        IN STMT   17  PROGRAM IS STOPPED.
```

Fig. 5-4   Program to generate a personalized form letter (cont'd.)

concepts in edited input and output. Finally in Sec. 5-4, the ideas presented in the chapter were illustrated in the solution of the application problems given in Chap. 5 of the main text.

In the next chapter the use of subprocedures or subprograms and functions is introduced.

EXERCISES FOR CHAPTER 5

1. Many programming languages, such as PL/I, permit the programmer to use blanks anywhere within certain parts of each statement of a program. The compiler of such a program would probably remove all the unnecessary blanks. Usually in these languages, there is a label field associated with each statement that is processed in a different manner. In the case of PL/I, the label is ended with a colon. Furthermore, the remaining part of the statement must lie within a fixed field, such as characters 2 through 72 in PL/I.
    Write a program that will

    (i) Read in a text of 80 characters.
    (ii) Delete the last eight of them.
    (iii) Delete any leading or following blanks from the label (if a label exists).
    (iv) Remove all blanks from the PL/I statement.
    (v) Print the modified text.

2. Write a program for converting Roman numerals to Arabic numerals. The input consists of a sequence of Roman numerals. For each of these Roman numerals, the corresponding Arabic numeral is to be generated. Table 5-1 gives the correspondence between the two number systems.

3. The usual way of writing a cheque requires five fields to be filled in, namely, the date, the person being paid, the amount as a number, the amount in words and the signature of the issuer. The amount is written twice for consistency and protection. Computer generated cheques sometimes do not generate the amount in words, since it is believed by some that a machine-printed amount is more difficult to change than its hand-written counterpart. Many companies have learned, however, that such is not the case and, consequently, these companies do print on each check the amount in words. Formulate a program which, given an integer amount, will print the amount in words. The integer amount lies in the range 100 through 99999 in pennies. Table 5-2 contains examples of numbers and their corresponding outputs.

Table 5-1

Roman symbol	Arabic equivalent
I	1
V	5
X	10
L	50
C	100
D	500
M	1000

Table 5-2

Input (in pennies)	Amount (in figures)	Amount in words
17573	$175.73	ONE HUNDRED SEVENTY-FIVE AND 73/100
2900	$ 29.00	TWENTY-NINE AND 00/100
48050	$480.50	FOUR HUNDRED EIGHTY AND 50/100
1362	$ 13.62	THIRTEEN AND 62/100

4. A coded message is received on punched cards in groups of five letters separated by a blank. The last groups of letters is followed by five 9's. The initial step in the decoding process is to replace each letter by another, according to a table which changes each day. This table precedes the coded message information and occupies one card.
For example, the string

ABCDEFGHIJKLMNOPQRSTUVWXYZ
'DEFGHIJKLMNOPQRSTUVWXYZABC'

represents a coding table in which D replaces A, E replaced B, F replaces C, . . . , B replaces Y, and C replaces Z. Using this code, the encoded message

WKHZRbUOGLYbFRPLQbJWRDKbHKGCCb99999

with 'b' interpreted as a blank, will be encoded as

THEWORLDISCOMINGTOANENDZZ

Formulate a program which inputs the given data and decodes the message.

CHAPTER

6

SUBPROGRAMS: FUNCTIONS AND PROCEDURES

Chapter 6 of the main text deals with the notion of the subalgorithm. Any large problem is more easily solved if first it is broken into a number of smaller subproblems. The notion of "subprograms" is important in the programming process.

PL/I supports the two forms of subprogram described in the main text — the function and the procedure. The use of functions and procedures in PL/I is the topic of this chapter.

6-1   FUNCTIONS IN PL/I

A PL/I function is a group of statements within a program which form a somewhat independent and separate block or component. This block of statements constitutes a subprogram which performs a particular set of operations on a supplied set of arguments and returns a single value. Each time the function is invoked, control transfers to the block of statements defined for that function. After these statements have been performed, execution returns to the statement from which the function was called or *invoked*. A similar type of subprogram block, the *procedure*, is discussed in the next section.

The block of statements belonging to a function is written as a *function definition* in PL/I and is usually included within the main program. A transfer of execution from outside the program statements to the function is caused by a function *invocation*, written in the form:

> *entry-name (argument1, argument2, ...)*

where *entry-name* is the name of the function being called. The arguments to be used by the function are listed in parentheses following the name of the function. Each argument may be any valid variable, constant, or expression.

In addition to the code comprising the statements to be executed, the definition of a function also includes the definition of its parameters. The general form of a function definition is as follows:

> *entry-name:*PROCEDURE(*parameter1, parameter2, ...*)RETURNS(*attributes*);
>   *parameter declarations*
>   *local variable declarations*
>   *function body*
> END *entry-name;*

The first statement is called the definition "head". Notice that even though a function is being defined, PL/I uses the keyword PROCEDURE to begin the definition. The *entry-name* portion of the head (also used in the closing END statement) is the name by which the particular function is known. This name must be a valid PL/I identifier, containing at most seven characters. Although the entry-name following the END keyword may be omitted, it is advisable to include it. The

> *(parameter1, parameter2, ...)*

portion of the head statement constitutes the *parameter list* for the function. It lists the parameters, each of which must be a valid PL/I variable name. The order of the list defines the order of correspondence with the arguments in the argument list of the invocation. That is, the first parameter in the parameter list will always correspond to the first argument in the argument list, the second parameter to the second argument, and so on. Therefore, the number of arguments in the invocation and parameters in the definition head must always be equal. If a particular function requires no parameters to be passed, then the list of arguments and the corresponding list of parameters are omitted, giving an invocation of the form:

entry-name

and a definition head of the form:

*entry-name:*PROCEDURE RETURNS(*attributes*);

The particular methods used by PL/I in allowing a parameter to be given the value of its corresponding argument are discussed in Sec. 6-3.

The RETURNS (*attributes*) clause of the head serves to indicate the type attributes of the value which the function returns. In PL/C, only numeric, character, and logical values are allowed to be returned by functions. Thus, the only type attributes permissible in the RETURNS clause attribute list are those pertaining to these data types. An example of a valid function definition head follows:

MAXIMUM: PROCEDURE (NUM1, NUM2, NUM3) RETURNS (FIXED);

The function name in this example is MAXIMUM, which uniquely identifies the particular function. Three parameters, NUM1, NUM2, and NUM3, are used by the function, and thus any invocation of MAXIMUM must supply three arguments. The value returned by the function is numeric, with attribute FIXED.

The definition head must be followed by the *parameter declarations*. These consist of valid type declarations for the function parameters, and should, for each parameter, define attributes which agree with those of the corresponding argument. In PL/C, if the attributes of the two differ even slightly, a different method of "passing" the argument value to the parameter is used (see Sec. 6-3). Parameter declarations differ in one respect from variable declarations. PL/C requires that for a character or bit string parameter, the length of the string must be given as the asterisk *, not as a value. Thus, the character attribute is written CHARACTER (*) or CHARACTER(*) VARYING. Furthermore, an argument passed may be an entire array, with just the array name given in the argument list, in which case the parameter receiving the array must have, in its declaration, the bounds of the dimensions replaced by asterisks, one for each dimension. Thus, for an array parameter MATRIX, with two dimensions and entries of type FLOAT, the declaration in the function definition is written:

DECLARE MATRIX(*, *) FLOAT;

The particular bounds on each dimension and, for a character or bit string parameter, the length or maximum length of the string will be the same as that of the corresponding argument in a given invocation.

Suppose that a function MAXIMUM with the definition head given earlier is, when invoked, to be supplied with three arguments of type FIXED. The parameter declarations required in the function defintion would then be written as follows:

DECLARE (NUM1, NUM2, NUM3) FIXED;

Parameter declarations must be followed by the declarations of the *local* variables; that is, the variables which are not parameters, but which are defined and used within the function. These cannot be used outside the function itself. All these declarations follow the same form as that for any variable declarations, as discussed in Chap. 2.

The actual statements of the function (i.e., the function body) appear next in the definition, and are composed of any valid PL/I statements. The programmer must, for one of these statements, specify the value to be returned by the function through a RETURN statement of the following form:

RETURN (*value*);

where *value* is any valid expression producing a single value. This value must have the same type attributes as indicated in the RETURNS clause of the head statement, or at least attributes which may be converted to those of the RETURNS clause. Note that an array may not be returned, since it contains more than one value. The RETURN statement causes the evaluation of the expression inside the parentheses. Execution of the function is then terminated and control is passed back to the point in the outside program from which the function was invoked. The value obtained in the RETURN statement is returned to the invocation point as the value of the function. Notice that the RETURN statement may be physically located at any point in the definition body.

The final statement of the function definition must always be an

END *entry-name*;

statement. It serves to indicate the *physical* termination of the statements belonging to the function (as distinct from the *logical* termination point marked by the RETURN statement). The label on the END statement provides a convenient reminder of this fact.

For example, suppose the complete definition of the function named MAXIMUM is as follows:

```
MAXIMUM: PROCEDURE(NUM1, NUM2, NUM3) RETURNS(FIXED);
      /* FIND THE MAXIMUM OF 3 NUMBERS */
      DECLARE (NUM1, NUM2, NUM3) FIXED;
      DECLARE MAX FIXED;
      IF NUM1 > NUM2
      THEN MAX = NUM1;
      ELSE MAX = NUM2;
      IF NUM3 > MAX
      THEN MAX = NUM3;
      RETURN (MAX);
END MAXIMUM;
```

An invocation of this function must supply three values as arguments; these are represented in the function by parameters NUM1, NUM2, and NUM3. The function compares these values, which are fixed-point numbers, and returns the largest of the three as the value of MAXIMUM. A local variable MAX is used, and, after the comparisons are completed, it holds the value of the largest number. Suppose the following invocation appears in a program which contains this function definition:

VALU = MAXIMUM (A, B, C);

where variables VALUE, A, B, and C have previously been declared as having type FIXED, and A, B, and C currently possess the values 37, 25, and 89, respectively. Execution of this statement causes control to jump to the function definition statements, where the argument values are passed to the parameters. The statements of the function are performed, leaving the value 89 in the local variable MAX. When the RETURN (MAX) statement is reached, execution of the function terminates, and control returns to the invocation point in the calling program. The value 89 is returned as the resulting value of MAXIMUM, and thus the variable VALU receives, through the assignment, the value 89. At this point the local variable MAX has ceased to exist.

Consider the result if the attributes in the RETURNS clause of the definition head were changed from FIXED to FLOAT, and also the variable VALU was declared to be FLOAT. Execution of the function statements would produce the value 89 for MAX, as before, and terminate with the RETURN statement. Before the value 89 may be returned to the point of invocation, however, the compiler compares the attributes of that value, and those indicated in the RETURNS clause. Since they are not the same, an automatic conversion of the 89 to the equivalent value 8.90000E 01 occurs, and the *converted* value is then returned as the value of the function. Thus, the value assigned to the variable VALU is 8.90000E01.

Function definitions, as discussed thus far, may be embedded inside a main program, and called from an invocation in the program. In PL/I this type of function is termed as *internal* function, since its definition is written within the bounds of the main program. For example, in the following program skeleton:

```
HELLO: PROCEDURE OPTIONS(MAIN);
       program statements
       AVERAGE: PROCEDURE (FIRST, SECOND) RETURNS (CHARACTER(8));
            function statements
       END AVERAGE;
       program statements
END HELLO;
```

the function named AVERAGE is internal to the main program, and may be invoked by a function call anywhere in the section marked *program statements*. If a function definition is not included in the main program, then it is said to be an *external* function. Further discussion of internal and external functions is found in Sec. 6-4.

Under certain conditions in PL/I, the main program requires that the function name be declared in an *entry-name declaration*. This serves to provide the main program with information concerning the function. The usual form of this declaration statement is

DECLARE *entry-name* ENTRY (*attribute1, attribute2, ...*) RETURNS (*attributes*);

where the RETURNS clause specifies the same attributes as those of the definition head. The *entry-name* entry gives the particular name of the function being declared. Following the name is the keyword ENTRY, and a parenthesized list of attribute entries, where the *i*th *attributes* entry indicates the type attributes of the ith parameter in the definition head parameter list. As in the parameter declarations in the function definition, character and bit strings lengths, and array bounds, are replaced by asterisk symbols. If the function being declared has no parameters and thus requires no arguments to be passed, the ENTRY(...) clause can always be omitted. In other cases, however, a problem may arise if the attributes of one of the arguments in an invocation disagree even slightly with those of the corresponding parameter. In this situation, PL/C causes a change in the method of passing the argument value to the parameter, and a warning message about the value conversion is printed. The warning message is usually not serious, however, and can almost always be ignored. In any event, the inclusion of an entry-name declaration, with the ENTRY clause attributes provided, suppresses the warning message.

The following program outline further illustrates the use of programmer-defined functions:

```
LIST: PROCEDURE OPTIONS(MAIN);
   DECLARE NAMES(50) CHARACTER(20),
     (CTR, A_B_NUM) FIXED,
     COUNT ENTRY ((*) CHAR(*)) RETURNS (FIXED);
   GET LIST ((NAMES (CTR) DO CTR = 1 TO 50));
     .
     .
     .
   A_B_NUM = COUNT (NAMES);
   PUT LIST (A_B_NUM, 'OF THE FOLLOWING NAMES BEGIN WITH LETTER A OR B');
   PUT LIST ((NAMES(CTR) DO CTR = 1 TO 50));
     .
     .
     .
   COUNT: PROCEDURE (ARR) RETURNS (FIXED);
     DECLARE ARR(*) CHARACTER (*);
     DECLARE (TALLY, J) FIXED;
     TALLY = 0;
     DO J = 1 TO 50;
       IF SUBSTR(ARR(J), 1, 1) = 'A' | SUBSTR(ARR(J), 1, 1) = 'B'
       THEN TALLY = TALLY + 1;
     END;
     RETURN (TALLY);
   END COUNT;
     .
     .
     .
END LIST;
```

The main program begins execution by reading a list of 50 names into the array NAMES. After some intervening statements, an invocation of the function COUNT is encountered, in the assignment A_B_NUM = COUNT (NAMES);. At this point, execution is transferred to the function COUNT. Note that the function name is declared in an entry-name declaration in the main program. The entire array NAMES is the only argument passed, and is represented in the function statements by the parameter ARR. The RETURNS clauses indicate that the value to be returned by the function is type FIXED. After the parameter ARR is declared, two local variables, TALLY and J, are also declared. Execution of the counted loop then occurs. This serves to count the number of names in the array which begin with the letter A or the letter B. This number is held in the variable TALLY. After termination of the loop, the RETURN statement is performed, causing the termination of the function and the transfer of control back to the invocation point in the assignment statement, where the value of TALLY is returned as the value of COUNT. The assignment to the variable A_B_NUM can now be completed, giving it the returned value. Execution of the main program statements now continues, in normal sequence, until the COUNT function definition statements are reached. Since function statements can only be "invoked," a jump around the definition occurs, with the next statement to be executed being the one immediately following the END COUNT;. Execution continues until the END LIST; statement is reached.

The ability to define functions and to call them from any point in a program is a powerful programming tool. First of all, it allows the programmer to defer writing certain program portions until later, while still being able to write the main part of the program. For example, in the previous outline example, the main program statements could have been written without also having to worry, at that time, about writing the statements for counting the names beginning with the letter A or the letter B. The programmer need only remember that, later, he or she will have to compose a function named COUNT to do this operation and then to include it inside the main program before it is run. This permits the programmer to concentrate on one task at a time, and thus one cause of error is eliminated. Second, if a particular operation or set of operations is required at several different points in a program, the programmer is spared having to write out the statements to perform the task each time. Instead, the operation statements may be written once, in the form of a single function to be included with the program, and an invocation to the function written at each point where the operation is required.

We turn now to a second type of subprogram available in PL/I, which provides the same programming enhancements in a slightly different way.

Exercises for Sec. 6-1

1. Design a function that takes a parameter x and returns the following value:

$$\frac{1}{x^5 \left(e^{\frac{1.432}{x}} - 1 \right)}$$

2. (i) In Chap. 2, built-in functions TRUNC and ROUND were introduced. Although convenient for programming, ROUND is actually redundant. Design a function to perform the action of ROUND using TRUNC.

   (ii) The function FLOOR(x) is defined as the largest integer value not exceeding x. This is not quite the same as the TRUNC function. For example, FLOOR (4.72) is 4, but FLOOR(-16.8) is -17. Use the built-in functions listed in Chap. 2 to design a function to compute FLOOR(x).

   (iii) The function MOD(x, y) is defined as the remainder that results from the division of x by y (x and y are both integers, as is the remainder). For example, MOD(8, 3) is 2. Formulate a function to compute

MOD(x, y).

3. Design functions MEANS and STD to compute the mean and standard deviation, respectively, of the N elements of a vector X, according to the following formulas:

$$MEAN \ (X) = \frac{1}{N} \sum_{i=1}^{N} x_i$$

$$STD \ (X) = \frac{1}{N} \sum_{i=1}^{N} (x_i - MEAN(x))^2$$

N is never greater than 25.

4. Design a string-valued function that takes as a parameter a card image (as a string) on which there appears some text. The purpose of the function is to remove all blanks from the text and return the string that results.

5. An expression involving a variable X such as

$$A(1)*X^1 + A(2)*X^2 + A(3)*X^3 + CONSTANT$$

can be evaluated for many values of X. For example, if

$$A(1) = 3, \ A(2) = 1, \ A(3) = 0.5 \text{ and } CONSTANT = 5.2,$$

then the value of the expression for X = 2 is

$$(3)*(2) + 1*(2)^2 + 0.5*(2)^3 + 5.2 = 19.2$$

Desired is a function that would calculate

$$A(1)*X^1 + A(2)*X^2 + A(3)*X^3 + ... + A(N)*X^N + CONSTANT$$

given the value of N, a particular set of coefficients (a vector A, never greater than 20), a CONSTANT and the value of X. Design a function EVAL that will accept the value of N, the CONSTANT, the coefficients (vector A) and a value for X. It will then evaluate the given expression for the value of X and return the resulting value to the point of call.

6-2 PROCEDURES IN PL/I

As we saw in the previous section, a function is a block of statements, which, when invoked, performs the specified operations, and returns a single value.

A procedure in PL/I is a block of statements similar to a function, but with two important differences. First, it is invoked in a different manner, using a CALL statement, as follows

CALL *entry-name (argument1, argument2, ...)*;

where *entry-name* is the name given to the procedure block. The list of arguments following it is identical to the argument list in a function invocation, serving to pass values to the corresponding procedure parameters. The execution of a CALL statement causes immediate transfer of control to the statements of the procedure's definiton (to be discussed later), and the establishment of the correspondence between arguments and parameters. After execution of the procedure statements, control is returned to the statement which immediately follows the CALL statement which invoked the procedure.

The second important difference is that no single value is returned by a procedure to the point of invocation. Instead, any number of values can be passed back to the main program through the parameters. Thus, the particular method used to set up the correspondence between arguments and parameters must allow "reverse" passing of values (that is, from parameters to arguments) as well as the usual passing of values from arguments to parameters (see Sec. 6-3).

To illustrate the use of "two-way" value passing between argument and parameter in a procedure, suppose a procedure named SORT has been defined, which sorts a given array. We wish to invoke it in the main program, to sort an array named NAMES, having N elements. A valid invocation would be:

CALL SORT (NAMES. N):

where the two arguments are the array itself, and the variable N, whose value is the number of elements in NAMES. The invocation transfers execution to the SORT definition statements, and passes the argument values to parameters of the procedure. After the sort operation has been performed on the parameter array the NAMES array in the main program should contain also the sorted array entries, (not the original, unsorted entries). In the next section we will examine methods of argument-parameter correspondence which result in this and other effects.

A procedure definition in PL/I is very similar to a function definition, but with a few differences. The definition head for a procedure does not contain a RETURNS clause, since no single value is returned as is the case for a definition head for a function. The parameters, listed in the definition head, are given the values of the corresponding arguments upon invocation of the procedure. Procedures which do not have any parameters may also be defined, with a definition head of the form:

entry-name: PROCEDURE;

and invocations of the form:

CALL *entry-name*;

The procedure parameters, listed in the parameter declarations, and local variable declarations are as before. The statements in the procedure perform the desired operations on the parameters, and usually pass values back to the main program through the parameters. Unlike functions, a RETURN (*value*) statement is not used in the procedure definition statements. Execution of a procedure is terminated by either reaching the END *entry-name* statement or by encountering a statement:

RETURN;

Several RETURN statements may appear in a definition, with the first execution of one causing termination. The following example is a procedure which when given two integer values returns the quotient and remainder produced by the division of the first integer by the second.

```
DIVIDE: PROCEDURE(DIVIDEND, DIVISOR, QUOTIENT, REMAINDER);
        DECLARE DIVIDEND FIXED,
                DIVISOR FIXED,
                QUOTIENT FIXED,
                REMAINDER FIXED;

        /*PERFORM INTEGER DIVISION*/
        QUOTIENT = DIVIDEND / DIVISOR;

        /*DETERMINE REMAINDER*/
        REMAINDER = DIVIDEND - QUOTIENT * DIVISOR;

        RETURN;
END DIVIDE;
```

As with functions in PL/I, an entry-name declaration for a procedure may be required in the main program if an invocation of the procedure appears with at least one of the arguments supplied having attributes differing from those of the corresponding parameter. The form of the entry-name declaration is the same as that for functions, except that no RETURNS clause is used.

Procedures may be defined inside or outside the main program body, yielding *internal* and *external* procedures, respectively. We will study added features of the use of internal procedures in Sec. 6-4.

Let us turn now to a more complete example of the use of a procedure. A program is required to input and sort a set of data cards concerning a store's employees. Each card contains two character strings — the name of an employee, and the employee's five-character identification code. The last card contains dummy data values of

'LAST_NAME' 'AOOOO'

The program must print two lists: first a sorted list of the employee names, and then a sorted list of the identification codes. A procedure SORT is used in the solution given in Fig. 6-1.

The main program begins by reading in the employee names and codes into separate vectors NAMES and CODES, counting them as they are read using the variable NUM. The first invocation of the procedure SORT is then encountered, with the NAMES array and the variable NUM as arguments. Control transfers immediately to the SORT procedure. The two parameters are LIST and COUNT, which receive the values of the NAMES array and NUM, respectively. Local variables and PASS are declared and created at the start of the procedure execution. A selection sort is then performed on the array parameter LIST. The COUNT parameter contains the value of NUM, and thus indicates the actual number of elements in the array being sorted. When the RETURN; statement is reached, the array is in sorted order. Execution of the procedure then terminates and control reverts to the main program statement following the first invocation, which turns out to be a second invocation with the argument NAMES now containing the array

```
EMP_EES: PROCEDURE OPTIONS (MAIN);
      DECLARE NAMES (50) CHARACTER (20) VARYING, /*EMPLOYEE NAMES LIST*/
            CODES (50) CHARACTER (5), /*IDENTIFICATION CODES LIST*/
            (NUM, K) FIXED;
      NUM = 1;
      GET LIST (NAMES(1), CODES(1));
      DO WHILE (NAMES(NUM ¬ = 'LAST_NAME');
            NUM = NUM + 1;
            GET LIST (NAMES(NUM), CODES(NUM));
      END;
      NUM = NUM - 1;

      /*SORT THE LIST OF EMPLOYEE NAMES INTO ASCENDING ORDER*/
      CALL SORT (NAMES, NUM);
      /*SORT THE LIST OF EMPLOYEE CODES INTO ASCENDING ORDER*/
      CALL SORT (CODES, NUM);

      /*PRINT OUT THE SORTED LISTS*/
      PUT LIST ('EMPLOYEE NAMES LIST:');
      PUT EDIT ((NAMES(K) DO K = 1 TO NUM)) ((NUM) (SKIP, COL(5), A));
      PUT SKIP(2) LIST ('EMPLOYEE CODES LIST:');
      PUT EDIT ((CODES(K) DO K = 1 TO NUM)) ((NUM) (SKIP, COL(5), A));

      SORT: PROCEDURE (LIST, COUNT);
      /*SORT THE GIVEN ARRAY INTO ASCENDING ORDER*/
            DECLARE LIST(*) CHARACTER(*) VARYING, /*ARRAY TO BE SORTED*/
                  COUNT FIXED; /*NUMBER OF ELEMENTS*/
            DECLARE TEMP CHARACTER (20) VARYING,
                  (MIN, POS, PASS) FIXED;

            DO PASS = 1 TO COUNT - 1;
                  MIN = PASS;
                  DO POS = PASS + 1 TO COUNT;
                        IF LIST(POS) < LIST(MIN) THEN MIN = POS;
                  END;

                  IF MIN ¬ = PASS
                  THEN DO;
                        TEMP = LIST(MIN);
                        LIST(MIN) = LIST(PASS);
                        LIST(PASS) = TEMP;
                        END;
            END;
            RETURN;
      END SORT;
      PUT EDIT('END OF PROGRAM')(SKIP, A);
END EMP_EES;
```

Fig. 6-1   Program EMP_PEES

in sorted order. On this second invocation, the first argument is the CODES array, and the second is again NUM (CODES also has NUM elements in it). Once again, control transfers to the SORT procedure, with the parameter LIST now corresponding to the CODES array. As a result, this execution of the SORT procedure causes the CODES array to be sorted. Termination of the second execution of SORT returns control to the statement following the second invocation, namely the first of the output statements. The two ordered lists are then printed. Since the procedure can be executed only by means of a call, control then skips around the SORT definition statements. The next statement performed is therefore the one following the END SORT; statement, which is the final output statement after which the program terminates. Notice that local variables TEMP, MIN, POS, and PASS are created and destroyed on two separate occasions, once for each execution of SORT. Note also the relationship between the parameter COUNT and the argument NUM to which it corresponds during both calls to the procedure. During procedure execution, if any change to its current value had occurred, the value of NUM would also be so altered, causing unexpected results on the second call of the procedure. Fortunately, however, the SORT operations never cause a change in the value given to COUNT.

We have seen, in this section, that a PL/I procedure is similar in many respects to a function. The major differences between the two forms of subprogram are the manner in which they are invoked, and the manner in which results are returned to the point of call. The programmer, in deciding what type to use in a particular program, must determine which is most suitable for the given application.

Exercises for Sec. 6-2

1. One of the earliest applications of computers was the calculation of shell trajectories. If a shell is fired with an initial velocity V (feet per second) at an angle of inclination B (radians), its position in the vertical x,y plane at time t (seconds) is calculated from the following:

    $$x = (V \cos\Theta) \, t$$
    $$y = (V \sin\Theta) \, t - \tfrac{1}{2}gt^2$$

    where $0 < \Theta < \pi/2$ and $g = 32$ feet per second^2.
    Design a procedure with parameters Θ and V that will list the x,y coordinates at intervals of 0.01 seconds for a particular firing, terminating the list when the shell hits the ground.

2. Design a procedure to center a title. The procedure takes as an input parameter a card image string, somewhere in which appears a title. The procedure is to produce a print line image string (of length 120) in which the input text (exluding leading and trailing blanks) is to be centered as nearly as possible within the string; that is, to within one blank, the number of blanks before the title is the same as the number after. This print line image is then to be returned to the point of call.

3. Design a procedure to accept as a parameter a vector which may contain

duplicate entries. The procedure is to replace each repeated value by –1 and return to the point of call the altered vector and the number of altered entries.

4. Design a procedure TRIM to accept as a parameter an arbitrary character string and return a string in which all the trailing blanks are removed. For example,

>Input   'JOHNbSTEEDbbb'
>Output   'JOHNbSTEED'

where 'b' represents a blank.

5. Design a procedure REVERSE to accept as a parameter an arbitrary character string and return a string of the same length in which the order of the characters is reversed. That is, the first character of the output string is the last character of the input string, and so on.

6-3 ARGUMENT-PARAMETER CORRESPONDENCE

An association or correspondence is formed between each argument and its parameter every time a procedure or function is invoked. Section 6-4 of the main text discusses two methods by which this correspondence can be achieved. These are known as call by value (or pass by value) and call as variable (or pass by reference). Both of these methods are available in PL/I.

Call by value simply involves assigning the value of the argument concerned, upon invocation of the procedure or function, to its parameter in the subprogram definition. The parameter is, in effect, a newly created independent variable, with its own memory location, that receives the value of the argument upon the start of the subprogram execution. Since the parameter and argument are independent variables, any change in the parameter that occurs during subprogram execution has no effect whatsoever on the value of the original argument. This means that when call by value is employed, the passing of values back to the point of invocation through the parameter is impossible. Call by value is, therefore, most useful for parameters where initial transmission of the argument value to the parameter is required upon invocation, to be followed by a severance of any further communication between argument and parameter. Upon termination of subprogram execution, the parameter variable is destroyed and the value(s) which it held lost. *Call by reference*, unlike call by value, does not involve creating a separate memory location for the parameter. Instead, invocation causes the passing of the *address* of the actual storage location where the value of the argument is held. The parameter, in effect, becomes merely another name for the same location already created for the argument value. This method of association implies, then, that each time the parameter name is encountered in the subprogram, the actual location which it references is precisely that of the argument. The effect of this is the passing of values in both directions between argument and parameter. That is, the parameter "receives" the current argument value at the time of invocation, and any subsequent assignment of new values to the parameter during subprogram execution causes that assignment to occur on the argument. Call by reference, then, is most useful for parameters where communication of value in both directions is required (for example, in Sec. 6-2, in the program EMP_EES, the array parameter LIST).

Both forms of correspondence apply to function calls as well as to procedure calls. A function, therefore, has the ability now to return values back to the main program in two ways — as the value of the function (as discussed in Sec. 6-1) and through parameters governed by call by reference parameter — argument correspondence. For procedures, as mentioned in Sec. 6-2, the latter method is available for the return of results.

How does the PL/I compiler decide which of the two types of correspondence to establish between a given argument-parameter pair? Also, how can the programmer ensure that the type which he or she desires for a given argument and parameter is actually used? The following rules summarize the actions taken by PL/I.

(1) If the given argument is a variable name and the type attributes of the argument match exactly those declared for the corresponding parameter, then call by reference is automatically used.

(2) If the given argument is a variable name and the type attributes of the argument differ even slightly from those of the parameter, then call by value is automatically used. The value of the argument at the time of invocation is assigned to the memory location created for the parameter, being converted first to the type of the parameter.

(3) If the given argument is a constant or an expression, then call by value is automatically used. The expression is evaluated, and assigned to the memory location created for the parameter. If the type attributes of the value obtained from the expression evaluation differ from those of the parameter, then type conversion of the value occurs before the assignment.

The following example illustrates these rules, and the effects of call by value and call by reference. Suppose a program is written which inputs a list of product codes, each being a string between one and six characters long. After some itnermediate processing, the program must sequence through the list of codes, counting the number of codes beginning with the character "0". As the search proceeds each character "0" beginning any code must be changed to the character '1'. A function BEGINS is used in the solution given in Fig. 6-2.

Notice in this example that the conditions required for call by reference are met for the argument CODES and parameter VALS in the function invocation, and thus, as desired, the VALS parameter is merely another name for the array stored in CODES. The function execution causes the required replacements to occur directly on the codes in the CODES array. The second argument in the invocation is an expression NBR − 1, meaning call by value is used. This implies the value obtained from evaluation of this simple expression is assigned to the location newly created in storage for parameter NUM. Upon completion of the function, the variable NUM, and its value, are destroyed.

Consider the effect if the declaration for the parameter VALS had been written instead as an array of nonvarying strings

DECLARE VALS (*) CHARACTER (*);

and the VARYING attribute excluded from those given for the first parameter in the

```
PRODUCT: PROCEDURE OPTIONS (MAIN);
        DECLARE CODES(30) CHARACTER (6) VARYING, /*PRODUCT CODES LIST*/
            REPLACE FIXED, /*NUMBER OF REPLACEMENTS*/
            NBR FIXED,
            END_IN BIT (1), /*END OF INPUT FLAG*/
            BEGINS ENTRY ((*) CHAR (*) VARYING, FIXED)
            RETURNS (FIXED);

        NBR = 1;
        END_IN = '1'B;
        /*INPUT LIST OF PRODUCT CODES*/
        ON ENDFILE (SYSIN) END_IN = '0'B;
        GET LIST (CODES (NBR));
        DO WHILE (END_IN = '1'B);
            NBR = NBR + 1;
            GET LIST (CODES (NBR));
        END;
            .
            .
            .

        /*REPLACE BEGINNING '0' BY '1' AND COUNT*/
        REPLACE = BEGINS (CODES, NBR - 1);
        PUT SKIP LIST (REPLACE, 'REPLACEMENTS WERE MADE');
            .
            .
            .

        BEGINS: PROCEDURE (VALS, NUM) RETURNS (FIXED DECIMAL);
        /*SUBSTITUTE ALL INITIAL '0' BY '1' AND COUNT*/
        /*FUNCTION VALUE THE NUMBER OF REPLACEMENTS REQUIRED*/
            DECLARE VALS (*) CHARACTER (*) VARYING,
                NUM FIXED;
            DECLARE (COUNT, /* NUMBER OF REPLACEMENTS*/
                K) FIXED;
            COUNT = 0;
            DO K = 1 TO NUM;
                IF SUBSTR (VALS (K), 1, 1) = '0'
                THEN DO;
                    COUNT = COUNT + 1;
                    SUBSTR (VALS (K), 1, 1) = '1';
                    END;
            END;
            RETURN (COUNT);
        END BEGINS;
            .
            .
            .

END PRODUCT;
```

Fig. 6-2   Program PRODUCT

ENTRY clause in the entry-name declaration. This would cause the attributes of the argument array CODES and of the parameter VALS to differ. The result is a call by value correspondence between the two, not the previous call by reference association. Thus, no replacements made in the VALS array by the function operations would be affected in the CODES array, and the contents of the latter following the execution of the function would remain unchanged from its contents prior to the invocation.

The programmer must always be cautious, when implementing subprograms, that the conditions required by PL/I for establishment of the type of correspondence he or she desires for a certain argument are met. Many confusing errors result when the programmer assumes one form of correspondence is instituted, when actually the other has been used.

In Sec. 6-1 and Sec. 6-2 a classification of functions and procedures into internal and external types was mentioned. These types are further examined in the section to follow, along with special features of each.

Exercises for Sec. 6-3

1. A procedure is desired to accept as a parameter an arbitrary vector of numeric elements. The procedure is to calculate certain statistics concerning the vector. The vector is to be returned unchanged, though the procedure in calculating the required statistics may change elements in the vector. What type of parameter passing is required? Why?

2. Consider the following procedure ADD, with parameters A and B, which calculates the sum of A and B rounded to the nearest integer and returns the value in B.

```
ADD: PROCEDURE (A, B);
     DECLARE (A, B) FLOAT;
     B = ROUND(A + B, 0);
     RETURN;
END ADD;
```

This procedure is invoked in the following program:

```
TEST: PROCEDURE OPTIONS(MAIN);
     DECLARE (A, B) FLOAT;
     GET LIST (A, B);
     CALL ADD (A, B);
     PUT LIST ('ROUNDED SUM IS', B);
END TEST;
```

Give the results of the PUT LIST statement, explaining in detail what happens. Suppose the declaration in the ADD procedure were changed to

```
DECLARE (A, B) FIXED;
```

How would this affect the execution of the program and procedure? What would be the result of the PUT LIST statement now?

6-4   INTERNAL AND EXTERNAL BLOCKS IN PL/I

We have already stated that both functions and procedures may be placed either inside or outside the statements of the main program, yielding, respectively, internal and external subprograms. The notions of internality and externality are examined in this section, illustrating important differences between the two. Also mentioned is another form of structure available in PL/I — the BEGIN block — which has somewhat similar properties to procedures and functions.

An internal subprogram is one which is defined within the main program statements, and thus one which is called by invocations in the main program. Internal subprograms may themselves contain definitions of other subprograms, which are called from within the outer subprogram. Thus, several levels of internal nesting are possible. The levels of nesting define where invocations can and cannot be made. In fact, the levels of nesting define what is known as the *scope* of a name. For example, consider the folowing program outline:

```
PGM: PROCEDURE OPTIONS (MAIN);
    .
    .
    .
       B1: PROCEDURE...;
          .
          .
          .
          B2: PROCEDURE...;
             .
             .
          END B2;
             .
             .
             .
       END B1;
    .
    .
    .
END PGM;
```

Two subprograms (functions or procedures) are present, named B1 and B2, and both are internal to the main program. Note, however, that B2 is itself internal to the B1 subprogram. The subprogram B1 may be invoked by an invocation in the main program statements, but, because of its nesting level, the subprogram B2 may only be invoked from within the B1 statements. That is, the main program cannot call the subprogram B2. The general rule is that reference is permitted to something within the current scope (or nesting level), or a scope *enclosing* the current scope, but not to something in an *enclosed* scope. This rule will be elaborated on shortly.

The use of internal subprograms permits another means through which communication between a subprogram and main program. (or, more generally, between two compatible scopes) can occur. This involves the use of *global variables*. To demonstrate global variables, consider the following outline:

```
PGM: PROCEDURE OPTIONS (MAIN);
     DECLARE VARI 1 FIXED,
         .
         .
         .

     SORT: PROCEDURE___;
           DECLARE VAR 2 FIXED;
               .
               .
               .

     END SORT;
         .
         .
         .

ENG PGM;
```

The subprogram SORT is internal to the main program PGM, and may be called by an invocation in PGM. The variable VAR 2 is *local* to the subprogram SORT, since it is declared within it. Thus it is known only to the subprogram SORT. It is created only when SORT is invoked and destroyed upon termination of an execution of SORT. Consider now the variable VAR1, which is declared in the main program. Because it is declared where it is (in an enclosing scope), VAR1 is said to be *global* to the internal subprogram SORT, meaning that it may be used not only in the main program, but also within the SORT statements. Generally, any variable name which is declared in a particular scope is global to all scopes which are internal to it. A global variable need not be redeclared inside a subprogram definition, unless the name is intended for reuse, that is, intended to represent a separate, local variable, not related to the variable of the same name in the invoking block. Note that if execution of an internal subprogram uses and alters the current value of one of the variables that are global to it, then the value of the variable, upon termination of the subprogram, is then the latest, and not the original value which it received. In this way, global variables can provide a simple method for communication of values in both directions between an internal subprogram and the main program (or block from which invocation occurred), but at the same time can lead to dangerous side effects for the unwitting programmer.

As an illustration of nested internal subprograms, and the use of global variables in subprograms, consider the modified version appearing in Fig. 6-3 of the program EMP_EES, first given in Sec. 6-2. The procedure SORT is internal to the main program EMP_EES, as before. The differences in this version are within the SORT block, where the switching of two elements in the array is now peformed by invoking another procedure EXCHNGE. Thus, EXCHNGE uses the variables TEMP, LIST, MIN, and PASS just as if they were declared within that procedure. After an execution of EXCHNGE, the two elements LIST(MIN) and LIST(PASS) have exchanged values, which in turn implies that those two elements in the main program have also switched values (by call by reference between NAMES and LIST). The program EMP_EES could further be rewritten to make more extensive use of the communication provided by global variables in internal subprograms. This is done in the third version of the same program given in Fig. 6-4. In this version, an

```
EMP_EES: PROCEDURE OPTIONS (MAIN);
     DECLARE NAMES (50) CHARACTER (20) VARYING, /*EMPLOYEE NAMES LIST*/
          CODES (50) CHARACTER (5), /*IDENTIFICATION CODES LIST*/
          (NUM, K) FIXED;
     NUM = 1;
     GET LIST (NAMES(1), CODES(1));
     DO WHILE (NAMES(NUM) ¬ = 'LAST_NAME');
          NUM = NUM + 1;
          GET LIST (NAMES(NUM), CODES(NUM));
     END;
     NUM = NUM − 1;

     /*SORT THE LIST OF EMPLOYEE NAMES INTO ASCENDING ORDER*/
     CALL SORT (NAMES, NUM);
     /*SORT THE LIST OF EMPLOYEE CODES INTO ASCENDING ORDER*/
     CALL SORT (CODES, NUM);

     /*PRINT OUT THE SORTED LISTS*/
     PUT LIST ('EMPLOYEE NAMES LIST:');
     PUT EDIT ((NAMES(K) DO K = 1 TO NUM)) ((NUM) (SKIP, COL(5), A));
     PUT SKIP(2) LIST ('EMPLOYEE CODES LIST:');
     PUT EDIT ((CODES(K) DO K = 1 TO NUM)) ((NUM) (SKIP, COL(5),A));

     SORT: PROCEDURE (LIST, COUNT);
     /*SORT THE GIVEN ARRAY INTO ASCENDING ORDER*/
          DECLARE LIST(*) CHARACTER(*) VARYING, /*ARRAY TO BE SORTED*/
               COUNT FIXED; /*NUMBER OF ELEMENTS*/
          DECLARE TEMP CHARACTER (20) VARYING,
               (MIN, POS, PASS) FIXED;

          DO PASS = 1 TO COUNT − 1;
               MIN = PASS;
               DO POS = PASS + 1 TO COUNT;
                    IF LIST(POS) < LIST(MIN) THEN MIN = POS;
               END;
               IF MIN ¬ = PASS
               THEN CALL EXCHNGE;
          END;

          EXCHNGE: PROCEDURE;
          /* EXCHANGE TWO ELEMENTS IN LIST ARRAY */
               TEMP = LIST(MIN);
               LIST(MIN) = LIST(PASS);
               LIST(PASS) = TEMP;
               RETURN;
          END EXCHNGE;
          RETURN;
     END SORT;
     PUT EDIT ('END OF PROGRAM')(SKIP, A);
END EMP_EES;
```

Fig. 6-3   Modified EMP_EES using nested internal subprograms

```
EMP_EES: PROCEDURE OPTIONS (MAIN);
     DECLARE NAMES (50) CHARACTER (20) VARYING, /*EMPLOYEE NAMES LIST*/
          CODES (50) CHARACTER (5), /*IDENTIFICATION CODES LIST*/
          (NUM, K) FIXED;
     GET LIST (NAMES(1), CODES(1));
     DO WHILE (NAMES(NUM) ¬ = 'LAST_NAME');
          NUM = NUM + 1;
          GET LIST (NAMES(NUM), CODES(NUM));
     END;
     NUM = NUM - 1;

     /*SORT THE LIST OF EMPLOYEE NAMES INTO ASCENDING ORDER*/
     CALL SORT (NAMES);
     /*SORT THE LIST OF EMPLOYEE CODES INTO ASCENDING ORDER*/
     CALL SORT (CODES);

     /*PRINT OUT THE SORTED LISTS*/
     PUT LIST ('EMPLOYEE NAMES LIST:');
     PUT EDIT ((NAMES(K) DO K = 1 TO NUM)) ((NUM) (SKIP, COL(5), A));
     PUT SKIP(2) LIST ('EMPLOYEE CODES LIST:');
     PUT EDIT ((CODES(K) DO K = 1 TO NUM)) ((NUM) (SKIP, COL(5), A));
     SORT: PROCEDURE (LIST);

     /*SORT THE GIVEN ARRAY INTO ASCENDING ORDER*/
          DECLARE LIST(*) CHARACTER(*) VARYING; /*ARRAY TO BE SORTED*/
          DECLARE TEMP CHARACTER (20) VARYING,
               (MIN, POS, PASS) FIXED;

          DO PASS = 1 TO NUM - 1;
               MIN = PASS;
               DO POS = PASS + 1 TO NUM;
                    IF LIST(POS) < LIST(MIN) THEN MIN = POS;
               END;
               IF MIN ¬ = PASS
               THEN CALL EXCHNGE;
          END;

          EXCHNGE: PROCEDURE;
          /*EXCHANGE TWO ELEMENTS IN LIST ARRAY*/
               TEMP = LIST(MIN);
               LIST(MIN) = LIST(PASS);
               LIST(PASS) = TEMP;
               RETURN;
          END EXCHNGE;

          RETURN;
     END SORT;
     PUT EDIT ('END OF PROGRAM')(SKIP, A);
END EMP_EES;
```

Fig. 6-4   Modified version of EMP_EES using global variables

invocation of the SORT procedure does not require the passing of a second argument, which previously was necessary to inform that procedure of the number of elements in the array to be sorted. This item of information, held in the variable NUM, is now communicated to SORT using the fact that NUM is global to the procedure. Thus, the variable name NUM is used directly in the SORT statements. When using internal subprograms, as in this case, the programmer is often faced with the decision of whether to establish communication between a variable in the invoking block and a variable in the subprogram by argument-parameter correspondence in the parameter list or by global variables. Although the latter method (use of global variable references) may appear to be less troublesome to implement than the former, we advocate that you consider its use very carefully since it decreases the modularity of the subprogram and can lead to errors that are very hard to detect.

Let us now look briefly at the second type of subprogram to be discussed in this section — external subprograms. These are subprograms which are not contained within the main program, nor within any other subprogram. Instead, the definition of an external subprogram appears at the end of the program, after the main program and preceding the data. Each external subprogram definition in PL/C must be preceded by a

    *PROCESS

card. An external subprogram may be invoked from the main program or from any internal or external subprogram. Global variables are not possible with external subprograms. That is, variables declared in the invoking program may not be referenced in the external subprogram. Thus, communication between the external subprogram, and the invoking program may only occur through argument-parameter correspondence and, if the subprogram is a function, by returning a value on the function name.

As an example of the use of external subprograms, consider the version of the program EMP_EES given in Fig. 6-5, this time utilizing only external subprograms. Note that the vector to be sorted and the number of elements in it are given to the external procedure SORT by correspondence with the parameters, and the sorted vector is communicated to the main program during execution of the procedure by the same means. Thus, all variables used in the procedure are local to it, as they must be for external subprograms.

The concept of scope is important in any programming language that has what is known as a *block structure*. PL/I, ALGOL, and PASCAL are all examples of block structured languages. To rephrase the basic rule, scopes are inherited inwards; that is any name (variable name or subprogram name) is known to any enclosed block where a block may be a subprogram or a BEGIN block, which will be discussed shortly. Figure 6-6 uses boxes to represent blocks. X, Y, Z represent names; S_1, S_2, and S_3 represent statements. Table 6-1 shows which variables can be referenced by which statements according to the rules of scope.

Notice that Y and Z cannot be referenced from outside the blocks in which they are defined; scopes are inherited *inward*. Notice also that there is no place where both Y and Z can be referenced. Their scopes are incompatible.

We now introduce a type of PL/I block which is slightly different from subprogram (procedure and function) blocks. A BEGIN block is merely a group of statements inside a program having the following outline:

```
EMP_EES: PROCEDURE OPTIONS (MAIN);
      DECLARE NAMES (50) CHARACTER (20) VARYING, /*EMPLOYEE NAMES LIST*/
            CODES (50) CHARACTER (5), /*IDENTIFICATION CODES LIST*/
            (NUM, K) FIXED;
      NUM = 1;
      GET LIST (NAMES(1), CODES(1));
      DO WHILE (NAMES(NUM)  ⌐= 'LAST_NAME');
            NUM = NUM + 1;
            GET LIST (NAMES(NUM), CODES(NUM));
      END;
      NUM = NUM - 1;

      /*SORT THE LIST OF EMPLOYEE NAMES INTO ASCENDING ORDER*/
      CALL SORT (NAMES, NUM);
      /*SORT THE LIST OF EMPLOYEE CODES INTO ASCENDING ORDER*/
      CALL SORT (CODES, NUM);

      /*PRINT OUT THE SORTED LISTS*/
      PUT LIST ('EMPLOYEE NAMES LIST:');
      PUT EDIT ((NAMES(K) DO K = 1 TO NUM)) ((NUM) (SKIP, COL(5), A));
      PUT SKIP(2) LIST ('EMPLOYEE CODES LIST:');
      PUT EDIT ((CODES(K) DO K = 1 TO NUM)) ((NUM) (SKIP, COL(5), A));
      PUT EDIT ('THE END OF THE PROGRAM')(SKIP, A);
END EMP_EES;

      *PROCESS
      SORT: PROCEDURE (LIST, COUNT);
      /*SORT THE GIVEN ARRAY INTO ASCENDING ORDER*/
            DECLARE LIST(*) CHARACTER(*) VARYING, /*ARRAY TO BE SORTED*/
                  COUNT FIXED; /*NUMBER OF ELEMENTS*/
            DECLARE TEMP CHARACTER (20) VARYING,
                  (MIN, POS, PASS) FIXED;

            DO PASS = 1 TO COUNT - 1;
                  MIN =PASS;

            DO POS = PASS  TO COUNT;
                  IF LIST(POS) < LIST(MIN) THEN MIN = POS;
            END;

            IF MIN⌐ = PASS
            THEN DO;
                  TEMP = LIST(MIN);
                  LIST(MIN) = LIST(PASS);
                  LIST(PASS) = TEMP;
                  END;
      END;
      RETURN;
END SORT;
```

Fig. 6-5   Modified EMP_EES using external subprograms

Table 6-1   Allowed References in Fig. 6-6

Statements	Names to which reference is permitted
S_1	X
S_2	X, Y
S_3	X, Z

> *block-name:* BEGIN;
>   *local variable declarations*
>   *block statements*
> END *block-name;*

Note that BEGIN blocks do not have parameters, and do not return a value. A BEGIN block must always be internal to a subprogram or main program. Any communication desired between the BEGIN block and the subprogram or main program in which it is contained must occur through the use of global variables. Furthermore, BEGIN blocks are not invoked. Instead, they are executed by having the normal program execution flow into it. After execution of such a block is completed, control continues with execution of the statement immediately following the END *block-name;* statement and the local variables created inside the block are destroyed.

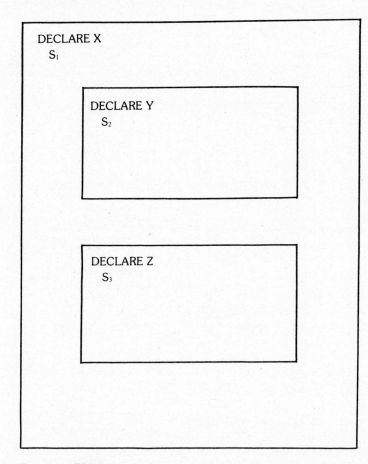

Fig. 6-6   Block structure

The most common use of BEGIN blocks is to postpone the creation of arrays until execution has determined the exact number of elements required for the array (recall from our earlier discussion that local varibles are not "created" until the subprogram or block in which they are declared is entered). For example, if a set of data is to be read into an array, it is not unusual first to input a number giving the number of data elements to be read in. A BEGIN block is then entered, where this number is then used to declare the array to have the correct number of elements required to fit the data. As an example of this usage, consider yet another version of the program EMP_EES given in Fig. 6-7. We now assume that the data containing the employee names and codes are as before, except that they are now preceded by a card giving the number of data cards to follow, and the dummy 'LAST_NAME' card at the end is not included (recall that this is counter-controlled input). In this version, the creation of the two arrays NAMES and CODES is not done until the exact number of employee names and codes to follow is input into NUM. Since the BEGIN block is internal to the main program, the variable NUM is global to it, and thus, is used in the block for the declaration of the arrays. The arrays are created to precisely accomodate NUM elements. Notice that in the original version of this program, the size of the arrays was arbitrarily declared to be 50, under the assumption that it was unlikely that more than 50 employee data cards would ever be presented as data. This policy of declaring arrays to have an arbitrarily large size for the expected amount of data to be assigned to it has the disadvantage that the array will require more storage space than needed, and much of it will be unused. The version, using a BEGIN block, to defer storage allocation until run-time needs are known, eliminates this problem.

In this section we have discussed several of the important issues involving the use of blocks in PL/I, where blocks may be either of the subprogram type or of the BEGIN block type. This concludes our consideration of the subprogram. In the next section, PL/C programs for the applications of Chap. 6 in the main text are developed and discussed.

Exercises for Sec. 6-4

1. Give the value of MAX following the execution of this program and sub-program, assuming

    (i) The subprogram is internal.
    (ii) The subprogram is external.

    Main program
```
        MAXI: PROCEDURE OPTIONS (MAIN);
              DECLARE (MAX, A, B) FIXED;
              A = 4;
              B = 3;
              CALL LARGE;
              PUT LIST (MAX);
        END MAX1;
```

    Subprogram
```
        LARGE: PROCEDURE;
              IF A > B
```

```
EMP_EES: PROCEDURE OPTIONS (MAIN);
     DECLARE NUM FIXED; /*NUMBER OF EMPLOYEES*/
     GET LIST (NUM);
     START: BEGIN;
          DECLARE NAMES(NUM) CHARACTER (20) VARYING, /*EMPLOYEE*/
          /*NAME*/
               CODES (NUM) CHARACTER (5), /*IDENTIFICATION CODES LIST*/
               K FIXED;
          GET LIST ((NAMES(K), CODES(K) DO K = 1 TO NUM));

          /*SORT THE LIST OE EMPLOYEE NAMES INTO ASCENDING ORDER*/
          CALL SORT (NAMES, NUM);
          /*SORT THE LIST OF EMPLOYEE CODES INTO ASCENDING ORDER*/
          CALL SORT (CODES, NUM);

          /*PRINT OUT THE SORTED LISTS*/
          PUT LIST ('EMPLOYEE NAMES LIST:');
          PUT EDIT ((NAMES(K) DO K = 1 TO NUM)) ((NUM) (SKIP, COL(5), A));
          PUT SKIP(2) LIST ('EMPLOYEE CODES LIST:');
          PUT EDIT ((CODES(K) DO K = 1 TO NUM)) ((NUM) (SKIP, COL(5), A)):

          SORT: PROCEDURE (LIST, COUNT);
          /*SORT THE GIVEN ARRAY INTO ASCENDING ORDER*/
          DECLARE LIST(*) CHARACTER(*) VARYING, /*ARRAY TO BE SORTED*/
                    COUNT FIXED; /*NUMBER OF ELEMENTS*/
               DECLARE TEMP CHARACTER (20) VARYING,
                    (MIN, POS, PASS) FIXED;

               DO PASS = 1 TO COUNT - 1;
                    MIN = PASS;
                    DO POS = PASS + 1 TO COUNT;
                         IF LIST(POS) < LIST(MIN) THEN MIN = POS;
                    END;

                    IF MIN ¬= PASS
                    THEN DO;
                         TEMP = LIST(MIN);
                         LIST(MIN) = LIST(PASS);
                         LIST(PASS) = TEMP;
                         END;
               END;

          END SORT;
     END START;
END EMP_EES;
```

Fig. 6-7 Modified version of EMP_EES using a block structure

```
                    THEN MAX = A;
                    ELSE MAX = B;
         END LARGE;
```

What if the call is written

```
         CALL LARGE(A, B);
```

and the subprogram begins

```
         LARGE: PROCEDURE(A, B);
                DECLARE (A, B) FIXED;
```

2. What are the advantages and disadvantages of using global variables?

3. Consider the following program outline:

```
         PGM1: PROCEDURE OPTIONS(MAIN);
               DECLARE (X, Y)
                .
                .
                .


               PGM2: PROCEDURE;
                     DECLARE (A, B, C)
                      .
                      .
                      .
               END PGM2;


                .
                .
                .


               PGM3: PROCEDURE;
                     DECLARE (M, N)
                      .
                      .
                      .


                     PGM4: PROCEDURE;
                           DECLARE (S, T)
                            .
                            .
                            .
                     END PGM4:

               END PGM3;

         END PGM1;
```

```
*PROCESS
PGM5: PROCEDURE;
        DECLARE (Z)
        .
        .
        .
    END PGM5;
```

Based on the preceding outline, answer the following questions:

(i) What variables are global to PGM2?
(ii) Is it possible for PGM3 to access the value of variable A?
(iii) List all the variables global to PGM4.
(iv) Draw a block diagram like the one given in Fig. 6-6 for the above program outline.

6-5 APPLICATIONS

This section presents PL/C program solutions to the application problems found in Sec. 6-5 of the main text.

6-5.1 Processing Symbol Tables

The program given in Fib. 6-8 is a solution to the symbol table problem presented in Sec. 6-5.1 of the main text. In order to illustrate programs that perform the functions of the subroutines described in the main text, a main program called TEST_R is used to call the routines. TEST_R uses the INSERT subprocedure to create a symbol table containing ten elements. Once the elements have been inserted, the contents of the symbol table are printed. Elements are then retrieved from the symbol table in a random order using the RETRIEVE procedure. The SEARCH subroutine is used in both the INSERT and RETRIEVE subprocedures. The following is a general outline of the TEST_R program.

1. Enter ten elements into the symbol table using the subprocedure INSERT.
2. Print the created symbol table.
3. Repeat thru step 6 for all remaining input.
4. Read name of variable sought.
5. Find the variable's type and position using the RETRIEVE procedure.
6. Print the variable's name, type, and address.

The following variables appear in the TEST_R program.

Variable Name	Type	Usage
NAME(10)	CHARACTER(31) VARYING	Vector of variable names
TYPE(10)	CHARACTER(7) VARYING	Vector of variable types
ADDRES(10)	FIXED	Vector of variable addresses
VARIABLE	CHARACTER(31) VARYING	Name of variable to be inserted or retrieved
VARIABLE_TYPE	CHARACTER(7) VARYING	Type of variable

VARIABLE_ADDRESS	FIXED	Address of variable
MAX_NUM	FIXED	Maximum number of table positions
NUMBER	FIXED	Number of elements inserted
END_FLAG	CHARACTER(3) VARYING	End of data flag
I	FIXED	Loop variable

Variables used in the INSERT subprocedure

VAR_NAME	CHARACTER(*) VARYING	Name of variable to be inserted

```
/* PROGRAM TO TEST SYMBOL TABLE ROUTINES, SEARCH, INSERT, AND  */

STMT LEVEL NEST BLOCK MLVL   SOURCE TEXT


                                 /* PROGRAM TO TEST SYMBOL TABLE ROUTINES, SEARCH, INSERT, AND  */
                                 /* RETRIEVE */
   1                             TEST_R: PROCEDURE OPTIONS(MAIN);
   2     1              1            DECLARE NAME(10) CHARACTER(31) VARYING, /* VECTOR OF VARIABLE */
                                                                       /* NAMES */
                                        TYPE(10) CHARACTER(7) VARYING,  /* VECTOR OF VARIABLE */
                                                                       /*TYPES */
                                        ADDRESS(10) FIXED, /* ADDRESS OF VARIABLES */
                                        VARIABLE CHARACTER(31) VARYING, /* VARIABLE TO BE */
                                                                       /*INSERTED OR RETRIEVED */
                                        VARIABLE_TYPE  CHARACTER(7) VARYING,   /* VARIABLE'S TYPE*/
                                        VARIABLE_ADDRESS FIXED,        /* VARIABLE'S ADDRESS */
                                        MAXNUM FIXED,    /* MAXIMUM NUMBER OF TABLE POSITIONS */
                                        NUMBER FIXED,        /* NUMBER OF ELEMENTS INSERTED */
                                        I FIXED,           /* LOOP VARIABLE */
                                        END_FLAG CHARACTER(3) VARYING,/* END OF DATA FLAG */
                                        SEARCH ENTRY ((*) CHARACTER(*) VARYING, FIXED,
                                           CHARACTER(*) VARYING)
                                                RETURNS (FIXED);

                                 /* INITIALIZE */
   3     1              1         NUMBER = 0;
   4     1              1         MAXNUM = 10;
   5     1              1         END_FLAG = 'OFF';
   6     1              1         ON ENDFILE(SYSIN) END_FLAG = 'ON';

                                 /* READ AND INSERT TEN ELEMENTS INTO THE SYMBOL TABLE VECTORS */
   8     2         1    2         DO I = 1 TO 10;
   9     1    1         1             GET LIST( VARIABLE, VARIABLE_TYPE, VARIABLE_ADDRESS);
  10     1    1         1             CALL INSERT( VARIABLE,VARIABLE_TYPE,VARIABLE_ADDRESS,NUMBER);
  11     1    1         1         END;

                                 /* PRINT OUT SYMBOL TABLE ENTRIES */
  12     1              1         PUT SKIP LIST (' ', 'SYMBOL TABLE ');
  13     1              1         PUT SKIP LIST ('VARIABLE', 'TYPE','ADDRESS');
  14     1              1         DO I = 1 TO NUMBER;
  15     1    1         1             PUT SKIP LIST(NAME(I), TYPE(I), ADDRESS(I));
  16     1    1         1         END;

                                 /* TEST RETRIEVE PROCEDURE */
                                 /* PRINT HEADINGS */
  17     1              1         PUT PAGE;
  18     1              1         PUT SKIP LIST('VARIABLE SOUGHT', 'TYPE', 'ADDRESS');
                                 /* RETRIEVE  INFORMATION */
  19     1              1         DO WHILE (END_FLAG = 'OFF');

                                     /* READ IN NAME OF VARIABLE SOUGHT */
  20     1    1         1             GET LIST(VARIABLE);
  21     1    1         1             IF END_FLAG = 'ON'
  22     1    1         1             THEN EXIT;

  23     1    1         1             CALL RETRIEVE(VARIABLE,VARIABLE_TYPE,VARIABLE_ADDRESS,NUMBER);
  24     1    1         1             PUT SKIP LIST(VARIABLE,VARIABLE_TYPE,VARIABLE_ADDRESS);
  25     1    1         1         END;
```

Fig. 6-8   Program for symbol table application

```
                              /* PROCEDURE TO INSERT A VARIABLE INTO A SYMBOL TABLE  */
                              /* NAME, TYPE, AND ADDRESS ARE GLOBAL VECTORS COMPRISING THE  */
                              /* SYMBOL TABLE */
26    1        1             INSERT: PROCEDURE(VAR_NAME, VAR_TYPE, VAR_ADDRESS, SIZE);

27    2        3                 DECLARE VAR_NAME CHARACTER(*) VARYING,  /* VARIABLE'S NAME */
                                         VAR_TYPE CHARACTER(*) VARYING,  /* VARIABLE'S TYPE */
                                         VAR_ADDRESS FIXED, /* ADDRESS OF VARIABLE */
                                         SIZE FIXED; /* NO. OF ENTRIES IN THE SYMBOL TABLE */

                                 /* CHECK IF VARIABLE HAS ALREADY BEEN DEFINED */
28    2        3                 IF SEARCH(NAME, SIZE, VAR_NAME) ¬= 0
29    2        3                 THEN DO;
30    2   1    3                     PUT SKIP LIST('***ERROR - VARIABLE',VAR_NAME,
                                         'HAS BEEN PREVIOUSLY DEFINED.');
31    2   1    3                     RETURN;
32    2   1    3                 END;

                                 /* COMPUTE THE NEXT AVAILABLE POSITION */
33    2        3                 SIZE = SIZE + 1;
34    2        3                 IF SIZE > MAXNUM
35    2        3                 THEN DO;  /* TABLE IS FULL */
36    2   1    3                     PUT SKIP LIST('***ERROR - TOO MANY VARIABLES DEFINED.');
37    2   1    3                     RETURN;
38    2   1    3                 END;

                                 /* MAKE INSERTION INTO THE POSITION FOUND */
39    2        3                 NAME(SIZE) = VAR_NAME;
40    2        3                 TYPE(SIZE) = VAR_TYPE;
41    2        3                 ADDRESS(SIZE) = VAR_ADDRESS;
42    2        3                 RETURN;

43    2        3             END INSERT;




                              /* PROCEDURE TO RETRIEVE THE TYPE AND ADDRESS OF A VARIABLE FROM */
                              /* A SYMBOL TABLE */
44    1        1             RETRIEVE: PROCEDURE(VAR_NAME,VAR_TYPE, VAR_ADDRESS, SIZE);
45    2        4                 DECLARE VAR_NAME CHARACTER(*) VARYING, /* VARIABLE NAME */

                                         VAR_TYPE CHARACTER(*) VARYING, /* VARIABLE TYPE */
                                         VAR_ADDRESS FIXED,            /* ADDRESS OF VARIABLE */
                                         SIZE FIXED;      /* NO. OF VARIABLES IN THE */
                                                          /* SYMBOL TABLE */
46    2        4                 DECLARE POS FIXED;  /* POSITION OF VARIABLE IN */
                                                          /* SYMBOL TABLE */

                                 /* CHECK IF VARIABLE IS IN TABLE */
47    2        4                 POS = SEARCH(NAME, SIZE, VAR_NAME);
48    2        4                 IF POS = 0
49    2        4                 THEN DO;        /* VARIABLE NOT IN TABLE */
50    2   1    4                     PUT SKIP LIST('***ERROR - VARIABLE', VAR_NAME,
                                         'HAS NOT BEEN DEFINED.');
51    2   1    4                     RETURN;
52    2   1    4                 END;

                                 /* IF THE VARIABLE IS FOUND, SUPPLY THE REQUIRED */
                                             /* INFORMATION */
53    2        4                 VAR_TYPE = TYPE(POS);
54    2        4                 VAR_ADDRESS = ADDRESS(POS);
55    2        4                 RETURN;

56    2        4             END RETRIEVE;
```

Fig. 6-8 Program for symbol table application (cont'd.)

VAR_TYPE	CHARACTER(*) VARYING	Type of variable to be inserted
VAR_ADDRESS	FIXED	Address of variable to be inserted
SIZE	FIXED	Number of entries in the symbol table

```
                                         /* PROCEDURE TO FIND AN ELEMENT IN A VECTOR */
 57    1         1           SEARCH: PROCEDURE(LIST, N, ELEMENT)
                                          RETURNS(FIXED);

 58    2         5              DECLARE LIST(*) CHARACTER(*) VARYING, /* LIST TO BE SEARCHED*/
                                       N FIXED,          /* NUMBER OF ELEMENTS IN THE LIST */
                                       ELEMENT CHARACTER(*) VARYING; /*ELEMENT SOUGHT */
 59    2         5              DECLARE I FIXED;           /* LOOP VARIABLE */

                                /* SEARCH THE VECTOR */
 60    2         5              DO I = 1 TO N;
 61    2    1    5                 IF LIST(I) = ELEMENT
 62    2    1    5                    THEN RETURN (I);
 63    2    1    5              END;

                                /* ELEMENT NOT FOUND */
 64    2         5              RETURN(0);
 65    2         5           END SEARCH;

 66    1         1        END TEST_R;
```

ERRORS/WARNINGS DETECTED DURING CODE GENERATION:

    WARNING: NO FILE SPECIFIED. SYSIN/SYSPRINT ASSUMED. (CGOC)

```
                           SYMBOL TABLE
VARIABLE              TYPE                ADDRESS
ALPHA                INTEGER              6030
BETA                 REAL                 6034
GAMMA                INTEGER              6038
LETTERS              STRING               7010
TOTAL                INTEGER              7124
AVERAGE              REAL                 7388
SUM                  INTEGER              7764
WORD                 STRING               7777
NAME                 STRING               7900
COUNT                INTEGER              7944
VARIABLE SOUGHT      TYPE                 ADDRESS
LETTERS              STRING               7010
WORD                 STRING               7777
BETA                 REAL                 6034
TOTAL                INTEGER              7124
SUM                  INTEGER              7764
```

IN STMT   22 PROGRAM IS STOPPED.

Fig. 6-8   Program for symbol table application (cont'd.)

Variables used in the RETRIEVE subprocedure

VAR_NAME	CHARACTER(*) VARYING	Name of variable sought
VAR_TYPE	CHARACTER(*) VARYING	Type of variable sought
VAR_ADDRESS	FIXED	Address of variable sought
SIZE	FIXED	Number of variables in the symbol table
POS	FIXED	Position of variable in the symbol table

Variables used in the SEARCH subprocedure

L(*)	CHARACTER(*) VARYING	List containing element sought
N	FIXED	Number of elements in the list
ELEMENT	CHARACTER(*) VARYING	Element sought
I	FIXED	Loop variable

The following input values were used during this run.

'ALPHA'	'INTEGER'	6030
'BETA'	'REAL'	6034
'GAMMA'	'INTEGER'	6038
'LETTERS'	'STRING'	7010
'TOTAL'	'INTEGER'	7124
'TOTAL'	INTEGER'	7124
'AVERAGE'	'REAL'	7388
'SUM'	'INTEGER'	7764
'WORD'	'STRING'	7777
'NAME'	'STRING'	7900
'COUNT'	'INTEGER'	7944
'LETTERS'		
'WORD'		
'BETA'		
'TOTAL'		
'SUM'		

Statements 3 and 4 initialize NUMBER and MAX_NUM to 0 and 10, respectively. In statement 8, a loop to read and insert ten elements is begun. Once this loop has been completed, statements 12 through 16 print the elements of the symbol table. A DO WHILE loop is then used to control the input of variable names and the retrieval of the corresponding type and address. Execution is terminated when the end of the input values have been reached.

6-5.2 The Transposition of Musical Scores

The program appearing in Fig. 6-9 is a solution to the problem of transposing musical scores given in Sec. 6-5.2 of the main text. The problem concerns shifting a score written in one key to a corresponding score in a different key. Both the original key and the new key are to be read in along with the musical score. The amount of shift between these two keys defines the amount of shift needed. The possible keys are represented by the following character string

'AbbBbCbbDbbEbFbbGbbAbbBbCbbDbbEbFbbGb'

The blanks between the notes, represented here by b's, denote the tones separating notes: a single blank represents a semitone and two blanks represent a full tone. Beside the shift between keys, sharps and flats must be taken into consideration as they imply a semitone shift. This means that to convert a chord that is a sharp or flat, 1 must be added (for a sharp) or subtracted (for a flat) to the amount of the shift to produce the correct shift. For example, suppose the following score was to be transposed from the key of E to C.

'E'
'A'
'G#'

According to the string of notes given previously, the shift from E to C is eleven. The transposed score would then be

```
/* PROGRAM TO TRANSPOSE CHORDS OF A MUSICAL SCORE */

STMT LEVEL NEST BLOCK MLVL   SOURCE TEXT


                                     /* PROGRAM TO TRANSPOSE CHORDS OF A MUSICAL SCORE */
   1                                 KEYS: PROCEDURE OPTIONS(MAIN);

   2     1              1            DECLARE NOTES CHARACTER(37), /* BASIC SCALE */
                                         ORIGINAL_KEY CHARACTER(2),/* ORIGINAL KEY OF THE MUSIC */
                                         KEY_DESIRED CHARACTER(2), /* DESIRED KEY OF THE MUSIC */
                                         POSITION FIXED,           /* POSITION OF NOTE IN SCALE */
                                         SHIFT FIXED,              /* NUMBER OF NOTES MUSIC */
                                                                   /* MUST BE SHIFTED */
                                         CHORD CHARACTER (5),
                                         END_FLAG CHARACTER(3) VARYING, /* END OF DATA FLAG */
                                         TRANSPOSE ENTRY (CHARACTER(*),FIXED)
                                                 RETURNS (CHARACTER(5) VARYING);

                                     /* INITIALIZE */
   3     1              1            NOTES = 'A  BC  D  E F  G  A  BC  D  E F  G ';
   4     1              1            END_FLAG = 'OFF';
   5     1              1            ON ENDFILE(SYSIN) END_FLAG = 'ON';

                                     /* READ KEYS */
   7     2              2            GET LIST (ORIGINAL_KEY, KEY_DESIRED);

                                     /* COMPUTE SHIFT */
   8     1              1            POSITION = INDEX(NOTES, SUBSTR(ORIGINAL_KEY,1,1));
   9     1              1            SHIFT = INDEX(SUBSTR(NOTES,POSITION+1), SUBSTR(KEY_DESIRED,1,1));

                                     /* CHECK IF ADJUSTMENT REQUIRED */
  10     1              1            IF SUBSTR(ORIGINAL_KEY, 2, 1) = '#'
  11     1              1            THEN SHIFT = SHIFT - 1;
  12     1              1            IF SUBSTR(ORIGINAL_KEY,2,1) = '!'
  13     1              1            THEN SHIFT = SHIFT + 1;
  14     1              1            IF SUBSTR(KEY_DESIRED, 2, 1) = '#'
  15     1              1            THEN SHIFT = SHIFT +1;
  16     1              1             IF SUBSTR(KEY_DESIRED, 2, 1) = '!'
  17     1              1            THEN SHIFT = SHIFT - 1;

                                     /* TRANSPOSE CHORDS OF COMPLETE SCORE */
  18     1              1            PUT SKIP LIST('ORIGINAL CHORD','TRANSPOSED CHORD');

  19     1              1            DO WHILE(END_FLAG = 'OFF');
  20     1    1         1                GET LIST (CHORD);
  21     1    1         1                IF END_FLAG = 'ON'
  22     1    1         1                THEN EXIT;
  23     1    1         1                PUT SKIP LIST(CHORD, TRANSPOSE(CHORD, SHIFT));
  24     1    1         1            END;
```

Fig. 6-9   Program for music transposition problem

'C'

'E'

'D#'

Note that in transposing the last chord, one was added to the basic shift of eleven. Variations of the basic chords such as minors or sevenths are simply concatenated to the transposed key. For example, Gm7 transposed to the key of D would be Dm7. Using this information the program given in Fig. 6-9 can be used to transpose simple musical scores. The variables used in this program are

Variable Name	Type	Usage
NOTES	CHARACTER(37)	Basic scale
ORIGINAL_KEY	CHARACTER(2)	Original key of the score
KEY_DESIRED	CHARCTER(2)	Desired key of the score

```
                                /* FUNCTION TO TRANSPOSE CHORDS */
   25    1        1         TRANSPOSE: PROCEDURE(IN_CHORD, DIST)
                                    RETURNS (CHARACTER(5) VARYING);
   26    2        3              DECLARE IN_CHORD CHARACTER(*),   /* CHORD TO BE TRANSPOSED */
                                        DIST FIXED;        /* DISTANCE CHORD IS TO BE */
                                                           /* SHIFTED */
   27    2        3              DECLARE (P1, P2) FIXED,       /* INDICES INTO THE STRING OF */
                                                              /* NOTES */
                                        OUT_CHORD CHARACTER(5) VARYING; /* TRANSPOSED CHORD */

                                /* FIND POSITION OF BASIC CHORD, SHIFTING IF NECESSARY FOR */
                                /* SHARP OR FLAT */
   28    2        3              P1 = INDEX(NOTES, SUBSTR(IN_CHORD, 1, 1));
   29    2        3              IN_CHORD = SUBSTR(IN_CHORD, 2);   /* REMOVE CHARACTER JUST */
                                                                  /* CONSIDERED */
   30    2        3              IF SUBSTR(IN_CHORD, 1, 1) = '#'
   31    2        3              THEN DO;
   32    2    1   3                  P1 = P1 + 1;
   33    2    1   3                  IN_CHORD = SUBSTR(IN_CHORD, 2);
   34    2    1   3                  END;
   35    2        3              IF SUBSTR(IN_CHORD, 1, 1) = '!'
   36    2        3              THEN DO;
   37    2    1   3                  P1 = P1 - 1;
   38    2    1   3                  IN_CHORD = SUBSTR(IN_CHORD, 2);
   39    2    1   3                  END;

                                /* DETERMINE TRANSPOSED CHORD */
   40    2        3              P2 = P1 + DIST;
   41    2        3              OUT_CHORD = SUBSTR(NOTES, P2, 1);
   42    2        3              IF OUT_CHORD = ' '       /* SHARP OR FLAT */
   43    2        3              THEN IF SUBSTR(NOTES, P2 + 1, 1) ¬= ' '
   44    2        3                   THEN OUT_CHORD = SUBSTR(NOTES, P2 + 1, 1) || '!';
   45    2        3                   ELSE IF SUBSTR(NOTES, P2 - 1, 1) ¬= ' '
   46    2        3                        THEN OUT_CHORD = SUBSTR(NOTES, P2 - 1, 1) || '#';
   47    2        3                        ELSE PUT SKIP LIST ('***ERROR***');

                                /* RETURN TRANSPOSED CHORD */
   48    2        3              OUT_CHORD = OUT_CHORD || IN_CHORD;
   49    2        3              RETURN(OUT_CHORD);

   50    2        3          END TRANSPOSE;

   51    1        1      END KEYS;
```

ERRORS/WARNINGS DETECTED DURING CODE GENERATION:

    WARNING: NO FILE SPECIFIED. SYSIN/SYSPRINT ASSUMED. (CGOC)

```
ORIGINAL CHORD         TRANSPOSED CHORD
C                      F
AM                     DM
F                      B!
G7                     C7
E!                     A!
D#M7                   G#M7
```

IN STMT 22 PROGRAM IS STOPPED.

Fig. 6-9 Program for music transposition problem (cont'd.)

POSITION	FIXED	Position of note in the scale
SHIFT	FIXED	Number of notes chords must be shifted
CHORD	CHARACTER(5)	Chord of score to be transposed
END_FLAG	CHARACTER(3) VARYING	End of data flag

The following input values were used in this run.

```
'C'        'F'
'C'
'AM'
'F'
'G7'
'E!'
'D#M7'
```

In statement 3, the variable NOTES is assigned the basic scale. The original key and the desired key are read. In statements 8 and 9, the position in the scale of the original key and the shift required to transpose the score to the desired key are calculated. Statements 10 through 17 perform any adjustment that may be required for a sharp or flat. In statement 19 a loop is begun which reads in each chord and, using the TRANSPOSE function, prints the original chord and its transposed counterpart.

6-5.3   Finding Paths in a Graph

The program given in Fig. 6-10 is a programmed solution to the problem of finding paths in a graph presented in Sec. 6-5.3 of the main text. The program is to determine if a path exists between the two points (read in) and to print the length of the path. The graph is represented in the program by an *adjacency matrix*. An adjacency matrix is a n x n matrix where n equals the number of nodes in the corresponding graph. The element in row i, column j is '0'B. One method of determining whether a path exists between two nodes i and j is the following. We first check if i and j are adjacent (i.e., there is an edge of the graph between i and j). If this is not true, a check is made to see if there is a vertex k such that there is a path from i to k to j. Again, if this is not true, we test whether there are two vertices, k and h, such that there is a path from i to k to h to j. This process continues until all possible paths have been checked or until a path between i and j has been found. This search can be done by a program that performs logical operations on the adjacency matrix of the graph. The logical operation "and" performed on the adjacency matrix and itself produces a new matrix A^2 in which the i, j entry is

$$a_{ij} = a_{i1} \mathbin{\&} a_{ij} \mid a_{i2} \mathbin{\&} a_{2j} \mid \ldots \mid a_{in} \mathbin{\&} a_{nj}$$

In other words $a_{ij} = $ '1' if there is a path from i to 1 to j, or i to 2 to j, or i to 3 to j,..., or i to n to j; that is, if a path of length two exists. Similarly, A^3 represents all paths of length three, A^4 represents all paths of length 4, etc. The program given in Fig. 6-10 uses this method to find a path between two nodes. The function POWER is used by this program to calculate the different powers of the adjacency matrix. The following variables appear in this solution.

Variable Name	Type	Usage
N	FIXED	Number of nodes in the graph
A(25, 25)	BIT(1)	Adjacency matrix of the graph
I	FIXED	End point of path sought
J	FIXED	End point of path sought
AL(25, 25)	BIT(1)	Array used for temporary results

```
/* PROGRAM TO  DETERMINE WHETHER OR NOT A PATH EXISTS BETWEEN TWO */

STMT LEVEL NEST BLOCK MLVL   SOURCE TEXT

                              /* PROGRAM TO  DETERMINE WHETHER OR NOT A PATH EXISTS BETWEEN TWO */
                              /* SPECIFIED NODES, I AND J, OF A 5 X 5 GRAPH, A */
  1                           PATHS: PROCEDURE OPTIONS(MAIN);
  2    1         1            DECLARE N FIXED,              /* NO. OF NODES IN THE GRAPH */
                                      A(25, 25) BIT(1),     /* ADJACENCY MATRIX OF THE GRAPH */
                                      (I, J) FIXED,         /* NODES BETWEEN WHICH A PATH IS  */
                                                            /* SOUGHT */
                                      AL(25, 25) BIT(1),    /* TEMPORARY ARRAY */
                                      T(25, 25) BIT(1),     /* TEMPORARY ARRAY */
                                      L FIXED,              /* POWER OF THE ADJACENCY MATRIX */
                                                            /* BEING COMPUTED */
                                      (G, H) FIXED;         /* LOOP VARIABLES */

                              /* INPUT DATA VALUES AND INITIALIZE TEMPORARY ARRAY */
  3    1         1            GET LIST(N);
  4    1         1            DO G = 1 TO N;
  5    1    1    1                DO H = 1 TO N;
  6    1    2    1                    GET LIST(A(G, H));
  7    1    2    1                    AL(G, H) = A(G, H);
  8    1    2    1                END;
  9    1    1    1            END;
 10    1         1            GET LIST(I, J);

                              /* DETERMINE ALL POSSIBLE PATHS IN THE GRAPH */
 11    1         1            DO  L = 1 TO N;
 12    1    1    1                IF AL(I, J) = '1'B
 13    1    1    1                THEN DO;
 14    1    2    1                    PUT SKIP LIST('A PATH OF LENGTH', L, 'EXISTS');
 15    1    2    1                    EXIT;
 16    1    2    1                END;
 17    1    1    1                CALL POWER(AL, A, T, N);
 18    1    1    1                DO G = 1 TO N;
 19    1    2    1                    DO H = 1 TO N;
 20    1    3    1                        AL(G, H) = T(G, H);
 21    1    3    1                    END;
 22    1    2    1                END;
 23    1    1    1            END;

                              /* NO PATH */
 24    1         1            PUT SKIP LIST('NO PATH EXISTS'):
                              /* PROCEDURE TO CALCULATE A & B FOR A AND B, BOTH N X N ARRAYS */

 25    1         1            POWER: PROCEDURE(A, B, C, N);
 26    2         2                DECLARE A(*,*) BIT(*),            /* INPUT BOOLEAN ARRAY */
                                          B(*,*) BIT(*),            /* INPUT BOOLEAN ARRAY */
                                          C(*,*) BIT(*),        /* RESULT OF A & B OPERATION */
                                          N FIXED;              /* NO. OF ROWS OR COLUMNS */
 27    2         2            DECLARE(I, J, K) FIXED;       /* LOOP VARIABLES */

                                  /* INITIALIZE RESULT ARRAY */
 28    2         2                C = '0'B;

                                  /* COMPUTE A & B */
 29    2         2                DO I = 1 TO N ;               /* COMPUTE ROW ELEMENTS */
 30    2    1    2                    DO J = 1 TO N;            /* COMPUTE COLUMN ELEMENTS */
 31    2    2    2                        DO K = 1 TO N;        /* COMPUTE I, J ELEMENT */
 32    2    3    2                            C(I,J) = C(I,J) ¦ (A(I,K) & B(K,J));
 33    2    3    2                        END;
 34    2    2    2                    END;
 35    2    1    2                END;
 36    2         2                RETURN;
 37    2         2            END POWER;

 38    1         1            END PATHS;

ERRORS/WARNINGS DETECTED DURING CODE GENERATION:

      WARNING: NO FILE SPECIFIED. SYSIN/SYSPRINT ASSUMED. (CGOC)
A PATH OF LENGTH               2                 EXISTS

IN STMT   15 PROGRAM IS STOPPED.
```

Fig. 6-10 Program to find paths in graphs

T(25, 25)	BIT(1)	Array used for temporary results
L	FIXED	Current power of the adjacency matrix
G	FIXED	Loop variable
H	Fixed	Loop variable

The following data values were used in this program.

5

'0'B	'1'B	'0'B	'0'B	'0'B
'1'B	'0'B	'0'B	'1'B	'0'B
'0'B	'0'B	'0'B	'1'B	'1'B
'0'B	'1'B	'1'B	'0'B	'1'B
'0'B	'0'B	'1'B	'1'B	'0'B
2	5			

In statement 3, the number of nodes in the graph is read. Using this information, statement 4 through 9 accomplish the input of the adjacency matrix of the graph into arrays A and AL. The values of the nodes between which a path is sought is read. A counted loop is then used to find the paths in the graph. The element in row i and column j of the adjacency matrix is inspected, and if it has a value of '1'B, a message is printed indicating a path has been found and the program is terminated. If, however, this condition is not true, the POWER subprogram is called to calculate the next power of the adjacency matrix. Statements 18 through 22 then copy the result into the temporary array AL. If all possible paths have been found (i.e., the counted loop has been completely executed) without a path between the two specified nodes being found, statement 24 prints a message indicating that no path between the nodes exists.

EXERCISES FOR CHAPTER 6

1. The scalar product (also called the inner or dot product) of two vectors A and B of length n is defined as

$$AB = \sum_{i=1}^{n} a_i b_i = a_1 b_1 + a_2 b_2 + \ldots + a_n b_n$$

(i) Design a function with three parameters A, B, and N that computes the scalar product according to this formula.
(ii) If the scalar product of two vectors is zero, the vectors are said to be orthogonal. Design a program that calls the function from part (i). If the value returned is less than .00001, the message ORTHOGONAL VECTORS is to be printed.

2. Design a function FACTORIAL(N) that computes the factorial of the argument N (sometimes written as N!).
   For an integer N, N! is by definition

   $$N! = N * (N - 1) * (N - 2) * \ldots * 1$$

Incorporate in your function the special case

> $0! = 1.$

3. Design a procedure to accept as a parameter an arbitrary string containing a series of words separated by one or more blanks and return to the point of call the average number of letters in each word.

4. Design a procedure to accept as a parameter an adjacency matrix for a graph (containing no more than ten nodes) and a length k, and return to the point of call the number of paths of *exactly* length k in the graph. Test your procedure on the adjacency matrix given in Sec. 6-4.3.

5. The Saskatoon Police Department requires a program to assist them in determining the identities of criminals from filed descriptions supplied by their victims. The police have cards describing known criminals. These cards have the following format:

> name   height (in inches)   weight (in pounds)   address

Example:

> 'BUGSY MALONE'   53   119   '68 TOWN ST.'

Design a program that first reads in the deck of cards giving the description of known criminals and prepares a table of information on "known criminals". This set of cards is terminated by a special card of the form

'***' 0 0 '***'

A second set of cards follows, containing descriptions of criminals participating in unsolved crimes. These cards have the format:

> description of crime   estimated height of criminal   estimated weight

Example:

> '21 JULY: MUGGING'   68   155

This second set of cards is terminated by a special card of the form

> '***' 0 0

For each of the unsolved crimes, call a procedure (which you must also write) to determine possible suspects for the crime. This determination is based on the estimated height and weight of the criminals as given by the victims of the crimes. If the height is within two inches *and* the weight is within ten pounds, the person is to be listed as a possible suspect for the crime involved. The parameters are to include the table of "known criminals" and the card image on which the current crime is described.

CHAPTER

7

PROGRAMMING STYLE IN PL/I PROGRAMS

The issue of programming style has been addressed informally throughout the first six chapters of this book. This chapter deals with the subject in more depth, and considers the effect of style on the production of programs. The first section provides an introduction and motivation. Section 2 looks at issues of control structures and introduces the notion of "structured programming" as it relates to the use of control structures. Section 3 deals with the proper use of variables in a program. Section 4 considers questions of the presentation of a program. The chapter concludes with some final reflections and an annotated bibliography of suggested readings.

7-1 INTRODUCTION

Chapter 7 of the main text deals with the issue of programming style. The programming profession is presently undergoing a critical review of its own practices, motivated largely by the fact that many programs are of a disappointingly poor quality. This is felt to be due less to the talents of the individual programmers than to the methods by which the programs have been produced. The past decade has seen an influx of techniques reputed to improve the production of programs. These run the gamut from systematic methodologies, to graphical aids, to informal guidelines. If there is an underlying theme in these suggestions, it could well be the importance of programming style to the quality of programs.

Chapter 7 looks at the issue of programming style from several vantage points. First, some thoughts are offered on what constitutes a good program. We then review the individual phases of the programming process: problem analysis, solution development, solution implementation as a program, testing and maintenance. Section 7-4 deals with a methodology for solution development that we refer to as top-down design. In Sec. 7-5, we consider the actual implementation or coding of programs and show that considerations of style at this stage can be very important. The chapter concludes with some thoughts on human elements and their effect on the programming process.

In this chapter, we look more closely at implementation issues, specifically as they relate to the PL/I programming language. The language used to implement programs has an undeniably profound effect on their quality. The PL/I language offers a rich set of capabilities with which high-quality programs can be produced. It is important to remember, though, that the appropriate design work must precede any implementation effort. One is hard-pressed to produce a good program, in any language, from an inadequate, ill-conceived or incomplete design. As the saying goes, you can't make a silk purse out of a sow's ear. Although we will not dwell on issues of solution design in this manual, we will assume throughout this chapter that a careful design process has preceded any implementation we will undertake. The reader is advised to be completely comfortable with these processes, as presented in Sec. 7-4 (and, to some extent, Sec. 7-5) of the main text, before proceeding with this chapter.

A single chapter cannot hope to do justice to this topic. As we did in the main text, we draw your attention to the books *The Elements of Programming Style*, by Kernighan and Plauger, and *Programming Proverbs*, by Ledgard, both of which contain numerous PL/I examples. Although we can only scratch the surface, we hope that our examples serve to start you thinking in the right direction and to whet your appetite for more. The ultimate style you choose to adopt is largely a personal thing; to convince you of the importance of style is our objective here.

7-2 CONTROL STRUCTURES AND STRUCTURED PROGRAMMING

As stated in the main text, the "structure" of a program is determined largely by the constructs used to direct the flow of control through its statements. One of the first principles of "structured programming" is a restriction on the type of control structure that can be used. In the main text, we advocate restricting yourself to the IF-THEN-ELSE and REPEAT algorithmic constructs and combinations of these. PL/I, fortunately, offers direct analogues of these constructs in the IF-THEN-ELSE and DO constructs, respectively, as introduced in Chap. 3. Programs written using only these constructs are structured as a series of nested *action modules*, each of which has a single point of entry and a single point of exit. This greatly enhances the understanding and verification of the code. The example shown in Fig. 7-1 illustrates the concept of action modules in a segment taken from the program PATHS produced in Chap. 6 to determine the paths of a graph. The action modules are indicated by boxes. The *structure* of the program (as distinct from its *logic*) is clearly shown by the orderly nesting of the boxes. The program code reads in a straightforward fashion from top-to-bottom and executes similarily without unnecessarily jumping about in the code. The controlling code (that is, the DO's and the IF's) is clearly seen as well.

One language construct that is generally to be avoided is the *GO TO* statement. The GO TO statement permits an immediate jump to the statement whose label is referred to by the GO TO statement. Unrestricted use of the GO TO can seriously compromise attempts to provide a sound structure for a program since it violates the natural nested structure of action modules imposed by the IF-THEN-ELSE and DO-WHILE constructs. Rather than the smooth top-to-bottom flow of control evident in Fig. 7-1 for example, the flow of control in programs in which the GO TO statement has been used excessively often resembles a plate of spaghetti. Such a program is depicted in Fig. 7-2.

The GO TO statement per se is not bad; but unrestricted use of it is. Its flaw is its virtually unbounded scope — it is possible to branch almost anywhere in a program (with a few exceptions). There are places, however, where an immediate branch is desirable. Usually these correspond to exceptional conditions in a program that require a special action. One of the most common of these situations occurs when, for some reason, you wish to terminate a loop. For example, a particular item being sought has been found, or the data have been found to contain an error. In neither of these cases do you wish normal looping to continue. The GO TO provides an immediate escape from the control of the loop. Such an escape could be effected by setting an exit flag and incorporating a test for this flag in the exit test, as is done, for example, in sentinel-controlled input. In many programs, however, this results in very clumsy code, code that is awkward and often difficult to understand. In such a case, the use of the GO TO statement may lead to a more elegant solution. Consider the following example:

```
        DO I = 1 TO END_LIST;
                    .
                    .
                    .

            IF X(I) < 0
            THEN GO TO EXIT;
                    .
                    .
                    .

        END;
    EXIT: PUT LIST ('NEGATIVE VALUE ENCOUNTERED.');
```

In this particular example, processing of the elements of the vector X is suspended immediately if one of them is found to be negative. In this case the statement labelled "EXIT" is executed next. Note that the loop has been terminated as a result.

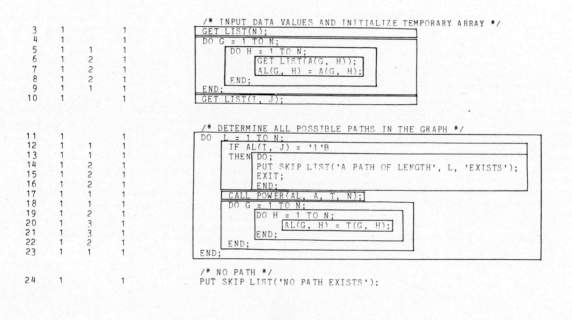

```
3   1        1        /* INPUT DATA VALUES AND INITIALIZE TEMPORARY ARRAY */
4   1        1        GET LIST(N);
5   1   1    1        DO G = 1 TO N;
6   1   2    1            DO H = 1 TO N;
7   1   2    1                GET LIST(A(G, H));
8   1   2    1                AL(G, H) = A(G, H);
9   1   1    1            END;
10  1        1        END;
                      GET LIST(I, J);

11  1        1        /* DETERMINE ALL POSSIBLE PATHS IN THE GRAPH */
12  1   1    1        DO L = 1 TO N;
13  1   1    1            IF AL(I, J) = '1'B
14  1   2    1            THEN DO;
15  1   2    1                PUT SKIP LIST('A PATH OF LENGTH', L, 'EXISTS');
16  1   2    1                EXIT;
17  1   1    1            END;
18  1   1    1            CALL POWER(AL, A, T, N);
19  1   2    1            DO G = 1 TO N;
20  1   3    1                DO H = 1 TO N;
21  1   3    1                    AL(G, H) = T(G, H);
22  1   2    1                END;
23  1   1    1            END;
                      END;

24  1        1        /* NO PATH */
                      PUT SKIP LIST('NO PATH EXISTS');
```

Fig. 7-1 Action modules in PL/I program

The GO TO statement in this particular case, offers a nice solution to a troublesome problem, while still preserving the "structure" of the code. As an exercise, try to produce this same effect using a flag.

Because PL/I offers a rich set of control structures, translation of the algorithmic constructs IF-THEN-ELSE and REPEAT presents no particular problems. Programmers in other languages, such as FORTRAN and BASIC, are normally not so fortunate. In some cases, it may be necessary to simulate the action of these constructs using more primitive control structures, such as the GO TO. We will not go into such simulations in this book.

As was pointed out in Sec. 7-5.2 of the main text, it is not sufficient to adhere to the *letter* of the law in producing structured programs; more important is a recognition of the *spirit* of the law in attempting to arrive at a clear, logical structure.

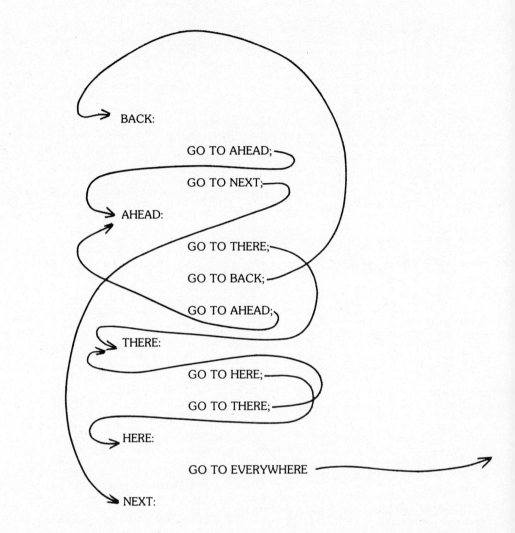

Fig. 7-2   Example of excessive use of the GO TO statement

This section is worth re-reading. Because of the similarity in control structures between the algorithmic language and PL/I, the comments in that section are highly pertinent.

Considerations of structure must be borne in mind throughout the development of a program not only in the coding phase, but also in the solution development phase. Good structure cannot be an afterthought. It must be seen as an important component of a good program that can aid as much in its creation as in its subsequent enhancements.

7-3 THE USE OF VARIABLES

Variables constitute an essential part of PL/I programming. It is important that they be employed to best advantage. PL/I offers the programmer considerable flexibility in the choice of variable names. This can be exploited to make PL/I programs largely self-documenting. This point is again made in the main text; namely, that variable names should be chosen to reflect the purpose of the variable in a program. This has a major impact on the readability of the code and also on its ability to be modified. Not only is it easier to understand the function of an individual statement when the variables in the statement are named so that their role in the program is clear, but also should a functional change be required in the program, it is easier to target on the variables involved. Figure 7-3 is a case in point. The first version of this program is identical to that given in Sec. 3-5 for processing orders in a university book store. The second version is the same program with single letter variable names. Which is easier to understand? Which would you rather modify?

Many PL/I compilers permit the programmer to omit the declaration of a variable. The compiler will create an *implicit* declaration for the variable at its first point of use. In many cases, no warning message is given.

Although this may enable a program to get into execution when otherwise it may have terminated with an error message, we feel this to be an undesirable feature for several reasons. First, as a matter of style, it is valuable to have declarations visibly present (see Fig. 7-3a, for example). This allows the reader of the program to survey the variables involved and also serves as a useful reference list, should the purpose or attributes of a particular variable be forgotten at some point. The remaining reasons for preferring *explicit* declarations are more technical. First, since no attributes have been supplied by the programmer, PL/I will be forced to assign default attributes. These may be other than what the programmer wishes, with unexpected consequences. Consider the following example

```
REP: PROCEDURE OPTIONS(MAIN);
       DECLARE (STRING, REPLACE, PATTERN) CHARACTER(30) VARYING;
       DECLARE (POSITION) FIXED;
       GET LIST (STRING, PATTERN, REPLACE);
       PUT LIST (STRING, PATTERN, REPLACE);
       POSITION = INDEX(STRING, PATTERN);
       IF POSITION = 0
       THEN RESULT = STRING;
       ELSE RESULT = SUBSTR(STRING, 1, POSITION–1) || REPLACE ||
            SUBSTR(STRING, POSITION+LENGTH(PATTERN));
       PUT LIST ( RESULT );
   END REP;
```

The purpose of this program is to read a string, a pattern, and a replacement pattern. If the pattern is found in the string, it is replaced accordingly; otherwise, the string is left intact. For example, if the input is

'MINICOMPUTER'   'NI'   'CRO'

```
/* PROGRAM TO DETERMINE THE PROFIT MARGIN ON BOOK ORDERS */

STMT LEVEL NEST BLOCK MLVL   SOURCE TEXT

                            /* PROGRAM TO DETERMINE THE PROFIT MARGIN ON BOOK ORDERS */

   1                        BSTORE: PROCEDURE OPTIONS (MAIN);

   2     1           1      DECLARE IDENT CHARACTER(6),   /* BOOK IDENTIFICATION NUMBER */
                               STOCK FIXED,               /* QUANTITY IN STOCK */
                               TYPE FIXED,                /* CLASSIFICATION OF THE BOOK */
                               ENROLMENT FIXED,           /* ESTIMATED COURSE ENROLMENT */
                               NEW FIXED,                 /* NEW TEXT OR USED PREVIOUSLY */
                               COST FLOAT,                /* WHOLESALE COST */
                               NUMBER REQUIRED FIXED,     /* NUMBER NEEDED */
                               ORDER FIXED,               /* NUMBER TO BE ORDERED */
                               PROFIT FLOAT,              /* PROFIT MARGIN ON BOOK */
                               TOTAL PROFIT FLOAT,        /* TOTAL PROFIT MARGIN */
                               END_FLAG CHARACTER(3) VARYING; /* END OF DATA FLAG */

                            /* INITIALIZE */
   3     1           1      TOTAL_PROFIT = 0.00;
   4     1           1      END_FLAG = 'OFF';

   5     1           1      ON ENDFILE (SYSIN) END_FLAG = 'ON';

                            /* PRINT REPORT HEADINGS */
   7     2           2      PUT SKIP LIST ('IDENTIFICATION', 'ON HAND', 'TO ORDER',
                               'PROFIT MARGIN');

                            /* PROCESS BOOKS */
   8     1           1      DO WHILE (END_FLAG = 'OFF');
                               /* READ INFORMATION FOR NEXT BOOK */
   9     1    1      1          GET LIST (IDENT, STOCK, TYPE, ENROLMENT, NEW, COST);
  10     1    1      1          IF END_FLAG = 'ON'
  11     1    1      1          THEN DO;
  12     1    2      1             PUT SKIP LIST ('TOTAL PROFIT', TOTAL_PROFIT);
  13     1    2      1             EXIT;
  14     1    2      1             END;

                            /* DETERMINE NUMBER OF COPIES REQUIRED */
  15     1    1      1          IF TYPE = 1
  16     1    1      1          THEN IF NEW = 1          /* PRESCRIBED TEXT */
  17     1    1      1             THEN NUMBER_REQUIRED = ROUND(0.85 * ENROLMENT, 0);
  18     1    1      1             ELSE NUMBER_REQUIRED = ROUND(0.60 * ENROLMENT, 0);
  19     1    1      1          ELSE IF NEW = 1          /* SUPPLEMENTARY READING */
  20     1    1      1             THEN NUMBER_REQUIRED = ROUND(0.40 * ENROLMENT, 0);
  21     1    1      1             ELSE NUMBER_REQUIRED = ROUND(0.25 * ENROLMENT, 0);

                            /* DETERMINE SIZE OF ORDER AND, IF NECESSSARY, ISSUE */
                            /* OVERSTOCKED NOTICE */
  22     1    1      1          ORDER = NUMBER_REQUIRED - STOCK;
  23     1    1      1          IF ORDER < 0
  24     1    1      1          THEN PUT SKIP LIST (IDENT, 'IS OVERSTOCKED:', ABS(ORDER),
                                   'COPIES TO RETURN');

                            /* DETERMINE PROFIT ON THIS BOOK */
  25     1    1      1          IF COST <= 10.00
  26     1    1      1          THEN PROFIT = NUMBER_REQUIRED * 0.25 * COST;
  27     1    1      1          ELSE PROFIT = NUMBER_REQUIRED * 0.20 * COST;

                            /* UPDATE TOTAL PROFIT STATISTIC */
  28     1    1      1          TOTAL_PROFIT = TOTAL_PROFIT + PROFIT;

                            /* PRINT LINE FOR THIS BOOK */
  29     1    1      1          PUT SKIP LIST (IDENT, STOCK, ORDER, PROFIT);
  30     1    1      1          END;

  31     1           1      END BSTORE;
```

Fig. 7-3 (a)   The importance of choice of variable names

```
/* PROGRAM TO DETERMINE THE PROFIT MARGIN ON BOOK ORDERS */
STMT LEVEL NEST BLOCK MLVL   SOURCE TEXT

                              /* PROGRAM TO DETERMINE THE PROFIT MARGIN ON BOOK ORDERS */
  1                           BSTORE: PROCEDURE OPTIONS (MAIN);
  2     1           1         DECLARE I CHARACTER(6),   /* BOOK IDENTIFICATION NUMBER */
                                       S FIXED,          /* QUANTITY IN STOCK */
                                       T FIXED,          /* CLASSIFICATION OF THE BOOK */
                                       E FIXED,        /* ESTIMATED COURSE ENROLMENT */
                                       N FIXED,         /* NEW TEXT OR USED PREVIOUSLY */
                                       C FLOAT,          /* WHOLESALE COST */
                                       R FIXED,      /* NUMBER NEEDED */
                                       O FIXED,         /* NUMBER TO BE ORDERED */
                                       P FLOAT,         /* PROFIT MARGIN ON BOOK */
                                       Q FLOAT,   /* TOTAL PROFIT MARGIN */
                                       F CHARACTER(3) VARYING; /* END OF DATA FLAG */

                              /* INITIALIZE */
  3     1           1         Q = 0.00;
  4     1           1         F = 'OFF';

  5     1           1         ON ENDFILE (SYSIN) F = 'ON';

                              /* PRINT REPORT HEADINGS */
  7     2           2         PUT SKIP LIST ('IDENTIFICATION', 'ON HAND', 'TO ORDER',
                                 'PROFIT MARGIN');

                              /* PROCESS BOOKS */
  8     1           1         DO WHILE (F = 'OFF');
                                  /* READ INFORMATION FOR NEXT BOOK */
  9     1     1     1             GET LIST (I, S, T, E, N, C);
 10     1     1     1             IF F = 'ON'
 11     1     1     1             THEN DO;
 12     1     2     1                 PUT SKIP LIST ('TOTAL PROFIT', Q);
 13     1     2     1                 EXIT;
 14     1     2     1                 END;

                                  /* DETERMINE NUMBER OF COPIES REQUIRED */
 15     1     1     1             IF T = 1
 16     1     1     1             THEN IF N = 1          /* PRESCRIBED TEXT */
 17     1     1     1                 THEN R = ROUND(0.85 * E, 0);
 18     1     1     1                 ELSE R = ROUND(0.60 * E, 0);
 19     1     1     1             ELSE IF N = 1          /* SUPPLEMENTARY READING */
 20     1     1     1                 THEN R = ROUND(0.40 * E, 0);
 21     1     1     1                 ELSE R = ROUND(0.25 * E, 0);

                                  /* DETERMINE SIZE OF ORDER AND, IF NECESSSARY, ISSUE */
                                  /* OVERSTOCKED NOTICE */
 22     1     1     1             O = R - S;
 23     1     1     1             IF O < 0
 24     1     1     1             THEN PUT SKIP LIST (I, 'IS OVERSTOCKED:', ABS(O),
                                     'COPIES TO RETURN');

                                  /* DETERMINE PROFIT ON THIS BOOK */
 25     1     1     1             IF C <= 10.00
 26     1     1     1             THEN P = R * 0.25 * C;
 27     1     1     1             ELSE P = R * 0.20 * C;

                                  /* UPDATE TOTAL PROFIT STATISTIC */
 28     1     1     1             Q = Q + P;

                                  /* PRINT LINE FOR THIS BOOK */
 29     1     1     1             PUT SKIP LIST (I, S, O, P);
 30     1     1     1             END;

 31     1           1         END BSTORE;
```

Fig. 7-3 (b)   The importance of choice of variable names (cont'd.)

the "NI" pattern in "MINICOMPUTER" will be replaced by "CRO" to yield "MICROCOMPUTER". The solution is a fairly straightforward program of nine statements. However, the program doesn't work. Instead, the following message results.

```
MINICOMPUTER              NI          CRO
***** ERROR IN STMT   9  ( INVALID CHARACTER(S) IN FIELD. 0 USED FOR EACH. ORIGINAL STRING IS MICROCOMPUTER FIRST BAD CHARACTER IS M (EX1D)
                                       0.00000E+00


IN STMT      11 PROGRAM RETURNS FROM MAIN PROCEDURE.
```

Why? The answer lies in the failure to declare the variable RESULT. Since there is no explicit declaration of RESULT, it is implicitly declared at its first occurrence to be a FLOAT variable (the default decision). This is, of course, imcompatible with the assignment of a string value.

The problem in this case was fairly easy to diagnose. In other situations, this is not so. Consider the case given in Fig. 7-4.

This appears to be the same program that worked correctly in Chap. 6. The key difference is that the declaration of the loop control variables in the procedure POWER has been omitted. Perhaps the programmer felt that these were not sufficiently important to warrant explicit declaration; and, besides, the compiler uses FIXED anyway. Well, as you can see, the consequences are fairly dramatic. Because variables I and J have been declared in an enclosing scope and there is no overriding local declaration, they are global to the procedure POWER. Thus, when the execution of the procedure POWER changes the values of I and J, the values in the main program are changed as well. The absence of an explicit declaration for the local loop control variables (although seemingly unimportant) was a direct cause of this problem. Could you have debugged this one?

In this section, we have offered some comments on the use of variables in PL/I programs. Although partly a matter of style and partly a matter of good programming practice, the thoughtful use of variables can make a significant contribution toward high quality computer programs.

7-4 PROGRAM PRESENTATION

Section 7-5.3 of the main text deals with two facets of the program presentation question: comments and paragraphing. As stated, the program code itself serves as the front line of documentation. It is essential that the code be easy to read. Comments and paragraphing play important roles to this end.

The PL/I comment facility provides for comments of various forms. Lengthy comments, extending perhaps over several lines, can be used to explain the purpose and assumptions of a section of code (for example, a procedure). Figure 7-5 shows the use of such a comment to describe the purpose and parameters of the program INSERT from Sec. 6-5. Notice also the presence of three additional comments before statements

```
IF SEARCH(NAME, SIZE, VAR_NAME) ¬= 0
SIZE = SIZE + 1;
```

and

```
NAME(SIZE) = VAR_NAME;
```

to describe the purpose of each of those sections of code. PL/I also allows comments to be placed on the same line as code, as for example in line 5 of Fig. 7-5. Normally, these might be considered as *elaborative* comments; that is, comments that elaborate on the piece of code on the same line, providing some information or insight not discernible from the code itself. Both types of comment are useful and important.

Section 7-5.3 contains some good material on the use of comments, much of it taken from the aforementioned books by Kernighan and Plauger and Ledgard, as well as an article entitled "Some Comments on Comments" by Sachs. In general, comments exist to explain and support program code. They should not be expected to improve bad code. Be wary of overcommenting, which serves only to add clutter to an already cluttered visual display. Do not just "parrot" the code by repeating it in comment form, but try to add something that will be of value to a reader trying to understand what is going on. Lastly, ensure that comments and code agree at all times. Too often, changes are made to code, without the corresponding changes to the related comments. This increases confusion immeasurably.

The writing of good comments can be as difficult as the writing of good code; yet, at the same time, it can also be as important. It is a skill that you will develop through practice, provided that you recognize it as important. It is.

Paragraphing is another important element of program presentation that is, again, well-supported by features of PL/I. PL/I is a free-format language, allowing the programmer to adopt a completely individual scheme for the positioning of statements on cards (and thus, the appearance of the source listing). If taken advantage of, this can offer valuable assistance in identifying structural and logical program units, as is done in the spacing of the algorithms in the main text. If abused, however, the free-format feature can increase confusion considerably. Figure 7-6 shows the same program presented in three ways: totally random alignment, linear alignment (that is, all statements start in the same column) and our preferred indentation scheme with blank cards judiciously placed to increase separation. The readability advantages are obvious.

Paragraphing is particularly valuable when nesting is employed. The program in Fig. 7-6c contains various types of nesting. In each case, the paragraphing scheme removes confusion by indicating clearly what corresponds to what. For example, in the program section beginning with the comment.

```
/*READ IN SCHEDULE OF FAMILY ALLOWANCE PAYMENTS*/
```

it is readily apparent that the loop

```
DO J = 0 TO 6;
```

is completely under control of the loop

```
DO I = 1 TO 9;
```

```
/* PROGRAM TO  DETERMINE WHETHER OR NOT A PATH EXISTS BETWEEN TWO */

STMT LEVEL NEST BLOCK MLVL   SOURCE TEXT


                              /* PROGRAM TO  DETERMINE WHETHER OR NOT A PATH EXISTS BETWEEN TWO */
                              /* SPECIFIED NODES, I AND J, OF A 5 X 5 GRAPH, A */

  1                           PATHS: PROCEDURE OPTIONS(MAIN);

  2    1         1            DECLARE N FIXED,              /* NO. OF NODES IN THE GRAPH */
                                      A(25, 25) BIT(1),     /* ADJACENCY MATRIX OF THE GRAPH */
                                      (I, J) FIXED,         /* NODES BETWEEN WHICH A PATH IS */
                                                            /* SOUGHT */
                                      AL(25, 25) BIT(1),    /* TEMPORARY ARRAY */
                                      T(25, 25) BIT(1),     /* TEMPORARY ARRAY */
                                      L FIXED,              /* POWER OF THE ADJACENCY MATRIX */
                                                            /* BEING COMPUTED */
                                      (G, H) FIXED;         /* LOOP VARIABLES */

                              /* INPUT DATA VALUES AND INITIALIZE TEMPORARY ARRAY */
  3    1         1            GET LIST(N);
  4    1         1            DO G = 1 TO N;
  5    1   1     1                DO H = 1 TO N;
  6    1   2     1                    GET LIST(A(G, H));
  7    1   2     1                    AL(G, H) = A(G, H);
  8    1   2     1                END;
  9    1   1     1            END;
 10    1         1            GET LIST(I, J);


                              /* DETERMINE ALL POSSIBLE PATHS IN THE GRAPH */
 11    1         1            DO L = 1 TO N;
 12    1   1     1                IF AL(I, J) = '1'B
 13    1   1     1                THEN DO;
 14    1   2     1                    PUT SKIP LIST('A PATH OF LENGTH', L, 'EXISTS');
 15    1   2     1                    EXIT;
 16    1   2     1                END;
 17    1   1     1                CALL POWER(AL, A, T, N);
 18    1   1     1                DO G = 1 TO N;
 19    1   2     1                    DO H = 1 TO N;
 20    1   3     1                        AL(G, H) = T(G, H);
 21    1   3     1                    END;
 22    1   2     1                END;
 23    1   1     1            END;

                              /* NO PATH */
 24    1         1            PUT SKIP LIST('NO PATH EXISTS');

                              /* PROCEDURE TO CALCULATE A & B FOR A AND B, BOTH N X N ARRAYS */

 25    1         1            POWER: PROCEDURE(A, B, C, N);
 26    2         2                DECLARE A(*,*) BIT(*),              /* INPUT BOOLEAN ARRAY */
                                          B(*,*) BIT(*),
                                          C(*,*) BIT(*),              /* RESULT OF A & B OPERATION */
                                          N FIXED;                    /* NO. OF ROWS OR COLUMNS */

                                  /* INITIALIZE RESULT ARRAY */
 27    2         2                C = '0'B;

                                  /* COMPUTE A & B */
 28    2         2                DO I = 1 TO N ;              /* COMPUTE ROW ELEMENTS */
 29    2   1     2                    DO J = 1 TO N;           /* COMPUTE COLUMN ELEMENTS */
 30    2   2     2                        DO K = 1 TO N;       /* COMPUTE I, J ELEMENT */
 31    2   3     2                            C(I,J) = C(I,J) | (A(I,K) & B(K,J));
 32    2   3     2                        END;
 33    2   2     2                    END;
 34    2   1     2                END;
 35    2         2                RETURN;
 36    2         2            END POWER;

 37    1         1            END PATHS;

ERRORS/WARNINGS DETECTED DURING CODE GENERATION:

      WARNING: NO FILE SPECIFIED. SYSIN/SYSPRINT ASSUMED. (CGOC)
```

Fig. 7-4   Path program with local declarations removed

```
***** ERROR IN STMT   12  AL(6,6)  HAS NOT BEEN INITIALIZED.   IT IS SET TO ZERO. (EX5D)
NO PATH EXISTS


IN STMT    37  PROGRAM RETURNS FROM MAIN PROCEDURE.
```

Fig. 7-4 Path program with local declarations removed (cont'd.)

In the section of code beginning with the comment

/*DETERMINE APPROPRIATE ROW SUBSCRIPT*/

the statement

R = TRUNC((INCOME – 1000) / 1000);

is clearly seen to be executed only when the value of INCOME is between 3000 and 10000 (including 3000).

As observed earlier in this book, the PL/I language is particularly confusing in its multiple use of the word "END". In Fig. 7-6c, there are in fact four END statements. Part of this confusion can be alleviated with paragraphing to indicate what, in particular, a given END is meant to close. This can be made even more clear through the use of operands on the END statements as in the final statement in Fig. 7-6c. The operand indicates the label on the first statement of the construct that the END is meant to close. Thus

END BENEFIT;

is meant to close the procedure name BENEFIT. Labels can also be placed on DO loops and BEGIN blocks, as in

READ: DO I = 1 TO NUM_VALUES;
      .

      .

      .
      GET LIST (VAL(I));
      .

      .

      .
END READ;
      and
INNER: BEGIN;
      .

      .

      .
END INNER;

```
                            /* PROCEDURE TO INSERT A VARIABLE INTO A SYMBOL TABLE  */
                            /* NAME, TYPE, AND ADDRESS ARE GLOBAL VECTORS COMPRISING THE  */
                            /* SYMBOL TABLE */

26    1        1            INSERT: PROCEDURE(VAR_NAME, VAR_TYPE, VAR_ADDRESS, SIZE);

27    2        3                DECLARE VAR_NAME CHARACTER(*) VARYING,  /* VARIABLE'S NAME */
                                        VAR_TYPE CHARACTER(*) VARYING,  /* VARIABLE'S TYPE */
                                        VAR_ADDRESS FIXED, /* ADDRESS OF VARIABLE */
                                        SIZE FIXED;  /* NO. OF ENTRIES IN THE SYMBOL TABLE */

                                /* CHECK IF VARIABLE HAS ALREADY BEEN DEFINED */
28    2        3                IF SEARCH(NAME, SIZE, VAR_NAME) ¬= 0
29    2        3                THEN DO;
30    2    1   3                    PUT SKIP LIST('***ERROR - VARIABLE',VAR_NAME,
                                        'HAS BEEN PREVIOUSLY DEFINED.');
31    2    1   3                    RETURN;
32    2    1   3                END;

                                /* COMPUTE THE NEXT AVAILABLE POSITION */
33    2        3                SIZE = SIZE + 1;
34    2        3                IF SIZE > MAXNUM
35    2        3                THEN DO;  /* TABLE IS FULL */
36    2    1   3                    PUT SKIP LIST('***ERROR - TOO MANY VARIABLES DEFINED.');
37    2    1   3                    RETURN;
38    2    1   3                END;

                                /* MAKE INSERTION INTO THE POSITION FOUND */
39    2        3                NAME(SIZE) = VAR_NAME;
40    2        3                TYPE(SIZE) = VAR_TYPE;
41    2        3                ADDRESS(SIZE) = VAR_ADDRESS;
42    2        3                RETURN;

43    2        3            END INSERT;
```

Fig. 7-5   The use of descriptive comments

This operand is, of course, completely optional.

As stated in the main text, issues of program presentation seldom *cause* errors, but they can play a large role in avoiding them. In addition to the pride felt when a program listing has a pleasing, professional appearance, the presentation of a program is a key determinant of its readability, and through this, of its quality.

7-5 REFLECTIONS

The theme in this chapter has been the role of programming style in the production of good programs. This is an important aspect, to be sure, but one must be careful not to interpret "style" in too restrictive a manner. There are many elements involved in the production of a program. Is the problem completely understood? Is the program adequately specified? Has the best algorithm been employed? Have the most appropriate data structures been used? And the list continues.

The purpose of this chapter has not been to suggest that good programs follow directly from attention to matters of style. That is certainly not the case; however, this can provide a suitable starting point. As much as anything, we are encouraging a mental attitude. It is our belief that if you care enough to do your best always, that you stand a good chance of succeeding as a programmer.

```
/* PROGRAM TO COMPUTE THE MONTHLY FAMILY ALLOWANCE PAYMENTS */

STMT LEVEL NEST BLOCK MLVL   SOURCE TEXT


                                /* PROGRAM TO COMPUTE THE MONTHLY FAMILY ALLOWANCE PAYMENTS */
   1                                        BENEFIT: PROCEDURE OPTIONS(MAIN);

   2    1           1        DECLARE SCHED(9, 0:6) FIXED, /* SCHEDULE OF PAYMENTS */
                                           INCOME FIXED,  /* FAMILY'S INCOME */
                                   CHILDREN FIXED,        /* NO OF CHILDREN */
                             END_FLAG CHARACTER(3) VARYING,        /* END OF DATA FLAG */
                                           R FIXED,    /* ROW SUBSCRIPT */
                                       C FIXED,             /* COLUMN SUBSCRIPT */
                             (I,J) FIXED;        /* LOOP VARIABLES */

                                       /*INITIALIZE */
   3    1           1            END_FLAG = 'OFF';
   4    1           1                        ON ENDFILE(SYSIN) END_FLAG = 'ON';

                                /* READ IN SCHEDULE OF FAMILY ALLOWANCE PAYMENTS */
   6    2           2                                DO I = 1 TO 9;
   7    1    1      1                        DO J = 0 TO 6;
   8    1    2      1                    GET LIST (SCHED(I, J));
   9    1    2      1                        END;
  10    1    1      1            END;

                                /* PROCESS FAMILIES */
  11    1           1                        DO WHILE (END_FLAG = 'OFF');

                                                /* READ DATA FOR NEXT FAMILY */
  12    1    1      1            GET LIST (INCOME, CHILDREN);
  13    1    1      1                        IF END_FLAG = 'ON'
  14    1    1      1                THEN EXIT;

                                /* DETERMINE APPROPRIATE ROW SUBSCRIPT */
  15    1    1      1                            IF INCOME < 3000
  16    1    1      1            THEN R = 1;
  17    1    1      1                    ELSE IF INCOME >= 10000
  18    1    1      1                THEN R = 9;
  19    1    1      1                    ELSE R = TRUNC((INCOME - 1000) / 1000);

                                /* DETERMINE APPROPRIATE COLUMN SUBSCRIPT */
  20    1    1      1                            IF CHILDREN >= 6
  21    1    1      1                THEN C = 6;
  22    1    1      1            ELSE C = CHILDREN;

                                /* SELECT CORRECT PAYMENT */
  23    1    1      1                        PUT SKIP LIST ('PAYMENT IS', SCHED(R, C));
  24    1    1      1                            END;
  25    1           1                        END BENEFIT;

ERRORS/WARNINGS DETECTED DURING CODE GENERATION:

      WARNING: NO FILE SPECIFIED. SYSIN/SYSPRINT ASSUMED. (CGOC)

PAYMENT IS              15
PAYMENT IS              21
PAYMENT IS               0
PAYMENT IS              17
PAYMENT IS              22
PAYMENT IS              17
PAYMENT IS              23
PAYMENT IS               9
PAYMENT IS               9
PAYMENT IS              19


IN STMT   14  PROGRAM IS STOPPED.
```

Fig. 7-6 (a)   Three program presentations

```
/* PROGRAM TO COMPUTE THE MONTHLY FAMILY ALLOWANCE PAYMENTS */

STMT LEVEL NEST BLOCK MLVL   SOURCE TEXT


                                    /* PROGRAM TO COMPUTE THE MONTHLY FAMILY ALLOWANCE PAYMENTS */

    1                               BENEFIT: PROCEDURE OPTIONS(MAIN);

    2    1              1           DECLARE SCHED(9, 0:6) FIXED,   /*SCHEDULE OF PAYMENTS */
                                    INCOME FIXED,                  /* FAMILY'S INCOME */
                                    CHILDREN FIXED,                /* NO. OF CHILDREN */
                                    END_FLAG CHARACTER(3) VARYING, /*END OF DATA FLAG */
                                    R FIXED,                       /* ROW SUBSCRIPT */
                                    C FIXED,                       /* COLUMN SUBSCRIPT */
                                    (I, J) FIXED;                  /* LOOP VARIABLE */

                                    /* INITIALIZE */
    3    1              1           END_FLAG = 'OFF';
    4    1              1           ON ENDFILE(SYSIN) END_FLAG = 'ON';

                                    /* READ IN SCHEDULE OF FAMILY ALLOWANCE PAYMENTS */
    6    2              2           DO I = 1 TO 9;
    7    1    1         1           DO J = 0 TO 6;
    8    1    2         1           GET LIST (SCHED(I, J));
    9    1    2         1           END;
   10    1    1         1           END;

                                    /* PROCESS FAMILIES */
   11    1              1           DO WHILE (END_FLAG = 'OFF');

                                    /* READ DATA FOR NEXT FAMILY */
   12    1    1         1           GET LIST (INCOME, CHILDREN);
   13    1    1         1           IF END_FLAG = 'ON'
   14    1    1         1           THEN EXIT;

                                    /* DETERMINE APPROPRIATE ROW SUBSCRIPT */
   15    1    1         1           IF INCOME < 3000
   16    1    1         1           THEN R = 1;
   17    1    1         1           ELSE IF INCOME >= 10000
   18    1    1         1           THEN R = 9;
   19    1    1         1           ELSE R = TRUNC((INCOME - 1000) / 1000);

                                    /*DETERMINE APPROPRIATE COLUMN SUBSCRIPT */
   20    1    1         1           IF CHILDREN >= 6
   21    1    1         1           THEN C = 6;
   22    1    1         1           ELSE C = CHILDREN;

                                    /* SELECT CORRECT PAYMENT */
   23    1    1         1           PUT SKIP LIST ('PAYMENT IS', SCHED(R, C));
   24    1    1         1           END;
   25    1              1           END BENEFIT;

ERRORS/WARNINGS DETECTED DURING CODE GENERATION:

     WARNING: NO FILE SPECIFIED. SYSIN/SYSPRINT ASSUMED. (CGOC)

PAYMENT IS                 15
PAYMENT IS                 21
PAYMENT IS                  0
PAYMENT IS                 17
PAYMENT IS                 22
PAYMENT IS                 17
PAYMENT IS                 23
PAYMENT IS                  9
PAYMENT IS                  9
PAYMENT IS                 19


IN STMT   14  PROGRAM IS STOPPED.
```

Fig. 7-6 (b)   Three program presentations (cont'd.)

```
/* PROGRAM TO COMPUTE THE MONTHLY FAMILY ALLOWANCE PAYMENTS */

STMT LEVEL NEST BLOCK MLVL  SOURCE TEXT


                            /* PROGRAM TO COMPUTE THE MONTHLY FAMILY ALLOWANCE PAYMENTS */

    1                       BENEFIT: PROCEDURE OPTIONS(MAIN);

    2    1         1        DECLARE SCHED(9, 0:6) FIXED, /* SCHEDULE OF PAYMENTS */
                                    INCOME FIXED,        /* FAMILY'S INCOME */
                                    CHILDREN FIXED,      /* NO OF CHILDREN */
                                    END_FLAG CHARACTER(3) VARYING,  /* END OF DATA FLAG */
                                    R FIXED,             /* ROW SUBSCRIPT */
                                    C FIXED,             /* COLUMN SUBSCRIPT */
                                    (I, J) FIXED;        /* LOOP VARIABLES */

                            /* INITIALIZE */
    3    1         1        END_FLAG = 'OFF';
    4    1         1        ON ENDFILE(SYSIN) END_FLAG = 'ON';

                            /* READ IN SCHEDULE OF FAMILY ALLOWANCE PAYMENTS */
    6    2         2        DO I = 1 TO 9;
    7    1    1    1            DO J = 0 TO 6;
    8    1    2    1                GET LIST (SCHED(I, J));
    9    1    2    1            END;
   10    1    1    1        END;

                            /* PROCESS FAMILIES */
   11    1         1        DO WHILE (END_FLAG = 'OFF');

                                /* READ DATA FOR NEXT FAMILY */
   12    1    1    1            GET LIST (INCOME, CHILDREN);
   13    1    1    1            IF END_FLAG = 'ON'
   14    1    1    1            THEN EXIT;

                                /* DETERMINE APPROPRIATE ROW SUBSCRIPT */
   15    1    1    1            IF INCOME < 3000
   16    1    1    1            THEN R = 1;
   17    1    1    1            ELSE IF INCOME >= 10000
   18    1    1    1                THEN R = 9;
   19    1    1    1                ELSE R = TRUNC((INCOME - 1000) / 1000);

                                /* DETERMINE APPROPRIATE COLUMN SUBSCRIPT */
   20    1    1    1            IF CHILDREN >= 6
   21    1    1    1            THEN C = 6;
   22    1    1    1            ELSE C = CHILDREN;

                                /* SELECT CORRECT PAYMENT */
   23    1    1    1            PUT SKIP LIST ('PAYMENT IS', SCHED(R, C));
   24    1    1    1        END;
   25    1         1        END BENEFIT;

ERRORS/WARNINGS DETECTED DURING CODE GENERATION:

PAYMENT IS             15
PAYMENT IS             21
PAYMENT IS              0
PAYMENT IS             17
PAYMENT IS             22
PAYMENT IS             17
PAYMENT IS             23
PAYMENT IS              9
PAYMENT IS              9
PAYMENT IS             19


IN STMT  14 PROGRAM IS STOPPED.
```

Fig. 7-6 (c)   Three program presentations (cont'd.)

BIBLIOGRAPHY

The items in this list deal with various issues in the practice of programming, some of which have been dealt with in this chapter; many of which have not. Comments are offered where they are felt to be appropriate

ACM: Computing Surveys, special issue on programming (edited by Peter J. Denning), 6, December, 1974.
This special issue contains a number of articles of varying degrees of readability. They range from articles of a general survey flavour to articles on specific technical topics, which are the most difficult.

Brooks, Frederick P. JR.: *The Mythical Man-Month*, Addison-Wesley, Reading, Mass., 1975.
This is a very entertaining and informative collection of essays on programming and the management of programming projects, specifically slanted to very large projects. The style is light and casual.

Dijkstra, Edsger W.: "The Humble Programmer," *Communications of the ACM*, 15, October, 1972, p. 859.
This article was the text of the author's Turing lecture to the Association of Computing Machinery. It offers some interesting insights on programming and the computing profession in an easy-to-read style.

Dijkstra, Edsger W.: *A Discipline of Programming*, Prentice-Hall Inc., Englewood Cliffs, N.J., 1976.
A major work, this book is difficult and is intended for the serious student of programming.

Jackson, Michael A.: *Principles of Program Design*, Academic Press, 1975.
The author offers a constructive and repeatable method for the design of correct programs that relies little on inspiration and insight on the designer's part. The approach differs from that which we have presented, but a comparison of the methods would certainly be valuable.

Kernighan, Brian W., and Plauger, P.J.: *The Elements of Programming Style*, McGraw-Hill Book Co., New York, 1974.
This is a concise, well-written and entertaining book that operates in a critical mode. Working from existing programs, the authors show how they can be improved through consideration of style.

Ledgard, Henry F.: *Programming Proverbs*, Hayden Book Company, Rochelle Park, New Jersey, 1975.
Written in a light, amusing style, this book contains many good programming tips with ample illustration.

Mills, Harlan D.: "Software Development", *Transactions on Software Engineering*, SE-2, 1976, p.265.
This is a good overview of the present state of software development. The article is well-written and very readable.

Sachs, Jon: "Some Comments on Comments," * (Systems Documentation
    Newsletter), 3, December, 1976.
    This easy-to-read article offers some good suggestions on the use of
comments in programs.

Weinberg, Gerald M.: *The Psychology of Computer Programming*,
    Van Nostrand Reinhold, New York, 1971.
    This is good reading for anyone interested in more than just the technical
issues of programming. Highly anecdotal in style, it offers very entertaining and
informative reading.

Wirth, Niklaus: "Program Development by Stepwise Refinement,"
    Communications of the ACM, 14, April 1971, p. 221.
    This article is a good discussion, complete with examples, of top-down
design. It may be somewhat heavy-going for the novice.

CHAPTER

NUMERICAL COMPUTATIONS

This chapter explains the programming aspects of numerical computations in PL/I. First the specifications of precision for PL/I arithmetic computations are given. Next we discuss the propagation of errors in such computations. Finally, programs for several numerical applications dealing with finding roots of equations, integration, solution of simultaneous equations, and least-squares curve fitting are presented.

8-1 ERRORS

This section discusses the specification of precision for variables in PL/I. Also, we discuss the precision of constants and intermediate results. Finally, a description of how the programmer can handle certain computational problems on the compiler is given.

8-1.1 The Specification of Precision in PL/I

Section 2-1.1 presented an introduction to the DECLARE statement in PL/I. The variable attributes given were only those most commonly used by novice programmers. This subsection contains a discussion of the declaration of variables for computational purposes which is more complete than that given previously.

The *precision* of a variable specifies the range of values that it can hold. From our discussion of errors in the main text, it is clear that a computer can represent numbers only within some finite precision. For many of the example programs given earlier, we have relied on default precisions associated with numeric variables. For the IBM 360/370 PL/C versions of programs, the following default precision values apply.

FIXED	DECIMAL	5 decimal digits plus sign (-99999 to $+99999$)
FLOAT	DECIMAL	6 decimal digits plus sign with a range of exponent values between 10^{-78} to 10^{+75} (approximately)
FIXED	BINARY	15 bits plus sign (-32768 to $+32767$)
FLOAT	BINARY	21 bits plus sign with a range of exponent values between 2^{-260} to 2^{+252} (approximately)

For certain calculations (and associated variables), however, it may be required that more than the standard (or default) number of digits be stored in the computer's memory. Such an approach reduces the effect of truncation for the variables in question. Clearly, there must be some maximum number of digits that can be carried in numerical computations. We now examine how this specification is denoted in PL/C.

Recall that three classes of attributes have been discussed in conjunction with the declaration of a numeric variable. The programmer (or the compiler in case of default) must choose one attribute from each class and include the appropriate keywords in the list of attributes for the variable. Also recall that the order of these three attributes is not important. The first class of attributes gives the number *base* of the numeric values which the variable will assume; namely, DECIMAL or BINARY. A variable which is declared to have a base attribute of DECIMAL is able to hold numbers of a decimal base, while the BINARY attribute defines the variable to accommodate only binary numbers. The second attribute class specifies the *mode* of the variable, REAL or COMPLEX, which specify whether the variable will hold real or complex numbers, respectively (the default mode attribute is REAL). The third attribute class gives the *scale* of a variable – FIXED or FLOAT. A FIXED variable can assume fixed-point values. A FLOAT variable, on the other hand, specifies a floating point value.

In addition to these attribute classes, a programmer can also specify a *precision* attribute. This attribute, unlike the three others, has no keyword associated with it, but is specified in the attribute list by one or two decimal integers enclosed in parentheses, depending on the scale attribute of the variable being declared. For example, the declaration statement:

DECLARE A FLOAT DECIMAL(4);

declares A to be a floating-point variable which can contain four significant digits.

For a FLOAT variable, the precision attribute consists of a single decimal integer constant, enclosed in parentheses, of form (p). The integer "p" specifies the total number of significant digits that are allowed for any floating-point value assigned to the variable. Assignment of a value to a variable which allows fewer significant digits than the variable contains causes the extra significant digits to be truncated, starting from the right. That is, the least significant digit is the first to be lost in the truncation process.

For FIXED variables, the precision attribute is a pair of decimal integers separated by a comma and enclosed in parentheses of the form (p, q). The first integer, "p", must be assigned and specifies, for any fixed point value assigned to the variable, the total number of digits that will be allowed in the value. The second integer, "q", may be assigned, and it indicates the number of digits to be kept to the right of the decimal (binary) point in each of the values that may be assigned to the variable. If the second integer in the precision attribute for a FIXED variable is omitted, then the compiler assumes a value of 0, thus limiting that variable to integer values. If a value contains more fractional digits than are allowed by the second integer (q) in the precision attribute for a certain FIXED variable, then the rightmost fractional digits are truncated, thus reducing the correct number of digits. If, on the other hand, a value containing less than the allowed number of digits is assigned to a variable, then the nonfractional part of the number is padded with leading zeros; similarly, the fractional part of the number is padded with trailing zeros. As an example, the declaration statement

DECLARE PAY FIXED DECIMAL(6, 2);

creates a variable PAY that can have values between −9999.99 and +9999.99. The execution of the assignment statement

PAY = 10.28;

assigns the value 0010.28 to the variable PAY. The declaration

DECLARE METER FIXED DECIMAL(5, −3);

contains a negative scale factor (−3) which is used to specify that three zeros are assumed to the immediate left of the decimal point. That is, the possible values for METER lie between −99999000 and +99999000.

Observe that the precision attribute is the only attribute whose position in the attribute list is significant. It *must* be written following one of the other three attributes, and thus may not appear as the first in the list. There also are precision restrictions on the values that numeric variables are allowed to have. These restrictions, however, are compiler dependent. For example, the IBM 360/370 PL/I F – level compiler has the following precision attributes:

FIXED	DECIMAL	15 digits plus sign
FLOAT	DECIMAL	16 decimal digits plus sign with a range of exponent values between 10^{-78} to 10^{+75} (approximately)
FIXED	BINARY	31 bits plus sign (equivalent to a maximum value of 2,147,483,647 in decimal)
FLOAT	BINARY	53 bits plus sign with a range of exponent values between 2^{-260} to 2^{+252} (approximately)

Often when a programmer declares a numeric variable, not all of the above need be stated explicitly. In such a case, the compiler must supply attributes by default. The following default rules apply:

1. If the scale attribute is omitted, the compiler assumes the scale attribute of FLOAT.
2. If the base attribute is absent, the compiler assumes it to be DECIMAL.
3. If the mode attribute is not given, the compiler assumes an attribute of REAL.
4. If a precision attribute is missing, the IBM PL/I 360/370 F – level compiler assumes the default values given at the beginning of this subsection.

The programmer will find the mode default attribute useful. Since numeric variables of mode REAL are much more commonly used than those of mode COMPLEX, the programmer is spared the need of declaring each numeric variable to be REAL. Instead, he or she relies on the compiler's default assumption of REAL. The programmer should be cautious, however, in depending on the compiler for default attribute selection.

Before terminating this section, a few comments are in order concerning the choice of precision specification. First, if the numeric data being manipulated have unpredictable sizes, then floating-point numbers should probably be used. Second, a result obtained through computations may require the carrying of extra digits in order to obtain a desired accuracy. Finally, care must be exercised in computations involving nonintegral fixed-point values. Additional high-order digits should be specified so that a larger than normal value will show up as a larger value, rather than as an error or some undetected (or "chopped") result. For example, the declaration

    DECLARE A FIXED DECIMAL(3, 2);

causes the value of 152.32 to be recorded as 2.32 in the variable A.

In this subsection we have examined briefly the use of the precision attribute in declaring variables. In the next subsection the problem of round-off in performing PL/I computations is explored.

8-1.2 The Precision of Numeric Constants and Intermediate Results

Thus far in our discussion of precision of variables in computer programs, we have had explicit control, through declarations, of the precisions of such variables. This explicit control, however, does not extend to constants and intermediate results or expressions. In this latter case, precisions are determined implicitly by certain rules.

In PL/I, numeric decimal constants have their precision specified by the following rules:

1. A fixed-point constant has a precision of (p, q), where p is the total number of digits in the constant and q is the number of fractional digits.
2. A floating-point constant has a precision of (p) where p is the total number of digits in the constant.

Consequently, the precisions of the following constants are:

> 2.71 has the precision (3, 2)
> 6.12343E3 has the precision (6)
> 0.120E–4 has the precision (4)
> –1 has the precision (1)
> 00.250 has the precision (5, 3)

The assignment of a numeric constant to a variable whose precision is sufficiently large to contain the given constant creates no problems. Such is not the case, however, when a constant is used directly in an arithmetic operation.

When ordinary arithmetic operations (+, –, *, /, and **) are performed on two floating point operands, the precision of the result is assumed to be that of the more precise of the two operands. As an example, the value of the expression

> 3.14E1 + 2.7128E1

is 5.8528E1. This intermediate result has the same precision as 2.7128E1, the more precise of the two operands. The result in this example is useful. Consider, however, the evaluation of the following expression which involves division

> 1E0 / 3E0.

The result of the division is .3E0, which is a very crude approximation to the true value. If this result is used in other computations, several problems in precision may result. An easy way out of this situation is to declare the variable ONE (with a value of 1E0) to have the precision desired of the result and to perform the division as in the expression

> ONE / 3E0.

The precision rules for fixed-point values are significantly more complex, as every attempt is made to retain all generated digits. In the addition and subtraction of fixed-point values, the result, in addition to allowing for a carry digit, has a digit in each position where either operand does. For example, the evaluation of the expression

> 2.7128 + 125.5

yields the value of 0128.2128. For multiplication, the total number of digits in the result is one greater than that of the sum of its operands. The scale factor of this result is given by the sum of the scale factors of the two operands. For example, the expression

6.5 * 0.25

yields a value of 001.625. Note that the total number of digits in a result cannot exceed the maximum number of digits allowed (see Sec. 8-1.1). This limit is sufficiently large to avoid most problems. The same, however, cannot be said for division. The total number of digits in the result is always equal to the maximum allowed (e.g., 15 decimal digits). The scale factor is given by the formula

$$15 - ((p_1 - q_1) + q_2)$$

where (p_1, q_1) and (p_2, q_2) specify the precision of the first and second operands, respectively. For example, the precision (p, q) of the result in performing the operation

18.636 / 3

is $(15, 15 - ((5 - 3) + 0) = (15, 13)$.

Observe that a change in the number of integer digits in the first operand (i.e., the dividend) or a change in the number of fractional digits in the second operand (i.e., the divisor) will change the precision of the result. As an example, the expressions

0018.636 / 3
18.636 / 3.00000

yield a precision of (15, 11) for the first expression and (15, 8) for the second. This phenomenon can cause an overflow condition to arise as the result of a computation which involves division. It should be emphasized at this point that these problems can arise in PL/I. In PL/C, however, few of these problems occur since the compiler has been written to avoid them. The next subsection examines how the programmer can handle problems that can arise in computations.

8-1.3 The Handling of Interruptions in Numeric Computations

During the execution of a PL/I program, various events can occur that cause the execution to be interrupted. An example of such an event was discussed in Sec. 3-3.3. This discussion dealt with the detection and handling of an end-of-input-data situation when executing a GET statement. In general, a PL/I programmer can specify how a program interrupt is to be handled through the use of an ON statement. Recall from Sec. 3-3.3 that the ON statement for detecting an end-of-file situation has the form

ON ENDFILE (SYSIN) *action*

where *action* may be a single statement such as a GO TO statement or a group of statements in a BEGIN block.

There are other events that can arise in input-output operations. In this subsection, however, we do not consider them. Instead, we concentrate on some events that occur when performing arithmetic operations. A partial list of these events include the following:

> FIXEDOVERFLOW
> OVERFLOW
> UNDERFLOW
> ZERODIVIDE
> SIZE

We now give a brief description of each of these events, or as they are referred to, *conditions*.

FIXEDOVERFLOW Condition. This condition arises when the total number of digits in a result obtained in a fixed-point operation exceeds the maximum size permitted (i.e., 15 decimal digits).

OVERFLOW Condition. This condition arises when the magnitude of a floating-point result exceeds the maximum value permitted in the language.

UNDERFLOW Condition. This condition arises when the magnitude of a floating-point result is less than the minimum value permitted in the language.

ZERODIVIDE Condition. This condition arises when an attempt is made to divide by zero. The condition arises for both floating-point and fixed-point divisions.

SIZE Condition. This condition arises when high-order digits are lost on an assignment of a value to a variable or an intermediate result. Such a loss occurs when the value assigned to an element exceeds the default or declared size of that element. This condition is not to be confused with the FIXEDOVERFLOW condition which arises when a value exceeds the maximum allowable value in the system.

A condition is said to be *enabled*, when its occurrence will cause a programmer-defined action or a default system action to take place. A condition which is not enabled is said to be *disabled*. Consequently, a disabled condition means that errors may not be detected. In PL/C, the five arithemtic conditions just discussed are always enabled.

The enabling and disabling of arithmetic conditions is accomplished by associating a *condition prefix* with an assignment statement. For example, the assignment statement

> (ZERODIVIDE): F = EXP (X) / X – 1.0;

contains the condition prefix (ZERODIVIDE) which indicates that the condition ZERODIVIDE is to be enabled for the execution of this statement. If the word NO precedes a condition name, then the specified condition is to be disabled. The following assignment statement disables the ZERODIVIDE condition:

> (NOZERODIVIDE): F = EXP (X) / X – 1.0;

An example of a program which contains a programmer-defined action to handle a division by zero is given in Fig. 8-1. The ON statement contains a ZERODIVIDE condition and a BEGIN block as its action. The block contains an appropriate message and a GO TO statement. The program contains a loop which computes a series of functional values. If an attempt is made to divide by zero in the assignment statement, then the ZERODIVIDE condition arises and execution transfers to the action specified by the ON statement. At that point, an appropriate

```
TEST_ZR:  PROCEDURE OPTIONS (MAIN);

STMT LEVEL NEST BLOCK MLVL  SOURCE TEXT


    1                           TEST_ZR:  PROCEDURE OPTIONS (MAIN);
                                /* THIS SHORT PROGRAM SHOWS THE USE OF THE ON ZERODIVIDE    */
                                /* CONDITION.                                               */

    2    1          1           DECLARE (F, X) FLOAT DECIMAL(15);

    3    1          1           ON ZERODIVIDE
    4    1          1               BEGIN;
    5    2          2                   PUT SKIP EDIT ('*** DIVIDING BY X = 0 ) (A);
    6    2          2                   GO TO ENDLOOP;
    7    2          2               END;

    8    1          1           PUT SKIP EDIT ('X', 'F(X)') (X(9), A, X(16), A);
    9    1          1           LOOP:    DO X = -1.0 TO 1.0 BY 0.125;
   10    1    1     1               (ZERODIVIDE):  F = (EXP (X) / X - 1.0);
   11    1    1     1               PUT SKIP EDIT (X, F) (E(15, 3), E(20, 6));
   12    1    1     1           ENDLOOP: END;
   13    1          1       END TEST_ZR;

ERRORS/WARNINGS DETECTED DURING CODE GENERATION:

    WARNING: NO FILE SPECIFIED. SYSIN/SYSPRINT ASSUMED. (CGOC)

        X               F(X)
    -1.000E+00      -1.367879E+00
    -8.750E-01      -1.476414E+00
    -7.500E-01      -1.629822E+00
    -6.250E-01      -1.856418E+00
    -5.000E-01      -2.213061E+00
    -3.750E-01      -2.832771E+00
    -2.500E-01      -4.115203E+00
    -1.250E-01      -8.059975E+00
*** DIVIDING BY X = 0
     1.250E-01       8.065188E+00
     2.500E-01       4.136102E+00
     3.750E-01       2.879977E+00
     5.000E-01       2.297443E+00
     6.250E-01       1.989194E+00
     7.500E-01       1.822667E+00
     8.750E-01       1.741572E+00
     1.000E+00       1.718282E+00


IN STMT   13 PROGRAM RETURNS FROM MAIN PROCEDURE.
```

Fig. 8-1   Program which handles an interrupt due to zero division

error message is printed and control transfers to the END statement of the loop.

The condition prefix may contain more than one condition name. An example of such a situation is given in the statement

(NOSIZE, NOUNDERFLOW, ZERODIVIDE): A = (B + C) / D;

where the conditions SIZE and UNDERFLOW are disabled and the condition ZERODIVIDE is enabled.

On occasion, it may be desired to disable and enable a condition for the entire execution of a procedure or a BEGIN block. In such an instance the prefix condition is appended to the front of the PROCEDURE statement. For example,

(NOSIZE, NOUNDERFLOW): PROCEDURE OPTIONS (MAIN);

specifies that the conditions SIZE and UNDERFLOW are to be disabled throughout the procedure.

The preceding discussion has been a brief introduction to the handling of program interrupts. For more details, the reader should refer to a more complete PL/I reference document.

Exercises for Sec. 8-1

1. Give the base, scale, and precision for the following:

   (a) 3.1415
   (b) 11.10101B
   (c) –110.011
   (d) 476.53E2

   (e) 81700
   (f) .5632E–7
   (g) –1.101E1B
   (h) 110101B

2. Determine the possible range of values for the following variable declarations:

   (a) DECLARE VALUE FIXED DECIMAL;
   (b) DECLARE QUOTIENT FIXED DECIMAL (8, 3);
   (c) DECLARE SUM FIXED BINARY (4, –2);
   (d) DECLARE PRECISION FLOAT BINARY (4);

3. Using the default attributes as specified in this subsection, what are the attributes for the following partial declarations?

   (a) DECLARE DIFFER FLOAT;
   (b) DECLARE PRODUCT;
   (c) DECLARE DENOM FIXED;
   (d) DECLARE ROOT DECIMAL (3);

   (e) DECLARE DERIV FIXED BINARY;
   (f) DECLARE SQUARE FLOAT
        DECIMAL;
   (g) DECLARE EXPONENT FIXED (8, 7);
   (h) DECLARE ABSOLUTE;

4. Match the following constants with their PL/I attributes:

   (a) 0101110B
   (b) 1010110
   (c) 14.62E3
   (d) 10.110E3B
   (e) 1.1101
   (f) 1.1101B
   (g) 10.110E3

   (1) FLOAT DECIMAL (4)
   (2) FLOAT DECIMAL (5)
   (3) FLOAT BINARY (5)
   (4) FIXED BINARY (7)
   (5) FIXED BINARY (5)
   (6) FIXED DECIMAL (5)
   (7) FIXED DECIMAL (7)

5. Given the following program segment:

   ```
   DECLARE A FIXED DECIMAL (4),
           B FIXED DECIMAL (4, 3),
           C FIXED;
       A = 1429;
       B = 1.250;
   ```

```
C = 12.5;
B = (C - 10 * B) + .2;
A = A - B;
```

What are the values of A, B, and C after execution? Check your answer by running the program.

8-2 FINDING THE ROOTS OF NONLINEAR FUNCTIONS

Recall that the root of a function of a single variable is the value of the variable that results in a value of zero for the function. While formulas exist for second-, third-, and fourth-degree polynomials, no general formulas exist for many other nonlinear equations. The *method of successive bisection* is one numerical procedure that can be used to find the root of a function.

To find the root of a function, we begin by choosing two values of x, x_1 and x_2, such that $f(x_1) * f(x_2) < 0$; in other words, two values of f having different signs. If a function never changes sign, the requirement cannot be met and this method of successive bisection cannot be applied. If we assume that $f(x)$ is continuous in the interval (x_1, x_2), there must exist a root between x_1 and x_2 that can be found by the method of successive bisection. The idea of this method is to reduce the size of each successive interval by a half for each iteration while keeping the root inside this interval.

The program given in Fig. 8-2 uses the method of successive bisection to find the solution of the function

$$f(x) = x^3 - x^2 - 2x + 1$$

given the initial boundaries $x_1 = 0.0$ and $x_2 = 1.0$. The variables used in the main program are:

Variable	Type	Usage
A	FLOAT	Initial lower bound of the interval
B	FLOAT	Initial upper bound of the interval
ACCURACY	FLOAT	Accuracy of the solution

Variables used in procedure SUC_BIS are:

X1	FLOAT	Lower bound of the interval
X2	FLOAT	Upper bound of the interval
ROOT	FLOAT	Estimated root of F(X)
ACCURACY	FLOAT	Accuracy of the solution required
F_ROOT	FLOAT	Value of F(ROOT)
F_X1	FLOAT	Value of F(X1)
I	FIXED	Counted loop variable

The main program initializes the boundary of the interval and the desired accuracy of the root. Procedure SUC_BIS is then called to find the root of the function. In this procedure, a loop is entered in statement 13 which causes the program to terminate if the root does not appear to converge within 30 iterations.

```
SUC_TST: PROCEDURE OPTIONS (MAIN);

STMT LEVEL NEST BLOCK MLVL   SOURCE TEXT


    1                              SUC_TST: PROCEDURE OPTIONS (MAIN);
                                   /* THIS PROGRAM CALLS SUC_BIS TO TEST THE SUCCESSIVE BISECTION   */
                                   /* PROGRAM. */

    2     1          1            DECLARE (A, B) FLOAT,   /* BOUNDARIES OF THE SOLUTION INTERVAL   */
                                          ACCURACY FLOAT; /* ACCURACY OF THE SOLUTION             */

    3     1          1            A = 0.0;
    4     1          1            B = 1.0;
    5     1          1            ACCURACY = 0.0001;
    6     1          1            CALL SUC_BIS (A, B, ACCURACY);
    7     1          1            END SUC_TST;

    8                             SUC_BIS: PROCEDURE (X1, X2, ACCURACY);
                                   /* GIVEN X1 AND X2, TWO X VALUES SUCH THAT F (X1) * F (X2) < 0,  */
                                   /* AND ACCURACY, THE DESIRED ACCURACY, THIS PROCEDURE FINDS      */
                                   /* ROOT, A VALUE OF X FOR WHICH F (X) = 0.                       */

    9     1          2            DECLARE X1 FLOAT,                /* FIRST ROOT APPROX. FOR F     */
                                          X2 FLOAT,                /* SECOND ROOT APPROXIMATION    */
                                          ACCURACY FLOAT,          /* DESIRED ACCURACY OF ROOT     */
                                          ROOT FLOAT,              /* DETERMINED ROOT OF F         */
                                          (F_ROOT, F_X1) FLOAT,    /* TEMPORARY FUNCTION VALUES    */
                                          I FIXED;                 /* ITERATIONS COUNTER           */

                                   /* F FUNCTION */
   10     1          2            DECLARE F ENTRY (FLOAT) RETURNS (FLOAT);

                                   /* PRINT A HEADING FOR THE ITERATIONS TABLE */
   11     1          2            PUT SKIP EDIT ('INTERVAL, (X1, X2)', 'MIDPOINT', 'F(ROOT)')
                                          (A, COL(26), A, COL(42), A);

   12     1          2            PUT SKIP;

                                   /* MAKE AT MOST 30 ITERATIONS */
   13     1          2            DO I = 1 TO 30 BY 1;

                                       /* FIND THE MIDPOINT OF THE INTERVAL */
   14     1    1     2                ROOT = (X1 + X2) / 2;

                                       /* ROOT FOUND? */
   15     1    1     2                F_ROOT = F (ROOT);

                                       /* OUTPUT THE RESULT OF THIS ITERATION */
   16     1    1     2                PUT SKIP EDIT ('(', X1, ',', X2, ')', ROOT, F_ROOT)
                                          (A, F(9, 6), A, F(9, 6), A, COL(25), F(9, 6), COL(40),
                                           F(9, 5));

   17     1    1     2                IF (F_ROOT = 0.0 | ABS (X2 - X1) < ACCURACY)
   18     1    1     2                THEN DO;
   19     1    2     2                        PUT SKIP (2) EDIT ('SOLUTION: ROOT = ', ROOT,
                                                  ';   F(ROOT) = ', F_ROOT)
                                                  (COL(10), A, F(12, 7), A, F(12, 7));
   20     1    2     2                        RETURN;
   21     1    2     2                     END;

                                       /* BISECT THE INTERVAL */
   22     1    1     2                F_X1 = F(X1);
   23     1    1     2                IF F_ROOT * F_X1 < 0.0
   24     1    1     2                THEN X2 = ROOT;
   25     1    1     2                ELSE X1 = ROOT;
   26     1    1     2            END;      /* OF 30 ITERATIONS */
                                   /* MORE THAN 30 ITERATIONS REQUIRED; PRINT MESSAGE */
   27     1          2            PUT SKIP (2) EDIT ('ROOT NOT FOUND IN 30 ITERATIONS.  ROOT SO FAR',
                                          ' IS ',  ROOT) (COL(10), A, A, F(12, 7));

                                   /* FINISHED */
   28     1          2            RETURN;

   29     1          2            END SUC_BIS;
```

Fig. 8-2 Program to find the root of a function using successive bisection

```
STMT LEVEL NEST BLOCK MLVL   SOURCE TEXT


*PROCESS

   30                               F: PROCEDURE (X) RETURNS (FLOAT);
                                    /* THIS FUNCTION RETURNS THE VALUE OF THE FUNCTION       */
                                    /*        F(X) = X**3 - X**2 - 2X + 1                    */

   31    1         3                DECLARE X FLOAT;

   32    1         3                RETURN (((X - 1) * X - 2) * X + 1);
   33    1         3           END F;

ERRORS/WARNINGS DETECTED DURING CODE GENERATION:

      WARNING: NO FILE SPECIFIED. SYSIN/SYSPRINT ASSUMED. (CGOC)

INTERVAL, (X1, X2)       MIDPOINT       F(ROOT)

( 0.000000, 1.000000)    0.500000      -0.12500
( 0.000000, 0.500000)    0.250000       0.45313
( 0.250000, 0.500000)    0.375000       0.16211
( 0.375000, 0.500000)    0.437500       0.01733
( 0.437500, 0.500000)    0.468750      -0.05423
( 0.437500, 0.468750)    0.453125      -0.01854
( 0.437500, 0.453125)    0.445313      -0.00062
( 0.437500, 0.445313)    0.441406       0.00835
( 0.441406, 0.445313)    0.443359       0.00386
( 0.443359, 0.445313)    0.444336       0.00162
( 0.444336, 0.445313)    0.444624       0.00050
( 0.444824, 0.445313)    0.445068      -0.00006
( 0.444824, 0.445068)    0.444946       0.00022
( 0.444946, 0.445068)    0.445007       0.00008
( 0.445007, 0.445068)    0.445038       0.00001


        SOLUTION: ROOT =    0.4450378;   F(ROOT) =      0.0000092



IN STMT    7  PROGRAM RETURNS FROM MAIN PROCEDURE.
```

Fig. 8-2   Program to find the root of a function using successive bisection (cont'd.)

Inside the loop, the midpoint of the interval is first computed and printed. If the accuracy of the root is within the specified tolerance, the procedure returns to the calling program in statement 20. Otherwise, statements 22 to 25 reduce the size of the interval where the midpoint becomes one of the boundaries. If the values of F (ROOT) and F (X1) are of the same sign, the lower bound (X1) is assigned the value of the midpoint of the interval, otherwise, the upper bound (X2) gets the value of the midpoint of the interval.

Another numerical procedure, called *Newton's method*, finds the root of a function based upon the equation

$$x_{n+1} = x_n - f(x_n)/f'(x_n)$$

where $f'(x_n)$ denotes the derivative of the function at the point x_n. Successive approximations using this formula are made until $f(x_n)$ is within a stated tolerance.

Figure 8-3 gives a program that finds the root of a function using Newton's method. The variables used in the main program are:

Variable	Type	Usage
GUESS	FLOAT	Initial estimate of the root
ACCURACY	FLOAT	Desired accuracy of the root

Variables used in the procedure NEWTON are:

Variable	Type	Usage
X	FLOAT	Value of x_n
ACCURACY	FLOAT	Desired accuracy of the root
ROOT	FLOAT	Calculated root of F
FVALUE	FLOAT	Value of the function F
DERIVATIVE	FLOAT	Value of the derivative of the function
I	FIXED	Counted loop variable

This program finds a root of the function

$$f(x) = x^3 - x^2 - 2x + 1$$

where the derivative of $f(x)$ is

$$f'(x) = 3x^2 - 2x - 2$$

The main program calls procedure NEWTON, with an initial value of 1.0 for the root of the function and the desired accuracy of the root to be 0.00001. In procedure NEWTON, the loop beginning in statement 13 stops execution of the procedure if no covergence of the root is obtained after 30 iterations. Statements 14 to 16 calculate the value of $x_n - f(x_n)/f'(x_n)$. If the newly computed root stored in the variable ROOT is such that F (ROOT) is within the stated tolerance, the procedure returns to the main program, otherwise, the new value of the root is set to X. The function F returns the value of the function $f(x)$, while DERIV_F returns the value of the derivative of $f(x)$.

Exercises for Sec. 8-2

1. Use the successive bisection program to compute a root of each of the following functions to an accuracy of 0.0001 on the interval [0, 1].

    (a) $f(x) = 10x^3 - 33x^2 + 29x - 6$
    (b) $f(x) = xe^x - 1$
    (c) $f(x) = x - 2^{-x}$

2. Use Newton's method to devise a program which will compute a root of each of the following functions to an accuracy of 0.0005 and with an initial approximation of $x = 1$.

    (a) $f(x) = x^3 - x - 1$
    (b) $f(x) = 3x^2 - e^x$
    (c) $f(x) = 4\cos x - e^x$

3. Construct a program which uses the method of successive bisection to compute the square root of a number N to an accuracy of five decimal places. Use x_0 = N as an initial approximation to the root.

4. Let $f_1 (x)$ and $f_2 (x)$ denote two functions in x. One method of obtaining their solution is by writing a third function g(x) as

$$g(x) = f_1 (x) - f_2 (x)$$

and solving for a root of g(x). Given $f_1 (x) = x^2 - 2x$ and $f_2 (x) = \sqrt{3x}$, write a program which uses the above method and the method of successive bisection to determine a point of intersection of the two functions. Use an accuracy of 0.0001 and run the program twice, once on the interval $-.5 \leqslant x \leqslant 1.5$ and once on the interval $1.0 \leqslant x \leqslant 3.5$.

5. The objective of this problem is to find the positive root of the following equation

$$x^4 - 2x^3 - x^2 - 7x - 4 = 0$$

You should try each of (i) the successive bisection method, (ii) the secant method (see main text), and (iii) Newton's method on the equation. Each of the methods should be implemented by means of a function.

    The evaluation of the function and its derivative should also be done by functional procedures (so that it would be simple to find the root of another equation by simply replacing these two procedures). Thus you should have five functional procedures; one for the successive bisection method, one for the secant method, one for Newton's method, one for the evaluation of the function, and one for the evaluation of the derivative of the function (i.e., the evaluation of $4x^3 - 6x^2 - 2x - 7$).

    For the successive bisection and secant methods try initial end points of both 0.0 and 5.0, and 2.5 and 4.0. For Newton's method try the initial guesses of 2.0 and 2.5. In all cases, continue the iterations until the functional value is less than 1.0×10^{-5} (this tolerance should be a parameter to the procedures) or until 25 iterations have been tried.

8-3 NUMERICAL INTEGRATION

    For several reasons, numerical integration on a computer may be required. A popular method of numerical integration, *Simpson's rule*, calculates the integral of a function by fitting second-degree polynomials to the curve of f(x). To approximate the integral of f(x), the interval (a, b) is subdivided into n equal subintervals where n is even. Then the integral of f(x) is approximately

$$\frac{h}{3} [f(x_0) + 4f(x_1) + 2f(x_2) + 4f(x_3) + \cdots + 2f(x_{n-2}) + 4f(x_{n-1}) + f(x_n)]$$

This formula is exact for all polynomials having a degree of three or lower. In most other cases, its error tends to be small.

    A program to compute the integral of a function using Simpson's rule is given in Fig. 8-4. The variables used in the main program are:

```
STMT LEVEL NEST BLOCK MLVL  SOURCE TEXT


  1                              NEWT: PROCEDURE OPTIONS (MAIN);
                                 /* THIS PROGRAM CALLS THE PROCEDURE NEWTON AND TESTS NEWTON'S   */
                                 /* METHOD OF FINDING THE ROOT OF A FUNCTION.                    */

  2    1           1             DECLARE GUESS FLOAT,    /* INITIAL ESTIMATE OF THE ROOT         */
                                         ACCURACY FLOAT; /* REQUIRED ACCURACY OF THE ROOT        */

  3    1           1             GUESS = 1.0;
  4    1           1             ACCURACY = 0.00001;
  5    1           1             CALL NEWTON (GUESS, ACCURACY);
  6    1           1             END NEWT;


  7                              NEWTON: PROCEDURE (X, ACCURACY);
                                 /* GIVEN X, AN INITIAL GUESS AT THE ROOT OF F(X), AND THE DESIRED */
                                 /* ACCURACY OF THE ROOT, ACCURACY, THIS PROCEDURE FINDS THE      */
                                 /* ROOT OF F(X).                                                */

  8    1           2             DECLARE X FLOAT,                  /* INITIAL GUESS AT F(X) ROOT */
                                         ACCURACY FLOAT,           /* DESIRED ACCURACY FOR ROOT  */
                                         ROOT FLOAT,               /* DETERMINED ROOT OF F       */
                                         (FVALUE, DERIVATIVE) FLOAT,/* TEMPORARY FUNCTION VALUES */
                                         I FIXED;                  /* ITERATIONS COUNTER         */
                                 /* F FUNCTION TO FIND ROOT OF */
  9    1           2             DECLARE F ENTRY (FLOAT) RETURNS (FLOAT);
                                 /* DERIVATIVE OF F FUNCTION */
 10    1           2             DECLARE DERIV_F ENTRY (FLOAT) RETURNS (FLOAT);
 11    1           2             PUT EDIT ('X', 'F(X)') (X(4), A, COL(17), A);
 12    1           2             PUT SKIP (2) EDIT (X, F(X)) (F(9, 6), X(5), F(9, 6));

                                 /* PERFORM AT MOST 30 ITERATIONS */
 13    1           2             DO I = 1 TO 30;

                                    /* CALCULATE IMPROVED ESTIMATE */
 14    1    1      2                FVALUE = F(X);
 15    1    1      2                DERIVATIVE = DERIV_F (X);
 16    1    1      2                ROOT = X - (FVALUE / DERIVATIVE);

                                    /* CONVERGENCE? */
 17    1    1      2                FVALUE = F (ROOT);
 18    1    1      2                PUT SKIP EDIT (ROOT, FVALUE) (F(9, 6), X(5), F(9, 6));
 19    1    1      2                IF (ABS (FVALUE) < ACCURACY)
 20    1    1      2                THEN DO;
 21    1    2      2                    PUT SKIP (2) EDIT ('ROOT = ', ROOT, '; F (ROOT) = ',
                                            FVALUE) (COL(10), A, F(11,6), A, F(11,6));
 22    1    2      2                    RETURN;
 23    1    2      2                  END;

                                    /* SAVE NEW ESTIMATE */
 24    1    1      2                X = ROOT;

 25    1    1      2             END;      /* OF 30 ITERATIONS */

                                 /* MORE THAN 30 ITERATIONS REQUIRED; PRINT MESSAGE */
 26    1           2             PUT SKIP (2) EDIT ('ROOT NOT FOUND IN 30 ITERATIONS.  ROOT SO FAR ',
                                    'IS ', ROOT) (COL(10), A, A, F(11, 6));

                                 /* FINISHED */
 27    1           2             RETURN;

 28    1           2             END NEWTON;


 29                              F: PROCEDURE (X) RETURNS (FLOAT);
                                 /* THIS FUNCTION RETURNS THE VALUE OF THE FUNCTION             */
                                 /*        F(X) = X**3 - X**2 - 2X + 1                          */

 30    1           3             DECLARE X FLOAT;

 31    1           3             RETURN (((X - 1.0) * X - 2.0) * X + 1.0);
 32    1           3             END F;
```

Fig. 8-3   Program to find the root of a function using Newton's method

```
   33                            DERIV_F: PROCEDURE (X)  RETURNS (FLOAT);
                                 /* THIS FUNCTION RETURNS THE VALUE OF THE DERIVATIVE OF THE    */
                                 /* FUNCTION F(X),  I.E.,                                       */
                                 /*          F´(X) = 3X**2 - 2X - 2                             */

   34   1      4                 DECLARE X FLOAT;

   35   1      4                   RETURN ((3.0 * X - 2.0) * X - 2.0);
   36   1      4                 END DERIV_F;

ERRORS/WARNINGS DETECTED DURING CODE GENERATION:

     WARNING: NO FILE SPECIFIED. SYSIN/SYSPRINT ASSUMED. (CGOC)

    X          F(X)

 1.000000    -1.000000
 0.000000     1.000000
 0.500000    -0.125000
 0.444444     0.001372
 0.445042     0.000000

        ROOT =    0.445042; F (ROOT) =    0.000000



IN STMT    6  PROGRAM RETURNS FROM MAIN PROCEDURE.
```

Fig. 8-3   Program to find the root of a function using Newton's method (cont'd.)

Variable	Type	Usage
A	FLOAT	Lower bound of the interval
B	FLOAT	Upper bound of the interval
ACCURACY	FLOAT	Desired accuracy of the result

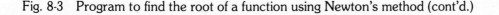

Variables used in the procedure SIMPSON are:

A	FLOAT	Lower bound of the interval
B	FLOAT	Upper bound of the interval
ACCURACY	FLOAT	Desired accuracy of the result
H	FLOAT	Length of the subinterval
LAST	FLOAT	Previous approximation of the integral
SUM	FLOAT	Sum of the areas under the curve
SIMP	FLOAT	Calculated value of the integral of F
N	FLOAT	Number of subintervals
I	FIXED	Counted loop variable
J	FIXED	Counted loop variable

The program computes the integral of $f(x) = 6x^5 - 3x^3$ over the interval (1, 2) to an accuracy of 0.0001.

The main program initializes the interval and accuracy required before calling the procedure SIMPSON. Within this procedure (SIMPSON), H is first set to half the size of the given interval. Then in statement 15, a loop which performs at most 20 iterations is entered. Thus, if the value of the integral doesn't converge within 20 iterations, execution of the procedure terminates. Within the loop, the

```
STMT LEVEL NEST BLOCK MLVL   SOURCE TEXT

  1                           SIMP:  PROCEDURE OPTIONS(MAIN);
                                /* THIS PROGRAM TESTS PROCEDURE SIMPSON FOR DETERMINING THE    */
                                /* INTEGRAL OF A GIVEN PROGRAMMER-DEFINED FUNCTION F(X).        */

  2    1          1           DECLARE (A, B) FLOAT,     /* INTERVAL OVER WHICH INTEGRAL OF F(X) */
                                                        /* IS DESIRED                          */
                                      ACCURACY FLOAT;   /* ACCURACY OF SOLUTION                */

  3    1          1           A = 1.0;
  4    1          1           B = 2.0;
  5    1          1           ACCURACY = 0.0001;
  6    1          1           CALL SIMPSON (A, B, ACCURACY);
  7    1          1           END SIMP;

  8                           SIMPSON: PROCEDURE (A, B, ACCURACY);
                                /* GIVEN PARAMETERS A, B AND ACCURACY, THIS PROCEDURE CALCULATES */
                                /* SIMP, THE SIMPSON'S RULE APPROXIMATION OF THE INTEGRAL FROM A */
                                /* TO B OF F(X)D(X), TO THE SPECIFIED ACCURACY BY A SERIES OF    */
                                /* ITERATIONS.  F(X) IS A PROGRAMMER-DEFINED FUNCTION.          */

  9    1          2           DECLARE A FLOAT,                /* LOWER LIMIT OF INTEGRAL      */
                                      B FLOAT,                /* UPPER LIMIT OF INTEGRAL      */
                                      ACCURACY FLOAT,         /* DESIRED ACCURACY OF INTEGRAL */
                                      H FLOAT,                /* LENGTH OF THE SUBINTERVAL    */
                                      LAST FLOAT,             /* PREVIOUSLY DETERMINED SIMP   */
                                      SUM FLOAT,              /* SUM OF AREAS UNDER THE CURVE */
                                      SIMP FLOAT,             /* DETERMINED INTEGRAL OF F     */
                                      N FLOAT,                /* NUMBER OF SUBINTERVALS USED  */
                                      (I, J) FIXED;           /* ITERATION COUNTERS           */
                                /* F FUNCTION TO INTEGRATE */
 10    1          2           DECLARE F ENTRY (FLOAT) RETURNS (FLOAT);

 11    1          2           SIMP = 0.0;
 12    1          2           H = (B - A) / 2;
 13    1          2           PUT LIST ('VALUE OF INTEGRAL');
 14    1          2           PUT SKIP (2) EDIT (SIMP) (X(2), F(12, 7));

                                /* PERFORM AT MOST 20 ITERATIONS */
 15    1          2           DO I = 1 TO 20;

                                  /* SAVE PREVIOUS APPROXIMATION */
 16    1    1     2               LAST = SIMP;

                                  /* CALCULATE NUMBER OF SUBINTERVALS TO BE USED */
 17    1    1     2               N = (B - A) / H;

                                  /* ACCUMULATE SUM */
 18    1    1     2               SUM = F (A) + 4 * F (A + H) + F (B);
 19    1    1     2               DO J = 2 TO (N-2) BY 2;
 20    1    2     2                   SUM = SUM + 2 * F (A + J * H) + 4 * F (A + (J + 1) * H);
 21    1    2     2               END;

                                  /* CALCULATE SIMPSON'S RULE APPROXIMATION */
 22    1    1     2               SIMP = H / 3 * SUM;
 23    1    1     2               PUT SKIP EDIT (SIMP) (X(2), F(12, 7));

                                  /* TEST ACCURACY */
 24    1    1     2               IF (ABS ((SIMP - LAST) / SIMP) < ACCURACY)
 25    1    1     2               THEN DO;
 26    1    2     2                   PUT SKIP (2) EDIT ('ANSWER IS ', SIMP, ';    TOLERANCE ',
                                              'MET IN ', 1, ' ITERATIONS.')
                                              (COL(10), A, F(12,7), A, A, F(2), A);
 27    1    2     2                       RETURN;
 28    1    2     2                   END;

                                  /* HALVE SIZE OF SUBINTERVALS FOR NEXT ITERATION */
 29    1    1     2               H = H / 2;
 30    1    1     2           END;    /* OF 20 ITERATIONS */
```

Fig. 8-4   Program to compute the integral of f(x) using Simpson's method

```
                                      /* NO CONVERGENCE */
   31     1          2                PUT SKIP (2) EDIT ('TOLERANCE WAS NOT MET AFTER 20 ITERATIONS. ',
                                          'CURRENT ANSWER IS ', SIMP) (COL(10), A, A, F(12, 7));

                                      /* FINISHED */
   32     1          2                RETURN;
   33     1          2             END SIMPSON;


   34                             F: PROCEDURE (X) RETURNS (FLOAT);
                                      /* THIS FUNCTION RETURNS THE VALUE OF F(X), WHERE F(X) IS THE    */
                                      /* FUNCTION  F(X) = 6X**5 - 3X**2                                */

   35     1          3                DECLARE X FLOAT;

   36     1          3                RETURN ((6 * (X ** 5)) - (3 * (X ** 2)));
   37     1          3             END F;
ERRORS/WARNINGS DETECTED DURING CODE GENERATION:

    WARNING: NO FILE SPECIFIED. SYSIN/SYSPRINT ASSUMED. (CGOC)

VALUE OF INTEGRAL

    0.0000000
   56.3750000
   56.0234375
   56.0014648
   56.0000916

       ANSWER IS   56.0000916;    TOLERANCE MET IN  4 ITERATIONS.


IN STMT    7  PROGRAM RETURNS FROM MAIN PROCEDURE.
```

Fig. 8-4   Program to compute the integral of f(x) using Simpson's method (cont'd.)

number of subintervals to be used is first calculated. Statements 18 to 21 compute the sum of the areas of the subintervals. The accuracy of this result is then determined and if its value is within the given requirement, the result is printed and the subprogram returns to the calling program. If this is not the case, statement 29 is used to halve the size of the subintervals for the next iteration.

Exercises for Sec. 8-3

1. Use the Simpson's rule program to approximate the following integrals to an accuracy of 0.0001 using the step sizes shown.

    (a) $\int_0^2 x^2 e^x dx$ with h = .25
    (b) $\int_0^{\pi/2} \sin^2 x dx$ with h = .10
    (c) $\int_1^{\pi} \frac{1 - \cos x}{x} dx$ with h = π / 9

2. Construct a program to compute the area in the first quadrant under the curve $y = x^2$ and inside the circle with unit radius. Use Simpson's rule with a step size of h = .05.

3. Formulate a program to compute the area of a circle with a radius of 2 units, whose center has coordinates (4, 4). Use Simpson's rule with a step size of h = .01.

8-4 SIMULTANEOUS LINEAR EQUATIONS

In this section, we examine two methods for solving sets of simultaneous linear equations. The first method, known as *Gaussian elimination*, solves equations of the form

$$a_{11}x_1 + a_{12}x_2 + \cdots + a_{1n}x_n = b_1$$
$$a_{21}x_1 + a_{22}x_2 + \cdots + a_{2n}x_n = b_2$$
$$\vdots \qquad\qquad\qquad\qquad \vdots$$
$$a_{n1}x_1 + a_{n2}x_2 + \cdots + a_{nn}x_n = b_n$$

by representing them as a matrix as described in the main text.

The process of Gaussian elimination consists of the two steps:

1. *Forward elimination:* starting from the top row, successively divide the row by its diagonal element, called the *pivot*, leaving a 1 on the diagonal, and then subtract a multiple of the row from each row below it, leaving zeros in the column below the diagonal 1.
2. *Back substitution:* subtract multiples of lower rows from the higher rows, leaving zeros in all positions but those on the diagonal, which contains 1's and the rightmost column.

The program given in Fig. 8-5 solves a system of linear equations using this approach. The variables used in the main program are:

Variable	Type	Usage
N	FIXED	Number of variables in the system
MATRIX(N, N + 1)	FLOAT	Augmented matrix for storing the linear equations
I	FIXED	Counted loop variable
J	FIXED	Counted loop variable

The variables used in the procedure GAUS_EL are:

ARRAY(*, *)	FLOAT	System of equations
N	FIXED	Number of rows in ARRAY
M	FIXED	Number of columns in ARRAY
PIVOT	FLOAT	Pivot for each row
I	FIXED	Counted loop variable
J	FIXED	Counted loop variable
K	FIXED	Counted loop variable

This program is used to solve the set of equations

$$
\begin{aligned}
1.0x_1 + 3.0x_2 - 2.0x_3 &= 7.0 \\
4.0x_1 - 1.0x_2 + 3.0x_3 &= 10.0 \\
-5.0x_1 + 2.0x_2 + 3.0x_3 &= 7.0
\end{aligned}
$$

The main program first inputs the system of equations. Procedure GAUS_EL is then called in statement 19 to solve this system of equations. Finally, the solution to this system of equations is printed.

Within the procedure GAUS_EL, statements 38 to 49 first perform forward elimination. For each row, the elements in that row are divided by the pivot element and a multiple of the row is subtracted from each lower row so that all values below the pivot are zero. Then back substitution is performed in statements 50 to 55, which makes all values above the diagonal zero.

A second method to solve a system of linear equations is called *Gauss-Seidel iteration*. The equations are each solved for one of the variables. For example, the set of equations

$$
\begin{array}{rcrcrcll}
5x_1 & + & x_2 & + & 3x_3 & = & 10 & \quad (1) \\
x_1 & + & x_2 & + & 5x_3 & = & 8 & \quad (2) \\
2x_1 & + & 4x_2 & + & x_3 & = & 11 & \quad (3)
\end{array}
$$

might be written as

$$
\begin{array}{rclclcll}
x_1 & = & 2.00 & - & 0.20x_2 & - & 0.60x_3 & \quad (1) \\
x_2 & = & 2.75 & - & 0.50x_1 & - & 0.25x_3 & \quad (3) \\
x_3 & = & 1.60 & - & 0.20x_1 & - & 0.20x_2 & \quad (2)
\end{array}
$$

and stored in an array as

$$
\begin{pmatrix}
2.00 & -0.20 & -0.60 \\
2.75 & -0.50 & -0.25 \\
1.60 & -0.20 & -0.20
\end{pmatrix}
$$

An initial estimate for the variables $x_1, x_2, ..., x_n$ is assigned. Zero is used in many cases. When calculating a new value for x_i, the new values for $x_1, x_2, ..., x_{i-1}$ are used as well as the old values for $x_{i+1}, x_{i+2}, ..., x_n$, rather than the entire set of old values, as is done in the *Jacobi method* (see main text). For each iteration, we solve these equations for better estimates of the variables. We stop when the errors are within a prescribed tolerance defined by

$$
\sum_{j=1}^{N} (x_j^i - x_j^{i-1})^2 < \epsilon
$$

where x_j^i is the ith estimation of the jth variable. The program for this method of solving linear equations is given in Fig. 8-6. The variables used in the main program are:

Variable	Type	Usage
N	FIXED	Number of equations
EQUATIONS(N, N)	FLOAT	Coefficients of the variables in the equations

```
STMT LEVEL NEST BLOCK MLVL   SOURCE TEXT


  1                                   TEST_GE: PROCEDURE OPTIONS (MAIN);
                                      /* THIS PROGRAM TESTS PROCEDURE GAUS_EL FOR SOLVING SETS OF     */
                                      /* SIMULTANEOUS LINEAR EQUATIONS.                               */

  2      1           1                DECLARE N FIXED;            /* SIZE OF MATRIX                    */

  3      1           1                GET LIST (N);

                                      /* DECLARE THE MATRIX */
  4      1           1                BEGIN;
  5      2           2                   DECLARE MATRIX (N, N + 1) FLOAT,   /* CONTAINS EQUATIONS     */
                                                  (I, J) FIXED;             /* ITERATION COUNTER      */

                                         /* INPUT THE SYSTEM */
  6      2           2                   DO I = 1 TO N;
  7      2      1    2                      DO J = 1 TO N + 1;
  8      2      2    2                         GET LIST (MATRIX(I, J));
  9      2      2    2                      END;
 10      2      1    2                   END;

                                         /* PRINT OUT THE ORIGINAL SYSTEM */
 11      2           2                   PUT SKIP EDIT ('ORIGINAL SYSTEM') (COL(35), A);
 12      2           2                   PUT SKIP (2) EDIT ('X1', 'X2', 'X3', 'RIGHT HAND SIDE')
                                                  (COL(15), A, COL(33), A, COL(51), A, COL(62), A);
 13      2           2                   DO I = 1 TO N;
 14      2      1    2                      PUT SKIP (2);
 15      2      1    2                      DO J = 1 TO N + 1;
 16      2      2    2                         PUT EDIT (MATRIX(I, J)) (X(9), F(9, 5));
 17      2      2    2                      END;
 18      2      1    2                   END;

                                         /* PERFORM GAUSSIAN ELEMINATION ON THE SYSTEM */
 19      2           2                   CALL GAUS_EL (N, MATRIX);

                                         /* PRINT OUT THE SOLUTION */
 20      2           2                   PUT SKIP (3) EDIT ('SOLUTION SYSTEM:') (COL(35), A);
 21      2           2                   PUT SKIP (2) EDIT ('X1', 'X2', 'X3', 'SOLUTION')
                                                  (COL(15), A, COL(33), A, COL(51), A, COL(65), A);
 22      2           2                   PUT SKIP (2);
 23      2           2                   DO I = 1 TO N;
 24      2      1    2                      PUT SKIP;
 25      2      1    2                      DO J = 1 TO N + 1;
 26      2      2    2                         PUT EDIT (MATRIX(I, J)) (X(9), F(9, 5));
 27      2      2    2                      END;
 28      2      1    2                   END;
 29      2           2                   PUT SKIP (3) LIST ('THE FINAL SOLUTION IS:');
 30      2           2                   DO I = 1 TO N;
 31      2      1    2                      PUT SKIP EDIT ('X', I, ':', MATRIX(I, N + 1))
                                                  (A, F(2), A, X(2), F(9, 5));
 32      2      1    2                   END;
 33      2           2                END;
 34      1           1                END TEST GE:
```

Fig. 8-5   Program to solve a system of linear equations using Gaussian elimination

SOLUTIONS(N)	FLOAT	Solution vector for the system
ACCURACY	FLOAT	Desired accuracy of the solutions
I	FIXED	Counted loop variable
J	FIXED	Counted loop variable

The variables used in the procedure GAUSS_S are:

N	FIXED	Number of equations in system
EQUATION(*, *)	FLOAT	Coefficients of the variables in the equations

```
 35                        GAUS_EL: PROCEDURE (N, ARRAY);
                              /* GIVEN PARAMETERS N AND MATRIX, THIS PROCEDURE FINDS THE    */
                              /* SOLUTION TO THE SIMULTANEOUS LINEAR EQUATIONS REPRESENTED IN */
                              /* MATRIX FORM AS:                                           */
                              /*                                                           */
                              /*           | A11 A12  . . .  A1N | B1 |                     */
                              /*           | A21 A22  . . .  A2N | B2 |                     */
                              /*           |     .         .  |  . |                       */
                              /*           |     .         .  |  . |                       */
                              /*           |     .         .  |  . |                       */
                              /*           | AN1 AN2  . . .  ANN | BN |                     */
                              /*                                                           */
                              /* THE CORRESPONDING SOLUTION ARRAY, WHERE A*X = B, IS        */
                              /*                                                           */
                              /*           | 1   0   . . .   0 | X1 |                       */
                              /*           | 0   1           0 | X2 |                       */
                              /*           |     .         .  |  . |                        */
                              /*           |     .         .  |  . |                        */
                              /*           |     .         .  |  . |                        */
                              /*           | 0   0           1 | XN |                       */
                              /*                                                           */

 36   1         3          DECLARE N FIXED,                    /* DIMENSION OF SQUARE MATRIX */
                                   ARRAY(*,*) FLOAT,            /* THE AUGMENTED MATRIX      */
                                   PIVOT FLOAT,                 /* PIVOT OF ROW              */
                                   M FIXED,                     /* # ROWS IN ARRAY:  N+1     */
                                   (I, J, K) FIXED;             /* SUBSCRIPTS AND COUNTERS   */

                              /* INITIALIZE M */
 37   1         3          M = N + 1;

                              /* FORWARD ELIMINATION */
 38   1         3          DO I = 1 TO N;

                                  /* DIVIDE EACH ELEMENT IN THE ROW BY THE PIVOT */
 39   1    1    3              PIVOT = ARRAY(I, I);
 40   1    1    3              DO J = I TO M;
 41   1    2    3                  ARRAY(I, J) = ARRAY(I, J) / PIVOT;
 42   1    2    3              END;

                                  /* SUBTRACT A MULTIPLE OF THE ROW FROM EACH LOWER ROW */
 43   1    1    3              DO K = I + 1 TO N;
 44   1    2    3                  PIVOT = ARRAY(K, I);
 45   1    2    3                  DO J = I TO M;
 46   1    3    3                      ARRAY(K, J) = ARRAY(K, J) - PIVOT * ARRAY(I, J);
 47   1    3    3                  END;
 48   1    2    3              END;
 49   1    1    3          END;      /* OF FORWARD ELIMINATION */

                              /* BACK SUBSTITUTION */
 50   1         3          DO I = N TO 2 BY -1;
 51   1    1    3              DO K = 1 TO I - 1;
 52   1    2    3                  ARRAY(K, M) = ARRAY(K, M) - ARRAY(K, I) * ARRAY(I, M);
 53   1    2    3                  ARRAY(K, I) = 0.0;
 54   1    2    3              END;
 55   1    1    3          END;

                              /* FINISHED */
 56   1         3          RETURN;
 57   1         3          END GAUS_EL;

ERRORS/WARNINGS DETECTED DURING CODE GENERATION:
```

Fig. 8-5   Program to solve a system of linear equations using Gaussian
elimination (cont'd.)

```
WARNING: NO FILE SPECIFIED. SYSIN/SYSPRINT ASSUMED. (CGOC)
                         ORIGINAL SYSTEM

        X1              X2              X3        RIGHT HAND SIDE

    1.00000          3.00000         -2.00000        7.00000

    4.00000         -1.00000          3.00000       10.00000

   -5.00000          2.00000          3.00000        7.00000


                        SOLUTION SYSTEM:

        X1              X2              X3          SOLUTION


    1.00000          0.00000          0.00000        1.50000
    0.00000          1.00000          0.00000        3.50000
    0.00000          0.00000          1.00000        2.50000


THE FINAL SOLUTION IS:
X 1:    1.50000
X 2:    3.50000
X 3:    2.50000



IN STMT   34  PROGRAM RETURNS FROM MAIN PROCEDURE.
```

Fig. 8-5   Program to solve a system of linear equations using Gaussian elimination (cont'd.)

X_VECTOR(*)	FLOAT	Solution vector
ACCURACY	FLOAT	Desired accuracy of the solution
SUM	FLOAT	Sum of the squares of the differences
OLD	FLOAT	Previous value of X_VECTOR(J)
I	FIXED	Counted loop variable
J	FIXED	Counted loop variable
K	FIXED	Counted loop variable
L	FIXED	Counted loop variable

The program in Fig. 8-6 solves the system of equations

$$
\begin{aligned}
x_1 &= -1.4 &+ 0.4x_2 &+ 0.6x_3 \\
x_2 &= 2.3333 &- 0.3333x_1 &+ 0.6666x_3 \\
x_3 &= 3.3333 &- 1.3333x_1 &+ 0.3333x_2
\end{aligned}
$$

The main program first reads the system of equations. Then the solution vector elements are initialized to 0.0. Procedure GAUSS_S is then called to solve this system of equations. In this procedure, no more than 30 iterations to find the required solution vector are allowed. Within this loop, a new set of approximations is computed in statements 29 to 35. A sum of the squared differences between the new value of X_VECTOR(J) and its previous value is updated in statement 36. Next the accuracy of the solution is tested and the program returns to the main program if the error is small enough.

Exercises for Sec. 8-4

1. Use the Gaussian elimination program to solve the following systems of equations:
   (a)

$$
\begin{aligned}
x_1 + 2x_2 + 3x_3 &= 5 \\
2x_1 - x_2 + x_3 &= 6 \\
x_1 + 3x_2 - 5x_3 &= 2
\end{aligned}
$$

   (b)

$$
\begin{aligned}
x_1 + 2x_2 + 3x_3 + 4x_4 &= 5 \\
2x_1 + 3x_2 + 4x_3 + 5x_4 &= 6 \\
3x_1 + 4x_2 + 5x_3 + 6x_4 &= 7 \\
4x_1 + 5x_2 + 6x_3 + 7x_4 &= 8
\end{aligned}
$$

2. Repeat exercise 1(a) using the iterative function Gauss-Seidel program. Use $x_1 = x_2 = x_3 = 0$ as the initial guesses and .005 as the accuracy. Compare your results with those obtained in exercise 1(a).

3. Repeat exercise 1(b) using the iterative Gauss-Seidel program. Use $x_1 = x_2 = x_3 = x_4 = 0$ as the initial guesses and .0001 as the accuracy. Compare your results with those obtained in exercise 1(b).

4. Recall that elimination with partial pivoting is a method in which roundoff errors are reduced by interchanging rows so that the largest number in magnitude is the next pivot. Formulate a program for Gaussian elimination with partial pivoting. Use the equations in exercise 1(a) to test your program.

8-5 CURVE FITTING BY LEAST-SQUARES APPROXIMATION

A curve which gives the best fit for a set of points is often required. Approximating the curve by a polynomial of degree n which minimizes the squares of the errors is called the *least-squares technique*. For the special case of linear approximations, which we will examine in this section, the method is known as *linear regression*. For example, to find an equation of the form

$$f(x) = a_0 + a_1 x$$

we must solve the set of equations

$$a_0 N + a_1 \sum_{i=1}^{N} x_i = \sum_{i=1}^{N} y_i$$

and

$$a_0 \sum_{i=1}^{N} x_i + a_1 \sum_{i=1}^{N} x_i^2 = \sum_{i=1}^{N} x_i y_i$$

```
STMT LEVEL NEST BLOCK MLVL  SOURCE TEXT


  1                              GAS_SED:  PROCEDURE OPTIONS(MAIN);
                                 /* THIS PROGRAM TESTS THE PROCEDURE GAUSS_S FOR SOLVING       */
                                 /* ITERATIVELY  SIMULTANEOUS LINEAR EQUATIONS.  THE FORMULA FOR */
                                 /* EACH X VALUE IS DEPENDENT UPON THE APPLICATION AND THUS MUST  */
                                 /* BE CHANGED FOR EACH DIFFERENT SYSTEM OF EQUATIONS.           */

  2    1         1              DECLARE N FIXED,         /* NUMBER OF EQUATIONS       */
                                        (I, J) FIXED,    /* INDEX VARIABLES          */
                                        ACCURACY FLOAT;  /* ACCURACY DESIRED         */

                                 /* INPUT THE SYSTEM OF EQUATIONS */
  3    1         1              GET LIST (N);
  4    1         1              BEGIN;
  5    2         2                  DECLARE EQUATIONS(N, N) FLOAT,      /* EQUATIONS */
                                            SOLUTIONS(N) FLOAT;         /* SOLUTION VECTOR */

  6    2         2                  DO I = 1 TO N;
  7    2   1     2                      DO J = 1 TO N;
  8    2   2     2                          GET LIST (EQUATIONS(I, J));
  9    2   2     2                      END;
 10    2   1     2                  END;

                                    /* INITIALIZE THE SOLUTION VECTOR */
 11    2         2                  DO I = 1 TO N;
 12    2   1     2                      SOLUTIONS(I) = 0;
 13    2   1     2                  END;

 14    2         2                  ACCURACY = 0.00001;
 15    2         2                  CALL GAUSS_S (N, EQUATIONS, SOLUTIONS, ACCURACY);
 16    2         2              END;
 17    1         1              END GAS_SED;
```

Fig. 8-6   Program to solve a system of equations using Gauss-Seidel iteration

for a_0 and a_1. The program for solving such a system of equations is given in Fig. 8-6. The variables used in the main program are:

Variable	Type	Usage
N	FIXED	Number of ordered pairs
X(N)	FLOAT	Vector of X values
Y(N)	FLOAT	Vector of Y values
SOLUTION(2)	FLOAT	Solution to the system
I	FIXED	Counted loop variable

The variables used in the procedure LINEAR are:

N	FIXED	Number of ordered pairs
X_VALS(*)	FLOAT	Vector of X values
Y_VALS(*)	FLOAT	Vector of Y values
COEFF(*)	FLOAT	Solution vector
SUM_X	FLOAT	Sum of X_VALS(x_i)
SUM_Y	FLOAT	Sum of Y_VALS(y_i)
SUM_XSQUARE	FLOAT	Sum of X_VALS squared (x_i^2)
SUM_XY	FLOAT	Sum of products ($x_i y_i$)
DENOM	FLOAT	Value of determinate for solving the two equations
I	FIXED	Counted loop variable

```
18                      GAUSS_S: PROCEDURE (N, EQUATION, X_VECTOR, ACCURACY);
                        /* GIVEN PARAMETERS N, X_VECTOR AND ACCURACY, THIS PROCEDURE    */
                        /* SOLVES THE GIVEN SET OF SIMULTANEOUS LINEAR EQUATIONS USING   */
                        /* GAUSS-SEIDEL ITERATION.                                       */

19   1        3         DECLARE N FIXED,                   /* # OF EQUATIONS IN THE SYSTEM*/
                                EQUATION(*, *) FLOAT,      /* EQUATION COEFFICIENTS       */
                                X_VECTOR(*) FLOAT,         /* SOLUTION VECTOR             */
                                ACCURACY FLOAT,            /* DESIRED ACCURACY OF SOLUTION*/
                                SUM FLOAT,                 /* SUM OF DIFFERENCE'S SQUARES */
                                OLD FLOAT,                 /* PREVIOUS X VALUE            */
                                (I, J, K, L) FIXED;        /* ITERATION COUNTERS          */

                        /* PRINT HEADING FOR THE ITERATIONS TABLE */
20   1        3         PUT SKIP EDIT ('X1', 'X2', 'X3') (COL(8), A, COL(20), A,
                              COL(32), A);
21   1        3         PUT SKIP;

                        /* LIMITED TO 30 ITERATIONS */
22   1        3         DO I = 1 TO 30;

23   1   1    3             PUT SKIP;
                            /* OUTPUT THIS RESULT */
24   1   1    3             DO I = 1 TO N;
25   1   2    3                 PUT EDIT (X_VECTOR(I)) (X(3), F(9, 5));
26   1   2    3             END;

                            /* CALCULATE NEW SET OF APPROXIMATIONS */
27   1   1    3             SUM = 0.0;

28   1   1    3             DO J = 1 TO N;
29   1   2    3                 OLD = X_VECTOR(J);
30   1   2    3                 X_VECTOR(J) = EQUATION(J, 1);
31   1   2    3                 DO L = 2 TO N;
32   1   3    3                     IF J >= L
33   1   3    3                     THEN X_VECTOR(J) = X_VECTOR(J) + EQUATION(J, L) *
                                          X_VECTOR(L - 1);
34   1   3    3                     ELSE X_VECTOR(J) = X_VECTOR(J) + EQUATION(J, L) *
                                          X_VECTOR(L);
35   1   3    3                 END;
36   1   2    3                 SUM = SUM + (X_VECTOR(J) - OLD) * (X_VECTOR(J) - OLD);
37   1   2    3             END;

                            /* TEST ACCURACY */
38   1   1    3             IF SUM < ACCURACY
39   1   1    3             THEN DO;
40   1   2    3                 PUT SKIP (2) EDIT ('ANSWER IS, FOR ', N, ' EQUATIONS,')
                                          (A, F(2), A);
41   1   2    3                 DO J = 1 TO N;
42   1   3    3                     PUT SKIP EDIT ('X', J, X_VECTOR(J))
                                          (COL(5), A, F(1), COL(15), F(9, 5));
43   1   3    3                 END;
44   1   2    3                 RETURN;
45   1   2    3             END;
46   1   1    3         END;        /* OF 30 ITERATIONS */

                        /* NO CONVERGENCE */
47   1        3         PUT SKIP (2) EDIT ('TOLERANCE NOT MET IN 3 ITERATIONS, ANSWER SO ',
                              'FAR IS') (A, A);
48   1        3         PUT SKIP;
49   1        3         DO I = 1 TO N;
50   1   1    3             PUT SKIP EDIT ('X', I, X_VECTOR(I))
                                      (COL(5), A, F(1), COL(15), F(9, 5));
51   1   1    3         END;

                        /* FINISHED */
52   1        3         RETURN;
53   1        3         END GAUSS_S;

ERRORS/WARNINGS DETECTED DURING CODE GENERATION:
```

Fig. 8-6   Program to solve a system of equations using Gauss-Seidel
           iteration (cont'd.)

```
WARNING: NO FILE SPECIFIED. SYSIN/SYSPRINT ASSUMED. (CGOC)

      X1            X2            X3

    0.00000       0.00000       0.00000
   -1.40000       2.79992       6.13313
    3.39985       5.28848       0.56293
    1.05315       2.35754       2.71490
    1.17196       3.75244       3.02142
    1.91383       3.70950       2.01797
    1.29458       3.24699       2.68946
    1.51247       3.62199       2.52393
    1.56315       3.49475       2.41395
    1.44627       3.46040       2.55834
    1.51916       3.53235       2.48514
    1.50402       3.48860       2.49074
    1.48988       3.49705       2.51240
    1.50626       3.50603       2.49356
    1.49855       3.49604       2.50051
    1.49873       3.50062       2.50181
    1.50133       3.50061       2.49833
    1.49924       3.49899       2.50057


ANSWER IS, FOR  3 EQUATIONS,
    X1            1.49994
    X2            3.50025
    X3            2.50006



IN STMT   17  PROGRAM RETURNS FROM MAIN PROCEDURE.
```

Fig. 8-6   Program to solve a system of equations using Gauss-Seidel iteration (cont'd.)

The data used by the program given in Fig. 8-7 are

X	Y
0.4501	3.0509
0.9802	1.5078
1.3376	1.0999
2.3999	0.9212
2.7936	1.0012
3.5805	2.2333
3.7201	3.2500

The main program after reading the set of points, calls procedure LINEAR to find the best-fit linear equation. Statements 10 and 11 print the resulting equation. Procedure LINEAR first computes the sums of x_i, y_i, x_i^2, and $x_i y_i$ and stores them in the variables SUM_X, SUM_Y, SUM_XSQUARE, and SUM_XY, respectively. Then the resulting equations

$$N * COEFF(0) + SUM\_X * COEFF(1) = SUM\_Y$$
$$SUM\_X * COEFF(0) + SUM\_XSQUARE * COEFF(1) = SUM\_XY$$

are solved in statements 23 to 25 for COEFF(0) and COEFF(1) by using determinants.

```
STMT LEVEL NEST BLOCK MLVL  SOURCE TEXT


     1                              LIN_REG:  PROCEDURE OPTIONS(MAIN);
                                    /* THIS PROGRAM TESTS PROCEDURE LINEAR FOR DETERMINING A LINEAR   */
                                    /* EQUATION TO FIT A GIVEN SET OF DATA.                           */

     2    1          1             DECLARE N FIXED,          /* NUMBER OF ORDERED PAIRS               */
                                           I FIXED;          /* INDEX VARIABLE                        */

                                    /* READ THE NUMBER OF ORDERED PAIRS */
     3    1          1             GET LIST (N);

                                    /* PROCESS THE SYSTEM */
     4    1          1             BEGIN;
     5    2          2                 DECLARE (X(N), Y(N)) FLOAT,  /* VECTORS TO STORE COORDINATES */
                                               SOLUTION(2) FLOAT;   /* SOLUTION TO SYSTEM           */

                                        /* READ VECTORS */
     6    2          2                 DO I = 1 TO N;
     7    2    1     2                     GET LIST (X(I), Y(I));
     8    2    1     2                 END;

                                        /* USE PROCEDURE LINEAR TO FIND THE PROPER EQUATION */
     9    2          2                 CALL LINEAR (N, X, Y, SOLUTION);

                                        /* PRINT THE SOLUTION */
    10    2          2                 PUT SKIP (3) EDIT ('THE RESULTING REGRESSION LINE IS')
                                              (COL(5), A);
    11    2          2                 PUT SKIP (2) EDIT ('Y = ', SOLUTION(1), ' + ', SOLUTION(2),
                                              'X') (COL(10), A, F(9,5), A, F(9,5), A);

    12    2          2             END;
    13    1          1             END LIN_REG;

    14                            LINEAR: PROCEDURE (N, X_VALS, Y_VALS, COEFF);
                                    /* THIS PROCEDURE DETERMINES THE LINEAR COEFFICIENTS FOR THE SET   */
                                    /* OF X AND Y VALUES GIVEN IN VECTORS X_VALS AND Y_VALS,           */
                                    /* RESPECTIVELY.  THE DETERMINED COEFFICIENTS ARE RETURNED TO THE  */
                                    /* CALLING PROCEDURE THROUGH PARAMETER COEFFICIENTS, WITH THE       */
                                    /* B COEFFICIENT FOLLOWED BY THE X COEFFICIENT.  N IS THE NUMBER   */
                                    /* OF X AND Y VALUES USED IN THE REGRESSION.                       */

    15    1          3             DECLARE N FIXED,               /* NUMBER OF ORDERED PAIRS           */
                                           X_VALS(*) FLOAT,       /* VECTOR OF X VALUES                */
                                           Y_VALS(*) FLOAT,       /* VECTOR OF Y VALUES                */
                                           COEFF(*) FLOAT,        /* SOLUTION VECTOR                   */
                                           SUM_X FLOAT,           /* SUM OF X_VALS                     */
                                           SUM_Y FLOAT,           /* SUM OF Y_VALS                     */
                                           SUM_XSQUARE FLOAT,     /* SUM OF X_VALS ** 2                */
                                           SUM_XY FLOAT,          /* SUM OF X_VALS * Y_VALS            */
                                           DENOM FLOAT,           /* VALUE OF DETERMINANT              */
                                           I FIXED;               /* COUNTED LOOP VARIABLE             */

                                    /* DETERMINE ALL THE REQUIRED SUMS */
    16    1          3             SUM_X, SUM_Y, SUM_XSQUARE, SUM_XY = 0;
    17    1          3             DO I = 1 TO N BY 1;
    18    1    1     3                 SUM_X = SUM_X + X_VALS(I);
    19    1    1     3                 SUM_Y = SUM_Y + Y_VALS(I);
    20    1    1     3                 SUM_XSQUARE = SUM_XSQUARE + (X_VALS(I)**2);
    21    1    1     3                 SUM_XY = SUM_XY + X_VALS(I) * Y_VALS(I);
    22    1    1     3             END;

                                    /* SOLVE USING DETERMINANTS (CRAMER'S RULE) */
    23    1          3             DENOM = N * SUM_XSQUARE - SUM_X * SUM_X;
    24    1          3             COEFF(1) = ((SUM_Y * SUM_XSQUARE) - (SUM_XY * SUM_X)) / DENOM;
    25    1          3             COEFF(2) = ((N * SUM_XY) - (SUM_X * SUM_Y)) / DENOM;
    26    1          3             RETURN;
    27    1          3             END LINEAR;

THE RESULTING REGRESSION LINE IS

    Y =   1.66088 +    0.09423X


IN STMT   13  PROGRAM RETURNS FROM MAIN PROCEDURE.
```

Fig. 8-7   Program to perform linear regression on a set of points

Exercises for Sec. 8-5

1. Write a program to compute the regression line for the data in Table 8-1. Plot the data and the computed regression line. Does your line appear to be a good approximation to the actual curve? Why or why not?

Table 8-1

X	Y
1.5603	3.6189
2.0157	2.4113
2.3399	1.1346
2.7568	0.5673
3.1346	1.2015
3.4799	2.5682
3.7521	3.3999

2. The midterm averages for a selected sample of freshman computer science students were recorded and tabulated along with their final high school averages. The results are given in Table 8-2.

Table 8-2

Student	Midterm Average	High School Average
ADAMS	73.5	78.2
BARNES	66.9	71.5
CAMPBELL	83.8	81.7
DOLBY	58.1	77.3
FRIESEN	77.1	85.6
HOOPER	44.3	65.8
JONES	35.8	70.3
MARSHALL	66.2	60.5
REMPEL	72.5	75.3
SCOTT	60.6	66.6
TURNER	85.8	85.2
WALSH	87.9	86.3

Write a program to compute the regression line for the data. Plot the regression line. Can you predict, with a reasonable degree of accuracy, the midterm average of a specific student given that student's high school average? Why or why not?

3. The purpose of this problem is to write a program to obtain the best-fit polynomial regression line of arbitrary degree for a given set of data. If we let n represent the order of the curve we are approximating and N the number of data points, then we wish to approximate the curve by a function of the form

$$f(x) = a_0 + a_1x + a_2x^2 + \cdots + a_nx^n$$

We can find these $n + 1$ unknowns $(a_0, a_1, ..., a_n)$ using Gaussian elimination on the $n + 1$ simultaneous equations given on pages 390 and 391 of the main text. Formulate a program for this purpose.

4. Use the program devised in exercise 3 to determine the best-fit polynomial regression line of degree 2 for the data in Table 8-7. Compare your results with those obtained in exercise 1 by plotting this regression line on your previous graph. Which line fits the data most accurately and why?

CHAPTER

9

ADVANCED STRING PROCESSING

The basic notions of string manipulation in PL/I were introduced in Chap. 5. These notions are extended to include three additional nonprimitive functions in this chapter. Also, programs for four string manipulation applications are presented. In particular these applications deal with lexical analysis, text editing, KWIC indexing, and the use of bit strings in information organization and retrieval.

9-1 BASIC FUNCTIONS

Chapter 5 discussed in some detail the PL/I programming aspects of string manipulation. The basic operation of concatenation (‖) and the two primitive functions LENGTH and SUBSTR were discussed in detail. Most other string-manipulation functions can be obtained from these primitives.

In this chapter we provide programs for the three additional functions – MATCH, SPAN, and BREAK – which are discussed in the main text. As was done in that discussion, we associate a *cursor* with the scanning process. The three programs presented in this section concern themselves with the maintenance and updating of the cursor mechanism.

The three PL/I functions which we present here all have the same six parameters. These parameters are the following:

SUBJECT	Subject string to be examined.
PATTERN	String sought within the subject string.
CURSOR	Character position in SUBJECT at which the pattern matching process is to begin.
MATCH_STR	Desired substring found in SUBJECT in the case of a successful pattern match.
REPLACE_FLAG	Flag indicating whether or not a replacement is required. A value of '1'B specifies a replacement and '0'B indicates no replacement.
REPLACE_STR	Replacement string for the matched substring.

Observe that in the following programs we have been forced to depart from making use of SUBSTR as a pseudo-variable. Although SUBSTR can be used as a pseudo-variable, its use is very restrictive. As mentioned earlier in Chap. 5, the substring being rewritten in the subject string must be replaced by a string of the same length.

Figure 9-1 presents a PL/I function for the MATCH function. This program corresponds closely to the algorithm MATCH in the main text. The differences which occur are due to the differences between the SUB and SUBSTR functions. In particular in statement 18, the replacement of MATCH_STR by REPLACE_STR is done by concatenating the substring of SUBJECT coming before MATCH_STR in front of REPLACE_STR and concatenating the substring of SUBJECT appearing after MATCH_STR behind REPLACE_STR.

Figure 9-2 is a PL/I implementation of the function SPAN. In statement 27 a check is made to see if the cursor is greater than the length of SUBJECT. If so, a value of *false* is returned. In the next statement, the VERIFY function is used to find the first occurrence of a character in SUBJECT which is not also in PATTERN. If the character indicated by the CURSOR is not in the PATTERN string (i.e., VERIFY returns a value of 1), SPAN returns the value *false*. If all the characters in SUBJECT from CURSOR on are in the PATTERN string (i.e., VERIFY returns a value of 0), then I is set to the length of SUBJECT plus one; otherwise, I is set to the position in SUBJECT containing the first character which is also in PATTERN. MATCH_STR is set to the substring of SUBJECT from the CURSOR position, up to but not including the character in position I. If replacement is indicated by a true value of REPLACE_FLAG, MATCH_STR is replaced by REPLACE_STR using the same method as that used in the MATCH function.

```
 9   1       1       MATCH: PROCEDURE (SUBJECT, PATTERN, CURSOR, MATCH_STR, REPLACE_FLAG,
                                        REPLACE_STR)
                            RETURNS (BIT(1));
10   2       2       DECLARE SUBJECT CHARACTER(*) VARYING, /* STRING TO BE EXAMINED */
                            PATTERN CHARACTER(*) VARYING, /* STRING SOUGHT WITHIN */
                                                         /* SUBJECT STRING */
                            CURSOR FIXED,        /* CHARACTER POSITION IN SUBJECT */
                                                 /* AT WHICH THE PATTERN MATCHING */
                                                 /* PROCESS IS TO BEGIN */
                            MATCH_STR CHARACTER(*) VARYING, /* DESIRED SUBSTRING */
                                                 /* FOUND IN SUBJECT */
                            REPLACE_FLAG BIT(*), /* FLAG INDICATING WHETHER */
                                                 /* REPLACEMENT IS REQUIRED */
                            REPLACE_STR CHARACTER(*) VARYING; /* STRING USED TO */
                                                 /* REPLACE MATCHED SUBSTRING */
                     /* DOES THE PATTERN FIT WITHIN THE SEARCH BOUNDS OF THE SUBJECT */
                     /* STRING? */
11   2       2       IF CURSOR + LENGTH(PATTERN) > LENGTH(SUBJECT) + 1
12   2       2       THEN RETURN('0'B);
                     /* PERFORM PATTERN MATCH */
13   2       2       IF SUBSTR(SUBJECT, CURSOR, LENGTH(PATTERN)) ¬= PATTERN
14   2       2       THEN RETURN('0'B);
                     /* SET MATCH_STR AND PERFORM INDICATED REPLACEMENT */
15   2       2       MATCH_STR = PATTERN;
16   2       2       IF REPLACE_FLAG
17   2       2       THEN DO;
18   2   1   2           SUBJECT = SUBSTR(SUBJECT, 1, CURSOR-1) || REPLACE_STR ||
                            SUBSTR(SUBJECT, CURSOR + LENGTH(PATTERN));
19   2   1   2           CURSOR = CURSOR + LENGTH(REPLACE_STR);
20   2   1   2           END;
21   2       2       ELSE CURSOR = CURSOR + LENGTH(PATTERN);
                     /* SUCCESSFUL RETURN */
22   2       2       RETURN('1'B);
23   2       2   END MATCH;
```

Fig. 9-1   PL/I program for the function MATCH

Finally, Fig. 9-3 contains a PL/I program for the function BREAK. The BREAK function is essentially the same as the corresponding algorithm given in the main text. Differences occur in the implementation of two parts of the function. Statements 51 through 59 search the SUBJECT string for the first occurrence of a character which is also in PATTERN. Since in the DO WHILE statement all conditions are evaluated at the same time, it is necessary in the implementation of the algorithm to break the *Repeat while* statement of the algorithm into two IF statements inside a DO WHILE statement. Again, as in the functions MATCH and SPAN, concatenation is used to replace the MATCH_STR by the REPLACE_STR when a replacement is indicated.

Now that programs for the functions MATCH, SPAN, and BREAK have been presented, we are ready to use them in a variety of string-manipulation applications. The next section examines four of these applications.

Exercises for Sec. 9-1

1. Write a PL/C function TRIM which will delete all trailing blanks of a given character string. Test your program on the following strings:

   'HELLObbbbb'

   and

```
24   1      1         SPAN: PROCEDURE (SUBJECT, PATTERN, CURSOR, MATCH_STR, REPLACE_FLAG,
                                  REPLACE_STR)
                          RETURNS (BIT(1));

25   2      3         DECLARE SUBJECT CHARACTER(*) VARYING, /* STRING TO BE EXAMINED */
                              PATTERN CHARACTER(*) VARYING, /* STRING SOUGHT WITHIN */
                                                            /* SUBJECT STRING */
                              CURSOR FIXED,        /* CHARACTER POSITION IN SUBJECT */
                                                   /* AT WHICH THE PATTERN MATCHING */
                                                   /* PROCESS IS TO BEGIN */
                              MATCH_STR CHARACTER(*) VARYING, /* DESIRED SUBSTRING */
                                                            /* FOUND IN SUBJECT */
                              REPLACE_FLAG BIT(*), /* FLAG INDICATING WHETHER */
                                                   /* REPLACEMENT IS REQUIRED */
                              REPLACE_STR CHARACTER(*) VARYING; /* STRING USED TO */
                                                            /* REPLACE MATCHED SUBSTRING */
26   2      3         DECLARE I FIXED;            /* TEMPORARY CURSOR */

                      /* DOES THE PATTERN FIT WITHIN THE BOUNDS OF THE SUBJECT STRING */
27   2      3         IF CURSOR > LENGTH(SUBJECT)
28   2      3         THEN RETURN('0'B);

29   2      3         I = VERIFY(SUBSTR(SUBJECT, CURSOR), PATTERN);

                      /* UNSUCCESSFUL PATTERN MATCH */
30   2      3         IF I = 1
31   2      3         THEN RETURN('0'B);
32   2      3         IF I = 0
33   2      3         THEN I = LENGTH(SUBJECT) + 1;
34   2      3         ELSE I = CURSOR + I - 1;
                      /* SET MATCH_STR AND PERFORM INDICATED REPLACEMENT */
35   2      3         MATCH_STR = SUBSTR(SUBJECT, CURSOR, I-CURSOR);
36   2      3         IF REPLACE_FLAG
37   2      3         THEN DO;
38   2   1  3              SUBJECT = SUBSTR(SUBJECT, 1, CURSOR-1) || REPLACE_STR ||
                              SUBSTR(SUBJECT, I);
39   2   1  3              CURSOR = CURSOR + LENGTH(REPLACE_STR);
40   2   1  3              END;
41   2      3         ELSE CURSOR = I;

                      /* SUCCESSFUL RETURN */
42   2      3         RETURN('1'B);
43   2      3         END SPAN;
```

Fig. 9-2   PL/I program for the function SPAN

'GOODBYEbbbbbbbbb'

where "b" represents blank spaces in the string.

2. The PL/C function REPEAT(*pattern, n*) produces a string containing $n + 1$
    copies of *pattern* (i.e., *pattern* concatenated with n copies of *pattern*). Design a
    PL/C function which acts in the same manner as the REPEAT function
    illustrated in the main text; that is, produce a string containing n replications of
    pattern.

9-2   APPLICATIONS

This section presents PL/C solutions to the application problems found in
Sec. 9-2 of the main text.

9-2.1   Lexical Analysis

The program given in Fig. 9-4 is a solution to the lexical analysis problem
discussed in Sec. 9-2.1 of the main text. The problem consists of designing a

```
44    1         1              BREAK: PROCEDURE(SUBJECT, PATTERN, CURSOR, MATCH_STR, REPLACE_FLAG,
                                      REPLACE_STR)
                                  RETURNS (BIT(1));
45    2         4              DECLARE SUBJECT CHARACTER(*) VARYING, /* STRING TO BE EXAMINED */
                                      PATTERN CHARACTER(*) VARYING, /* STRING SOUGHT WITHIN */
                                                                    /* SUBJECT STRING */
                                      CURSOR FIXED,        /* CHARACTER POSITION IN SUBJECT */
                                                           /* AT WHICH THE PATTERN MATCHING */
                                                           /* PROCESS IS TO BEGIN */
                                      MATCH_STR CHARACTER(*) VARYING, /* DESIRED SUBSTRING */
                                                                     /* FOUND IN SUBJECT */
                                      REPLACE_FLAG BIT(*), /* FLAG INDICATING WHETHER */
                                                           /* REPLACEMENT IS REQUIRED */
                                      REPLACE_STR CHARACTER(*) VARYING; /* STRING USED TO */
                                                                       /* REPLACE MATCHED SUBSTRING */
46    2         4              DECLARE I FIXED,           /* TEMPORARY CURSOR */
                                      NOT_FOUND BIT(1);
                               /* DOES THE PATTERN FIT WITHIN THE SEARCH BOUNDS OF THE  SUBJECT */
                               /* STRING? */
47    2         4              IF CURSOR > LENGTH(SUBJECT)
48    2         4              THEN RETURN('0'B);
                               /* INITIALIZE PATTERN MATCH */
49    2         4              I = CURSOR;
                               /* IS CHARACTER I IN THE PATTERN STRING? */
50    2         4              NOT_FOUND = '1'B;
51    2         4              DO WHILE(NOT_FOUND);
52    2    1    4                  IF I <= LENGTH(SUBJECT)
53    2    1    4                  THEN DO;
54    2    2    4                      IF INDEX(PATTERN, SUBSTR(SUBJECT, I, 1)) = 0
55    2    2    4                      THEN I = I + 1;
56    2    2  · 4                      ELSE NOT_FOUND = '0'B;
57    2    2    4                      END;
58    2    1    4                  ELSE NOT_FOUND = '0'B;
59    2    1    4              END;
                               /* SUCCESSFUL PATTERN MATCH? */
60    2         4              IF I = LENGTH(SUBJECT) + 1
61    2         4              THEN RETURN('0'B);
                               /* SET MATCH_STR AND PERFORM INDICATED REPLACEMENT */
62    2         4              MATCH_STR = SUBSTR(SUBJECT, CURSOR, I-CURSOR);
63    2         4              IF REPLACE_FLAG
64    2         4              THEN DO;
65    2    1    4                  SUBJECT = SUBSTR(SUBJECT, 1, CURSOR-1) || REPLACE_STR ||
                                          SUBSTR(SUBJECT, I);
66    2    1    4                  CURSOR = CURSOR + LENGTH(REPLACE_STR);
67    2    1    4                  END;
68    2         4              ELSE CURSOR = I;
                               /* SUCESSFUL RETURN */
69    2         4              RETURN('1'B);
70    2         4          END BREAK;
```

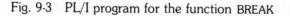

Fig. 9-3   PL/I program for the function BREAK

scanner that is able to isolate words or tokens of an assignment statement and separate them into classes to be used by a syntactic analyzer. For this example, we assume that the allowable tokens in the assignment statement are identifiers; integers; the addition, subtraction, multiplication, division, exponentiation, and assignment operators; and left and right parentheses. The exponentiation operator in this example is assumed to be the exclamation punctuation mark (i.e., !). In addition to these tokens, the scanner must also be able to handle blanks within the assignment statement. Table 9-1 lists the name of the classes, the tokens in the classes, and the number assigned to each class.

The following variables appear in this program:

Variable	Type	Usage
SOURCE	CHARACTER(256) VARYING	Statement to be scanned

Table 9-1 Tokens of an assignment statement

Name	Tokens	Number
Identifier	Valid PL/C identifier	1
Integer	String of digits	2
Addition and subtraction operators	+ and −	3
Multiplication and division operators	* and /	4
Exponentiation operator	!	5
Assignment operator	=	6
Left parenthesis	(	7
Right parenthesis	)	8

CHAR	CHARACTER(1) VARYING	Current character being examined
TOKEN	CHARACTER(256) VARYING	Current token being isolated
REP_NO	FIXED	Representation number of a token
LETTERS	CHARACTER(26) VARYING	Letters of the alphabet
DIGITS	CHARACTER(10) VARYING	Digits 0 thru 9
CURSOR	FIXED	Position of character in SOURCE currently being examined
DUMMY	BIT(1)	Temporary variable
F	FIXED	Temporary variable
T	FIXED	Temporary variable
ALPHA	CHARACTER(36) VARYING	All characters and digits

The program uses the following input data:

$$'A1 = A + 5'$$

In the first part of the program, the variables representing the letters and digits are initialized. The variable CURSOR is also initialized to one. The statement to be analyzed is then read and assigned to the variable SOURCE. After the statement to be analyzed is printed, a loop is begun to separate the tokens of the statement and print a copy of the tokens preceded by their classifications. The function SPAN is used to move the CURSOR to the next nonblank character of SOURCE. A number of nested if statements are then used to determine the classification of the token consisting of (or begun by, in the case of an identifier or digit) the character found and to print the appropriate message. When the end of the statement has been reached, the program terminates.

9-2.2 Keyword-In-Context (KWIC) Indexing

KWIC indexing is a popular method of indexing which produces a listing of all the lines in a document that contain any of a particular list of keywords. In the program presented in Fig. 9-5 of this section, KWIC indexing is applied to a list of titles. The program consists of two subprograms. The first subprogram called KWIC_C creates the KWIC index by scanning each title for keywords which specify the meaning of the document. (The words "a", "an", "and", "its", "the", "to" and

```
STMT LEVEL NEST BLOCK MLVL  SOURCE TEXT

 1                              SCAN: PROCEDURE OPTIONS(MAIN);

 2    1          1             DECLARE SOURCE CHARACTER(256) VARYING, /* SOURCE STATEMENT */
                                  CHAR CHARACTER(1) VARYING, /* CURRENT CHARACTER BEING */
                                                             /* EXAMINED */
                                  TOKEN CHARACTER(256) VARYING,  /* CURRENT TOKEN BEING */
                                                                 /* ISOLATED */
                                  REP NO FIXED,          /* REPRESENTATION NUMBER OF A TOKEN */
                                  LETTERS CHARACTER(26) VARYING, /* LETTERS OF THE ALPHABET*/
                                  DIGITS CHARACTER(10) VARYING,  /*DIGITS 0 THRU 9 */
                                  CURSOR FIXED,          /* POSITION OF CHARACTER BEING */
                                                         /* EXAMINED IN SOURCE */
                                  DUMMY BIT(1),          /* DUMMY VARIABLE */
                                  F FIXED,               /* TEMPORARY VARIABLE */
                                  T CHARACTER(256) VARYING, /* TEMPORARY VARIABLE */
                                  ALPHA CHARACTER(36) VARYING, /* STRING CONTAINING ALL */
                                                               /* LETTERS AND DIGITS */
                                  SPAN ENTRY(CHARACTER(*) VARYING, CHARACTER(*) VARYING,
                                        FIXED, CHARACTER(*) VARYING, BIT(*),
                                        CHARACTER(*) VARYING)
                                        RETURNS (BIT(1));

                               /* INITIALIZE */
 3    1          1             LETTERS = 'ABCDEFGHIJKLMNOPQRSTUVWXYZ';
 4    1          1             DIGITS = '0123456789';
 5    1          1             CURSOR = 1;
 6    1          1             ALPHA = LETTERS ¦¦ DIGITS;

                               /* INPUT SOURCE STATEMENT */
 7    1          1             GET LIST (SOURCE);

                               /* OUTPUT SOURCE STATEMENT */
 8    1          1             PUT SKIP LIST (SOURCE);
```

Fig. 9-4   Program to perform a lexical scan of an assignment statement

"with" are considered to be ordinary words and are ignored in the creation of KWIC index.) For each keyword found in the title of a document, an entry is made in the vector T_INDEX which indicates the title's position in the vector TITLE.

The second subprogram called KWIC_G uses the T_INDEX entries of each of the keywords in order to produce a listing of the KWIC index. In listing the KWIC index, each line is permuted so that the keyword appears first. The following variables are used in the main program KWIC:

Variable	Type	Usage
ORD_WORD(7)	CHARACTER(4) VARYING	Vector of ordinary words
TITLE(50)	CHARACTER(100) VARYING	Document titles
KEYWORD(100)	CHARACTER(20) VARYING	Document keywords
LAST_KEY	FIXED	Index of last keyword
T_INDEX(100)	CHARACTER(50) VARYING	Title indices for a particular keyword

Variables for procedure KWIC_C:

LAST_TITLE	FIXED	Index of last title
WORD	CHARACTER(20) VARYING	Current word being processed

```
                                         /* SCAN SOURCE STATEMENT */
  9   1        1                          DO WHILE (CURSOR <= LENGTH(SOURCE));

                                             /*OBTAIN NEXT TOKEN */
 10   1        1        1                     IF ¬ SPAN(SOURCE, ' ', CURSOR, T, '0'B, '') /* CHECK FOR */
                                                                               /* NONBLANK SYMBOL */
 11   1   1   1                              THEN DO;
 12   1   2   1                                 CHAR = SUBSTR(SOURCE, CURSOR, 1);  /* ISOLATE NEXT CHAR*/
 13   1   2   1                                 IF INDEX(LETTERS,CHAR) ¬= 0 /* CHECK FOR IDENTIFIER */
 14   1   2   1                                 THEN DO;
 15   1   3   1                                    DUMMY=SPAN(SOURCE, ALPHA, CURSOR, TOKEN, '0'B, '');
 16   1   3   1                                    PUT SKIP LIST(1, TOKEN);  /* OUTPUT IDENTIFIER */
 17   1   3   1                                    END;
 18   1   2   1                                 ELSE IF INDEX(DIGITS, CHAR) ¬= 0 /* CHECK FOR INTEGER*/
 19   1   2   1                                    THEN DO;
 20   1   3   1                                       DUMMY = SPAN(SOURCE, DIGITS, CURSOR, TOKEN,
                                                          '0'B,'');
 21   1   3   1                                       PUT SKIP LIST(2, TOKEN);
 22   1   3   1                                       END;
 23   1   2   1                                    ELSE DO;
 24   1   3   1                                       F = INDEX('+*!=()', CHAR);/* CHECK FOR +, *,*/
                                                                               /* !, =, (, OR ) */
 25   1   3   1                                       IF F ¬= 0
 26   1   3   1                                       THEN DO;
 27   1   4   1                                          REP_NO = F + 2;
 28   1   4   1                                          PUT SKIP LIST (REP_NO, CHAR);/* OUTPUT */
                                                                               /* OPERATOR */
 29   1   4   1                                          END;
 30   1   3   1                                       ELSE DO;
 31   1   4   1                                          F = INDEX('-/', CHAR);/* CHECK FOR - OR */
                                                                               /* / */
 32   1   4   1                                          IF F ¬= 0
 33   1   4   1                                          THEN DO;
 34   1   5   1                                             REP_NO = F + 2;
 35   1   5   1                                             PUT SKIP LIST (REP_NO, CHAR);
                                                             /* OUPUT OPERATOR */
 36   1   5   1                                             END;
 37   1   4   1                                          ELSE PUT SKIP LIST ('ILLEGAL CHARACTER',
                                                                CHAR);
 38   1   4   1                                          END;
 39   1   3   1                                       CURSOR = CURSOR + 1;
 40   1   3   1                                       END;
 41   1   2   1                                 END;
 42   1   1   1                              END;
```

Fig. 9-4   Program to perform a lexical scan of an assignment statement (cont'd.)

KEYIND	FIXED	Index of keyword
BLANKS	CHARACTER(80) VARYING	Temporary string
DUMMY	BIT(1)	Temporary variable
CHAR_NO	CHARACTER(256) VARYING	Character string of title index number
NUM	FIXED	Temporary variable
PHRASE	CHARACTER(80) VARYING	Input title
END_FLAG	BIT(1)	End of data flag

Variables for procedure KWIC_G:

KEYSTRING	CHARACTER(256) VARYING	String of title indices
KWIC_LINE	CHARACTER(256) VARYING	Line of output
INDEX_NO	FIXED	Particular title index
I	FIXED	Counter variable
J	FIXED	Counter variable

```
43   1   1        SPAN: PROCEDURE (SUBJECT, PATTERN, CURSOR, MATCH_STR, REPLACE_FLAG,
                                    REPLACE_STR)
                        RETURNS (BIT(1));
44   2   2        DECLARE SUBJECT CHARACTER(*) VARYING, /* STRING TO BE EXAMINED */
                          PATTERN CHARACTER(*) VARYING, /* STRING SOUGHT WITHIN */
                                                        /* SUBJECT STRING */
                          CURSOR FIXED,          /* CHARACTER POSITION IN SUBJECT */
                                                 /* AT WHICH THE PATTERN MATCHING */
                                                 /* PROCESS IS TO BEGIN */
                          MATCH_STR CHARACTER(*) VARYING, /* DESIRED SUBSTRING */
                                                 /* FOUND IN SUBJECT */
                          REPLACE_FLAG BIT(*),  /* FLAG INDICATING WHETHER */
                                                 /* REPLACEMENT IS REQUIRED */
                          REPLACE_STR CHARACTER(*) VARYING; /* STRING USED TO */
                                                 /* REPLACE MATCHED SUBSTRING */
45   2   2        DECLARE I FIXED;               /* TEMPORARY CURSOR */
                  /* DOES THE PATTERN FIT WITHIN THE BOUNDS OF THE SUBJECT STRING */
46   2   2        IF CURSOR > LENGTH(SUBJECT)
47   2   2        THEN RETURN('0'B);
48   2   2        I = VERIFY(SUBSTR(SUBJECT, CURSOR), PATTERN);
                  /* UNSUCCESSFUL PATTERN MATCH */
49   2   2        IF I = 1
50   2   2        THEN RETURN('0'B);
51   2   2        IF I = 0
52   2   2        THEN I = LENGTH(SUBJECT) + 1;
53   2   2        ELSE I = CURSOR + I -1;
                  /* SET MATCH STR AND PERFORM INDICATED REPLACEMENT */
54   2   2        MATCH_STR = SUBSTR(SUBJECT, CURSOR, I-CURSOR);
55   2   2        IF REPLACE_FLAG
56   2   2        THEN DO;
57   2   1   2        SUBJECT = SUBSTR(SUBJECT, 1, CURSOR-1) || REPLACE_STR ||
                              SUBSTR(SUBJECT, I);
58   2   1   2        CURSOR = CURSOR + LENGTH(REPLACE_STR);
59   2   1   2        END;
60   2   2        ELSE CURSOR = I;
                  /* SUCCESSFUL RETURN */
61   2   2        RETURN('1'B);
62   2   2   END SPAN;
63   1   1   END SCAN;
```

ERRORS/WARNINGS DETECTED DURING CODE GENERATION:

   WARNING: NO FILE SPECIFIED. SYSIN/SYSPRINT ASSUMED. (CGOC)

```
A1 = A + 5
 1                A1
     6            =
 1                A
     3            +
 2                5
```

IN STMT   63 PROGRAM RETURNS FROM MAIN PROCEDURE.

Fig. 9-4   Program to perform a lexical scan of an assignment statement (cont'd.)

| DUMMY | CHARACTER(256) VARYING | Dummy variable |
| POS | FIXED | Temporary variable |

The sample input data used in the program consist of the following titles:

'AN INTRODUCTION TO COMPUTER SCIENCE AN ALGORITHMIC APPROACH'
'STRUCTURED PL/I PROGRAMMING'
'STRUCTURED WATFIV-S PROGRAMMING'
'PL/I PROGRAMMING WITH APPLICATIONS'
'AN INTRODUCTION TO PASCAL PROGRAMMING'

The main program KWIC initializes the ORD_WORD vector to seven ordinary words and then calls the two subprograms KWIC_C and KWIC_G to create and generate the KWIC index. In the first part of the KWIC_C procedure, the counters LAST_TITLE and LAST_KEY are initialized to zero. A loop is then begun to read in all the titles. Once a title is read, any initial blanks are removed using the SPAN function and the end marker // is appended to the end of the title. The title is then added to the TITLE vector. Statements 26 through 43 define a loop which is used to process all the words in the current title. First a check is made to see if the word is one of the ordinary words. The function ORD_SEARCH returns a value of zero if the word is not one of the words in ORD_WORD; otherwise, it returns the position of the word in the ORD_WORD vector. If the word is not ordinary, the function KEY_SEARCH is used to find the position of the word in the keyword vector. If the word is not present in KEYWORD, the function KEY_SEARCH adds the word to the vector preserving the lexical ordering of KEYWORD. The index of the title from which the keyword comes is then concatenated to the element of T_INDEX which corresponds to the keyword. If this is the first time the keyword appears, then the initial blank is removed from T_INDEX. Once all the titles have been processed, the procedure KWIC_G is called to print the KWIC index. The T_INDEX entry corresponding to each keyword is used to find the titles containing that keyword. The corresponding titles are permuted so that the keyword is at the beginning of the title. The titles are then printed.

9-2.3 The Application of Bit Strings to Information Retrieval

The program presented in Fig. 9-6 uses bit strings to represent information gathered about a number of students. Each bit of the bit string represents a student, with the first bit representing the first student, the second bit the second student, and so on. The information concerning the students is contained in eleven bit strings, representing the sex, college and marital status of the students. A bit of a particular bit string is '1'B if the student represented by that bit falls into the category represented by the bit string. The program consists of two subprograms: the first builds the bit strings from information read concerning the students and the second prints information concerning the students based on queries made in the main program. The variables used in this program are:

Variable	Type	Usage
N	FIXED	Number of students
NUMBER(100)	CHARACTER(6)	Student number
NAME(100)	CHARACTER(20) VARYING	Student name
SEX(100)	FIXED	Student sex
COLLEGE(100)	FIXED	Student college
MARITAL_STATUS(100)	FIXED	Student marital status
SEX_WORD(2)	CHARACTER(6) VARYING	Name of sex
COLLEGE_WORD(6)	CHARACTER(16) VARYING	Name of college
STATUS_WORD(3)	CHARACTER(7) VARYING	Name of status
SEX_FILE(2)	BIT(100)	Bit string of students' sexes
COLLEGE_FILE(6)	BIT(100)	Bit string of students' colleges
STATUS_FILE(3)	BIT(100)	Bit string of students' marital statuses

```
STMT LEVEL NEST BLOCK MLVL  SOURCE TEXT

  1                          KWIC: PROCEDURE OPTIONS(MAIN);

  2    1          1          DECLARE ORD_WORD(7) CHARACTER(4) VARYING, /* ORDINARY WORDS */
                                  TITLE(50) CHARACTER(100) VARYING, /* DOCUMENT TITLES */
                                  KEYWORD(100) CHARACTER(20) VARYING, /* DOCUMENT KEYWORDS */
                                  LAST_KEY FIXED,       /* INDEX OF LAST KEYWORD */
                                  T_INDEX(100) CHARACTER(50) VARYING; /* INDICES OF TITLES*/

  3    1          1          ORD_WORD(1) = 'A';
  4    1          1          ORD_WORD(2) = 'AN';
  5    1          1          ORD_WORD(3) = 'AND';
  6    1          1          ORD_WORD(4) = 'ITS';
  7    1          1          ORD_WORD(5) = 'THE';
  8    1          1          ORD_WORD(6) = 'TO';
  9    1          1          ORD_WORD(7) = 'WITH';
 10    1          1          CALL KWIC_C(ORD_WORD, TITLE, KEYWORD, T_INDEX);
 11    1          1          CALL KWIC_G;


                            /* PROGRAM TO CREATE THE VECTORS TITLE, KEYWORD, AND T_INDEX */

 12    1          1          KWIC_C: PROCEDURE(ORD_WORD, TITLE, KEYWORD, T_INDEX);

 13    2          2          DECLARE ORD_WORD(*) CHARACTER(*) VARYING,/* ORDINARY WORD VECTOR */
                                  TITLE(*) CHARACTER(*)  VARYING, /* TITLE VECTOR */
                                  KEYWORD(*) CHARACTER(*)  VARYING,/* KEYWORD VECTOR */
                                  T_INDEX(*) CHARACTER(*) VARYING; /* VECTOR OF INDICES */
                                                      /* OF TITLES CONTAINING KEYWORDS */
 14    2          2          DECLARE LAST_TITLE FIXED,    /*INDEX OF THE LAST TITLE TO BE */
                                                      /*ADDED TO TITLE */
                                  WORD CHARACTER(20) VARYING, /* CURRENT WORD BEING */
                                                      /* PROCESSED */
                                  KEYIND FIXED,  /* INDEX FOR VECTOR KEYWORD */
                                  BLANKS CHARACTER(80) VARYING, /*TEMPORARY STRING */
                                  DUMMY BIT(1),          /*TEMPORARY VARIABLE */
                                  CHAR_NO CHARACTER(256) VARYING, /* STRING CONTAINING */
                                                      /* TITLE INDEX NO */
                                  NUM FIXED, /* TEMPORARY VARIABLE */
                                  PHRASE CHARACTER(80) VARYING,  /* INPUT TITLE */
                                  END_FLAG BIT(1), /* END OF DATA FLAG */
                                  ORD_SEARCH ENTRY   (CHARACTER(*) VARYING)
                                          RETURNS(FIXED),
                                  KEY_SEARCH ENTRY   (CHARACTER(*) VARYING)
                                          RETURNS(FIXED),
                                  SPAN ENTRY(CHARACTER(*) VARYING, CHARACTER(*) VARYING,
                                          FIXED, CHARACTER(*) VARYING, BIT(*),
                                          CHARACTER(*) VARYING)

                                      RETURNS (BIT(1));

                            /* INITIALIZE */
 15    2          2          ON ENDFILE(SYSIN) END_FLAG= '1'B;
 17    3          3          LAST_TITLE = 0;
 18    2          2          LAST_KEY = 0;
 19    2          2          END_FLAG = '0'B;
```

Fig. 9-5   Program to generate a KWIC indexing system

Variables used in subprogram BUILD:

| I | FIXED | Index variable |

Variables used in subprogram OUTPUT:

| TITLE | CHARACTER(*) | Title of report |
| STRING | BIT(*) | Bit string of students who satisfy the query |

```
                                    /* PROCESS ALL TITLES */
20   2        2         DO WHILE (END_FLAG = '0'B);
21   2   1    2             GET LIST (PHRASE);

                                /* REMOVE ANY LEADING BLANKS AND APPEND END MARKERS // TO */
                                /* STORE CURRENT DOCUMENT TITLE */
22   2   1    2             DUMMY = SPAN(PHRASE, ' ', 1, BLANKS, '1'B, '');
23   2   1    2             PHRASE = PHRASE || '//';
24   2   1    2             LAST_TITLE = LAST_TITLE + 1;
25   2   1    2             TITLE(LAST_TITLE) = PHRASE;

                                /* PROCESS ALL WORDS IN CURRENT TITLE */
26   2   1    2             DO WHILE(SUBSTR(PHRASE,1,2) ¬= '//');
                                    /* SCAN AND REMOVE NEXT WORD FROM CURRENT TITLE */
27   2   2    2                 WORD = SUBSTR(PHRASE, 1, INDEX(PHRASE, ' ') - 1);
28   2   2    2                 PHRASE = SUBSTR(PHRASE, INDEX(PHRASE, ' ') + 1);

                                    /* IS WORD A KEYWORD? */
29   2   2    2                 IF ORD_SEARCH(WORD) = 0
30   2   2    2                 THEN DO;
31   2   3    2                     KEYIND = KEY_SEARCH(WORD);

                                        /* CONVERT INDEX NO INTO CHARACTER STRING */
32   2   3    2                     NUM = LAST_TITLE;
33   2   3    2                     CHAR_NO = '';
34   2   3    2                     DO WHILE(NUM > 0);
35   2   4    2                         CHAR_NO = SUBSTR('0123456789',
                                            NUM - TRUNC(NUM / 10.0) * 10 + 1, 1) ||
                                                CHAR_NO;
36   2   4    2                         NUM = TRUNC(NUM / 10.0);
37   2   4    2                     END;
38   2   3    2                     T_INDEX(KEYIND) = T_INDEX(KEYIND) || ' ' ||
                                            CHAR_NO;
                                        /* REMOVE INITIAL BLANK FROM  T_INDEX(KEYIND) */
39   2   3    2                     IF SUBSTR(T_INDEX(KEYIND), 1, 1) = ' '
40   2   3    2                     THEN T_INDEX(KEYIND) = SUBSTR(T_INDEX(KEYIND), 2);
41   2   3    2                     END;
42   2   2    2                 END;
43   2   1    2             END;

                                /*FINISHED*/
44   2        2             RETURN;


                        /* FUNCTION TO SEARCH THE GLOBAL VECTOR ORD_WORD  TO DETERMINE */
                        /* WHETHER OR NOT A WORD IN A PARTICULAR TITLE IS AN  ORDINARY WORD */
45   2        2         ORD_SEARCH: PROCEDURE(WORD)
                                RETURNS(FIXED);

46   3        4             DECLARE WORD CHARACTER(*) VARYING;
47   3        4             DECLARE I FIXED;

48   3        4             DO I = 1 TO 7;
49   3   1    4                 IF ORD_WORD(I) = WORD
50   3   1    4                 THEN RETURN(I);  /* SUCESSFULL MATCH */
51   3   1    4             END;
52   3        4             RETURN(0);    /* WORD IS NOT IN ORD_WORD */
53   3        4         END ORD_SEARCH;
```

Fig. 9-5 Program to generate a KWIC indexing system (cont'd.)

The data used in this program are:

Number	Name	Sex	College	Marital Status
'596426'	'LARRY R BROWN'	1	2	2
'600868'	'ROY B ANDERSON'	1	4	2

```
                        /* FUNCTION TO SEARCH THE GLOBAL VECTOR KEYWORD TO DETERMINE WHETHER */
                        /*OR NOT A KEYWORD HAS PREVIOUSLY BEEN ENCOUNTERED IN THE TITLES */
                        /* LAST KEY IS A GLOBAL VARIABLE THAT CONTAINS THE INDEX OF THE */
                        /* LAST KEYWORD IN KEYWORD */

54    2       2         KEY_SEARCH: PROCEDURE(WORD)
                                    RETURNS(FIXED);

55    3       5             DECLARE WORD CHARACTER(*) VARYING;
56    3       5             DECLARE I FIXED,
                                    J FIXED;

                           /* SEARCH KEYWORD VECTOR FOR WORD */
57    3       5             DO I = 1 TO LAST_KEY;
58    3   1   5                 IF KEYWORD(I) = WORD
59    3   1   5                 THEN RETURN(I);    /* SUCCESSFUL MATCH */
60    3   1   5                 ELSE IF KEYWORD(I) > WORD
61    3   1   5                      THEN DO;       /* WORD IS NOT IN KEYWORD VECTOR */
                                          /* MOVE REMAINING  KEYWORDS  ONE POSITION */
                                          /* IN THE KEYWORD VECTOR */
62    3   2   5                           DO J = LAST_KEY TO I BY -1;
63    3   3   5                               KEYWORD(J+1) = KEYWORD(J);
64    3   3   5                               T_INDEX(J+1) = T_INDEX(J);
65    3   3   5                           END;
66    3   2   5                           KEYWORD(I) = WORD;
67    3   2   5                           LAST_KEY = LAST_KEY + 1;
68    3   2   5                           T_INDEX(I) = '';
69    3   2   5                           RETURN(I);
70    3   2   5                           END;
71    3   1   5                 END;

                           /* PLACE NEW KEYWORD AT THE END OF THE KEYWORD VECTOR */
72    3       5             LAST_KEY = LAST_KEY + 1;
73    3       5             KEYWORD(LAST_KEY) = WORD;
74    3       5             T_INDEX(LAST_KEY) = '';
75    3       5             RETURN(LAST_KEY);
76    3       5         END KEY_SEARCH;


77    2       2         SPAN: PROCEDURE (SUBJECT, PATTERN, CURSOR, MATCH_STR, REPLACE_FLAG,
                                         REPLACE_STR)
                              RETURNS (BIT(1));

78    3       6         DECLARE SUBJECT CHARACTER(*) VARYING, /* STRING TO BE EXAMINED */
                                PATTERN CHARACTER(*) VARYING, /* STRING SOUGHT WITHIN */
                                                              /* SUBJECT STRING */
                                CURSOR FIXED,      /* CHARACTER POSITION IN SUBJECT */
                                                   /* AT WHICH THE PATTERN MATCHING */
                                                   /* PROCESS IS TO BEGIN */
                                MATCH_STR CHARACTER(*) VARYING, /* DESIRED SUBSTRING */
                                                                /* FOUND IN SUBJECT */
                                REPLACE_FLAG BIT(*), /* FLAG INDICATING WHETHER */
                                                     /* REPLACEMENT IS REQUIRED */
                                REPLACE_STR CHARACTER(*) VARYING; /* STRING USED TO */
                                                                  /* REPLACE MATCHED SUBSTRING */
79    3       6         DECLARE I FIXED;              /* TEMPORARY CURSOR */

                        /* DOES THE PATTERN FIT WITHIN THE BOUNDS OF THE SUBJECT STRING */
80    3       6         IF CURSOR > LENGTH(SUBJECT)
81    3       6         THEN RETURN('0'B);

82    3       6         I = VERIFY(SUBSTR(SUBJECT, CURSOR), PATTERN);

                        /* UNSUCCESSFUL PATTERN MATCH */
83    3       6         IF I = 1
84    3       6         THEN RETURN('0'B);
85    3       6         IF I = 0
86    3       6         THEN I = LENGTH(SUBJECT) + 1;
87    3       6         ELSE I = CURSOR + I -1;
```

Fig. 9-5   Program to generate a KWIC indexing system (cont'd.)

```
 88  3      6            /* SET MATCH_STR AND PERFORM INDICATED REPLACEMENT */
 89  3      6            MATCH_STR = SUBSTR(SUBJECT, CURSOR, I-CURSOR);
 90  3      6            IF REPLACE_FLAG
 91  3   1  6            THEN DO;
                              SUBJECT = SUBSTR(SUBJECT, 1, CURSOR-1) || REPLACE_STR ||
                                  SUBSTR(SUBJECT, I);
 92  3   1  6                  CURSOR = CURSOR + LENGTH(REPLACE_STR);
 93  3   1  6                  END;
 94  3      6            ELSE CURSOR = I;

                         /* SUCCESSFUL RETURN */
 95  3      6            RETURN('1'B);
 96  3      6        END SPAN;
 97  2      2        END KWIC_C;


                     /* PROCEDURE TO GENERATE A KWIC INDEX ORDERED LEXICALLY BY KEYWORDS */

 98  1      1        KWIC_G: PROCEDURE;
 99  2      7            DECLARE KEYSTRING CHARACTER(256) VARYING, /* STRING OF TITLE */
                                                                  /* INDICES */
                                INDEX_NO FIXED,   /*PARTICULAR TITLE VECTOR INDEX */
                                KWIC_LINE CHARACTER(256) VARYING, /* LINE OF OUTPUT */
                                I FIXED,             /* COUNTER VARIABLE */
                                J FIXED,               /* COUNTER VARIABLE */
                                DUMMY CHARACTER(256) VARYING, /* DUMMY VARIABLE */
                                POS FIXED;          /* TEMPORARY VARIABLE */

                         /* PROCESS EACH KEYWORD IN KEYWORD */
100  2      7            DO I = 1 TO LAST_KEY;

                             /* OBTAIN INDEX LIST FOR CURRENT KEYWORD */
101  2   1  7                KEYSTRING = T_INDEX(I) || ' ';

                             /* PROCESS ALL TITLE INDICES IN KEYSTRING */
102  2   1  7                DO WHILE(LENGTH(KEYSTRING) > 1);

                                 /* OBTAIN AND DELETE NEXT TITLE INDEX */
103  2   2  7                    DUMMY = SUBSTR(KEYSTRING, 1, INDEX(KEYSTRING, ' ') - 1);
104  2   2  7                    IF LENGTH(KEYSTRING) = INDEX(KEYSTRING, ' ')
105  2   2  7                    THEN KEYSTRING = '';
106  2   2  7                    ELSE KEYSTRING = SUBSTR(KEYSTRING, INDEX(KEYSTRING,' ')
                                             + 1);

                                 /* CONVERT CHARACTER STRING TO INTEGER */
107  2   2  7                    INDEX_NO = 0;
108  2   2  7                    DO J = 1 TO LENGTH(DUMMY);
109  2   3  7                        INDEX_NO = INDEX_NO * 10 + (INDEX('0123456789',
                                         SUBSTR(DUMMY, J, 1)) - 1);
110  2   3  7                    END;

                                 /* OBTAIN AND OUTPUT KWIC LINE */
111  2   2  7                    KWIC_LINE = TITLE(INDEX_NO);
112  2   2  7                    POS = INDEX(KWIC_LINE, KEYWORD(I));
113  2   2  7                    IF POS ¬= 0
114  2   2  7                    THEN DO;
115  2   3  7                        KWIC_LINE = KEYWORD(I) || SUBSTR(KWIC_LINE, POS +
                                               LENGTH(KEYWORD(I))) || ' '
                                               || SUBSTR(KWIC_LINE, 1, POS-1);
116  2   3  7                        PUT SKIP LIST(KWIC_LINE);
117  2   3  7                        END;
118  2   2  7                    ELSE PUT SKIP EDIT ('ERROR - KEYWORD NOT FOUND IN ',
                                         'TITLE') (A, A);
119  2   2  7                    END;
120  2   1  7                END;
121  2      7            RETURN;
122  2      7        END KWIC_G;
123  1      1        END KWIC;
    ERROR IN STMT    14  DECLARATION FOR ENTRY SPAN DOES NOT AGREE WITH CORRESPONDING PROCEDURE OR ENTRY POINT.  DECLARATION
IGNORED. (SY46)
```

ERRORS/WARNINGS DETECTED DURING CODE GENERATION:

    WARNING: NO FILE SPECIFIED. SYSIN/SYSPRINT ASSUMED. (CGOC)

Fig. 9-5   Program to generate a KWIC indexing system (cont'd.)

```
ALGORITHMIC APPROACH // AN INTRODUCTION TO COMPUTER SCIENCE AN
APPLICATIONS // PL/I PROGRAMMING WITH
APPROACH // AN INTRODUCTION TO COMPUTER SCIENCE AN ALGORITHMIC
COMPUTER SCIENCE AN ALGORITHMIC APPROACH // AN INTRODUCTION TO
INTRODUCTION TO COMPUTER SCIENCE AN ALGORITHMIC APPROACH // AN
INTRODUCTION TO PASCAL PROGRAMMING // AN
PASCAL PROGRAMMING // AN INTRODUCTION TO
PL/I PROGRAMMING // STRUCTURED
PL/I PROGRAMMING WITH APPLICATIONS //
PROGRAMMING // STRUCTURED PL/I
PROGRAMMING // STRUCTURED WATFIV-S
PROGRAMMING WITH APPLICATIONS // PL/I
PROGRAMMING // AN INTRODUCTION TO PASCAL
SCIENCE AN ALGORITHMIC APPROACH // AN INTRODUCTION TO COMPUTER
STRUCTURED PL/I PROGRAMMING //
STRUCTURED WATFIV-S PROGRAMMING //
WATFIV-S PROGRAMMING // STRUCTURED
```

IN STMT 123 ·PROGRAM RETURNS FROM MAIN PROCEDURE.

Fig. 9-5   Program to generate a KWIC indexing system (cont'd.)

'621655'	'DAVID N PARKER'	1	3	2
'640621'	'JOHN M BROWN'	1	1	2
'652079'	'PATRICIA L FOX'	2	1	2
'672915'	'JOE E WALL'	1	3	3
'672919'	'LINDA R GARDNER'	2	2	2
'683369'	'SUSAN C FROST'	2	1	3
'690528'	'SUSAN L WONG'	2	5	2
'703062'	'JAKE L FARMER'	1	6	1

The main program initializes the vectors SEX_WORD, STATUS_WORD, and COLLEGE_WORD. The subprogram BUILD is then called to create the bit strings for the eleven categories. Information concerning each of the students is read in, and using this information the bit corresponding to this student is set to '1'B in the appropriate bit strings. After the completion of the procedure BUILD, the OUTPUT subprogram is then called four times to produce reports for the following four queries: all students, female students, science students, and unmarried students in science.

9-2.4   Text Editing

The program presented in this section is a solution to the text editing problem discussed in Sec. 9-2.4 of the main text. The text editor interprets a number of commands to format textual material. Each command is preceded by "##" and is associated with a code which is used by the text editor. A summary of the commands is given in Table 9-2.

The program given in Fig. 9-7 consists of a main program (TEXT_ED) and four procedures — namely, FORMATOR, SCANNER, PRINT_U, and PRINT_J. The main procedure TEXT_ED reads in the line width and calls the subprogram FORMATOR, which produces the edited version of the text with the line width just read. To produce the edited line of text, the FORMATOR uses the subprograms SCANNER, PRINT_U, and PRINT_J. The SCANNER finds the next item in the text and determines its type. If the end of an input line has been reached, SCANNER inputs

Table 9-2 Summary of commands for the text editor

Command	Code	Description
##JS	2	Right justify text
##NJ	3	Do not right justify
##NP	4	Begin a new paragraph
##CN/.../	5	Center the text between the two slashes
##BL n	6	Add n blank lines
##ED	7	End of text

another line of text. In determining the next line of text, SCANNER uses the two functions SPAN and BREAK. PRINT_U and PRINT_J are used to print an unadjusted line and an adjusted line of text, respectively.

The following variable is used in the main program TEXT_ED:

Variable	Type	Usage
WIDTH	FIXED	Length of edited line

Variables used in the procedure FORMATOR:

Variable	Type	Usage
INPUT_LINE	CHARACTER(81) VARYING	Line currently being processed
CURSOR	FIXED	Current character position
WORDS(100)	CHARACTER(20) VARYING	Vector of words to be printed
NO_WORDS	FIXED	Number of words in WORDS vector
LINE_LENGTH	FIXED	Length of unedited line
ITEM	CHARACTER(80) VARYING	Current item
TYPE	FIXED	Type of command
BLANK_LINE	CHARACTER(80) VARYING	Sequence of blanks
NO_LINES	FIXED	Number of blank lines
JUSTIFY	BIT(1)	Flag for justification
PADDING	CHARACTER(256) VARYING	Padding for edited line
I	FIXED	Loop variable

Variables used in the procedure SCANNER:

Variable	Type	Usage
DUMMY	BIT(1)	Temporary variable
BLANKS	CHARACTER(80) VARYING	Variable to hold any leading blanks

Variables used in the procedure PRINT_U:

Variable	Type	Usage
LINE	CHARACTER(80) VARYING	Line to be output
I	FIXED	Index variable

Variables used in the procedure PRINT_J:

Variable	Type	Usage
TOTAL_PAD	FIXED	Number of additional blanks needed

```
STMT LEVEL NEST BLOCK MLVL   SOURCE TEXT

  1                                STUDENT: PROCEDURE OPTIONS(MAIN);
  2    1         1                     DECLARE N FIXED, /* NUMBER OF STUDENTS */
                                           NUMBER(100) CHARACTER(6), /* STUDENT NUMBER */
                                           NAME(100) CHARACTER(20) VARYING, /*STUDENTS NAMES */
                                           SEX(100) FIXED, /* STUDENTS' SEX */
                                           COLLEGE(100) FIXED, /* STUDENTS' COLLEGE */
                                           MARITAL_STATUS(100) FIXED, /* STUDENTS' MARITAL STATUS */
                                           SEX_WORD(2) CHARACTER(6) VARYING, /* MALE OR FEMALE */
                                           COLLEGE_WORD(6) CHARACTER(16) VARYING, /* NAME OF */
                                                                               /* COLLEGE */
                                           STATUS_WORD(3) CHARACTER(7) VARYING, /* NAME OF STATUS */
                                           SEX_FILE(2) BIT(100), /* BIT STRING OF STUDENTS' SEX */
                                           COLLEGE_FILE(6) BIT(100), /* BIT STRING OF STUDENTS' */
                                                                             /* COLLEGE*/
                                           STATUS_FILE(3) BIT(100); /* BIT STRING OF STUDENTS' */
                                                                         /* MARITAL STATUS */

                                       /* INITIALIZE */
  3    1         1                     SEX_WORD(1) = 'MALE';
  4    1         1                     SEX_WORD(2) = 'FEMALE';
  5    1         1                     STATUS_WORD(1) = 'SINGLE';
  6    1         1                     STATUS_WORD(2) = 'MARRIED';
  7    1         1                     STATUS_WORD(3) = 'OTHER';
  8    1         1                     COLLEGE_WORD(1) = 'SCIENCE';
  9    1         1                     COLLEGE_WORD(2) = 'COMMERCE';
 10    1         1                     COLLEGE_WORD(3) = 'ENGINEERING';
 11    1         1                     COLLEGE_WORD(4) = 'GRADUATE STUDIES';
 12    1         1                     COLLEGE_WORD(5) = 'HOME ECONOMICS ';
 13    1         1                     COLLEGE_WORD(6) = 'AGRICULTURE';

                                       /* BUILD THE BIT STRINGS */
 14    1         1                     CALL BUILD;
                                       /* PROCESS THE QUERIES */
 15    1         1                     CALL OUTPUT('ALL STUDENTS', SEX_FILE(1) | SEX_FILE(2));
 16    1         1                     CALL OUTPUT('FEMALE STUDENTS', SEX_FILE(2));
 17    1         1                     CALL OUTPUT('SCIENCE STUDENTS',COLLEGE_FILE(1));
 18    1         1                     CALL OUTPUT('UNMARRIED STUDENTS IN SCIENCE', COLLEGE_FILE(1)
                                                                          &¬STATUS_FILE(2));
                                   /* PROGRAM TO CONSTRUCT A MASTER FILE CONTAINING THE NUMBER,NAME, */
                                   /* SEX, COLLEGE, AND MARITAL_STATUS */
 19    1         1                 BUILD: PROCEDURE;
 20    2         2                     DECLARE I FIXED; /* INDEX VARIABLE */
                                       /* INITIALIZE */
 21    2         2                     DO I = 1 TO 2;
 22    2    1    2                         SEX_FILE(I) = REPEAT('0'B, 100);
 23    2    1    2                     END;
 24    2         2                     DO I = 1 TO 6;
 25    2    1    2                         COLLEGE_FILE(I) = REPEAT('0'B, 100);
 26    2    1    2                     END;
 27    2         2                     DO I = 1 TO 3;
 28    2    1    2                         STATUS_FILE(I) = REPEAT('0'B, 100);
 29    2    1    2                     END;
                                       /* INPUT NUMBER OF STUDENT RECORDS */
 30    2         2                     GET LIST(N);
                                       /* PROCESS THE STUDENT RECORDS */
 31    2         2                     DO I = 1 TO N;
                                           /*INPUT A STUDENT RECORD */
 32    2    1    2                         GET LIST(NUMBER(I), NAME(I), SEX(I), COLLEGE(I),
                                                   MARITAL_STATUS(I));
                                           /* UPDATE BIT-STRING VECTORS */
 33    2    1    2                         SUBSTR(SEX_FILE(SEX(I)),I, 1) = '1'B;
 34    2    1    2                         SUBSTR(COLLEGE_FILE(COLLEGE(I)), I, 1) = '1'B;
 35    2    1    2                         SUBSTR(STATUS_FILE(MARITAL_STATUS(I)), I, 1) = '1'B;
 36    2    1    2                     END;
 37    2         2                     RETURN;
 38    2         2                 END BUILD;
```

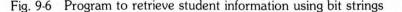

Fig. 9-6   Program to retrieve student information using bit strings

```
                              /*PROCEDURE TO PRODUCE A REPORT LISTING ALL STUDENT INFORMATION */
                              /*PERTAINING TO A QUERY */
  39   1      1               OUTPUT: PROCEDURE(TITLE, STRING);
  40   2      3                  DECLARE TITLE CHARACTER(*),    /* TITLE OF REPORT */
                                         STRING BIT(*);        /* BIT STRING OF THOSE STUDENTS WHO*/
                                                               /* SATISFY THE QUERY */
  41   2      3                  DECLARE I FIXED; /* INDEX VARIABLE */
                                  /* OUTPUT TITLE OF REPORT */
  42   2      3                  PUT SKIP LIST (TITLE);
                                  /* GENERATE THE DETAILS OF THE REPORT */
  43   2      3                  DO WHILE(INDEX(STRING, '1'B) ¬= 0);
                                      /* OBTAIN POSITION OF NEXT STUDENT TO BE OUTPUT */
  44   2   1  3                     I = INDEX(STRING, '1'B);
                                      /* CHANGE THE CORRESPONDING BIT IN STRING TO '0'B */
  45   2   1  3                     SUBSTR(STRING,I,1) = '0'B;
                                      /*OUTPUT DETAILS OF NEXT STUDENT */
  46   2   1  3                     PUT SKIP LIST(NUMBER(I), NAME(I), SEX_WORD(SEX(I)),
                                             COLLEGE_WORD(COLLEGE(I)),
                                             STATUS_WORD(MARITAL_STATUS(I)));
  47   2   1  3                     END;
  48   2      3                  RETURN;
  49   2      3               END OUTPUT;
  50   1      1            END STUDENT;
```

ERRORS/WARNINGS DETECTED DURING CODE GENERATION:

     WARNING: NO FILE SPECIFIED. SYSIN/SYSPRINT ASSUMED. (CGOC)

```
ALL STUDENTS
596426            LARRY R BROWN       MALE        COMMERCE           MARRIED
600868            ROY B ANDERSON      MALE        GRADUATE STUDIES   MARRIED
621656            DAVID N PARKER      MALE        GRADUATE STUDIES   MARRIED
640621            JOHN M BROWN        MALE        SCIENCE            MARRIED
652079            PATRICIA L FOX      FEMALE      SCIENCE            MARRIED
672915            JOE E WALL          MALE        ENGINEERING        OTHER
672919            LINDA R GARDNER     FEMALE      COMMERCE           SINGLE
683369            SUSAN C FROST       FEMALE      SCIENCE            OTHER
690528            SUSAN L WONG        FEMALE      HOME ECONOMICS     MARRIED
703062            JAKE L FARMER       MALE        AGRICULTURE        SINGLE
FEMALE STUDENTS
652079            PATRICIA L FOX      FEMALE      SCIENCE            MARRIED
672919            LINDA R GARDNER     FEMALE      COMMERCE           SINGLE
683369            SUSAN C FROST       FEMALE      SCIENCE            OTHER
690528            SUSAN L WONG        FEMALE      HOME ECONOMICS     MARRIED
SCIENCE STUDENTS
640621            JOHN M BROWN        MALE        SCIENCE            MARRIED
652079            PATRICIA L FOX      FEMALE      SCIENCE            MARRIED
683369            SUSAN C FROST       FEMALE      SCIENCE            OTHER
UNMARRIED STUDENTS IN SCIENCE
```

IN STMT 50 PROGRAM RETURNS FROM MAIN PROCEDURE.

Fig. 9-6   Program to retrieve student information using bit strings (cont'd.)

AV_PAD	FIXED	Number of blanks to be inserted between each pair of words
EXTRA_BLANKS	FIXED	Number of extra blanks that must be distributed
PADDING	CHARACTER(256) VARYING	Padding between words
J	FIXED	Loop variable
LINE	CHARACTER(80) VARYING	Output line of text
I	FIXED	Index variable

The data used in this program are:

```
/* PROGRAM TO PRODUCE AN EDITED VERSION OF INPUT TEXT */

STMT LEVEL NEST BLOCK MLVL  SOURCE TEXT


                                    /* PROGRAM TO PRODUCE AN EDITED VERSION OF INPUT TEXT */
     1                              TEXT_ED: PROCEDURE OPTIONS(MAIN);
     2    1         1                   DECLARE WIDTH FIXED;  /* LENGTH OF EDITED LINE */
                                        /* INPUT LINE WIDTH */
     3    1         1                   GET LIST (WIDTH);
                                        /* INVOKE FORMATOR ROUTINE */
     4    1         1                   CALL FORMATOR(WIDTH);




                                    /* PROCEDURE TO CONTROL THE OUTPUT OF THE TEXT EDITOR */
     5    1         1               FORMATOR: PROCEDURE(WIDTH);
     6    2         2                   DECLARE WIDTH FIXED; /* LENGTH OF EDITED LINE */
     7    2         2                   DECLARE INPUT_LINE CHARACTER(81) VARYING, /* CURRENT LINE BEING */
                                            /* PROCESSED */
                                        CURSOR FIXED, /* CURRENT CHARACTER POSITION */
                                        WORDS(100) CHARACTER(20)VARYING, /* WORDS TO BE OUTPUT */
                                        NO_WORDS FIXED, /* NUMBER OF WORDS IN WORDS */
                                        LINE_LENGTH FIXED, /* LENGTH OF UNEDITED LINE */
                                        ITEM CHARACTER(80) VARYING, /* CURRENT ITEM */
                                        TYPE FIXED,        /* TYPE OF COMMAND */
                                        BLANK_LINE CHARACTER(80) VARYING, /* SEQUENCE OF BLANK */
                                        NO_LINES FIXED,  /* NO OF BLANK LINES */
                                        JUSTIFY BIT(1),  /* FLAG FOR JUSTIFICATION */
                                        PADDING CHARACTER(256) VARYING,
                                        I FIXED;         /* LOOP VARIABLE */
                                    /* INITIALIZE */
     8    2         2               INPUT_LINE = '';
     9    2         2               CURSOR = 1;
    10    2         2               JUSTIFY = '1'B;
    11    2         2               LINE_LENGTH = 0;
    12    2         2               NO_WORDS = 0;
                                    /* EDIT THE GIVEN TEXT */
    13    2         2               DO WHILE('1'B);
    14    2    1    2                   CALL SCANNER(INPUT_LINE, CURSOR, TYPE, ITEM);
                                        /* PROCESS CURRENT WORD OR COMMAND */
    15    2    1    2                   IF TYPE = 1
    16    2    1    2                   THEN IF LINE_LENGTH + LENGTH(ITEM) + 1 <= WIDTH
    17    2    1    2                        THEN DO;  /* ADD THE WORD TO THE CURRENT LINE */
    18    2    2    2                             NO_WORDS = NO_WORDS + 1;
    19    2    2    2                             WORDS(NO_WORDS) = ITEM;
    20    2    2    2                             IF NO_WORDS = 1
    21    2    2    2                             THEN LINE_LENGTH = LENGTH(ITEM);
    22    2    2    2                             ELSE LINE_LENGTH = LINE_LENGTH + LENGTH(ITEM) + 1;
    23    2    2    2                             END;
    24    2    1    2                        ELSE DO;  /* PRINT PREVIOUS LINE AND USE NEW ITEM TO */
                                                 /* START NEW LINE */
    25    2    2    2                             IF JUSTIFY
    26    2    2    2                             THEN CALL PRINT_J(WORDS,NO_WORDS,LINE_LENGTH,
                                                           WIDTH);
    27    2    2    2                             ELSE CALL PRINT_U(WORDS, NO_WORDS);
    28    2    2    2                             WORDS(1) = ITEM;
    29    2    2    2                             NO_WORDS = 1;
    30    2    2    2                             LINE_LENGTH = LENGTH(ITEM);
    31    2    2    2                             END;
    32    2    1    2                   ELSE IF TYPE = 2
    33    2    1    2                        THEN JUSTIFY = '1'B;   /* RIGHT-JUSTIFY TEXT */
    34    2    1    2                        ELSE IF TYPE = 3
    35    2    1    2                             THEN JUSTIFY = '0'B;  /* DO NOT RIGHT-JUSTIFY TEXT*/
    36    2    1    2                             ELSE IF TYPE = 4
    37    2    1    2                                  THEN DO;
    38    2    2    2                                       IF LINE_LENGTH ¬= 0
                                                           THEN  /* PRINT THE PREVIOUS LINE AND A */
                                                                 /* BLANK LINE AND INDENT THE FIRST*/
                                                                 /* WORD ON THE NEXT LINE */
    39    2    2    2                                            CALL PRINT_U(WORDS, NO_WORDS);
    40    2    2    2                                       PUT SKIP LIST (BLANK_LINE);
    41    2    2    2                                       CALL SCANNER(INPUT_LINE, CURSOR,
                                                                   TYPE, ITEM);
```

Fig. 9-7   Program for a text editing system

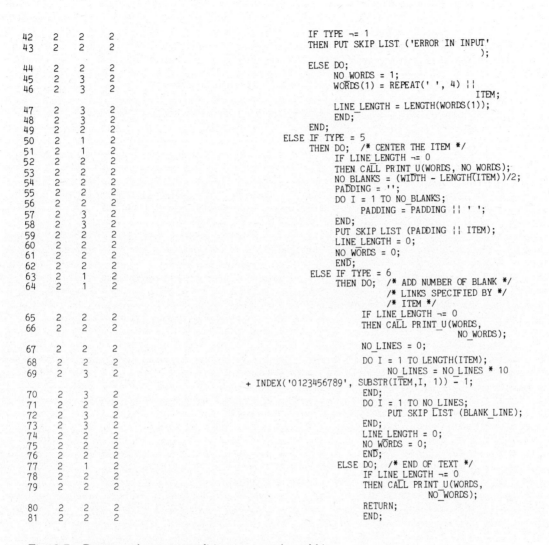

```
42   2   2   2              IF TYPE ¬= 1
43   2   2   2              THEN PUT SKIP LIST ('ERROR IN INPUT'
                                                         );
44   2   2   2              ELSE DO;
45   2   3   2                  NO_WORDS = 1;
46   2   3   2                  WORDS(1) = REPEAT(' ', 4) ||
                                                         ITEM;
47   2   3   2                  LINE_LENGTH = LENGTH(WORDS(1));
48   2   3   2                  END;
49   2   2   2          END;
50   2   1   2      ELSE IF TYPE = 5
51   2   1   2      THEN DO;   /* CENTER THE ITEM */
52   2   2   2          IF LINE_LENGTH ¬= 0
53   2   2   2          THEN CALL PRINT_U(WORDS, NO_WORDS);
54   2   2   2          NO_BLANKS = (WIDTH - LENGTH(ITEM))/2;
55   2   2   2          PADDING = '';
56   2   2   2          DO I = 1 TO NO_BLANKS;
57   2   3   2              PADDING = PADDING || ' ';
58   2   3   2          END;
59   2   2   2          PUT SKIP LIST (PADDING || ITEM);
60   2   2   2          LINE_LENGTH = 0;
61   2   2   2          NO_WORDS = 0;
62   2   2   2          END;
63   2   1   2      ELSE IF TYPE = 6
64   2   1   2      THEN DO;   /* ADD NUMBER OF BLANK */
                               /* LINKS SPECIFIED BY */
                               /* ITEM */
65   2   2   2          IF LINE_LENGTH ¬= 0
66   2   2   2          THEN CALL PRINT_U(WORDS,
                                          NO_WORDS);
67   2   2   2          NO_LINES = 0;
68   2   2   2          DO I = 1 TO LENGTH(ITEM);
69   2   3   2              NO_LINES = NO_LINES * 10
         + INDEX('0123456789', SUBSTR(ITEM,I, 1)) - 1;
70   2   3   2          END;
71   2   2   2          DO I = 1 TO NO_LINES;
72   2   3   2              PUT SKIP LIST (BLANK_LINE);
73   2   3   2          END;
74   2   2   2          LINE_LENGTH = 0;
75   2   2   2          NO_WORDS = 0;
76   2   2   2          END;
77   2   1   2      ELSE DO;   /* END OF TEXT */
78   2   2   2          IF LINE_LENGTH ¬= 0
79   2   2   2          THEN CALL PRINT_U(WORDS,
                                          NO_WORDS);
80   2   2   2          RETURN;
81   2   2   2          END;
```

Fig. 9-7 Program for a text editing system (cont'd.)

```
##JS
THIS LINE ILLUSTRATES THE USE OF THE JUSTIFY TEXT COMMAND.
##NP
THIS IS THE START OF A NEW PARAGRAPH.
##CN/THIS IS CENTERED./
##BL 5
THE ##BL COMMAND HAS BEEN USED TO LEAVE FIVE BLANK LINES.
THE FOLLOWING LINE HAS NOT BEEN JUSTIFIED.
##NJ
##NP
ALL THE WORLD LOVES A TEXT EDITING COMPUTER.
##ED
```

The main program TEXT_ED reads the width of the line to be used in formatting the text. The FORMATOR is then called to process the text. In the

```
                              /* PROCEDURE TO SCAN INPUT TEXT, ISOLATE NEXT ITEM AND DETERMINE ITS */
                              /* TYPE*/
82   2   1   2                SCANNER: PROCEDURE(INPUT_LINE, CURSOR, TYPE, ITEM);
83   3   1   3                    DECLARE INPUT_LINE CHARACTER(*) VARYING, /* INPUT LINE OF TEXT */
                                      CURSOR FIXED,     /* CURRENT CHARACTER POSITION BEING */
                                                        /* EXAMINED */
                                      TYPE FIXED,       /* TYPE OF ITEM ISOLATED */
                                      ITEM CHARACTER(*) VARYING; /* ISOLATED ITEM */
84   3   1   3                    DECLARE DUMMY BIT(1), /* TEMPORARY VARIABLE */
                                      BLANKS CHARACTER(80) VARYING, /* VARIABLE TO HOLD ANY */
                                                        /* LEADING BLANKS */
                                      BREAK ENTRY(CHARACTER(*) VARYING, CHARACTER(*)
                                          VARYING, FIXED, CHARACTER(*) VARYING, BIT(*),
                                        CHARACTER(*) VARYING)
                                          RETURNS (BIT(1)),
                                      SPAN ENTRY(CHARACTER(*) VARYING, CHARACTER(*) VARYING,
                                          FIXED, CHARACTER(*) VARYING, BIT(*),
                                            CHARACTER(*) VARYING)
                                          RETURNS (BIT(1));
                                  /* SCAN ANY LEADING BLANK CHARACTERS */
85   3   1   3                    DUMMY = SPAN(INPUT_LINE, ' ', CURSOR, BLANKS, '0'B, '');
                                  /* HAS THE CURRENT LINE BEEN ENTIRELY SCANNED? */
86   3   1   3                    IF CURSOR > LENGTH(INPUT_LINE)
87   3   1   3                    THEN DO;
88   3   2   3                        GET SKIP EDIT(INPUT_LINE)(A(80));
89   3   2   3                        INPUT_LINE = INPUT_LINE || ' ';
90   3   2   3                        CURSOR = 1;
91   3   2   3                        DUMMY = SPAN(INPUT_LINE, ' ', CURSOR, BLANKS, '0'B, '');
92   3   2   3                        DUMMY = BREAK(INPUT_LINE, ' ', CURSOR, ITEM, '0'B, '');
93   3   2   3                        IF SUBSTR(INPUT_LINE, 1, 4) = '##JS'
94   3   2   3                        THEN TYPE = 2;
95   3   2   3                        ELSE IF SUBSTR(INPUT_LINE, 1, 4) = '##NJ'
96   3   2   3                            THEN TYPE = 3;
97   3   2   3                            ELSE IF SUBSTR(INPUT_LINE, 1, 4) = '##NP'
98   3   2   3                                THEN TYPE = 4;
99   3   2   3                                ELSE IF SUBSTR(INPUT_LINE, 1, 4) = '##CN'
100  3   2   3                                    THEN DO;
101  3   3   3                                        TYPE = 5;
102  3   3   3                                        ITEM = SUBSTR(INPUT_LINE, 6, INDEX(
                                                            SUBSTR(INPUT_LINE,.6), '/') - 1);
103  3   3   3                                        CURSOR = LENGTH(INPUT_LINE) + 1;
104  3   3   3                                        END;
105  3   2   3                                    ELSE IF SUBSTR(INPUT_LINE, 1, 4) = '##BL'
106  3   2   3                                        THEN DO;
107  3   3   3                                            TYPE = 6;
108  3   3   3                                            ITEM = SUBSTR(INPUT_LINE, 6,
                                                        INDEX(SUBSTR(INPUT_LINE, 6), ' ') - 1);
109  3   3   3                                            CURSOR = LENGTH(INPUT_LINE) + 1;
110  3   3   3                                            END;
111  3   2   3                                        ELSE IF SUBSTR(INPUT_LINE, 1, 4) = '##ED'
112  3   2   3                                            THEN TYPE = 7;
113  3   2   3                                            ELSE TYPE = 1;
114  3   2   3                        RETURN;
115  3   2.  3                        END;
                                  /* OBTAIN ORDINARY WORD OF TEXT */
116  3   1   3                    DUMMY = BREAK(INPUT_LINE, ' ', CURSOR, ITEM, '0'B, '');
117  3   1   3                    TYPE = 1;
118  3   1   3                    RETURN;
```

Fig. 9-7   Program for a text editing system (cont'd.)

FORMATOR, INPUT_LINE is initially set to the empty string. A loop is then begun to process the input text. At the beginning of the loop, SCANNER is called to isolate the next item in the input text. In SCANNER if the CURSOR is greater than the length of INPUT_LINE (as is the case when the loop in FORMATOR is first executed), then a line of text is read. A blank is then concatenated to the end of the input line, and CURSOR is reset to one. The functions SPAN and BREAK are then called to remove initial blanks from the input line and place the next item in INPUT_LINE into ITEM,

```
119   3   1   3       SPAN: PROCEDURE (SUBJECT, PATTERN, CURSOR, MATCH_STR, REPLACE_FLAG,
                                      REPLACE_STR)
                            RETURNS (BIT(1));

120   4   1   4       DECLARE SUBJECT CHARACTER(*) VARYING, /* STRING TO BE EXAMINED */
                              PATTERN CHARACTER(*) VARYING, /* STRING SOUGHT WITHIN */
                                                           /* SUBJECT STRING */
                              CURSOR FIXED,        /* CHARACTER POSITION IN SUBJECT */
                                                   /* AT WHICH THE PATTERN MATCHING */
                                                   /* PROCESS IS TO BEGIN */
                              MATCH_STR CHARACTER(*) VARYING, /* DESIRED SUBSTRING */
                                                           /* FOUND IN SUBJECT */
                              REPLACE_FLAG BIT(*), /* FLAG INDICATING WHETHER */
                                                   /* REPLACEMENT IS REQUIRED */
                              REPLACE_STR CHARACTER(*) VARYING; /* STRING USED TO */
                                                           /* REPLACE MATCHED SUBSTRING */
121   4   1   4       DECLARE I FIXED;               /* TEMPORARY CURSOR */

                      /* DOES THE PATTERN FIT WITHIN THE BOUNDS OF THE SUBJECT STRING */
122   4   1   4       IF CURSOR > LENGTH(SUBJECT)
123   4   1   4       THEN RETURN('0'B);

124   4   1   4       I = VERIFY(SUBSTR(SUBJECT, CURSOR), PATTERN);

                      /* UNSUCCESSFUL PATTERN MATCH */
125   4   1   4       IF I = 1
126   4   1   4       THEN RETURN('0'B);
127   4   1   4       IF I = 0
128   4   1   4       THEN I = LENGTH(SUBJECT) + 1;
129   4   1   4       ELSE I = CURSOR + I -1;

                      /* SET MATCH_STR AND PERFORM INDICATED REPLACEMENT */
130   4   1   4       MATCH_STR = SUBSTR(SUBJECT, CURSOR, I-CURSOR);
131   4   1   4       IF REPLACE_FLAG
132   4   1   4       THEN DO;
133   4   2   4           SUBJECT = SUBSTR(SUBJECT, 1, CURSOR-1) || REPLACE_STR ||
                                  SUBSTR(SUBJECT, I);
134   4   2   4           CURSOR = CURSOR + LENGTH(REPLACE_STR);
135   4   2   4           END;
136   4   1   4       ELSE CURSOR = I;

                      /* SUCCESSFUL RETURN */
137   4   1   4       RETURN('1'B);
138   4   1   4       END SPAN;
139   3   1   3       BREAK: PROCEDURE(SUBJECT, PATTERN, CURSOR, MATCH_STR, REPLACE_FLAG,
                                       REPLACE_STR)
                            RETURNS (BIT(1));
140   4   1   5       DECLARE SUBJECT CHARACTER(*) VARYING, /* STRING TO BE EXAMINED */
                              PATTERN CHARACTER(*) VARYING, /* STRING SOUGHT WITHIN */
                                                           /* SUBJECT STRING */
                              CURSOR FIXED,        /* CHARACTER POSITION IN SUBJECT */
                                                   /* AT WHICH THE PATTERN MATCHING */
                                                   /* PROCESS IS TO BEGIN */
                              MATCH_STR CHARACTER(*) VARYING, /* DESIRED SUBSTRING */
                                                           /* FOUND IN SUBJECT */
                              REPLACE_FLAG BIT(*), /* FLAG INDICATING WHETHER */
                                                   /* REPLACEMENT IS REQUIRED */
                              REPLACE_STR CHARACTER(*) VARYING; /* STRING USED TO */
                                                           /* REPLACE MATCHED SUBSTRING */
141   4   1   5       DECLARE I FIXED,               /* TEMPORARY CURSOR */
                              NOT_FOUND BIT(1);
                      /* DOES THE PATTERN FIT WITHIN THE SEARCH BOUNDS OF THE  SUBJECT */
                      /* STRING? */
142   4   1   5       IF CURSOR > LENGTH(SUBJECT)
143   4   1   5       THEN RETURN('0'B);
                      /* INITIALIZE PATTERN MATCH */
144   4   1   5       I = CURSOR;
                      /* IS CHARACTER I IN THE PATTERN STRING? */
145   4   1   5       NOT_FOUND = '1'B;
146   4   1   5       DO WHILE(NOT_FOUND);
147   4   2   5           IF I <= LENGTH(SUBJECT)
148   4   2   5           THEN DO;
149   4   3   5               IF INDEX(PATTERN, SUBSTR(SUBJECT, I, 1)) = 0
150   4   3   5               THEN I = I + 1;
151   4   3   5               ELSE NOT_FOUND = '0'B;
152   4   3   5               END;
```

Fig. 9-7 Program for a text editing system (cont'd.)

```
153   4   2   5              ELSE NOT_FOUND = '0'B;
154   4   2   5          END;
                         /* SUCCESSFUL PATTERN MATCH? */
155   4   1   5          IF I = LENGTH(SUBJECT) + 1
156   4   1   5          THEN RETURN('0'B);
                         /* SET MATCH STR AND PERFORM INDICATED REPLACEMENT */
157   4   1   5          MATCH_STR = SUBSTR(SUBJECT, CURSOR, I-CURSOR);
158   4   1   5          IF REPLACE_FLAG
159   4   1   5          THEN DO;
160   4   2   5              SUBJECT = SUBSTR(SUBJECT, 1, CURSOR-1) || REPLACE_STR ||
                                  SUBSTR(SUBJECT, I);
161   4   2   5              CURSOR = CURSOR + LENGTH(REPLACE_STR);
162   4   2   5          END;
163   4   1   5          ELSE CURSOR = I;
                         /* SUCESSFUL RETURN */
164   4   1   5          RETURN('1'B);
165   4   1   .5     END BREAK;
166   3   1   3      END SCANNER;
                     /* PROCEDURE TO OUTPUT A LINE OF TEXT IN UNJUSTIFIED FORM */
167   2   1   2      PRINT_U: PROCEDURE(WORDS, NO_WORDS);
168   3   1   6          DECLARE WORDS(*) CHARACTER(*) VARYING, /* WORDS TO BE OUTPUT */
                             NO_WORDS FIXED;   /* NUMBER OF WORDS */
169   3   1   6          DECLARE LINE CHARACTER(80) VARYING, /* LINE TO BE OUTPUT */
                             I FIXED;   /* INDEX VARIABLE */
                         /* OBTAIN THE CURRENT LINE IN UNJUSTIFIED FORM */
170   3   1   6          LINE = WORDS(1);
171   3   1   6          DO I=2 TO NO_WORDS;
172   3   2   6              LINE = LINE || ' ' || WORDS(I);
173   3   2   6          END;
                         /* OUTPUT CURRENT LINE */
174   3   1   6          PUT SKIP LIST(LINE);
                         /* FINISHED */
175   3   1   6          RETURN;
176   3   1   6      END PRINT_U;

                     /* PROCEDURE TO OUTPUT A JUSTIFIED LINE OF TEXT */
177   2   1   2      PRINT_J: PROCEDURE(WORDS, NO_WORDS, LINE_LENGTH, WIDTH);
178   3   1   7          DECLARE WORDS(*) CHARACTER(*) VARYING, /* WORDS TO BE OUTPUT */
                             NO_WORDS FIXED,   /* NUMBER WORD */
                             LINE_LENGTH FIXED, /* LENGTH OF UNEDITED LINE */
                             WIDTH FIXED;   /* LENGTH OF EDITED LINE */
179   3   1   7          DECLARE TOTAL_PAD FIXED, /* NUMBER OF ADDITIONAL BLANKS NEEDED */
                             AV_PAD FIXED, /* NUMBER OF BLANKS TO BE INSERTED BETWEEN */
                                           /* EACH PAIR OF WORDS */
                             EXTRA_BLANKS FIXED, /* NUMBER OF EXTRA BLANKS THAT MUST */
                                                 /* DISTRIBUTED */
```

Fig. 9-7 Program for a text editing system (cont'd.)

respectively. Then a number of IF statements are used to determine if the input line begins with a command. If this is true, then TYPE is set to the command's corresponding code number. If the first item on the input line is not a command, however, then TYPE is assigned the value one. The SCANNER then returns to the FORMATOR procedure.

On the other hand, if the CURSOR is less than or equal to the length of INPUT_LINE, then the function BREAK is used to place the next item of the line into ITEM. TYPE is set to one, and SCANNER returns to the FORMATOR.

After the SCANNER has isolated the next item and determined its type, a number of nested IF statements are used to handle the different types of items. If TYPE equals one (i.e., a word of text), then a check is made to see if the word fits on the current line. If this test is true, the word is added to the WORDS vector and NO_WORDS and LINE_LENGTH are updated appropriately; otherwise, either the

```
                                    PADDING CHARACTER(256) VARYING,
                                    J FIXED,
                                    LINE CHARACTER(80) VARYING, /* OUTPUT LINE OF TEXT */
                                    I FIXED; /* INDEX VARIABLE */
                                 /* COMPUTE TOTAL NUMBER OF BLANKS TO BE INSERTED */
   180    3    1    7            TOTAL_PAD = WIDTH - LINE_LENGTH;
                                 /* COMPUTE AVERAGE NUMBER OF BLANKS TO BE PADDED BETWEEN EACH */
                                                                       /* WORD */
   181    3    1    7            AV_PAD = TRUNC(TOTAL_PAD / (NO_WORDS - 1));
                                 /* COMPUTE EXTRA BLANKS TO BE DISTRIBUTED BETWEEN CERTAIN WORDS */
   182    3    1    7            EXTRA_BLANKS = MOD(TOTAL_PAD, NO_WORDS - 1);
                                 /* OBTAIN OUTPUT LINE */
   183    3    1    7            LINE = WORDS(1);
   184    3    1    7            PADDING = '';
   185    3    1    7            DO J = 1 TO AV_PAD + 1;
   186    3    2    7                PADDING = PADDING || ' ';
   187    3    2    7            END;
   188    3    1    7            DO I = 2 TO NO_WORDS - EXTRA_BLANKS;
   189    3    2    7                LINE = LINE || PADDING || WORDS(I);
   190    3    2    7            END;
   191    3    1    7            PADDING = '';
   192    3    1    7            DO J = 1 TO AV_PAD + 2;
   193    3    2    7                PADDING = PADDING || ' ';
   194    3    2    7            END;
   195    3    1    7            DO I = NO_WORDS - EXTRA_BLANKS+1 TO NO_WORDS;
   196    3    2    7                LINE = LINE || PADDING || WORDS(I);
   197    3    2    7            END;
                                 /* OUTPUT LINE */
   198    3    1    7            PUT SKIP LIST(LINE);
                                 /* FINISHED */
   199    3    1    7            RETURN;
   200    3    1    7        END PRINT_J;
   201    2    1    2     END FORMATOR;
   202    1         1  END TEXT_ED;
```

ERRORS/WARNINGS DETECTED DURING CODE GENERATION:

    WARNING: NO FILE SPECIFIED. SYSIN/SYSPRINT ASSUMED. (CGOC)

THIS LINE ILLUSTRATES THE USE OF THE
JUSTIFY TEXT COMMAND.

    THIS   IS   THE   START   OF   A   NEW
PARAGRAPH.
            THIS IS CENTERED.

THE ##BL COMMAND HAS BEEN USED TO LEAVE
FIVE BLANK LINES. THE FOLLOWING LINE HAS
NOT BEEN JUSTIFIED.

    ALL THE WORLD LOVES A TEXT-EDITING
COMPUTER.

IN STMT 202 PROGRAM RETURNS FROM MAIN PROCEDURE.

Fig. 9-7 Program for a text editing system (cont'd.)

procedure PRINT_J or PRINT_U is used to print the line, depending upon the value of JUSTIFY. If TYPE equals two (i.e., the justify command) or three (i.e., the unjustify command), then the logical variable JUSTIFY is set to *true* or *false*, respectively. A TYPE value of four (i.e., begin a new paragraph) causes the current line to be printed without justification, and a call to SCANNER to input the next line of text. If the next input item is not a word, then the message "ERROR IN INPUT" is printed; otherwise,

NO_WORDS is set to one, five blanks are concatenated to the beginning of the item which is assigned to WORDS(1), and the LINE_LENGTH is set to the length of WORDS(1). If TYPE is equal to five (i.e., center the following item), then the previous line is printed using the PRINT_U procedure. The item is then centered on the following line. A TYPE value of six indicating blank lines, causes the current line to be printed unjustified. The number of lines given by the variable ITEM are then skipped. Finally, TYPE value of seven indicates the end of the text, and the FORMATOR procedure ends. The program is then ended.

EXERCISES FOR CHAPTER 9

1. Modify the program SCAN given in Sec. 9-2.1 so that it can handle a sample language which contains real numbers. A real number is defined to be a sequence of digits (possibly empty) followed by a period (.) followed by a (nonempty) sequence of digits. Test your program on the values:

    > 3.456
    > 45.9
    > .99999
    > 1.2

2. Alter the program KWIC given in Sec. 9-2.2 so that it prints only the titles containing keywords which appear as data following the document titles. You may assume that the keywords given as data are in alphabetic order.

3. A company is computerizing its payroll and accounting procedures. The employee file for the company is to contain the following information:

    1. Employee's social insurance number (SIN) — a nine-digit field.
    2. Employee's name (NAME) — a 25-character field.
    3. Employee's sex (SEX) — a one-character field coded as 'M' for male and 'F' for female.
    4. Employee's type of work (TYPE) — a one-character field with 'A' denoting agent, 'D' denoting driver, 'H' denoting driver's helper, and 'P' denoting payroll.
    5. Employee's wage (WAGE) — a one-digit field where 1 denotes $4.00/hour, 2 denotes $4.80/hour, 3 denotes $6.00/hour, and 4 denotes $7.00/hour.
    6. Employee's location (LOCATION) — a one-character field where 'B' denotes Banff, 'J' denotes Jasper, and 'L' denotes Lake Louise.

    The following list of employee records is to be used.

Soc. In. No.	Name	Sex	Type	Wage	Location
693121053	LEW ARCHER	M	D	2	J
686725001	NANCY DREW	F	D	2	B
591146235	ARCHIE GOODWIN	M	H	1	B
661301964	PHILIP MARLOWE	M	A	3	J
529270792	JANE MARPLE	F	P	2	B
637263675	TRAVIS MCGEE	M	P	3	J

Write a PL/C procedure (similar to the procedure BUILD) to build a master file containing 13 bit strings, representing the sex, type of work, wage category, and location of the employees.

4. Write a PL/C program that will use the bit strings built by the program in exercise 3 to print a list of employees for the following categories: all employees earning $6.00 per hour, all drivers in Lake Louise, and all female employees in Jasper.

CHAPTER

10

LINEAR
DATA
STRUCTURES

Our programming discussion of data structures thus far has been concerned with the programming aspects of simple structures such as numbers, strings, vectors, and arrays. In this chapter we discuss the programming aspects of linear lists. These programming details fall into two categories which deal with the sequential-allocation and linked-allocation methods of storage for linear lists.

The chapter contains a basic discussion of an address. Also present is a description of the PL/I notation of a structure and an array of structures. A structure is important because it can be used to represent the structural relationship of the constituent parts of an element in a linear list. Programming details of stacks and queues are given. These programming details are exemplified in several applications such as recursion, the translation of expressions to Polish, simulation, and hash-table methods.

10-1 POINTERS IN PL/I

In PL/I a *pointer* is an address or reference to a data structure or one of its elements. A pointer is sometimes called a *link*. Recall that in PL/I, a pointer is considered to be a primitive data structure. The following declaration statement declares the pointer variable P.

DECLARE P POINTER:

Since the PL/I programmer does not know the precise location in memory where data structures are stored, he or she cannot assign a constant value to a pointer variable as can be done, for example, for a numeric or string variable. Although the programmer can control *when* a pointer variable receives a value (i.e., an address), it is the compiler that controls *what* specific value is assigned to that variable. Such programmer control is discussed throughout this chapter and, in particular, in Secs. 10-4 and 10-8.

A pointer in PL/I occupies one-half word (or two bytes) of memory. Since all pointers require the same storage space, the referencing of any data structure, regardless of its complexity, is made in a uniform manner.

Finally, since the actual value received by a pointer variable is under compiler control, PL/I does not allow the reading and writing of addresses for pointer variables.

10-2 STRUCTURES

Thus far we have encountered PL/I data types such as strings, integers, real numbers, and arrays. We now introduce nonhomogeneous data aggregates called *structures*. We first introduce the notion of a structure through the use of a simple example — a complex number. Although PL/I contains a COMPLEX data type and associated built-in operations (such as addition and subtraction) on complex numbers, it is instructive to simulate complex arithmetic by using PL/I structures.

The declaration statement

```
DECLARE 1 Z,
          2 REAL FLOAT DECIMAL,
          2 IMAG FLOAT DECIMAL;
```

creates a structure which consists of the two real variables REAL and IMAG. This structure is a hierarchical collection of three names. The hierarchical information is given by the level numbers (1 and 2 in our example). The name of the entire collection (specified by a level number of 1) is Z. The names at the bottom of the hierarchy (specified by a level number of 2) are REAL and IMAG. The structure Z is interpreted as a complex number with the variables REAL and IMAG representing the real and imaginary parts of a complex number, respectively. For example, for the complex number $-1.5 + 2.3i$, where $i = \sqrt{-1}$, the following sequence of assignment statements

```
REAL = -1.5;
IMAG = 2.3;
```

assigns the complex number $-1.5 + 2.3i$ to the structure Z.

Suppose that we declare two additional complex number structures called X and Y in the following statement

```
DECLARE 1 X,
           2 REAL FLOAT DECIMAL,
           2 IMAG FLOAT DECIMAL,
        1 Y,
           2 REAL FLOAT DECIMAL,
           2 IMAG FLOAT DECIMAL;
```

Now assume that we want to refer to the variable REAL in structure X. How can this be accomplished? If we simply refer to REAL, there is an ambiguity since REAL is a variable name in the three structures X, Y, and Z. In order to make the desired reference unambiguous or unique, the *qualified* name X.REAL specifies that structure X is being selected. The period separates the qualifier (X) from the variable being qualified (REAL). This name-qualification approach avoids the necessity of having to create variable names for essentially the same class of items, each item of which may be associated with a different but similar hierarchical structure.

It is an interesting exercise to formulate a procedure for simulating the subtraction of two complex numbers. Let us assume that this procedure is to have three structure variables, as previously described, called A, B, and C. The following procedure simulates the desired subtraction:

```
CSUB: PROCEDURE (A, B, C);
       /*THIS PROCEDURE SUBTRACTS THE COMPLEX NUMBERS*/
       /*A AND B, WHICH ARE STORED IN STRUCTURES*/
       /*AND RETURNS THE DIFFERENCE THROUGH THE PARAMETER C.*/
       DECLARE 1 A,
                  2 R FLOAT DECIMAL,
                  2 I FLOAT DECIMAL,
               1 B,
                  2 R FLOAT DECIMAL,
                  2 I FLOAT DECIMAL,
               1 C
                  2 R FLOAT DECIMAL,
                  2 I FLOAT DECIMAL;
       C.R = A.R - B.R;
       C.I = A.I - B.I;
END CSUB;
```

The mainline statement

```
CALL CSUB (X, Y, Z);
```

invokes the procedure and the desired result is placed in the REAL and IMAG parts of the structure Z. Similar procedures can be written to simulate other complex arithmetic operations.

The structures just described each have two component variables which are of the same type. This is not always the case. As an example, the following statement creates a simplified structure for an employee

```
DECLARE 1 EMPLOYEE,
         2 NAME,
           3 FIRST CHARACTER (10),
           3 M_I CHARACTER (1),
           3 LAST CHARACTER (19),
         2 ADDRESS,
           3 STREET CHARACTER (20),
           3 CITY CHARACTER (20),
           3 PROVINCE CHARACTER (15),
         2 DEDUCTIONS,
           3 NO_OF_DED FIXED DECIMAL,
           3 DEDUCTION_NAME(5) CHARACTER(10),
           3 AMOUNT(5) FIXED DECIMAL;
```

The name of the structure is EMPLOYEE. Such a structure is called a *major structure*. It can be used to refer to the whole structure. EMPLOYEE.NAME refers to the part of the structure dealing with the employee's name and is called a *minor structure*. EMPLOYEE.NAME.FIRST, EMPLOYEE.NAME.M_I, and EMPLOYEE.NAME.LAST refer to first name, middle initial, and last name of an employee, respectively, and are called *elementary items*. Elementary items cannot be further subdivided. Similarly, EMPLOYEE.ADDRESS is a minor structure which refers to the employee's address. Finally, EMPLOYEE.DEDUCTIONS refers to a minor structure consisting of three elementary items (NO_OF_DED, DEDUCTION_NAME, and AMOUNT) which describes an employee's deductions. Note that two parts of the DEDUCTIONS structure are arrays. The first array (DEDUCTION_NAME) is a character array; while the second (AMOUNT) is a numeric array. Observe that unlike an array, a structure does not require all of its constituent parts to be of the same type. The qualified name of the deduction array is

EMPLOYEE.DEDUCTIONS.DEDUCTION_NAME

To refer to the Ith deduction of this array, we use

EMPLOYEE.DEDUCTIONS.DEDUCTION_NAME(I).

Observe that only elementary items have attributes. In other words, major and minor structures cannot have attributes. Also note that the hierarchy of the items shown in the previous example can be viewed as having different levels. At the highest level (i.e., level 1) is the major structure name. At an intermediate level are *substructures* or minor structures. Each substructure name at a deeper level is given a greater number to specify the level depth. Elementary items within a minor structure must be given a higher level number than that of the structure. Finally, the indentation of level numbers in the declaration of a structure is used only to improve the readability of the structure. Moreover, the level numbers do not have to be successive. Each item, however, must be assigned a higher number than that of the level it is subdividing. As an example, the following declaration is valid:

```
DECLARE 1 A,
          3 B,
          3 C,
            5 D,
            5 E,
              7 F;
```

The notion of a structure is easily extended to arrays of structures. This is done in the next section.

Exercises for Sec. 10-2

1. A western farm currently produces several feed grains. In particular, wheat, barley, oats, rape seed, and flax are produced. The production level (in bushels) and the price per bushel (in dollars and cents) received during the year are recorded. Use a structure to describe the data.

2. A university book store maintains a list of up to twenty requests for any book which is currently out of stock. The information kept for such a book consists of the book title (80 characters), book price (in dollars and cents), and the requests for the book. Each request consists of a person's name (40 characters) and address (100 characters). Use a structure to describe a book with its associated information.

3. Use a PL/I structure to represent each of the following documents:

    a)   Airline ticket
    b)   Blue Cross or Medicare card
    c)   Gasoline credit card
    d)   Driver's license
    e)   Student identification card

Make realistic assumptions about the contents of each document.

4. Given the following program segment

```
DECLARE 1 A,
          2 B,
            3 C FIXED,
            3 D FIXED,
          2 E,
            3 F,
              4 G FIXED(4, 2),
              4 C FIXED(5, 1),
          2 H,
            3 I FIXED,
            3 J FIXED;
     GET LIST(A);
```

and the data

105	63	20.25	1800.5	-76	38

Obtain:

a) The value of B · C.
b) The sum of B and H.
c) The element that contains 1800.5.
d) The sum of B · C and F · C.

5. A liquor store has the following kinds of alcoholic beverages on hand:

> 60 brands of wine of which:
> > 10 brands are champagne
> > 5 brands are sherry
> > 20 brands are red
> > 10 brands are white
> > 5 brands are sparkling
>
> 15 brands of whiskey of which:
> > 6 brands are rye
> > 6 brands are scotch
> > 3 brands are bourbon
>
> 10 brands of rum
> 5 brands of cognac
> 7 brands of gin
> 5 brands of vodka

Design a structure to store this information.

10-3 ARRAYS OF STRUCTURES

The notion of an array was introduced in Chap. 4. Its use has been illustrated widely throughout the book. In PL/I, arrays are stored in row-major order. For example, a two-dimensional array is stored row by row. A sometimes undesirable property of an array is that all of its elements must be of the same data type attribute. As mentioned in the previous section, the parts of a structure can be nonhomogeneous, i.e., they can be of different data types. In this section we extend the notion of a structure to include arrays of structures.

An *array of structures* is simply an array whose elements are structures. These elements have identical names, levels, and subparts. For example, if a structure MONTH_SALES were used to represent the sales performance of a salesperson for each month of the year, it might be declared as follows:

```
DECLARE 1 MONTH_SALES(12),
            2 SALESPERSON,
              3 NAME CHARACTER (30),
              3 REGION CHARACTER(5),
            2 SALES_DETAIL,
              3 QUOTA FIXED DECIMAL,
              3 SALES FIXED DECIMAL,
              3 COMMISSION FIXED DECIMAL;
```

Thus, we can refer to the sales data for the month of May by specifying

MONTH_SALES(5). Parts of the May sales are referred to by SALESPERSON(5) and SALES_DETAIL(5). SALES_DETAIL.SALES(2)(or equivalently, SALES_DETAIL(2).SALES), which refers to the sales for the month of February, is called a *subscripted qualified name*.

As an application of an array of structures, let us consider a simplified system for gathering and reporting student grades. Let us assume that the data comprise two parts. The first part contains the number of all students enrolled in courses followed by the details (such as student name, student number, and address) for each student in student number order. The second part of the data specifies the number of courses whose examination results are being reported, followed by the examination results for each course. The results of each course contain the course name and the course enrollment. A list of student descriptions (with grades) follows its course description. For example, the data which follow describe a total of 100 students enrolled in three courses:

100 (number of students)
'LYLE OPSETH' 1 '120 2ND AVE' 'MELFORT' 'SASK' 'S0E1A0'

.

.   student details in student number order

.

'MURRAY MAZER' 100 '17 MAZE AVE' 'SASKATOON' 'SASK' 'S5J1B2'
3 (number of courses)
'CMPT 180A' 60   (first course)
1 'LYLE OPSETH' 91

.

.

72 ' JACK COOPER' 73
'CMPT 181B' 40   (second course)
3 'MARY SMITH' 62

.

.

90 'JOE BLACK' 55
'CMPT 212A' 25   (third course)
17 'JIM BROWN' 25

.

.

75 'JANE FORD' 76

The following declaration statement defines an array of structures for representing students and course data:

```
DECLARE 1 STUDENT(NO_OF_STUDENTS),
          2 NAME CHARACTER (20),
          2 NUMBER FIXED DECIMAL,
          2 ADDRESS,
            3 STREET CHARACTER (20),
```

```
          3 CITY CHARACTER (15),
          3 PROVINCE CHARACTER (15),
          3 POSTAL_CODE CHARACTER (6),
      2 TRANSCRIPT,
          3 NUMBER_OF_COURSES FIXED DECIMAL,
          3 COURSE_NAME(5) CHARACTER (10),
          3 GRADE(5) FIXED DECIMAL;
```

Observe that the number of elements in the array of structures is specified by the number of students taking courses. Also, the transcript associated with each student consists of the number of courses he or she has taken (NO_OF_COURSES) and the course descriptions. Each course description contains a course name and a grade for that course. We assume that each student cannot take more than five courses. The vectors COURSE_NAME and GRADE represent the course names and the associated grades, respectively.

A general algorithm for constructing the array of structures from the input data given in the form described earlier follows:

1. Input number of students
2. Repeat for each student
    input student's name, number, and address
    initialize transcript portion of the student's record
3. Input number of courses
4. Repeat thru step 6 for each course
5. Input course title and class size
6. Repeat for each student in this class
    input student in this class
    update transcript portion of student's record
7. Output student file

For convenience, we assume that the student numbers are sequentially ordered from 1 to NO_OF_STUDENTS. In this way a particular student number can be used to access directly that student's record in the array of structures.

Figure 10-1 is a PL/I program which performs the required task. The list of variables used is as follows:

NO_OF_STUDENTS	Number of students
STUDENT	Array of structures
COURSES	Number of courses being reported
COURSE_TITLE	Title or name of course
CLASS_SIZE	Number of students in a class
STUDENT_#	Student number of student in a particular course
STUDENT_NAME	Student name of student in a particular course
TEMP	Stores number of courses a student is taking
I	Index to access a particular student
J	Index to access a particular course

Note that the program contains a BEGIN block. The first statement in this block declares the array of structures to contain NO_OF_STUDENTS elements. Next, the data on enrolled students are read and placed into the array of structures in

```
STMT LEVEL NEST BLOCK MLVL  SOURCE TEXT

  1                          GRADE: PROCEDURE OPTIONS (MAIN);
                               /* THIS PROGRAM INPUTS A SERIES OF STUDENTS AND THE COURSE LISTS  */
                               /* FOR THE STUDENTS, STORING THE STUDENTS STATISTICS IN AN ARRAY  */
                               /* OF STRUCTURES.                                                 */
  2     1           1        DECLARE NO_OF_STUDENTS FIXED,          /* NUMBER OF STUDENTS */
                                     COURSE_TITLE CHARACTER (10),   /* TITLE OF COURSE */
                                     CLASS_SIZE FIXED,              /* SIZE OF CLASS */
                                     STUDENT_# FIXED,               /* STUDENT NUMBER */
                                     STUDENT_NAME CHARACTER (20),   /* STUDENT NAME */
                                     MARK FIXED,                    /* STUDENT GRADE */
                                     COURSES FIXED,                 /* NO OF COURSES OFFERED  */
                                     TEMP FIXED,                    /* NUMBER OF COURSES */
                                                                    /* STUDENT IS TAKING */
                                     (I, J) FIXED;                  /* COUNTED LOOP VARIABLES */

  3     1           1        GET LIST (NO_OF_STUDENTS);

  4     1           1        BEGIN;
                               /* DECLARE THE ARRAY OF STRUCTURES FOR THE STUDENTS */
  5     2           2        DECLARE 1 STUDENT (NO_OF_STUDENTS),
                                       2 NAME CHARACTER (20) VARYING,
                                       2 NUMBER FIXED,
                                       2 ADDRESS,
                                         3 STREET CHARACTER (20) VARYING,
                                         3 CITY CHARACTER (15) VARYING,
                                         3 PROVINCE CHARACTER (15) VARYING,
                                         3 POSTAL_CODE CHARACTER (6),
                                       2 TRANSCRIPT,
                                         3 NO_OF_COURSES FIXED,
                                         3 COURSE_NAME(5) CHARACTER (10),
                                         3 GRADE(5) FIXED;

                               /* INPUT ENROLLED STUDENTS */
  6     2           2        DO I = 1 TO NO_OF_STUDENTS;
  7     2     1     2            GET LIST (NAME(I), NUMBER(I), STREET(I), CITY(I),
                                          PROVINCE(I), POSTAL_CODE(I));
  8     2     1     2            STUDENT(I).NO_OF_COURSES = 0;
  9     2     1     2            DO J = 1 TO 5;
 10     2     2     2                STUDENT(I).TRANSCRIPT.COURSE_NAME(J) = ´ ´;
 11     2     2     2                STUDENT(I).TRANSCRIPT.GRADE(J) = 0;
 12     2     2     2            END;
 13     2     1     2        END;

                               /* PROCESS COURSES OFFERED */
 14     2           2        GET LIST (COURSES);
 15     2           2        DO I = 1 TO COURSES;
 16     2     1     2            GET LIST (COURSE_TITLE, CLASS_SIZE);

                               /* PROCESS STUDENTS TAKING CLASS */
 17     2     1     2            DO J = 1 TO CLASS_SIZE;
 18     2     2     2                GET LIST (STUDENT_#, STUDENT_NAME, MARK);
 19     2     2     2                STUDENT(STUDENT_#).NO_OF_COURSES =
                                           STUDENT(STUDENT_#).NO_OF_COURSES + 1;
 20     2     2     2                TEMP = STUDENT(STUDENT_#).NO_OF_COURSES;
 21     2     2     2                STUDENT(STUDENT_#).COURSE_NAME(TEMP) = COURSE_TITLE;
 22     2     2     2                STUDENT(STUDENT_#).GRADE(TEMP) = MARK;
 23     2     2     2            END;
 24     2     1     2        END;
```

Fig. 10-1 A program to store the courses students are taking

statement 7. Then the grades of the students are initialized to zero and the course titles to blanks. Statements 14 and 15 control reading the courses offered.

Exercises for Sec. 10-3

1. The following declaration statement defines an array of structures:

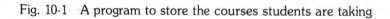

```
                              /* OUTPUT ARRAY OF STRUCTURES */
25  2      2              DO I = 1 TO NO_OF_STUDENTS;
26  2  1   2                  PUT SKIP (3) EDIT ('NAME: ', NAME(I), 'STUDENT NUMBER: ',
                                  NUMBER(I)) (A, A, COL(30), A, F(5));
27  2  1   2                  PUT SKIP EDIT ('ADDRESS: ', STREET(I)) (A, A);
28  2  1   2                  PUT SKIP EDIT (CITY(I), ', ', PROVINCE(I), POSTAL_CODE(I))
                                  (COL(10), A, A, A, X(3), A);
29  2  1   2                  PUT SKIP (2) EDIT ('COURSE NAME', 'GRADE')
                                  (COL(10), A, COL(25), A);
30  2  1   2                  DO J = 1 TO STUDENT(I).NO_OF_COURSES;
31  2  2   2                      PUT SKIP EDIT (STUDENT(I).COURSE_NAME(J),
                                      STUDENT(I).GRADE(J)) (COL(10), A, COL(26), F(3));
32  2  2   2                  END;
33  2  1   2              END;
34  2      2          END;
35  1      1      END GRADE;
```

```
         NAME: LYLE OPSETH          STUDENT NUMBER:    1
         ADDRESS: 120 2ND AVE
                 MELFORT, SASK   SOE1AO

                 COURSE NAME    GRADE
                 CMPT 180A      91
                 CMPT 212A      79
                 CMPT 228B      87
                 CMPT 313B      69


         NAME: MURRAY MAZER         STUDENT NUMBER:    2
         ADDRESS: 17 MAZE AVE
                 SASKATOON, SASK   M5J1B2

                 COURSE NAME    GRADE
                 CMPT 180A      85
                 CMPT 181B      79
                 CMPT 212A      93
                 CMPT 220B      77
                 CMPT 313B      98


         NAME: MARY SMITH           STUDENT NUMBER:    3
         ADDRESS: 2 MADISON CRES
                 PRINCE ALBERT, SASK   M3K4P7

                 COURSE NAME    GRADE
                 CMPT 181B      54
                 CMPT 220B      66
                 CMPT 377A      68


         NAME: JOE BLACK            STUDENT NUMBER:    4
         ADDRESS: 43 ARCADIA DRIVE
                 SASKATOON, SASK   S7K2P3

                 COURSE NAME    GRADE
                 CMPT 181B      49


         NAME: JANE FORD            STUDENT NUMBER:    5
         ADDRESS: 1137 117TH STRREET
                 TORONTO, ONTARIO   P3J7F6

                 COURSE NAME    GRADE
                 CMPT 180A      73
                 CMPT 181B      77
                 CMPT 220B      83


         IN STMT   35  PROGRAM RETURNS FROM MAIN PROCEDURE.
```

Fig. 10-1   A program to store the courses students are taking (cont'd.)

```
DECLARE 1 SALES(200),
          2 SALESPERSON CHARACTER(30),
            3 CITY CHARACTER(10),
            3 DISTRICT FIXED,
          2 RECORD,
            3 YEAR_TO_DATE,
              4 QUOTA FIXED,
              4 SALES FIXED,
              4 COMMISSION FIXED,
            3 CURRENT_MONTH,
              4 QUOTA FIXED,
              4 SALES FIXED,
              4 COMMISSION FIXED;
```

a)   How many elementary items does this structure have?

b)   Write a PUT statement to output the information associated with the 50th salesperson.

c)   Assuming a commission rate of 10%, give a statement to compute and store each salesperson's commission for the current month.

2.   The Honest John Motor Corporation has six dealerships of motor vehicle sales. Each dealership markets cars and trucks. The cars are classified into three categories as follows:

Small	Mid-size	Full
Futura	Fairmont	Lincoln
Zephyr	Mustang	Thunderbird
Bobcat	Granada	LTD1
Fiesta		LTD2

The trucks are broken down into the two following classes:

Pick-up	Freight
Courier	F600
F100	F700
F150	F800
F250	
F350	

Each time a vehicle is sold, a card containing the following information is filed:

```
type
model name
month purchased (1 to 12)
dealership (1 to 6)
purchase price (to the nearest dollar)
```

Construct a PL/I program that outputs the following:

a)   The total number of cars sold and total sales in each month.

b)   The total number of cars sold and total sales in each dealership in each month.

c)   The most popular pick-up sold overall.

d)   The region with the most cars and trucks sold in a given month.

e)   The most popular small car sold overall.

10-4 STACKS

The notion of a stack is introduced in Sec. 10-4 of the main text. In particular, a vector is used to simulate a stack structure. Using this representation, algorithms for pushing an element onto a stack and popping an element from a stack are developed. Note that these algorithms require a special variable to keep track of the topmost element in the stack. As mentioned in the main text, the update of the top element index of a stack is a burden to the programmer. This burden can be avoided if the programming language being used allows a "pure" representation of a stack. We present such a representation of a stack in this section.

PL/I allows explicit control through program statements of when and how much storage is to be allocated for certain variables in a program. Storage which can be controlled in this manner is called CONTROLLED storage in PL/I. Whenever an additional instance of a stack element is required, it can be created by a special statement called an ALLOCATE statement. The new element created by such a statement can then be assigned one or more data values. The only element which is accessible in such a stack-like structure is the most recently created one. Alternatively, when the element on top of the stack is no longer required, it can be deleted from the stack by executing another special statement called a FREE statement. In both the ALLOCATE and FREE statements, the top element index of the stack is handled automatically by the compiler. Let us now consider an example which illustrates how these programming constructs are used. We emphasize at this point that these programming constructs are available in PL/I but not in PL/C.

Suppose in a PL/I program we declare a structure variable STUDENT which contains two fields or components, a student's name (NAME) and a student's number (NUMBER). The following declaration statement places the storage allocation of STUDENT under direct programmer control:

```
DECLARE 1 STUDENT CONTROLLED,
         2 NAME CHARACTER (20),
         2 NUMBER FIXED DECIMAL;
```

To create a new element of STUDENT, we use the statement

```
ALLOCATE STUDENT;
```

Observe that this ALLOCATE statement only provides storage for the new element it creates, and that the fields NAME and NUMBER have no values at this point. Assignment of values can be achieved through the execution of assignment statements such as

```
NAME = 'LYLE OPSETH'; NUMBER = 74283;
```

Let us now consider what happens if, following these assignment statements, another ALLOCATE statement plus two more assignment statements are executed. Assume that these additional statements are the following:

ALLOCATE STUDENT;
NAME = 'JUDY RICHARDSON'; NUMBER = 73645;

At this point in time the stack structure STUDENT contains two elements (i.e., 'LYLE OPSETH' and 'JUDY RICHARDSON'). After the execution of the last group of statements, any reference to NAME and NUMBER would yield the values assigned to the last element created (i.e., the values 'JUDY RICHARDSON' and 73645). Note that the storage associated with 'LYLE OPSETH' is not destroyed or lost; however, it is not accessible at this point. To access this student requires that the latest element be released. This release is achieved through the execution of the following statement

FREE STUDENT;

At this point a reference to NAME would yield the value 'LYLE OPSETH'. If a second FREE STUDENT; statement is executed, then the storage associated with the first element is released, and any subsequent reference to NAME and NUMBER would result in an error.

The reader has probably noticed that the allocating and freeing of CONTROLLED storage is performed in a "last-in, first-out" manner. Elements are inserted onto and deleted from a stack in the same manner and, consequently, it is easy to effect the operations of a stack using the ALLOCATE and FREE statements. To push an element onto a stack, say, S (which must be declared to be of storage type CONTROLLED), involves the following sequence of PL/I statements:

```
/*PUSH (S, X) – PUSH ELEMENT X ONTO STACK S*/
ALLOCATE S;
S = X;
```

To pop an element from the stack S involves the statements:

```
/*POP (S) – REMOVE TOP ELEMENT FROM S*/
FREE S;
```

The empty stack condition can be determined by using the PL/I built-in function ALLOCATION. This function returns the value *false* when the stack is empty. For a nonempty stack the function returns a value of *true*.

The following program segment controls the emptying and printing of a stack S whose element is a character variable:

```
STACK: PROCEDURE OPTIONS(MAIN);
       DECLARE S CHARACTER(20) VARYING CONTROLLED;
       DECLARE P CHARACTER(20) VARYING;
```

```
        DO WHILE (ALLOCATION (S));
              P = S;
              FREE S;
              PUT SKIP LIST (P);
        END;
                  .
                  .
                  .
        END STACK;
```

Note that the location of the top element in a stack represented in CONTROLLED storage is handled implicitly by the PL/I compiler. That is, variable S yields the value of the top element of the stack.

In closing, we wish to emphasize that there are major differences between representing a stack with CONTROLLED storage as opposed to a vector representation. The notion of a stack as a possible multiple-element data structure is less apparent when using controlled allocation. The declaration of a "stacklike" structure involves the declaration of a prototype element which is used in allocating and freeing CONTROLLED storage for each instance of the declared variable. Not only can elements be inserted onto or deleted from the top of the stack, but only the top element can be referenced in a CONTROLLED storage representation. Several applications of CONTROLLED storage pervade the remainder of the book. The next section examines some of these.

10-5 APPLICATIONS OF STACKS

This section describes the programming aspects associated with the three application areas discussed in Sec. 10-5 of the main text. The first application deals with recursion. Several programming examples of recursion are given. The second application of stacks involves the compilation of arithmetic expressions to machine code. The last application pertains to the use of a stack in performing a sort.

10-5.1 Recursion

Thus far in this book we have encountered instances of a procedure calling another procedure. We now consider the case of a recursive procedure; that is, a procedure which calls itself.

Consider the following recursive formulation of the factorial function:

$$n! = \begin{cases} 1 & \text{if } n = 0 \\ n\,(n - 1) & \text{if } n > 0 \end{cases}$$

A recursive PL/I procedure for this function and an associated main test procedure are given in Fig. 10-2. Note that any recursive procedure must be declared to have the RECURSIVE attribute.

The following recursive definition specifies the nth Fibonacci number:

$$FIB(n) = \begin{cases} 0 & \text{if } n = 1 \\ 1 & \text{if } n = 2 \\ FIB(n - 1) + FIB(n - 2) & \text{if } n > 2 \end{cases}$$

```
STMT LEVEL NEST BLOCK MLVL  SOURCE TEXT


  1                             RUNFACT: PROCEDURE OPTIONS(MAIN);
                                /* THIS PROGRAM TESTS THE RECURSIVE FACTORIAL FUNCTION. */

  2    1             1          DECLARE FACT ENTRY (BINARY FIXED (31)) RETURNS (BINARY FIXED (31)),
                                   I BINARY FIXED (31);

  3    1             1          DO I = 2 TO 8 BY 3;
  4    1    1        1            PUT SKIP (2) EDIT ('FACTORIAL(', I, ') IS', FACT (I))
                                     (A(10), F(1), A(5), F(5));
  5    1    1        1          END;

  6    1             1          FACT: PROCEDURE (N) RECURSIVE RETURNS (BINARY FIXED(31));
                                /* THIS FUNCTION RETURNS THE FACTORIAL OF N. */

  7    2             2          DECLARE (M, N) BINARY FIXED (31);

  8    2             2          IF N = 0
  9    2             2          THEN RETURN (1);
 10    2             2          ELSE DO;
 11    2    1        2            M = N - 1;
 12    2    1        2            RETURN (N * FACT (M));
 13    2    1        2          END;
 14    2             2          END FACT;
 15    1             1          END RUNFACT;
```

ERRORS/WARNINGS DETECTED DURING CODE GENERATION:

    WARNING: NO FILE SPECIFIED. SYSIN/SYSPRINT ASSUMED. (CGOC)

FACTORIAL(2) IS   2

FACTORIAL(5) IS   120

FACTORIAL(8) IS 40320

IN STMT   15 PROGRAM RETURNS FROM MAIN PROCEDURE.

Fig. 10-2   Recursive formulation of the factorial function

Figure 10-3 contains the PL/I recursive procedure which performs the required evaluation.

    As a final example, Fig. 10-4 contains a PL/I recursive procedure which performs a binary search for the element X in the vector K. The remaining parameters, TOP and BOTTOM, define the current search interval.

Exercises for Sec. 10-5.1

1. A well-known algorithm for finding the greatest common divisor of two integers is *Euclid's algorithm*. The greatest common divisor function is defined by the following:

$$GCD(M,N) = \begin{cases} GCD(N,M), & \text{if } N > M \\ M, & \text{if } N = 0 \\ GCD(N,MOD(M,N)), & \text{if } N > 0 \end{cases}$$

where MOD(M, N) is M modulo N – the remainder on dividing M by N.

```
STMT LEVEL NEST BLOCK MLVL   SOURCE TEXT


    1                          RUNFIB: PROCEDURE OPTIONS(MAIN);
                                  /* TEST THE RECUSIVE FIBONACCI NUMBER FUNCTION */

    2    1          1          DECLARE FIB ENTRY (FIXED) RETURNS (FLOAT),
                                      I BINARY FIXED;

    3    1          1          DO I = 2 TO 12 BY 5;
    4    1    1     1              PUT SKIP (2) EDIT ('FIBONACCI (', I, ') IS', FIB (I))
                                      (A(11), F(2), A(5), F(5));
    5    1    1     1          END;

    6    1          1          FIB: PROCEDURE (N) RECURSIVE RETURNS (FLOAT);

    7    2          2              DECLARE N FIXED;

                                  /*  RETURN FIBONACCI NUMBER OF N */
    8    2          2              IF N = 1
    9    2          2              THEN RETURN (0);
   10    2          2              ELSE IF N = 2
   11    2          2                  THEN RETURN (1);
   12    2          2                  ELSE RETURN (FIB (N - 1) + FIB (N - 2));
   13    2          2              END FIB;
   14    1          1          END RUNFIB;

ERRORS/WARNINGS DETECTED DURING CODE GENERATION:

    WARNING: NO FILE SPECIFIED. SYSIN/SYSPRINT ASSUMED. (CGOC)

FIBONACCI ( 2) IS    1

FIBONACCI ( 7) IS    8

FIBONACCI (12) IS    89


IN STMT   14  PROGRAM RETURNS FROM MAIN PROCEDURE.
```

Fig. 10-3   Recursive function for computing Fibonacci numbers

Construct a recursive-function procedure for this problem and obtain GCD(20, 6).

2. The usual method used in evaluating a polynomial of the form

$$p_n(x) = a_0 x^n + a_1 x^{n-1} + a_2 x^{n-2} + \cdots + a_{n-1} x + a_n$$

is by using the technique known as *nesting* or *Horner's rule*. This is an iterative method which is described as follows:

$$b_0 = a_0 \quad b_{i+1} = x \cdot b_i + a_{i+1}; \quad i = 0, 1, \ldots, n-1$$

from which one can obtain

$$b_n = p_n(x)$$

An alternate solution to the problem is to write

```
STMT LEVEL NEST BLOCK MLVL   SOURCE TEXT


  1                           RUN_BSR: PROCEDURE OPTIONS(MAIN);
                              /* THIS PROGRAM TESTS THE RECURSIVE BINARY SEARCH PROCEDURE */

  2    1           1          DECLARE (VECTOR(10),          /* VECTOR TO BE SEARCHED */
                                       VALUE) FLOAT,        /* VALUE TO SEARCH FOR */
                                      (TOP, BOTTOM) FIXED,  /* TOP AND BOTTOM OF VECTOR */
                                       NUM FIXED,           /* POSITION OF ELEMENT SEARCHED FOR */
                                       I FIXED,             /* COUNTED LOOP VARIABLE */
                                       B_S_R ENTRY ((*)FLOAT, FLOAT, FIXED, FIXED) RETURNS (FIXED);

                              /* INPUT VECTOR */
  3    1           1          PUT SKIP LIST ('VECTOR READ IN IS');
  4    1           1          DO I = 1 TO 10;
  5    1     1     1              GET LIST (VECTOR(I));
  6    1     1     1              PUT EDIT (VECTOR(I)) (X(5), F(2));
  7    1     1     1          END;

                              /* TEST B_S_R ON SEVERAL INPUT ITEMS */
  8    1           1          PUT SKIP (2);
  9    1           1          DO I = 1 TO 5;
 10    1     1     1              TOP = 1;   BOTTOM = 10;
 12    1     1     1              GET LIST (VALUE);
 13    1     1     1              NUM = B_S_R (VECTOR, VALUE, TOP, BOTTOM);
 14    1     1     1              PUT SKIP EDIT ('POSITION OF ', VALUE, ' IS ', NUM)
                                      (A, F(2), A, F(2));
 15    1     1     1          END;

 16    1           1          B_S_R: PROCEDURE (K, X, TOP, BOTTOM) RECURSIVE RETURNS (FIXED);
                              /* THIS RECURSIVE FUNCTION RETURNS THE POSITION OF THE       */
                              /* ELEMENT X IN THE SORTED VECTOR X.                         */

 17    2           2          DECLARE K(*) FLOAT,           /* VECTOR TO BE SEARCHED */
                                      X FLOAT,              /* ELEMENT TO BE SEARCHED FOR */
                                     (TOP, BOTTOM) FIXED,   /* TOP AND BOTTOM OF INTERVAL */
                                      MIDDLE FIXED;         /* MIDDLE OF SEARCH INTERVAL */

                              /* CHECK IF UNSUCCESSFUL SEARCH */
 18    2           2          IF TOP = BOTTOM & K(TOP) ¬= X
 19    2           2          THEN DO;
 20    2     1     2              PUT SKIP (2) LIST ('SEARCH IS UNSUCCESSFUL');
 21    2     1     2              RETURN (0);
 22    2     1     2          END;

                              /* DETERMINE MIDDLE ELEMENT AND NEW TOP OR BOTTOM OF */
                              /* SEARCH VECTOR */
 23    2           2          MIDDLE = TRUNC ((TOP + BOTTOM) / 2);
 24    2           2          IF K (MIDDLE) = X
 25    2           2          THEN DO;
 26    2     1     2              PUT SKIP (2) LIST ('SEARCH IS SUCCESSFUL');
 27    2     1     2              RETURN (MIDDLE);
 28    2     1     2          END;
 29    2           2          ELSE IF K(MIDDLE) < X
 30    2           2                  THEN RETURN (B_S_R (K, X, MIDDLE + 1, BOTTOM));
 31    2           2                  ELSE RETURN (B_S_R (K, X, TOP, MIDDLE - 1));
 32    2           2          END B_S_R;
 33    1           1          END RUN_BSR;

ERRORS/WARNINGS DETECTED DURING CODE GENERATION:

   WARNING: NO FILE SPECIFIED. SYSIN/SYSPRINT ASSUMED. (CGOC)
```

Fig. 10-4   Recursive function for performing a binary search

$$p_n(x) = x \cdot p_{n-1}(x) + a_0$$

where

$$p_{n-1}(x) = a_0 x^{n-1} + a_1 x^{n-2} + \cdots + a_{n-2}x + a_{n-1}$$

```
VECTOR READ IN IS        7    12    15    42    56    59    67    88    89    93


SEARCH IS SUCCESSFUL
POSITION OF 67 IS  7

SEARCH IS SUCCESSFUL
POSITION OF 59 IS  6

SEARCH IS SUCCESSFUL
POSITION OF 12 IS  2

SEARCH IS SUCCESSFUL
POSITION OF  7 IS  1

SEARCH IS UNSUCCESSFUL
POSITION OF  9 IS  0


IN STMT   33  PROGRAM RETURNS FROM MAIN PROCEDURE.
```

Fig. 10-4   Recursive function for performing a binary search (cont'd.)

which is the recursive formulation of the problem. Formulate a recursive-function procedure for this problem. Test this procedure with the data

$$n = 3, a_0 = 1, a_1 = 3, a_2 = 3, a_3 = 1, \text{ and } x = 3.$$

3.   Consider the set of all valid, completely parenthesized, infix arithmetic expressions consisting of single-letter variable names, a digit, and the four operators +, −, *, and /. The following recursive definition specifies the set of valid expressions:

   1.   Any single-letter variable (A – Z) or a digit is a valid infix expression.
   2.   If α and β are valid infix expressions, then $(\alpha + \beta)$, $(\alpha - \beta)$, $(\alpha * \beta)$, and (α / β) are all valid infix expressions.
   3.   The only valid infix expressions are those defined by steps 1 and 2.

Formulate a recursive-function procedure that will input a string of symbols and output either VALID EXPRESSION for a valid infix expression or INVALID EXPRESSION otherwise. Use the following strings as test data:

   '(((A*B)−C)+D)'
   '((A+B*C)*D)'
   '(((A*X)+B)*X)+C)'
   '(A−B)*C'

4.   Write a recursive-function procedure to compute the square root of a number. Read in triples of numbers N, A, and E, where N is the number for which the square root is to be found, A is an approximation of the square root, and E is the allowable error in the result. Use as your function

$$ROOT(N,A,E) = \begin{cases} A, & \text{if } |A^2 - N| < E \\ ROOT(N, \dfrac{A^2 + N}{2A}, E), & \text{otherwise} \end{cases}$$

Use the following triples as test data:

2	1.0	.001
3	1.5	.001
8	2.5	.001
225	14.2	.001

5. An important theoretical function, known as *Ackerman's function*, is defined as

$$A(M, N) = \begin{cases} N + 1, & \text{if } M = 0 \\ A(M - 1, 1), & \text{if } N = 0 \\ A(M - 1, A(M, N - 1)), & \text{otherwise} \end{cases}$$

Obtain a recursive-function procedure for this function. As test data, use the values $M = 2$ and $N = 2$.

6. Recursion can be used to generate all possible permutations of a set of symbols. For example, there are six permutations of the set of symbols A, B, and C; namely, ABC, ACB, BAC, BCA, CBA, and CAB. The set of permutations of N symbols is generated by taking each symbol in turn and prefixing it with all the permutations which result from the remaining $N - 1$ symbols. Formulate a recursive procedure for this problem.

7. Certain applications require a knowledge of the number of different partitions of a given integer N; that is, how many different ways N can be expressed as a sum of integer summands. For example, $N = 5$ yields the partitions

$$1 + 1 + 1 + 1 + 1, \ 5, \ 1 + 2 + 2, \ 3 + 1 + 1, \ 2 + 3, \ 1 + 4, \ \text{and } 1 + 1 + 1 + 2$$

If we denote by Q_{MN} the number of ways in which an integer M can be expressed as a sum, each summand of which no larger than M, then the number of partitions of N is given by Q_{NN}. The function Q_{MN} is defined recursively as

$$Q_{MN} = \begin{cases} 1, & \text{if } M = 1 \text{ and for all } N \\ 1, & \text{if } N = 1 \text{ and for all } M \\ Q_{MN}, & \text{if } M < N \\ 1 + Q_{M,M-1}, & \text{if } M = N \\ Q_{M,N-1} + Q_{M-N,N}, & \text{if } M > N \end{cases}$$

Formulate a recursive-function procedure for this problem and generate Q_{33} and Q_{55}.

10-5.2 Polish Expressions and Their Compilation

The problem of converting a partially-parenthesized infix expression to suffix Polish form and then converting this intermediate form to object code is

Table 10-1   Input and stack-precedence values for arithmetic expressions

| | Precedence | | Rank |
Symbol	Input Function(F)	Stack Function(G)	Function(R)
+ –	1	2	–1
* /	3	4	–1
@	6	5	–1
single-letter variables	7	8	1
(	9	0	–
)	0	–	–

discussed in Sec. 10-5.2 of the main text. Table 10-1 summarizes the input and stack precedence values associated with arithmetic expressions. The table also contains the rank value of each symbol. Note that, for convenience, the exponentiation operator (↑) is represented by the symbol @.

A general algorithm for the conversion of partially-parenthesized infix expressions to suffix Polish follows:

1. Place a left parenthesis onto the stack and initialize the rank count of the expression to zero
2. Obtain the leftmost symbol in the given infix expression and denote this symbol the current input symbol
3. Repeat thru step 6 while the current symbol is not empty
4. Repeat while the input precedence of the current input symbol is less than the stack precedence of the stack symbol
   pop and output the stack top symbol
   add the rank of this symbol to the rank count of the expression
   if the rank count is less than one then the infix expression is invalid and exit
5. If the current input symbol is a left parenthesis and the stack top symbol is a right parenthesis
   then pop the stack
   else push the current input symbol onto the stack
6. Set the new current input symbol to the next input symbol
7. If the stack is not empty or the rank count is not equal to one
   then the infix expression is invalid
   else the infix expression is valid
   exit

A program to perform this conversion process appears in Fig. 10-5. In addition to a main program segment, the program contains the procedure SUFFIX and the functions F, G, and R. The sample infix expressions used in this program are:

    (A+B*C)*(D+E@F@A))
    A+B)*C*(D+E))
    (A+B@C@D)*(E+FD))

```
 1            CONVERT: PROCEDURE OPTIONS (MAIN);
                 /* THIS PROGRAM INPUTS SEVERAL INFIX EXPRESSIONS AND CONVERTS    */
                 /* THESE EXPRESSIONS TO THEIR SUFFIX EQUIVALENT.                  */

 2                DECLARE INFIX CHARACTER (30) VARYING,
                                     /* INFIX EXPRESSION TO BE CONVERTED */
                          POLISH CHARACTER (30) VARYING,
                                     /* RESULTING POLISH EXPRESSION */
                          NUM FIXED,       /* NUMBER OF INFIX EXPRESSIONS TO READ */
                          I FIXED,         /* COUNTED LOOP VARIABLE */
                          F ENTRY (CHARACTER (*)) RETURNS (FIXED DEC),
                          G ENTRY (CHARACTER (*)) RETURNS (FIXED DEC),
                          R ENTRY (CHARACTER (*)) RETURNS (FIXED DEC);

                  /* INPUT NUMBER OF EXPRESSIONS */
 3                GET LIST (NUM);

                  /* INPUT AND CONVERT EACH EXPRESSION */
 4                DO I = 1 TO NUM;
 5                    GET LIST (INFIX);
 6                    PUT SKIP (3) EDIT ('INFIX STRING READ IS ', INFIX) (A);
 7                    CALL SUFFIX (INFIX, POLISH);
 8                    IF POLISH ¬= ''
 9                    THEN PUT SKIP EDIT ('POLISH FORM IS ', POLISH) (A, A);
10                END;


11            SUFFIX: PROCEDURE (INFIX, POLISH);
                 /* GIVEN AN INPUT STRING (INFIX) CONTAINING AN INFIX           */
                 /* EXPRESSION WHICH HAS BEEN PADDED ON THE RIGHT WITH A RIGHT*/
                 /* PARENTHESIS, THIS PROCEDURE CONVERTS INFIX INTO SUFFIX     */
                 /* NOTATION AND PLACES THE RESULT IN THE STRING POLISH.       */

12                DECLARE (INFIX, POLISH) CHARACTER (*) VARYING,
                          S CHARACTER (1) CONTROLLED,
                                          /* STACK */
                          TEMP CHARACTER (1),     /* TEMPORARY CHARACTER STRING */
                          CURRENT CHARACTER (1);/* SYMBOL BEING EXAMINED */

                  /* INITIALIZE STACK */
13                ALLOCATE S;
14                S = '(';

                  /* INITIALIZE OUTPUT STRING AND RANK COUNT */
15                POLISH = '';
16                RANK = 0;

                  /* GET FIRST INPUT SYMBOL */
17                CURRENT = SUBSTR (INFIX, 1, 1);
18                INFIX = SUBSTR (INFIX, 2);

                  /* TRANSLATE THE INFIX EXPRESSION */
19                DO WHILE (CURRENT ¬= '');

                      /* REMOVE SYMBOLS WITH GREATER PRECEDENCE FROM STACK */
20                    IF ¬ ALLOCATION (S)
21                    THEN DO;
22                        PUT SKIP LIST ('INVALID');
23                        POLISH = '';
24                        RETURN;
25                        END;
26                    DO WHILE (F (CURRENT) < G (S));
27                        TEMP = S;
28                        FREE S;
29                        POLISH = POLISH || TEMP;
30                        RANK = RANK + R (TEMP);
31                        IF RANK < 1
32                        THEN DO;
33                            PUT SKIP LIST ('INVALID');
34                            POLISH = '';
35                            RETURN;
36                            END;
37                        END;
```

Fig. 10-5 PL/I program to convert from infix to suffix Polish notation

```
                              /* ARE THERE MATCHING PARENTHESES? */
38                            IF F (CURRENT) ¬= G (S)
39                            THEN DO;
40                                ALLOCATE S;
41                                S = CURRENT;
42                                END;
43                            ELSE FREE S;

                              /* GET NEXT INPUT SYMBOL */
44                            IF LENGTH (INFIX) > 0
45                            THEN DO;
46                                CURRENT = SUBSTR (INFIX, 1, 1);
47                                INFIX = SUBSTR (INFIX, 2);
48                                END;
49                            ELSE CURRENT = ´´;
50                          END;

                            /* IS THE EXPRESSION VALID? */
51                          IF ALLOCATION (S) ¦ RANK ¬= 1
52                          THEN DO;
53                              PUT SKIP LIST (´INVALID´);
54                              POLISH = ´´;
55                              END;
56                          ELSE PUT SKIP LIST (´VALID´);
57                  END SUFFIX;

58          F: PROCEDURE (TOKEN) RETURNS (FIXED DEC);
                  /* THIS FUNCTION RETURNS THE INPUT PRECEDENCE VALUE FOR THE */
                  /* CHARACTER GIVEN IN TOKEN. */

59                DECLARE TOKEN CHARACTER (*);

                  /* RETURN PRECEDENCE VALUE */
60                IF TOKEN = ´+´ ¦ TOKEN = ´-´
61                THEN RETURN (1);
62                ELSE IF TOKEN = ´*´ ¦ TOKEN = ´/´
63                    THEN RETURN (3);
64                    ELSE IF TOKEN = ´@´
65                        THEN RETURN (6);
66                        ELSE IF TOKEN = ´(´
67                            THEN RETURN (9);
68                            ELSE IF TOKEN = ´)´
69                                THEN RETURN (0);
70                                ELSE RETURN (7);
71          END F;

72          G: PROCEDURE (TOKEN) RETURNS (FIXED DEC);
                  /* THIS FUNCTION RETURNS THE STACK PRECEDENCE VALUE FOR THE */
                  /* SYMBOL CONTAINED IN TOKEN. */

73                DECLARE TOKEN CHARACTER (*);

                  /* RETURN STACK PRECEDENCE VALUE */
74                IF TOKEN = ´+´ ¦ TOKEN = ´-´
75                THEN RETURN (2);
76                ELSE IF TOKEN = ´*´ ¦ TOKEN = ´/´
77                    THEN RETURN (4);
78                    ELSE IF TOKEN = ´@´
79                        THEN RETURN (5);
80                        ELSE IF TOKEN = ´(´
81                            THEN RETURN (0);
82                            ELSE RETURN (8);
83          END G;

84          R: PROCEDURE (TOKEN) RETURNS (FIXED DEC);
                  /* THIS FUNCTION RETURNS THE RANK VALUE FOR THE SYMBOL */
                  /* CONTAINED IN TOKEN. */

85                DECLARE TOKEN CHARACTER (*);

                  /* RETURN RANK VALUE */
86                IF INDEX (´ABCDEFGHIJKLMNOPQRSTUVWXYZ´, TOKEN) ¬= 0
87                THEN RETURN (1);
88                ELSE RETURN (-1);
89          END R;
90      END CONVERT;
```

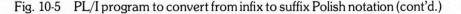

Fig. 10-5   PL/I program to convert from infix to suffix Polish notation (cont'd.)

```
INFIX STRING READ IS (A+B*C)*(D+E@F@A))
VALID
POLISH FORM IS ABC*+DEFA@@+*


INFIX STRING READ IS A+B)*C*(D+E))
INVALID


INFIX STRING READ IS (A+B@C@D)*(E+F/D))
VALID
POLISH FORM IS ABCD@@+EFD/+*
```

Fig. 10-5   PL/I program to convert from infix to suffix Polish notation (cont'd.)

Note that each expression is padded on the right with a right parenthesis. The variables used in the main program are:

Variable	Type	Usage
INFIX	CHARACTER(30) VARYING	Infix expression
POLISH	CHARACTER(30) VARYING	Suffix Polish output string
NUM	FIXED	Number of infix expressions to be converted
I	FIXED	Counted loop variable

Variables used in the procedure SUFFIX are:

INFIX	CHARACTER(*) VARYING	Infix expression
S	CHARACTER(1) CONTROLLED	Stack
TEMP	CHARACTER(1)	Contains stack top symbol
POLISH	CHARACTER(*)	Suffix Polish output string
CURRENT	CHARACTER(1)	Current input symbol
RANK	FIXED	Rank of infix expression

Variables used in the functions F, G, and R are:

TOKEN	CHARACTER(*) VARYING	An expression symbol

The main program inputs the infix expressions, and in statement 7 calls procedure SUFFIX to convert the expression to its suffix Polish form. In SUFFIX, a left parenthesis is placed on the stack in statement 14. Then the output string Polish and the rank count are initialized. Statements 19 to 50 perform the desired translation of the given expression. Statements 26 to 37 add all stack symbols with a precedence value greater than the input symbol's value to POLISH. A rank of less than one implies an invalid expression. The current symbol is then pushed onto the stack if it is not a right parenthesis; otherwise, the left parenthesis is popped from the stack. Finally, statements 31 to 36 check the validity of the expression. The function F determines the input precedence value of the current symbol contained in TOKEN as given in Table 10-1. The function G returns the stack precedence value of TOKEN, while R determines the rank value of TOKEN.

Table 10-2   Sample assembly-language instruction set

Operation	Meaning
LOD A	load: copy the value of the word addressed by A into the accumulator.
STO A	store: copy the value of the accumulator into the word addressed by A.
ADD A	add: replace the present value of the accumulator with the sum of its present value and the value of the word addressed by A.
SUB A	subtract: replace the present value of the accumulator with the result obtained by subtracting from its present value the value of the word addressed by A.
MUL A	multiply: replace the present value of the accumulator with the result obtained by multiplying its present value by the value of the word addressed by A.
DIV A	divide: replace the present value of the accumulator with the result obtained by dividing its present value by the value of the word addressed by A.

We now turn to translating a suffix Polish expression to object code. For our purposes we assume that the object code desired is in the form of hypothetical assembly-language instructions. As a matter of convenience, we also assume that the object computer which will execute the object code produced by the translation process is a single-address single-accumulator machine whose memory is sequentially organized into words. Such a computer was described in Sec. 2-1 of the main text. In this subsection we assume a simple assembly-language representation for the machine language instructions introduced there. A summary of these assembly instructions is given in Table 10-2. Note that we have added two new instructions — multiplication (MUL) and division (DIV).

An informal algorithm for the evaluation of a suffix string is given in Sec. 10-5.2.1 of the main text. Let us consider a program for converting suffix expressions consisting of the four basic arithmetic operators and single-letter variables to assembly language. Finally, assume that the basic arithmetic operators generate the following code:

a + b (ab+)	LOD	a
	ADD	b
	STO	T_i
a – b (ab–)	LOD	a
	SUB	b
	STO	T_i
a * b (ab*)	LOD	a
	MUL	b
	STO	T_i
a / b (ab/)	LOD	a
	DIV	b
	STO	T_i

Note that each operator generates three assembly-language instructions. The third instruction in each group is of the form STO T_i, where T_i denotes the address of a location (word) in the computer's memory that is to contain the value of the intermediate result. These addresses are to be created by the desired suffix-to-assembly-language program.

A straightforward algorithm involves the use of a stack. This entails the scanning of the suffix expression in a left-to-right manner. Each variable name in the input must be placed on the stack. On encountering an operator, the topmost two operands are unstacked and used (along with the operator) to generate the desired sequence of assembly instructions. The intermediate result corresponding to the operator in question is also placed on the stack. A general algorithm based on this approach follows:

1. Repeat thru step 3 while there still remains an input symbol
2. Obtain the current input symbol
3. If the current input symbol is a variable
   then push this variable on the stack
   else remove the two topmost operands from the stack
         generate the sequence of assembly-language instructions which corresponds to the current arithmetic operator
         stack the intermediate result

A program to perform the required translation appears in Fig. 10-6. In addition to a main-program segment the program contains the procedure CODE. The sample suffix expressions used in this program are:

```
AB*C+DEF/+*
AB+CEF/-*
AB/CD+/
```

The variables used in the main program are:

Variable	Type	Usage
EXPRESSION	CHARACTER (20) VARYING	Suffix expression
NUM	FIXED	Number of suffix expressions to process
I	FIXED	Counted loop variable

Variables used in the procedure CODE are:

Variable	Type	Usage
SUFFIX	CHARACTER (*) VARYING	Input suffix expression
CURRENT	CHARACTER (1)	Current input symbol
S	CHARACTER (20) VARYING CONTROLLED	Stack which contains operands
OPCODE	CHARACTER (4) VARYING	Contains assembly op-code for current instruction
TEMP	CHARACTER (4) VARYING	Intermediate result
LEFT	CHARACTER (4) VARYING	Left operand of current operator
RIGHT	CHARACTER (4) VARYING	Right operand of current operator
I	FIXED	Counter that keeps track of temporary storage
J	FIXED	Index associated with suffix string

The main program inputs the suffix expressions and calls the procedure CODE to generate the assembly-language instructions for each expression. In the procedure CODE, statement 11 initializes the temporary storage index. Statement 12 controls the loop to perform the translation process for each symbol in SUFFIX. If the current symbol is a variable name, then the name is pushed onto the stack; otherwise, in statements 20 to 26, the symbol is an operator so the correct operator is determined. Next, two operands are unstacked. The left operand is used with a load instruction while the right instruction is used with the operator generated in statements 20 to 26. The resulting instructions are printed. Finally, a temporary storage instruction is generated after the storage index is generated in statement 33. This storage location is then pushed onto the stack.

Exercises for Sec. 10-5.2

1. Modify the procedure SUFFIX presented in this section so that it will handle the PL/I relational operators:

   $$<, <=, =, \neg=, >, \text{ and } >=$$

   Recall that the relational operators should have a lower priority than the arithmetic operators. Note that the procedures F, G, and R must also change.

2. Alter procedure CODE given in this section such that it will generate more efficient code when the commutativity of the operators + and * is taken into consideration.

3. Modify the procedure obtained in exercise 2 so that the required number of temporary positions is reduced.

4. Modify the procedure obtained in exercise 3 so that it will handle the unary minus operator.

5. Using the general algorithm given in the main text, formulate a PL/I function (PREFIX) for converting an infix expression (INFIX) to its equivalent prefix form. Use the following data in checking your procedure:

   '(A+B)*(C–D+E)'
   'A*B*C(C+D)'
   '(A+B)(C+D)'
   'A+BD'

6. Formulate a procedure similar to procedure CODE for generating code for prefix expressions.

7. Modify the procedure obtained in exercise 6 so that the advantage of the commutative operators + and * is taken into consideration.

```
1              ASEMBLY: PROCEDURE OPTIONS (MAIN);
                 /* THIS PROGRAM TESTS PROCEDURE CODE ON SEVERAL SUFFIX EXPRESSIONS*/
                 /* IN ORDER TO GENERATE THEIR ASSEMBLY LANGUAGE INSTRUCTIONS.     */

2              DECLARE EXPRESSION CHARACTER (20) VARYING,
                                   /* SUFFIX EXPRESSION */
                 NUM FIXED,        /* NUMBER OF SUFFIX EXPRESSIONS TO READ */
                 I FIXED;          /* COUNTED LOOP VARIABLE */

               /* READ NUMBER OF EXPRESSIONS */
3              GET LIST (NUM);

               /* INPUT AND CONVERT EACH EXPRESSION */
4              DO I = 1 TO NUM;
5                  GET LIST (EXPRESSION);
6                  PUT SKIP (2) EDIT ('THE ASSEMBLY CODE FOR ', EXPRESSION, ' IS')
                       (A);
7                  CALL CODE (EXPRESSION);
8              END;

9              CODE: PROCEDURE (SUFFIX);
                 /* GIVEN A STRING (SUFFIX) REPRESENTING A SUFFIX EXPRESSION  */
                 /* EQUIVALENT TO A VALID INFIX EXPRESSION, THIS PROCEDURE    */
                 /* TRANSLATES THE STRING SUFFIX TO ASSEMBLY LANGUAGE         */
                 /* INSTRUCTIONS.                                             */

10             DECLARE SUFFIX CHARACTER (*) VARYING,
                 CURRENT CHARACTER (1),/* SYMBOL BEING EXAMINED */
                 S CHARACTER (20) VARYING CONTROLLED,
                                   /* STACK */
                 (LEFT, RIGHT) CHARACTER (4) VARYING,
                                   /* CURRENT OPERANDS */
                 OPCODE CHARACTER (4) VARYING,
                                   /* OPERATION CODE */
                 TEMP CHARACTER (4) VARYING,
                                   /* TEMPORARY STORAGE */
                 (NUM, DIGIT) FIXED,    /* USED TO CONVERT I TO STRING */
                 I FIXED,               /* TEMPORARY STORAGE INDEX */
                 J FIXED;               /* COUNTED LOOP VARIABLE */

               /* INITIALIZE */
11             I = 0;

               /* PROCESS THE SUFFIX EXPRESSION */
12             DO J = 1 TO LENGTH (SUFFIX);

                   /* OBTAIN AND PROCESS CURRENT INPUT SYMBOL */
13                 CURRENT = SUBSTR (SUFFIX, J, 1);
14                 IF CURRENT >= 'A' & CURRENT <= 'Z'
                   THEN /* PUSH CURRENT VARIABLE ONTO THE STACK */
15                     DO;
16                         ALLOCATE S;
17                         S = CURRENT;
18                     END;
19                 ELSE /* PROCESS CURRENT OPERATOR */
19                     DO;
20                         IF CURRENT = '+'
21                         THEN OPCODE = 'ADD ';
22                         ELSE IF CURRENT = '-'
23                             THEN OPCODE = 'SUB ';
24                             ELSE IF CURRENT = '*'
25                                 THEN OPCODE = 'MUL ';
26                                 ELSE OPCODE = 'DIV ';

                           /* UNSTACK TWO OPERANDS */
27                         RIGHT = S;
28                         FREE S;
29                         LEFT = S;
30                         FREE S;

                           /* OUTPUT LOAD INSTRUCTION */
31                         PUT SKIP LIST ('LOD ' || LEFT);
```

Fig. 10-6 PL/I program to convert from suffix to object code

```
                                   /* OUTPUT ARITHMETIC INSTRUCTION */
32                                 PUT SKIP LIST (OPCODE || RIGHT);
33                                 I = I + 1;  /* TEMPORARY STORAGE INDEX */
34                                 NUM = I;
35                                 TEMP = '';
36                                 DO WHILE (NUM > 0);
37                                     DIGIT = NUM / 10;
38                                     DIGIT = NUM - DIGIT * 10;
39                                     NUM = NUM / 10;
40                                     TEMP = SUBSTR ('0123456789', DIGIT + 1, 1)
                                           || TEMP;
41                                 END;
42                                 TEMP = 'T' || TEMP;

                                   /* TEMPORARY STORE INSTRUCTION */
43                                 PUT SKIP LIST ('STO ' || TEMP);
44                                 ALLOCATE S;  /* STACK INTERMEDIATE RESULT */
45                                 S = TEMP;
46                         END;
47              END;
48          END CODE;
49        END ASEMBLY;
```

```
THE ASSEMBLY CODE FOR AB*C+DEF/+* IS
LOD A
MUL B
STO T1
LOD T1
ADD C
STO T2
LOD E
DIV F
STO T3
LOD D
ADD T3
STO T4
LOD T2
MUL T4
STO T5


THE ASSEMBLY CODE FOR AB+CEF/-* IS
LOD A
ADD B
STO T1
LOD E
DIV F
STO T2
LOD C
SUB T2
STO T3
LOD T1
MUL T3
STO T4


THE ASSEMBLY CODE FOR AB/CD+/ IS
LOD A
DIV B
STO T1
LOD C
ADD D
STO T2
LOD T1
DIV T2
STO T3
```

Fig. 10-6 PL/I program to convert from suffix to object code (cont'd.)

10-5.3   Partition-Exchange Sorting

For the third and final application of a stack structure, we now consider a sorting technique which performs well on large tables. The approach is to place initially a particular record in its final position within the sorted table. Once this is done, all records which precede this record have smaller keys, while all records that follow it have larger keys. This technique partitions the original table into two subtables. The same process is then applied to each of these subtables and repeated until all records are placed in their final positions.

As an example of this approach to sorting, let us consider the placement of 73 in its final position in the following key set:

| 73 | 65 | 52 | 24 | 83 | 17 | 35 | 96 | 41 | 9 |

We now use two index variables I and J with initial values of 2 and 10, respectively. The two keys 73 and K[I] are compared and, if an exchange is required (i.e., $K[I] < 73$), then I is incremented by 1 and the process is repeated. When $K[I] \geqslant 73$, we proceed to compare keys K[J] and 73. If an exchange is required, then J is decremented by 1 and the process is repeated until $K[J] \leqslant 73$. At this point, the keys K[I] and K[J] (i.e., 83 and 9) are interchanged. The entire process is then repeated with J fixed and I being incremented once again. When $I \geqslant J$, the desired key is placed in its final position by interchanging the keys 73 and K[J].

Figure 10-7 contains a main program and a recursive procedure QUICK which performs the required sort. The sample input data used in this program are the key set

| 73 | 65 | 52 | 24 | 83 | 17 | 35 | 96 | 41 | 9 |

The variables used in the main program are:

Variable	Type	Usage
VECTOR(20)	FLOAT	Vector to be sorted
N	FIXED	Number of elements in table
NUM	FIXED	Number of tables to be sorted
I	FIXED	Counted loop variable
J	FIXED	Counted loop variable

Variables used in the procedure QUICK are:

Variable	Type	Usage
K(*)	FLOAT	Vector to be sorted
LB	FIXED	Lower bound of subtable
UB	FIXED	Upper bound of subtable
FLAG	BIT(1)	Variable to specify the end of splitting table into two subtables
KEY	FLOAT	Key to be placed in its final position
TEMP	FLOAT	Temporary variable in exchange process
I	FIXED	Index to subtable
J	FIXED	Index to subtable

The main program reads the number of tables to be sorted in statement 3. Then, for each table, the number of elements in the table and the individual elements are read. Statement 13 gives a value for the (n + 1)th element that is greater than all values in the table. The next statement calls the procedure QUICK to sort the table. Finally, the sorted table is printed.

The procedure QUICK first initializes FLAG to *true*. Then if there is more than one element in the subtable (i.e., LB < UB), the sort is performed. KEY is given the value of the first element in the subtable. Then, the keys are scanned from left to right until KEY has a value less than or equal to the Ith element, and from right to left until the Jth key is greater than KEY. If I is less than J, then the two records for these two indices can be interchanged; otherwise, the position where the table can be broken up into two subtables has been found and FLAG is set to *false* in order to exit the loop. Finally the Jth record is interchanged with the record at the lower bound of the table, and the procedure QUICK is called twice to sort the two smaller subtables.

Exercise for Sec. 10-5.3

1. Obtain an iterative PL/I procedure for the partition-exchange method of sorting. Use as data the key set

    42 23 74 11 65 58 94 36 99 87

10-6 QUEUES

As mentioned in the main text a queue structure is a linear list in which insertions are performed at the rear and elements are deleted from the front of the structure. Recall that elements in such a structure are processed on a first-come, first-served basis. A convenient and popular way of representing a FCFS queue is to use a vector. If we assume that the elements in such a vector are arranged in a circular fashion, that is, its first and last elements are logically adjacent to each other, then a circular queue structure results.

The following PL/I procedure, CQINS, performs an insertion into a FCFS circular queue which is represented as a vector.

```
CQINS: PROCEDURE (Q, N, F, R, X);
       /*THIS PROCEDURE INSERTS ELEMENT X INTO THE REAR OF THE */
       /*CIRCULAR QUEUE Q WHICH IS REPRESENTED AS A VECTOR OF*/
       /*SIZE N. F AND R POINT TO THE FRONT AND REAR OF THE */
       /*QUEUE, RESPECTIVELY. */
       DECLARE Q(*) CHARACTER (*) VARYING,
               N FIXED,
               (F, R) FIXED,
               X CHARACTER (*) VARYING;

       /* RESET REAR POINTER, IF NECESSARY */
       IF R = N
       THEN R = 1;
       ELSE R = R + 1;
```

```
STMT LEVEL NEST BLOCK MLVL  SOURCE TEXT

  1                          SORT: PROCEDURE OPTIONS (MAIN);
                             /* THIS PROGRAM INPUTS SEVERAL UNSORTED TABLES AND SORTS THEM BY  */
                             /* CALLING THE RECURSIVE PROCEDURE QUICK.                         */

  2    1          1          DECLARE NUM FIXED,       /* NUMBER OF TABLES TO BE SORTED */
                                 (I, J) FIXED,    /* COUNTED LOOP VARIABLES */
                                 N FIXED,         /* NUMBER OF ELEMENTS IN TABLE */
                                 VECTOR(20) FLOAT;/*UNSORTED TABLE */

                             /* READ NUMBER OF TABLES TO BE SORTED */
  3    1          1          GET LIST (NUM);

                             /* PROCESS THE TABLES */
  4    1          1          DO I = 1 TO NUM;

                                 /* INPUT UNSORTED TABLE */
  5    1    1     1          GET LIST (N);
  6    1    1     1          PUT SKIP (3) LIST ('UNSORTED TABLE IS');
  7    1    1     1          PUT SKIP (2);
  8    1    1     1          DO J = 1 TO N;
  9    1    2     1              GET LIST (VECTOR(J));
 10    1    2     1              PUT EDIT (VECTOR(J)) (X(5), F(2));
 11    1    2     1          END;

                                 /* SORT VECTOR */
 12    1    1     1          J = 1;
 13    1    1     1          VECTOR(N + 1) = 9999;
 14    1    1     1          CALL QUICK (VECTOR, J, N);

                                 /* OUTPUT SORTED VECTOR */
 15    1    1     1          PUT SKIP (3) LIST ('SORTED TABLE IS');
 16    1    1     1          PUT SKIP (2);
 17    1    1     1          DO J = 1 TO N;
 18    1    2     1              PUT EDIT (VECTOR(J)) (X(5), F(2));
 19    1    2     1          END;
 20    1    1     1      END;
```

Fig. 10-7   Program for a partition-exchange sort

```
                    /* OVERFLOW CONDITION */
                    IF F = R THEN CALL Q_OVER;

                    /* INSERT NEW ELEMENT */
                    Q(R) = X;

                    /* IS F PROPERLY SET? */
                    IF F = 0 THEN F = 1;
                    RETURN;
                END CQINS;
```

The second conditional statement of the procedure checks for an overflow situation. If an overflow occurs, then the procedure Q_OVER is invoked. Although this procedure is application dependent, usually its invocation signifies that more storage for the queue is required and that the program must be re-run. Observe that the last conditional statement in the program checks for an insertion into an empty queue. In such an instance F is set to 1.

The following PL/I procedure, CQDEL, performs a deletion from a circular queue structure which is represented by a vector.

```
21    1       1               QUICK: PROCEDURE (K, LB, UB) RECURSIVE;
                                      /* GIVEN A TABLE K OF N RECORDS, THIS RECURSIVE PROCEDURE   */
                                      /* SORTS THE TABLE INTO ASCENDING ORDER BY THE PARTITION-   */
                                      /* EXCHANGE SORT.                                           */

22    2       2               DECLARE K(*) FLOAT,
                                      (LB, UB) FIXED,        /* LOWER AND UPPPER BOUNDS */
                                      FLAG BIT(1),           /* INDICATES PLACING RECORD IN */
                                                             /* ITS FINAL POSITION */
                                      (I, J) FIXED,          /* INDEX VARIABLES */
                                      KEY FLOAT,             /* KEY VALUE BEING PLACED IN */
                                                             /* FINAL POSITION */
                                      M FIXED,               /* TEMPORARY VARIABLE */
                                      TEMP FLOAT;            /* USED TO EXCHANGE RECORDS */

                               /* INITIALIZE */
23    2       2               FLAG = '1'B;

                               /* PERFORM SORT */
24    2       2               IF LB < UB
25    2       2               THEN DO;
26    2    1  2                       I = LB;
27    2    1  2                       J = UB + 1;
28    2    1  2                       KEY = K(LB);
29    2    1  2                       DO WHILE (FLAG);
30    2    2  2                           I = I + 1;

                                          /* SCAN THE KEYS FROM LEFT TO RIGHT */
31    2    2  2                           DO WHILE (K(I) < KEY);
32    2    3  2                               I = I + 1;
33    2    3  2                           END;
34    2    2  2                           J = J - 1;

                                          /* SCAN THE KEYS FROM RIGHT TO LEFT */
35    2    2  2                           DO WHILE (K(J) > KEY);
36    2    3  2                               J = J - 1;
37    2    3  2                           END;
38    2    2  2                           IF I < J
39    2    2  2                           THEN DO;  /* INTERCHANGE RECORDS */
40    2    3  2                                   TEMP = K(J);
41    2    3  2                                   K(J) = K(I);
42    2    3  2                                   K(I) = TEMP;
43    2    3  2                               END;
44    2    2  2                           ELSE FLAG = '0'B;
45    2    2  2                       END;

                               /* INTERCHANGE RECORDS */
46    2    1  2                       TEMP = K(LB);
47    2    1  2                       K(LB) = K(J);
48    2    1  2                       K(J) = TEMP;
49    2    1  2                       M = J - 1;
50    2    1  2                       CALL QUICK (K, LB, M);          /* SORT 1ST SUBTABLE */
51    2    1  2                       M = J + 1;
52    2    1  2                       CALL QUICK (K, M, UB);          /* SORT 2ND DUBTABLE */
53    2    1  2                   END;
54    2       2               END QUICK;
55    1       1           END SORT;
```

ERRORS/WARNINGS DETECTED DURING CODE GENERATION:

   WARNING: NO FILE SPECIFIED. SYSIN/SYSPRINT ASSUMED. (CGOC)

   UNSORTED TABLE IS

       73   65   52   24   83   17   35   96   41   9

   SORTED TABLE IS

        9   17   24   35   41   52   65   73   83   96

   IN STMT   55 PROGRAM RETURNS FROM MAIN PROCEDURE.

Fig. 10-7   Program for a partition-exchange sort (cont'd.)

```
CQDEL: PROCEDURE (Q, N, F, R, X);
        /* THIS PROCEDURE DELETES THE FRONT ELEMENT OF THE QUEUE AND */
        /* PLACES IT INTO THE ELEMENT X. F AND R DENOTE THE FRONT */
        /* AND REAR OF THE QUEUE, RESPECTIVELY. */
        DECLARE Q(*) CHARACTER (*) VARYING,
                N FIXED,
                (F, R) FIXED,
                X CHARACTER (*) VARYING;

        /* UNDERFLOW? */
        IF F = 0 THEN CALL Q_UNDER;

        /* DELETE FRONT ELEMENT */
        X = Q(F);

        /* IS QUEUE NOW EMPTY? */
        IF F = R
        THEN DO;
            F = 0;
            R = 0;
            RETURN;
            END;

        /* INCREMENT F */
        F = F + 1;
        IF F > N THEN F = 1;
        RETURN;
END CQDEL;
```

The first conditional statement in the program checks for an underflow situation. If an underflow occurs, then procedure Q_UNDER is invoked. Although this procedure is also application dependent, an attempt to delete from an empty queue may be valid. The second conditional statement checks for an empty queue after deletion. In such a case the front and rear pointers are set to zero. An alternate representation of a queue, which reflects its variable-size property, is given in Sec. 10-9. The next section examines the applications of queues to the area of simulation.

10-7 SIMULATION

In this section, we consider the design of a simulation model of the loading of jobs into main memory by a hypothetical operating system. This application of queues, as well as the nature of simulation, is discussed in Sec. 10-7 of the main text. Prior reading of that discussion is assumed in this section. Recall that a very straightforward scheme for memory allocation is used in this application. Three queues are required, the descriptions of which are provided below. Notice the new organization of these queues, which in turn necessitates new procedures for handling queues of this new type.

The first queue contains information about available memory space and is a *priority queue*; that is, the elements are arranged in *decreasing order* of memory

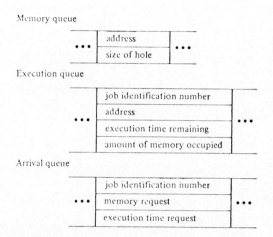

Fig. 10-8   The queues of the simulation model

hole size. The elements stored in the queue are the address and size of the memory holes.

Another priority queue is required to simulate execution of the jobs so that they leave the system in the proper order. This queue, however, is arranged in *increasing order* of execution time remaining. This is because the execution times of the jobs may vary, so they will not necessarily depart the system at the same relative time. Elements of the execution queue have four components; namely, a job identification number, the load address of this job in memory, the amount of execution time remaining, and the amount of memory occupied by this job. All execution times are assumed to be multiples of one minute to simplify job processing.

The final queue required is a straightforward first-in, first-out (FIFO) queue to represent the arrival of jobs to the system. Elements of this queue consist of three fields; a job identification number, a memory size request, and an execution time request. Again for simplicity, we assume a new job arrives every minute for 30 minutes. Figure 10-8 gives a summary of these queues.

Any computer simulation is the study of the behavior of some system over some time period. Our time simplifications ensure that no accuracy is lost in the state of the memory allocation system. This is because the passage of time is handled by updating the state of the system at regular one minute intervals, while changes occur only at time units which are multiples of one minute. If events in the system occurred irregularly, more elaborate mechanisms would be required to model the passage of time.

In specifying the current model, we use a simple naming convention to illustrate the multiple-component queue entries. Each component will actually be a separate vector, which enables us to use some of the procedures developed in Sec. 10-6 of the main text. The procedures used will be QINSERT and QDELETE, for rear insertion and front deletion, respectively, from a linear queue. These procedures operate on the same principles as CQINS and CQDEL in Sec. 10-6 of this text, except that CQINS and CQDEL are for circular queues.

Table 10-3 describes the vectors involved in each queue and their respective queue pointers. Note that the similarities in names indicate each respective queue. Assume that all queue values are integer.

Table 10-3   Queue naming conventions

Queue	Name of Vector	Queue Pointers	Component
Memory queue	MEM_Q_ADDR	MF1, MR1	Address of hole
	MEM_Q_SIZE	MF2, MR2	Size of hole
Execution queue	EXEC_Q_ID	EF1, ER1	Job identification number
	EXEC_Q_ADDR	EF2, ER2	Address of job (after loading)
	EXEC_Q_TIME	EF3, ER3	Remaining execution time
	EXEC_Q_SIZE	EF4, ER4	Memory occupied by job
Arrival queue	ARR_Q_ID	AF1, AR1	Job identification number
	ARR_Q_MEM	AF2, AR2	Memory request
	ARR_Q_TIME	AF3, AR3	Execution time request

The model clearly requires mechanisms for insertion and deletion analogous to those given in Sec. 10-6 of the main text, but for priority queues. The deletion is accomplished simply by procedure QDELETE, since we will delete from the front of the queue in all cases. Insertion is more complicated, however. Because of the priority considerations, a new element may be inserted somewhere in the middle of the queue instead of strictly at the rear, as in procedure QINSERT. Also, different orderings may be imposed on a priority queue; the queue elements may be in either descending or ascending order. Procedure QFILE accomplishes the insertion task on a single vector for both orderings by shifting the other elements, if necessary, and inserting the new element in its appropriate position.

Procedure QFILE accommodates only those queues that are represented by a single vector. However, because the position of the inserted element is returned through parameter P, the procedure can easily be used for queues with multiple components, where one of these components is the ordering key. This multiple-component insertion is accomplished as follows. First, procedure QFILE is used to insert into the ordering criterion vector; then the returned value of P is used to place the remaining components in parallel positions in their respective vectors by calling procedure QPLACE for each remaining component vector. This latter procedure simply shifts elements in the vector as required and then inserts the new element in the newly freed position P.

We are now ready to give the complete simulation model. Assume a memory of 10,000 words, which is initially one big hole. Therefore, the memory queue has one initial entry with address 0000 (assuming four-digit addresses) and size 10,000. As previously stated, we assume the simulation is to run for 30 minutes, with a new job arriving each minute, and that the characteristics of each job (memory and time requests) are read from the input stream at the time of its arrival. In the simulation, the time of arrival is used as the job identification number, and we will count the number of jobs completed.

A general algorithm to perform the simulation follows:

1. Initialize the completions counter, all queue pointers, and all queues to zero.
2. Insert the full memory size available (10,000) and the initial load address (0000) into the memory queue.
3. Repeat thru step 7 for 30 minutes by steps of one minute.
4. Input and print a memory size request and a corresponding execution time request.
5. Insert the new request at the rear of the arrivals queue.
6. If the largest available memory size is sufficient to handle
   the next memory request of the FIFO arrivals queue,
   then remove the first job from the arrivals queue, adjust the
       memory hole accordingly, file the new hole in the memory
       queue and put the job in the execution queue.
7. Take one minute off the remaining time for each job in the execution queue (*parallel processing*), and if a job is finished, increment the completions counter, delete the job from the execution queue and return the newly completed job's memory to the memory queue.
8. Print out the number of completions and exit.

The program MEM_SIM given in Fig. 10-9 performs this simulation. The variables used in this program are:

Main program MEM_SIM (excluding queues and pointers)

Variable	Type	Usage
MEM_REQUEST	FIXED	Requested size of the memory hole
TIME_REQUEST	FIXED	Execution time requested corresponding to the memory requested in MEM_REQUEST
COMPLETIONS	FIXED	Number of jobs completely executed
MINUTE	FIXED	Present time in the simulation
HOLE_SIZE	FIXED	Largest available memory size
ADDR	FIXED	Address of memory hole examined
ID	FIXED	Identification number of job examined
MEM	FIXED	Memory size request of job examined
TIME	FIXED	Execution time request of job examined
P, J	FIXED	Temporary counter variables

All the queues are declared as integer vectors, each containing 100 elements. All queue pointers are also FIXED.

The variables used in the procedure QINSERT are:

Q(*)	FIXED	Vector from queue for rear insertion

F	FIXED	Front pointer of Q
R	FIXED	Rear pointer of Q
X	FIXED	Element to insert at the rear of Q

The variables used in the procedure QDELETE are:

Q(*)	FIXED	Vector from queue for front deletion
F	FIXED	Front pointer of Q
R	FIXED	Rear pointer of Q
X	FIXED	Contains deleted element

The variables used in the procedure QFILE are:

Q(*)	FIXED	Vector from the priority queue for insertion
F	FIXED	Front pointer of Q
R	FIXED	Rear pointer of Q
X	FIXED	Element to insert
P	FIXED	Position of insertion of X
D	FIXED	Direction indicator of Q ordering (ascending or descending)
L	FIXED	Temporary counter variable

The variables used in the procedure QPLACE are:

Q(*)	FIXED	Vector from the priority queue for insertion
F	FIXED	Front pointer of Q
R	FIXED	Rear pointer of Q
X	FIXED	Element to insert
P	FIXED	Position of insertion of X
L	FIXED	Temporary counter variable

A statement of purpose for each of the procedures is as follows:

QINSERT	inserts an element at the rear of a queue (vector).
QDELETE	deletes an element from the front of a queue (vector).
QFILE	inserts an element into a priority queue (vector). The queue is maintained in either descending or ascending order, depending on a parameter value.
QPLACE	inserts into a priority queue (vector) an element corresponding to that used in QFILE above. The same ordering is used for corresponding calls of QFILE and QPLACE.
Q_OVERF	prints an error message and halts the program if a queue (vector) overflow occurs.
Q_UNDER	prints an error message and halts the program if a queue (vector) underflow occurs.

The 30 data values used are:

Memory Request	Time request
500	1
300	4
9200	2
600	4
400	10
500	4
300	5
350	6
400	1
1000	4
200	6
600	2
800	5
300	2
100	5
300	2
400	2
800	5
400	6
253	2
632	2
250	5
321	1
342	2
325	2
123	3
325	8
522	3
3422	10
322	3

The program works as follows. First, the count of completed jobs and all 18 queue pointers are initialized. Then the execution and arrivals queues are initialized, followed by the initialization of the memory queue to contain the entire memory as one hole with address 0000. Note the use of the two procedures QFILE and QPLACE, communicating through a common value of P, to insert the two components of the memory queue entry.

The timing loop for the simulation is engaged in statement 15; the loop is to run for 30 minutes in steps of one minute each, and it contains statements 16 through 56.

In statements 16 through 20, each new job arrives and is inserted into the FIFO arrivals queue. The time of arrival provides a unique identification for the job. Statements 21 through 41 embody the memory management strategy. If the first element in the ascending memory queue is sufficiently large to handle the first job in the arrivals queue, then that memory hole is allocated to the job and the hole's size is adjusted accordingly. The loaded job is then removed from the arrivals queue and inserted into the execution queue.

Statements 42 through 55 simulate the execution of the jobs in the execution queue by parallel processing. One minute is subtracted from the time

```
STMT LEVEL NEST BLOCK MLVL  SOURCE TEXT


  1                                  MEM_SIM:  PROCEDURE OPTIONS (MAIN);


                                     /* THIS PROGRAM IS A SIMULATION MODEL OF MEMORY MANAGEMENT IN A   */
                                     /* HYPOTHETICAL COMPUTER SYSTEM.  QUEUES ARE USED TO CONTROL      */
                                     /* AVAILABILITY OF MEMORY, JOB EXECUTION AND JOB ARRIVALS.        */
                                     /* PROCEDURES QINSERT, QDELETE, QFILE AND QPLACE ARE USED FOR     */
                                     /* QUEUE MANIPULATION.  ASSUME A MEMORY OF 10,000 WORDS, SO THAT  */
                                     /* THE MEMORY QUEUE HAS ONE ENTRY WITH ADDRESS 0000 (FOUR DIGIT   */
                                     /* ADDRESSES) AND SIZE 10,000.  THE OTHER TWO QUEUES ARE EMPTY    */
                                     /* INITIALLY.  ASSUME THE SIMULATION IS TO BE FOR 30 MINUTES,     */
                                     /* WITH A NEW JOB ARRIVING EVERY MINUTE.  TIME OF ARRIVAL IS USED */
                                     /* AS THE JOB IDENTIFICATION NUMBER.  EACH JOB'S CHARACTERISTICS  */
                                     /* ARE READ FROM THE INPUT STREAM AT THE TIME OF ARRIVAL.         */


  2    1        1                    DECLARE (MEM_Q_ADDR,                     /* ADDRESS OF HOLE QUEUE  */
                                             MEM_Q_SIZE) (100) FIXED,        /* SIZE OF MEMORY HOLE Q  */
                                             (EXEC_Q_ID,                     /* EXEC. JOB I.D. NUMBER Q*/
                                             EXEC_Q_ADDR,                    /* LOADED JOB'S ADDRESS Q */
                                             EXEC_Q_TIME,                    /* REMAINING EXEC. TIME Q */
                                             EXEC_Q_SIZE) (100) FIXED,       /* JOB'S MEMORY SIZE Q    */
                                             (ARR_Q_ID,                      /* ARRIVAL JOB I.D. # Q   */
                                             ARR_Q_MEM,                      /* ARRIVAL MEM. REQUEST Q */
                                             ARR_Q_TIME) (100) FIXED,        /* ARRIVAL EXEC. TIME Q   */
                                             MEM_REQUEST FIXED,              /* INPUT MEMORY SIZE AND  */
                                             TIME_REQUEST FIXED,             /* EXEC. TIME REQUESTS    */
                                             COMPLETIONS FIXED,              /* NUMBER JOBS COMPLETED  */
                                             MINUTE FIXED,                   /* TIMING LOOP CONTROLLER */
                                             HOLE_SIZE FIXED,                /* LARGEST MEM. HOLE SIZE */
                                             (MF1, MR1, MF2, MR2) FIXED,     /* MEMORY QUEUE POINTERS  */
                                             (EF1, ER1, EF2, ER2,            /* FRONT AND REAR POINTERS*/
                                             EF3, ER3, EF4, ER4) FIXED,      /* FOR EXECUTION QUEUE    */
                                             (AF1, AR1, AF2, AR2,            /* FRONT AND REAR POINTERS*/
                                             AF3, AR3) FIXED,                /* FOR ARRIVALS QUEUE     */
                                             ADDR FIXED,                     /* ADDRESS OF MEMORY HOLE */
                                             ID FIXED,                       /* ARRIVALS Q FIRST JOB ID*/
                                             MEM FIXED,                      /* ARRIVALS Q FIRST JOB   */
                                                                             /* MEMORY SIZE REQUEST    */
                                             TIME FIXED,                     /* ARRIVALS Q FIRST JOB   */
                                                                             /* EXECUTION TIME REQUEST */
                                             (P, J) FIXED;                   /* POSITION IN QUEUE AND  */
                                                                             /* TEMPORARY VARIABLES    */


                                     /* INITIALIZE COUNTER, ALL QUEUE POINTERS AND ALL QUEUES */
  3    1        1                    COMPLETIONS = 0;
  4    1        1                    MF1, MR1, EF1, ER1, AF1, AR1 = 0;
  5    1        1                    MF2, MR2, EF2, ER2, AF2, AR2 =0;
  6    1        1                    EF3, ER3, AF3, AR3 = 0;
  7    1        1                    EF4, ER4 = 0;
  8    1        1                    MEM_Q_ADDR, MEM_Q_SIZE = 0;
  9    1        1                    EXEC_Q_ID, EXEC_Q_ADDR, EXEC_Q_TIME, EXEC_Q_SIZE = 0;
 10    1        1                    ARR_Q_ID, ARR_Q_MEM, ARR_Q_TIME = 0;

 11    1        1                    CALL QFILE (MEM_Q_SIZE, MF2, MR2, 10000, P, -1);
 12    1        1                    CALL QPLACE (MEM_Q_ADDR, MF1, MR1, 00000, P);

                                     /* PRINT A HEADING FOR OUTPUT */
 13    1        1                    PUT SKIP EDIT ('MEMORY REQUEST', 'TIME REQUEST') (A, COL(25), A);
 14    1        1                    PUT SKIP;
```

Fig. 10-9 Program MEM_SIM: simulation of memory allocation

remaining for each job to account for their execution during the period since the last update. (Note that execution of the jobs in parallel may not be physically possible on many systems, but it is a useful simplification for our purposes.) Any job completions are counted, and the memory occupied is once again made available by insertion into the memory queue.

```
                              /* ENGAGE TIMING LOOP */
15    1        1              DO MINUTE = 1 TO 30 BY 1;

                                  /* READ INFORMATION FOR NEXT ARRIVAL AND FILE IN ARRIVALS  */
                                  /*       QUEUE                                             */
16    1    1   1                  GET LIST (MEM_REQUEST, TIME_REQUEST);

                                  /* OUTPUT THE PRESENT REQUESTS */
17    1    1   1                  PUT SKIP EDIT (MEM_REQUEST, TIME_REQUEST)
                                     ( COL(4), F(5), COL(27), F(5) );

18    1    1   1                  CALL QINSERT (ARR_Q_ID, AF1, AR1, MINUTE);    /* FIFO QUEUE */
19    1    1   1                  CALL QINSERT (ARR_Q_MEM, AF2, AR2, MEM_REQUEST);
20    1    1   1                  CALL QINSERT (ARR_Q_TIME, AF3, AR3, TIME_REQUEST);

                                  /* IS ENOUGH MEMORY AVAILABLE TO SATISFY FIRST JOB IN      */
                                  /*       ARRIVALS QUEUE?                                   */
21    1    1   1                  CALL QDELETE (MEM_Q_SIZE, MF2, MR2, HOLE_SIZE);  /* LARGEST */
                                                                                   /* HOLE  */
22    1    1   1                  CALL QDELETE (MEM_Q_ADDR, MF1, MR1, ADDR);
23    1    1   1                  MEM_REQUEST = ARR_Q_MEM (AF2);

24    1    1   1                  IF HOLE_SIZE >= MEM_REQUEST
25    1    1   1                  THEN DO;   /* REMOVE FIRST JOB FROM ARRIVALS QUEUE */

26    1    2   1                          CALL QDELETE (ARR_Q_ID, AF1, AR1, ID);
27    1    2   1                          CALL QDELETE (ARR_Q_MEM, AF2, AR2, MEM);
28    1    2   1                          CALL QDELETE (ARR_Q_TIME, AF3, AR3, TIME);

                                          /* ADJUST HOLE ACCORDINGLY */
29    1    2   1                          HOLE_SIZE = HOLE_SIZE - MEM;
30    1    2   1                          ADDR = ADDR + MEM;

                                          /* FILE NEW HOLE IN MEMORY QUEUE AND JOB IN        */
                                          /*       EXECUTION QUEUE                           */
31    1    2   1                          CALL QFILE  (MEM_Q_SIZE, MF2, MR2, HOLE_SIZE, P, -1);
32    1    2   1                          CALL QPLACE (MEM_Q_ADDR, MF1, MR1, ADDR, P);
33    1    2   1                          CALL QFILE  (EXEC_Q_TIME, EF3, ER3, TIME, P, +1);
34    1    2   1                          CALL QPLACE (EXEC_Q_ID, EF1, ER1, ID, P);
35    1    2   1                          CALL QPLACE (EXEC_Q_ADDR, EF2, ER2, ADDR - MEM, P);
36    1    2   1                          CALL QPLACE (EXEC_Q_SIZE, EF4, ER4, MEM, P);
37    1    2   1                  END;
38    1    1   1                  ELSE DO;   /* REINSERT FREE BLOCK */
39    1    2   1                          CALL QFILE  (MEM_Q_SIZE, MF2, MR2, HOLE_SIZE, P, -1);
40    1    2   1                          CALL QPLACE (MEM_Q_ADDR, MF1, MR1, ADDR, P);
41    1    2   1                  END;


                                  /* TAKE 1 MINUTE OFF TIME REMAINING FOR EACH EXECUTING JOB  */
                                  /*       AND PROCESS ANY COMPLETIONS                        */
42    1    1   1                  DO J = EF3 TO ER3 BY 1 WHILE (EF3 ¬= 0);
43    1    2   1                          EXEC_Q_TIME (J) = EXEC_Q_TIME (J) - 1;       /* ASSUME */
                                                                                  /* PARALLEL PROCESSING */

44    1    2   1                          IF EXEC_Q_TIME (J) = 0
45    1    2   1                          THEN DO;
46    1    3   1                                  COMPLETIONS = COMPLETIONS + 1;
                                                  /* DELETE THIS JOB FROM EXEC QUEUE */
47    1    3   1                                  CALL QDELETE (EXEC_Q_ID,   EF1, ER1, ID);
48    1    3   1                                  CALL QDELETE (EXEC_Q_ADDR, EF2, ER2, ADDR);
49    1    3   1                                  CALL QDELETE (EXEC_Q_TIME, EF3, ER3, TIME);
50    1    3   1                                  CALL QDELETE (EXEC_Q_SIZE, EF4, ER4, MEM);
51    1    3   1                                  PUT SKIP(2) EDIT ('JOB ', ID, ' IS COMPLETED ',
                                                      'AT TIME ', MINUTE) (A, F(2), A, A, F(2));
52    1    3   1                                  PUT SKIP;

                                                  /* RETURN NEWLY COMPLETED JOB'S MEMORY TO     */
                                                  /*       MEMORY QUEUE                         */
53    1    3   1                                  CALL QFILE  (MEM_Q_SIZE, MF2, MR2, MEM, P, -1);
54    1    3   1                                  CALL QPLACE (MEM_Q_ADDR, MF1, MR1, ADDR, P);
55    1    3   1                                  END;
56    1    2   1                  END;    /* OF PARALLEL PROCESSING */
57    1    1   1              END;    /* OF TIMING LOOP */
```

Fig. 10-9   Program MEM_SIM: simulation of memory allocation (cont'd.)

```
                                        /* END OF SIMULATION */
58    1         1      PUT SKIP(3) EDIT ('NUMBER OF JOBS PROCESSED: ', COMPLETIONS)
                                   (COL(5), A, F(3) );
                                        /* FINISHED */
59    1         1      END MEM_SIM;
60                 QINSERT:  PROCEDURE (Q, F, R, X);
                                   /* GIVEN VECTOR Q AND FRONT AND REAR POINTERS F AND R, THIS      */
                                   /* PROCEDURE INSERTS X AT THE REAR OF THE QUEUE.  AN EMPTY QUEUE */
                                   /* IS SIGNALLED BY F AND R BOTH HAVING A VALUE OF ZERO.          */

61    1         2      DECLARE Q (*) FIXED,                /* QUEUE FOR INSERTION  */
                              F FIXED,                     /* FRONT POINTER OF Q   */
                              R FIXED,                     /* REAR POINTER OF Q    */
                              X FIXED;                     /* ELEMENT FOR INSERTION */


                                        /* OVERFLOW CONDITION? */
62    1         2      IF R >= 100
63    1         2      THEN CALL Q_OVERF;

                                        /* INCREMENT REAR POINTER */
64    1         2      R = R + 1;

                                        /* INSERT NEW ELEMENT */
65    1         2      Q (R) = X;

                                        /* IS THE FRONT POINTER PROPERLY SET? */
66    1         2      IF F = 0
67    1         2      THEN F = 1;

                                        /* FINISHED */
68    1         2      RETURN;

69    1         2      END QINSERT;
70                 QDELETE:  PROCEDURE (Q, F, R, X);
                                   /* GIVEN VECTOR Q AND FRONT AND REAR POINTERS F AND R, THIS       */
                                   /* PROCEDURE DELETES THE FRONT ELEMENT FROM THE QUEUE AND PLACES  */
                                   /* THAT ELEMENT INTO X.  AN EMPTY QUEUE IS SIGNALLED BY F AND R   */
                                   /* BOTH HAVING A VALUE OF ZERO.                                   */

71    1         3      DECLARE Q (*) FIXED,                /* QUEUE FOR DELETION   */
                              F FIXED,                     /* FRONT POINTER OF Q   */
                              R FIXED,                     /* REAR POINTER OF Q    */
                              X FIXED;                     /* HOLDS DELETED ELEMENT */


                                        /* UNDERFLOW CONDITION? */
72    1         3      IF F = 0
73    1         3      THEN CALL Q_UNDER;

                                        /* DELETE FRONT ELEMENT */
74    1         3      X = Q (F);

                                        /* IS QUEUE NOW EMPTY? */
75    1         3      IF F = R
76    1         3      THEN DO;
77    1    1    3          F = 0;
78    1    1    3          R = 0;
79    1    1    3          RETURN;
80    1    1    3          END;

                                        /* INCREMENT FRONT POINTER AND RETURN */
81    1         3      F = F + 1;
82    1         3      RETURN;

83    1         3      END QDELETE;
```

Fig. 10-9   Program MEM_SIM: simulation of memory allocation (cont'd.)

```
84                       QFILE:  PROCEDURE (Q, F, R, X, P, D);
                         /* GIVEN A VECTOR Q AND FRONT AND REAR POINTERS F AND R, THIS    */
                         /* PROCEDURE INSERTS X IN THE APPROPRIATE PLACE IN THE PRIORITY  */
                         /* QUEUE REPRESENTED BY Q.  P POINTS TO THE PLACE AT WHICH X IS  */
                         /* INSERTED.  D IS AN INTEGER PARAMETER SPECIFYING THE ORDERING  */
                         /* DIRECTION FOR THE QUEUE.  IF D > 0, THE QUEUE IS ASSUMED TO BE */
                         /* IN ASCENDING ORDER FROM FRONT TO REAR; IF D < 0, THE QUEUE IS */
                         /* ASSUMED TO BE IN DECREASING ORDER.                            */
                         /* AN EMPTY QUEUE IS SIGNALLED BY F AND R BOTH HAVING A VALUE OF */
                         /* ZERO.                                                         */

85      1      4         DECLARE Q (*) FIXED,              /* THE PRIORITY QUEUE     */
                                 F FIXED,                  /* FRONT POINTER FOR Q    */
                                 R FIXED,                  /* REAR POINTER FOR Q     */
                                 X FIXED,                  /* ELEMENT FOR INSERTION  */
                                 P FIXED,                  /* POSITION OF INSERTION  */
                                 D FIXED,                  /* DIRECTION OF Q ORDERING*/
                                 L FIXED;                  /* TEMPORARY COUNTER      */


                         /* OVERFLOW CONDITION? */
86      1      4         IF R >= 100
87      1      4         THEN CALL Q_OVERF;

                         /* INCREMENT REAR POINTER TO ACCOMODATE INSERTION OF NEW ELEMENT */
88      1      4         R = R + 1;

                         /* FIND APPROPRIATE POSITION FOR NEW ELEMENT */
89      1      4         IF F = 0
90      1      4             THEN P = 1;
91      1      4             ELSE P = F;

                         /* IN WHICH DIRECTION IS THE QUEUE TO BE ORDERED? */
92      1      4         IF D > 0                /* ASCENDING ORDER */
93      1      4         THEN DO WHILE ( X > Q (P)  &  P < R );
94      1   1  4             P = P + 1;
95      1   1  4             END;
96      1      4         ELSE DO WHILE ( X < Q (P)  &  P < R );
97      1   1  4             P = P + 1;
98      1   1  4             END;

                         /* SHIFT REMAINING ELEMENTS ONE POSITION */
99      1      4         DO L = R TO P+1 BY -1;
100     1   1  4             Q (L) = Q (L-1);
101     1   1  4         END;

                         /* INSERT NEW ELEMENT */
102     1      4         Q (P) = X;

                         /* IS FRONT POINTER PROPERLY SET? */
103     1      4         IF F = 0
104     1      4         THEN F = 1;

                         /* FINISHED */
105     1      4         RETURN;

106     1      4         END QFILE;
```

Fig. 10-9 Program MEM_SIM: simulation of memory allocation (cont'd.)

When 30 minutes have elapsed, control passes to statement 58, and the final result is printed.

Several points should be noted about the given program. First, the simulation is run for only 30 minutes, so one would expect a maximum queue size of 30. However, the queues are all declared to be size 100. This is due to the nature of the memory queue. The execution and arrivals queues will have a maximum of 30 entries, because a job is entered only once into each of those queues. However, memory holes are constantly deleted, split up and re-inserted, which forces the

```
107                        QPLACE:  PROCEDURE (Q, F, R, X, P);
                           /* GIVEN A VECTOR Q AND FRONT AND REAR POINTERS F AND R, THIS     */
                           /* PROCEDURE INSERTS X AT POSITION P IN THE PRIORITY QUEUE        */
                           /* REPRESENTED BY Q.  THE QUEUE IS ASSUMED TO BE IN ASCENDING     */
                           /* ORDER FROM FRONT TO REAR.  AN EMPTY QUEUE IS SIGNALLED BY F    */
                           /* AND R BOTH HAVING A VALUE OF ZERO.                             */

108    1        5          DECLARE Q (*) FIXED,                      /* THE PRIORITY QUEUE   */
                                   F FIXED,                          /* FRONT POINTER FOR Q  */
                                   R FIXED,                          /* REAR POINTER FOR Q   */
                                   X FIXED,                          /* ELEMENT FOR INSERTION */
                                   P FIXED,                          /* POSITION FOR INSERTION */
                                   L FIXED;                          /* TEMPORARY COUNTER    */


                           /* OVERFLOW CONDITION? */
109    1        5          IF R >= 100
110    1        5          THEN CALL Q_OVERF;

                           /* ADJUST ELEMENT POSITIONS ACCORDINGLY */
111    1        5          R = R + 1;
112    1        5          DO L = R TO P+1 BY -1;
113    1    1   5              Q (L) = Q (L-1);
114    1    1   5          END;

                           /* INSERT NEW ELEMENT AT POSITION P */
115    1        5          Q (P) = X;

                           /* IS FRONT POINTER PROPERLY SET? */
116    1        5          IF F = 0
117    1        5          THEN F = 1;

                           /* FINISHED */
118    1        5          RETURN;

119    1        5          END QPLACE;
120                        Q_OVERF:  PROCEDURE;
                           /* Q_OVERF IS INVOKED IF THE QUEUE IN QUESTION DURING AN          */
                           /* INSERTION IS FULL                                             */

121    1        6          PUT SKIP(2) EDIT ('*** AN ERROR OCCURS DURING INSERTION INTO THE ',
                                            'QUEUE.') (A,A);
122    1        6          PUT SKIP EDIT ('THE VECTOR IS FULL PRIOR TO INSERTION.') (COL(7),A);
123    1        6          STOP;

124    1        6          END Q_OVERF;
125                        Q_UNDER:  PROCEDURE;
                           /* Q_UNDER IS INVOKED IF THE QUEUE IN QUESTION DURING A DELETION  */
                           /* IS EMPTY.                                                      */

126    1        7          PUT SKIP(2) EDIT ('*** AN ERROR OCCURS DURING DELETION FROM THE ',
                                            'QUEUE.') (A,A);
127    1        7          PUT SKIP EDIT ('THE VECTOR IS EMPTY PRIOR TO DELETION.') (COL(7),A);
128    1        7          STOP;

129    1        7          END Q_UNDER;
```

Fig. 10-9 Program MEM_SIM: simulation of memory allocation (cont'd.)

memory queue pointers farther down the queue. Thus, with 30 jobs being considered, *at least 30 different* memory holes will be inserted into the memory queue. The size of the memory queue is somewhat dependent upon the data used, so a queue large enough to handle all kinds of data is used (i.e., size 100).

Second, procedures Q_OVERF and Q_UNDER are purely application-dependent. That is, one may wish to perform many different actions upon queue overflow or underflow, depending on the course of action specified in the application. We are required only to print out an error message and stop the program.

MEMORY REQUEST	TIME REQUEST
500	1

JOB 1 IS COMPLETED AT TIME 1

300	4
9200	2
600	4

JOB 3 IS COMPLETED AT TIME 4

| 400 | 10 |

JOB 2 IS COMPLETED AT TIME 5

500	4
300	5
350	6

JOB 4 IS COMPLETED AT TIME 8

| 400 | 1 |
| 1000 | 4 |

JOB 9 IS COMPLETED AT TIME 10

JOB 6 IS COMPLETED AT TIME 10

| 200 | 6 |
| 600 | 2 |

JOB 7 IS COMPLETED AT TIME 12

| 800 | 5 |
| 300 | 2 |

JOB 12 IS COMPLETED AT TIME 14

JOB 10 IS COMPLETED AT TIME 14

JOB 8 IS COMPLETED AT TIME 14

| 100 | 5 |

JOB 5 IS COMPLETED AT TIME 15

| 300 | 2 |

JOB 14 IS COMPLETED AT TIME 16

| 400 | 2 |

JOB 11 IS COMPLETED AT TIME 17

| 800 | 5 |

JOB 16 IS COMPLETED AT TIME 18

JOB 13 IS COMPLETED AT TIME 18

| 400 | 6 |

JOB 17 IS COMPLETED AT TIME 19

| 253 | 2 |

JOB 15 IS COMPLETED AT TIME 20

| 632 | 2 |
| 250 | 5 |

JOB 20 IS COMPLETED AT TIME 22

| 321 | 1 |

JOB 21 IS COMPLETED AT TIME 23

JOB 18 IS COMPLETED AT TIME 23

| 342 | 2 |

JOB 23 IS COMPLETED AT TIME 24

| 325 | 2 |

JOB 19 IS COMPLETED AT TIME 25

| 123 | 3 |

JOB 24 IS COMPLETED AT TIME 26

| 325 | 8 |

JOB 25 IS COMPLETED AT TIME 27

JOB 22 IS COMPLETED AT TIME 27

| 522 | 3 |
| 3422 | 10 |

JOB 26 IS COMPLETED AT TIME 29

| 322 | 3 |

NUMBER OF JOBS PROCESSED: 26

Fig. 10-9   Program MEM_SIM: simulation of memory allocation (cont'd.)

Third, in statement 42 of the main program MEM_SIM, an interesting iterative statement is used:

DO J = EF3 TO ER3 BY 1 WHILE (EF3 ⌐= 0);

The internal evaluation of this instruction proceeds as follows. First, J is assigned the value EF3. Then, if any of the following conditions fail, we exit from the loop:

(i) (J ⩽ ER3 with a positive increment)
(ii) (J ⩾ ER3 with a negative increment)
(iii) (EF3 ⌐= 0)

Otherwise, the statements in the loop are performed, J is updated to J + 1, and the above three conditions are again tested.

Condition (i) implies that the "do" increment is positive while the object value is less than the start value. In such a case, no iterations of the loop should be performed. For example, consider

DO J = 10 TO 5 BY 1 WHILE (EF3 ⌐= 0);

Condition (ii) corresponds to a negative increment with an object value greater than the start value; again, no iterations should be done. An example of this condition is

DO J = 5 TO 10 BY –1 WHILE (EF3 ⌐= 0);

The third case implies that the "while" condition test fails; this should cause an exit from the loop. If none of these three conditions are true, the loop is iterated.

In this section, we have attempted to convey the flavor of computer simulation. It is a very broad subject, one that can be studied in considerable depth, and we have clearly only scratched the surface. Armed with this brief introduction, though, you should be prepared for a more complete treatment of the subject should the need arise. We have also introduced in this section the important concept of priority queues, along with procedures for manipulating them. Priority queues are very common in simulation applications, but they have many important applications beyond the realm of simulation as well.

Exercise for Sec. 10-7

1. A grocery store firm is considering the addition of a new service counter in one of its stores. Currently, the store has three checkouts, but the customer volume has increased to the point where a new counter is warranted. To determine whether the new counter should be a regular counter or an express counter (i.e., eight items or less), a simulation of customer flow through the checkout area is required.

    Our initial simulation is of a checkout area consisting of one express counter and three regular checkouts. All customers with eight or fewer items are assumed to proceed to the express counter. Customers with more than eight items go to the standard checkout with the shortest waiting line.

    Customers enter the checkout area randomly, with the time of next-arrival determined by adding to the present time a random number chosen from the range [0, 360] seconds. (0 is interpreted as the simultaneous arrival of two customers.) The number of items bought by each customer can also be approximated by selecting a random number in the range [1, 40]. The time taken for a customer to proceed through a checkout once the cashier begins "ringing up" his or her groceries can be calculated by assuming an average rate of 30 seconds per item (ringing plus wrapping time).

    In PL/C the built-in function RAND(X) generates a random number. X should be of type FLOAT and must have a value in the range

$$0 < X < 1$$

The initial value of X should contain nine significant digits and be odd. This function is invoked as follows:

    X = RAND(X);

Transformations are required to obtain random numbers from ranges other than (0, 1). For example, a random number in the range of [0, 360] is obtained by performing the multiplication 360 * X. A similar approach can be used to obtain a number in the range [1, 40]. The function RAND is not available in standard PL/I.

In setting up the simulation we should realize that prior to bringing a new customer into the checkout area, we must ensure that all customers who have had their groceries processed are removed from the waiting lines. Assume that no more than 10 customers are waiting in line at any one time for a regular checkout, and no more than 15 are waiting in line at any one time for an express checkout.

You are to formulate a program which simulates the checkout service just described. The desired output should contain the number of customers going through the checkout per hour, the total number of customers handled per hour, the average waiting time at each checkout, the overall average waiting time in minutes, the number of items processed at each checkout per hour, and the total number of items processed per hour. The waiting time is the time the customer spends in the checkout area.

Output having the following format is desirable:

	1	2	3	Express	Total
No. customers/hr	10	11	14	20	55
Avg. waiting time	2.80	3.01	2.96	0.22	1.94
Items processed/hr	192	261	210	65	728

Simulate the situation in which there are four standard checkouts, using the same method of generating arrival times and number of items purchased. Your program should be designed so that the second simulation can be performed with very few changes to the original program.

10-8 LINKED LINEAR LISTS

Thus far, we have used the sequential allocation method to represent data structures in the computer's memory. Using this method of allocation, the address or location of an element in memory is obtained through direct computation.

An alternate storage-allocation approach is to use pointers or links (see Sec. 10-1) to refer to elements of a linear list. Recall from Sec. 10-8 of the main text that the approach is to store the address of the successor of a particular element in that element. This method of allocating storage is called *linked allocation*. In this section we examine the programming aspects of using linked lists in PL/I. Such programming details cover the creation and manipulation of linked linear lists. These programming constructs, however, are not available in PL/C.

As an aid in introducing certain programming details related to linked allocation, let us consider a simple student registration application at a university. The information associated with each student can be represented by a record. Associated with each record is a set of properties such as student number, student name, and year of study. For a particular student, each property has a certain value. For example, a certain student might have a name of 'LYLE OPSETH', a student number of 75250 and a year of study of 1979. Conceptually, all the properties or fields in a record belong together, thus reflecting their relationship to one another. The structures discussed in Sec. 10-2 can be used to represent such a relationship.

In PL/I, each programmer can create a *template* for a record structure by declaring a structure to be of the BASED storage class. This facility permits the programmer to specify what fields are to be grouped together and in what order. This declaration also gives a name to the grouping or record.

For example, the statement

```
DECLARE 1 STUDENT BASED (P),
          2 NAME CHARACTER (20),
          2 NUMBER FIXED DECIMAL,
          2 YEAR FIXED DECIMAL;
```

declares a record structure, with the name STUDENT which consists of the fields NUMBER, NAME, and YEAR. Such a declaration results in the definition of the node or record structure only. It does not allocate storage for the fields named. The declaration simply indicates the makeup of the record structure. The creation of actual records is controlled by using subsequent ALLOCATE (see Sec. 10-4) statements elsewhere in the program. Specifically a record is created by the programmer in the following way:

```
ALLOCATE STUDENT;
```

This statement allocates storage space for the three fields — NUMBER, NAME, and YEAR. Since many instances of the BASED structure can be created in this way, a field name such as NAME is not enough for unambiguously specifying the name field. We must be able to reference, by the use of an address or pointer, a certain field within a particular record. This reference designator is a pointer variable which has as its value the address of the record in question. The variable P, following BASED, in the declaration for STUDENT is implicitly defined as a pointer variable. P automatically receives the address of the most recently created record. The referencing of a particular record of a BASED structure or of a field within this record is accomplished by using pointer qualification. For example, P -> STUDENT denotes the record generated by the last ALLOCATE statement. The fields are referenced as P -> NAME, P -> NUMBER, and P -> YEAR. (The imitation arrow is a minus sign followed immediately by a greater than sign.) The PL/I notation corresponds to the algorithmic notation STUDENT(P), NAME(P), NUMBER(P), and YEAR(P) of the main text.

The sequence of assignment statements

```
P -> NAME = 'LYLE OPSETH';
P -> NUMBER = 75250;
P -> YEAR = 1979;
```

initializes NAME, NUMBER, and YEAR of the created record to values of 'LYLE OPSETH', 75250, and 1979, respectively.

It is important to differentiate here between BASED storage and CONTROLLED storage. All elements or structures in BASED storage are accessible. However, only the last created element in CONTROLLED storage is accessible. This is an important distinction. The programmer, when using BASED storage, must ensure that the address of each created element be saved in a pointer variable.

Having created a record as in the previous ALLOCATE statement and placed its address (implicitly) into a pointer variable, the programmer is now in a position to use or change the values of the fields in the record. The following simple PL/I program, which creates a record, assigns values to the three fields NAME, NUMBER, and YEAR, and outputs the results, illustrates this:

```
SAMPLE: PROCEDURE OPTIONS (MAIN);
/* PROGRAM TO CREATE AND OUTPUT A RECORD */
        DECLARE 1 STUDENT BASED (P),
                  2 NAME CHARACTER (20),
                  2 NUMBER FIXED DECIMAL,
                  2 YEAR FIXED DECIMAL;

        ALLOCATE STUDENT;
        P -> NAME = 'JUDY BLACK';
        P -> NUMBER = 79100;
        P -> YEAR = 1979;
        PUT SKIP EDIT ('NAME IS', P -> NAME) (A, A);
        PUT SKIP EDIT ('NUMBER IS', P -> NUMBER) (A, F(5));
        PUT SKIP EDIT ('YEAR IS', P -> YEAR) (A, F(4));
END SAMPLE;
```

```
NAME IS JUDY BLACK
NUMBER IS 79100
YEAR IS 1979
```

PL/I not only allows the allocation of BASED structures, it also permits the freeing of such structures to available storage. This is accomplished by the statement

```
FREE P -> STUDENT;
```

when the record indicated by pointer P is to be restored to the availability area.

Pointer variables usually specify a memory address. An exception occurs when a pointer variable is assigned the special value returned by PL/I's built-in NULL function. This special value is not the address of some location in memory and, therefore, a record. NULL returns the same value on each invocation and, consequently, it can be used as an end-of-list delimiter. The only comparisons which can be made between NULL and a pointer variable or between two pointer variables are those of "equal" and "not equal".

As another example involving pointers, consider the following problem. It is required to write a program which reads in N sets of data consisting of employee number, employee name, hourly wage, and hours worked. A record is created for

```
PAYROLL  PROCEDURE OPTIONS (MAIN);
    /* SAMPLE PAYROLL PROGRAM */

    DECLARE 1 EMPLOYEE BASED (P), /* REQUIRED DATA STRUCTURE CLASS */
              2 NAME CHARACTER (20),
              2 RATE FLOAT DECIMAL,
              2 HOURS FLOAT DECIMAL,
              2 PAY FLOAT DECIMAL,
            MEMBER (50) POINTER,   /* REFERENCE ARRAY FOR EMPLOYEES */
            NUMBER FIXED DECIMAL,  /* EMPLOYEE NUMBER */
            N FIXED DECIMAL,       /* NUMBER OF EMPLOYEES TO READ */
            I FIXED DECIMAL;       /* COUNTED LOOP VARIABLE */

    /* READ THE NUMBER OF EMPLOYEES TO INPUT */
    GET LIST (N);
    PUT EDIT ('NUMBER', 'EMPLOYEE NAME', 'WAGE RATE', 'HOURS',
        'GROSS PAY') (A, COL(10), A, COL(35), A, COL(50), A, COL(60),
          A);
    PUT SKIP;

    /* PROCESS EMPLOYEES */
    DO I = 1 TO N;

        /* CREATE A NODE */
        ALLOCATE EMPLOYEE;

        /* READ AN EMPLOYEE CARD */
        GET LIST (NUMBER, P -> NAME, P -> RATE, P -> HOURS);

        /* PLACE ADDRESS OF CREATED NODE INTO ARRAY AND COMPUTE PAY */
        MEMBER (NUMBER) = P;
        P -> PAY = P -> HOURS * P -> RATE;
        PUT SKIP EDIT (NUMBER, P -> NAME, P -> RATE, P -> HOURS,
            P -> PAY) (COL(3), F(2), COL(10), A, COL(37), F(5, 2),
              COL(51), F(2), COL(61), F(7, 2));
    END;
END PAYROLL;


NUMBER   EMPLOYEE NAME          WAGE RATE     HOURS     GROSS PAY

  5      LYLE OPSETH              3.50          50        175.00
 17      JUDY RICHARDSON          4.00          20         80.00
 20      MURRAY MAZER             3.75          10         37.50
```

Fig. 10-10   Payroll Program using BASED storage

each set of data consisting of an input set and an additional field denoting gross pay. The addresses of the created records are to be stored in a pointer array which is indexed by employee number. Assume that the employee numbers in the input are unique and that their values are between one and fifty. A program which performs the desired task for the following input is given in Fig. 10-10.

Employee Number	Employee Name	Rate	Hours
5	'LYLE OPSETH'	3.50	50
17	'JUDY RICHARDSON'	4.00	20
20	'MURRAY MAZER'	3.75	10

The first DECLARE statement of this program declares a file whose record structure consists of four fields having names of NAME, RATE, HOURS, and PAY. The second declaration statement creates a 50-element pointer vector named MEMBER whose associated subscript is any valid employee number.

The ALLOCATE statement creates a record and stores its address in the pointer variable P. This address is then used to assign values to the four fields of the newly created record. The subscript of the vector element is given by the employee number read in. For the data of the three employees given earlier, three records whose addresses are stored into vector elements MEMBER(5), MEMBER(17), and MEMBER(20) are created. The program also outputs all related employee information.

Let us now discuss the representation of linked linear lists. This is accomplished by having a pointer field in a record contain the address of its successor. When BASED structures are used, all available space is allocated by the compiler. Similarly, the return of an unused record from a linked list to the availability area of memory is also handled by the compiler. We are therefore not concerned with available storage in the discussion to follow.

In the example programs to follow we assume the record structure is defined by the following declaration statement

```
DECLARE 1 NODE BASED (P),
          2 INFO CHARACTER (5) VARYING,
          2 LINK POINTER;
```

The following PL/I function inserts a new record or node at the front of a linked list. The function has two parameters - FIRST and X. FIRST denotes the address of the first record in the list while X contains the information contents of the new record.

```
LFRONT: PROCEDURE (FIRST, X) RETURNS (POINTER);
        /* INSERT A NODE OR RECORD IN THE LINKED LIST WHICH */
        /* WILL IMMEDIATELY PRECEDE THE RECORD WHOSE */
        /* ADDRESS IS DESIGNATED BY FIRST. RETURN THE */
        /* POINTER TO THE NEW RECORD. */
        DECLARE FIRST POINTER,
                X CHARACTER (*) VARYING;

        /* CREATE A NODE */
        ALLOCATE NODE;

        /* INITIALIZE INFORMATION AND LINK FIELDS */
        P -> INFO = X;
        P -> LINK = FIRST;

        /* RETURN ADDRESS OF NEW NODE */
        RETURN (P);
END LFRONT;
```

This function can be invoked repeatedly, resulting in the construction of a linked linear list. Initially, we begin with an empty list. On each invocation of LFRONT, a new node is inserted at the front of the existing linked list. The following sequence of five assignment statements in which LIST is a pointer variable creates a linked list of four records in a stack like manner. That is, 'RICK' and 'BOB' become the information contents of the fourth record and first record, respectively.

```
LIST = NULL;
LIST = LFRONT (LIST, 'RICK');
LIST = LFRONT (LIST, 'PAUL');
LIST = LFRONT (LIST, 'GRANT');
LIST = LFRONT (LIST, 'BOB');
```

We can also create a linked list by inserting a new record at the end of the existing list. To perform such an insertion first requires that the end of the existing list be found. That is, we must chain through that list until a LINK field with a value of NULL is found. At this point the new node can be inserted. The following PL/I program segment in which SAVE and FIRST are pointer variables performs the required task:

```
SAVE = FIRST;
DO WHILE (SAVE -> LINK ⌐= NULL);
    SAVE = SAVE -> LINK;
END;
SAVE -> LINK = NEW;
```

This program segment becomes part of the following function:

```
LEND: PROCEDURE (FIRST, X) RETURNS (POINTER);
    /* INSERT A NODE OR RECORD AT THE END OF A LINKED */
    /* LIST WHOSE FRONT NODE IS DENOTED BY FIRST. */
    /* RETURN THE ADDRESS OF THE FRONT NODE OF THE */
    /* UPDATED LIST. */
    DECLARE FIRST POINTER,
            X CHARACTER;
    DECLARE SAVE POINTER;

    /* CREATE A NEW NODE */
    ALLOCATE NODE;

    /* INITIALIZE CONTENTS OF NEW NODE */
    P -> INFO = X;
    P -> LINK = NULL;

    /* IS THE ORIGINAL LIST EMPTY? */
    IF FIRST = NULL THEN RETURN (P);

    /* SEARCH FOR THE LAST NODE OF THE LIST */
    /* AND PERFORM INSERTION */
    SAVE = FIRST;
    DO WHILE (SAVE -> LINK ⌐= NULL);
        SAVE = SAVE -> LINK;
    END;
    SAVE -> LINK = P;

    /* RETURN FIRST NODE POINTER */
    RETURN (FIRST);
END LEND;
```

The following program segment creates the linked list of four records described earlier.

```
LIST = NULL;
LIST = LEND (LIST, 'BOB');
LIST = LEND (LIST, 'GRANT');
LIST = LEND (LIST, 'PAUL');
LIST = LEND (LIST, 'RICK');
```

Note that the performance of the function LEND degenerates progressively as the list gets larger. The traversal of such a long list to perform the next insertion can be avoided by keeping the address of the last inserted node. Using this approach, an insertion operation involves changing the link field of the last node (which has the value NULL) of the existing list to the address of the new node being inserted. The following function incorporates this modification to inserting a new record at the end of a list.

```
LLAST: PROCEDURE (FIRST, LAST, X) RETURNS (POINTER);
        /* INSERT A NODE OR RECORD AT THE END OF A LINKED LIST */
        /* WHOSE FRONT NODE IS DENOTED BY FIRST. LAST IS A */
        /* POINTER WHICH CONTAINS THE ADDRESS OF THE LAST NODE */
        /* IN THE LIST BEFORE INSERTION. */
        DECLARE (FIRST, LAST) POINTER,
                X CHARACTER (*);

        /* CREATE A NEW NODE */
        ALLOCATE NODE;

        /* INITIALIZE CONTENTS OF NEW NODE */
        P -> INFO = X;
        P -> LINK = NULL;

        /* IS LIST EMPTY? */
        IF FIRST = NULL
        THEN DO;
             LAST = NEW;
             RETURN (P);
             END;

        /* INSERT NODE AT END OF NONEMPTY LIST */
        LAST -> LINK = P;
        LAST = P;
        RETURN (FIRST);
END LLAST;
```

Now that a number of insertion programs have been given, let us look at another equally important operation — that of deleting a record from a linked linear list. There are several ways of specifying which record is to be deleted. For example, we can denote the record to be deleted by giving its address. Another approach is to specify the INFO value of the record to be deleted. The procedure given in Fig. 10-11 is an implementation of the deletion operation for the latter approach.

Statement 3 saves the value of the pointer which points to the front of the list. In statement 4, a check is made for a deletion from an empty list. If the list is not empty, the procedure checks whether the first element in the list is the one to be deleted, and deletes it if it can. Otherwise, a search is made in the list for the desired element. The address of the current node being examined is stored in NEXT, while the address of the previous node that was examined is saved in the pointer variable PRED. Finally, the appropriate record is deleted from the list in statement 24, if it is found; otherwise, an error message is printed.

The link field of the last record in a linked linear list can be changed from its NULL value to point to the first record in the list. The resulting circular structure is called a *circular list*. Since the processing of such a circular structure can result in an infinite loop, it is desirable to add a list head record (with an address of HEAD) to a circular list. In so doing, a circular list can never be empty. An empty list is denoted by having HEAD -> LINK = HEAD. Usually, the INFO field of the list head is not used in processing a circular list. The following PL/I procedure inserts a record in a circular list with a list head.

```
CIFRONT: PROCEDURE (HEAD, X);
        /* INSERT A RECORD WITH INFO X AT THE FRONT OF A */
        /* CIRCULAR LINKED LIST WHOSE HEAD RECORD IS */
        /* DENOTED BY HEAD. */
        DECLARE HEAD POINTER,
                X CHARACTER (*);

        /* CREATE A NEW RECORD */
        ALLOCATE NODE;

        /* PERFORM INSERTION AND RETURN */
        P -> INFO = X;
        P -> LINK =  HEAD -> LINK;
        HEAD -> LINK = P;
        RETURN;
END CIFRONT;
```

Certain applications require that the predecessor as well as the successor of a node or record in a linear list be known. Also, many of these applications require that the linear list be traversed not only from left to right but right to left as well. The node or record structure is expanded to easily accommodate these requirements. Such an expansion involves adding an additional pointer field to a record which gives the address of the predecessor of that record. The expanded record structure now becomes

```
DECLARE 1 NODE BASED (NEW),
            2 LPTR POINTER,
            2 INFO CHARACTER (1),
            2 RPTR POINTER;
```

where LPTR and RPTR are pointer fields which denote the predecessor and successor of a given node, respectively. Recall that NEW is implicitly declared to be a pointer variable. Such a linear list structure is called a *doubly linked linear list*. As

```
1                    DELETE: PROCEDURE (FIRST, X);
                         /* FIND AND DELETE A RECORD WITH INFORMATION CONTENTS X FROM */
                         /* A LINKED LIST POINTED TO BY THE VARIABLE FIRST.          */
2                        DECLARE FIRST POINTER,
                                 X CHARACTER (*),
                                 (PRED, NEXT, SAVE) POINTER;

3                        SAVE = FIRST;
4                        IF FIRST = NULL
5                        THEN DO;  /* INDICATE THAT LIST IS EMPTY */
6                            PUT SKIP LIST ('LIST UNDERFLOW');
7                            RETURN;
8                            END;
9                        IF FIRST -> INFO = X
10                       THEN DO;  /* DELETE FIRST RECORD */
11                           FIRST = FIRST -> LINK;

                             /* RESTORE FRONT RECORD TO AVAILABILITY AREA */
12                           FREE SAVE -> NODE;
13                           RETURN;
14                           END;

                         /* INITIALIZE SEARCH FOR X */
15                       PRED = FIRST;
16                       NEXT = PRED -> LINK;

                         /* PERFORM SEARCH FOR X */
17                       DO WHILE (NEXT ¬= NULL & NEXT -> INFO ¬= X);
18                           PRED = NEXT;
19                           NEXT = NEXT -> LINK;
20                           END;

                         /* DELETE INDICATED RECORD, IF FOUND */
21                       IF NEXT ¬= NULL
22                       THEN DO;
23                           PRED -> LINK = NEXT -> LINK;

                             /* RESTORE RECORD WITH INFO X TO AVAILABILITY AREA */
24                           FREE NEXT -> NODE;
25                           END;
26                       ELSE /* RECORD NOT FOUND */
27                           PUT SKIP LIST ('RECORD NOT FOUND');
28                       RETURN;
29                    END DELETE;
```

Fig. 10-11   PL/I procedure for deleting a record from a linked list

was done for a circular linear list, it is very desirable to have the doubly linked circular list with a list head record. Such a structure is called a *circularly doubly linked linear list.* An empty doubly linked list has the following property for the pointers of its list head record:

LPTR -> HEAD = HEAD and RPTR -> HEAD = HEAD

The following PL/I procedure inserts a new record into a doubly linked list to the immediate right of the specified record with address M. X contains the information contents of the new record.

```
DOUBLEI: PROCEDURE (HEAD, M, X);
         /* INSERT A NEW RECORD TO THE IMMEDIATE RIGHT */
         /* OF RECORD M IN A DOUBLY LINKED LINEAR LIST */
         /* WHOSE HEAD NODE IS DENOTED HEAD. */
```

```
            DECLARE (HEAD, M) POINTER,
                    X CHARACTER (*),
                    TEMP POINTER;

            /* CREATE NEW RECORD */
            ALLOCATE NODE;

            /* INSERT NEW RECORD */
            NEW -> INFO = X;
            NEW -> LPTR = M;
            NEW -> RPTR = M -> RPTR;
            TEMP = M -> RPTR;
            TEMP -> LPTR = NEW;
            M -> RPTR = NEW;
            RETURN;
    END DOUBLEI;
```

Observe the use of a local pointer variable (TEMP) in this program. We need this variable since PL/I does not allow pointer references such as

M -> RPTR -> LPTR or (M -> RPTR) -> LPTR

In such instances M -> RPTR must be copied into a temporary pointer variable.

The following procedure performs the deletion of the node specified by OLD in a doubly-linked linear list.

```
    DOUBLED: PROCEDURE (HEAD, OLD);
            /* DELETE THE RECORD SPECIFIED BY OLD FROM A DOUBLY */
            /* LINKED CIRCULAR LIST WHOSE HEAD NODE IS DENOTED */
            /* BY HEAD. */
            DECLARE (HEAD, OLD) POINTER,
                    (PRED, SUC) POINTER;

            /* DELETE INDICATED RECORD */
            PRED = OLD -> LPTR;
            SUC = OLD -> RPTR;
            PRED -> RPTR = SUC;
            SUC -> LPTR = PRED;

            /* RETURN RECORD TO AVAILABILITY LIST */
            FREE OLD -> NODE;
            RETURN;
    END DOUBLED;
```

Again observe the need for the temporary pointer variables PRED and SUC that denote the addresses of the predecessor and successor records, respectively, of the node marked for deletion.

In this section we have presented the PL/I basics of representing linear lists using BASED storage. The next section gives PL/I programs for several applications of linked linear lists.

Exercises for Sec. 10-8

1. Given a singly-linked list whose node structure is declared as follows:

        DECLARE 1 NODE BASED(P),
                  2 INFO CHARACTER(20),
                  2 LINK POINTER;

   write a function which counts the number of nodes in the list. The function is to contain one parameter (FIRST) which contains the address of the front node in the list.

2. Write a procedure which performs an insertion to the immediate left of the Kth node in a linked linear list. K = 0 specifies that a node is to be inserted into an empty list. The procedure is to have three parameters; namely,

        FIRST - address of the front node in the linear list.
        K - the Kth node in the existing list.
        X - information content of the new node.

   Assume the same node structure as in exercise 1.

3. Given two linked lists whose front nodes are denoted by the pointers FIRST and SECOND, respectively, obtain a function that concatenates two lists. The front node address of the new list is to be returned by the function. Assume the node structure declaration given in exercise 1.

4. Obtain a procedure which will deconcatenate (or split) a given linked list into two separate linked lists. The first node of the original linked list is denoted by the pointer variable FIRST. SPLIT denotes the address of the node which is to become the first node of the second linked list. Assume the node declaration structure in exercise 1.

5. Write a procedure which inserts a node at the end of a circular list with a list head node, i.e., between the node which points to the list head and the list head node. The procedure is to have two parameters - HEAD, which denotes the head node, and X, which specifies the information content of the new node.

6. Formulate a procedure which deletes from a circular list with a list head (HEAD), a node whose information content is given by the string variable X.

7. An unknown number of cards are punched, each of which contains a student record with the following information: student number, name, college, sex, and year of study. Each field is separated by at least one blank, and the fields are in the order listed above. The sex is punched as M (male) or F (female). A trailer card with student number of 999999 and "dummy" information in the other four fields is placed at the end of the deck of cards.
   The college and year of study of a student may change. A series of update cards follows the initial deck. Update cards contain information on students who have made changes. The update deck is also followed by a trailer

card having student number 999999 and dummy information in the other two fields. The update deck is then followed by a series of cards on which a college name is punched.

Construct a program to create a linked list of the student records which is ordered by student numbers (smallest to largest). Then read the update cards and update this list. Once all update cards have been read, read the college names and output a well-organized report of all students in that college in alphabetical order. Do this for each college name read in. List the student number, name, sex and year of study for each of these students.

Note that neither the original file cards nor the student cards are ordered, and it is possible that there may be an update card for a student who is not in the original file, in which case an appropriate error message is to be printed.

10-9   APPLICATIONS OF LINKED LINEAR LISTS

This section discusses three applications of linked linear lists and their associated PL/I programs. The first application deals with the symbolic addition of polynomial expressions. The second topic describes the application of hashing functions to the operations of searching and sorting. The third and final application is an application of linked queues to radix sorting.

All of the applications are described in detail in Sec. 10-10 of the main text.

10-9.1   Polynomial Manipulation

In this section we concentrate on the symbolic addition of polynomials in three variables. For example, the addition of polynomial $x^2 + xy + x + y^2 + 2z^2$ to polynomial $2x^2 - 2xy + 3x - y^2 + yz$ yields the result $3x^2 - xy + 4x + yz + 2z^2$. A suitable representation of a polynomial in the three variables x, y, and z is given in the following declaration statement.

```
DECLARE 1 TERM BASED (NEW),
            2 POWER_X FIXED DECIMAL,
            2 POWER_Y FIXED DECIMAL,
            2 POWER_Z FIXED DECIMAL,
            2 COEFF FLOAT,
            2 LINK POINTER;
```

We assume that the terms in the linked list that represent a polynomial are ordered. More specifically a term with address P precedes another term with address Q, if P -> POWER_X > Q -> POWER_X; or if these powers are equal, then P -> POWER_Y must be greater than Q -> POWER_Y; or, if these y powers are equal, then P -> POWER_Z must be greater than Q -> POWER_Z.

Two polynomials ordered in this way are added by scanning each of their terms only once. For example, a polynomial term $D_1 x^{A_1} y^{B_1} z^{C_1}$ in the first polynomial is added to its corresponding term $D_2 x^{A_2} y^{B_2} z^{C_2}$ in the second term if $A_1 = A_2$, $B_1 = B_2$, and $C_1 = C_2$. In this case the coefficient of the sum term is $D_1 + D_2$.

A general algorithm which uses the functions POLY_INSERT, for inserting a term into a polynomial such that its order is maintained, and POLY_LAST, which inserts a term at the end of a polynomial, and the procedures POLY_ADD, which adds two polynomials, and PRINT_POLY, which prints the resulting polynomial follows:

1. Repeat thru step 6 for all pairs of polynomials
2. Initialize the pointers to the polynomials to NULL
3. Repeat for each term of the first polynomial
       Call POLY_INSERT to build linked list representing the polynomial
4. Repeat for each term of the second polynomial
       Call POLY_INSERT to build linked list representing the polynomial
5. Call POLY_ADD to add the two polynomials
6. Call PRINT_POLY to print the answer

Figure 10-12 is a PL/I program that adds pairs of polynomials. The sample infix expressions used for this program are

$$7x^5y^4z^2 + 7x^5y^4z + 8x^2y^3 + 16xy^3z$$
$$19x^6y^4z + 23x^6y^4 + 3x^5y^4z^2 + 3x^2y^3 + 16xy^3z^2$$

and

$$x^2 + xy + x + y^2 + 2z^2$$
$$2x^2 - 2xy + 3x - y^2 + yz$$

For convenience, we assume that each term of the polynomials is given as four numbers, where the first number denotes the value of the coefficient, while the second, third, and fourth give the values of the exponents x, y, and z, respectively. The end of the polynomials is denoted by a final term which has a coefficient value of zero.

The variables used in the main program are:

Variable	Type	Usage
POLY1	POINTER	Points to the first node of the first polynomial
POLY2	POINTER	Points to the first node of the second polynomial
POLY3	POINTER	Points to the first node of sum polynomial
X	FIXED	Exponent value of x
Y	FIXED	Exponent value of y
Z	FIXED	Exponent value of z
C	FLOAT	Coefficient of term
LAST	POINTER	Points to last node of polynomial
END_FLAG	CHARACTER(3)	End of file flag
NODE	BASED (POINT)	Structure used to store term of polynomial
POWER_X	FIXED	Exponent of x in term of polynomial
POWER_Y	FIXED	Exponent of y in term of polynomial

```
1                 POLY: PROCEDURE OPTIONS (MAIN);
                  /* GIVEN THE PROCEDURES POLY_ADD, POLY_INSERT, POLY_LAST, AND */
                  /* PRINT_POLY, THIS ALGORITHM INPUTS TWO POLYNOMIALS AND PRINTS   */
                  /* THEIR SUM.                                                      */

2                 DECLARE (POLY1, POLY2, POLY3) POINTER,    /* FRONT TERMS OF THE */
                                                            /* POLYNOMIALS */
                    (X, Y, Z) FIXED,                        /* POWERS OF X, Y, AND Z */
                    C FLOAT,                                /* COEFFICIENT VALUE OF */
                                                            /* INPUT TERM */
                    LAST POINTER,                           /* LAST TERM IN POLYNOMIAL*/
                    1 NODE BASED (POINT),                   /* TERM OF POLYNOMIAL */
                      2 LINK POINTER,                       /* POINTER TO NEXT TERM */
                      2 POWER_X FIXED,                      /* EXPONENT OF X */
                      2 POWER_Y FIXED,                      /* EXPONENT OF Y */
                      2 POWER_Z FIXED,                      /* EXPONENT OF Z */
                      2 COEFF FLOAT,                        /* COEFFICIENT OF TERM */
                    END_FLAG CHARACTER (3),                 /* END OF INPUT FLAG */
                    POLY_INSERT ENTRY (FIXED, FIXED, FIXED, FLOAT, POINTER)
                         RETURNS (POINTER),
                    POLY_LAST ENTRY (FIXED, FIXED, FIXED, FLOAT, POINTER)
                         RETURNS (POINTER);

3                 ON ENDFILE (SYSIN) EXIT;
5                 END_FLAG = 'NO';

                  /* PROCESS ALL POLYNOMIALS */
6                 DO WHILE (END_FLAG = 'NO');

                      /* INITIALIZE */
7                     POLY1, POLY2 = NULL;

                      /* INPUT AND CONSTRUCT FIRST POLYNOMIAL */
8                     GET LIST (X, Y, Z, C);
9                     DO WHILE (C ¬= 0);
10                        POLY1 = POLY_INSERT (X, Y, Z, C, POLY1);
11                        GET LIST (X, Y, Z, C);
12                    END;
13                    PUT SKIP (3) LIST ('FIRST POLYNOMIAL IS');
14                    CALL PRINT_POLY (POLY1);

                      /* INPUT AND CONSTRUCT SECOND POLYNOMIAL */
15                    GET LIST (X, Y, Z, C);
16                    DO WHILE (C ¬= 0);
17                        POLY2 = POLY_INSERT (X, Y, Z, C, POLY2);
18                        GET LIST (X, Y, Z, C);
19                    END;
20                    PUT SKIP (2) LIST ('SECOND POLYNOMIAL IS');
21                    CALL PRINT_POLY (POLY2);

                      /* ADD POLYNOMIALS */
22                    CALL POLY_ADD (POLY1, POLY2, POLY3);
23                    PUT SKIP (2) LIST ('SUM OF POLYNOMIALS IS');
24                    CALL PRINT_POLY (POLY3);

                  /* FINISHED */
25                END;
```

Fig. 10-12 Program to sum two polynomials

POWER_Z	FIXED	Exponent of z in term of polynomial
COEFF	FLOAT	Value of coefficient of term
LINK	POINTER	Points to next term in polynomial

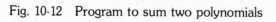

Variables used in the function POLY_INSERT are:

```
26              POLY_INSERT: PROCEDURE (NX, NY, NZ, NCOEFF, FIRST)
                    RETURNS (POINTER);
                /* GIVEN AN ORDERED SINGLY LINKED LINEAR LIST WHERE FIRST    */
                /* DENOTES THE ADDRESS OF THE FIRST TERM OF THE POLYNOMIAL,  */
                /* THIS FUNCTIONAL PROCEDURE INSERTS A NEW TERM INTO THE     */
                /* LINKED LIST AND PRESERVES ITS ORDER.  NX, NY, NZ, AND     */
                /* NCOEFF CORRESPOND TO THE EXPONENTS FOR X, Y, AND Z AND    */
                /* THE COEFFICIENT VALUE OF THE TERM.                        */

27              DECLARE (NX, NY, NZ) FIXED,
                    NCOEFF FLOAT,
                    FIRST POINTER,
                    (NEW, SAVE, TEMP) POINTER, /* TEMP POINTER VARIABLES */
                    (A, B, C) FIXED;           /* TEMP INTEGER VARIABLES */

                /* CREATE A NEW NODE */
28              ALLOCATE NODE;
29              NEW = POINT;

                /* COPY INFO INTO NEW NODE */
30              NEW -> POWER_X = NX;
31              NEW -> POWER_Y = NY;
32              NEW -> POWER_Z = NZ;
33              NEW -> COEFF = NCOEFF;

                /* IS THE LIST EMPTY? */
34              IF FIRST = NULL
35              THEN DO;
36                  NEW -> LINK = NULL;
37                  RETURN (NEW);
38                  END;

                /* DOES NEW NODE PRECEDE FIRST NODE OF LIST? */
39              A = FIRST -> POWER_X;
40              B = FIRST -> POWER_Y;
41              C = FIRST -> POWER_Z;
42              IF (A < NX | (A = NX & B < NY) | (A = NX & B = NY & C < NZ))
43              THEN DO;
44                  NEW -> LINK = FIRST;
45                  RETURN (NEW);
46                  END;

                /* INITIALIZE TEMPORARY POINTER */
47              SAVE = FIRST;

                /* SEARCH FOR PREDECESSOR AND SUCCESSOR OF NEW NODE */
48              DO WHILE (SAVE -> LINK ¬= NULL);
49                  TEMP = SAVE -> LINK;
50                  A = TEMP -> POWER_X;
51                  B = TEMP -> POWER_Y;
52                  C = TEMP -> POWER_Z;
53                  IF (A > NX | (A = NX & B > NY) | (A = NX & B = NY
                        & C > NZ))
54                  THEN SAVE = SAVE -> LINK;
55                  ELSE DO;  /* INSERT NEW NODE */
56                      NEW -> LINK = SAVE -> LINK;
57                      SAVE -> LINK = NEW;
58                      RETURN (FIRST);
59                      END;
60              END;
                /* INSERT NEW NODE AT END OF LIST */
61              NEW -> LINK = NULL;
62              SAVE -> LINK = NEW;
63              RETURN (FIRST);
64          END POLY_INSERT;
```

Fig. 10-12   Program to sum two polynomials (cont'd.)

```
65              POLY_ADD: PROCEDURE (P, Q, R);
                    /* GIVEN TWO POLYNOMIALS STORED IN LINKED LISTS AND WHOSE    */
                    /* FIRST TERMS ARE DENOTED BY THE POINTER VARIABLES P AND Q, */
                    /* THIS PROCEDURE SYMBOLLICALLY ADDS THESE POLYNOMIALS AND    */
                    /* STORES THE ORDERED SUM AS A LINKED LIST WHOSE FIRST NODE   */
                    /* IS DENOTED BY THE POINTER VARIABLE R.                      */

66                  DECLARE (P, Q, R) POINTER,
                        (PSAVE, QSAVE) POINTER,      /* TEMP POINTER VARIABLES */
                        (A1, A2, B1, B2, C1, C2)     /* TEMPORARY EXPONENT */
                          FIXED,                     /* VARIABLES */
                        (D1, D2) FLOAT;              /* TEMPORARY COEFFICIENT */
                                                     /* VARIABLES */

                    /* INITIALIZE */
67                  R = NULL;
68                  PSAVE = P;
69                  QSAVE = Q;

                    /* END OF ANY POLYNOMIAL? */
70                  DO WHILE (P ¬= NULL & Q ¬= NULL);

                        /* OBTAIN FIELD VALUES FOR EACH TERM */
71                      A1 = P -> POWER_X;
72                      A2 = Q -> POWER_X;
73                      B1 = P -> POWER_Y;
74                      B2 = Q -> POWER_Y;
75                      C1 = P -> POWER_Z;
76                      C2 = Q -> POWER_Z;
77                      D1 = P -> COEFF;
78                      D2 = Q -> COEFF;

                        /* COMPARE TERMS */
79                      IF A1 = A2 & B1 = B2 & C1 = C2
                        THEN /* CORRESPONDING TERMS */
80                          IF P -> COEFF + Q -> COEFF ¬= 0
81                          THEN DO;
82                              R = POLY_LAST (A1, B1, C1, D1 + D2, R);
83                              P = P -> LINK;
84                              Q = Q -> LINK;
85                              END;
86                          ELSE DO;
87                              P = P -> LINK;
88                              Q = Q -> LINK;
89                              END;
90                      ELSE /* TERMS DO NOT MATCH */
90                          IF (A1 > A2) ¦ (A1 = A2 & B1 > B2)
                                ¦ (A1 = A2 & B1 = B2 & C1 > C2)
91                          THEN DO; /* OUTPUT TERM FROM POLYNOMIAL P */
92                              R = POLY_LAST (A1, B1, C1, D1, R);
93                              P = P -> LINK;
94                              END;
95                          ELSE DO; /* OUTPUT TERM FROM POLYNOMIAL Q */
96                              R = POLY_LAST (A2, B2, C2, D2, R);
97                              Q = Q -> LINK;
98                              END;
99                      END;

                    /* IS POLYNOMIAL P PROCESSED? */
100                 IF P ¬= NULL
101                 THEN LAST -> LINK = P;
102                 ELSE IF Q ¬= NULL
103                     THEN LAST -> LINK = Q;

                    /* RESTORE INITIAL POINTER VALUES FOR P AND Q */
104                 P = PSAVE;
105                 Q = QSAVE;

                    /* FINISHED */
106                 RETURN;
107             END POLY_ADD;
```

Fig. 10-12   Program to sum two polynomials (cont'd.)

```
108         POLY_LAST: PROCEDURE (NX, NY, NZ, NCOEFF, FIRST) RETURNS (POINTER);
                    /* GIVEN AN ORDERED SINGLY LINKED LINEAR LIST, WHERE FIRST   */
                    /* DENOTES THE ADDRESS OF THE FIRST TERM OF THE POLYNOMIAL   */
                    /* THIS FUNCTIONAL PROCEDURE PERFORMS AN INSERTION AT THE    */
                    /* END OF THE LIST.  NX, NY, NZ, AND NCOEFF CORRESPOND TO    */
                    /* THE EXPONENTS FOR X, Y, AND Z AND THE COEFFICIENT VALUE   */
                    /* OF THE TERM.                                             */

109                 DECLARE (NX, NY, NZ) FIXED,
                            NCOEFF FLOAT,
                            FIRST POINTER,
                            NEW POINTER;          /* TEMPORARY POINTER VARIABLE */

                    /* CREATE NEW NODE */
110                 ALLOCATE NODE;
111                 NEW = POINT;

                    /* INITIALIZE FIELDS OF NEW NODE */
112                 NEW -> POWER_X = NX;
113                 NEW -> POWER_Y = NY;
114                 NEW -> POWER_Z = NZ;
115                 NEW -> COEFF = NCOEFF;
116                 NEW -> LINK = NULL;

                    /* IS THIS LIST EMPTY? */
117                 IF FIRST = NULL
118                 THEN DO;
119                     LAST = NEW;
120                     RETURN (NEW);
121                     END;

                    /* INSERT NEW NODE AT END OF NONEMPTY LIST */
122                 LAST -> LINK = NEW;
123                 LAST = NEW;
124                 RETURN (FIRST);
125         END POLY_LAST;

126         PRINT_POLY: PROCEDURE (FIRST);
                    /* THIS PROCEDURE PRINTS OUT A POLYNOMIAL WHICH IS STORED AS */

                    /* A LINKED LINEAR LIST WHOSE FIRST TERM IS POINTED TO BY    */
                    /* FIRST.                                                   */

127                 DECLARE FIRST POINTER,
                            SAVE POINTER;    /* TEMPORARY POINTER VARIABLE */

                    /* INITIALIZE */
128                 SAVE = FIRST -> LINK;

                    /* PRINT FIRST TERM */
129                 PUT SKIP EDIT (FIRST -> COEFF, ' * (X**', FIRST -> POWER_X,
                        ') * (Y**', FIRST -> POWER_Y, ') * (Z**', FIRST ->
                        POWER_Z, ')') (F(3), A, F(2), A, F(2), A, F(2), A);

                    /* PRINT REMAINING TERMS */
130                 DO WHILE (SAVE ¬= NULL);
131                     PUT EDIT (' + ', SAVE -> COEFF, ' * (X**', SAVE ->
                            POWER_X, ') * (Y**', SAVE -> POWER_Y, ') * (Z**',
                            SAVE -> POWER_Z, ')') (A, F(3), A, F(2), A, F(2), A,
                            F(2), A);
132                     SAVE = SAVE -> LINK;
133                     END;
134         END PRINT_POLY;

135     END POLY;
```

Fig. 10-12   Program to sum two polynomials (cont'd.)

```
FIRST POLYNOMIAL IS
  7 * (X** 5) * (Y** 4) * (Z** 2) +   7 * (X** 5) * (Y** 4) * (Z** 1) +   8 * (X** 2) * (Y** 3) * (Z** 0) +  16 * (X** 1
) * (Y** 3) * (Z** 1)

SECOND POLYNOMIAL IS
 19 * (X** 6) * (Y** 4) * (Z** 1) + 23 * (X** 6) * (Y** 4) * (Z** 0) +   3 * (X** 5) * (Y** 4) * (Z** 2) +   3 * (X** 2
) * (Y** 3) * (Z** 0) +  16 * (X** 1) * (Y** 3) * (Z** 2)

SUM OF POLYNOMIALS IS
 19 * (X** 6) * (Y** 4) * (Z** 1) + 23 * (X** 6) * (Y** 4) * (Z** 0) +  10 * (X** 5) * (Y** 4) * (Z** 2) +   7 * (X** 5
) * (Y** 4) * (Z** 1) +  11 * (X** 2) * (Y** 3) * (Z** 0) +  16 * (X** 1) * (Y** 3) * (Z** 2) +  16 * (X** 1) * (Y** 3)
* (Z** 1)


FIRST POLYNOMIAL IS
  1 * (X** 2) * (Y** 0) * (Z** 0) +   1 * (X** 1) * (Y** 1) * (Z** 0) +   1 * (X** 1) * (Y** 0) * (Z** 0) +   1 * (X** 0
) * (Y** 2) * (Z** 0) +   2 * (X** 0) * (Y** 0) * (Z** 2)

SECOND POLYNOMIAL IS
  2 * (X** 2) * (Y** 0) * (Z** 0) +  -2 * (X** 1) * (Y** 1) * (Z** 0) +   3 * (X** 1) * (Y** 0) * (Z** 0) +  -1 * (X** 0
) * (Y** 2) * (Z** 0) +   1 * (X** 0) * (Y** 1) * (Z** 1)

SUM OF POLYNOMIALS IS
  3 * (X** 2) * (Y** 0) * (Z** 0) +  -1 * (X** 1) * (Y** 1) * (Z** 0) +   4 * (X** 1) * (Y** 0) * (Z** 0) +   1 * (X** 0
) * (Y** 1) * (Z** 1) +   2 * (X** 0) * (Y** 0) * (Z** 2)
```

Fig. 10-12   Program to sum two polynomials (cont'd.)

NX	FIXED	Exponent of x of term to be inserted
NY	FIXED	Exponent of y of term to be inserted
NZ	FIXED	Exponent of z of term to be inserted
NCOEFF	FIXED	Coefficient of term to be inserted
FIRST	POINTER	Points to the first term of the polynomial
NEW	POINTER	Points to the term to be inserted
SAVE	POINTER	Temporary pointer variable
TEMP	POINTER	Temporary pointer variable
A	FIXED	Value of the exponent of x of the term being examined
B	FIXED	Value of exponent of y
C	FIXED	Value of exponent of z

Variables used in the procedure POLY_ADD are:

P	POINTER	Points to the first term of the first polynomial
Q	POINTER	Points to the first term of the second polynomial
R	POINTER	Points to the first term of the sum polynomial
PSAVE	POINTER	Points to the first term of the first polynomial
QSAVE	POINTER	Points to the first term of the second polynomial

A1	FIXED	Exponent value of x from the first polynomial
A2	FIXED	Exponent value of x from the second polynomial
B1	FIXED	Exponent value of y from the first polynomial
B2	FIXED	Exponent value of y from the second polynomial
C1	FIXED	Exponent value of z from the first polynomial
C2	FIXED	Exponent value of z from the second polynomial
D1	FLOAT	Coefficient value of the term from the first polynomial
D2	FLOAT	Coefficient value of the term from the second polynomial

Variables used in the procedure POLY_LAST are:

NX	FIXED	Value of exponent of x
NY	FIXED	Value of exponent of y
NZ	FIXED	Value of exponent of z
NCOEFF	FLOAT	Coefficient value of term
FIRST	POINTER	Points to head of polynomial

Variables used in the procedure PRINT_POLY are:

| FIRST | POINTER | Points to the head of polynomial |
| SAVE | POINTER | Temporary pointer variable |

Statement 6 of the main program controls the processing of all the pairs of the polynomials to be added. Statements 8 to 12 and 15 to 19 read the terms of the two polynomials and call the function POLY_INSERT to build the two polynomials. Then, in statement 22, POLY_ADD is invoked to add the two polynomials.

In the function POLY_INSERT, a new node is created first and the values of the coefficient and exponents are copied into its elementary items. Note that POINT implicitly receives the address of this new node. Then a search is made to find where the new term goes in the polynomial. Statement 34 determines whether the list is empty. If the list is not empty, a check is made to see if the new term precedes the first term of the linked list. If not, a search is made in statements 48 to 60, and the new term is placed in its correct position.

Procedure POLY_ADD first stores the addresses of the two polynomials in temporary pointer variables. Then a loop is entered which is used to add the terms of the polynomials until the end of either polynomial is reached. Inside the loop, the current terms of the polynomals are compared. If the terms correspond, the coefficients are added and if the resulting value is not zero, this term is added to the end of the sum polynomial. This is done by calling the function POLY_LAST. Otherwise, the term that precedes the other term of the two polynomials is added to the end of the new polynomial. After exiting the loop, the unprocessed terms of the remaining polynomial are appended to the end of the new polynomial in statements 100 to 103.

The function POLY_LAST creates and initializes a new term. Then, in statements 117 to 121, the list to which the polynomial is to be added is checked for being null. If it is, the address of the new node is returned; otherwise, the node is inserted at the end of the list and the address of the first node of the list is returned. Procedure PRINT_POLY prints the terms of the polynomial. Statement 129 prints the first term, while statements 130 to 133 print the remaining terms of the polynomial.

10-9.2   Hash-Table Techniques

This subsection examines the programming aspects of a class of search techniques based on computing the position of a record in a table through the use of a hashing function. Such a function associates the key of a record with a particular position in the table. Since more than one key can be mapped into the same table position; collisions occur. These collisions can be resolved using two classes of collision-resolution techniques; namely, open addressing and chaining. We examine the programming aspects of both methods in this subsection. The notions of hashing are also applicable to the operation of sorting. A program for sorting by address calculation is given.

Recall that a *key-to-address transformation* problem is a mapping or *hashing function* (HASH), that maps the key space (KEY) into an address space. This address space is usually an address to an element in a table. *Preconditioning* is often necessary to convert a key consisting of alphanumeric characters into a form that allows arithmetic or logical manipulation. Usually, the key space is larger than the address space, which often results in collisions between records.

Preconditioning is most efficiently performed by using the numerically coded representations of the characters in the key. The PL/I built-in function UNSPEC is used to convert characters into their arithmetic forms. The function call has the form

UNSPEC(s)

where s is any PL/I expression. UNSPEC returns the bit string that represents the internal representation of s. For example, UNSPEC('B') returns '11000010'B which is the EBCDIC representation of the character 'B'. Note that each EBCDIC character requires 8 bits. UNSPEC ('AN'), on the other hand, returns the bit string of length 16 '1100000111010101'B. Once we have the numeric representation of the alphanumeric characters, arithmetic or logical manipulation can easily be done on the characters.

Two hashing functions are required to generate an address. First, the preconditioned value of the key must be computed, and second, the mapping of the key into a table location is performed. These two hashing functions are often combined into one hashing function.

The *division method* of hashing, which is defined as

$$H(x) = x \bmod m + 1$$

can be implemented in PL/I using the built-in function MOD (X, M) which returns the remainder after dividing X by M. Thus, MOD (37, 11) is 4. Before the division method can be used, preconditioning of the key may be required. One method that can be used is a length-dependent hashing function.

Figure 10-13 gives a hashing function using the *length-dependent method*. With this method, the length of the key is used along with some portion of the key to produce a table address directly, or an intermediate key which is used with, say, the division method to produce the final table address. It is often difficult to convert alphanumeric characters directly to a table address; thus, in Fig. 10-13, the length-dependent method is only used for preconditioning. The hashing function obtains the internal binary representation of the first and last characters of the key and sums them along with the length of the key shifted left four binary places. The binary representations of the first and last characters are obtained by using the UNSPEC function. The length of the key shifted over four places is obtained by multiplying the key's length by 16. Finally, the division method is used to compute the final table address. In this hashing function, SIZE stores the size of the address space, and should be a prime number.

Recall that hashing functions often map several keys into the same address. Collision-resolution techniques are required so that the colliding records can be stored and accessed. Open addressing and chaining are two classes of collision resolution used to resolve these conflicts. Open addressing searches for a free location in a table if the location that the key was hashed into is occupied.

Because of difficulties in deleting records with open addressing, a special value (DELETE) is used to denote that a record has been deleted. Recall that for look-ups, difficulty occurs when records have been deleted between the position where the record was hashed and where it is finally stored in the table.

One method of open addressing, called *linear probing*, uses the following sequence of locations for a table of m entries:

$$d, d + 1 ..., m - 1, m, 1, 2, ..., d - 1$$

where d denotes the initial hash position of the input key. Insertions fail if no unoccupied location is found and look-ups fail if either an empty position is reached without finding the record in question, or if the entire table has been searched.

Figure 10-14 gives a program that performs look-ups and insertions using the function OPENLP. The variables used in the main program are:

Variable	Type	Usage
HASH_TABLE(100)		Array of structures storing records
K	CHARACTER (10) VARYING	Key field of record
DATA	CHARACTER (20) VARYING	Information field of record
FLAG	CHARACTER (1)	Denotes whether record location is empty, occupied, or deleted
KEY	CHARACTER (10) VARYING	Key of record to be inserted or looked-up
INFO	CHARACTER (20) VARYING	Information field of record to be inserted or looked-up
M	FIXED	Size of the hash table
NUM	FIXED	Number of records to be inserted
INSERT	BIT (1)	Logical flag for insertion or look-up
POS	FIXED	Position of record looked-up
I	FIXED	Counted loop variable

Variables used in function OPENLP are:

```
HASH: PROCEDURE (SYMBOL, SIZE) RETURNS (FIXED DECIMAL);
     /* THIS FUNCTION COMPUTES THE HASH VALUE OF THE STRING SYMBOL*/
     /* BY USING THE LENGTH-DEPENDENT METHOD.                    */
     DECLARE SYMBOL CHARACTER (*) VARYING,
                                  /* STRING TO BE HASHED */
             SIZE FIXED,          /* SIZE OF TABLE */
             (FIRST_CHAR, LAST_CHAR) /* FIRST AND LAST CHARACTERS */
               CHARACTER (1),     /* OF SYMBOL */
             VALUE FIXED;         /* PRECONDITIONED VALUE */

     /* GET FIRST AND LAST CHARACTERS OF SYMBOL */
     FIRST_CHAR = SUBSTR (SYMBOL, 1, 1);
     LAST_CHAR = SUBSTR (SYMBOL, LENGTH (SYMBOL));

     /* COMPUTE PRECONDITIONED RESULT */
     VALUE = UNSPEC (FIRST_CHAR) + UNSPEC (LAST_CHAR) +
         16 * LENGTH (SYMBOL);

     /* RETURN HASHED VALUE */
     RETURN (MOD (VALUE, SIZE) + 1);
END HASH;
```

Fig. 10-13   Example of a length-dependent hashing function

X	CHARACTER (*) VARYING	Key value to be hashed for look-up or insertion
INFO	CHARACTER (*) VARYING	Information field
INSERT	BIT (*)	Specifies look-up or insertion
D	FIXED	Hashed value of key
I	FIXED	Counted loop variable
STOP_INSERT	FIXED	Position of last record in table to look at during search

The main program first initializes the hash table locations to empty. Then a loop is entered which calls the function OPENLP to insert the records into the table. Finally, look-ups are performed in statements 20 to 27.

In OPENLP, the initial position of the record in the table is calculated. The hash function used for this purpose is the one given in Fig. 10-13. Next, a scan of the table is made starting at the initial position. If the key value matches the key in the table, the position is returned if a look-up is required. For insertions, a negated index is returned if the record is already present. Then if the table location either is empty or contains a deleted record, the record is inserted if required. An empty location for a look-up indicates that the search key is not found and a negated index is, therefore, returned. Finally, if statement 54 is reached, either the table is full, or the search key was not found.

This program was tested on the following data. The keys 'FROG', 'WHALE', 'LYNX', 'SNAKE', 'BLUEJAY', 'BEETLE', and 'SALMON' were inserted. Look-ups were performed on 'LYNX', 'BLUEJAY', 'SALMON', 'JACKFISH', 'LADYBUG', and 'SNAKE'. Note that 'JACKFISH' and 'LADYBUG' were not previously inserted into the table.

Because of primary clustering, the efficiency of look-ups and insertions in the table decreases as the table becomes full. For a table, the probability of an insertion into any location increases as the number of locations immediately preceding that location that are contiguously occupied increases. This problem can be solved by using *random probing*. A random sequence of positions is generated rather than an ordered sequence. Such a random sequence can be generated by the PL/I statement

Y = MOD (Y + C, M);

where Y is the previous position of the random sequence, C is a constant, and M is the size of the address space. C and M should be relatively prime to each other.

The program of Fig. 10-14 was rerun using the same data except that function OPENRP was used in place of function OPENLP. Figure 10-15 gives the function OPENRP and shows results obtained when the program was run. The variables used in OPENRP are:

Variable	Type	Usage
X	CHARACTER (*) VARYING	Key field to be hashed for insertion or look-up
INFO	CHARACTER (*) VARYING	Information field
INSERT	BIT (*)	Determines if look-up or insertion required
D	FIXED	Hashed value of key
J	FIXED	Index for random probing
Y	FIXED	Index for random probing
C	FIXED	Constant used to generate next random position

First the initial position is calculated in the function OPENRP. It uses the hashing function described earlier. Then an initial probe is made into the table. If an insertion is required, and the position is empty or a deleted record is in this location, the new record is inserted. For a look-up, if the search key and the key in the table match, the position is found. If this position is empty, a negated position is returned. Otherwise, a loop is entered in statement 48 to perform a search through the table. Each location in the table is scanned by computing the next location to be examined in statements 49 and 50. If the new position to be examined is the original position, an overflow or look-up error occurs, and the negated position is returned. In statements 59 to 61 an insertion, if required, is performed into an empty location or in a location that contains a deleted record. For look-ups, if the record position is empty, a negated position is returned since the search key was not found in the table. If it is found, the location of the record is returned.

While random probing solves the problem of *primary clustering*, it creates the problem of *secondary clustering*. All keys hashed into the same location generate the same random sequence. Another approach to solving this problem, called *double hashing*, requires two independent hashing functions. For example, if $H_1(x_1) = H_1(x_2)$ for $x_1 \neq x_2$, we can have a second hashing function H_2 such that $H_2(x_1) \neq H_2(x_2)$. An example of a double hashing procedure is given in Fig. 10-16. Only the functions OPENDH, HASH1, and HASH2 are given, and the output. The main program and data used are the same as in Fig. 10-14. Procedure OPENDH is the same as procedure OPENRP given in Fig. 10-15 except that statement 30 has been replaced by two statements that call two independent hashing functions. The function HASH1 is the same as HASH which was used in previous programs. HASH2, on the other hand is used to generate a random constant value for C. In HASH2, the statement VALUE = MOD(X, SIZE) + 1; is replaced by VALUE = MOD (X, SIZE – 2) + 1; thus giving an independent hashing function.

```
STMT LEVEL NEST BLOCK MLVL  SOURCE TEXT

  1                         PROBE: PROCEDURE OPTIONS (MAIN);
                            /* THIS PROGRAM INPUTS RECORDS AND KEYS AND PERFORMS THE REQUIRED */
                            /* LOOK-UPS AND INSERTIONS.  THE PROCEDURE OPENLP IS USED TO      */
                            /* PERFORM OPEN ADDRESSING USING LINEAR PROBING.                  */

  2     1       1           DECLARE 1 HASH_TABLE(17),              /* STRUCTURE OF HASH TABLE */
                                2 K CHARACTER (10) VARYING,  /* KEY FIELD */
                                2 DATA CHARACTER (20) VARYING,
                                                            /* INFORMATION FIELD */
                                2 FLAG CHARACTER (1),         /* DENOTES IF RECORD LOCA- */
                                   /* TION IS EMPTY 'E', OCCUPIED 'I', OR DELETED 'D' */
                                KEY CHARACTER (10) VARYING,    /* KEY FIELD OF RECORD */
                                INFO CHARACTER (20) VARYING,   /* INFORMATION FIELD */
                                M FIXED,                       /* SIZE OF HASH TABLE */
                                I FIXED,                       /* COUNTED LOOP VARIABLE */
                                NUM FIXED,                     /* NO OF RECORDS TO INSERT */
                                INSERT BIT (1),                /* LOGICAL FLAG FOR INSER- */
                                                               /* TION OR LOOK-UP */
                                POS FIXED,                     /* POSITION OF RECORD */
                                END_FLAG CHARACTER (3),        /* END OF FILE FLAG */
                                OPENLP ENTRY (CHARACTER (*) VARYING, CHARACTER (*) VARYING,
                                   BIT (*)) RETURNS (FIXED),
                                HASH ENTRY (CHARACTER (*) VARYING, FIXED) RETURNS (FIXED);

                            /* INITIALIZE HASH TABLE AND VARIABLES */
  3     1       1           M = 17;
  4     1       1           DO I = 1 TO M;
  5     1   1   1               FLAG(I) = 'E';
  6     1   1   1           END;
  7     1       1           END_FLAG = 'NO';
  8     1       1           ON ENDFILE (SYSIN) END_FLAG = 'YES';
 10     2       2           INSERT = '1'B;

                            /* INSERT REQUIRED RECORDS */
 11     1       1           GET LIST (NUM);
 12     1       1           PUT LIST ('INSERTED RECORDS ARE');
 13     1       1           PUT SKIP (2) EDIT ('KEY', 'INFORMATION FIELD', 'POSITION')
                                   (A, COL(10), A, COL(33), A);
 14     1       1           DO I = 1 TO NUM;
 15     1   1   1               GET LIST (KEY, INFO);
 16     1   1   1               PUT SKIP EDIT (KEY, INFO, OPENLP (KEY, INFO, INSERT))
                                       (A, COL(10), A, COL(36), F(2));
 17     1   1   1           END;

                            /* PERFORM REQUIRED LOOK-UPS */
 18     1       1           PUT SKIP (3) LIST ('POSITIONS OF LOOK-UP RECORDS ARE');
 19     1       1           PUT SKIP (2) EDIT ('KEY', 'POSITION') (A, COL(10), A);
 20     1       1           GET LIST (KEY);
 21     1       1           DO WHILE (END_FLAG = 'NO');
 22     1   1   1               POS = OPENLP (KEY, INFO, ¬INSERT);
 23     1   1   1               IF POS > 0
 24     1   1   1               THEN PUT SKIP EDIT (K(POS), POS) (A, COL(13), F(2));
 25     1   1   1               ELSE PUT SKIP EDIT ('INVALID KEY IS ', KEY) (A, A);
 26     1   1   1               GET LIST (KEY);
 27     1   1   1           END;
```

Fig. 10-14 Program to enter records into a table using linear probing

Recall that there are three main difficulties with open addressing. Colliding records tend to cluster. Also, table overflows are difficult to resolve, which requires a total reorganization of the table. Finally, record deletions are difficult. *Separate chaining* is one method that may be used to handle overflow records. Colliding records are chained in an *overflow area* which is distinct from the *prime area*. Thus, all records that are hashed into the same location are maintained in a linked list. Figure 10-17 gives a program using this approach. Note that the hash table

```
28   1     1          OPENLP: PROCEDURE (X, INFO, INSERT) RETURNS (FIXED);
                             /* THIS FUNCTION PERFORMS THE TABLE LOOK-UP AND INSERTION    */
                             /* OPERATIONS, AND RETURNS THE POSITION OF THE RECORD GIVEN  */
                             /* BY X, IF SUCCESSFUL.  OTHERWISE, A NEGATED POSITION IS    */
                             /* RETURNED, INDICATING AN ERROR.  THE HASHING FUNCTION HASH */
                             /* IS USED TO CALCULATE AN INITIAL POSITION.                 */

29   2     3          DECLARE X CHARACTER (*) VARYING,
                              INFO CHARACTER (*) VARYING,
                              INSERT BIT (*),        /* LOOK-UP OR INSERTION */
                              D FIXED,               /* HASHED VALUE */
                              I FIXED,               /* COUNTED LOOP VARIABLE */
                              FINISHED FIXED;        /* TERMINATES LOOP */

                             /* CALCULATE INITIAL POSITION */
30   2     3          D = HASH (X, M);

                             /* PERFORM INDICATED OPERATION IF LOCATION IS FOUND */
31   2     3          I = D;
32   2     3          FINISHED = D - 1;
33   2     3          DO WHILE (I ¬= FINISHED);
34   2   1 3              IF X = K(I)
35   2   1 3                 THEN IF ¬INSERT & FLAG(I) = 'I'
36   2   1 3                    THEN RETURN (I);      /* POSITION OF RETRIEVED RECORD*/
37   2   1 3                    ELSE RETURN (- I);  /* ERROR IN INSERTION */
38   2   1 3              IF FLAG(I) = 'E' ¦ FLAG(I) = 'D'
39   2   1 3                 THEN IF INSERT
40   2   1 3                    THEN DO;  /* PERFORM INDICATED INSERTION */
41   2   2 3                       K(I) = X;
42   2   2 3                       DATA(I) = INFO;
43   2   2 3                       FLAG(I) = 'I';
44   2   2 3                       RETURN (I);
45   2   2 3                       END;
46   2   1 3                    ELSE IF FLAG(I) = 'E'
47   2   1 3                       THEN RETURN (- I);  /* ERROR I LOOK-UP */
48   2   1 3              IF I = M
49   2   1 3                 THEN I = 1;
50   2   1 3                 ELSE I = I + 1;
51   2   1 3              END;

                             /* TABLE OVERFLOW */
52   2     3          PUT SKIP LIST ('OVERFLOW OR LOOK-UP ERROR');
53   2     3          RETURN (0);
54   2     3          END OPENLP;
```

```
INSERTED RECORDS ARE

KEY        INFORMATION FIELD     POSITION
FROG       AMPHIBIAN                3
WHALE      MAMMAL                  15
LYNX       MAMMAL                  14
SNAKE      REPTILE                 11
BLUEJAY    BIRD                    12
BEETLE     INSECT                  13
SALMON     FISH                     9


POSITIONS OF LOOK-UP RECORDS ARE

KEY        POSITION
LYNX          14
BLUEJAY       12
SALMON         9
INVALID KEY IS JACKFISH
INVALID KEY IS LADYBUG
SNAKE         11


IN STMT   62  PROGRAM RETURNS FROM MAIN PROCEDURE.
```

Fig. 10-14 Program to enter records into a table using linear probing (cont'd.)

```
28    1         1              OPENRP: PROCEDURE (X, INFO, INSERT) RETURNS (FIXED);
                               /* THIS FUNCTION PERFORMS THE TABLE LOOK-UP AND INSERTION    */
                               /* OPERATIONS AND RETURNS THE POSITION OF THE RECORD IN      */
                               /* QUESTION, IF SUCCESSFUL.  OTHERWISE, A NEGATED POSITION   */
                               /* IS RETURNED.                                              */

29    2         3              DECLARE X CHARACTER (*) VARYING,
                                       INFO CHARACTER (*) VARYING,
                                                            /* INFORMATION FIELD */
                                       INSERT BIT (*),      /* LOOK-UP OR INSERTION */
                                       D FIXED,             /* HASHED VALUE */
                                       (J, Y) FIXED,        /* INDICES FOR RANDOM PROBE */
                                       C FIXED;             /* RANDOM PROBE CONSTANT */

                               /* CALCULATE INITIAL POSITION */
30    2         3              D = HASH (X, M);

                               /* FIRST PROBE? */
31    2         3              IF INSERT
32    2         3              THEN IF FLAG(D) = 'D' | FLAG(D) = 'E'
33    2         3                  THEN DO;
34    2    1    3                      K(D) = X;
35    2    1    3                      DATA(D) = INFO;
36    2    1    3                      FLAG (D) = 'I';
37    2    1    3                      RETURN (D);
38    2    1    3                      END;
39    2         3                  ELSE IF X = K(D)
40    2         3                      THEN RETURN (-D);
41    2         3                      ELSE;
42    2         3              ELSE IF K(D) = X & FLAG(D) = 'I'
43    2         3                  THEN RETURN (D);
44    2         3                  ELSE IF FLAG(D) = 'D' | FLAG(D) = 'E'
45    2         3                      THEN RETURN (-D);

                               /* PERFORM SEARCH */
46    2         3              Y = D - 1;
47    2         3              C = 7;
48    2         3              DO WHILE ('1'B);

                                   /* SCAN NEXT ENTRY */
49    2    1    3                  Y = MOD (Y + C, M);
50    2    1    3                  J = Y + 1;

                                   /* OVERFLOW? */
51    2    1    3                  IF J = D
52    2    1    3                  THEN DO;
53    2    2    3                      PUT SKIP LIST ('OVERFLOW OR LOOK-UP ERROR');
54    2    2    3                      RETURN (0);
55    2    2    3                      END;

                                   /* PERFORM LOOK-UP OR INSERTION */
56    2    1    3                  IF INSERT
57    2    1    3                  THEN IF FLAG(J) = 'D' | FLAG(J) = 'E'
58    2    1    3                      THEN DO;
59    2    2    3                          K(J) = X;
60    2    2    3                          DATA(J) = INFO;
61    2    2    3                          FLAG(J) = 'I';
62    2    2    3                          RETURN(J);
63    2    2    3                          END;
64    2    1    3                      ELSE IF K(J) = X
65    2    1    3                          THEN RETURN (-J);
66    2    1    3                          ELSE;
67    2    1    3                  ELSE IF FLAG(J) = 'E'
68    2    1    3                      THEN RETURN (-J);
69    2    1    3                      ELSE IF K(J) = X
70    2    1    3                          THEN RETURN (J);
71    2    1    3                  END;
72    2         3              END OPENRP;
```

Fig. 10-15   Program to resolve record collisions using random probing

```
INSERTED RECORDS ARE

KEY        INFORMATION FIELD      POSITION
FROG       AMPHIBIAN                11
WHALE      MAMMAL                    2
LYNX       MAMMAL                    1
SNAKE      REPTILE                   9
BLUEJAY    BIRD                      7
BEETLE     INSECT                    4
SALMON     FISH                      8


POSITIONS OF LOOK-UP RECORDS ARE

KEY        POSITION
LYNX          1
BLUEJAY       7
SALMON        8
INVALID KEY IS JACKFISH
INVALID KEY IS LADYBUG
SNAKE         9



IN STMT   80  PROGRAM RETURNS FROM MAIN PROCEDURE.
```

Fig. 10-15 Program to resolve record collisions using random probing (cont'd.)

merely becomes a vector of pointers to the linked lists. A value of NULL in any position of the hash table means that the corresponding linked list is empty.

The variables used in the main program are:

Variable	Type	Usage
HASH_TABLE(100)	POINTER	Pointer vector representing hash table
RECORD	BASED (NEW)	Structure for storing records
KEY	CHARACTER (20)	Key field of record
DATA	CHARACTER (20)	Information field of record
LINK	POINTER	Pointer to next record in linked list
POS	POINTER	Pointer for printing linked lists
X	CHARACTER (20)	Key field of record to be inserted or looked-up
INFO	CHARACTER (20)	Information field of record
M	FIXED	Size of hash table
END_FLAG	CHARACTER (3)	End of file flag
I	FIXED	Counted loop variable

The variables used in procedure ENTER are:

X	CHARACTER (20)	Key field of record to be inserted or looked-up
INFO	CHARACTER (20)	Information field of record
RANDOM	FIXED	Hashed value of key
P	POINTER	Temporary pointer variable

```
28    1    1              OPENDH: PROCEDURE (X, INFO, INSERT) RETURNS (FIXED);
                              /* THIS FUNCTION PERFORMS THE TABLE LOOK-UP AND INSERTION   */
                              /* OPERATIONS USING DOUBLE HASHING, AND RETURNS THE POSITION */
                              /* OF THE KEY X, IF SUCCESSFUL.  OTHERWISE, A NEGATED OR     */
                              /* ZERO POSITION IS RETURNED.  HASH1 GIVES THE FIRST HASH    */
                              /* VALUE WHILE HASH2 IS AN INDEPENDENT HASHING FUNCTION FOR  */
                              /* THE SECOND HASHED VALUE.                                  */

29    2    3              DECLARE X CHARACTER (*) VARYING,
                                  INFO CHARACTER (*) VARYING,
                                                      /* INFORMATION FIELD */
                                  INSERT BIT (*),     /* LOOK-UP OR INSERTION */
                                  D FIXED,            /* HASH1 VALUE OF X */
                                  (J, Y) FIXED,       /* INDICES FOR RANDOM PROBE */
                                  C FIXED;            /* SECOND HASHED VALUE */

                          /* CALCULATE INITIAL POSITION */
30    2    3              D = HASH1 (X, M);
31    2    3              C = HASH2 (X, M);

                          /* FIRST PROBE? */
32    2    3              IF INSERT
33    2    3              THEN IF FLAG(D) = 'D' | FLAG(D) = 'E'
34    2    3                  THEN DO;
35    2  1 3                      K(D) = X;
36    2  1 3                      DATA(D) = INFO;
37    2  1 3                      FLAG (D) = 'I';
38    2  1 3                      RETURN (D);
39    2  1 3                      END;
40    2    3                  ELSE IF X = K(D)
41    2    3                      THEN RETURN (-D);
42    2    3                      ELSE;
43    2    3              ELSE IF K(D) = X & FLAG(D) = 'I'
44    2    3                  THEN RETURN (D);
45    2    3                  ELSE IF FLAG(D) = 'D' | FLAG(D) = 'E'
46    2    3                      THEN RETURN (-D);

                          /* PERFORM SEARCH */
47    2    3              Y = D - 1;
48    2    3              DO WHILE ('1'B);

                              /* SCAN NEXT ENTRY */
49    2  1 3                  Y = MOD (Y + C, M);
50    2  1 3                  J = Y + 1;
                              /* OVERFLOW? */
51    2  1 3                  IF J = D
52    2  1 3                  THEN DO;
53    2  2 3                      PUT SKIP LIST ('OVERFLOW OR LOOK-UP ERROR');
54    2  2 3                      RETURN (0);
55    2  2 3                      END;

                              /* PERFORM LOOK-UP OR INSERTION */
56    2  1 3                  IF INSERT
57    2  1 3                  THEN IF FLAG(J) = 'D' | FLAG(J) = 'E'
58    2  1 3                      THEN DO;
59    2  2 3                          K(J) = X;
60    2  2 3                          DATA(J) = INFO;
61    2  2 3                          FLAG(J) = 'I';
62    2  2 3                          RETURN(J);
63    2  2 3                          END;
64    2  1 3                      ELSE IF K(J) = X
65    2  1 3                          THEN RETURN (-J);
66    2  1 3                          ELSE;
67    2  1 3                  ELSE IF FLAG(J) = 'E'
68    2  1 3                      THEN RETURN (-J);
69    2  1 3                      ELSE IF K(J) = X
70    2  1 3                          THEN RETURN (J);
71    2  1 3                  END;
72    2    3              END OPENDH;
```

Fig. 10-16 Program to perform double hashing

```
73    1    1        HASH1: PROCEDURE (SYMBOL, SIZE) RETURNS (FIXED);
                        /* THIS HASHING FUNCTION RETURNS THE HASH VALUE OF THE STRING*/
                        /* SYMBOL BY USING THE LENGTH-DEPENDENT METHOD.            */

74    2    4            DECLARE SYMBOL CHARACTER (*) VARYING,
                            SIZE FIXED,            /* SIZE OF TABLE */
                            (FIRST_CHAR, LAST_CHAR) /* FIRST AND LAST CHARACTERS */
                                CHARACTER (1),     /* OF SYMBOL */
                            VALUE FIXED;           /* PRECONDITIONED RESULT */

                        /* GET FIRST AND LAST CHARACTERS OF SYMBOL */
75    2    4            FIRST_CHAR = SUBSTR (SYMBOL, 1, 1);
76    2    4            LAST_CHAR = SUBSTR (SYMBOL, LENGTH (SYMBOL));

                        /* COMPUTE PRECONDITIONED RESULT */
77    2    4            VALUE = UNSPEC (FIRST_CHAR) + UNSPEC (LAST_CHAR) +
                                16 * LENGTH (SYMBOL);

                        /* RETURN HASHED VALUE */
78    2    4            RETURN (MOD (VALUE, SIZE) + 1);
79    2    4        END HASH1;

80    1    1        HASH2: PROCEDURE (SYMBOL, SIZE) RETURNS (FIXED);
                        /* THIS FUNCTION IS AN INDEPENDENT HASHING FUNCTION THAT    */
                        /* RETURNS THE HASHED VALUE OF X WHICH IS TO BE USED AS THE */
                        /* CONSTANT FOR RANDOM PROBING.                            */

81    2    5            DECLARE SYMBOL CHARACTER (*) VARYING,
                            SIZE FIXED,            /* SIZE OF TABLE */
                            (FIRST_CHAR, LAST_CHAR) /* FIRST AND LAST CHARACTERS */
                                CHARACTER (1),     /* OF SYMBOL */
                            VALUE FIXED;           /* PRECONDITIONED RESULT */

                        /* GET FIRST AND LAST CHARACTERS OF SYMBOL */
82    2    5            FIRST_CHAR = SUBSTR (SYMBOL, 1, 1);
83    2    5            LAST_CHAR = SUBSTR (SYMBOL, LENGTH (SYMBOL));

                        /* COMPUTE PRECONDITIONED RESULT */
84    2    5            VALUE = UNSPEC (FIRST_CHAR) + UNSPEC (LAST_CHAR) +
                                16 * LENGTH (SYMBOL);

                        /* RETURN HASHED VALUE */
85    2    5            RETURN (MOD (VALUE, SIZE - 2) + 1);
86    2    5        END HASH2;
```

```
INSERTED RECORDS ARE

KEY       INFORMATION FIELD       POSITION
FROG      AMPHIBIAN                 11
WHALE     MAMMAL                     2
LYNX      MAMMAL                     1
SNAKE     REPTILE                    9
BLUEJAY   BIRD                       8
BEETLE    INSECT                     4
SALMON    FISH                       7


POSITIONS OF LOOK-UP RECORDS ARE

KEY       POSITION
INVALID KEY IS DUCK
INVALID KEY IS BIRD
INVALID KEY IS MONKEY
INVALID KEY IS MAMMAL
LYNX        1
BLUEJAY     8
SALMON      7
INVALID KEY IS JACKFISH
INVALID KEY IS LADYBUG
SNAKE       9


IN STMT   87  PROGRAM RETURNS FROM MAIN PROCEDURE.
```

Fig. 10-16   Program to perform double hashing (cont'd.)

The main program first initializes the hash table to NULL. Then statements 12 to 16 read the records and call procedure ENTER to insert them into the appropriate linked list. Finally, the program outputs the linked lists formed by procedure ENTER.

In procedure ENTER, the hash value of the key X is first computed. Then statement 31 checks whether or not the linked list where the record is to be inserted is empty. The hash table position will have a NULL value if it is empty. If the linked list is not empty a search is made to determine if the new record is already present. If not, in statements 46 to 50 the new record is inserted at the front of the linked list.

The hashing function is essentially the same as the one discussed near the beginning of this section. Since the key fields are of fixed length, it is necessary to search for the end of the key field which is assumed to be the last nonblank character in this field. This is done in statements 55 to 59.

So far we have been concerned with searching using hashing functions. next, we look at a method of sorting that uses an order-preserving hashing function.

Address-Calculation Sorting

An order-preserving hashing function has the property

$$x_1 < x_2 \text{ implies that } HASH(x_1) \leqslant HASH(x_2)$$

The variables used in the program are:

Variable	Type	Usage
RECORD	BASED (NEW)	Structure representing records
K	CHARACTER (20)	Key field of record
DATA	CHARACTER (20)	Information field of record
LINK	POINTER	Points to next record in list
KEY	CHARACTER (20)	Key field of record read
INFO	CHARACTER (20)	Information field of record read
HASH_TABLE(13)	POINTER	Vector of pointers representing hash table
M	FIXED	Size of record table
RANDOM	FIXED	Hashed value of key
I	FIXED	Counted loop variable
P	POINTER	Pointer to insert record into hash table
S	POINTER	Pointer to insert record into hash table
HEAD	POINTER	Points to head of sorted linked list
END_FLAG	CHARACTER (3)	End of file flag

Variables used in the function HASH are:

KEY	CHARACTER (*)	Key which is to be hashed
CHAR	CHARACTER (1)	Stores first character of key
VALUE	FIXED	Hashed value of key

The program initializes all elements in the hash table to NULL. The first record is read in statement 11. Then a loop is entered to sort the records. First a new record is allocated and initialized. Then the key is hashed and the record is inserted into the appropriate linked list. Statement 21 determines whether the record is to be inserted into a null linked list. If not, a search is made through the list and the record is inserted such that the order of the keys are preserved in increasing order. Then in statement 45, the next record is read. After all the records have been processed, the nonempty linked lists are concatenated. Finally, the sorted table is printed in statements 65 to 71.

The function HASH returns a value that is order preserving by computing the position in the alphabet that the first character of the key is found. Then this preconditioned value is mapped into the address space.

10-9.3 Radix Sorting

The notion of radix sorting was introduced in the exercises at the end of Chap. 4 in the main text, and discussed further in Sec. 10-10.3 of the main text. In radix sorting, there are 10 pockets, one for each digit value. Each digit position is sorted, where all records having the same digit in the same position in the key field are placed into the same pocket. All digits are processed in turn, starting with the lowest-order digit.

For example, the table

73, 65, 52, 77, 24, 83, 17, 35, 96, 62, 41, 87, 09, 11

is first sorted by the low-order digits, giving

```
                                87
            11  62  83      35  17
            41  52  73  24  65  96  77      09
Pocket:  0   1   2   3   4   5   6   7   8   9
```

This results, after placing the contents of the 0 pocket at the bottom and the 9 pocket on top, in the table:

41, 11, 52, 62, 73, 83, 24, 65, 35, 96, 77, 17, 87, 09

After sorting on the high-order digit, we obtain:

```
            17                  65  77  87
        09  11  24  35  41  52  62  73  83  96
Pocket:  0   1   2   3   4   5   6   7   8   9
```

giving the sorted table

09, 11, 17, 24, 35, 41, 52, 62, 65, 73, 77, 83, 87, 96

A general algorithm to sort the keys containing m digits follows. Note that m successive passes are required.

```
1              CHAIN: PROCEDURE OPTIONS (MAIN);
                    /* THIS PROGRAM INPUTS A SERIES OF RECORDS AND ENTERS THEM INTO A */
                    /* HASH TABLE USING SEPARATE CHAINING.  PROCEDURE ENTER IS        */
                    /* USED TO PERFORM THE INSERTION.                                 */

2              DECLARE HASH_TABLE(11) POINTER,     /* POINTER VECTOR REPRESENTING */
                                                   /* THE HASH TABLE */
                       1 RECORD BASED (NEW),       /* RECORD STRUCTURE */
                         2 KEY CHARACTER (20),     /* KEY FIELD */
                         2 DATA CHARACTER (20),    /* INFORMATION FIELD */
                         2 LINK POINTER,           /* POINTER TO NEXT RECORD */
                       POS POINTER,                /* USED TO PRINT LINKED LISTS */
                       X CHARACTER (20),           /* KEY FIELD OF NEW RECORD */
                       INFO CHARACTER (20),        /* INFORMATION FIELD */
                       M FIXED,                    /* SIZE OF HASH TABLE */
                       END_FLAG CHARACTER (3),     /* END OF FILE FLAG */
                       I FIXED,                    /* COUNTED LOOP VARIABLE */
                       HASH ENTRY (CHARACTER (*), FIXED) RETURNS (FIXED);

               /* INITIALIZE HASH TABLE AND VARIABLES */
3              M = 11;
4              DO I = 1 TO M;
5                   HASH_TABLE(I) = NULL;
6              END;

               /* INPUT VARIABLES TO ENTER INTO TABLE */
7              END_FLAG = 'NO';
8              ON ENDFILE (SYSIN) END_FLAG = 'YES';
10             PUT LIST ('RECORDS HASHED TO');
11             PUT SKIP;
12             GET LIST (X, INFO);
13             DO WHILE (END_FLAG = 'NO');
14                  CALL ENTER (X, INFO);
15                  GET LIST (X, INFO);
16             END;

               /* PRINT OUT LINKED LISTS */
17             PUT SKIP (3) LIST ('LINKED LISTS FORMED BY PROCEDURE ENTER');
18             PUT SKIP;
19             DO I = 1 TO M;
20                  POS = HASH_TABLE(I);
21                  PUT SKIP EDIT ('ROW ', I) (A, F(2));
22                  DO WHILE (POS ¬= NULL);
23                       PUT EDIT (POS -> KEY) (X(2), A);
24                       POS = POS -> LINK;
25                  END;
26             END;
```

Fig. 10-17   Program to resolve collisions using separate chaining

1. Repeat thru step 3 for each digit
2. Initialize the pointers to the front and rear of the linked lists for each pocket to NULL
3. Repeat for each node in the linked list
     Obtain the jth digit of the key
     If the list for the appropriate pocket is empty, set the front and rear pointers to the address of the new node in the linked list,
     else add it to the end of the list
4. Find the first nonempty pocket and concatenate the nonempty pockets together

A main program and the procedure RADIX_SORT are given in Fig. 10-19. The program sorted the tables

73, 65, 52, 77, 24, 83, 17, 35, 96, 62, 41, 87, 09, 22

```
27                  ENTER: PROCEDURE (X, INFO);
                        /* GIVEN A POINTER VECTOR HASH_TABLE REPRESENTING A HASH   */
                        /* TABLE, EACH ELEMENT OF WHICH CONTAINS A POINTER TO A    */
                        /* LINKED LIST OF COLLIDING RECORDS, AND A HASHING FUNCTION */
                        /* HASH, THIS PROGRAM APPENDS THE GIVEN KEY (X) AND THE    */
                        /* INFORMATION FIELD (INFO) TO THE FRONT OF THE APPROPRIATE */
                        /* LINKED LIST IF IT IS NOT ALREADY THERE.                 */

28                      DECLARE (X, INFO) CHARACTER (20),
                                RANDOM FIXED,          /* HASHED VALUE OF KEY */
                                P POINTER;             /* TEMPORARY POINTER VARIABLE */
                        /* COMPUTE THE HASH NUMBER */
29                      RANDOM = HASH (X, M);

                        /* IS LINKED LIST TO WHICH X BELONGS EMPTY? */
30                      PUT SKIP EDIT (X, ' HASHED INTO ', RANDOM) (A, A, F(2));
31                      IF HASH_TABLE(RANDOM) = NULL
32                      THEN DO;
33                          ALLOCATE RECORD;
34                          HASH_TABLE(RANDOM) = NEW;
35                          NEW -> KEY = X;
36                          NEW -> DATA = INFO;
37                          NEW -> LINK = NULL;
38                          RETURN;
39                          END;

                        /* PERFORM SEARCH FOR X */
40                      P = HASH_TABLE(RANDOM);
41                      DO WHILE (P ¬= NULL);
42                          IF X = P -> KEY
43                          THEN RETURN;  /* X IS ALREADY PRESENT */
44                          ELSE P = P -> LINK;
45                      END;

                        /* X IS NOT IN THE TABLE */
46                      ALLOCATE RECORD;
47                      NEW -> KEY = X;
48                      NEW -> DATA = INFO;
49                      NEW -> LINK = HASH_TABLE(RANDOM);
50                      HASH_TABLE(RANDOM) = NEW;
51                      RETURN;
52                  END ENTER;

53              HASH: PROCEDURE (SYMBOL, SIZE) RETURNS (FIXED DECIMAL);
                        /* THIS FUNCTION COMPUTES THE HASH VALUE OF THE STRING SYMBOL*/
                        /* BY USING THE LENGTH-DEPENDENT METHOD.                   */
54                      DECLARE SYMBOL CHARACTER (*), /* STRING TO BE HASHED */
                                SIZE FIXED,          /* SIZE OF TABLE */
                                (FIRST_CHAR, LAST_CHAR) /* FIRST AND LAST CHARACTERS */
                                  CHARACTER (1),     /* OF SYMBOL */
                                M FIXED,             /* SIZE OF KEY */
                                VALUE FIXED;         /* PRECONDITIONED VALUE     */

                        /* GET FIRST CHARACTER AND LAST NONBLANK CHARACTER OF SYMBOL */
55                      FIRST_CHAR = SUBSTR (SYMBOL, 1, 1);
56                      M = LENGTH (SYMBOL);
57                      DO WHILE (SUBSTR (SYMBOL, M, 1) = ' ');
58                          M = M - 1;
59                      END;
60                      LAST_CHAR = SUBSTR (SYMBOL, M);

                        /* COMPUTE PRECONDITIONED RESULT */
61                      VALUE = UNSPEC (FIRST_CHAR) + UNSPEC (LAST_CHAR) +
                                16 * M;

                        /* RETURN HASHED VALUE */
62                      RETURN (MOD (VALUE, SIZE) + 1);
63                  END HASH;
64              END CHAIN;
```

Fig. 10-17   Program to resolve collisions using separate chaining (cont'd.)

```
RECORDS HASHED TO

FROG                HASHED INTO 11
LION                HASHED INTO  5
PELICAN             HASHED INTO  2
WHALE               HASHED INTO  2
LYNX                HASHED INTO  1
SNAKE               HASHED INTO  9
BLUEJAY             HASHED INTO 11
BEETLE              HASHED INTO  4
SALMON              HASHED INTO  8
DUCK                HASHED INTO  9
MONKEY              HASHED INTO  2
WOLF                HASHED INTO  9


LINKED LISTS FORMED BY PROCEDURE ENTER

ROW  1  LYNX
ROW  2  MONKEY              WHALE               PELICAN
ROW  3
ROW  4  BEETLE
ROW  5  LION
ROW  6
ROW  7
ROW  8  SALMON
ROW  9  WOLF                DUCK                SNAKE
ROW 10
ROW 11  BLUEJAY             FROG
```

Fig. 10-17   Program to resolve collisions using separate chaining (cont'd.)

and

    38, 52, 59, 53, 11, 76

This program assumes that the key field is read as a character string so that single digits can easily be removed from the keys. The variables used in the main program are:

Variable	Type	Usage
NODE	BASED (P)	Table of records
K	CHARACTER (10) VARYING	Key field
LINK	POINTER	Pointer to next node in list
N	FIXED	Number of records in table
KEY	CHARACTER (10) VARYING	Key of record read
M	FIXED	Size of key field
I	FIXED	Counted loop variable
J	FIXED	Counted loop variable
FIRST	POINTER	Pointer to first node in table
PREV	POINTER	Pointer used to build sorted table

Variables used in procedure RADIX_SORT are:

N	FIXED	Number of records in table
M	FIXED	Size of key field
FIRST	POINTER	Head of list to be sorted

T(0:9)	POINTER	Pointers to first nodes in the linked lists of the pockets
B(0:9)	POINTER	Pointers to last nodes in the linked lists of the pockets
I	FIXED	Counted loop variable
J	FIXED	Counted loop variable
TEMP	FIXED	Index variable
R	POINTER	Pointer to current node in list
NEXT	POINTER	Pointer to next node in list
PREV	POINTER	Used to combine the pockets at the end of a pass
POINT	POINTER	Temporary pointer variable
D	CHARACTER (1)	Current digit used to sort record
D_INT	FIXED	Integer value of digit D

In the main program, statement 3 controls a loop that sorts the tables. The next statement reads the number of records in the table and the key size. Next, the table is read and built as a linked list. Procedure RADIX_SORT is called in statement 20 to sort the table. Finally, statements 21 to 29 print the sorted table.

In procedure RADIX_SORT, statement 33 controls the passes for each digit in the key. First the pointers for the pockets are initialized to NULL. Then statement 39 controls a loop to distribute each record into the appropriate pocket. The jth digit is obtained and converted into its integer value. Then, the record is appended to the end of the appropriate pocket. Once all records have been placed into the appropriate pockets, the resulting linked lists are concatenated. Statements 57 and 58 search for the first nonempty pocket. Then the pointer to the last node of each nonempty pocket is set to the address of the first node of the next nonempty pocket. The pointer variable FIRST is set to the address of the first record of the sorted linked list.

EXERCISES FOR CHAPTER 10

1. Write a PL/I program to subtract two polynomials in three variables.

2. Write a PL/I program to multiply two polynomials in three variables.

3. Formulate a PL/I program for evaluating a polynomial of three variables which is represented by a linked list. The values for x, y, z are given as a, b, and c, respectively.

4. Using the division method of hashing with m = 101 and the UNSPEC function in PL/I, obtain the hash values for the following set of keys:

    'NAME'
    'RATE'
    'DATE'
    'NUM'

5. Write a PL/I function procedure for the mid-square hashing method which extracts the middle N bits of the square of a five-digit key. The procedure is to have two parameters:

```
1        ADD_CAL: PROCEDURE OPTIONS (MAIN);
            /* THIS PROGRAM INPUTS RECORDS AND SORTS THEM BASED ON AN ADDRESS */
            /* CALCULATION WITH A SEPARATE OVERFLOW AREA USING AN ORDER       */
            /* PRESERVING HASHING FUNCTION.                                   */

2        DECLARE 1 RECORD BASED (NEW),        /* USED TO SORT RECORDS */
                2 K CHARACTER (20),           /* KEY */
                2 DATA CHARACTER (20),        /* INFORMATION FIELD */
                2 LINK POINTER,
                (KEY,                         /* KEY OF RECORD */
                 INFO) CHARACTER (20),        /* INFORMATION FIELD OF RECORD */
                M FIXED,                      /* SIZE OF TABLE */
                RANDOM FIXED,                 /* HASHED VALUE OF KEY */
                I FIXED,                      /* LOOP COUNTER VARIABLE */
                (P, S) POINTER,               /* USED TO INSERT ELEMENTS */
                HASH_TABLE(13) POINTER,       /* POINTS TO OVERFLOW AREAS */
                HEAD POINTER,                 /* HEAD OF SORTED LINKED LIST */
                END_FLAG CHARACTER (3);       /* END OF FILE FLAG */
3        DECLARE HASH ENTRY (CHARACTER (*)) RETURNS (FIXED);

         /* INITIALIZE HASH TABLE */
4        M = 13;
5        DO I = 1 TO M;
6            HASH_TABLE(I) = NULL;
7        END;
8        END_FLAG = 'NO';
9        ON ENDFILE (SYSIN) END_FLAG = 'YES';

         /* INPUT AND INSERT RECORDS INTO APPROPRIATE LINKED LISTS */
11       GET LIST (KEY, INFO);
12       PUT LIST ('UNSORTED TABLE IS');
13       PUT SKIP;
14       DO WHILE (END_FLAG = 'NO');
15           PUT SKIP EDIT (KEY, INFO) (A, X(2), A);
16           ALLOCATE RECORD;
17           NEW -> K = KEY;
18           NEW -> DATA = INFO;
19           NEW -> LINK = NULL;
20           RANDOM = HASH (KEY);

             /* INSERT RECORD INTO APPROPRIATE LINKED LIST */
21           IF HASH_TABLE(RANDOM) = NULL
22           THEN DO;  /* INSERT RECORD INTO EMPTY LINKED LIST */
23               NEW -> LINK = NULL;
24               HASH_TABLE(RANDOM) = NEW;
25               END;
26           ELSE DO;  /* INSERT RECORD IN MIDDLE OR AT END OF LIST */
27               P = HASH_TABLE(RANDOM);
28               S = P;
29               DO WHILE (S -> LINK ¬= NULL & S -> K < KEY);
30                   P = S;
31                   S = S -> LINK;
32                   END;
33               IF S = HASH_TABLE(RANDOM) & KEY <= S -> K
34               THEN DO;  /* INSERT AT FRONT */
35                   HASH_TABLE(RANDOM) = NEW;
36                   NEW -> LINK = S;
37                   END;
38               ELSE IF S -> LINK = NULL & KEY > S -> K
                     THEN /* INSERT AT END */
39                       S -> LINK = NEW;
40                   ELSE DO;  /* INSERT IN MIDDLE */
41                       P -> LINK = NEW;
42                       NEW -> LINK = S;
43                       END;
44               END;
45           GET LIST (KEY, INFO);
46       END;

         /* FIND FIRST NON-EMPTY LINKED LIST */
47       I = 1;
48       DO WHILE (HASH_TABLE(I) = NULL & I < M);
49           I = I + 1;
50       END;
```

Fig. 10-18   Program to perform address-calculation sort

```
51                      HEAD = HASH_TABLE(I);
52                      J = I + 1;

                        /* CONCATENATE THE NON-EMPTY LINKED LISTS */
53                      DO WHILE (J <= M);
54                          IF HASH_TABLE(J) ¬= NULL
55                          THEN DO;  /* FIND TAIL OF LINKED LIST */
56                              P = HASH_TABLE(I);
57                              DO WHILE (P -> LINK ¬= NULL);
58                                  P = P -> LINK;
59                              END;

                                /* LINK END OF THIS LINKED LIST TO THE HEAD OF THE NEXT */
60                              P -> LINK = HASH_TABLE(J);
61                              I = J;
62                          END;
63                          J = J + 1;
64                      END;

                        /* PRINT LINKED LIST */
65                      PUT SKIP (3) LIST ('SORTED LIST IS');
66                      PUT SKIP;
67                      P = HEAD;
68                      DO WHILE (P ¬= NULL);
69                          PUT SKIP EDIT (P -> K, P -> DATA) (A, X(2), A);
70                          P = P -> LINK;
71                      END;

72                      HASH: PROCEDURE (KEY) RETURNS (FIXED);
                            /* THIS ORDER PRESERVING HASHING FUNCTION RETURNS A HASH    */
                            /* VALUE OF KEY.                                            */
73                          DECLARE KEY CHARACTER (*),
                                    CHAR CHARACTER (1),    /* FIRST CHARACTER OF KEY */
                                    VALUE FIXED;           /* HASHED VALUE OF KEY */

                            /* COMPUTE HASHED VALUE OF KEY */
74                          CHAR = SUBSTR (KEY, 1, 1);
75                          VALUE = INDEX ('ABCDEFGHIJKLMNOPQRSTUVWXYZ', CHAR);
76                          VALUE = CEIL (VALUE / 2.0);
77                          RETURN (VALUE);
78                      END HASH;
79                  END ADD_CAL;


UNSORTED TABLE IS

CAT                 FELIS CATUS
DOG                 CANIS FAMILIARIS
PIKE                ESOX LUCIUS
CANADA GOOSE        BRANTA CANADENSIS
DOLPHIN             DELPHINUS DELPHIS
MAN                 HOMO SAPIENS
MALLARD DUCK        ANAS BOSCAS
HORSE               EQUUS CABALLUS
CANARY              SERINUS CANARIUS


SORTED LIST IS

CANADA GOOSE        BRANTA CANADENSIS
CANARY              SERINUS CANARIUS
CAT                 FELIS CATUS
DOG                 CANIS FAMILIARIS
DOLPHIN             DELPHINUS DELPHIS
HORSE               EQUUS CABALLUS
MALLARD DUCK        ANAS BOSCAS
MAN                 HOMO SAPIENS
PIKE                ESOX LUCIUS
```

Fig. 10-18   Program to perform address-calculation sort (cont'd.)

```
1               SORT: PROCEDURE OPTIONS (MAIN);
                  /* THIS PROGRAM INPUTS TABLES OF VALUES CONSISTING OF 2 DIGIT   */
                  /* NUMBERS (WHICH ARE READ AS STRINGS) AND SORTS THEM BY USING  */
                  /* PROCEDURE RADIX_SORT.                                        */

2                 DECLARE 1 NODE BASED (P),    /* TABLE OF RECORDS */
                            2 K CHARACTER (10), /* KEY FIELD */
                            2 LINK POINTER,     /* POINTER FIELD */
                          N FIXED,              /* NUMBER OF RECORDS IN TABLE */
                          KEY CHARACTER (10),   /* RECORD KEY WHICH IS READ IN */
                          M FIXED,              /* SIZE OF KEY FIELD */
                          (I, J) FIXED,         /* COUNTED LOOP VARIABLES */
                          FIRST POINTER,        /* ADDRESS OF FIRST NODE IN TABLE */
                          PREV POINTER;         /* USED TO BUILD TABLE */

                  /* PROCESS EACH TABLE */
3                 DO I = 1 TO 2;

                     /* INPUT NUMBER OF RECORDS IN TABLE AND SIZE OF KEY */
4                    GET LIST (N, M);

                     /* INPUT TABLE */
5                    PUT SKIP (3) LIST ('UNSORTED TABLE IS');
6                    PUT SKIP;
7                    FIRST = NULL;
8                    PREV = NULL;
9                    DO J = 1 TO N;
10                      GET LIST (KEY);
11                      ALLOCATE NODE;
12                      P -> K = KEY;
13                      P -> LINK = NULL;
14                      IF PREV = NULL
15                      THEN FIRST = P;
16                      ELSE PREV -> LINK = P;
17                      PREV = P;
18                      PUT EDIT (KEY) (A(6));
19                    END;

                     /* SORT THE TABLE */
20                   CALL RADIX_SORT (N, M, FIRST);

                     /* PRINT THE TABLE AND FREE THE NODES FOR THE NEXT TABLE */
21                   PUT SKIP (2) LIST ('SORTED TABLE IS');
22                   PUT SKIP;
23                   PREV = FIRST;
24                   DO WHILE (PREV ¬= NULL);
25                      PUT EDIT (PREV -> K) (A(6));
26                      FIRST = PREV -> LINK;
27                      FREE PREV -> NODE;
28                      PREV = FIRST;
29                   END;
30                END;
```

Fig. 10-19 Program to sort records using the radix sort

KEY - numerical key
N - number of bits to be extracted

The function is to return the hash value obtained in the computation.

6. Write a PL/I function for the folding method of hashing. Assume that a three digit address (000 – 999) is required. The function, which has one parameter, is to return the desired hash value.

7. Compare the results of applying the division, midsquare, and folding hashing functions to a fixed set of keys. Make sure the ranges of these three functions

```
31             RADIX_SORT: PROCEDURE (N, M, FIRST);
                     /* GIVEN A TABLE OF N RECORDS ARRANGED AS A LINKED LIST     */
                     /* WHERE EACH NODE CONSISTS OF A KEY FIELD (K) OF M DIGITS   */
                     /* AND A POINTER FIELD (LINK), THIS PROCEDURE PERFORMS A      */
                     /* RADIX SORT.                                                */
32                   DECLARE (N, M) FIXED,

                             FIRST POINTER,                /* HEAD OF LIST */
                             (T(0:9), B(0:9)) POINTER,     /* ADDRESSES OF REAR AND   */
                                                           /* FRONT RECORDS IN QUEUES*/
                             (I, J, TEMP) FIXED,           /* INDEX VARIABLES */
                             R POINTER,                    /* ADDRESS OF CURRENT WORD*/
                             NEXT POINTER,                 /* ADDRESS OF NEXT WORD    */
                             PREV POINTER,                 /* USED TO COMBINE POCKETS*/
                                                           /* AT END OF PASS */
                             POINT POINTER,                /* TEMP POINTER VARIABLE */
                             D CHARACTER (1),              /* DIGIT BEING EXAMINED */
                             D_INT FIXED;                  /* INTEGER VALUE OF D */

                     /* PERFORM SORT */
33                   DO J = 1 TO M;

                         /* INITIALIZE PASS */
34                       DO I = 0 TO 9;
35                           T(I) = NULL;
36                           B(I) = NULL;
37                       END;
38                       R = FIRST;

                         /* DISTRIBUTE EACH RECORD INTO THE APPROPRIATE POCKET */
39                       DO WHILE (R ¬= NULL);

                             /* OBTAIN JTH DIGIT OF KEY K(R) */
40                           D = SUBSTR (R -> K, M - J + 1, 1);
41                           D_INT = INDEX ('0123456789', D) - 1;
42                           NEXT = R -> LINK;
43                           IF T(D_INT) = NULL
44                           THEN DO;
45                               T(D_INT) = R;
46                               B(D_INT) = R;
47                               END;
48                           ELSE DO;
49                               POINT = T(D_INT);
50                               POINT -> LINK = R;
51                               T(D_INT) = R;
52                               END;
53                           R -> LINK = NULL;
54                           R = NEXT;
55                       END;

                         /* COMBINE POCKETS */
56                       TEMP = 0;
57                       DO WHILE (B(TEMP) = NULL);
58                           TEMP = TEMP + 1;
59                       END;
60                       FIRST = B(TEMP);
61                       DO I = TEMP + 1 TO 9;
62                           PREV = T(I - 1);
63                           IF T(I) ¬= NULL
64                           THEN PREV -> LINK = B(I);
65                           ELSE T(I) = PREV;
66                       END;
67                   END;
68             END RADIX_SORT;
69         END SORT;
```

Fig. 10-19   Program to sort records using the radix sort (cont'd.)

```
UNSORTED TABLE IS
73   65   52   77   24   83   17   35   96   62   41   87   09   22

SORTED TABLE IS
09   17   22   24   35   41   52   62   65   73   77   83   87   96


UNSORTED TABLE IS
38   52   59   53   11   76

SORTED TABLE IS
11   38   52   53   59   76
```

Fig. 10-19   Program to sort records using the radix sort (cont'd.)

are the same or almost the same for the keyset used. Which method distributes the keys most uniformly over the elements of the range?

8. Write a program, based on the linear probe method, for deleting a record from a hash table. This algorithm is not to use a special value of DELETE. That is, each record position is to be either occupied or empty.

     One approach that can be used is first to mark the deleted record as empty. An ordered search is then made for the next empty position. If a record, say, y, is found whose hash value is not between the position of the record just marked for deletion and that of the present empty position, then record y can be moved to replace the deleted record. Then the position for record y is marked as empty and the entire process is repeated, starting at the position occupied by y.

CHAPTER

11

TREES

So far, we have been concerned with the programming aspects of linear data structures. In this chapter we examine the programming details associated with tree structures. In particular, the BASED method of storage allocation in PL/I is used to give linked representations of tree structures. Also, programs for the application of trees to the area of symbolic manipulation of expressions, searching, and sorting are given.

11-1   INTRODUCTION

The notation and concepts of tree structures are given in the main text. In this section we summarize these notations.

A tree consists of a set of nodes and a set of lines or branches. A node which does not have any branches emanating from it is called a *terminal node* or *leaf node*. A nonleaf node is called a *branch node*. The following is a recursive definition of a tree.

A *tree* is a finite set of one or more nodes such that:
1. There is a specially designated node called a *root*.
2. The remaining nodes are partitioned into disjoint subsets T_0, T_1, T_2, ..., and T_n ($n \geqslant 0$), each of which is a tree. Each T_i ($0 \leqslant i \leqslant n$) is called a *subtree* of the root.

Another important notational convenience in dealing with trees is that of the *level* of a node. The level of the root node of a tree is 1. Otherwise, the level of any other node is 1 plus its distance from the root node. It is also convenient to define the degree of a node. The *degree* of a node is simply its number of subtrees.

If we order, say, from left to right, the children of a node at each level in the tree, the resulting tree is said to be *ordered*. A set of disjoint ordered trees is called a *forest*.

Finally, it is useful to restrict trees so that the degree of each node is at most 2. Also, it is convenient to distinguish between the left and right subtrees of each node. The following recursive definition specifies a binary tree:

A *binary tree* is a finite set (possible empty) of nodes consisting of a root node which has two disjoint binary subtrees called the left subtree and the right subtree.

An *empty binary tree* is a binary tree of zero nodes.

With this brief summary of tree notation, we proceed to examine how trees might be represented in the computer's memory. This is the topic of the next section.

11-2   STORAGE REPRESENTATION AND MANIPULATION OF BINARY TREES

The previous chapter was concerned with the storage representation of linear lists within the computer's memory. We will now extend these concepts to the representation of binary tree structures.

Although both linked and sequential storage allocation techniques can be used to represent binary trees, in this section we will emphasize the programming of linked storage structures in PL/I. In Sec 11-3.3, however, a sequential storage structure will be used to represent a tree for the purpose of sorting.

First, PL/I BASED structures are used to implement a linked representation of binary trees in memory. Based on this approach, several programs, such as those for traversing and creating trees are presented. Second, the programming aspects of threaded binary trees are introduced. Finally, a program for the conversion of a general tree to a binary tree is presented.

11-2.1   Linked Storage Representation

As mentioned in the main text, an obvious representation of a binary tree involves storage nodes whose components are given by the following declaration statement:

```
DECLARE 1 NODE BASED,
          2 LPTR POINTER,
          2 INFO CHARACTER(1),
          2 RPTR POINTER;
```

where LPTR and RPTR are pointer variables which denote the addresses of the root nodes of the left and right subtrees, respectively, of a particular node. An empty subtree has an address of NULL.

Recall that the *preorder traversal* of a binary tree consists of the following steps:

1. Process the root node.
2. Traverse the left subtree in preorder.
3. Traverse the right subtree in preorder.

The following PL/I recursive procedure traverses in preorder a given binary tree with the node structure just given:

```
RPREORDER: PROCEDURE (T) RECURSIVE;
    /*GIVEN A BINARY TREE WHOSE ROOT NODE */
    /*ADDRESS IS GIVEN BY A POINTER VARIABLE T, */
    /*THIS PROCEDURE RECURSIVELY DESCENDS THE TREE */
    /* IN PREORDER. */

    DECLARE T POINTER;

    IF T □= NULL
    THEN DO;

            /* PROCESS THE ROOT NODE */
            PUT LIST(T -> INFO);

            /* PROCESS THE LEFT SUBTREE */
            CALL RPREORDER(T -> LPTR);

            /*PROCESS THE RIGHT SUBTREE */
            CALL RPREORDER(T -> RPTR);
            END;

        /* FINISHED */
        RETURN;
    END RPREORDER;
```

Observe that the preceding program also works for an empty binary tree (i.e., a tree that contains no nodes).

Similarly, the inorder traversal of a binary tree involves executing the following steps:

1. Traverse the left subtree in inorder.
2. Process the root node.
3. Traverse the right subtree in inorder.

A PL/I recursive procedure for this traversal order is the following:

```
RINORDER: PROCEDURE(T) RECURSIVE;
        /* GIVEN A BINARY TREE WHOSE ROOT NODE */
        /* ADDRESS IS GIVEN BY A POINTER VARIABLE */
        /* T, THIS PROCEDURE TRAVERSES RECURSIVELY */
        /* THE TREE IN INORDER */

        DECLARE T POINTER;

        IF T □= NULL
        THEN DO;

                /* PROCESS THE LEFT SUBTREE */
                CALL RINORDER(T -> LPTR);

                /* PROCESS THE ROOT NODE */
                PUT LIST(T -> INFO);

                /* PROCESS THE RIGHT SUBTREE */
                CALL RINORDER(T -> RPTR);

                END;

        /* FINISHED */
        RETURN;
END RINORDER;
```

Of course, it is also possible to program the traversals of a binary tree in an iterative manner. In such an approach we require a stack to save upward-pointing information which will permit the ascent of the certain parts of the tree. Figure 11-1 illustrates this approach for preorder traversal. In this program a vector is used to simulate a stack.

The notion of CONTROLLED allocation (see Sec. 10-4) can also be used in defining a stack structure. The program of Fig. 11-2 replaces the vector representation of the stack in the previous program by a "true" stack structure. Note the use of the built-in function ALLOCATION in determining whether or not the stack is empty.

Frequently, a binary tree may be destroyed during its processing. Consequently, a duplicate copy of the given binary tree, prior to such processing, may be required. Figure 11-3 exemplifies a PL/I recursive function for the copying of a binary tree.

We terminate this section with a program for deleting an arbitrary node from a lexically-ordered tree. Recall that the general algorithm for deleting a node is the following:

1. Determine the parent of the node marked for deletion, if it exists; note that it will not exist if we are deleting the root node
2. If the node being deleted has either an empty left or right subtree,
   then append the nonempty subtree to its grandparent node (that is, the node found in step 1) and exit

```
IPREORDER: PROCEDURE (T);
        /* GIVEN A BINARY TREE WHOSE ROOT NODE ADDRESS IS GIVEN BY A */
        /* POINTER VARIABLE T, THIS PROCEDURE ITERATIVELY TRAVERSES  */
        /* THE TREE IN PREORDER.                                     */

        DECLARE T POINTER,
                P POINTER,        /* CURRENT NODE IN THE TREE */
                S(50) POINTER,    /* STACK */
                TOP FIXED;        /* TOP INDEX OF STACK */

        /* INITIALIZE */
        IF T = NULL
        THEN DO;
                PUT LIST ('EMPTY TREE');
                RETURN;
                END;
        ELSE DO;            /* INITIALIZE STACK */
                TOP = 1;
                S(TOP) = T;
                END;

        /* PROCESS EACH STACKED BRANCH ADDRESS */
        DO WHILE (TOP > 0);

                /* GET STORED ADDRESS AND BRANCH LEFT */
                P = S(TOP);
                TOP = TOP - 1;
                DO WHILE (P ¬= NULL);
                    PUT LIST (P -> INFO);
                    IF P -> RPTR ¬= NULL
                    THEN DO;
                        /* STORE ADDRESS OF NONEMPTY RIGHT SUBTREE */
                        TOP = TOP + 1;
                        S(TOP) = P -> RPTR;
                        END;
                    P = P -> LPTR;       /* BRANCH LEFT */
                END;
        END;

        /* FINISHED */
        RETURN;
END IPREORDER;
```

Fig. 11-1   Iterative preorder traversal of a binary tree (vector representation)

3. Obtain the inorder successor of the node to be deleted. Append the right subtree of this successor node to its grandparent. Replace the node to be deleted by its inorder successor.

> This is accomplished by appending the left and right subtrees (with the aforementioned successor node) of the node marked for deletion to the successor node. Also the successor node is appended to the parent of the node just deleted (that is, the node obtained in step 1).

A PL/I procedure which follows the general algorithm appears in Fig. 11-4. This procedure has one parameter that denotes the information contents of the node marked for deletion.

The procedure given in this figure first initializes the pointer P to the root node of the tree. If the tree is empty, a message that the node to be deleted is not found is printed and the procedure returns to the calling program. In statement 13, a loop is entered which searches for the desired node. The root of the current subtree is compared with the record to be deleted. If it is greater than the record to

```
CPREORDER: PROCEDURE (T);
         /* GIVEN A BINARY TREE WHOSE ROOT NODE ADDRESS IS GIVEN BY  */
         /* THE VARIABLE T, THIS PROCEDURE ITERATIVELY TRAVERSES THE */
         /* TREE IN PREORDER, USING CONTROLLED ALLOCATION.           */

         DECLARE T POINTER,
                 P POINTER,              /* CURRENT NODE IN THE TREE */
                 S POINTER CONTROLLED; /* STACK */

         /* INITIALIZE */
         IF T = NULL
         THEN DO;
              PUT SKIP LIST ('EMPTY TREE');
              RETURN;
              END;
         ELSE DO;
              ALLOCATE S;
              S = T;
              END;

         /* PROCESS EACH STACKED BRANCH ADDRESS */
         DO WHILE (ALLOCATION (S));

              /* GET STORED ADDRESS AND BRANCH LEFT */
              P = S;
              FREE S;
              DO WHILE (P ¬= NULL);
                   PUT LIST (P -> INFO);
                   IF P -> RPTR ¬= NULL
                   THEN DO;

                        /* STORE ADDRESS OF NONEMPTY RIGHT SUBTREE */
                        ALLOCATE S;
                        S = P -> RPTR;
                        END;
                   P = P -> LPTR;
              END;
         END;

         /* FINISHED */
         RETURN;
END CPREORDER;
```

Fig. 11-2   Iterative preorder traversal of a binary tree using CONTROLLED
            allocation

be deleted, a branch to the left subtree is made in statements 16 to 18; otherwise, a comparison is made to see if the root node is less than that of the given key. If this is the case, a branch to the right subtree occurs. If the node to be deleted has been found, the procedure first checks whether either subtree of this node is empty. If one subtree is empty, the pointer variable Q is set to the nonempty subtree of the marked node. Otherwise Q is set to the inorder successor of the node to be deleted. The two subtrees are then combined in statements 44 to 47. Finally, in statements 50 to 53, the pointer which points to the node to be deleted is set to the new subtree which has been formed. If statement 57 is reached, the record to be deleted was not found in the tree.

11-2.2   Threaded Storage Representation

The storage representation of binary trees introduced in the last subsection suffers two drawbacks:

1. It contains many NULL links.
2. The traversal of such a tree structure requires a stack. This requirement is wasteful in terms of time and memory space.

```
COPY: PROCEDURE (T) RECURSIVE RETURNS (POINTER);
        /* GIVEN A BINARY TREE WHOSE ROOT NODE ADDRESS IS GIVEN BY   */
        /* THE POINTER VARIABLE T, AND A NODE STRUCTURE (NODE), THIS  */
        /* RECURSIVE FUNCTION GENERATES A COPY OF THE TREE AND        */
        /* RETURNS THE ADDRESS OF ITS ROOT NODE.                      */

        DECLARE T POINTER,
                NEW POINTER;      /* TEMPORARY POINTER VARIABLE */

        /* NULL POINTER? */
        IF T = NULL
        THEN RETURN (NULL);

        /* CREATE A NEW NODE */
        ALLOCATE NODE;
        NEW = P;

        /* COPY INFORMATION FIELD */
        NEW -> INFO = T -> INFO;

        /* SET THE STRUCTURAL LINKS */
        NEW -> LPTR = COPY (T -> LPTR);
        NEW -> RPTR = COPY (T -> RPTR);

        /* RETURN ADDRESS OF NEW NODE */
        RETURN (NEW);
END COPY;
```

Fig. 11-3   Recursive procedure to copy a binary tree

The NULL links in this storage representation can be replaced by threads. A *thread* is a pointer which gives information about either the predecessor or successor of a given node in the tree. We "thread" a binary tree with a particular traversal order in mind. For the inorder traversal of a binary tree, threads are pointers that point to higher nodes in the tree. These threads permit us to ascend the tree directly without having to store the addresses of nodes in a stack.

Since the left and right links of a node can be either a structural link or a thread, we must be able to distinguish between them. One way of doing this is to use a separate Boolean flag for each of the left and right pointers. The node or record structure using this approach is declared as:

        DECLARE 1 NODE BASED(P),
                    2 LPTR POINTER,
                    2 LFLAG BIT(1),
                    2 INFO CHARACTER (20),
                    2 RFLAG BIT(1),
                    2 RPTR POINTER;

where LFLAG and RFLAG are Boolean indicators associated with the left and right pointers, respectively. In particular, the following coding scheme distinguishes between a structural link and a thread:

        LFLAG = '1' B   denotes a left structural link
        LFLAG = '0' B   denotes a left thread link
        RFLAG = '1' B   denotes a right structural link
        RFLAG = '0' B   denotes a right thread link

```
1                            TREE_DELETE: PROCEDURE (X, HEAD);
                                /* GIVEN A LEXICALLY ORDERED BINARY TREE, THIS PROCEDURE   */
                                /* DELETES THE NODE WHOSE INFORMATION FIELD IS EQUAL TO X.  */
                                /* THE TREE IS ASSUMED TO HAVE A LIST HEAD WHOSE ADDRESS IS */
                                /* GIVEN BY HEAD.                                           */
2                            DECLARE X CHARACTER (20),
                                     HEAD POINTER,
                                     P POINTER,             /* NODE TO BE DELETED */
                                     PARENT POINTER,        /* PARENT OF NODE TO BE DELETED*/
                                     (PRED, SUC) POINTER,   /* USED TO FIND INORDER SUCCES-*/
                                                            /* SOR OF NODE P */
                                     Q POINTER,             /* USED TO DELETE NODE P */
                                     D CHARACTER (1);       /* DIRECTION FROM PARENT NODE */
                                                            /* TO NODE TO BE DELETED */

                             /* INITIALIZE */
3                            IF HEAD -> LPTR -= NULL
4                            THEN DO;
5                                P = HEAD -> LPTR;
6                                PARENT = HEAD;
7                                D = 'L';
8                                END;
9                            ELSE DO;
10                               PUT SKIP LIST ('NODE NOT FOUND');
11                               RETURN;
12                               END;
```

Fig. 11-4   PL/I procedure for deleting an arbitrary node from a binary tree

Given the inorder threaded representation of a binary tree, the PL/I function of Fig. 11-5 returns the address of the successor of a designated node X. The first assignment statement in this program initializes P to the right link of X. If the RFLAG of node X has the value '0'B (i.e., if it denotes a thread link), then the inorder successor of X has been obtained and the contents of P is returned. If the test fails, however, we enter a loop which repeatedly branches left until a left thread is obtained. The function terminates with the return of this pointer value.

A similar PL/I function for obtaining the inorder predecessor of a given node is given in Fig. 11-6. This program is similar to the program just given in the sense that the roles of LPTR and RPTR are interchanged.

By repeatedly using function INS of Fig. 11-5, a threaded binary tree is easily traversed in inorder. A program which accomplishes this task is given in Fig 11-7. Note that the DO WHILE statement appears to set up an infinite loop. This loop, however, will terminate when the inorder successor of a node becomes the list head node. At this point the traversal of the given tree is complete. Observe that the program first obtains the inorder successor of the list head node. In order for the right node to be found, the right link of the list head node must be a structural link which points to itself.

Up to this point, we have conveniently assumed that a threaded binary tree exists. We next examine programming modules which can be used to construct a threaded tree. The first programming module inserts a node between a given node, say, X, and the X -> LPTR. The required program appears in Fig. 11-8. Observe that two cases can arise. The first case involves the insertion of a new node as the left subtree of the designated node. The second case inserts the new node between the given node X and the node X -> LPTR. In this case the right link of the inorder predecessor of X before insertion is set to a thread link which points to a new node. Also note that the pointer variable P (which is global to this procedure) receives implicitly the address of the new node created by the ALLOCATE statement.

```
                         /* SEARCH FOR AND DELETE THE MARKED NODE */
13                       DO WHILE (P ¬= NULL);
14                           IF X < P -> INFO
15                           THEN DO; /* BRANCH LEFT */
16                               PARENT = P;
17                               P = P -> LPTR;
18                               D = 'L';
19                           END;
20                           ELSE IF X > P -> INFO
21                                THEN DO; /* BRANCH RIGHT */
22                                    PARENT = P;
23                                    P = P -> RPTR;
24                                    D = 'R';
25                                END;
26                                ELSE DO; /* INDICATED NODE HAS BEEN FOUND */
27                                    IF P -> LPTR = NULL
                                     THEN /* EMPTY LEFT SUBTREE */
28                                       Q = P -> RPTR;
29                                     ELSE IF P -> RPTR = NULL
                                          THEN /* EMPTY RIGHT SUBTREE */
30                                            Q = P -> LPTR;
31                                          ELSE DO; /* CHECK RIGHT SON */
32                                              PRED = P -> RPTR;
33                                              IF PRED -> LPTR = NULL
34                                              THEN DO;
35                                                  PRED -> LPTR = P -> LPTR;
36                                                  Q = PRED;
37                                              END;
38                                              ELSE DO;
                                                  /* SEARCH FOR SUCCESSOR OF P */
39                                                  SUC = PRED -> LPTR;
40                                                  DO WHILE (SUC -> LPTR ¬= NULL);
41                                                      PRED = SUC;
42                                                      SUC = PRED -> LPTR;
43                                                  END;

                                                  /* CONNECT SUCCESSOR */
44                                                  PRED -> LPTR = SUC -> RPTR;
45                                                  SUC -> LPTR = P -> LPTR;
46                                                  SUC -> RPTR = P -> RPTR;
47                                                  Q = SUC;
48                                              END;
49                                          END;
50                                     IF D = 'L'
51                                     THEN PARENT -> LPTR = Q;
52                                     ELSE PARENT -> RPTR = Q;
53                                     FREE P -> NODE;
54                                     RETURN;
55                                END;
56                        END;

                         /* SEARCH FOR INDICATED NODE HAS FAILED */
57                       PUT SKIP LIST ('NODE NOT FOUND');
58                   END TREE_DELETE;
```

Fig. 11-4 PL/I procedure for deleting an arbitrary node from a binary
tree (cont'd.)

An analogous programming module is easily obtained for performing an insertion to the right of a designated node (say, between X and X -> RPTR). Such a program appears in Fig. 11-9. Note that the roles of LPTR and RPTR have been interchanged. Furthermore, the successor of the designated node (X) is required instead of its predecessor.

These two programming modules are used in the next program which inserts a given node into a lexically-ordered threaded binary tree. The insertion is to be performed at the leaf level, if no duplicate of that node already exists in the tree. The program which performs such an insertion appears in Fig. 11-10.

The program first initializes T to contain the address of the list head node of the tree. The program then, through a DO WHILE construct, controls the descent

```
INS: PROCEDURE (X) RETURNS (POINTER);
        /* GIVEN X, THE ADDRESS OF A PARTICULAR NODE IN A THREADED   */
        /* BINARY TREE, THIS FUNCTION RETURNS THE ADDRESS OF THE      */
        /* INORDER SUCCESSOR OF THIS NODE.                            */

        DECLARE X POINTER,
                P POINTER;          /* TEMPORARY POINTER VARIABLE */

        /* A THREAD? */
        P = X -> RPTR;
        IF - X -> RFLAG      /* FALSE DENOTES A RIGHT THREAD LINK */
        THEN RETURN (P);

        /* BRANCH LEFT? */
        DO WHILE (P -> LFLAG);
            P = P -> LPTR;
        END;

        /* RETURN ADDRESS OF SUCCESSOR */
        RETURN (P);
END INS;
```

Fig. 11-5   PL/I procedure for obtaining the inorder successor of a given node

```
INP: PROCEDURE (X) RETURNS (POINTER);
        /* GIVEN X, THE ADDRESS OF A PARTICULAR NODE IN A THREADED   */
        /* BINARY TREE, THIS FUNCTION RETURNS THE ADDRESS OF THE      */
        /* INORDER PREDECESSOR OF THIS NODE.                          */

        DECLARE X POINTER,
                P POINTER;          /* TEMPORARY POINTER VARIABLE */

        /* A THREAD? */
        P = X -> LPTR;
        IF ¬ X -> LFLAG THEN RETURN (P);

        /* BRANCH RIGHT? */
        DO WHILE (P -> RFLAG);
            P = P -> RPTR;
        END;

        /* RETURN ADDRESS OF PREDECESSOR */
        RETURN (P);
END INP;
```

Fig. 11-6   PL/I procedure for obtaining the inorder predecessor of a given node

through the trees. A branch left is attempted if X is lexically smaller than the INFO field of the current node. If the left pointer of this node is a flag procedure LEFT is called to insert a new node with information contents given by X as the left son of the current node; otherwise, the branch left is performed. If X is lexically greater than the information contents of the current node and the right pointer is not a flag the branch is made; otherwise procedure RIGHT is invoked to insert the new node as a right son of the current node. If the information contents of the node equals that of X, then a message indicating that a node already exists in the tree is printed and the procedure returns to the calling program. The loop is repeated until either a new node is inserted into the tree or a node with the same information contents as X is found.

The previous procedures (INP, INS, LEFT, RIGHT, INSERT_NODE and TINORDER) are all brought together in the main program given in Fig. 11-11. This

```
TINORDER: PROCEDURE (HEAD);
        /* GIVEN THE ADDRESS OF THE LIST HEAD OF A BINARY TREE (HEAD)*/
        /* WHICH HAS BEEN THREADED FOR INORDER TRAVERSAL, THIS      */
        /* PROCEDURE TRAVERSES THE TREE IN INORDER.                 */

        DECLARE HEAD POINTER,
                P POINTER;        /* TEMPORARY POINTER VARIABLE */

        /* INITIALIZE */
        P = HEAD;

        /* TRAVERSE THE THREADED TREE IN INORDER */
        DO WHILE ('1'B);
            P = INS(P);
            IF P = HEAD
            THEN RETURN;
            ELSE PUT LIST (P -> INFO);
        END;
END TINORDER;
```

Fig. 11-7   PL/I procedure for the inorder traversal of a threaded tree

```
LEFT: PROCEDURE (HEAD, X, DATA);
        /* GIVEN THE ADDRESS OF THE HEAD NODE OF AN INORDER THREADED */
        /* BINARY TREE (HEAD), THE ADDRESS OF A DESIGNATED NODE X,    */
        /* AND THE INFORMATION ASSOCIATED WITH A NEW NODE (DATA),     */
        /* THIS PROCEDURE INSERTS A NEW NODE TO THE LEFT OF THE       */
        /* DESIGNATED NODE.                                           */

        DECLARE (HEAD, X) POINTER,
                DATA CHARACTER (20),
                NEW POINTER,    /* DENOTES ADDRESS OF NODE */
                                /* TO BE INSERTED */
                TEMP POINTER;   /* TEMPORARY POINTER VARIABLE */

        /* CREATE NEW NODE */
        ALLOCATE NODE;
        NEW = P;
        NEW -> INFO = DATA;

        /* ADJUST POINTER FIELDS */
        NEW -> LPTR = X -> LPTR;
        NEW -> RPTR = X;
        X -> LPTR = NEW;
        NEW -> LFLAG = X -> LFLAG;
        NEW -> RFLAG = '0'B;
        X -> LFLAG = '1'B;

        /* RESET PREDECESSOR THREAD, IF NECESSARY */
        IF NEW -> LFLAG
        THEN DO;
            TEMP = INP (NEW);
            TEMP -> RPTR = NEW;
            TEMP -> RFLAG = '0'B;
            END;

        /* FINISHED */
        RETURN;
END LEFT;
```

Fig. 11-8   Procedure to make a left insertion into a threaded tree

program creates and traverses a lexically-ordered threaded binary tree. The following input data were used:

'DEER', 'DOG', 'RAT', 'DODO', and 'MOUSE'.

```
RIGHT: PROCEDURE (HEAD, X, DATA);
       /* GIVEN THE ADDRESS OF THE HEAD NODE OF AN INORDER THREADED */
       /* BINARY TREE (HEAD), THE ADDRESS OF A DESIGNATED NODE X,   */
       /* AND THE INFORMATION ASSOCIATED WITH A NEW NODE (DATA),    */
       /* THIS PROCEDURE INSERTS A NEW NODE TO THE RIGHT OF THE     */
       /* DESIGNATED NODE.                                          */

       DECLARE (HEAD, X) POINTER,
               DATA CHARACTER (20),
               NEW POINTER,       /* ADDRESS OF NODE TO BE INSERTED */
               TEMP POINTER;      /* TEMPORARY POINTER VARIABLE */

       /* CREATE NEW NODE */
       ALLOCATE NODE;
       NEW = P;
       NEW -> INFO = DATA;

       /* ADJUST POINTER FIELDS */
       NEW -> RPTR = X -> RPTR;
       NEW -> LPTR = X;
       X -> RPTR = NEW;
       NEW -> RFLAG = X -> RFLAG;
       NEW -> LFLAG = '0'B;
       X -> RFLAG = '1'B;

       /* RESET SUCCESSOR THREAD, IF NECESSARY */
       IF NEW -> RFLAG
       THEN DO;
           TEMP = INS (NEW);
           TEMP -> LPTR = NEW;
           TEMP -> LFLAG = '0'B;
       END;

       /* FINISHED */
       RETURN;
END RIGHT;
```

Fig. 11-9   Procedure to make a right insertion into a threaded tree

Figure 11-11 also gives the inorder traversal output.

Thus far, we have been concerned exclusively with binary trees. In the next subsection, the conversion of a general tree to an equivalent binary tree is examined.

11-2.3   Conversion of General Trees to Binary Trees

Recall that the natural correspondence conversion process converts a general tree (or, more generally, a forest) to a unique equivalent binary tree. The conversion process requires that a parent node be connected to its left offspring. Furthermore, all siblings at the same level within the same tree must be connected from left to right. This subsection presents a program which performs the required conversion.

As was done in the main text, we choose the level-number method to specify a general tree (or forest). The input of each tree is given in preorder.

A general algorithm for the required conversion consists of the following steps:

1. Create a list head node and stack its address and level number.
2. Repeat through step 6 while there still remains an input node.
3. Input a node description.

```
INSERT_NODE: PROCEDURE (HEAD, X);
    /* THIS PROCEDURE INSERTS A NODE WITH INFORMATION CONTENTS X */
    /* AS A LEAF NODE IF IT IS NOT ALREADY THERE.              */

    DECLARE HEAD POINTER,
            X CHARACTER (20),
            NEW POINTER,      /* ADDRESS OF NEW NODE */
            T POINTER;        /* ADDRESS OF CURRENT NODE */

    /* INITIALIZE */
    T = HEAD;

    /* PERFORM INDICATED INSERTION IF REQUIRED */
    DO WHILE (T ¬= NULL);

        /* FIND THE LOCATION AND APPEND NEW NODE */
        IF X < T -> INFO
        THEN    /* BRANCH LEFT */
            IF T -> LFLAG
            THEN DO;
                T = T -> LPTR;
                END;
            ELSE DO;  /* APPEND NEW NODE AS A LEFT SUBTREE */
                CALL LEFT (HEAD, T, X);
                RETURN;
                END;
        ELSE IF X > T -> INFO
            THEN IF T -> RFLAG
                THEN DO;   /* BRANCH RIGHT */
                    T = T -> RPTR;
                    END;
                ELSE DO;
                    /* APPEND NEW NODE AS A RIGHT SUBTREE */
                    CALL RIGHT (HEAD, T, X);
                    RETURN;
                    END;
            ELSE DO;  /* NODE ALREADY THERE */
                PUT SKIP EDIT ('DUPLICATE NODE', X)
                    (A, X(2), A);
                RETURN;
                END;
    END;
END INSERT_NODE;
```

Fig. 11-10   Procedure for inserting a node into a lexically-ordered threaded tree

4. Create a tree node and initialize its contents.
5. If the level number of the input node is greater than the level number of the stack-top node
   then connect the parent to its left offspring
   else while the level number of the stack-top node is greater than
       the level number of the input node
           pop the stack
           connect the siblings together
6. Push input node onto the stack.
7. Exit.

      Figure 11-12 contains a program for the required conversion process. The variables used in the main program are:

Variable	Type	Usage
NODE	BASED(P)	Nodes of the tree

```
THREAD: PROCEDURE OPTIONS (MAIN);
      /* THIS PROGRAM USES PROCEDURES INSERT_NODE AND TINORDER TO      */
      /* CONSTRUCT AND TRAVERSE A THREADED BINARY TREE.                */
      DECLARE 1 NODE BASED (P),           /* TREE NODE */
               2 LPTR POINTER,            /* LEFT POINTER */
               2 LFLAG BIT (1),           /* THREAD FLAG FOR LPTR */
               2 INFO CHARACTER (20),     /* INFORMATION FIELD */
               2 RFLAG BIT (1),           /* THREAD FLAG FOR RPTR */
               2 RPTR POINTER,            /* RIGHT POINTER */
              DATA CHARACTER (20),        /* INFORMATION TO ADD TO TREE */
              HEAD POINTER,               /* HEAD OF TREE */
              END_FLAG CHARACTER (3),     /* END OF FILE FLAG */
              INS ENTRY (POINTER) RETURNS (POINTER),
              INP ENTRY (POINTER) RETURNS (POINTER);

      /* BUILD HEAD OF TREE */
      ALLOCATE NODE;
      P -> LPTR = P;
      P -> RPTR = P;

      /* INITIALIZE */
      END_FLAG = 'NO';
      ON ENDFILE (SYSIN) END_FLAG = 'YES';
      P -> INFO = 'ZZZZ';
      P -> LFLAG = '0'B;
      P -> RFLAG = '1'B;
      HEAD = P;

      /* BUILD TREE */
      GET LIST (DATA);
      DO WHILE (END_FLAG = 'NO');
          CALL INSERT_NODE (HEAD, DATA);
          GET LIST (DATA);
      END;

      /* TRAVERSE TREE */
      PUT SKIP LIST ('TREE IN INORDER IS');
      PUT SKIP;
      CALL TINORDER (HEAD);

      END;
```

```
TREE IN INORDER IS
CAT                    DEER              DODO              DOG              MOOSE
MOUSE                  RAT
```

Fig. 11-11   Main program for constructing and traversing a threaded tree

LPTR	POINTER	Pointer to the left subtree of the node
INFO	CHARACTER (10)	Information field of the node
RPTR	POINTER	Pointer to the right subtree of the node
T	POINTER	Pointer to the head of the tree

Variables used in the procedure CONVERT are:

HEAD	POINTER	Head node of the tree
STACK	CONTROLLED	Stack structure
NUMBER	FIXED	Level number of nodes
LOC	POINTER	Address of node in the tree
LEVEL	FIXED	Level number of input node
NAME	CHARACTER (10)	Name of input node

PRED_LEVEL	FIXED	Level number of the previous node
PRED_LOC	POINTER	Address of the previous node
NEW	POINTER	Temporary pointer variable
END_FLAG	CHARACTER (3)	End of file flag

Procedures RPREORDER and RINORDER which are used to print the binary tree are similar to the ones given in Sec. 11-2.1. The stack used in the program uses controlled allocation. Thus, the push and pop routines can be performed by using the ALLOCATE and FREE statements of PL/I.

The main program calls procedure CONVERT to build the trees. Then it calls procedures RINORDER and RPREORDER to print the tree that has been built. In procedure CONVERT, the head node to the tree and the stack are first initialized. Then a loop is entered which processes all nodes from the forest of trees. First, a node's name and level are read. Then a tree node for this node is created and initialized. The level of this node is compared with the level of the top node on the stack. If its level is greater than that of the node on the top of the stack, this node is connected to the previous node's left offspring; otherwise, the top node on the stack is deleted from the stack and has the right pointer of the new node on the stack set to the new tree node location. If the level of this node is actually less than the level of the node on the stack, the input has not been read in its proper order and the procedure terminates. Finally, the level of the node just read, and its location are pushed onto the stack.

The input data used for the program are:

First tree		Second tree	
Name	*Level*	*Name*	*Level*
'ANDY'	1	'FLORENCE'	1
'BRIAN'	2	'GAIL'	2
'CLARENCE'	2	'ILENE'	3
'DONALD'	2	'JANICE'	3
'EMILE'	3	'HEATHER'	2

The first tree is read in the order shown before the second tree is read.

Now that we have introduced the basics of programming tree structures, we are ready to apply these programming techniques to a variety of applications.

Exercises for Sec. 11-2

1. Given a pointer variable T which denotes the address of the root node of a binary tree, obtain a recursive PL/I procedure for its postorder traversal.

2. Using CONTROLLED allocation, formulate a recursive PL/I procedure for the iterative inorder traversal of a given binary tree with root node address T.

3. Given a threaded binary tree for inorder traversal, write a PL/I function which computes the number of leaf nodes in that tree. Assume that the address of the tree's root node is given by the pointer variable T.

```
1          TEST: PROCEDURE OPTIONS (MAIN);
              /* THIS PROGRAM USES SUBPROCEDURE CONVERT TO BUILD A BINARY TREE  */
              /* FROM A FOREST OF TREES.  SUBPROCEDURES IINORDER AND RPREORDER   */
              /* PRINT THE REULTING TREE.                                        */
2             DECLARE 1 NODE BASED (P),          /* TREE NODE */
                       2 LPTR POINTER,           /* LEFT POINTER */
                       2 INFO CHARACTER (10),    /* INFORMATION FIELD */
                       2 RPTR POINTER,           /* RIGHT POINTER */
                     T POINTER;                  /* HEAD OF TREE */

              /* BUILD TREE */
3             CALL CONVERT (T);

              /* PRINT OUT TREE */
4             PUT LIST ('TREE IN INORDER IS');
5             PUT SKIP;
6             CALL IINORDER (T);
7             PUT SKIP (2) LIST ('TREE IN PREORDER IS');
8             PUT SKIP;
9             CALL RPREORDER (T);
```

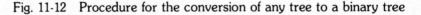

Fig. 11-12   Procedure for the conversion of any tree to a binary tree

4. Given a binary tree T which has been threaded for preorder traversal, construct PL/I functions for obtaining the preorder predecessor and successor of a designated node.

5. Write a recursive procedure for converting a forest into an equivalent binary tree.

6. This problem concerns the operations of subtree insertion and deletion, as applied to general trees. Remember that a general tree can be converted to a binary tree using the natural correspondence algorithm discussed in the main text.

   It is most natural to discuss insertion or deletion of a subtree in terms of its relation to a parent node. Thus we define our two operations as follows:

   DELETE (N, I)
   INSERT (N, I, T)

   DELETE deletes the Ith subtree of the node given by N. INSERT inserts the tree, with root T, as the new Ith subtree of the node given by N. For illustration consider the general tree

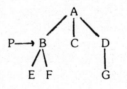

   If we execute

   INSERT (P, 2, Q)

```
10              CONVERT: PROCEDURE (HEAD);
                /* GIVEN A FOREST OF TREES WHOSE INPUT FORMAT IS OF THE FORM    */
                /* DESCRIBED, THIS PROCEDURE CONVERTS THE FOREST INTO AN EQUIVA- */
                /* LENT BINARY TREE WITH LIST HEAD (HEAD).                       */

11                  DECLARE HEAD POINTER,
                            1 STACK CONTROLLED,
                                2 NUMBER FIXED,  /* LEVEL NUMBER OF NODES */
                                2 LOC POINTER,   /* ADDRESS OF NODE */
                            LEVEL FIXED,         /* LEVEL NUMBER OF INPUT NODE */
                            NAME CHARACTER(10), /* NAME OF INPUT NODE */
                            PRED_LEVEL FIXED,    /* LEVEL NUMBER OF PREVIOUS NODE */
                            PRED_LOC POINTER,    /* ADDRESS OF PREVIOUS NODE */
                            NEW POINTER,         /* TEMPORARY POINTER VARIABLE */
                            END_FLAG CHARACTER (3);
                                                 /* END OF FILE FLAG */

                    /* INITIALIZE */
12                  ALLOCATE NODE;
13                  HEAD = P;
14                  HEAD -> LPTR, HEAD -> RPTR = NULL;
15                  ALLOCATE STACK;
16                  NUMBER = 0;
17                  LOC = HEAD;
18                  END_FLAG = 'YES';
19                  ON ENDFILE (SYSIN) END_FLAG = 'NO';

                    /* PROCESS THE INPUT */
21                  DO WHILE ('1'B);

                        /* INPUT A NODE */
22                      GET LIST (LEVEL, NAME);
23                      IF END_FLAG = 'NO' THEN RETURN;

                        /* CREATE A TREE NODE */
25                      ALLOCATE NODE;
26                      NEW = P;
27                      NEW -> LPTR, NEW -> RPTR = NULL;

28                      NEW -> INFO = NAME;

                        /* COMPARE LEVELS */
29                      PRED_LEVEL = NUMBER;
30                      PRED_LOC = LOC;
31                      IF LEVEL > PRED_LEVEL

                        /* THEN CONNECT PARENT TO ITS LEFT OFFSPRING */
32                      THEN PRED_LOC -> LPTR = NEW;
33                      ELSE DO;      /* REMOVE NODES FROM STACK */
34                          DO WHILE (PRED_LEVEL > LEVEL);
35                              FREE STACK;
36                              PRED_LEVEL = NUMBER;
37                              PRED_LOC = LOC;
38                          END;
39                          IF PRED_LEVEL < LEVEL
40                          THEN DO;
41                              PUT SKIP LIST ('MIXED LEVEL NUMBERS');
42                              RETURN;
43                              END;

                            /* CONNECT SIBLINGS TOGETHER */
44                          PRED_LOC -> RPTR = NEW;
45                          FREE STACK;
46                          END;

                        /* PUSH A NEW NODE IN THE STACK */
47                      ALLOCATE STACK;
48                      NUMBER = LEVEL;
49                      LOC = NEW;
50                  END;

51              END CONVERT;
```

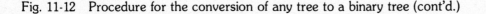

Fig. 11-12 Procedure for the conversion of any tree to a binary tree (cont'd.)

```
52              IINORDER: PROCEDURE (T); ·
                /* GIVEN A BINARY TREE WHOSE ROOT NODE ADDRESS IS GIVEN BY A      */
                /* POINTER VARIABLE T, THIS PROCEDURE TRAVERSES THE TREE IN       */
                /* INORDER, IN AN ITERATIVE MANNER. */

53                  DECLARE T POINTER,
                        P POINTER,          /* CURRENT NODE IN THE TREE */
                        S(50) POINTER,      /* STACK */
                        TOP FIXED;          /* TOP INDEX OF STACK */

                    /* INITIALIZE */
54                  IF T = NULL
55                  THEN DO;
56                      PUT LIST ('EMPTY TREE');
57                      RETURN;
58                      END;
59                  ELSE DO;
60                      TOP = 0;
61                      P = T;
62                      END;

                    /* TRAVERSE THE TREE IN INORDER */
63                  DO WHILE ('1'B);

                        /* STACK ADDRESSES ALONG A LEFT CHAIN */
64                      DO WHILE (P ¬= NULL);
65                          TOP = TOP + 1;
66                          S(TOP) = P;
67                          P = P -> LPTR;
68                          END;

                        /* PROCESS NODE AND RIGHT BRANCH */
69                      IF TOP > 0
70                      THEN DO;
71                          P = S(TOP);
72                          TOP = TOP - 1;
73                          PUT LIST (P -> INFO); ·
74                          P = P -> RPTR;
75                          END;
76                      ELSE RETURN;
77                      END;
78              END IINORDER;

79              RPREORDER: PROCEDURE (T) RECURSIVE;
                /* GIVEN A BINARY TREE WHOSE ROOT NODE ADDRESS IS GIVEN BY A      */
                /* POINTER VARIABLE T, THIS PROCEDURE TRAVERSES THE TREE IN       */
                /* PREORDER. */

80                  DECLARE T POINTER;

                    /* PROCESS THE ROOT NODE */
81                  IF T ¬= NULL
82                  THEN PUT LIST (T -> INFO);

                    /* PROCESS THE LEFT SUBTREE */
83                  IF T -> LPTR ¬= NULL
84                  THEN CALL RPREORDER (T -> LPTR);

                    /* PROCESS THE RIGHT SUBTREE */
85                  IF T -> RPTR ¬= NULL
86                  THEN CALL RPREORDER (T -> RPTR);

                    /* FINISHED */
87                  RETURN;
88              END RPREORDER;
89          END TEST;
```

Fig. 11-12 Procedure for the conversion of any tree to a binary tree (cont'd.)

```
TREE IN INORDER IS
BRIAN               CLARENCE            EMILE               DONALD              ANDY
ILENE               JANICE              GAIL                HEATHER             FLORENCE


TREE IN PREORDER IS
        ANDY            BRIAN           CLARENCE            DONALD
EMILE           FLORENCE        GAIL            ILENE               JANICE
HEATHER
```

Fig. 11-12   Procedure for the conversion of any tree to a binary tree (cont'd.)

where Q identifies the tree

then we obtain the tree

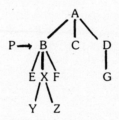

The complementary operation for restoring our original tree is then

> DELETE (P, 2)

It is required to formulate PL/I procedures for the operations of INSERT and DELETE assuming that we are given the binary tree equivalent to the general tree. It would be helpful if you examined what happens to the binary-tree equivalent of the general tree when these operations are performed.

11-3   APPLICATIONS OF TREES

In this section, we will look at four applications of trees. The first application considers the evaluation of an algebraic expression which is stored symbolically. Next, searching a binary tree is examined. In the third application, we study complete binary trees used for sorting. Finally, we examine the applicability of general trees to searching.

11-3.1   The Symbolic Manipulation of Expressions

In the previous section, we discussed the manipulation of polynomial expressions which were represented by linked lists. Binary trees, on the other hand, will allow us to add, subtract, multiply, etc., algebraic expressions symbolically.

Recall that nonleaf nodes in a binary tree are used for representing operators and that the left and right subtrees are the left and right operands of that operator. Unary operators, which have only one operand, have only a right subtree. Each node in the tree has three fields, a left pointer, an information field, and a right pointer. The values of the information field are

0, 1, 2, 3, 4, 5, 6, and 7

which correspond to constants, variables, and the operations $+$, $-$, $*$, $/$, θ, and $\uparrow$, respectively. θ represents the unary minus operator. A leaf node of a tree is either a variable or a constant, and its right pointer points to the position in the symbol table which gives the value of the variable or constant.

With this representation for an algebraic expression, we can evaluate this expression. A recursive algorithm for this problem is easy to formulate and is given as follows:

1. If the current node being examined is a constant or variable,
   then return the value of the node which comes from the symbol table
2. Return the values of the two subtrees of the node which are applied to the operator given by the information field

A PL/I program to accomplish this task is given in Fig. 11-13. The variables used by this program are:

Variable	Type	Usage
NODE	BASED(P)	Tree node
LPTR	POINTER	Pointer to the left subtree
TYPE	FIXED	Information field
RPTR	POINTER	Pointer to the right subtree
TABLE	BASED (Q)	Symbol table
VALUE	FLOAT	Value of the constant or variable
E	POINTER	Address of the current node in the tree
F	POINTER	Pointer to a value in the symbol table

Note that the declarations for the structure NODE do not appear in the function EVAL since they are used as global variables.

The function EVAL is basically a series of IF ... THEN statements. Each IF statement tests the value of TYPE to determine what operation is required, or if the node represents a constant or variable. If TYPE has the value 0 or 1, then the address of the node containing the value of the constant or variable is set to F. Finally, the value of this node is returned. Otherwise, EVAL is called recursively with the operation represented in TYPE applied to the subtrees of this node. If TYPE has a value other than 0 through 7, an error message is printed and the value 0 is returned.

```
EVAL: PROCEDURE (E) RECURSIVE RETURNS (FLOAT);
/* GIVEN AN EXPRESSION WHICH IS REPRESENTED BY A BINARY TREE WITH A   */
/* ROOT-NODE ADDRESS OF E, THIS FUNCTION RETURNS THE VALUE OF THE     */
/* GIVEN EXPRESSION. */

   DECLARE (E,              /* ROOT-NODE ADDRESS OF TREE OR SUBTREE  */
            F) POINTER;     /* TEMPORARY POINTER VARIABLE */

   /* EVALUATE EXPRESSION RECURSIVELY */
   IF E -> TYPE = 0
   THEN DO;
        F = E -> RPTR;
        RETURN (F -> VALUE);
        END;
   IF E -> TYPE = 1
   THEN DO;
        F = E -> RPTR;
        RETURN (F -> VALUE);
   END;
   IF E -> TYPE = 2
   THEN RETURN (EVAL(E -> LPTR) + EVAL(E -> RPTR));
   IF E -> TYPE = 3
   THEN RETURN (EVAL(E -> LPTR) - EVAL(E -> RPTR));
   IF E -> TYPE = 4
   THEN RETURN (EVAL(E -> LPTR) * EVAL(E -> RPTR));
   IF E -> TYPE = 5
   THEN RETURN (EVAL(E -> LPTR) / EVAL(E -> RPTR));
   IF E -> TYPE = 6
   THEN RETURN (- EVAL(E -> RPTR));
   IF E -> TYPE = 7
   THEN RETURN (EVAL(E -> LPTR) ** EVAL(E -> RPTR));

   /* INVALID EXPRESSION */
   PUT SKIP LIST ('INVALID EXPRESSION');
   RETURN (0);
END EVAL;
```

Fig. 11-13   Function to evaluate algebraic expressions

11-3.2 Binary Search Trees

Recall that binary trees are *lexicographically* (or *lexically*) ordered if for any given record in the tree, all records in its left subtree have values less than that of the root of the given tree or subtree, and all records in its right subtree have values greater than that of the root node. Insertions and searching can easily be performed on such a tree if it is stored using linked allocation. A new entry is inserted as a leaf node in the tree such that the tree's order is preserved. Note that to find a record in a tree, or the position where one is to be inserted, is merely a matter of comparing the value of the record with that of the root of the tree or subtree we are examining and branching right or left.

Since a search is required for insertions the two algorithms of searching and inserting into a binary tree can easily be combined. Such an example is the following algorithm:

1. Repeat thru step 2.
2. If the value of the given record is less than that of the root of the subtree
   then branch left
        if the subtree is empty
        then if we are performing a search
             then the desired record was not found
             else create a new leaf and append it as the new left subtree

else if the value of the given record is greater than that of the root of the subtree

> then branch right
> > if the subtree is empty
> > then if we are doing a search
> > > then the record being searched for was not found
> > > else create a new leaf and append it as the new right subtree

> else return the position of the record found

A procedure to perform this operation appears in Fig. 11-14. Note that for failures of insertions or look-ups, the pointer value NULL is returned. The variables used in the procedure are:

Variable	Type	Usage
NODE	BASED (P)	Node structure of tree
LPTR	POINTER	Pointer to left subtree of node
INFO	CHARACTER (20)	Information field of the record
RPTR	POINTER	Pointer to the right subtree of the node
HEAD	POINTER	Head node of the tree
INSERT	BIT (*)	Denotes whether an insertion or look-up is required
ITEM	CHARACTER (*) VARYING	Record to be searched for or inserted
PARENT	POINTER	Address of the parent node of the record to be inserted
T	POINTER	Temporary pointer variable

In the procedure the pointer T is set to the head of the tree. Then a loop is entered to perform the search. The given record is compared with the root of the current subtree. If its value is less than that of the root node, a branch is made to the left subtree; otherwise, in statement 21, a branch is made to the right subtree. After the branch is made, a check is made to see if the new subtree is empty. If it is and a look-up is required, the record is not in the table and the NULL value is returned. Otherwise, for an insertion, a new node is allocated and inserted as the appropriate left or right subtree. If the keys are equal, statement 37 is executed. For look-ups, the position of the record is returned. For insertions, the record was already present in the tree, thus the NULL pointer value is returned.

11-3.3 Tree Sorts

In the previous section, we introduced a method of sorting using binary trees. A more efficient method, called a *heap sort,* uses a special form of a full binary tree called a *heap.* The root of the tree is the largest key in the tree. The next two largest keys are the left and right offspring of the root. Similar relationships exist for the remaining keys of the table. In general, a heap which represents a table K of n records satisfies the following property:

$$K_j \leqslant K_i \text{ for } 2 \leqslant j \leqslant n \text{ and } i = \text{TRUNC } (j/2)$$

```
1    BINTREE: PROCEDURE (HEAD, INSERT, ITEM) RECURSIVE RETURNS (POINTER);
          /* THIS RECURSIVE FUNCTION PERFORMS THE REQUESTED OPERATIONS     */

          /* ON THE TREE STRUCTURE. */
2         DECLARE HEAD POINTER,          /* HEAD NODE OF TREE OR SUBTREE */
                  INSERT BIT (*),        /* INSERTION OR LOOK-UP? */
                  ITEM CHARACTER(*) VARYING,
                                         /* INFORMATION TO BE INSERTED OR */
                                         /* FOUND */
                  T POINTER,             /* TEMPORARY POINTER VARIABLE */
                  PARENT POINTER;        /* ADDRESS OF PARENT NODE OF NEW ITEM
                                            TO BE INSERTED */

          /* INITIALIZE SEARCH VARIABLE */
3         T = HEAD;

          /* PERFORM INDICATED OPERATION */
4         DO WHILE (T ¬= NULL);

              /* COMPARE GIVEN ITEM WITH ROOT ENTRY  OF THE SUBTREE */
5             IF ITEM < T -> INFO
6             THEN DO;        /* BRANCH LEFT */
7                  PARENT = T;
8                  T = T -> LPTR;
9                  IF T = NULL
10                 THEN IF ¬INSERT
11                      THEN RETURN (NULL);       /* SEARCH UNSUCCESSFUL */
12                      ELSE DO;

                            /* CREATE A NEW LEAF AND INSERT AS A */
                            /* LEFT SUBTREE */
13                          ALLOCATE NODE;
14                          P -> INFO = ITEM;
15                          P -> LPTR, P -> RPTR = NULL;
16                          PARENT -> LPTR = P;
17                          RETURN (P);
18                      END;
19                 ELSE;
20            END;
21            ELSE IF ITEM > T -> INFO
22                 THEN DO;        /* BRANCH RIGHT */
23                      PARENT = T;
24                      T = T -> RPTR;
25                      IF T = NULL
26                      THEN IF ¬INSERT
27                           THEN RETURN (NULL);  /* SEARCH UNSUCCESSFUL */
28                           ELSE DO;

                                 /* CREATE A NEW LEAF AND INSERT AS A */
                                 /* RIGHT SUBTREE */
29                               ALLOCATE NODE;
30                               P -> INFO = ITEM;
31                               P -> LPTR, P -> RPTR = NULL;
32                               PARENT -> RPTR = P;
33                               RETURN (P);
34                           END;
35                      ELSE;
36                 END;
                   ELSE    /* A MATCH HAS OCCURRED */
37                      IF INSERT
38                      THEN RETURN (NULL);
39                      ELSE RETURN (T);
40            END;
41    END BINTREE;
```

Fig. 11-14 Program to perform look-ups and insertions on a binary tree

Note that a heap can easily be represented by using a vector. The positions of the left and right sons of record in position i are 2i and 2i + 1, respectively. The position of the parent of record in position i is TRUNC (i/2) if the ith record is not the root node. Thus, any path in the tree can easily be traversed.

To sort a table, we require two algorithms. The first algorithm must create a heap from the table. To do this, we can use the following high-level algorithm:

1. Repeat thru step 3 for q = 2, 3, ..., n
2. Obtain the parent of the qth record
3. Repeat while the key of the qth record is greater than that of its parent
   exchange the records
   obtain the next parent of this record

Once we have created a heap, it is easy to obtain the largest key in the table. We can exchange this record, which is always the root of the heap, with the last record in the heap and re-sort the new heap which now has one less record in it. This is done in the following algorithm:

1. Repeat thru step 4 for q = n, n–1, ..., 2
2. Exchange the first record in the heap with the qth record
3. Compute the index of the largest son of the first record
4. Repeat while the son having the largest key is greater than that of the record
   exchange the records
   compute the index of the next largest son

These two algorithms can easily be combined into one program, which is given in Fig. 11-15. Note that the procedure CREATE is called by the main program to build a heap. After this, the main program performs a sort on the heap. The variables used in the main program are:

Variable	Type	Usage
K(50)	FIXED	The table to be sorted
N	FIXED	Number of elements in the table
KEY	FIXED	Key of record to be swapped
Q	FIXED	Pass index variable
I	FIXED	Index variable
J	FIXED	Index variable of the largest son of the record
TEMP	FIXED	Used to exchange the records

Variables used in the procedure CREATE are:

K(*)	FIXED	Table of keys for which to create a heap
N	FIXED	Number of elements in the table
KEY	FIXED	Key of the record to be inserted
Q	FIXED	Number of insertions into the heap
I	FIXED	Index variable
J	FIXED	Index of the parent key

The following table was sorted by the program in Fig. 11-15:

52, 14, 89, 56, 42, 3, 25, 78, 42, 11, 56, 23, and 58.

The main program first reads the table and calls procedure CREATE to create the initial heap. Then a loop is entered in statement 8 to perform the sort. The first and last records are exchanged for the current size of the heap, which is given by the value of Q. This places the largest key in the heap at the back of the heap. Then the heap is rebuilt. Statement 19 controls a loop which exchanges the record that was swapped previously with its son having the greatest key value if possible. This is done by exchanging the record if possible, and obtaining the index of the son having the largest key.

In the procedure CREATE, statement 36 controls a loop that builds the heap. This is done by considering heaps of size 2, then 3, and so on up to a size of n. For each heap, a new element is added at the back of the heap. This record ascends the heap until its key becomes smaller than its parent. The loop in statement 40 is used to control this process. Within the loop, the record is exchanged with its parent and the new parent of the record is computed.

In the next section, we examine the use of m-ary trees for searching. This involves using a trie structure.

11-3.4 Trie Structures

This section examines the application of m-ary trees ($m \geqslant 2$) for searching. A trie structure is a complete m-ary tree in which each node consists of m components, where each component may contain either a character string or the address to another node in the structure. The method of searching tries is analogous to digital searching which was described in Chap. 10.

A trie structure can be represented by a 27 x n array of character strings. The keys of the records are stored in the elements of this array. The 27 rows represent the blank character and the letters A through Z, respectively. The n columns represent the nodes in the trie structure. Note that node 1 is the root of the tree.

To access a node given a search key, we examine the first letter of the key. This gives the position (i.e., 1 through 27) of the component in the node that we should examine. If this node contains the key searched for, the search is finished; otherwise, if the entry is a number, we go to the node that corresponds to that number. This process is repeated for the next letter in the key. Note that the blank symbol is used to denote the end of a word during the scan of a key.

Figure 11-16 gives an example of a main program that calls procedure TRIE_SH to perform searching in a trie structure. The variables used in the main procedure are:

Variable	Type	Usage
TRIE(27,15)	CHARACTER (20) VARYING	Trie structure
NAME	CHARACTER (20) VARYING	Key to search for in the trie structure
N	FIXED	Number of nodes in the trie structure
ROW	FIXED	Row NAME is found in TRIE
COL	FIXED	Column NAME is found in TRIE
I	FIXED	Counted loop variable
J	FIXED	Counted loop variable

```
STMT LEVEL NEST BLOCK MLVL  SOURCE TEXT


  1                            HEAP: PROCEDURE OPTIONS (MAIN);
                               /* THIS PROGRAM READS A TABLE INTO THE VECTOR K AND SORTS IT INTO*/
                               /* ASCENDING ORDER.                                            */

  2    1            1          DECLARE (K(50),       /* CONTAINS THE KEYS OF THE RECORDS */
                                       N,            /* NUMBER OF ELEMENTS OF VECTOR K */
                                       Q,            /* PASS INDEX */
                                       I, J,         /* INDEX VARIABLES */
                                       KEY,          /* CONTAINS VARIABLE CONTAING KEY OF */
                                                     /* THE RECORD BEING SWAPPED */
                                       TEMP) FIXED;  /* TEMPORARY VARIABLE */

                               /* READ THE KEYS */
  3    1            1          GET LIST (N);
  4    1            1          DO I = 1 TO N;
  5    1      1     1              GET LIST (K(I));
  6    1      1     1          END;

                               /* CREATE INITIAL HEAP */
  7    1            1          CALL CREATE (K, N);

                               /* PERFORM SORT */
  8    1            1          DO Q = N TO 2 BY -1;

                                   /* OUTPUT AND EXCHANGE RECORD */
  9    1      1     1              PUT SKIP LIST (K(1));
 10    1      1     1              TEMP = K(1);
 11    1      1     1              K(1) = K(Q);
 12    1      1     1              K(Q) = TEMP;

                                   /* INITIALIZE PASS */
 13    1      1     1              I = 1;
 14    1      1     1              KEY = K(1);
 15    1      1     1              J = 2;

                                   /* OBTAIN INDEX OF LARGEST SON OF NEW RECORD */
 16    1      1     1              IF J + 1 < Q
 17    1      1     1              THEN IF K(J + 1) > K(J)
 18    1      1     1                  THEN J = J + 1;

                                   /* RECONSTRUCT THE NEW HEAP */
 19    1      1     1              DO WHILE (J <= Q - 1 & K(J) > KEY);

                                       /* INTERCHANGE RECORD */
 20    1      2     1                  K(I) = K(J);

                                       /* OBTAIN NEXT LEFT SON */

 21    1      2     1                  I = J;
 22    1      2     1                  J = 2 * I;

                                       /* OBTAIN INDEX OF NEXT LARGEST SON */
 23    1      2     1                  IF J + 1 < Q
 24    1      2     1                  THEN IF K(J + 1) > K(J)
 25    1      2     1                      THEN J = J + 1;
 26    1      2     1                      ELSE;

                                       /* CHECK IF J SUBSCRIPT OUT OF BOUNDS */
 27    1      2     1                  ELSE IF J > N
 28    1      2     1                      THEN J = N;

                                       /* COPY RECORD INTO ITS PROPER PLACE */
 29    1      2     1                  K(I) = KEY;
 30    1      2     1              END;
 31    1      1     1          END;

                               /* FINISHED */
 32    1            1          PUT SKIP LIST (K(1));
 33    1            1          END HEAP;
```

Fig. 11-15　Program to sort a table by using a heap sort

```
34                          CREATE: PROCEDURE (K, N);
                            /* GIVEN A VECTOR K OF N ELEMENTS, THIS PROCEDURE CREATES AN    */
                            /* INITAL HEAP.                                                 */

35   1       2              DECLARE K(*) FIXED,      /* VECTOR OF ELEMENTS */
                                    (N,              /* NUMBER OF ELEMENTS IN VECTOR */
                                    Q,               /* NUMBER OF INSERTIONS */
                                    J,               /* INDEX OF PARENT KEY */
                                    I,               /* INDEX VARIABLE */
                                    KEY) FIXED;      /* KEY OF RECORD BEING INSERTED */

                            /* BUILD HEAP */
36   1       2              DO Q = 2 TO N;

                                    /* INITIALIZE CONSTRUCTION PHASE */
37   1   1   2                      I = Q;
38   1   1   2                      KEY = K(Q);

                                    /* OBTAIN PARENT OF NEW RECORD */
39   1   1   2                      J = TRUNC (I / 2);

                                    /* PLACE NEW RECORD IN EXISTING HEAP */
40   1   1   2                      DO WHILE (I > 1 & KEY > K(J));

                                            /* INTERCHANGE RECORD */
41   1   2   2                              K(I) = K(J);

                                            /* OBTAIN NEXT PARENT */
42   1   2   2                              I = J;
43   1   2   2                              J = TRUNC (I / 2);

                                            /* CHECK IF J SUBSCRIPT OUT OF BOUNDS */
44   1   2   2                              IF J < 1
45   1   2   2                              THEN J = 1;
46   1   2   2                      END;

                                    /* COPY NEW RECORD INTO ITS PROPER PLACE */
47   1   1   2                      K(I) = KEY;
48   1   1   2              END;

                            /* FINISHED */
49   1       2              RETURN;
50   1       2              END CREATE;
```

ERRORS/WARNINGS DETECTED DURING CODE GENERATION:

   WARNING: NO FILE SPECIFIED. SYSIN/SYSPRINT ASSUMED. (CGOC)

```
89
78
58
56
56
52
42
42
25
23
14
11
 3
```

IN STMT   33   PROGRAM RETURNS FROM MAIN PROCEDURE.

Fig. 11-15   Program to sort a table by using a heap sort (cont'd.)

```
STMT LEVEL NEST BLOCK MLVL   SOURCE TEXT

  1                              TRIETST: PROCEDURE OPTIONS (MAIN);
                                 /* THIS PROGRAM READS IN A TRIE STRUCTURE AND CALLS PROCEDURE   */
                                 /* TRIE_SH TO PERFORM SEARCHES ON THE TRIE STRUCTURE.           */
  2    1           1             DECLARE TRIE (27, 15) CHARACTER (20) VARYING,
                                                               /* TRIE STRUCTURE */
                                    NAME CHARACTER (20) VARYING,
                                                               /* KEY TO SEARCH FOR */
                                    (ROW, COL) FIXED,          /* POSITION OF KEY IN STRUCTURE*/
                                    N FIXED,                   /* NUMBER OF NODES IN STRUCTURE*/
                                    (I, J) FIXED;              /* COUNTED LOOP VARIABLES */

                                 /* READ N */
  3    1           1             ROW = 0; COL = 0;
  5    1           1             GET LIST (N);
  6    1           1             DO I = 1 TO 27;
  7    1     1     1                 DO J = 1 TO N;
  8    1     2     1                     GET LIST (TRIE(I, J));
  9    1     2     1                 END;
 10    1     1     1             END;

                                 /* PERFORM SEARCH */
 11    1           1             ON ENDFILE (SYSIN) STOP;
 13    2           2             DO WHILE ('1'B);
 14    1     1     1                 GET LIST (NAME);
 15    1     1     1                 PUT SKIP (4) EDIT ('NAME SEARCHED FOR IS ', NAME) (A, A);
 16    1     1     1                 CALL TRIE_SH (NAME, TRIE, ROW, COL);
 17    1     1     1                 PUT SKIP EDIT ('NAME IS IN ROW', ROW, 'AND COLUMN', COL)
                                        (A, F(3), X(1), A, F(3));
 18    1     1     1             END;
 19    1           1             END TRIETST;
```

Fig. 11-16 Program to perform trie search

Variables used in the procedure TRIE_SH are:

NAME	CHARACTER (*) VARYING	Key to search for in trie structure
TRIE(*, *)	CHARACTER (*) VARYING	Trie structure
ROW	FIXED	Component being examined
COL	FIXED	Node being examined
K	FIXED	Index variable
CHAR	CHARACTER (2) VARYING	Used to convert string numbers to fixed
NUMBER	CHARACTER (2) VARYING	Used to convert string numbers to fixed

In the main program statement 5 reads the number of nodes in the trie structure. Then the elements of the trie structure are read. Next, a loop is entered which inputs a series of keys and calls procedure TRIE_SH to find the position of the key in the table.

In the procedure TRIE_SH, COL is initialized to 1 because the first node is the root node. Then a loop is entered which examines every character of the key (NAME). ROW is set to the value which corresponds to the letter being examined. The IF statement in statement 25 determines whether an empty position is found and returns if this position is empty. If the position corresponding to the search key is found, the program returns; otherwise, a check is made to see if the element contains a number. If not, another name has been found and the search terminates.

```
20                              TRIE_SH: PROCEDURE (NAME, TRIE, ROW, COL);
                                   /* THIS PROCEDURE SEARCHES FOR NAME IN TRIE, THE TRIE STRUCTURE, */
                                   /* RETURNING ITS POSITION THROUGH ROW AND COL.                   */
21    1          3                 DECLARE (NAME,          /* NAME BEING SEARCHED FOR */
                                            TRIE(*, *))    /* ARRAY OF ELEMENTS */
                                               CHARACTER (*) VARYING,
                                            (ROW, COL)     /* ROW AND COLUMN INDICES */
                                               FIXED,
                                            K FIXED,            /* INDEX VARIABLE */
                                            (CHAR, NUMBER)   /* USED TO CONVERT NUMBER IN TRIE ARRAY */
                                               CHARACTER (2) VARYING;    /* TO AN INTEGER */

                                   /* INITIALIZE */
22    1          3                 COL = 1;

                                   /* PERFORM SEARCH */
23    1          3                 DO K = 1 TO LENGTH (NAME);
24    1    1     3                      ROW = INDEX (' ABCDEFGHIJKLMNOPQRSTUVWXYZ',
                                                      SUBSTR (NAME, K, 1));
25    1    1     3                      IF TRIE(ROW, COL) = '-'
26    1    1     3                      THEN DO;

                                            /* MISSING NAME */
27    1    2     3                          PUT SKIP LIST ('NAME NOT FOUND');
28    1    2     3                          ROW, COL = 0;
29    1    2     3                          RETURN;
30    1    2     3                          END;
31    1    1     3                      ELSE DO;
32    1    2     3                          IF TRIE(ROW, COL) = NAME
33    1    2     3                          THEN RETURN;
34    1    2     3                          IF INDEX ('0123456789', SUBSTR (TRIE(ROW, COL), 1, 1))
                                               = 0
35    1    2     3                          THEN DO;
36    1    3     3                              PUT SKIP EDIT ('UNEXPECTED', TRIE(ROW, COL),
                                                     'FOUND') (A, X(1), A, X(1), A);
37    1    3     3                              ROW, COL = 0;
38    1    3     3                              RETURN;
39    1    3     3                              END;
40    1    2     3                          ELSE DO;

                                                /* CONVERT COLUMN TO AN INTEGER */
41    1    3     3                              NUMBER = TRIE(ROW, COL);
42    1    3     3                              COL = 0;
43    1    3     3                              IF LENGTH (NUMBER) = 2
44    1    3     3                              THEN DO;
45    1    4     3                                  CHAR = SUBSTR (NUMBER, 1, 1);
46    1    4     3                                  COL = (INDEX ('0123456789', CHAR) - 1) * 10;
47    1    4     3                                  NUMBER = SUBSTR (NUMBER, 2);
48    1    4     3                                  END;
49    1    3     3                              COL = COL + INDEX ('0123456789', NUMBER) - 1;
50    1    3     3                              END;
51    1    2     3                          END;
52    1    1     3                      END;

                                   /* MISSING NAME */
53    1          3                 PUT SKIP LIST ('NAME NOT FOUND');
54    1          3                 ROW, COL = 0;
55    1          3                 RETURN;
56    1          3                 END TRIE_SH;

ERRORS/WARNINGS DETECTED DURING CODE GENERATION:

    WARNING: NO FILE SPECIFIED. SYSIN/SYSPRINT ASSUMED. (CGOC)
```

Fig. 11-16 Program to perform trie search (cont'd.)

```
NAME SEARCHED FOR IS CANARY
NAME IS IN ROW  2 AND COLUMN  2


NAME SEARCHED FOR IS EAGLE
NAME IS IN ROW  2 AND COLUMN  3

NAME SEARCHED FOR IS HELLO
UNEXPECTED HAWK FOUND
NAME IS IN ROW  0 AND COLUMN  0

NAME SEARCHED FOR IS ZERO
NAME NOT FOUND
NAME IS IN ROW  0 AND COLUMN  0

NAME SEARCHED FOR IS SNOB
NAME NOT FOUND
NAME IS IN ROW  0 AND COLUMN  0

IN STMT   12  PROGRAM IS STOPPED.
```

Fig. 11-16   Program to perform trie search (cont'd.)

The number is converted to its integer form and COL is set to the new trie node that is to be examined. If the program reaches statement 53 the key was not found. ROW and COL are, therefore, set to zero before the procedure returns to the calling program.

EXERCISES FOR CHAPTER 11

1. A familiar example of symbol manipulation is finding the derivative of a formula with respect to a variable, say, x.

   The following rules define the derivative of a formula with respect to x where u and v denote functions of x:
   1. $D(x) = 1$
   2. $D(a) = 0$, if a is a constant or a variable other than x
   3. $D(\# u) = D(u) / u$, where # denotes the natural logarithm
   4. $D(-u) = -D(u)$
   5. $D(u + v) = D(u) + D(v)$
   6. $D(u - v) = D(u) - D(v)$
   7. $D(u * v) = D(u) * v + u * D(v)$
   8. $D(u / v) = D(u) / v - (u * D(v)) / v^2$
   9. $D(v ** u) = (v ** u) * (u * D(v) / v + D(u) * \# v)$

   These rules permit evaluation of the derivative $D(y)$ for any formula y composed of the preceding operators. Based on the binary tree representation of an expression given in the text, formulate a program which differentiates a given expression according to the differentiation rules 1 through 9.

2. If we apply the differentiation rules of the previous exercise to a formula, certain simplifications can be made to the resulting derivative. In particular, certain redundant operations such as multiplications by 0 or 1 and

exponentiation to the first power can be avoided. Modify the program obtained in the previous exercise so that these simplifications are realized.

3. Construct a program which uses the function BINARY_TREE repeatedly to perform a sequence of insertions and/or searches. Use the following sequence of inputs:

    '1'B   'THEN'
    '1'B   'DECLARE'
    '1'B   'ELSE'
    '1'B   'GET'
    '0'B   'ELSE'
    '1'B   'PUT'
    '1'B   'FREE'
    '0'B   'ALLOCATE'

4. Construct a program for the deletion of an element from a trie structure whose organization is that given in the text.

APPENDIX

**A
REFERENCE
SUMMARY
FOR
PL/I AND PL/C**

This appendix is an attempt to collect, in a form convenient for quick reference, many details of the PL/I language. As described in the preface, the terms of reference are somewhat fuzzy because of the many implementations of PL/I. The information in this appendix is drawn primarily from two sources: a book by R. Conway and D. Gries [1979] that is based on release 7.6 of PL/C, and the IBM reference summary for the Checkout and Optimizing compilers [1976].

Section A — Notation

To permit a simple and precise description of language features and constructs, we employ what is known as a "metalanguage." In the metalanguage certain symbols, not part of the language itself, are used to describe how one forms valid elements of the language.

1. Square brackets, "[" and "]", are used to denote optional entities. For example,

    SKIP [(n)]

means that the item "(n)" is optional in the writing of the SKIP input/output option; that is, either of the following forms is legal in PL/I

    SKIP
    SKIP (n)

2. Curly brackets (or braces), "{" and "}", are used to denote an item that can be repeated any number of times (including 0 times, unless information to the contrary is given). For example,

    array-name [(subscript {, subscript})]

says that any of the following can be legal in PL/I

    array-name
    array-name (subscript)
    array-name (subscript, subscript)
    and so forth...

Note that although "subscript" can in theory be replicated any number of times (according to the specification given), in practice a limit will normally be imposed.

3. Uppercase words will be used to denote keywords in the PL/I language; lowercase words denote general classes of entities that will be replaced by a specific element of that class in an actual PL/I construct. For example, the model of an IF statement is

    IF condition
    THEN statement1
    [ELSE statement2]

Section B — Basic Concepts

1. A Program

A PL/I program has the following basic form:

```
entry-name: PROCEDURE OPTIONS (MAIN);
           { declaration }
           { statement  }
           END [entry-name];
```

If present, the "entry-name" given on the END statement must be the same as the label of the PROCEDURE statement. The set of "declarations" may include the declaration and definition of procedure or function subprograms. The declarations and statements themselves are described elsewhere in this appendix.

2.   Variable Names and Keywords

A variable name (or identifier) in PL/I consists of a string of alphanumeric characters beginning with a letter (or one of the special characters \$, @, or #). The remaining characters in the name (up to a maximum of 31 in PL/C) can be any combination of letters, digits, or the special characters \$, @, #, or _. No blanks are allowed within a variable name.

Some compilers may forbid the use of certain keywords of the PL/I language (sometimes referred to as *reserved* words) as variable names. Whether it is allowed or not, such use of keywords is to be avoided purely as a matter of good programming style. The following are the reserved keywords of PL/C:

ALLOCATE BEGIN BY CALL CHECK DECLARE (DCL) DELETE DO ELSE END ENTRY EXIT FLOW FORMAT FREE GET GO GOTO IF NOCHECK NOFLOW ON OPEN PROCEDURE (PROC) PUT READ RETURN REVERT REWRITE SIGNAL STOP THEN TO WHILE WRITE

3.   Comments

A comment in PL/I is any sequence of characters delimited by "/*" and "*/" (for obvious reasons the comment itself may not include the characters "*/"). Comments are intended to make the program more understandable and have no effect whatsoever on either the compilation or the execution of the program. Although in theory a comment can comprise any length of text, some compilers (PL/C for one) restrict the length of an individual comment to one card.

4.   Constants in PL/I

The following are available in PL/I:

Decimal fixed point constant (with or without decimal point) — examples: 435 980.78 –0.00087

Decimal floating point constant — "E" notation used. Examples: 435E0 76.98E-5 –.00086E13

Logical constant — "true" or "false". In PL/I these are written as bit strings '1'B and '0'B respectively.

String constant (or literal) — a sequence of characters enclosed in delimiting quotes ('). Examples: 'THE FINAL SUM IS' 'NAME   ADDRESS   PHONE NO.' '1221 AVE OF THE AMERICAS'

Bit string constant — a sequence of 0's and 1's enclosed in delimiting quotes (') and followed by a "B". Examples: '010001'B '100010'B '1'B '0'B

Others — other types of constants that are beyond the scope of this book include binary fixed point and binary floating point, imaginary decimal and imaginary binary, and label constants.

Section C — Executable Statements

In this section the executable statements of PL/I are described in alphabetical order. While we attempt to be reasonably complete, we make no attempt to be exhaustive. A number of statements that are beyond the scope of this book have been omitted. In PL/I any executable statement can be given one or more labels. To avoid repeating this in our specifications of the individual statements we will assume a general form as follows:

{label :} statement

ALLOCATE

The ALLOCATE statement is used to allocate new storage for a data item that is declared to be CONTROLLED or BASED. Its form is as follows:

ALLOCATE item-name ;

Controlled and based storage are described in more detail in Chapters 10 and 11, respectively.

Assignment

The assignment statement is used to assign values to variables. Its basic form is the following:

variable-name = expression ;

In general, the value of the expression on the right-hand side of the assignment operator "=" is assigned to the variable named on the left-hand side. Variations of the assignment operation include assignment to arrays and assignment to structures, which can include (optionally) the BY NAME qualifier. Also possible is the multiple assignment, of the form

var-name , var-name {, var-name} = expression ;

which is interpreted as a series of simple assignments.

BEGIN

The BEGIN statement is used to indicate the start of a BEGIN block of the following form:

```
[label :] BEGIN;
        {declaration}
        {statement  }
        END [label] ;
```

The use of BEGIN blocks is described in Sec. 6-4

CALL

The CALL statement is used to transfer control to a procedure. Its basic form is the following:

```
CALL procedure-name [ (argument {, argument}) ] ;
```

The arguments of a procedure call can be variables, constants, expressions, entry names, or built-in functions. They must agree in number and type with the parameters of the procedure definition. The rules of correspondence can be quite complex. These are summarized in Sec. 6-3. In general, call by reference is used whenever the argument is a variable whose type matches that of the parameter; call by value is used otherwise. The same rules apply to function calls as well.

DECLARE, DCL

This is **not** an executable statement. See Section D.

DO

The DO statement controls iteration and comes in several flavors. First there are the two most familiar forms:

```
Form 1: DO WHILE (logical expression) ;
            {statement}
        END;
```

```
Form 2: DO var = exp1 TO exp2 [BY exp3] ;
            {statement}
        END;
```

Form 1 of the DO is used to control a conditional loop, that is, a loop whose termination is based on the truth or falsity of a particular logical expression. In the PL/I "WHILE" loop, iteration continues as long as the specified logical expression is true. The test itself is made at the top of the loop; thus it is possible to execute the range of the loop zero times.

Form 2 of the DO loop is used to control a counted loop, that is, a loop that is to be executed a stated number of times. The range of the loop is executed for a sequence of values of the control variable, beginning with the value given by "exp1" and proceeding in increments of "exp3" until the value exceeds that given by "exp2".

Any real values are allowed for "exp1" "exp2", and "exp3" (positive, negative, or zero). If "BY exp3" is omitted, "exp3" is assumed to be +1. Again, the loop is top-tested.

Two other forms of DO are possible in PL/I. These have the following forms:

```
Form 3: DO var = exp { , exp } ;
            {statement}
        END ;

Form 4: DO var = spec { , spec } ;
            {statement}
        END;
```

Form 3 is similar to Form 2 in that the control variable assumes a sequence of values on iterations through the range of the loop. The difference is that there is no automatic incrementing involved. The entire sequence of values is specified *explicitly* in the DO statement. The loop terminates when this list is exhausted.

Form 4 is really a combination of Forms 1, 2, and 3. Each specification (spec) has the following form:

```
exp1 [TO exp2] [BY exp 3] [WHILE (logical expression) ]
```

END

This is *not* an executable statement. Rather, it is used to terminate the BEGIN block, the procedure block, the DO block, and the compound statement (or, DO group). If a label follows the END, it must be the same as that on the statement to which the END refers; any missing END's between these points will automatically be inserted.

EXIT

In PL/C, EXIT causes execution of the program to terminate and it is equivalent to STOP.

FORMAT

This is *not* an executable statement. See Section F.

FREE

This statement causes the storage that had previously been allocated for data items declared as CONTROLLED or BASED to be freed (see Chapters 10 and 11). Its form is as follows:

```
FREE item-name ;
```

This statement is the companion to the ALLOCATE.

GET

This statement controls the reading of data. Data can be read in three ways: through list-directed input, through data-directed input, and through edit-directed input. Complete descriptions are given in Sec. 2-3 (for list-directed and data-directed) and Sec. 5-3 (for edit-directed).

GOTO (or GO TO)

This statement is used to alter the normal flow of control in a program. The execution of a statement

GOTO label ;

causes an immediate (unconditional) branch to the statement whose label is specified. This *must* be an executable statement and cannot be within a block not currently being executed.

IF

This statement normally causes the execution of one of a specified pair of alternatives based on the evaluation of a given condition. It has the following basic form:

IF condition
THEN statement1
[ELSE statement2]

"statement1" is executed if the "condition" evaluates to "true"; otherwise "statement2" is executed. In the event that IF statements are nested, an ELSE relates back to the nearest preceding THEN for which no ELSE is specified.

ON

The specifications of an "On-unit" permits a programmer to take action should particular events take place during the execution of his or her program. An ON statement has the following basic form:

ON condition On-unit

The On-unit can be any unlabelled statement except a DO statement (or DO group), an IF statement, a RETURN statement, or another ON statement. It can be an unlabelled BEGIN block. Examples of conditions that can be specified in an ON statement are the following:

data conversion error (CONVERSION)
end of file (ENDFILE)
end of page on a print file (ENDPAGE)
fixed point arithmetic overflow (FIXEDOVERFLOW)
floating point arithmetic overflow (OVERFLOW)
subscript out of bounds (SUBSCRIPTRANGE)
floating point arithmetic underflow (UNDERFLOW)
division by zero (ZERODIVIDE)

Any of these conditions can be *enabled* (to permit checking via ON statements) or *disabled* for part or all of a given program.

PROCEDURE, PROC

This is *not* an executable statement, but rather marks the beginning of a procedure definition. See Section F.

PUT

The execution of this statement causes data to be written as output. The same methods apply here as with the GET statement: namely, list-directed output, data-directed output, and edit-directed output. These are described in detail in Sec. 2-3 (list-directed and data-directed) and Sec. 5-3 (edit-directed).

RETURN

There are two forms of the RETURN statement, for use respectively in procedure subprograms and function subprograms.

    Form 1: RETURN ;
    Form 2: RETURN [(expression)] ;

Each of these forms causes an immediate transfer of control back to the point from where the subprogram was invoked. When Form 2 is used to return from a function, a value can be returned as the value of the function.

SIGNAL

This statement is used in conjunction with the ON statement. It has the following format:

    SIGNAL condition ;

Execution of a SIGNAL statement raises the condition and, if it is enabled, the On-unit for that condition is executed.

STOP

This statement causes execution of the program to terminate. It has the following form:
    STOP;

Other statements

A number of statements have not been considered in this summary. These include the following:

ASSERT CHECK CLOSE DEFAULT DELAY DELETE DISPLAY FETCH FLOW HALT

LEAVE LOCATE NOCHECK NOFLOW OPEN READ RELEASE REVERT REWRITE SELECT UNLOCK WAIT WRITE

Section D — Declarations

Declarations are not executable statements in PL/I. They are used instead to describe things. These "things" include simple scalar variables, arrays, structures, procedures and procedure entry points, and parameters to procedures. Since they are not executable, declarations may in theory be placed anywhere within a block or procedure; however, as a matter of good style it is advisable to group declarations together, preferably at the beginning of the block or procedure, as has been our convention throughout this book. In this section, we discuss general notions of declaration. A discussion of attributes is contained in Sec. D.1.

Declaration of simple scalar variables

Format: DECLARE (var-name $\{$, var-name$\}$) attribute ;

1. Parentheses are not necessary when only one variable is being declared.

2. Typical attributes, together with their meaning in PL/C, are the following:

FIXED [DECIMAL] The variable can contain integers internally stored in decimal format with a range of –99999 to +99999.

FIXED BINARY The variable can contain integers internally stored in binary format with a range (in decimal) of –32767 to +32767.

FLOAT [DECIMAL] The variable can contain floating point numbers with 6 significant digits and a range of exponent values (powers of 10) of approximately –78 to +75.

CHARACTER(n) where n is an integer constant between 1 and 256. The variable can contain a string of n characters.

CHARACTER(n) VARYING where n is an integer constant between 1 and 256. The variable can contain a string of characters where the total length is between 0 and n characters.

BIT(n) where n is an integer constant between 1 and 256. The variable can contain a string of n bits.

BIT(n) VARYING where n is an integer constant between 1 and 256. The variable can contain a string of bits where the total length is between 0 and n bits.

3. Two or more declarations may be grouped under a single DECLARE, as in the following example:

```
DECLARE (S, P, Q) FIXED,
         R FLOAT;
```

4.   Although PL/I permits the implicit declaration of variables, we advise that each variable used in a program be explicitly declared. Failure to do so can lead to unexpected errors as is discussed in Sec. 7-3. Likewise it is advisable to specify all the attributes for each variable. A description of attributes, and a list of defaults, is given in Section D.1.

Declaration of arrays

The declaration of arrays is very similar to the declaration of simple scalar variables, and consequently the preceding remarks apply here as well. In the event that an array is being declared, the range of subscript values for each dimension must be specified, as in the following:

array-name ([exp1:] exp2 $\{$, [exp1:] exp2 $\}$)

In this specification, "exp1" gives the lower bound for the subscript, and "exp2", the upper bound. If "exp1" is omitted, it is assumed to be +1. Notice that the array has as many dimensions as there are "exp1:exp2" pairs.

The following example shows how declarations of simple scalars and arrays can be combined under a single DECLARE.

```
DECLARE (X, Y(3:27,-5:+5)) CHARACTER(20) VARYING,
         AGE(24) FIXED BINARY;
```

Declaration of structures

The concept of a structure as a hierarchical aggregation of data is introduced in Chapter 10. The declaration of a structure is a straightforward extension to the ideas of the preceding two sections. Rather than repeat a lengthy discussion at this point, we refer you instead to the discussion in Sec. 10-2.

Others

There are a number of other elements in a PL/I program that might require declaration. The most important omission is files. Since files are not required for this book, however, they will be discussed no further.

Section D.1 — Attributes

In this section we present a brief summary of the most important attributes that might appear in the declaration of a variable. We will also indicate defaults where applicable.

Any variable in a PL/I program has attributes of *type, scope* and *storage,* and, perhaps, an *initial* attribute as well.

1.   Type attributes

a) For numeric variables, type attributes fall into the following classes:

- A *base* attribute: DECIMAL or BINARY.
- A *scale* attribute: FIXED or FLOAT (one of these should always be given).
- A *precision* attribute: describes the number of digits to be retained in the internal representation. This determines both the accuracy and the range of values for the numeric variable. In general, the default precisions are adequate.

b) For character-string variables, the attribute is CHARACTER (and, perhaps, VARYING).

c) For bit-string variables, the attribute is BIT (and, perhaps, VARYING).

d) For pointer variables, the attribute is POINTER. Pointer variables are not presently available in PL/C.

2. Scope attributes

The possibilities for scope attributes are INTERNAL and EXTERNAL. These help in indicating where in the program the variable can be referenced. The default is INTERNAL.

3. Storage class attribute

This helps to indicate when and where the variable is to be created and destroyed. The main possibilities are AUTOMATIC and STATIC (default AUTOMATIC). The attributes BASED and CONTROLLED are available for variables for which the programmer wishes to have more direct control over the allocation of storage. BASED and CONTROLLED are not presently available in PL/C.

4. INITIAL attribute

The purpose of the INITIAL attribute is to give an initial value to a variable at the time of its declaration. The specified value must be a constant in PL/C.

5. A further word on defaults

The influence of the FORTRAN era is evident in the assigning of defaults for some of the attributes defining a variable. For someone not familiar with FORTRAN conventions these defaults appear somewhat capricious. In particular, the defaults for base, mode, and type depend on the variable name. For variables whose names begin with one of the letters I through N, the default is FIXED BINARY (15,0). For variables whose names begin with any other valid symbol, the default is FLOAT DECIMAL (6).

In the event of a partial specification of attributes, the full picture is completed by default. Should either BINARY or DECIMAL be specified by itself, FLOAT is assumed. Should either FIXED or FLOAT be specified by itself, DECIMAL is assumed. With such a confusing state of affairs you can see why we advocate full declaration.

We will now consider the major attributes in more detail.

AUTOMATIC, STATIC, CONTROLLED, and BASED

Storage is allocated for a variable declared with the AUTOMATIC attribute on entry to the block in which the variable is declared, and released upon exit from the block. In a sense the variable declared with the AUTOMATIC attribute is "created" whenever the block is entered and "destroyed" when it is left. STATIC variables are created when the program begins executing, and are destroyed only when the program terminates. This is not to be confused with the *scope* of the variable. A static variable cannot be referenced outside the block in which it is declared even though it retains both its storage and its value. In fact there may be several STATIC variables with the same name in a program.

The attributes BASED and CONTROLLED both specify that full control over the allocation and releasing (or freeing) of storage is to be in the hands of the programmer. For a CONTROLLED variable successive allocations without intervening freeings will cause the generations of the variable to be stacked. For BASED variables these are not stacked, but are instead referenced through the use of a pointer. The use of CONTROLLED and BASED variables is described in Chapters 10 and 11, respectively.

Normally the default storage class is AUTOMATIC.

BASED

See AUTOMATIC.

BINARY and DECIMAL

These attributes control the internal representation of the numeric values of the variables declared. Unless additional precision attributes are specified, default precisions take effect. These depend on the attributes of the variable in the following way:

FIXED BINARY   15 binary digits (plus sign). The range (in decimal) is –32767 to +32767.

FIXED DECIMAL   5 decimal digits (plus sign). The range is –99999 to +99999.

FLOAT DECIMAL   6 decimal digits (plus sign) for the mantissa (or fraction). The approximate range for the exponent (as a power of 10) is –78 to +75.

See also "Precision attribute."

BIT, CHARACTER, and VARYING

Format: BIT(length) [VARYING]
        CHARACTER(length) [VARYING]

These attributes are used to specify bit and character strings, respectively. These may be fixed or varying. The "length" specified for character-string variables is in characters (or bytes); for bit-string variables it is in bits. In each case the expression supplied is converted to an integer value when storage is allocated for the variable.

CHARACTER

See BIT.

CONTROLLED

See AUTOMATIC.

DECIMAL

See BINARY.

Dimension attribute

See "Declaration of arrays" in Section D.

ENTRY

The ENTRY attribute is used to designate a name as an entry point to a procedure or function, and to describe the attributes of the parameters of the entry point. In PL/C it is only *necessary* for a parameter of a function or procedure that is itself a function or procedure. In PL/I it may also be necessary to force conversion when the arguments of a call do not match exactly the parameters of a procedure.

> Format: ENTRY [(attribute {, attribute})]

The "attribute"s given here refer to the parameters of the entry point. For example,

> DECLARE SORT ENTRY ((*,*) FLOAT, FIXED);

indicates that procedure SORT has two parameters: the first is a two-dimensional array of type FLOAT, the second is a scalar of type FIXED. Any arguments are converted to conform, if required.

FIXED and FLOAT

The FIXED and FLOAT attributes specify the scale of the numeric variable being declared. FIXED specifies that the values are to be kept in fixed-point form (typically integer, but see "Precision attribute" for more information). FIXED alone is equivalent to FIXED DECIMAL.

FLOAT specifies that the values are to be kept in floating-point form (again see "Precision attribute"). FLOAT alone is equivalent to FLOAT DECIMAL.

See also the comments on defaults at the beginning of this section.

FLOAT

See FIXED.

INITIAL

The INITIAL attribute is used to specify a constant, expression, or function reference whose value is to be assigned to the declared data item when storage is allocated for it. In PL/C, only constants are permitted. The general form is the following:

INITIAL (item {, item })

The INITIAL attribute can be associated with scalar variables or with arrays. The multiple "item"s are for the initialization of arrays. The assignment of initial values to an array takes place in row-major order. If there are fewer initial values than array elements, the remaining array elements are uninitialized; if there are more initial values than array elements, excess initial values are ignored.

It is possible to abbreviate a sequence of identical initial values through the use of an "iteration factor." For example, the item (3) 0 is equivalent to 0, 0, 0. The iteration factor is any expression that can be evaluated and converted to an integer value. If an asterisk follows the iteration factor, then the specified number of elements are skipped in the assignment of initial values.

Length attribute

See BIT.

POINTER

The POINTER attribute describes a variable used to identify a particular generation of a BASED variable. The value of a pointer variable can be set in a number of ways: by an ALLOCATE statement, by assignment of another pointer variable, or by assignment of the built-in functions ADDR or NULL (see Sec. G). The values of pointer variables cannot be used in any way other than to identify storage; for example, they cannot be read or written. Pointer variables are not available at present in PL/C.

Precision attribute

The precision attribute is used to specify the precision of a numeric variable (the minimum number of significant digits to be maintained for its values), and also the scale factor (the assumed position of the binary or decimal point).

Format: (number-of-digits [, scale-factor])

The "number-of-digits" is an unsigned decimal integer constant, and the "scale-factor" is a signed or unsigned decimal integer constant. For the sake of brevity in the following description, we express the precision attribute specification as (p, q).

The precision attribute must follow immediately (that is, with no intervening keywords or names) one of the attributes FIXED, FLOAT, DECIMAL, or BINARY at the same factoring level. The scale factor q may be specified for fixed-point variables only; it must be in the range –128 to +127. If it is omitted, 0 is assumed and the variable is an integer variable. A negative scale factor $(-q)$ always specifies integers with the point assumed to be located q places to the *right* of the rightmost actual digit. A positive scale factor that is larger than the number of digits always specifies a fraction, with the point assumed to be located q places to the *left* of the rightmost actual digit. In either case, intervening zeroes are assumed (but not stored).

The standard defaults for precision are:

(5,0) for FIXED DECIMAL [max digits 15]
(15,0) for FIXED BINARY [max digits 31]
(6) for FLOAT DECIMAL [max digits 33]

STATIC

See AUTOMATIC.

VARYING

See BIT.

Section E - Variables and Expressions

In this section we consider how variables are used in a program. For information on how they are declared we refer you to Section D.

1. Scope of Names

That part of a program in which an entity may be referenced by its name is known as the *scope* of the entity. The scope of an entity has nothing to do with the time when storage for the entity is allocated or released, or when the entity gets valid values; instead it indicates only where one is permitted to refer to the entity by its name. The scope of an entity depends on where it is declared (in the case of a variable) or defined (in the case of an entry point or label) relative to the block structure of the program.

The rules of scope are basically quite simple. The scope of an entity is the block in which its declaration or definition appears, including any contained blocks, except those blocks (and blocks internal to them) in which the name is redefined. As a general principle scopes are inherited inward; that is, within any block one can refer to all names accessible to the containing block that are not redefined in the present block. Examples of scopes are given in Sec. 6-4.

2. Rules of Reference

Within the scope of declaration, references are made according to the following rules:

a) A *scalar variable* is referenced simply by its name (for example, X, SUM, SCALAR_VARIABLE).

b) An entire *array* is referenced simply by its name (for example, TOTALS, TABLE). Individual elements of arrays are referenced using subscripts (see part c).

c) *Subscripted variables* are referenced in the following manner:

array-name (exp $\{$, exp $\}$)

where the number of "exp"s is equal to the number of dimensions declared for the array. The particular element is identified by evaluating the "exp" subscripts and converting them to integers (left to right).

d) An *array cross section* is indicated by using an asterisk to indicate an entire dimension (that is, the entire range of values for that subscript). For example, suppose that we have the following array declarations:

    DECLARE (A(5, 5), B(3, 3, 3), C(5, 3, 5) FIXED;

A(*, 1) represents the "vector cross section" obtained by taking the entire first column of the array A (that is, A(1, 1), A(2, 1), ..., A(5, 1)). By the same token, B(2, *, *) represents a "table cross section" of the three-dimensional array B. Notice that B(*, *, *) denotes the entire array B.

The following program statement copies a table cross section of array C into array A.

    A(*, *) = C(*, 1, *);

e) An entire *structure* is referenced simply by its name (for example, EMPLOYEE, STUDENT_RECORD). References to individual parts of structures require qualified names (see part f).

f) *Portions of structures* are referenced using qualified names. A qualified name defines a unique "path" to the part of the structure that is desired. It is formed as a sequence of identifiers beginning with the name of the structure, and proceeding down through the levels to the part desired, separated by periods (for example, STUDENT_RECORD.COLLEGE.CLASS). A fully-qualified name is not always necessary, as long as the amount of information supplied is sufficient to identify the particular element uniquely. For a more complete discussion of structures (with examples), see Sec. 10-2.

g) A *function* is referenced by giving the name and the list of arguments, if any, for the particular invocation. For example,

    STR = SUBSTR(NAME, 3, 7);

h) A *pseudo-variable* is a built-in function that can be used as the left-hand side of an assignment statement. Examples are SUBSTR and UNSPEC.

3. Expressions

An expression is something that produces a value upon evaluation. It can be composed of constants, references to variables, or function calls, combined by various operators. The operators fall into the following categories:

a) **Numeric (or arithmetic) operators**

These have only numeric operands. Normally the resulting value is given the same attributes as the operand(s). Exceptions occur when the operands have different attributes, in which case one of the operands is converted prior to the operation. The particulars of these conversions are described in subsection 4. The set of numeric operators in PL/I is the following:

+   addition, or unary plus (sign)
−   subtraction, or unary minus (sign)
*   multiplication
/   division
** exponentation

b) Character (and bit) string operator

PL/I provides only a single operator that takes character (or bit) strings as operands.

|| concatenation

Other operations are provided through built-in functions, of which LENGTH, SUBSTR and INDEX are examples.

c) Relational operators

Relational operators always yield one of two values: "true" ('1'B) or "false" ('0'B). Relations can be applied either to numeric operands or to string operands. When comparing string operands of different lengths, the shorter string is first extended on the right (with blanks for character strings, zeroes for bit strings) until the lengths are equal. For character strings, the EBCDIC coding scheme defines the collating sequence.

The complete set of relational operators is the following:

<   less than
>   greater than
=   equal
<= less than or equal
>= greater than or equal
¬= not equal
¬< not less than
¬> not greater than

d) Logical (bit string) operators

These operators always take bit strings as operands, and yield bit string results. They are not to be confused with the relational operators. The logical operators available are the following:

¬ negation ("not")
| disjunction ("or")
& conjunction ("and")

Priority of Operators

The evaluation order of a complex expression is governed by the priorities of the operators that comprise it. The following table summarizes the priorities of the PL/I operators (operators on the same line have equal priority):

(unary) − (unary) + ¬ **   (highest priority)
*   /

```
  _   +
  ||
  <  ⌐<  <=  =  ⌐=  >=  >  ⌐>
  &
  |                                              (lowest priority)
```

In the evaluation of an expression, operators are taken from left to right in order of decreasing priority. Where parentheses are used, operators are taken in order of decreasing depth of parentheses.

4. Data Conversion

Data conversions occur often in PL/I — when evaluating expressions, during assignment operations, when processing procedure arguments, and so forth. The actual rules of data conversion can be quite complex because of the way precision attributes are defined and used. Since beginning programmers rarely need to take explicit notice of precision attributes we will not go into the full complexity of data conversions. Instead, we will give general notions as they apply to PL/C. Since PL/C retains as many significant digits as possible, this greatly simplifies matters. Throughout this discussion we will assume that default precisions are used at all times.

During the evaluation of an arithmetic operation in which the attributes of the operands do not match exactly, some conversion must take place. The rules governing this conversion are the following:

a) If one operand is binary and the other is decimal, the decimal operand is converted to binary. The result is binary.

b) If one operand is fixed point and the other is floating point, the fixed-point operand is converted to floating point. The result is floating point. There is an exception to this rule in the case of exponentiation. In an expression like x**y, if x is floating point and y is fixed point, then no conversion is necessary; the result will be floating point. If, on the other hand, both x and y are fixed point, then x is converted to floating point *unless y is an unsigned integer constant.*

A couple of remarks on the *results* of conversion are in order. In the conversion from bit string to character string each 1 bit becomes the character 1 and each 0 bit, the character 0. In the conversion in the reverse direction each character 1 becomes the bit 1 and each character 0, the bit 0. The presence of any other character raises the CONVERSION condition and causes an error message to be printed. In each case, the length of the result is the same as the length of the original value.

Converting from fixed point to floating point causes no problem since the floating point representation allows for more digits than the fixed point representation. When converting from floating point to fixed point, it is important to remember that truncation, not rounding, is performed. Thus, any fractional digits are lost. Converting from FIXED DECIMAL to FIXED BINARY, however, can result in the loss of *significant* digits, again due to truncation. In this case it is a range problem — FIXED DECIMAL numbers have a much larger range. If a significant digit is lost, the SIZE condition is raised and an error message is printed.

A final point to note is that decimal constants, such as 3.14, are actually represented as FIXED DECIMAL values. This may cause some problems due to conversions.

Section F - Procedures

1. Definition

Format: entry-name: PROCEDURE[(parameter{, parameter})]
           [OPTIONS(MAIN)]
           [RECURSIVE]
           [RETURNS(attribute)]
                { parameter declaration }
                { declaration }
                { statement }
           END [entry-name];

The "entry-name" is used to invoke the procedure, either by a CALL statement or by means of a function call. At the time of the call, arguments are supplied to correspond to the parameters of the definition. The precise nature of this correspondence is described in the next subsection.

Parameter declarations are similar in appearance to normal variable declarations except that the length of a string or bounds of an array may be specified as *, in which case the actual value is taken from the argument passed. The declaration of a parameter does not indicate what attributes it expects the corresponding argument to have.

The execution of a RETURN statement causes control to be returned to the point of invocation. The execution of the last statement of the procedure has the same effect.

OPTIONS (MAIN) designates the main procedure that is called to begin execution. RECURSIVE must be specified if the procedure is to be called recursively (see Sec. 10-5.1). The RETURNS phrase is used only if the procedure is to be called as a function. The attributes specified in the RETURNS phrase describe the value that is to be returned as the value of the function. A function can only return simple scalar quantities.

It is possible to define other procedure within a procedure (as, indeed, one does in the main procedure). Such procedures are known as *internal* procedures and can only be called from within the procedure in which they are defined. In other words, standard rules of scope apply to entry names as well as to variable names.

2. Argument-Parameter Correspondence

The basic concepts of correspondence are considered in Sec. 6.3. The purpose of this subsection is to describe what actually happens in more detail.

The argument-parameter correspondence is established before the execution of the statements of the procedure begins. Once established, it is not changed for the duration of the procedure execution. The exact nature of the correspondence depends on the attributes of both parties, that is, both the argument and the parameter. We will examine what happens from the point of view of the parameter.

a) Scalar parameter

The parameter denotes a variable that is neither an array nor a structure. The argument can be any expression (constant, scalar variable, or more general expression) with a scalar value. If the argument is a simple or subscripted variable whose data attributes match those of the parameter *exactly*, then call by reference is used; that is, the parameter and argument are assumed to have the same address. Note that this is done *prior* to the execution of any statements of the procedure. If the argument is a subscripted variable, the subscripts are evaluated (just once) to determine which element of the subscripted variable is being passed to the procedure.

If the argument is anything else (a constant, an expression that is not a variable, a variable with attributes different from the parameter), then call by value is used. The argument in question is evaluated and its value is placed in a dummy variable with attributes that match those of a parameter. Once again it is important to note that this is done prior to the execution of any statements of the procedure. Thus this value cannot change during the course of the procedure.

If either the parameter or the argument is a fixed-length string and the other is a VARYING string, this is treated as a case of unmatched attributes. What happens depends on the particular circumstances and the compiler being used. In PL/I if a VARYING string argument is passed to a fixed-length string parameter whose length is undefined (that is, specified by an asterisk), the current length of the argument is passed to the procedure. When the argument is a varying-length string array and the parameter is declared as a non-varying undefined-length string array then only one length is passed, namely the maximum length. In PL/C one must use asterisk notation for all string parameters. The length passed in PL/C for a varying string argument is always the maximum length.

b) Array parameter

If the parameter is an array, the corresponding argument can be either an array expression or a scalar expression. PL/C permits only the case where the argument is an array expression. We will deal with that case first.

When both the parameter and the argument are arrays, the specified number of dimensions must be the same. If the argument is in fact an array expression, the operands of the expression must have the same number of dimensions as the parameter. If the argument is an array (or cross section of an array) whose attributes match those of the parameter exactly, then the correspondence is call by reference. In any other case a dummy array is created and call by value results.

As stated, it is possible in PL/I to pass a scalar argument to an array parameter. In order to allow this the programmer must have specified an entry declaration for this procedure in which the bounds of the parameter array are specified as decimal integer constants. In this case a dummy array is created, and each element of the dummy array is assigned the value of the scalar argument. Again, this facility is not available in PL/C.

c) Structure parameter

If the parameter is a structure, the argument may be either a structure expression or a scalar expression (PL/C permits only structure expressions). The correspondence is similar to that described in part b for array parameters. If the parameter is an *array of structures,* the argument can be any one of a scalar expression, an array expression, a structure expression, or an array of structures expression. The expected generalizations apply.

d) Entry-name parameter

If the parameter is an entry name, the argument must be an entry name (that is, the name of a function or procedure). This can be a programmer-defined entry name or one of the mathematical built-in functions such as SIN. Notice that other built-in functions cannot be passed. For entry-name parameters to be permitted, an entry-name declaration of the parameter must be given (see Sec. D.1). The number of parameters and their attributes must match those of the argument.

Section G - Built-in Functions

The built-in functions of PL/I can be classified according to the PL/I features they are intended to provide. In this book we are not concerned with all the possible classes (nor with all the functions). Instead we restrict ourselves to the following classes and functions within them:

String-handling built-in functions

These functions provide capabilities for processing bit and character strings. The functions that we consider are the following:

BIT CHAR INDEX LENGTH REPEAT SUBSTR UNSPEC VERIFY

Arithmetic built-in functions

These functions perform operations such as base, scale, or mode conversion. Other arithmetic operations are also included. We consider the following functions from this class:

ABS CEIL DECIMAL FIXED FLOAT FLOOR MOD ROUND TRUNC

Mathematical built-in functions

These functions provide standard mathematical operations. We consider the following:

COS COSD EXP LOG LOG10 LOG2 RAND SIN SIND SQRT TAN TAND

Array-handling built-in functions

The functions in this class all operate on array arguments and return a single value property of the array. We consider the following members of this class:

DIM HBOUND LBOUND

Based storage built-in functions

Several functions are useful for working with based storage. We consider only the following:

ADDR NULL

Miscellaneous built-in functions

Other useful functions include the following:

DATE TIME

We now proceed to a more detailed description of these functions. To provide a consistent perspective for the discussion we will deal with the PL/C implementations of the functions wherever possible. There may be slight variations in other implementations, but the basics should be much the same.

ABS (x)

The result is the absolute value of the numeric expression x. The attributes are the same as the attributes of the argument.

ADDR (x)

The result is a pointer value identifying the location at which a given variable x has been allocated. This function is not available in PL/C.

BIT (exp, [length])

The "exp" is converted to a bit string of length "length". If "length" is omitted, the length of the result is determined from the attributes of "exp". In PL/C "exp" cannot be numeric. (One must use PUT STRING to convert a numeric quantity to a string in PL/C.)

CEIL (x)

The result is the smallest integer that is greater than or equal to the numeric argument x.

CHAR (exp, [length])

The "exp" is converted to a character string of length "length" representing the same value. If "length" is omitted the length of the result is determined by the attributes of "exp". As with BIT, CHAR cannot be used in PL/C to convert numeric quantities to strings.

COS (x)

COS returns a floating-point value that represents the cosine of x (expressed in radians) .

COSD (x)

COSD returns a floating-point value that represents the cosine of x (expressed in degrees).

DATE

DATE returns the current date as a character string of length 6, with the form yymmdd (e.g., 790418).

DIM (x, n)

The result is a fixed binary integer giving the "extent" of the nth dimension of the array x. The extent is defined as the upper bound minus the lower bound, plus 1.

DECIMAL (x)

The argument x is converted to base DECIMAL.

EXP (x)

EXP returns a floating-point value that is given by $e^{**}x$, where e is the base of the natural logarithm system.

FIXED (x)

The argument x is converted to fixed point.

FLOAT (x)

The argument x is converted to floating point.

FLOOR (x)

The result is the largest integer less than or equal to x.

HBOUND (x, n)

The result is the upper bound of the nth dimension of the array x.

INDEX (string, config)

Arguments "string" and "config" can be either bit or character strings. The result is a fixed binary integer giving the leftmost position in "string" where "config" begins. If "config" does not appear within "string", 0 is returned.

LBOUND (x, n)

The result is the lower bound of the nth dimension of the array x.

LENGTH (string)

The result is a fixed binary integer giving the length of the argument "string".

LOG (x)

LOG returns a floating-point value that is the natural (base e) logarithm of x. The value of x must be greater than 0.

LOG 10 (x)

LOG 10 returns a floating-point value that is the common (base 10) logarithm of x. The value of x must be greater than 0.

LOG2 (x)

LOG2 returns a floating-point value that is the base 2 logarithm of x. The value of x must be greater than 0.

MOD (x, y)

The result is the remainder upon dividing x by y. If x and y differ in sign, the operation is performed on their absolute values, and the result is then ABS (y) - remainder.

NULL

NULL returns a null pointer value, that is, a value that cannot identify any generation of a based variable. The NULL function is not available in PL/C.

RAND (x)

The RAND function generates a sequence of pseudo-random floating-point values, yielding a new one each time it is called. The argument x should be floating point (or it will be converted to floating point), and must have a value between 0 and 1 (exclusive). Prior to the first call to RAND, x should be given an odd value with 9 significant digits to produce a sequence with maximum period. Normally RAND is used in an assignment statement of the form X=RAND(X);. (Note: RAND is based on the method of Coveyou and Macpherson in ACM Journal, Vol. 14, 1967, pp. 100-119. It is not included in standard PL/I.)

REPEAT (string, i)

The result is "string" concatenated to itself "i" times. In PL/C, i must be a decimal integer constant.

ROUND (x, n)

ROUND returns the given value x rounded to the nth digit to the right of the decimal (or binary) point. n must be a (signed or unsigned) integer constant. If n is 0, x is rounded to the nearest integer. If n is less than zero, x is rounded as the (n+1)th digit to the left of the decimal (or binary) point.

SIN (x)

SIN returns a floating-point value that represents the sine of x, where x is expressed in radians.

SIND(x)

SIND returns a floating-point value that represents the sine of x, where x is expressed in degrees.

SQRT(x)

SQRT returns a floating-point value that is the square root of x. The value of x must not be less than 0.

SUBSTR (string, i[, j])

The result is a substring of the argument string "string". The substring extracted begins at position i in the argument string and comprises the next j positions. If j is not specified, the substring is assumed to extend to the end of the argument string.

TAN(x)

TAN returns a floating-point value that represents the tangent of x, where x is expressed in radians.

TAND(x)

TAND returns a floating-point value that represents the tangent of x, where x is expressed in degrees.

TIME

TIME returns the current time as a character string of length 9, in the form hhmmssttt (ttt denotes the number of milliseconds).

TRUNC(x)

TRUNC returns an integer that is the truncated form of the given value x. If x is negative, the result is CEIL(x); if x is positive, the result is FLOOR(x).

UNSPEC(x)

The argument x can be any expression. UNSPEC returns a bit string containing the internal representation of x. The length of the result is determined by the attributes of x.

VERIFY (string, config)

The arguments "string" and "config" are both strings (character or bit). VERIFY returns a fixed binary integer that indicates the position of the first character in "string" not found in "config". If all elements of "string" are in "config", the result is 0.

Section - H Format Items

GET EDIT and PUT EDIT statements require programmer-defined format items to control the form and layout of the data involved. The use of format items is discussed in Sec. 5-3. In this section we present a brief summary of format items.

We will consider two major categories of format items: data format items and control format items. A data format item is used to describe the external format of a single data item. Control format items are used to specify the layout of the data. The following is a list of data format items:

Fixed-point format item	F
Floating-point format item	E
Bit-string format item	B
Character-string format item	A

The following is a list of control format items:

Paging format item	PAGE
Line skipping format item	SKIP
Line position format item	LINE
Column position format item	COLUMN
Spacing format item	X

We now consider each of these in more detail.

A format item

The A format item is:

A [(w)]

The A format item is used for reading or writing character strings. For input, the next w columns of input data are read from the input stream. For output, the character string value is printed, left-justified, in the next w columns of the output stream. The value is truncated if it is too long. For output, w can be omitted, in which case the number of columns of output is determined directly from the length of the string being printed.

B format item

The B format item is:

B [(w)]

The B format item is used for reading and writing bit strings. For input, the next w columns of the input stream are read. Only 1's and 0's are allowed within the value, and there must be no imbedded blanks. For output, the bit string value is printed, left-justified, in the next w columns of the output stream. The value is truncated if it is too long. As with the A-format item, w can be omitted, in which case the number of columns of output is determined directly from the length of the string being printed.

COLUMN format item

The COLUMN format item is:

COLUMN (p)

The COLUMN format item causes the current pointer to be positioned at position p of the current input card or output line. For input, the columns skipped over are ignored; for output, they are filled with blanks. If the current position is already past position p, the pointer is positioned at position p of the following card or line.

E format item

The E format item is:

E(w, d [, s])

The E format item is used for reading or printing a floating-point number, in the next w columns. The value of w must be large enough to include all parts of the number, including sign and exponent. If the actual variable involved is not floating point, an appropriate conversion will take place. s denotes the number of significant digits and d, the number of fractional digits. If s is omitted it is assumed to be d+1. If necessary, the number is rounded to fit the format specified.

F format item

The F format item is:

F(w, d[, s])

The F format item is used for reading or printing a fixed-point decimal number, in the next w columns. If the actual variable involved is not fixed decimal, an appropriate conversion will take place. For input, the number is an optionally-signed decimal fixed-point constant. It can contain no imbedded blanks. If the entire field is blank, the value 0 is read. If the number contains no decimal point, an implied decimal point is inserted d digits from the right of the number. If s is supplied in the format item, the number is multiplied by 10**s, after it is read but before being assigned to the variable.

For output, the value to be printed is first converted to fixed-decimal representation. It is printed, right-justified, in the next w columns in the output stream (rounded, if necessary, to fit). If no d is specified, the integer part of the number is written with no decimal point. If d is specified, d digits will be printed to the right of the decimal point. If s is specified, the value is multiplied by 10**s prior to printing.

LINE format item

The LINE format item is:

LINE(n)

The LINE format item causes blank lines to be inserted in the output stream so that the next output will take place on the nth line on the page. If the current line number already exceeds n, the ENDPAGE condition is raised.

PAGE format item

The PAGE format item is:

> PAGE

The PAGE format item causes a new output page to be started.

SKIP format item

The SKIP format item is:

> SKIP[(n)]

The SKIP format item causes n cards or lines to be skipped, with the current card or line counting as 1 skip. If n is not specified, 1 is assumed. On output if n is less than or equal to 0, the column pointer will be repositioned to column 1 of the current line. This can be used to cause overprinting of characters. Notice that SKIP may cause the ENDPAGE condition to be raised.

X format item

The X format item is:

> X(w)

The X format item causes w columns to be skipped on input, or w blank characters to be inserted on output.

Section I - Major Differences between PL/C and PL/I

PL/C was designed to be an "upward compatible" subset of PL/I, meaning that a program that runs without error messages on the PL/C compiler should run under PL/I and produce the same results. PL/C is not quite a proper subset of PL/I since a few features have been added; however most of these are in the nature of debugging and testing aids — not language incompatibilities. The version of PL/C described in this appendix is designated "Release 7.6" as documented in the book by R. Conway and D. Gries [1979] that is cited in the references. The purpose of this section is to provide a summary of the major differences between this version of PL/C and IBM-supported PL/I as they pertain to the level of the language presented in this book.

1. **PL/I Features Not Present in PL/C**

- Controlled and based storage, and list processing.
- A small number of built-in functions.

2. **Additional Restrictions Imposed by PL/C**

- A total of 33 statement keywords and 6 auxiliary keywords are reserved and cannot be used as identifiers.

- Although the names of built-in functions and pseudo-variables are not reserved, they must be redeclared if they are to be used as identifiers.
- String constants and comments must normally be confined to a single source card.
- String constants cannot have repetition factors.
- There are restrictions on the following statements: END, ENTRY, FORMAT, PROCEDURE, READ, and WRITE.
- There are restrictions on the following attributes: dimension, ENTRY, INITIAL, and length.
- Not all defaults under PL/C are the same as under PL/I.

3. Differences in Internal Representation of Data

PL/C performs all floating point arithmetic in double-precision, adopting programmer-specified precisions only for output. This can produce results that are more precise than those obtained in PL/I.

PL/C assigns a full word of storage to all FIXED BINARY variables and a double word of storage to all FIXED DECIMAL variables, no matter what precision the programmer has declared. This means that PL/C variables can hold larger values than their PL/I counterparts. However, the raising of the SIZE condition is set in such a way that situations which would give different results are detected.

More storage is consumed by PL/C for bit strings and character strings.

Decimal-base values in PL/C are maintained internally in floating point binary form, and are converted on output.

4. Limits in the PL/C Compiler

The internal structure of the PL/C compiler made it necessary to impose certain limits on the dimensions of source programs. This is unlikely to affect "normal" programs. The following limits have been imposed:

- A maximum nesting depth of IF statements of 12.
- A maximum static nesting of PROCEDURE, BEGIN, and DO statements of 11.
- A maximum nesting of factors for a DECLARE of 6.
- A maximum nesting depth for parentheses in expressions of 14.
- A maximum number of identifiers in a factor or structure of a DECLARE of 88.
- A maximum number of symbols in any single expression of 256.

Section J - References

The material for this appendix was collected primarily from two sources:

CONWAY, R. and GRIES, D.: *An Introduction to Programming: A Structured Approach Using PL/I and PL/C,* Third Edition, Winthrop Publishers, Inc., Cambridge, Massachusetts, 1979.

IBM: *OS PL/I Checkout and Optimizing Compilers: Language Reference Manual,* IBM Corp., GC33-0009-4, 1976.

INDEX